Section Five
ACCOUNTING, COMPUTERS, AND
INFORMATION MANAGEMENT

Section Six
FINANCIAL MANAGEMENT

Section Eight
THE BUSINESS ENVIRONMENT

Section Seven
PERSPECTIVES ON THE
SCOPE OF BUSINESS

1984 Update

INTRODUCTION TO BUSINESS
A Contemporary View

FOURTH EDITION

John A. Reinecke
University of Southern Mississippi

William F. Schoell
University of Southern Mississippi

Allyn and Bacon, Inc. Boston London Sydney Toronto

For Gladys and Rosie

Library of Congress Cataloging in Publication Data

Reinecke, John A., 1931–
 Introduction to business.

 Includes index.
 1. Business. 2. Industrial management. I. Schoell, William F. II. Title.
HD31.R4417   1983   658.4   82–11329
ISBN 0-205-07845-1

Printed in the United States of America
10 9 8 7 6 5 4 3 2   87 86 85 84

Production Editor: Elaine Ober

Credits

Photo Research by Laurel Anderson. The authors would like to acknowledge the contributions of the following authors, publishers, companies, and photographers who granted permission to reproduce their materials.

Four-color insert: p. 1—Agency: FCB-Honig, photo by Frank Cowan, Reprinted courtesy of Levi Strauss & Company. p. 2—Courtesy of Fabergé, Inc. Photo courtesy of Neal Barr. p. 3—Courtesy of Lenox China and Crystal. p. 4—Courtesy of Knoll International.

Section One: SO Duotone p. 1—Harry Wilkes/Stock, Boston.

Chapter One: Photo p. 5—Christopher Brown/Stock, Boston. Ad p. 6—Courtesy of Westinghouse Corporation. p. 9—*Economic Indicators*, March, 1983, p. 1. p. 10—Monthly Labor Review, July 1983, p. 66 (Washington, D.C.: U.S. Department of Labor). Cartoon (*bottom*)—Pepper . . . and Salt: From *The Wall Street Journal*, permission—Cartoon Features Syndicate. p. 11—From *The United Nations 1979–1981 Statistical Yearbook*, Copyright United Nations, 1981, pp. 693–696. Reproduced by permission. Photo p. 19—The Ford Archives.

Chapter Two: p. 38—*Monthly Tax Features*, (Washington, D.C.: Tax Foundation, Inc.) June—July, 1982, p. 1. Cartoon p. 39—*pepper . . . and Salt:* From *The Wall Street Journal*, permission—Cartoon Features Syndicate. Photo p. 42—Courtesy "Couples Inc." Photo p. 50—Lionel Delevingne/Stock, Boston. p. 53—*Statistical Abstract of the United States 1982–3*, 103rd edition (Washington, D.C.: Bureau of the Cenus, 1982), p. 546. Ad p. 54—Courtesy of the American Council of Life Insurance. Photo p. 55—David Strickland/Picture Cube.

Chapter Three: Photo p. 64—William Koechling. Photo p. 65—Marsha Fall Stuart/Global Focus. Ad p. 70—Courtesy of Amax, Inc. p. 75—Courtesy of the State of Mississippi. Photo p. 76—Arthur Grace/Stock, Boston. p. 77—Courtesy of Amax, Inc. p. 81—*Statistical Abstract, 1981*, p. 535. p. 82—*Statistical Abstract 1981*, p. 534. p. 83—From "The Fortune 500," *Fortune*, May 2, 1983, pp. 228–229. © 1982 Time Inc.

(Credits continue on p. 699.)

CONTENTS

SECTION 2   **Management and Organization** 95

CHAPTER 11

**Promotion and
Pricing**   310

CHAPTER 12

Accounting   342

PREFACE

Introduction to Business: A Contemporary View, Fourth Edition, reveals the excitement, the meaning, and the challenge that is found in modern business. Its goal is to convey a basic understanding of contemporary business concepts and how they are applied in the real world.

Major Improvements in the Fourth Edition

The material in the Fourth Edition has been significantly reorganized in order to provide a larger number of sections, each of which has a smaller number of more carefully integrated chapters than the Third Edition. Whereas the Third Edition contained 18 chapters organized into 5 sections, the Fourth Edition has 21 chapters organized into 8 sections. This reorganization permits a reduction in the total length of the book and in the length of each chapter as well. Breaking the discussion into more digestible units should improve the text for the instructor and for the students.

Section Features

Each section is preceded by a brief introduction to the chapters that comprise it. The introduction helps to link the chapters that are included in each section. At the end of each section there is a case study, a discussion of career opportunities related to the section topics, and a career profile. The case study provides an opportunity for case analysis of a realistic business situation. The discussion of career opportunities includes practical career planning information which supplements the "careers chapter" (Chapter 21). The career profile features a young man or woman who has chosen a job related to the major section topic. These three features introduce a stronger real-world orientation to the text to stimulate career interest and motivation.

Chapter Features

Besides the section material described above, the chapter provides all of the following teaching and learning features.

Learning Objectives. The list of learning objectives at the beginning of each chapter ties the text, the Study Guide, and the Instructor's Manual together. Each chapter in the Study Guide contains a programmed review section that provides two or more exercises for testing student mastery of the learning objectives. Each item in the Test Bank is also linked to a specific and identified learning objective.

Key Concepts. The list of key concepts at the beginning of each chapter identifies the most important terms in the chapter and is designed to help build business vocabulary. Each key concept is defined in bold face type in the text and appears in color in the margin. Each chapter in the Study Guide contains a Test Yourself Business Vocabulary feature to reenforce vocabulary building. Each key concept is also defined in the expanded Glossary at the end of the text, along with many other important terms.

Real-World Examples. A real-world example of a contemporary business practice or problem follows the list of key concepts for each chapter. In addition to this attention getting feature, numerous other references are made to actual firms and their business practices throughout every chapter. Both help to build interest and to tie the chapter content to contemporary business practices. In addition, the incidents, or short cases, that appear at the end of each chapter focus on issues in contemporary business. Their real-world orientation helps to build analytical skills.

Boxed Inserts. Three types of boxed inserts are used to elaborate on the discussion in each chapter. *What Do You Think?* boxes require a decision on a contemporary business problem. *Point of View* boxes present various perspectives on contemporary business issues. *Authors' Commentary* boxes present the authors' opinions and/or predictions about current business questions.

Advertisements, Cartoons, Photographs, and Business Documents. Reproductions of contemporary advertisements are used to dramatize major business concepts and practices. Cartoons, photos, and reproductions of actual business documents also liven up the presentation and help to give it an added visual dimension.

Summary and Look Ahead. The Summary and Look Ahead feature summarizes the chapter in a concise manner. It also introduces the subject matter that follows in the next chapter or section. This continues the strategy of tying together the major ideas from chapter to chapter and from section to section.

Review and Discussion Questions. The review questions at the end of each chapter relate directly to the chapter's factual material. The discussion questions encourage the student to explore and analyze issues contained in the chapter.

The Study Guide

We, along with Alvin J. Williams and Thomas S. O'Connor, have prepared a comprehensive Study Guide. Each chapter contains: 1) a summary of the text chapter, 2) a vocabulary testing exercise, 3) a programmed review section for self-testing to determine if the student can accomplish each of the learning objectives, 4) multiple-choice questions and true-false statements for the student to test himself or herself, and 5) five additional exercises, including real-world incidents, or short cases, crossword puzzles, and completion exercises. Answers are provided in the Study Guide for all items (along with references to the pages in the text where the answers appear) except three of the exercises. Instructors may use these exercises as supplementary outside assignments to be submitted for grading.

Acknowledgments

We owe special thanks to our production editor, Elaine Ober, and to our series editor, Jack Peters, for their dedicated efforts toward helping us to meet our goal of significantly improving the Third Edition. We also want to thank Carlyle Carter for developmental work, Julie Heyd for clerical assistance, and Judith Gimple and Carole Feinberg for helping in securing permissions. Thanks also to our families for bearing with us, and encouraging us, throughout the revision process.

Many changes from the previous edition were inspired by its readers. We want to continue to learn from our readers, as they are our best possible critics.

The following people helped in reviewing our manuscript and/or graciously offered suggestions, either on their own or by replying to questionnaires distributed by the Allyn and Bacon sales representatives. Their comments were gratefully received, carefully read, and implemented wherever possible.

Phyllis C. Alderdice, West Virginia State College;
Mary Andersen, Frostburg State College;
David J. Auer, Western Washington University;
William J. Baker, Lake Michigan College;
Phyllis J. Baldwin, Lake Michigan College;
Andrew M. Bonacic, Adirondack Community College;
Theordore B. Borecki, Hofstra University;
Daniel R. Boyd, Middle Tennessee State University;
William B. Boyles, Washington and Jefferson College;
Sonya K. Brett, Macomb County Community College;
William R. Brown, Towson State University;
Business Department Faculty, Grand Rapids Junior College;
Aaron C. Carpenter, Grambling State University;
Michael Cicero, Highland Community College;
Jack Cichy, Davenport College;
Margaret Cipcic, Waynesburg College;
Linda Collins, Jordan College;
Gerry Conner, Linn-Benton Community College;
J. H. Denson, Fullerton College;
Arnold DiSilvestri, Davis and Elkins College;
Lillie D. Ensley, Grambling State University;
Ransom A. Evans, State University of New York at Cobleskill;
Keith Flearson, West Liberty State College;
James M. Fordyce, Michigan State University;
R. J. Franz, Illinois Central College;
M. Gaines, Glenville State University;
Gerald R. Garst, Central Ohio Technical College;
Quintin W. Guerin, University of Wisconsin-Parkside;
Ray L. Hamb, Davenport College of Business;
J. M. Hartley, San Diego City College;
Sanford B. Helman, Middlesex Community College;
Clarence O. Hill, Fullerton College;
Jack A. Hill, University of Nebraska at Omaha;
Harold K. Hilson, Southern Illinois University;
K. Hirshl, Community College of Allegheny County;
John Holdorf, Union College;
R. A. Johannsen, Miami-Dade Community College;
Fran Jones, Cypress College;
Warren Keller, Grossmont College;
Ed Kiel, Spokane Falls Community College;
Kiyoshi Kubota, Ventura College;
Edward B. Lee, Community College of Allegheny County;
Susan A. Lee, American International College;

Richard Ligault, Southeastern Massachusetts
University;

Allen B. Lindsley, Foothill College;

Andrew Lionyo, Macomb County Community
College;

John W. Lloyd, Monroe Community College;

Paul J. Londrigan, Charles S. Mott Community
College;

Bernard J. Londwehr, West Liberty State College;

William P. Lovell, Cayough Community College;

Stuart L. Mandell, University of Lowell;

John Martin, Mt. San Antonio College;

Judith S. May, Humboldt State College;

Catherine C. McElroy, Bucks County Community
College;

Kenneth A. McKnight, Spokane Community College;

Kenneth R. Meisinger, University of Colorado;

Judy Mier, McNeese State University;

Mary M. Miller, Mississippi Gulf Coast Community
College;

Craig C. Milnor, Clark College;

R. W. Mitchel, Orange Coast College;

Jim Lee Morgan, West Los Angeles College;

Pete Moutsatson, Montcalm County College;

W. Gale Mueller, Spokane Community College;

Robert A. Myers, St. Petersburg Junior College;

Lee H. Neumann, Bucks County Community
College;

Dwight L. Packard, Morningside College;

Joseph Platts, Miami-Dade Community College;

Roderick Powers, Iowa State University;

Richard Randall, Nassau Community College;

Kenneth A. Reed, University of Colorado at Boulder;

Peter W. Replogle, Orange County Community
College;

Elizabeth Robinson, West Liberty State College;

John V. Ryan, Montgomery College;

Donald W. Satterfield, Memphis State University;

J. Herbert Scheer, Canisius College;

Jim Silverberg, Nicholls State University;

G. R. Smith, Loyola University;

W. Nye Smith, Clarkson College;

M. Sonfield, Hofstra University;

Carl J. Sonntag, Pikes Peak Community College;

Ronald Steele, Sacramento City College;

S. D. Steigmaan, Indiana University of Pennsylvania;

Richard Stewart, Mississippi Gulf Coast Community
College;

Richard M. Stone, Cuesta College;

Fred Tesch, Western Connecticut State College;

G. G. Titlow, St. Petersburg Junior College;

A. R. Uguado, Los Angeles Mission College;

Janna P. Vice, Eastern Kentucky University;

J. L. VonHatten, Hanover College;

Larry L. Waldort, Boise State University;

Clark Wheeler, Santa Fe Community College;

Luther G. White, Marshall University;

Onida White, Mississippi Gulf Coast Community
College;

Bill Williams, Henderson State University;

Peter Wright, Southeastern Louisiana University;

William F. Wright, Mt. Hood Community College;

Rodney E. Wyse, Central State University.

TO THE STUDENT

Introduction to Business: A Contemporary View, Fourth Edition, has been written with you in mind. We think you'll find it an up-to-date, practical, and exciting text. It reads smoothly and is comprehensive enough to give you a good overall view of the nature of business and the career opportunities it offers.

Take time to read the introductory materials in each chapter. They are designed to help you to do a more effective job of studying. The boxed material will help to get you involved in the book—to respond to questions, to see a situation from a different point of view, and to do a little looking into the future. You will also have many opportunities to put yourself in the shoes of a decision maker at companies that are familiar to you. Read and think about the questions raised in the incidents at the end of the chapters.

Most importantly, try to derive the maximum benefit from your first course in business by becoming familiar with the language of business and the challenges business offers. This course lays the foundation upon which your other business courses will build. Make the commitment to do your best in the course and keep up with developments in the business world. You will become an important part of that world in the not too distant future. Good luck in the course and in your future in business!

John A. Reinecke

William F. Schoell

SECTION 1

Our Business System

Our study of business begins with a discussion of its economic setting, the reasons business firms exist, and the forms of business ownership.

In Chapter 1 we examine what an economic system is and why it exists. The main purpose of any economic system is to enable people to cope with the economic problem—how to satisfy their unlimited wants with their limited resources. Two vastly different types of economic systems are collectivism and capitalism. We compare and contrast them both in their "pure forms" and in their "real-world forms."

In Chapter 2, we look at the reasons business firms exist. The business firm is the basic building block for organizing production activity in a capitalist economic system. In a capitalist nation such as the United States, most economic activity is channeled through business firms.

Chapter 3 describes the forms of business ownership. Although many people think mainly of corporations when they think of business firms, there are other forms of ownership. In fact, the majority of American firms are not corporations, although corporations conduct most of the business activity in the United States.

CHAPTER 1

Approaching the Economic Problem

OBJECTIVES:

After reading this chapter, you should be able to

1. Define the economic problem and discuss how we cope with it.
2. Describe ways in which the performance of an economic system is measured.
3. Define utility and explain the concept of value in exchange.
4. List and define the factors of production.
5. State the basic purpose of an economic system and give examples of economic systems that reflect this basic purpose.
6. Compare and contrast the collectivist and capitalist economic systems.
7. List and discuss the chief characteristics of a capitalist economic system.
8. Explain why real-world economic systems are not pure and give examples.
9. Define business and discuss the role of profit in business activity.
10. Describe a postindustrial economy.

KEY CONCEPTS:

Look for these terms as you read the chapter

the economic problem

specialization

exchange

standard of living

Gross National Product (GNP)

inflation

Disposable Personal Income (DPI)

utility

value in exchange

factors of production

land

labor

capital

entrepreneurship

entrepreneur

mercantilism

laissez faire

capitalism

private enterprise

collectivism

central planning

individualism

the Protestant ethic

capital formation

consumer power

consumerism

business

profit

All economic systems share the problem that human wants are unlimited while the resources with which to satisfy them are limited. You confront this problem every day and cope with it by assigning priorities to your wants and spending your limited income accordingly. In our economic system, business firms try to anticipate what their target customers want and produce goods and services that they hope will satisfy these wants. Business people can profit if they produce things consumers want, but they assume the risk of losing their investment if they produce things that consumers do not want.

A different situation exists in some other types of economic systems. Although these economic systems must also cope with unlimited human wants and limited productive resources, they allow individual consumers and business people very little voice in coping with the economic problem. In the Soviet Union, for example, the State Planning Committee (GOSPLAN) sets a plan every five years to govern the workings of the economic system. The Committee determines what goods and services will be produced and the prices at which they will be sold. It also sets production quotas for workers, in effect telling each citizen how much of which good or service he or she must produce. The central planners decide what will be produced and what will be available for consumers to buy.

If consumers want products and services that are not being produced by state-owned enterprises, the only alternative source is the black market. This underground economy includes individual black marketers and larger, privately owned businesses that supply consumers with what they want but cannot buy from the state-owned enterprises. These people are in business to make a profit but are sent to prison if they are caught engaging in profit-making activities.

The problem of dealing with limited resources to satisfy unlimited wants is not new. Human beings have always been "wanting" animals. Even the early cave dwellers' unlimited needs and wants had to be satisfied with the limited resources available to them.

Although the cave people lived in small, independent groups, modern people live with others in large, interdependent social and economic systems. In advanced systems we learn to want many more things than we really need in order to survive. Our natural resources, however, have not increased to the same degree as our wants. Thus the economic problem has been brought into sharper focus.

By specializing and exchanging, we can satisfy more wants with our limited resources. This raises our standard of living because we have more goods and services to consume. Recently more people have been questioning whether we really are better off. They question whether a greater output of goods and services really improves the quality of life.

An economic system is a framework for satisfying human wants. Collectivism and capitalism are two different types of systems. We will discuss both in their pure and real world forms. One major difference between these systems is the role of profit-seeking business firms in the economy. One major similarity between the two systems is that both must cope with general economic problems.

THE ECONOMIC PROBLEM

the economic problem

Because human wants are unlimited while productive resources are limited, we face a problem. It is **the economic problem—how to satisfy these unlimited wants with limited resources.** This problem exists for nations, individual consumers, business firms, and nonprofit organizations.

In recent years, for example, Congress has faced tough problems trying to balance the federal budget. It has to allocate its limited funds among a variety of departments and agencies. Should it provide for more spending on space exploration or for more spending on medical research and education? Is the Department of Health and Human Services using its funds in the best way possible or should it expand some programs and cut back others?

What about individual consumers who are faced with an almost endless variety of products and services to buy? Because their buying power is limited, they cannot have them all. Like Congress, consumers also must make choices about how they will spend their funds.

Business firms also face the economic problem. Should a company increase spending on advertising its present products or should it spend more to research and develop new products? Nonprofit organizations also have to decide how they will use their resources. For example, should the American Cancer Society invest more in research to find a cure for cancer or spend more to educate people about self-detection of cancer?

But what are "scarce resources"? One example is natural resources. Some of these are renewable (forests) but some are not renewable (petroleum). With proper forest management, timber is a renewable natural resource. But no matter how well petroleum resources are "managed," they eventually will run out. Critical decisions must be made about how increasingly scarce natural resources will be used. To meet our energy needs, we must decide the roles that coal, petroleum, solar power, geothermal power, and nuclear power will play.

The concept of resources does not mean just natural resources, however. It includes all productive resources, as we will see later in the discussion of the factors of production.

The economic problem has always existed and will continue to exist. The early cave people, in their struggle to survive, had to satisfy basic needs for food, clothing, and shelter by finding and preparing food, making clothing, and finding a cave. If a man and a woman shared these tasks, each one's economic fate as a producer and a consumer became tied to that of the other. They still faced the same economic problem, but the number of options for solving it increased. In other words, the family unit made it easier for them to cope with the economic problem because of specialization and exchange.

Ensuring that trucks run only with full loads is one way to manage our petroleum resources

Specialization

Sharing the task of providing their basic needs meant that neither person had to provide for all his or her needs alone. **Specialization means concentrating on a specific (specialized) task in-**

specialization

An ad that focuses on the importance of productivity to American industry

stead of dividing one's efforts among a greater number of tasks. Each person can make better use of his or her limited time and talents (that is, become more efficient in performing a specialized task) when there is specialization. For the cave dwellers this meant one person would specialize in hunting and the other would specialize in cooking.

A modern example of specialization is the assembly line in an automobile plant. Each worker on the assembly line performs a highly specialized task. In extreme cases a worker may tighten only one or two bolts. As we will see in several later chapters, very simple and routine tasks or chores can cause workers to become bored and less productive. Humanizing the assembly line has become a big challenge for management in a variety of businesses. In some businesses computerized robots are used to perform many tasks that humans would consider dull and boring. Many companies, such as Westinghouse, are striving to increase employee productivity through selected application of robotic equipment. As we will see later in this book, business firms consider increasing productivity to be a major goal.

Exchange

Specialization is pointless, however, unless specialists can exchange. **Exchange means trade, or giving up one thing to get another thing.**

exchange

Let's assume that our caveman specializes in hunting and the woman specializes in cooking. The man exchanges part of his hunt for part of the meal prepared by the woman. Specialization and exchange, of course, extend beyond the family unit in modern economies. Over time we have come to live in larger groups. From the single family, we have evolved to more complex groups such as tribes, villages, towns, cities, and nations with increasing dependence on specialization and exchange.

Production has become organized in shops, stores, and factories. Even your local McDonald's or Burger King restaurants practice specialization. The fast service you are used to would not be possible if one person had to raise, harvest, and deliver the beef, lettuce, and tomatoes, take your order, prepare the food, package it, and collect payment for it.

The specialization and exchange process, therefore, now includes a great many people. It is a fact of life in modern economic systems that people are dependent on other people to satisfy their wants. Specialists are economically interdependent. The process of exchange organizes people into groups and an economic system is the result. Although there are many different types of economic systems, all have one element in common—they exist to satisfy human wants.

NEEDS AND WANTS

People have basic survival needs, such as food, clothing, and shelter. When people relate to other people, specialization and exchange begin and they learn new wants. Satisfaction of needs is necessary for survival. Satisfaction of wants helps to make life more enjoyable.

A person's need for food may be satisfied by eating wild berries. But he or she may learn, as a result of coming into contact with other people, to want fancy cuts of meat and pastries. No one really needs a TV, a trash compactor, or a backyard swimming pool for survival, but life would be rather dull if we focused only on satisfying our most basic survival needs. As we will see, some people question how far we should go in creating new wants and how important consumption should be in our lives. One of the tools business firms use to make us want more is advertising, which is often attacked for contributing to what critics call our overly materialistic lifestyle.

In some cases conflict arises over *who* is the best judge of what is good for us. How far should individuals be permitted to go in satisfying their own wants regardless of the effects of their consumption on the rest of society? Even after gasoline prices skyrocketed, some people still wanted big cars that got few miles per gallon of gas; and car makers were willing to cater to their desire. Congress responded by passing laws requiring new cars to meet certain miles-per-gallon standards.

Advances in transportation and communications have led to even wider contact among people. The most remote cities of the world are seconds away by phone and only hours away by jet. Communications satellites help broadcast live TV specials and news programs to people around the world. Not only does such contact increase the number of people to whom sellers can sell their products but it also encourages greater specialization. It has led too, to the learning of still more wants. Who would have thought that French Perrier water and West German Adidas and Puma running shoes would be so popular in the United States or that many people in Paris would eat McDonald's hamburgers?

Measuring an Economy's Performance

As we have said, the purpose of an economic system is to satisfy human wants. It is, therefore, desirable to measure its performance. Comparisons of different systems may be made by a measure called the standard of living. **The standard of living is a relative measure of economic well-being that helps us compare the well-being of one society with that of another society and to observe change in well-being over time.**

    There are several approaches to measuring the standard of living. **One measure is Gross National Product (GNP). This is the sum of the market values of all final goods and services produced by a nation during a given year.** (See Figure 1-1.)

    The United States measures its GNP in trillions of dollars. It took 200 years for our GNP to reach the trillion dollar mark but little more than seven years to reach the second trillion dollar mark in 1978. It is projected to cross the $4 trillion mark in 1985. Keep in mind that a trillion is a thousand billion, or a million million. If someone were to distribute a trillion dollars, each man, woman, and child in the United States would get $4,415.

    The numbers themselves are staggering but much of the increase in dollar GNP is due in inflation. **Inflation means an increase in the prices of goods and services over a period of time that effectively reduces the purchasing power of a nation's currency.** It has been a very serious problem in the United States and in most other countries in recent years. Inflation is one reason that the prices of new homes and new cars are so high. (See Table 1-1 on page 10.)

    GNP reached the third trillion dollar mark by January, 1982. To measure the actual growth in GNP undistorted by inflation, however, we must express GNP in real terms. Between the third quarter of 1977 and the end of 1981, real GNP grew at an average annual rate

standard of living

Gross National Product (GNP)

inflation

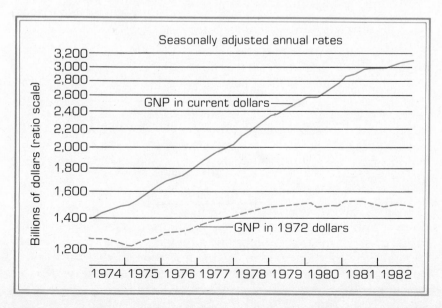

FIGURE 1-1

Gross National Product of the United States

TABLE 1-1

Purchasing power of
the consumer dollar
(1967 = $1.00)

1967	$1.00
1968	0.960
1969	0.911
1970	0.860
1971	0.824
1972	0.798
1973	0.751
1974	0.677
1975	0.620
1976	0.587
1977	0.551
1978	0.512
1979	0.459
1980	0.387
1981	0.356
1982	0.342
(April) 1983	0.339

of only 2.1 percent. Roughly $200 billion of the third trillion dollars
of GNP was accounted for by additional goods and services. That
means that about $800 billion was due simply to higher prices of
those goods and services.

A country's GNP minus net property income from abroad is its
Gross Domestic Product (GDP). Most countries use per capita GDP
(GDP divided by population) to measure the well-being of the average citizen. Figure 1-2 compares our per capita GDP with that of
several other countries.

**Disposable Personal
Income (DPI)**

Some people think that **Disposable Personal Income (DPI)** is a
more accurate measure of the people's welfare. **DPI is what remains
of our current incomes after we have paid our taxes.** Thus if a household's current income in a given year is $24,000 and it pays $4,000
in taxes, its disposable income is only $20,000.

Measures such as GNP and DPI, however, do not indicate the
quality of life in a nation. There are side effects of high production
activity that are not measured by GNP—pollution, congested cities,
rapid depletion of basic natural resources, and so on. Are we really
better off simply because we produce more goods and services or do
we also have to look beyond quantity and consider the overall quality of our lives?

There is some evidence that some of us are becoming more
conscious of and concerned with the quality of life. Some businesses,
for example, are finding it harder to transfer employees to other
areas, even if it means a promotion and a pay raise. Part of the reason,
of course, is the high cost of buying a house and the difficulty of
selling an old house. Inflation, high interest rates, and rising con-

"Sure, you're raising
my allowance. But am I
actually gaining any
purchasing power?"

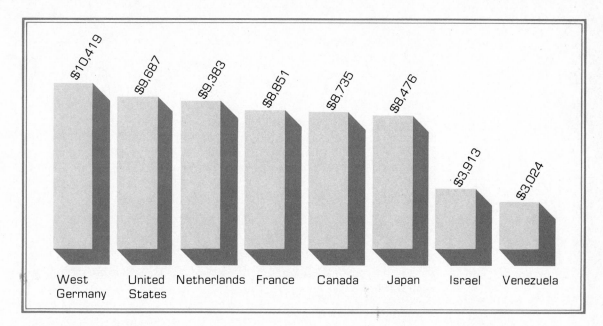

FIGURE 1-2

Per capita Gross Domestic Product for selected countries (in U.S. dollars)

struction costs all combine to make the monthly mortgage payment on a house very high.

Satisfaction of Wants

If a product or a service can satisfy a certain want, then it has **utility. Utility means usefulness in satisfying wants.** Because people have different wants, different products have different degrees of utility for different persons. Even if two people have the same want, we cannot assume that a certain product that satisfies the want would have the same utility to both people. But if a product has utility for someone, it is valuable to that person. The concept of value is very important.

Because all of us must breathe, air has value to all of us. But people ordinarily will not pay anything for it because it is too plentiful. It has *value in use* but no value in exchange. **Something has value in exchange when it can command something else in return for it. It can be swapped for something else.**

An example will help to illustrate the meaning of value in exchange. Mr. Smith has some apples and Ms. Green has some oranges. Suppose they both want apples and oranges. Mr. Smith can exchange some apples for some oranges. Ms. Green can exchange some oranges for some apples. Exchange would occur if both parties thought that they could benefit from it. Mr. Smith, since he already

utility

value in exchange

has apples, values apples less than Ms. Green, who has none. Ms. Green, since she already has oranges, values oranges less than Mr. Smith, who has none.

The exchange does *not* involve things of equal value. Mr. Smith's apples are worth less to him than the oranges he gets in return. Ms. Green's oranges are worth less to her than the apples she gets in return. In other words, how much anything is worth to you depends partly on how much of it you already have. The more you have of it, the less you want (and the less you are willing to pay) to get more units. This is the principle of *diminishing marginal utility*.

THE FACTORS OF PRODUCTION

factors of production

Limited resources must be used wisely to achieve a high level of production. **The following limited resources are the factors of production:**

- **land**
- **labor**
- **capital**
- **entrepreneurship**

The factors of production are the *inputs* of the productive system. The goods and services produced in order to satisfy human wants are the *outputs* of the system. (See Figure 1-3.)

Land

land

Land as a factor of production means all natural resources. Examples are petroleum, iron ore, and farm land. In the long run, all natural resources can run out. But, as we said earlier, with proper management some will last for a very long time (air, water, forests). Others, however, will run out (petroleum, uranium, other metals). We have a choice between thoughtless, rapid use of our resources and carefully planned use.

FIGURE 1-3

The productive system's inputs and outputs

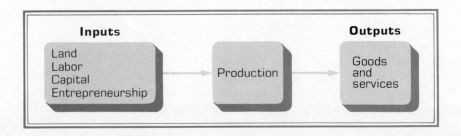

During our frontier days, as settlers used up the natural resources in one area, they moved westward to new areas where the
resources were plentiful. This type of resource use has been called
a "cowboy economy." During the last several decades, however, the
"cowboy economy" has become the "spaceship economy." A crew
on a spaceship must conserve and recycle the resources on board.
We must do the same for the natural resources here on earth!

Although the United States has a large share of many of the
most important resources, we are also the greatest user of natural
resources in the world. In the case of oil and some other materials,
we are dependent on other nations to help supply our needs.

Labor

Labor means human mental and physical effort. Much of our   labor
economic progress is the result of substituting mental effort for
physical effort. Mental effort leads to technological "breakthroughs" that result in greater output from the same or less
physical effort. If such progress enables us to get 10 percent more
energy from a ton of coal, the effect is the same as increasing the
coal supply by 10 percent.

As we said earlier, one of the major challenges in businesses
today is increasing productivity. When labor productivity remains

---

WHAT DO YOU THINK?

How Should We Deal with Technological Unemployment?

Recently we have witnessed a tremendous growth in automation. The age of the workerless factory, for example, is rapidly
approaching as computer-aided design and computer-aided
manufacturing (CAD/CAM) techniques along with computerized robots are changing our ideas and approaches to
manufacturing products. Automation is also affecting our service industries. For example, automated teller machines enable us to conduct banking activities twenty-four hours a day.

A major social problem associated with automation is
technological unemployment. People who lose their jobs as a
result of automation often face rather dim prospects for
finding suitable work elsewhere unless they receive intensive
retraining. Tens of thousands of people in the United States
are now unemployed because their skills have, in effect, become obsolete. How should we deal with technological unemployment? WHAT DO YOU THINK?

stable or decreases while wages go up, consumers must pay more for the products they buy. There is also a lot of talk about declining American productivity as a reason why some American firms have started producing in foreign countries. This trend is having an effect on American business, as we will see in Chapter 18.

Capital

capital

Capital as a factor of production means tools and machinery or anything made by humans that aids in producing and distributing goods and services. It is human-made productive capacity.
Machinery can help make labor more productive. In some cases, machinery displaces labor—machines take over the jobs of human workers. Although this is a major reason for increased productivity, it also has been a major issue in some strikes by labor unions.

An economy must produce more than it currently consumes in order to add to its capital equipment. How much of its output a country can devote to its productive facilities depends heavily on the willingness and ability of its people to postpone consumption, or save. This is a major problem in the world's poorer countries because most of the output must be consumed by the citizens. These countries can ill afford to invest in new plants and equipment when people are starving.

Lack of savings has been a problem in the United States in recent years as well. The average American, for example, saves a much smaller percentage of his or her income than the average West German or Japanese. Congress passed the Economic Recovery Tax Act in 1981 in the hope that it would enable consumers to save more money, part of which businesses could borrow to finance new investment and, thereby, increase productivity.

Entrepreneurship

entrepreneurship

entrepreneur

Bringing land, labor, and capital together and managing them productively to produce a good or service to make a profit is entrepreneurship. An entrepreneur is a person who assumes the risk of organizing and managing a business in the hope of making a profit.
People who go into business for themselves have no guarantee of earning a profit. They assume the risk of losing what they invest in their firms. Their willingness to assume the risk depends a lot on how healthy they think the economy will be in the future, the past political stability of the country, and their expected profit from undertaking the risk.

The three advertisements on these pages are based upon several of the major concepts introduced in Chapter One and discussed in greater detail in several subsequent chapters in the text.

It Makes Plain Common Sense

Conservation does.

It's common sense to conserve our precious natural resources. Natural gas, for example. With care this clean, efficient, easily-transportable fuel will continue to be the energy base of the industrial Gulf South, from today to the year 2000 and way beyond.

There's little sign that any other source of energy will take its place as the most economical fuel ever found in great quantities. Actually it was the "cheap" fuel that spurred on the Gulf South's economic development.

When gas cost a nickel per MCF (1000 cubic feet), waste was measured in pennies. Now it's measured in dollars and hundreds of dollars.

Daily, as this company buys long-term supplies of gas for distribution to the Gulf South, it faces steadily increasing prices. As much as any company, United Gas knows the cost of waste. Conserve whenever, and wherever you can. The natural gas we save today will be needed tomorrow.

This ad focuses on the need to conserve our increasingly scarce supplies of natural gas.

Rockwell International know-how:
It goes into the Space Shuttle.
It's in everything we do.

Rockwell International is NASA's prime contractor for the Space Shuttle Orbiters and their Rocketdyne main engines, and we're one of the principal contractors for the Space Transportation System's launch and landing operations.

Only a company with the know-how to combine advanced technology with outstanding engineering and management skills can successfully meet the unprecedented challenges of making space flight routine. That know-how goes into our aerospace business and into everything we do at Rockwell.

In electronics: where virtually every airliner in the free world relies on one or more of our Collins avionics systems for navigation, communications, instrumentation or flight control.

In the automotive industry: where we are addressing our customers' operating need for lower cost per mile through the application of state-of-the-art technology in such areas as materials, manufacturing and quality control processes and innovative systems designs.

In general industries: where advancements such as electronic press controls and total production systems have made our Goss presses a world leader in offset newspaper printing.

We're a $7.4 billion company where science gets down to business in four diverse areas. And that diversity has helped us achieve seven consecutive years of record earnings and impressive growth.

If you are interested in any of the products of Rockwell International or want to learn more about us, write: Rockwell International, Department 815F-18, 600 Grant Street, Pittsburgh, Pennsylvania 15219.

Rockwell International

...where science gets down to business

Aerospace/Electronics
Automotive/General Industries

This ad from InterNorth discusses the company's participation in a joint effort with several other large corporations to encourage the development of strong, market-oriented economies in the Caribbean Basin.

America's best export is America.

InterNorth and several other large American corporations have been engaged in a unique business-to-business relationship for five years in nations of the Caribbean Basin. Called Caribbean-Central American Action, it is the initiative of an international partnership to encourage development of strong, market-oriented economies.

The freedom and stability of the Western Hemisphere will depend largely upon the economic models its nations choose to adopt. The cooperative role of U.S. businesses can do much to ensure that those models provide productive freedom and a better way of life for the people of the region.

Balance-of-trade figures tell only part of the story of America's success in international business. The rest of the story is the incalculable benefit in sharing the best of America with other nations.

Americans don't export just goods and services. We also send abroad the compelling evidence of how well our system works, and the inspiring model of what free people can achieve for themselves in a free system.

That's why our InterNorth International company and other international companies take pride in sharing the best of America with the rest of the world. Our most valuable export is our nation's 200-year-old success story.

InterNorth is a diversified, energy-based corporation involved in natural gas, liquid fuels, petrochemicals, and exploration and production of gas and oil.

INTERNORTH
We work
for America.

The factors of production can be combined and used in many ways to produce many different things. The amount and variety of goods and services produced depend mainly on the way economic life is organized.

THE PURPOSE OF AN ECONOMIC SYSTEM

The purpose of an economic system is to provide a framework for satisfying human needs and wants. In our system, most productive economic activities (producing and selling goods and services) are channeled through business firms that operate in a *market* system. There are other types of economic systems, however, in which business firms play a lesser role in satisfying human needs and wants.

In ancient Greece, for example, producing goods for sale was not common. Agriculture was the main economic activity. Business activity and profit seeking were considered acceptable but lowly activities.

During the Middle Ages, the Church taught that people should not seek economic betterment but should concentrate on salvation. Although there was a great deal of business activity, it was looked upon as worldly, and often sinful.

The next major "age," as far as economic philosophy is concerned, was the age of mercantilism. **Mercantilism was an economic philosophy that advocated building strong national states (nations) from warring feudal kingdoms. A major goal was to increase the government's holdings of precious metals, such as gold and silver.** The nation with the greatest supply of precious metals was considered the most powerful. This is why mercantilist nations favored building their export trade. The greater the volume of products a country sold to people in other countries, the more gold and silver it received in payment. The citizens could be poor but as long as there was gold in the state treasury the state was considered wealthy.

Mercantilism was followed by a period of laissez-faire economics in Europe and, later, in the United States. **Laissez faire means let people do as they please. When applied to business, it means let the owners of business set the rules of competition without government regulation or control.**

This new economic philosophy began in France, although it was first presented in complete form by an Englishman, Adam Smith, in his book *The Wealth of Nations* (1776). Smith believed in free competition and capitalism. If each person sought to improve

mercantilism

laissez faire

his or her economic well-being, Smith believed, the economic well-being of the entire nation would be improved. He believed that government should interfere with the operation of individual self-interest only when it is necessary to protect society. Even today, there is a great deal of controversy in capitalist countries about government "interference" in business affairs.

capitalism

Capitalism is an economic system based on private ownership of the factors of production. The major features of capitalism are

- individualism
- private property
- profit incentive
- consumer power
- freedom to compete
- occupational freedom
- freedom of contract
- limited role of government

private enterprise

Our economic system is essentially a capitalist system based on private enterprise. **Private enterprise means private ownership of firms that make and sell goods and services.** But we do *not* have a purely capitalistic system or a purely private enterprise system. Our economic system has changed over time. It contains many of the ideas of capitalism and also certain concepts borrowed from collectivist systems. Perhaps it can be described best as a *mixed economy.* The Soviet Union's economic system also can be described as a mixture of collectivism and capitalism. Let's discuss the pure collectivist system and the pure capitalist system.

COLLECTIVISM

collectivism

In a purely collectivist system, the government controls social and economic decision making. **Collectivism means government ownership of the factors of production and government control of all economic activities.** There is little or no private property. The government determines the economy's rate of growth, the amount of investment, how resources will be used, and how goods and services will be divided among the people.

The government also uses direct means to achieve the desired results. For example, if it is decided that the output of military equipment should be increased, the government could order a reduction in the output of consumer products such as refrigerators and cars. The resources used in producing these products are shifted to producing military equipment. Wage rates and prices of products also are set by the government.

Governments in collectivist countries also practice central planning. **Central planning means that the government drafts a master plan of what it wants to accomplish and directly manages the economy to achieve the plan's goals.** Government fixes the total supply of products and services available for household consumption and distributes them to households in limited amounts and at fixed prices. There is no guarantee that the goods and services produced are what consumers want. Consumers, therefore, spend their fixed incomes on fixed amounts of fixed goods and services at fixed prices.

central planning

Collectivism is often accompanied by a totalitarian government (there is only one political party) that allows very little individual freedom to its people. The system seeks to achieve what it alleges to be the "greatest good for the greatest number of people." People contribute to the system on the basis of their abilities and receive from it on the basis of their needs. The individual is less important than the system, and the government determines each person's role in the system.

Collectivist systems seek to eliminate differences in economic welfare among people of different occupations, races, and backgrounds. A uniform standard of living is sought in order to eliminate friction among the various classes of people. Collectivist systems *in their pure form* are egalitarian systems.

CAPITALISM

Individualism

The basic idea underlying capitalism is individualism. **Individualism is the idea that the group, the society, and the government are necessary but are less important than the individual's self-determination.** The ancient Greeks valued the dignity and uniqueness of the individual. Although people lost sight of this value during some periods of history since ancient Greece, the idea of individualism remains a cornerstone of most Western democracies. It stands at the center of the Constitution of the United States.

individualism

Capitalism, as we have seen, recognizes the strength of individual self-interest. A person, if left alone, will seek economic betterment. Given certain political conditions, this leads to efficient and economical use of resources.

The full development of individual initiative required a shift in Christian philosophy from the medieval stress on spiritual matters and distrust of business to the more practical Protestant ethic. **The Protestant ethic is a tradition that stresses the value of hard work,**

the Protestant ethic

accumulation of property, and self-reliance. The most extreme form of the Protestant ethic existed in the United States during the nineteenth century, when the notion of the survival of the economically fittest was added to it. Thus the seal of Christian respectability was given to the rugged individualists who dominated America's economic growth in the latter half of the nineteenth century.

Private Property

Related to individualism is the right of *private property*. This is a person's right to acquire, use, accumulate, and dispose of things of value. Individual initiative would be greatly limited if a person could not own and accumulate property.

Although our legal system strongly defends the right of private property, private ownership of property cannot be an absolute right. In any society, certain limits must be placed on the right of own-

Egalitarianism in the United States

POINT OF VIEW

Collectivist systems are egalitarian in that they seek to equalize incomes and to achieve a uniform standard of living for their people.

Egalitarians in the United States want to do the same. They denounce laissez-faire economics and strongly criticize business. They see the government's social programs as the equalizing and leveling force in society. Through those programs, they believe, the "have nots" will have more and the "haves" will have less. This redistribution of income and wealth would continue until there is total equality. Although egalitarians are a minority in the United States, the egalitarian movement has a lot of appeal to some groups in our society.

Critics of egalitarianism argue that an egalitarian system cannot exist in a capitalist economy because equal wealth would destroy the profit incentive. In a political democracy each person has an equal voice in choosing elected officials because each person has one vote. The critics of egalitarianism question whether the voters will elect politicians who favor laws to equalize incomes because, in a capitalist system, people's incomes are not equal. These critics wonder if the United States can have a political democracy while also having a capitalist economic system.

ership so that one person's property cannot be used to hurt others. For example, a person who owns a house cannot use it to conduct illegal acts. Nor can the owner set fire to it if that would endanger other people. A balance is struck between the individual's private property rights and the society's common good. Federal, state, and local governments, for example, can use eminent domain proceedings to force property owners to sell their property when it is needed for highways or other public uses. Even in these cases the owner has the right to challenge the government's proposed action in court.

A basic aspect of private property is that people can accumulate it and use it as they please within the broad limits set by society. This concept is at the heart of the profit incentive.

Profit Incentive

One reason for our high standard of living is that many people use their private property to generate more property. They invest it to make a profit. The incentive to invest lies in the chance of getting a return—*making a profit*—from it. If people could not profit, they would have little reason to use their property in such a way. Instead, they would use up, or consume, their property.

The right to pursue profit involves *risk.* The degree of risk depends mainly on the use to which the property is put. As we'll see in Chapter 17, every year thousands of Americans go into

American business grew rapidly during the nineteenth century through the efforts of people such as Thomas Edison, Henry Ford, and Harvey Firestone

business for themselves. Many risk their accumulated savings, sell their homes, and go into debt in order to get started. They do so to try to make a profit. This process of putting money into business firms in order to try to make more money is called *investment.*

Investment is necessary for a nation's economic growth. It makes possible all the new goods and services that appear on the market every year. It also creates jobs and provides tax revenues for governments. **Capital formation is another way to describe the process of investment. Capital formation is the process of adding to the productive capacity of an economy.**

Certain institutions have been developed to help this process of capital formation. The corporation, which is discussed in Chapter 3, helps to make possible capital formation on a large scale. IBM, General Motors, General Electric, and American Telephone and Telegraph are examples of multibillion dollar corporations. Chapter 14 discusses banks and other financial institutions that help in this process.

capital formation

Consumer Power

Unless a firm can cultivate a group of customers, it will not survive. It must have buyers for its goods or services. In our system the consumer enjoys a position of great influence. **The consumer power concept means that, because consumers are free to do business with whomever they choose, businesses must consider consumer needs and wants in making decisions.** By doing this, businesses may earn a profit. Consumers, therefore, decide the economic fate of a firm through their individual decisions to buy from one firm or another. This is another way in which individualism is so important in our economic system. (See Table 1-2.)

consumer power

Consumerism has become a deep-seated force in our business system. **Basically, this movement is concerned with enhancing consumers' power relative to that of sellers.** Examples of consumerist concerns are product safety and truth in advertising. Several government agencies have been set up to protect consumers. Examples are the Consumer Product Safety Commission, the National Highway Traffic Safety Administration, the Food and Drug Administration, and the Federal Trade Commission's Bureau of Consumer Protection.

consumerism

Perhaps you have heard the concept of consumer power expressed in terms of "casting dollar votes in the marketplace." Firms that do not provide want-satisfying goods and services will not receive "dollar votes" from consumers. Consumers will not buy what these firms offer for sale and they will lose out in the struggle for customers.

Collectivism	*Capitalism*
1. Government practices central planning.	1. Individual consumers make independent choices by exercising their consumer power.
2. Central planning determines how resources will be used.	2. Consumer choices determine how resources will be used.
3. Resources are allocated to achieve the goals set by government planners.	3. Resources are allocated in response to decisions made by individual consumers.
4. Government planners determine • what will be produced • how it will be produced • how much will be produced • how the products and services will be distributed	4. Consumers influence • what will be produced • how it will be produced • how much will be produced • how the products and services will be distributed

TABLE 1-2

Government versus consumer control over economic decision making

Businesses, of course, do what they can to influence our buying decisions. American firms, for example, spend billions of dollars every year on advertising to inform us about their products and to persuade us to buy them.

Freedom to Compete

People who are free to compete can risk their private property in the hope of earning a profit. Within very broad limits, a person can go into any business, however much the existing competitors may like to keep the field to themselves.

Competition among firms benefits consumers and firms. For consumers, it usually results in higher-quality products, greater variety, better service, and lower prices. For firms, it provides an incentive to remain efficient and please their customers. If a firm does not, it may lose customers to rival firms.

Occupational Freedom

Still another aspect of capitalism is the freedom of occupational choice. You are free to start up a new firm—go into business for yourself—or to work for someone else. Individuals make this choice guided by their own best economic interests and within the limits of their talents and education.

In some economic systems, however, central planning determines the need for persons to fill various job categories. People are trained for and assigned to those jobs. The choice of a job is made by the government, not the individual.

Freedom of Contract

Freedom of contract enables a person to enter into contracts with other people. Examples of contracts include installment contracts, such as those involved in financing the purchase of a new car by making monthly payments; insurance policies; apartment leases; employment contracts; and partnership agreements. As long as the contract is legal, it is protected by law and is legally enforceable in court. We will discuss contracts in greater detail in Chapter 19.

Limited Role of Government

Americans generally dislike excessive government interference in their personal and business lives. Although what is considered to be government interference has changed over the years, the basic tradition of economic freedom still is very much a part of our system.

FIGURE 1-4

The purpose of an economic system

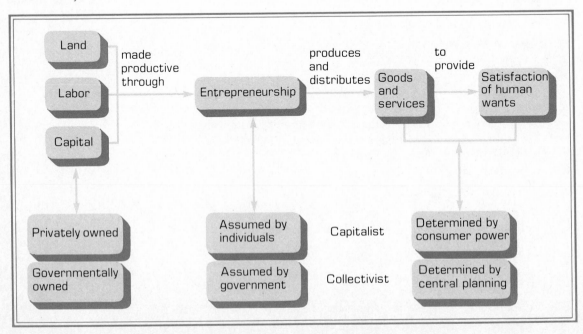

In general, the government is permitted to step in only when the welfare of citizens is threatened by business action or by the failure of business to act. We generally accept this regulatory role of government in the economy, but there is a difference of opinion over the manner in which government should exercise its regulatory role. Examples of government action from recent years include dealing with inflation, unemployment, energy, and health insurance. As we will see in this book, there has been considerable government deregulation of business in recent years, beginning in 1978 with the deregulation of the airline industry.

Figure 1-4 depicts the purpose of an economic system. Notice the contrasts between the capitalist and collectivist systems even though both systems seek to cope with the same economic problem. Table 1-3 outlines the basic ideas underlying the two economic systems.

Capitalism

1. The individual is of primary importance
2. Private property
3. Profit incentive
4. Consumer power
5. Freedom to compete
6. Occupational freedom
7. Freedom of contract
8. Limited role of government

Collectivism

1. The individual is less important than the system, which seeks equality for all of its citizens
2. No private property
3. No recognition of profit
4. Central control over social and economic decision making
5. Competition results in economic waste
6. Central planning determines the need for various types of occupations
7. Little freedom of contract
8. The government is the primary decision maker

TABLE 1-3

Basic ideas underlying capitalism and collectivism

MODERN COLLECTIVISM

Just as our economic system is not purely capitalist, neither are the economic systems of most communist countries purely collectivist. Pure collectivism involves setting exact rates of growth, exact allocations of capital, and exact prices.

In some forms of collectivism, instead of setting an exact wage rate or the exact price at which a product will sell, planners set minimum and maximum levels of wages and prices. Market forces, such as supply and demand, determine the exact level of prices within the range set by the minimum and maximum.

In Hungary, many farm workers farm small plots of land after they leave their regular jobs working on state and cooperative farms, and can keep any profit they make from farming these plots. Likewise, although the government owns all businesses, there are some examples of profit-making ventures. Some small restaurants, for example, are managed by people who pay a monthly fee to the government for use of the buildings and equipment. The managers, however, can keep any profit they make after meeting those expenses and paying their employees' wages.

In Cuba, government-owned food markets sell food at prices that are fixed at the level they were in the 1960s and supplies are rationed among consumers. Recently, however, the government has permitted farmers to sell crops in excess of their government mandated quotas on their own at prices that are basically determined by market forces of supply and demand.

Polish workers formed the free and independent Solidarity union federation in 1980 after the nation had experienced numerous labor strikes. Strikes, of course, are illegal in Soviet Bloc countries and many people feared that the Soviet Union would invade Poland to suppress the union. Among the major goals of Solidarity was an agreement with the government that would give self-management to local workers' councils at state-owned enterprises. Instead of having plant managers at those enterprises appointed by the government, workers wanted to choose their own managers.

MODERN CAPITALISM

The socioeconomic systems of some Western European nations can be classified as social democracies. These nations have adopted some rather severe restrictions of the classic capitalist freedoms. In Great Britain the practice of medicine and ownership of certain basic industries such as coal and steel are in the hands of the government. The French and Italian governments own auto manufacturing companies. Other economic activities also are highly regulated by government in many social democracies. Advertising may be severely restricted and consumption of some products is controlled by rationing. Taxation is much heavier than it is in the United States.

France's socialist President Mitterrand was elected in 1981. In his presidential campaign, Mitterrand promised to nationalize France's big banks and firms in a number of industries such as chemicals, electronics, aircraft, and steel. This marked the biggest effort of any government in Europe since the end of World War II to take over (buy out) privately owned businesses. It was undertaken in the hope of stimulating economic growth, increasing employment, and lowering the inflation rate.

Even in the United States, we are far from the pure ideal of capitalism. The basic belief in individualism has probably eroded somewhat during the past four or five decades. The Great Depression of the 1930s caused many Americans to rethink their basic distrust of "big government." As we will see later in our book, many laws were passed during the 1930s limiting what businesses can do. Labor legislation made it illegal for employers to fire or threaten to fire employees who try to organize a labor union, and it also set the normal working week of 40 hours. Other legislation was aimed at helping small business survive in the competitive struggle with big businesses, notably small grocery stores and huge supermarket chains. Unemployment benefits and the entire social security program sprang from the depression era.

Private property still is at the heart of our economic system but there are many laws pertaining to the use of private property. For example, a firm that serves the general public, such as a restaurant, cannot refuse to serve a customer because of race or national origin. Zoning laws also regulate the use of private property.

What about the tax, inheritance, and estate law changes in 1981? What about welfare reform? Some people wonder if the progressive federal income tax damages our individual initiative. Under our taxation system, your tax rate rises as your income rises. Did passage of the tax cut mean that some people believed that high tax rates may reduce the willingness of some people to work overtime or to invest their money in the hope of earning a profit? Likewise, were inheritance and estate taxes cut because of their potentially negative effect on the incentive to accumulate property? Were welfare reforms made because some people believe that a big welfare system can reduce some people's incentive to work?

What about consumerism? If consumers have so much power, would consumer affairs be such an issue in our system? Would government agencies and commissions have to be in the business of consumer protection?

What about freedom to compete? Even more basic, what is

competition? In some cases, the law protects small and inefficient firms against competition from bigger and more efficient firms. Is this desirable?

The Small Business Administration (SBA) was set up by the federal government to give various types of financial and management assistance to small firms. Should our government be in the business of helping people go into business? Should the biggest customer in the world, the United States government, limit its choice of suppliers in some buying situations to only small firms?

What about occupational freedom? Our government and private businesses sponsor programs to develop our nation's human resources. In some cases, the government grants tax incentives to firms that hire disadvantaged or handicapped workers. Is this desirable? How far should government go in passing laws that relate to job safety and health?

Freedom of contract also has come under more government regulation. Does the federal minimum wage increase unemployment of marginally qualified workers? Does the minimum wage make it harder for a teenager to find a part-time job? In some states new employees are required to join a labor union if there is one representing the employer's workforce whether or not the new employee wants to join the union.

Finally, how limited is the role of government in our economy today? Some of the biggest economic problems facing us in recent years have been high interest rates, lagging productivity, inflation, and unemployment. The government's role in seeking solutions to these problems is a major one, although it is dictated by the voters. Over the past several decades, consumers and business people have tended to look more and more to the government to solve economic problems.

There is little doubt that many forms of government regulation and taxation further distinguish the United States today from the capitalist ideal. Capitalism has been modified at least as much as collectivism since 1930. The process of modification is ongoing and dynamic. Thus in recent years we have seen considerable deregulation in the oil, banking, communications, trucking, railroad, and airline industries. The pricing mechanism, which we will discuss in the next chapter, is being relied upon to a greater extent than in past decades to keep our system working.

WHAT IS BUSINESS?

We purposely have put off defining *business* until we had developed some of the basic ideas that underlie our type of economic system. **In our economic system, business is all profit-directed eco-nomic activities that are organized and directed to provide goods and services.**

Notice the term *profit* in our definition. Profit is the basic motivator of business activities in our system. It is the major driving force. **To business people, profit is what remains of the sales reve-nues they receive from selling their goods or services after they deduct the costs incurred in producing and selling those goods and services.**

Sales Revenues	$150,000
Less Expenses	− 125,000
Profit (before tax)	$ 25,000

Businesses earn sales revenues by selling want-satisfying prod-ucts and services to their customers. A firm can survive over the long run only if it continues to satisfy and serve its customers. This allows the firm to make a profit while serving its customers. Mean-while, the firm is also serving society. For example, profitable firms pay taxes that help support public education and county hospitals. As we will see later in the book, businesses must be *managed effec-tively* to survive the competition of rival firms.

Many businesses produce and sell tangible (physical) products like cameras, cars, furniture, trucks, and farm machinery. Some firms, however, provide intangible services. Examples are the Met-ropolitan Life Insurance Company, Holiday Inn, Hertz, and United Air Lines. The services sector of our economy has been growing rapidly during recent decades.

Finally there are many organizations in our economy that en-gage in activities very similar to those of business firms. The big difference between them and business firms is that they are not seeking to earn a profit for owners. Examples of these nonprofit organizations are charities, political parties, state universities and colleges, and government units, such as police and fire departments and the Department of Defense.

THE POSTINDUSTRIAL SERVICES ECONOMY

During the 1950s and 1960s, the United States economy began undergoing a basic change from an industrial economy based on the manufacture of tangible products to a *postindustrial economy* based on the creation of intangible services. The effects of this change still are being felt in our economy.

Improving
Productivity in
the Postindustrial
Services Economy

AUTHORS' COMMENTARY

As we have seen in this chapter, a lot of attention has been paid in recent years to increasing the productivity of American businesses. Computerized robots are increasingly being used to improve productivity in a variety of manufacturing operations in many industries.

Basic manufacturing activities, however, are accounting for a declining proportion of the GNP in our postindustrial services economy. If the overall productivity of our labor force is to increase, more attention will have to focus on non-manufacturing operations. For example, some progress has been made in automating the work of clerical workers in offices. We can expect growing use of products like desk-top word and data processing terminals and electronic mail systems by clerical workers. Beyond that, we can expect greater focus on improving the productivity of executives and professionals like attorneys, accountants, and physicians through office automation.

The tremendous growth of our economy during the 1950s and 1960s contributed to record high levels of disposable personal income, and American consumers began buying huge amounts of intangible services. Recreation, entertainment, travel, and other service industries began growing faster than many of our manufacturing industries. One of the most dramatic examples of this growth in service industries is the fantastic spread of fast-food restaurants, such as Burger King and Kentucky Fried Chicken.

We will discuss the implications of this shift from an industrial to a postindustrial economy at several places in this book.

SUMMARY AND LOOK AHEAD

Economic systems help us to satisfy our unlimited wants with our limited resources. Because our wants are so varied and because our resources in many instances have become more scarce, the economic problem today is more complex than it was in the past.

Several basic concepts (utility, value, specialization, exchange, standard of living, diminishing marginal utility, and the factors of production) are relevant in any type of economic system, whether it is a capitalist or a collectivist economic system.

The major ideas underlying the U.S. private-enterprise system are individualism, private property, profit incentive, consumer power, freedom to compete, occupational freedom, freedom of contract, and the limited role of government.

The type of economic system most unlike the private-enterprise, or capitalist, system is the collectivist system. In this type of system, private property and the other institutions and ideas of the private enterprise system are largely absent. Central planning by the government replaces individual freedom and initiative.

Most economic systems in the world today fall somewhere between the two extremes of pure capitalism and pure collectivism. Our system has adopted some collectivist ideas. Our social security system, for example, would not exist in a purely capitalist system. However, collectivist systems also have adopted some capitalist ideas. The use of the profit incentive to get more production from the Hungarian farmer is an example.

Business, in our economy, includes all profit-directed economic activities that are organized and directed to provide the goods and services that contribute to our standard of living.

In the next chapter we will see how people use the freedoms provided by our economic system to form business firms, and we will discuss why business firms exist.

FOR REVIEW . . .

1. Has the economic problem become more complex in modern times than it was in earlier times? Explain.

2. Discuss the processes of specialization and exchange and their relationship to the economic problem.

3. Distinguish between needs and wants.

4. Should comparisons of the standards of living in different countries be based on per capita GNP? Explain.

5. What is the basic purpose of a) a capitalist economic system and b) a collectivist economic system?

6. List and define the factors of production.

7. List and discuss the major features of capitalism.

8. In what ways does pure capitalism differ from pure collectivism?

9. In what ways has our economic system changed over the last century?

10. Capital formation is necessary for fuller economic development. How does it occur in the absence of private property and profit incentive?

11. What is the basic motivation for business firms to produce want-satisfying products and services for consumers?

. . . FOR DISCUSSION

1. How do you as an individual cope with the economic problem?

2. Should future generations of people be considered when we cope with the economic problem?

3. Individual initiative is important in our system. What factors determine a person's initiative?

4. Does consumer power guarantee that consumer welfare is maximized?

5. One of the features of capitalism is freedom to compete. When should limitations be placed on this freedom?

6. What is profit? What determines how much profit a business firm will make?

INCIDENTS

The Cost of Clean Air

The Clean Air Act was passed in 1967. Amendments in 1970 and 1977 raised air quality standards even higher. As the air becomes cleaner, the cost of making it even cleaner increases. For example, one study conducted for the Environmental Protection Agency showed that it costs twenty-six cents per kilogram to remove 90 percent of the pollutants from a carbon steel plant. To remove 99 percent, it would cost $32.20 per kilogram.

QUESTIONS

1. Does this incident give any hint of an economic problem for business? Explain.

2. Does this incident give any hint of an economic problem for government? Explain.

3. How does the Clean Air Act affect the quality of life in the United States?

4. When the Clean Air Act came up for renewal in 1981, many firms were having financial problems because of high interest rates, recession, and foreign competition. Suppose you directed a firm that was spending millions of dollars to reduce the amount of pollutants it released into the air. Would you have favored revising the Clean Air Act's rules to make them less stringent? Why or why not?

Chrysler's Federally Guaranteed Loans

Chrysler Corporation incurred operating losses in many recent years. In 1980, for example, the firm lost $1.7 billion; in 1979 it lost $1.1 billion.

Chrysler, however, succeeded in getting $1.5 billion in federally guaranteed loans in June, 1980 and another $400 million in February, 1981. The guarantees were necessary in order for Chrysler to avoid bankruptcy.

QUESTIONS

1. Should the federal government guarantee loans to firms that are having trouble staying in business?

2. Why do you think the federal government decided to make the loan guarantees?

3. Could this happen in a purely capitalistic economic system? Explain.

A Changing French Economy

In 1982, one year after France's President Mitterrand was elected, changes were being made in his cabinet. In an effort to make French industries more competitive with those in Japan and the United States, the socialist government decided to make a major commitment to technological development.

For example, the minister of research and technology was also given the post of minister of industry. With nationalization of basic industries achieved, the industry minister was made responsible for restructuring those state-owned industries. He also was made responsible for disbursing massive government research and development funds, in addition to disbursing outright government subsidies to the nationalized industries.

At a June 1982 conference of economists in Paris, the minister expressed the need for the democratization of labor (see the *What Do You Think?* box on page 80 of the text) and the need to reinvigorate the entrepreneurial spirit in France.

QUESTIONS

1. Has the French economy become more collectivistic or more capitalistic since President Mitterrand's election? Explain.

2. On page 25 of the text, we said that one of the reasons the Mitterrand government undertook the nationalization program was to stimulate economic growth. How do you think the minister of industry, research, and technology can help in stimulating economic growth?

3. Is the concept of central planning being implemented by the Mitterrand government? Explain.

4. Do government research and development funds and outright government subsidies to nationalized industries contribute to capital formation in the French economy? Why or why not?

5. Do you think that the Mitterrand government is taking actions that will reinvigorate the entrepreneurial spirit in France? Discuss.

CHAPTER 2

The Market Economy and the Business Firm

OBJECTIVES:

After reading this chapter, you should be able to

1. Explain what a market economy is and how it works.
2. Define the law of demand and explain why it is valid.
3. Identify and describe the major factors that influence the overall demand for goods and services in an economy.
4. Define the law of supply and explain why it is valid.
5. Explain the major factors that influence the overall supply of goods and services in an economy.
6. Draw a demand curve and a supply curve and explain the significance of their intersection on a graph.
7. Distinguish between a change in demand and a change in quantity demanded.
8. Distinguish between a change in supply and a change in quantity supplied.
9. Discuss the importance of profit opportunity to business firms.
10. Explain why business owners assume risk.

KEY CONCEPTS:
Look for these terms as you read the chapter

market economy

price

demand

law of demand

discretionary income

real income

supply

law of supply

demand curve

supply curve

business opportunity

risk

In our market economy, business firms seek to identify market opportunity and to use their resources and capabilities to profit from it. Apple Computer, Inc., the personal computer company founded in 1975, is a good example. Steven Jobs and Stephen Wozniak, the entrepreneurs who started the company, recognized opportunity in the computer field despite the fact that the industry was dominated by giants like IBM. Jobs and Wozniak started the personal computer industry.

Recognizing market opportunity is an important requirement for business success. Business people must remain alert to recognize it. Consider, for example, how changes in our lifestyles can create problems and opportunities for business. Color TV was a growth industry during much of the 1960s but growth slowed toward the end of the decade. Most Americans who wanted and could afford a color TV had bought one and were spending their "entertainment dollars" away from home—dining out, going to theaters, traveling, and so on.

Recently, high inflation, advances in technology, and the higher price of gasoline have been causing many Americans to spend more money on in-home entertainment. Thus the TV set is becoming more than a receiver for network and local programming. This change did not go unnoticed. Atari, Home Box Office, and marketers of video cassette recorders and video disc players recognized a market opportunity in our changing lifestyle.

Because there are not enough resources to satisfy our unlimited wants, we must choose what will and what will not be produced. These choices determine how resources will be used. Under our economic system, independent decisions made by consumers and producers guided by the price system determine how resources are allocated.

The business firm is the basic building block for the production of goods and services in our system. Most economic activity is channeled through business firms, which gather and organize resources for production. They do so in the hope of making a profit. In other words, businesses seek to make a profit in our market economy by supplying products that their present and potential customers want. Doing so, however, requires that they be willing to assume the risk of going into business. Let's begin with a look at how a market economy works.

THE MARKET ECONOMY

The term *market* has many meanings. To some people it might mean the place where they shop for groceries. To other people it might mean the stock market. To a manufacturer of women's dresses it might mean the current level of demand for dresses.

In this chapter we will think of a market as a set of economic forces (supply and demand) which together form a price. Supply forces tend to bring goods and services into production. Demand forces tend to result in consumption of those goods and services. Supply and demand interact to form a price. Since markets play a large role in our economy, we say we have a market economy.

market economy   **A market economy is an economic system in which prices determine how resources will be allocated and how the goods and services produced will be distributed.** Markets exist to form prices.

Prices

Prices induce or limit production and consumption. Were it not for the price consumers have to pay to get things, they could consume as much as they want. Since consumers have limited income and limited buying power, however, they must limit the amount they buy. The supplier of an item, on the other hand, would have no incentive to supply it without being paid for it. Price, therefore, must be at a level such that some producers are willing to produce goods and services for sale and some consumers are willing to buy them for consumption.

In a very simple economy, prices as we know them would not exist. One person might trade potatoes for oranges produced by someone else. The two traders would agree on a rate of exchange of potatoes for oranges. This simple type of trading is called *barter*. Goods and services are exchanged directly for other goods and services. Barter still exists. Some airlines that are short of cash have bartered airline tickets for jet fuel. Individuals also sometimes barter goods and services in order to avoid the need for cash transactions.

Nevertheless, money facilitates or simplifies exchange by serving as a medium of exchange; it is the common measure of value for potatoes and oranges and thousands of other goods and services. **Price, therefore, is the quantity of money (or other goods and services) that is paid in exchange for something else.**   price

All economic systems must have a way of determining

- which goods and services will be produced
- how much of each will be produced
- the methods of producing them
- how they will be divided among the people

In a market economy these decisions are made through a pricing process in markets. The prices of different goods and services determine how resources will be allocated among alternative ends. Those prices also determine the kinds of goods and services that will be produced, their quantities, and the amounts that are made available to customers. A market economy, therefore, also can be called a *price system.* To understand how all this works, let's study the forces of demand and supply.

Demand

As we have seen, the basic human needs are for food, clothing, and shelter. We express these needs when we demand to buy a can of Green Giant peas, a red coat, or a new house.

Because your income is limited, you must choose which wants you will try to satisfy. Price helps you choose. By comparing prices of different things, you decide how much of item A must be given up to get one unit of item B. Price is the yardstick for comparisons. It is a major guide to production and consumption decisions.

In a modern economy new wants are always appearing and new goods and services are always being offered to satisfy those wants. Suppliers of these goods and services try to get consumers to spend money on them. In this way the consumer's desire for want satisfaction and the supplier's desire for profit are supposed to be satisfied.

In business demand means much more than desire on the part of a would-be buyer. For example, perhaps everyone in your class would like to own a new Corvette. But General Motors will not rush into the production of Corvettes for you and your classmates, because GM is concerned with demand in the economic sense, not desire by itself.

demand

Demand for a good or a service exists when there are people who

- **desire the good or service**
- **have the buying power to purchase it**
- **are willing to part with some buying power in order to buy it**

Each of these requirements must be met in order for effective demand (or a market) to exist for a good or a service.

As we will see in the marketing chapters, firms do what they can to increase the demand for their goods and services. They use advertising to build desire and willingness to spend. They often offer credit to increase consumer buying power.

For most products a greater number of units are demanded at a lower price than at a higher price. One of the reasons for this is the principle of diminishing marginal utility, mentioned in Chapter 1. A third pair of boots, for example, gives you less additional satisfaction than the first one did. You may be better off with three pair of boots than with only one, but you probably are not three times better off. As additional units lose something (marginal utility, or usefulness), you are willing to pay less and less to get them. One reason is that your buying power is limited. **The inverse relationship between**

law of demand

price and quantity demanded is the "law of demand"—as price goes up, the quantity demanded goes down.

We can talk about demand from different points of view. The overall demand for all goods and services in an economy is called *aggregate demand*. We also can refer to the total demand for a specific product class, such as the demand for cars. Narrowing it further, we could discuss the demand for a specific brand, such as Chevrolet Corvettes. An especially important distinction is *industry* and *firm demand*. The demand for cars is an example of industry demand, and the demand for GM cars is an example of firm demand.

The concept of demand, however, involves more than a relationship between quantity and price. Among the many nonprice factors underlying demand are

- buying power
- willingness to spend
- population changes
- population shifts

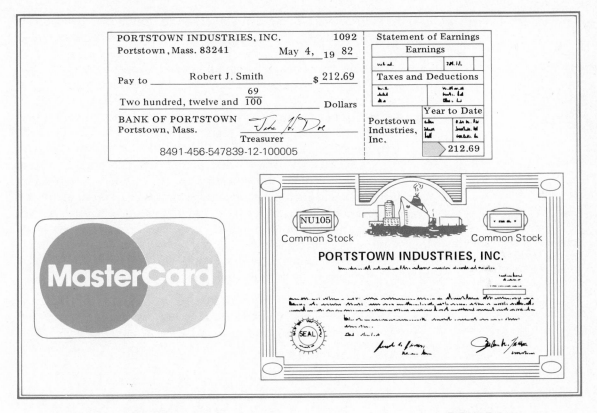

FIGURE 2-1

Current income, credit, and accumulated wealth are the three major sources of buying power

- changes in tastes and cultural values
- presence and price of substitute goods and services

Buying Power

As Figure 2-1 shows, buying power comes from

- current income
- accumulated wealth
- credit

Current income is the major source of buying power for Americans. Your current income is your salary or wages plus interest on savings accounts, rental income, dividends on stock, and interest on bonds. But you cannot spend it all because you have to pay taxes. Disposable income is your current income minus the taxes you pay. **Discretionary income is what remains of your disposable income after you have bought your necessities.** It is available to spend on "luxuries." **Finally your real income is your income expressed in terms of buying power; it is your income adjusted for the decline in buying power due to inflation.** Suppose your income doubles over a

discretionary income

real income

10-year period. Unless you could buy twice as much at the end of the period as you could at the beginning, your real income did not really double.

Table 2-1 shows that the median U.S. family earned an estimated $23,895 before taxes in 1982. The corresponding figure in 1972 was $11,152. When we adjust the $23,895 figure for federal income tax, social security tax, and inflation, it becomes $8,543. This is disposable income expressed in real terms.

Our federal income tax also has a big effect on the way income is *distributed* in our country. The income tax takes money from higher-income people and redistributes it, through government spending, to lower-income people. This results in less demand for luxuries and more demand for basic food, clothing, and shelter. Aggregate consumer demand, however, increases because people with lower incomes tend to spend a greater proportion of their income than people with higher incomes. People with higher incomes tend to save a greater proportion of their income.

TABLE 2-1

Median family incomes before and after direct federal taxes and inflation 1972–1984

Year	Median family income[a]	Direct Federal taxes			After-tax income	
		Income tax[b]	Social security	Total	Current dollars	1971 dollars[c]
1972	$11,152	$ 982	$ 468	$1,450	$ 9,702	$9,702
1973	11,895	1,098	632	1,730	10,165	9,569
1974	13,004	1,267	761	2,028	10,976	9,311
1975	14,156	1,172	825	1,997	12,159	9,451
1976	15,016	1,388	878	2,266	12,750	9,370
1977	15,949	1,466	933	2,399	13,550	9,355
1978	17,318	1,717	1,048	2,765	14,553	9,332
1979	19,048	1,881	1,168	3,049	15,999	9,221
1980	20,586	2,163	1,262	3,425	17,161	8,712
1981	22,410[d]	2,477	1,490	3,967	18,443	8,483
1982	23,895[d]	2,502[e]	1,601[e]	4,103	19,792	8,543
1983	25,329[d]	2,522[e]	1,697[e]	4,219	21,110	8,596
1984	26,848[d]	2,616[e]	1,799[e]	4,415	22,433	8,617

[a]Median income for all families with one earner employed full-time, year-round.
[b]Married couple filing joint return, two children.
[c]Adjusted by Consumer Price Index of the Bureau of Labor Statistics.
[d]Estimated by Tax Foundation.
[e]Assumes no change in current law.
Source: U.S. Department of Commerce, Bureau of Labor Statistics; Treasury Department, Internal Revenue Service; and Tax Foundation computations.

Accumulated wealth can be liquid or nonliquid. Liquid wealth can be converted quickly into a known amount of cash for making purchases. Money in regular savings accounts is an example. It can be withdrawn easily and quickly to buy or make down payments on major purchases such as homes, cars, and home appliances. United States savings bonds are another example of liquid wealth.

An example of nonliquid wealth is the equity in a home, the difference between its current market value and what is owed on the mortgage. You can look at your bank book and determine how much money you have on deposit. It is much harder to put a dollar value on the equity in a house because its true current market value must be determined. Loan companies, banks, and savings and loan associations often are willing to grant loans to people on the basis of their equity in their homes. This frees this nonliquid wealth for current use.

There are two basic types of credit. *Installment credit* involves making regular monthly payments (installments) on credit purchases. It is very important in the purchase of consumer durables such as cars. *Noninstallment credit* involves paying in full for your charge purchases at the end of the credit period, usually thirty days. Both types of credit have expanded greatly in our economy during recent years, especially installment credit. In fact, ours often is referred to as a credit economy. Without credit, millions of Americans would have a much lower standard of living.

Willingness to Spend

How much income and other types of buying power people have affects their ability to buy. But we also have to consider their willingness to buy. In general, consumers are more willing to buy when they have confidence in the economy. When they lack confidence, they tend to spend less and to save more. During recent years, however, this general pattern has not always held true.

Periods of low consumer confidence have been accompanied by high levels of consumer spending. Part of the explanation for this is the very high rate of inflation during recent years. When consumers expect inflation to continue, they reason that tomorrow's prices will be even higher than today's. This is called *inflationary psychology*. Saving money loses much of its appeal. Since the buying power of the dollar declines, many consumers prefer to buy products they hope will increase in value. Thus they may buy jewelry, furs, silverware, antiques, and fine china. They look upon these purchases as investments that will increase in value.

On the other hand, the onset of a recession is often accompanied by a decline in consumer willingness to spend. Consumers postpone some purchases, particularly purchases of durable goods, in

Price Changes and
Our Lifestyles

AUTHORS' COMMENTARY

Changes in the prices of goods and services can affect our lifestyles and the way firms do business. Consider the housing industry. During much of the 1960s and 1970s, inflation and fixed interest rates on long-term mortgages helped make the purchase of a new home a good investment. Interest charges on mortgages are deductible for federal income tax purposes and homebuyers reasoned they were paying a fixed monthly note for an asset that was increasing fairly rapidly in value.

Between 1971 and 1981 the median price of newly constructed one-family homes rose from $25,000 to $68,000, an increase of 172 percent. Mortgage interest rates reached record high levels in 1981. A typical $60,000 mortgage at 18 percent interest meant the homebuyer had a monthly note of $904. New housing starts fell to the lowest level in years.

Savings and loan associations were developing new financing plans to help would-be home buyers. Instead of a fixed interest rate, many started offering variable interest rate mortgages. The hope was that as inflation and high interest rates came down, the mortgage interest rate the homebuyer

the hope that prices will come down in the future. This contributes to lengthening the recession because consumer spending accounts for two-thirds of our gross national product.

Population Changes

Population changes also affect demand. Sellers of essential goods and services tend to experience increased demand when the population increases. A declining birthrate, on the other hand, means a decline in the demand for baby food. Changes in the age distribution of the population also affect demand. For example, the proportion of children and teenagers in our population will decline during the coming decades. This means a decline in demand for child-oriented toys and elementary and secondary education. A decline in the number of teenagers could mean declining sales of soft drinks because teenagers are the biggest consumers of soft drinks.

The proportion of people 65 years old and older will increase. This means increased demand for digestive aids, decaffeinated coffee, and bran cereals. By the year 2000 the median age of Americans is projected to be 35, up from 28 in 1970 and 30 in 1980. (The median is the middle number of a group of numbers ranked from the small-

paid would be reduced. Homebuilders also searched for new ways to cut building costs. Assembly-line construction methods were replacing many on-site construction activities. Meanwhile, zoning officials in many communities were having to rethink their minimum square-footage requirements as many of the newer homes were much smaller than the typical home of past years.

Homebuilders also noticed some changes in the housing market. Some people were buying and renovating older homes instead of buying new homes. Some people who could not afford to buy their own homes were teaming up with other unrelated individuals to buy homes and share ownership. Some realtors referred to the market for such houses as the "mingles market."

Whereas the aging of the baby boom generation—those people born between 1946 and 1964—was expected to contribute to a big increase in homebuyers during the 1980s, many of these people were unable to buy homes because of the high prices and interest rates. Some people who could afford new housing were buying lower-cost mobile homes instead of conventional homes. A growing number of young people decided to live with their parents.

est to the largest.) Perhaps you also have noticed that older people are being featured more in commercials and advertisements.

Changes in the ethnic makeup of the population also affect demand. Recently, the growing number of Hispanics in our population has increased the demand for Hispanic-oriented goods and services. Hispanic foods are appearing in supermarkets and Spanish-language TV programs are becoming commonplace in certain areas.

Population Shifts

Population shifts also can affect demand. During recent years there has been some movement of people and industry from the older industrialized East-North Central and Mid-Atlantic states to the Sunbelt states in the South and Southwest. This regional shift is increasing the demand for outdoor recreation equipment and housing in the Sunbelt states. There also are major shifts within our Standard Metropolitan Statistical Areas (SMSAs). An SMSA is an area that includes a central city (or twin cities) with a population of 50,000 or more and the surrounding counties that are economically and socially integrated with it.

In many SMSAs, the central cities are losing population to their suburbs. In fact over half of the people in our SMSAs now live in the suburbs. This trend has increased the demand for lawn-care products, outdoor swimming pools, and tennis courts. At the same time it has decreased sales for the merchants in downtown shopping areas. In very recent years, however, there is evidence that some people, especially older persons, are moving back into our central cities, many of which are experiencing increased demand for medical services, nursing homes, and apartment buildings as a result. Some younger people also are buying and modernizing older homes in central cities. The increase in demand for do-it-yourself books, tools, and clinics is due, in part, to this shift. Finally some SMSA dwellers are moving to smaller towns and rural areas to escape big-city problems such as high taxes, congestion, crime, and pollution. The demand for home canning equipment, rural land, and pick-up trucks has increased as a result.

Changes in Tastes and Cultural Values

Changes in consumer tastes and cultural values also can affect demand. Recently, the demand for products like beef, sugar, and tennis racquets has declined. Many people who used to consume large quantities of sugar and beef have reduced their consumption, in part because of reports that those products allegedly contribute to health problems. Tennis has lost some of its popularity while racquetball has gained popularity.

The growing acceptance of a singles lifestyle has increased the demand for goods and services designed for the "singles market." Examples include Campbell's Soup for One and housemate matching agencies for singles who want to share living space.

The rising divorce rate creates two households in place of one and increases the demand for housing and household appliances. The women's rights movement has increased the demand for child-care centers, business clothing, and convenience foods. We will discuss other changes in our cultural values and how they affect business in Chapter 20.

Presence and Price of Substitutes

Finally the presence of substitute products and services and their prices can affect the demand for a product or a service. The demand for dry cleaning, butter, train tickets, tooth powder, and shaving soap declined when new clothing fabrics, margarine, air travel, toothpaste, and electric shavers were introduced. There have been some big shifts in demand for some goods and services in recent years due to shortages of some basic resources and big price jumps. The high cost of electricity and natural gas has increased the demand for

Videotape/computer introduction centers are one of many new services catering to singles

wood-burning stoves and home-insulation materials. In some cases, firms that market products that are in short supply have, in effect, to ration them among their customers in an effort to reduce demand.

Supply

The other half of the price system is supply. **The supply of a good or a service results from the effort of producers. The quantity supplied is the number of units of a good or a service that producers will offer for sale at a certain price.**

supply

In most cases, a greater number of units will be offered for sale at a higher price than at a lower price. A higher price leads producers to supply more units than a lower price would because they perceive more profit potential. Price and quantity vary in the same direction. **This is the "law of supply"—as price goes up, the quantity supplied goes up.**

law of supply

Like the concept of demand, the concept of supply involves much more than a relationship between quantity and price. Among the many factors underlying supply are

- the outlook for the economy
- the outlook for the industry
- the firm's objectives
- technological progress
- expected profitability of producing other goods and services
- the nature of competition
- government spending policies and regulations
- other environmental factors

area of risk

The Outlook for the Economy

The aggregate supply of all goods and services is affected by many of the same things that affect overall demand. For example, producers who expect consumer buying power to increase may step up production in order to satisfy the expected increase in demand. When economic forecasters predict good times ahead, producers are optimistic and are willing to produce in anticipation of orders from customers.

The Outlook for the Industry

The outlook for a particular industry affects supply in that industry. For example, if November and December car sales indicate that consumers are not in a buying mood, car makers will cut back on

Demand versus
Supply
Management

POINT OF VIEW

Between the 1930s and the presidential election of 1980, the most popular view of the workings of an economic system was based on Keynesian economics. According to the late British economist, John Maynard Keynes, the key to managing an economic system is to manage demand. The basic idea is that an economy can be managed by adjusting the demand side of the supply-and-demand equation. Thus to reduce inflation, Keynesians favor tax hikes in order to reduce demand (consumer spending). To reduce unemployment, Keynesians favor tax cuts to increase demand (consumer spending).

During the early 1970s, however, an economic condition known as stagflation existed. Both inflation and unemployment were simultaneously at unacceptably high rates. Thus some economists started talking about supply-side economics. The basic idea is that an economy can be managed by adjusting the supply side of the supply-and-demand equation. Tax cuts would leave consumers with more money to spend and business people with more money to invest. Thus the economy would expand, employment would increase, supply would increase, demand would adjust to supply, and prices would stabilize. The election of President Reagan brought supply-side economics to the forefront.

Part of the theory of supply-side economics involves the widely discussed Laffer curve, named for its developer, Professor Arthur B. Laffer. The basic idea that the curve purports to show is that a lower tax rate can generate as much tax revenue or more tax revenue than a higher rate.

production. They will not produce as many units as they would have if the buying response were greater. When car makers cut back on production, they cut back on their orders for steel and the many other products that are used to make cars.

The Firm's Objectives

A firm's objectives also affect how much it is willing to supply. A firm's market share is the percentage of total sales it has in its industry. Some firms have an objective of increasing their market share by producing and selling in large volumes, often at prices that are lower than those charged by their competitors. Other firms are more concerned with building an image among consumers for providing high-quality products. They may offer fewer units for sale in order to help build a reputation for "quality rather than quantity."

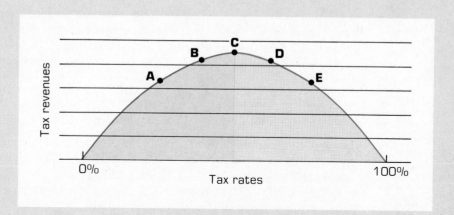

The Laffer curve portrays the presumed relationship between tax rates and tax revenues. Revenues are zero, of
course, when the tax rate is zero. But they are also zero when
tax rates rise to 100%; the tax base depends upon production
and income, and at a 100% tax rate there would be no incentive to produce. Revenues are maximized at some intermediate point, labeled "C" in the diagram. Beyond that point,
in the zone shaded orange, rising taxes discourage effort to
such an extent that revenues fall—the higher rates are more
than offset by reduced output. The curve is hypothetical, and
nobody knows either its shape or the location of point C.
These will vary with the type of tax; it is not likely either that
the true curve is symmetrical or that the point of maximum
revenue will lie at a tax rate halfway between 0% and 100%.[1]

Technological Progress

Technological progress also affects supply. From both a cost and a
quality standpoint, color TVs can be made more efficiently today
than 15 years ago. The same is true for computers, pocket calculators, and photocopying machines. This induces suppliers to supply more.

Expected Profitability of Producing Other
Products and Services

The supply of a product will decrease when a firm thinks it can
make more profit by shifting its resources to another product. This
is especially true when a firm can easily switch from making one
product to making another. General Electric stopped making many

types of small appliances, RCA and General Electric stopped making computers, and General Motors stopped making home appliances because they believed they could make more profit by making other products. In recent years Exxon has entered the office of the future market with products such as electronic word processors.

The Nature of Competition

The nature of competition in an industry also affects supply. When only three or four firms produce essentially the same product, the firms tend to recognize their interdependence. They know if they flood the market, all of them could end up with less profit because price will tend to fall due to excess supply.

Government Spending Policies and Regulations

Government spending policies and regulations also can stimulate or depress the supplies of some products and services. Increased defense spending stimulates production in the defense industries while cutbacks in federal loan guarantees for producers of synthetic fuels reduce the output of synthetic fuels. Tax incentives might induce oil companies to search harder for new oil reserves and steel companies to build new plants that are more efficient. Many home insulation producers expanded their production capacity when Congress approved tax credits for homeowners who added insulation to their houses.

Supply-side economics has received a lot of attention recently. People who accept this view argue that high tax rates discourage effort. Tax cuts, they believe, will induce people to work harder and business firms to invest more in modernizing their plants. For this to work, tax cuts must be accompanied by cuts in government spending.

Other Environmental Factors

Other environmental factors can also affect supply. Mounting product liability risk, for example, has led some drug manufacturers to stop producing certain types of live virus for diseases like measles and mumps. The cost of product liability insurance is high and, in some cases, potential suppliers of high-risk products prefer not to offer them for sale.

THE DETERMINATION OF MARKET PRICES

To see how supply and demand determine prices, let us study the supply and demand for plastic rulers. Table 2-2 shows the relationship between price and quantity supplied. Table 2-3 shows the relationship between price and quantity demanded. Putting the law of supply and the law of demand into graphical form gives us Figure 2-2 on page 48.

The demand curve (D) shows how many units are demanded at various prices. **A demand curve is a line that shows the number of units that will be demanded (bought) at each price at a given point in time. Fewer units are demanded at higher prices than at lower prices.**

demand curve

The supply curve (S) shows how many units are supplied at various prices. **A supply curve is a line that shows the number of units that will be supplied (offered for sale) at each price at a given point in time. Fewer units are supplied at lower prices than at higher prices.**

supply curve

The supply and demand curves in Figure 2-2 cross at a price of 50 cents per unit. Only at this price is the quantity suppliers are willing to offer (300 units) exactly equal to the quantity buyers are willing to buy (300 units). This is the *equilibrium price* because the quantity demanded and the quantity supplied are in balance. At higher prices, suppliers would be willing to supply more units than

Price (cents per unit)	Quantity supplied (units)
6	100
28	200
50	300
67	400
89	500
As price increases . . .	. . . quantity supplied increases

TABLE 2-2

Price and quantity supplied

Price (cents per unit)	Quantity demanded (units)
75	100
62	200
50	300
37	400
25	500
As price decreases . . .	. . . quantity demanded increases

TABLE 2-3

Price and quantity demanded

FIGURE 2-2

Determination of
market price

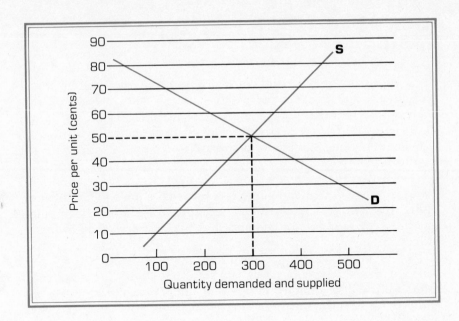

buyers would be willing to buy. At lower prices, buyers would be
willing to buy more units than suppliers would be willing to supply.

The situation shown in Figure 2-2 is oversimplified, however.
For example, the amount of money available in an economy (the
money supply) also affects prices. If there is too much money in
relation to goods and services, prices will rise. Such price inflation is
due to too much money chasing too few goods and services.

Government regulations and policies also can interfere with
the forces of supply and demand. For example, government policy
makers debated for years the effect of price controls on the supply
and demand for natural gas and crude petroleum. When the Organization of Petroleum Exporting Countries (OPEC) raised the price
of their oil, the government did not allow American oil producers to
follow suit. The price of American oil from old wells was kept below
the OPEC price. Some people say this reduced the incentive for
American oil producers to pump more oil, which contributed to the
deregulation of oil prices. The government's various attempts at
price supports for farmers also interfere with the natural workings of
the forces of supply and demand. The same is true when city governments practice rent control.

Nevertheless, Figure 2-2 does give us a basic insight into the
nature of price. Whether we are talking about the price we pay for
hamburgers or cars, the price we get for our labor (wage), or the price
we pay to borrow money (interest), the forces of supply and demand
are at work.

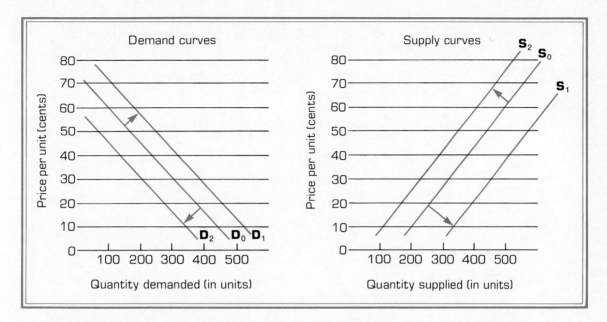

FIGURE 2-3

Changes (or shifts) in
demand and supply
curves

Figure 2-3 shows changes (or shifts) in the demand and supply curves. The shifts are due to changes in the underlying forces of supply and demand. A shift from D_0 to D_1 means that, at any given price, demand is *greater* than it was before the shift. One reason a firm advertises its product or service is the hope that it will shift its demand curve up and to the right. More units will be demanded at any given price.

A shift from D_0 to D_2 means that, at any given price, demand is *smaller* than it was before the shift. Over the years, the demand curves for men's hats, 78-RPM records, dial telephones, and tooth-powder have shifted to the left. Fewer units are demanded at any given price.

A shift from S_0 to S_1 means that, at any given price, supply is *greater* than it was before the shift. More units are supplied at any given price. The entry of so many firms, especially Japanese producers, into the microwave oven market has caused more microwave ovens to be for sale at any given price than were available when the product was first introduced to consumers.

A shift from S_0 to S_2 means that, at any given price, supply is *smaller* than it was before the shift. Fewer units are supplied at any given price. The high cost of liability insurance for pharma-ceutical manufacturers, for example, has led some of them to stop making certain types of drugs.

Study Table 2-4 carefully. A change in demand or a change in supply involves shifts in demand or supply curves. New curves have

TABLE 2-4

Demand and supply concepts

Change in demand   means that a greater or lesser number of units is bought without changing price. This means a *shift* in the demand curve. If it shifts up and to the right, a greater number of units is demanded at any given price. If it shifts down and to the left, a lesser number of units is demanded at any given price.

Change in supply   means that a greater or lesser number of units is supplied without changing price. This means a *shift* in the supply curve. If it shifts up and to the left, a lesser number of units is supplied at any given price. If it shifts down and to the right, a greater number of units is supplied at any given price.

Change in quantity demanded   means that a greater or lesser number of units is bought because of a change in price. An increase in quantity demanded means that a greater number of units is bought because the price has been lowered. We are moving down a *particular demand curve.* A decrease in quantity demanded means that a lesser number of units is bought because the price has been raised. We are moving up a particular demand curve.

Change in quantity supplied   means that a greater or lesser number of units is supplied because of a change in price. An increase in quantity supplied means that a greater number of units is supplied because the price has been raised. We are moving up a *particular supply curve.* A decrease in quantity supplied means that a lesser number of units is supplied because the price has been lowered. We are moving down a particular supply curve.

Rising energy costs have stimulated demand for alternative sources and methods of power

to be drawn to show the shifts. A change in quantity demanded or a change in quantity supplied does not involve any shifts in demand or supply curves. These changes can be shown without having to draw new curves.

THE BUSINESS FIRM

Demand gives a firm an opportunity to provide want-satisfying goods and services. Supply results from efforts by business firms to profit from this demand.

The business firm is the basic building block for organizing production in our system. Through it, resources are organized for production. Land, labor, and capital must be gathered and converted into goods and services that can be sold. This business activity must be directed and guided by the management of business firms.

Business activity requires decision making to produce and sell goods and services. It requires buying as well as selling. Thus the market plays a role. How resources are used depends basically on choices made by firms and consumers. Both are guided by market prices. The firm is the key to the market's operation. It guides the flow of resources through the marketplace. The firm is an input-output system. The inputs are productive resources that the firm buys in the marketplace. The outputs are the products and services it produces and sells in the marketplace. Both input and output depend on market prices. (See Figure 2-4.)

Resources and the goods and services produced from them are all scarce, which is why they command prices. The firm's costs of doing business (converting resources from one form to another) must be less than the sales revenues it receives from selling its output if it is to earn a profit. To determine how profitable it is, a firm must keep records of its costs and sales. The process of accounting traces the effects of resource flows on a firm's profits. We will discuss this in detail in Chapter 12. Figure 2-5 on the next page describes the essential elements of business activity.

FIGURE 2-4

Economic decision making in capitalist economic systems is guided by price

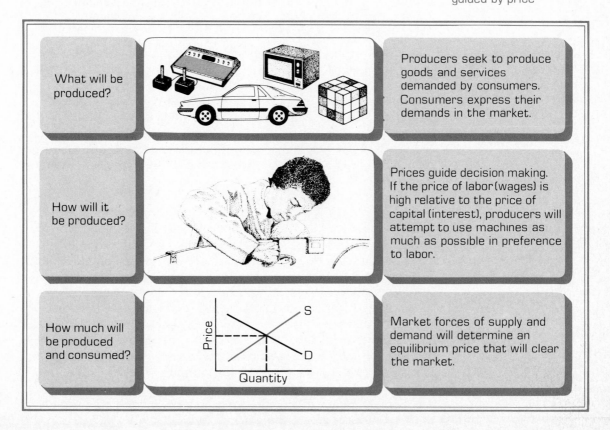

Effort	is exerted to exploit	Opportunity
Supply	is created to satisfy	Demand
Prices	are determined in	Markets
Entrepreneurship	is concerned with	Risk assumption
Risk	is assumed in the hope of	Profit
Profit	involves a recognition of	Costs
Decision making	is necessary because of the	Choice process
Production activity	is guided by the	Price system
Land Labor Capital }	are made productive through	Entrepreneurship
Factors of production (inputs)	are converted to	Marketable products and services (outputs)
Marketing activity	is guided by the	Price system
Markets	exist because of	Specialization and exchange

FIGURE 2-5

The nature of business activity

The Motivation of the Firm

People form business firms to produce and sell want-satisfying goods and services in the hope of profit. Profit, however, does not appear until it is earned. In our system there is no guarantee that a firm will make a profit. By providing goods and services that satisfy customers, a firm may make a profit.

Suppose Tommy Fields, age seven, opens a lemonade stand because he hopes to make a profit. During the first week he sells 20 cups of lemonade at five cents per cup. Is his profit for the week one dollar?

The answer depends on many things. If the cost of sugar, lemons, and cups is two cents per cup, Tommy's profit is not one dollar but sixty cents—the difference between one dollar in sales revenues and forty cents in costs (two cents per cup times 20 cups). If his parents wanted to be paid for whatever they supplied him, Tommy would realize that his supplies are scarce resources. His profit is sales revenues minus the cost of doing business.

If sales revenues are greater than costs, a profit is earned. A firm may increase its profit by raising prices, lowering costs, or selling more units. But most firms cannot raise prices very much without reducing sales. Most of them try to increase profit by cutting costs and/or increasing the number of units sold.

If a firm's sales revenues and costs are equal, it earns no profit. It only breaks even. Very few people go into business to break even. This is especially true if there is no "owner's salary" included in the firm's list of expenses. Firms that only break even give their owners no economic return for being in business.

Any *after-tax profit* that is earned by the firm is reinvested in the firm and/or is distributed to the owners. For many firms, reinvested profit is the major source of funds to finance their growth.

WHAT DO YOU THINK?

How Important Is Profit to You?

Samuel Gompers, head of the American Federation of Labor from 1886 to 1924, recognized the vital role of profit to American workers when he said, "The worst crime against working people is a company that fails to make a profit."

Profits reinvested in firms for growth create jobs. Profit not only rewards a firm's current owners, but it also attracts new investors. This stimulates investment, creates more jobs, and raises our standard of living.

Business profits also are a major source of federal, state, and local government tax revenues. These tax payments help to pay for schools, hospitals, and other social services.

Profitable firms can afford to set up programs to train people who want to work but cannot find jobs because they lack job skills. Profitable firms can afford to invest in costly pollution control devices, support the arts, participate in efforts to rebuild our deteriorating cities, and so on. Unprofitable firms cannot afford this.

But in recent years the word *profit* to some people has come to mean something ugly—like greed. There is a lot of misunderstanding of profit in our country. In public polls, the average American tends to overestimate the profits that the average company makes. Below are figures for manufacturing corporations that show the relation of profits after taxes to stockholders' equity (the financial interest of the owners of the corporation) and to sales for selected years:

Year	Ratio of profits after taxes to stockholders' equity (percent)	Profits after taxes per dollar of sales (cents)
1976	14.0	5.4
1977	14.2	5.3
1978	15.0	5.4
1979	16.5	5.7
1980	13.9	4.9
1981	13.6	4.8

How important is profit to you? WHAT DO YOU THINK?

Idealism vs. Investment.

Can you name the only industry that publishes an annual report of the money it invests to improve the quality of life in America?

The life insurance industry is the only business that publishes, each year, details on its investments for the betterment of our citizens and our communities. As one of our country's major sources of new capital, our industry has the means to invest in ways that will improve the quality of life for all Americans.

The state of our economy is interwoven with the well-being of the society it serves. To stimulate a healthier society, the life insurance companies in America are committed to make certain investments based on the merits of their social significance, as well as their potential for investment yield.

We are caretakers of the funds of 147 million policyholders who count on us for financial protection. These funds are invested for anticipated returns in the best interest of fulfilling guarantees to our policyholders. These same funds provide opportunities to respond to needs for improvement throughout our society, and that responsibility is a factor in many of our investment decisions.

From minority business loans to major urban revitalization, from housing for the elderly to day care centers for the young, the insurance industry is committed to funding programs for the benefit of our nation's citizens as well as our nation's economy.

American Council of Life Insurance

The owners, in effect, are willing to reinvest their profit in the firm rather than take it out for personal use. Congress passed the Economic Recovery Tax Act of 1981 because it wanted individual taxpayers to be able to keep more of their earnings to save, invest, or spend as they desired. Congress also wanted to make it possible and more attractive for businesses to reinvest more of their earnings in their firms for modernization and expansion.

That firms seek profit is an accepted fact in capitalist economies. There is some argument, however, whether profit should be their *only* objective. Do businesses owe something to people other than their owners and their customers?

Businesses pay federal, state, and sometimes city taxes on their profits. They also pay property taxes and licensing fees. Businesses hire employees who earn wages and salaries. They provide jobs to our people. Some people believe that as long as businesses provide jobs and want-satisfying products and services to their customers and pay taxes, the firms are contributing to society's well-being.

Other people, however, believe that businesses owe more to society. For example, a firm may be providing goods and services that satisfy its customers but in the process it may be creating problems for the rest of society. Soft drinks and beer may be packaged in aluminum cans to satisfy drinkers who want this convenience, but society in general has to pay for cleaning up the litter that some users of these cans create. Thus aluminum can producers are spending money to educate consumers about the need for proper disposal of used cans. In other words, some people believe that firms are accountable to society in general, not only to their customers and owners.

Whether businesses or communities will pay for recycling programs remains an unanswered question

This concept of the *social responsibility of business* is discussed at several places in this book. The issue of the social responsibility of business arises in such areas as the hiring of the handicapped, job-training for other disadvantaged people, cleaning up pollution, helping in the battle against inflation, supporting community projects, and complying with affirmative action guidelines to recruit and hire women and minorities. General Mills has a position entitled head of public responsibility. This person's job is to identify social problems in which the firm can invest its management skills and money.

Profit Opportunity and Organized Effort

One fact remains, however. A firm cannot survive over the long run if it does not earn a profit from its operations. It must find a way to use its scarce resources and convert them into saleable goods and services. It must both identify an opportunity for profit and use its resources to try to make that profit.

business opportunity

Before an opportunity can be exploited, it must exist and be recognized. **A business opportunity exists where there is a set of circumstances that may enable a firm to make a profit.** This set of circumstances can be the result of decisions made by persons inside or outside the firm or it can be mostly good luck.

Dr. E. H. Land's dedication to research and development enabled him to enter an industry that had been dominated for years by Kodak. He created the instant photography industry. IBM's dedication to research and development enabled it to become the dominant firm in the computer industry. Opportunity for these firms resulted from their decision to invest money and time in research and development.

Volkswagen's decision to begin manufacturing Volkswagens in New Stanton, Pennsylvania, created opportunity for many firms. Some firms, for example, built houses for the new residents who moved there to work in the plant. Their opportunity was the result of a decision made by Volkswagen.

The deregulation of the airline industry which began in 1978 led some major airlines to abandon their short-haul routes. This helped create opportunity for smaller regional airlines like Texas-based Southwest Airlines and California-based PSA, Inc.

A lot of opportunity is the result of being in the "right place at the right time." This is as true for businesses as it is for individuals. How many health food stores struggled to survive for years serving a handful of customers before eating health foods became a nationwide fad for thousands of Americans?

At any rate, the framework for evaluating opportunity is the *marketplace*. A firm searches the marketplace for unsatisfied wants that the firm, with its resources and capabilities, could satisfy at a profit. If it can accomplish this, it creates customers for the product or service it offers.

Exploiting opportunity need not involve developing new products. Today the fastest-growing part of the retail food industry is convenience stores. Minit Markets, Li'l General, and 7-Eleven stores recognized an opportunity to profit from serving the wants of people who want the ultimate in shopping convenience (nearby stores with extended shopping hours, easy parking, no long lines) and are willing to pay prices that are above those in supermarkets.

Exploiting opportunity, however, requires a keen ability to stay in tune with customer wants. In recent years some alert grocers have recognized opportunity in catering more carefully to consumers who are willing to forego some grocer services for lower food prices. Warehouse stores carry a full line of popular brands but customers must mark prices, bag, and carry their groceries out of the store. Box

stores are similar but they stock fewer items, carry a greater proportion of their own brands, and generally do not stock products that
require refrigeration.

Finally, exploiting opportunity requires an ability to meet it
with organized effort and productive resources. Since a firm's resources and capabilities are limited, they must be used to best advantage. Even if two firms have the same kind and amount of resources,
one may be able to develop more capability than the other through
better management. Superior strength in resources and capabilities
enables a firm to take a broader view of what constitutes market
opportunity.

The Role of Risk

It is the hope of profit that motivates people to go into business.
Because hopes are not always realized, risk is present. **Risk is the**   risk
chance of loss. The hope of profit explains risk-assumption. The
person thinks the expected profit is worth the risk involved. The
greater the reward a business owner expects, the more risk he or she
is likely to take.

People, however, see risk differently. What one person sees as
a very risky investment, another may see as quite safe. This perception of risk is important in understanding why people are willing to
risk their money in the hope of profit.

Much of our material progress is due to our highly stable political and economic systems. That stability helps to reduce the risk
seen in a possible investment. Thus a person is more likely to invest
in the United States than in a foreign country where frequent and
violent revolutions occur. This is one reason that in recent years
there has been a great increase in foreign investment in our country.
Business people and individual investors overseas are setting up
firms here and buying stocks and bonds in American corporations.

The nature of risk and how businesses handle it are discussed
at several places in this book. For now, it is enough to know that risk
is *always* present in business and any other type of human activity.

SUMMARY AND LOOK AHEAD

Ours is a market economy in which relative prices determine
how limited resources will be used to satisfy unlimited wants. Because resources are limited, choices must be made about what will
be produced. These choices are made by consumers and producers
working through the price system.

Prices induce or limit production and consumption. The price system helps firms decide which goods and services will be produced, how much will be produced, how they will be produced, and how they will be distributed. These decisions are not made by a central planning agency. They are made by millions of consumers and producers through the price-formulating process of a market.

The law of demand means that more of a given product or service is demanded at lower prices than at higher prices. The law of supply means that more of a given product or service is offered for sale at higher prices than at lower prices. These forces of supply and demand work to determine prices.

The business firm is the basic building block for organizing production in our economy. It gathers productive resources (inputs) and converts them into saleable goods or services (outputs). Both input and output depend on the price system.

The hope of profit motivates people to go into business. They earn profit from identifying business opportunity and exploiting it through organized effort. But risk is always present.

Now that we know what a firm is and why it exists, we can go on to discuss the different forms of ownership of business firms.

FOR REVIEW . . .

1. What is a market economy? Is it the same as a price system? Explain.

2. Contrast demand and quantity demanded, state the "law of demand," and draw a demand curve.

3. What are the three main sources of buying power?

4. Contrast disposable income, discretionary income, and real income.

5. Contrast supply and quantity supplied, state the "law of supply," and draw a supply curve.

6. What is the significance of (a) the intersection of a supply curve and a demand curve on a graph, and (b) shifts in demand and supply curves?

7. Are supply and demand forces the only ones that affect prices? Explain.

8. What can a firm do to increase its profits?

9. In what two basic ways can a firm use its after-tax profit?

10. What is "business opportunity"?

11. Why is risk present in business activity?

. . . FOR DISCUSSION

1. Can goods or services really be overpriced?

2. Is the concept of the social responsibility of business at odds with its need to make a profit?

3. What is a "favorable business climate"?

4. The chapter said that the hope of profit is the main reason business people undertake risk. What other reasons for going into business can you identify?

5. Are there any types of business opportunity in your community that are not being exploited? If there are, why are they not being exploited?

6. Why do people perceive risk differently?

7. Is it true that all businesses must serve their customers if they are to survive?

INCIDENTS

Supply and Demand in the Cattle Industry

The cattle industry provides a good example of how the laws of supply and demand work. When beef is plentiful, the price drops and some consumers will want to buy more beef. Ranchers, however, will want to supply less beef because of the low price and they will start sending their breeding cows to slaughterhouses. This means that beef supplies will become tighter and the price of beef will start to rise. Ranchers also will be encouraged to rebuild their herds. This cycle tends to repeat itself every eight years.

QUESTIONS

1. When the price of beef drops and consumers want to buy more, is this an increase in demand for beef or an increase in the quantity demanded of beef?

2. In the cycle we have described, what encourages ranchers to want to supply more beef or less beef?

3. In the cycle we have described, what encourages consumers to demand more beef or less beef? What other factors might underlie consumer demand for beef?

4. Is any risk present in the cattle industry? Discuss.

Indexing Federal Income Taxes

Suppose a household's income in one year is $20,000 and it pays $2,000 in federal income taxes. It pays 10 percent of its income in income taxes.

Now, assume that the Consumer Price Index (CPI) for the next year shows that consumer prices rose 12 percent. Further, assume that the household's income rises 12 percent to keep up with inflation.

Theoretically, the household will be able to buy the same quantity of goods and services it could have bought in the previous year. At the end of the year the household will find that its 12 percent increase in income paid for the higher prices of the goods and services it bought.

If the 12 percent increase in income shifted the household to a higher tax bracket, it will end up having less buying power than it did in the previous year. Although it may have broken even by using its 12 percent increase in income to pay prices that were 12 percent higher, it is also in a higher tax bracket, which means that it will pay more than 10 percent of its income in income taxes.

The Economic Recovery Tax Act of 1981 provides that indexation will take effect on January 1, 1985. Tax brackets, the personal exemption, and the standard deduction will be adjusted for inflation as reflected by the previous year's Consumer Price Index.

QUESTIONS

1. What effect will indexation of federal income taxes have on a household's real income?

2. How will indexing federal income taxes probably affect a typical household's willingness to spend?

3. Is indexing federal income taxes a good idea? Why or why not?

$$\boxed{\textbf{CHAPTER 3}}$$

Forms of Business Ownership

OBJECTIVES:
> **After reading this chapter, you should be able to**

1. Identify the reasons for and give examples of the growth of public ownership in the United States.
2. Identify the three most common forms of private ownership in the United States.
3. List and compare the relative advantages and disadvantages of the three major forms of ownership of business firms.
4. Outline the basic procedures involved in forming and operating a corporation.
5. Discuss the relative importance of the three major forms of ownership in terms of the number of firms, sales revenues received, and profit earned.
6. Identify and discuss the relative advantages and disadvantages of large-scale operations.
7. Explain the concept of countervailing power.
8. List and discuss other forms of business ownership that are modifications of the three basic forms of ownership.

KEY CONCEPTS:
Look for these terms as you read the chapter

sole proprietorship

unlimited liability

partnership

partnership agreement

corporation

stockholders

Subchapter S Corporation

corporate charter

common stock

preferred stock

cumulative voting

proxy

board of directors

corporation bylaws

professional managers

countervailing power

limited partnership

joint venture

business trust

cooperative association

mutual company

Big corporations are always in the news because their actions help to make the news. Consider all the attention U.S. Steel (the biggest American steel producer) and Mobil (the second biggest American petroleum company) received in late 1981 when they were bidding against each other to buy Marathon Oil Company (the seventeenth biggest American petroleum company). U.S. Steel won the bidding war and acquired Marathon. Shortly thereafter Mobil announced that it might buy a big chunk of stock in U.S. Steel.

Both U.S. Steel and Mobil were criticized during the bidding war which lasted for weeks. Some people criticized U.S. Steel for buying Marathon rather than using its money to modernize its steel mills to compete more effectively against imported Japanese steel. Some people criticized Mobil for wanting to become too dominant in the petroleum industry. Interestingly, Mobil had been criticized several years earlier for buying Montgomery Ward and Company instead of keeping its money invested in the oil business.

This chapter takes a close look at the issue of ownership of business firms. We will look at the sole proprietorship, the partnership, and the corporation. We will also examine other, less common, forms of private ownership.

Private ownership is the rule in the United States; government ownership is the exception. Our government sometimes undertakes ownership of organizations that provide goods and services to consumers and businesses. For example, some cities are served by publicly owned transit companies. Let's begin by focusing on the issue of public versus private ownership.

PUBLIC VERSUS PRIVATE OWNERSHIP

In the capitalist system a person has the right to save and to invest money to make more money. Persons, alone or in groups, can risk their money by going into business to try to make a profit. Private ownership of business firms is a basic part of the capitalist system.

Private ownership is not the only form of ownership in our business system. Public, or government, ownership also exists. Public ownership may be undertaken for many reasons:

- The investment required may be too great for private investors, or the potential payoff may be too far off and intangible, making private investors unwilling to assume the risk.

- Public ownership may be the only option left when privately owned firms fail.

- Public ownership may be needed to stimulate competition among privately owned firms.

- Services are believed to be too important to society's welfare to be left up to private businesses.

In some cases the investment required may be too great for private investors. For example, the Federal Deposit Insurance Corporation (FDIC) is a government agency that insures the deposits in banks that meet the FDIC's requirement for coverage. Some banks that are nonmembers have insurance with private firms but, in some cases, these firms have been unable to pay off depositors when the banks have failed.

When the United States entered the space race, the government set up the National Aeronautics and Space Administration (NASA).

The amount of the required investment was too great and the potential payoff on the investment was too far off and intangible for private investors to assume the risk alone.

Several years ago a swine flu epidemic threatened the United States and drug makers rushed into the production of vaccines. Privately owned insurance companies were unwilling to provide liability insurance to these manufacturers because of the great risk involved. As a result the federal government had to provide it.

Privately owned businesses that provide needed services sometimes do fail, and government may step in to ensure that the services are still provided. Thus, the federal government has set up the National Railroad Passenger Corporation (Amtrak) and the Consolidated Rail Corporation (Conrail).

Public ownership may also be undertaken to stimulate competition among firms in an industry. Canada's government-owned Canadian National Railroad competes with the privately owned Canadian Pacific Railroad. Some people believe that the United States government should own and operate shipyards to compete with privately owned shipyards.

Finally the federal government is in the mail and the social security "businesses" and local governments are in the water, sewage, and garbage collection "businesses" because these services are felt to be too important to the public welfare to be left to private firms. In recent years many people have argued that even these public services should be turned over to private firms, especially in states and cities where the voters have turned down proposals for property tax increases. Thus in some communities trash collection is handled by private firms.

Private ownership is the main type of ownership in the United States. The three most common forms of private ownership are

- the sole proprietorship
- the partnership
- the corporation

THE SOLE PROPRIETORSHIP

The sole proprietorship is the oldest and the most common form of ownership in the United States. **A sole proprietorship is a business owned and managed by one person. That person, however, may have help from others in running the business.** The sole proprietor is the classic example of the entrepreneur.

sole proprietorship

Advantages of the Sole Proprietorship

Farms are often sole proprietorships

Suppose Alice Stone wanted to go into the florist business. She might find that the sole proprietorship is the easiest way for her to start. There are no general laws that regulate the setting up of a sole proprietorship. Of course, the business activity must be legal and there may be local and state laws that require licenses and permits. Usually the sole proprietor is required to register the firm's name at the county courthouse. This prohibits two firms from operating under the same name. Other license and permit requirements are discussed in Chapter 17. Otherwise, Alice can go into business any time she pleases. Simplicity in starting the business is a major advantage of the sole proprietorship.

As sole owner, Alice owns the firm outright. She is the sole owner of any profits (or losses). Alice may get personal satisfaction out of seeing her firm grow under her direct guidance. She does what she believes is best for her firm and makes decisions without required approval from anyone else.

Because Alice is the firm, she pays only personal income taxes on the firm's profits. There is no income tax on the firm as a separate entity. If Alice wants to go out of business, she simply sells her inventory and equipment. She needs permission from no one. A sole proprietorship is easy to dissolve.

The sole proprietorship's major advantages, therefore, are

- simplicity in starting the business
- ownership of all the profits
- enjoyment gained from a great deal of personal involvement and satisfaction from being one's own boss
- the ability to make management decisions without required approval from anyone else
- no tax on profits of the business as a separate entity, only on the owner's personal income
- simplicity in dissolving the business

Disadvantages of the Sole Proprietorship

unlimited liability

Because Alice is the firm, she is legally liable for all its debts. She has unlimited liability. **Unlimited liability means that a proprietor is liable for claims against the business that go beyond the value of his or her ownership in the firm. The liability extends to his or her personal property (furniture, car, and personal savings) and, in some cases, real property (home and other real estate).** If Alice goes out of

the entire corporation subject to "rubber stamp" approval by the board.

Thus the distinctions between the board and the corporate officers often are blurred. In some corporations the chairperson of the board is also the company's president. The corporation's other top managers also may be on the board. In such a case the board members who are not corporate officers are called *outside directors.*

Board members have certain legal obligations. They must act in the best interest of the stockholders and be reasonable and prudent in doing their jobs. They must be as careful in managing the corporation's affairs as they are in managing their personal affairs. In the past, board members have been held liable for illegal acts and fraud, but not for poor judgment. More recently, however, some courts have held directors liable for using what the courts consider to be poor judgment.

ANALYSIS OF AMERICAN BUSINESS FIRMS ACCORDING TO FORM OF OWNERSHIP

The sole proprietorship has traditionally been the most common form of business ownership in the United States. Today, sole

TABLE 3-3
Number of businesses operating in principal industries in the United States

Industry	Number of firms (in thousands)		
	Proprietorships	Active partnerships	Active corporations
Agriculture, forestry, and fisheries	3,177	121	67
Mining	71	22	19
Construction	994	69	216
Manufacturing	224	28	230
Transportation and public utilities	385	17	84
Trade	2,264	193	674
Wholesale	307	29	239
Retail	1,862	164	433
Finance, insurance, and real estate	895	476	434
Services	3,302	227	514
All industries	11,346	1,153	2,241

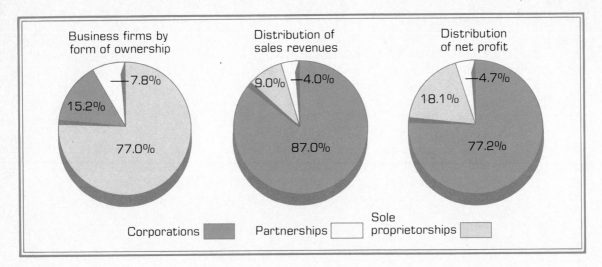

FIGURE 3-5

Percentages of American business firms by form of ownership and relative percentage distribution of sales revenues and net profit

proprietorships comprise 77% of all our business firms. Table 3-3 shows that in the United States there are

- 11.3 million sole proprietorships
- 1.2 million partnerships
- 2.2 million corporations

There are more than five times as many sole proprietorships as corporations. However, the sole proprietorships include many small retailers and service establishments. Thus sole proprietorships do not account for a proportionally high percentage of sales revenues and net profit. Figure 3-5 shows that

- sole proprietorships receive 9.0 percent of all sales revenues and 18.1 percent of all net profit of American firms
- partnerships receive 4.0 percent of all sales revenues and 4.7 percent of all net profit of American firms
- corporations receive 87.0 percent of all sales revenues and 77.2 percent of all net profit of American firms

THE EFFECTS OF SIZE

So far we have discussed the relative advantages of the three forms of ownership as they relate basically to the form of ownership. There are also advantages and disadvantages to large-scale business operations unrelated to the form of ownership.

Advantages of Large-Scale Operation

The larger a firm, the more likely it can justify setting up research and development, product testing, marketing research, and advertising departments and hire specialists such as engineers, chemists, market researchers, and advertising copywriters to staff them. A small firm usually cannot afford this degree of specialization. It may have one manager in charge of all production oper-

TABLE 3-4

The ten largest industrial corporations in the United States (ranked by sales) 1982

Rank	Company	Sales ($000)	Assets ($000)	Net income ($000)	Employees (number)	Net income as percent of sales
1	Exxon (New York	97,172,523	62,288,550	4,185,932	173,000	4.3
2	General Motors (Detroit)	60,025,600	41,397,800	962,700	657,000	1.6
3	Mobil (New York)	59,946,000	36,439,000	1,380,000	188,000	2.3
4	Texaco (Harrison, New York)	46,986,000	27,114,000	1,281,000	60,330	2.7
5	Ford Motor (Dearborn, Mich.)	37,067,200	21,961,700	(657,800)	379,229	—
6	International Business Machines (Armonk, NY)	34,364,000	32,541,000	4,409,000	364,796	12.8
7	Standard Oil of California (San Francisco)	34,362,000	23,490,000	1,377,000	41,726	4.0
8	E. I. du Pont de Nemours (Wilmington, Delaware)	33,331,000	24,343,000	894,000	165,013	2.7
9	Gulf Oil (Pittsburgh)	28,427,000	20,436,000	900,000	51,500	3.2
10	Standard Oil (Indiana) (Chicago)	28,073,000	24,289,000	1,826,000	57,810	6.5

ations instead of separate managers for warehousing, traffic, production scheduling, and product quality control.

Large firms are often able to borrow more money and get favorable interest rates. The prime interest rate reported in the news is the rate banks charge their most credit-worthy customers—the big corporations. It is lower than the rate most smaller firms pay to borrow money.

Large firms also have access to more investment money than small firms. For example, some of the money in employee pension plans is used to buy stock in big corporations. Employees who participate in the pension plan become indirect owners of the corporation whose stock is bought with their pension fund money. Smaller firms ordinarily do not attract this type of investment.

Large firms tend to be more permanent, which helps them in hiring managers and workers who value permanence in employment. **Professional managers are people whose profession or career is management. Such a person participates in managing a firm in which he or she is not a major owner.** Sole proprietors, partners, and the owners of small corporations usually are *owner-managers*. Only larger firms can afford to hire professional managers. Partners in successful partnerships, however, can attract high-quality personnel who might expect to be offered a chance to buy into the firm. This practice is common in law and accounting firms.

professional managers

The advantages of large-scale operation, regardless of the form of ownership, are

- greater opportunity for specialization by workers and managers
- greater borrowing power
- greater access to investment money
- greater availability of managerial talent

Table 3-4 identifies the ten largest industrial corporations in the United States.

Disadvantages of Large-Scale Operation

Some economists, government regulators, small business owners, politicians, and labor leaders believe that business can be too big. Large size can result in reduced competition and greater concentration of economic power in certain sectors of the economy.

Big labor and government are also part of our business system. **The overall balancing of power between big business, big labor, and government is called countervailing power.** The offsetting size and power of each of these three supposedly will prevent any one of them from becoming too powerful and dominant in our society.

countervailing power

AUTHORS' COMMENTARY

AT&T and IBM Will Become Major Rivals

On January 8, 1982 the U.S. Department of Justice announced it was dropping its antitrust suit against IBM and had reached a settlement with AT&T on the government's antitrust case against it. These two giant corporations grew up under very different circumstances. Whereas AT&T, as a utility company, was heavily regulated by the government, IBM was not. The settlement with the Department of Justice apparently would allow AT&T for the first time to grow in new directions upon divesting itself of its twenty-two local telephone companies.

AT&T and IBM will most likely become major rivals in the information processing business. Each will be striving to outdo the other in merging communications and computer technologies. AT&T will take on more of the characteristics of a high technology company like IBM as it moves far beyond its traditional role as a utility company.

In any large organization there is some tendency toward impersonality. The lack of personal contact between workers and managers tends to make the workers feel uninvolved with the business. There is more personal contact in small firms.

The sole proprietor who assumes risk stands to gain all the rewards. In smaller corporations the accomplishments of managers can be observed more easily than in large corporations, where there are many levels of managers. These hired managers stand to gain fewer of the rewards from risk assumption. Some may become overly conservative and avoid taking risks, even when that may be best for the firm.

The disadvantages of large-scale operation, regardless of the form of ownership, are

- the potential for too much concentration of economic power
- the potential for reduced management efficiency
- some tendency toward impersonality
- the potential for overconservatism in management

"The secret of staying in business is making something people really need . . . profit!"

OTHER FORMS OF BUSINESS OWNERSHIP

The sole proprietorship, the partnership, and the corporation are the three major forms of ownership of business firms. Over the years some modifications of these three basic forms have been made in order to overcome some of their disadvantages. Examples are

- limited partnerships
- joint ventures
- business trusts
- cooperative associations
- mutual companies

Limited Partnerships

The previous discussion of the partnership focused on the general partnership in which all partners are co-owners and each has unlimited liability for the firm's debts. This liability also is a joint liability.

limited partnership

In a limited partnership there is at least one general partner and one or more limited partners. A limited partner's liability is limited to his or her financial investment in the firm. This feature helps general partners to attract investment dollars from people who do not want to assume unlimited financial liability or participate in managing the firm. Under the law, partners are assumed to be general partners unless it is made known that they are limited partners. If a limited partner does participate in managing the firm, that person's limited liability must be disclosed to the firm's creditors.

Other types of partners are described in Table 3-5.

TABLE 3-5
Types of partners*

1. silent partner—a partner who does not actively participate in managing the firm but whose name is identified with the firm.
2. secret partner—a partner who actively participates in managing the firm but whose identity is not disclosed to the public.
3. dormant (sleeping) partner—a person who does not actively participate in managing the firm and whose identity is not disclosed to the public.
4, nominal partner—a person who is not an actual partner but whose name is identified with the firm because he or she is a well-known personality. Use of the name gives the firm promotional benefits and the person usually is paid a fee for the use of his or her name.
*These partners can be general or limited partners but the dormant partner most often is a limited partner.

Joint Ventures

The joint venture is a special type of temporary partnership arrangement. It is set up for a specific purpose and it ends when that purpose is accomplished. A partner's death or withdrawal does not end the joint venture. Usually, one general partner manages the venture and the others have limited financial liability.

This arrangement has been popular in real estate during recent years. Several people may pool their funds and talents to buy an older home, remodel it, and sell it. They divide the profit they make and the joint venture ends. Another example is a group of brokerage firms that get together to sell a new stock issue for a corporate client. These firms make up an underwriting syndicate.

joint venture

Business Trusts

In a business trust the trustee holds the property, runs the business, and accepts funds from investors. The trustee makes all management decisions, including how any profit will be divided. The investors have no say in management but they do have limited financial liability. They receive trust shares but they do not vote for the people who manage the trust. An example is a mutual fund that accepts funds from investors. The trustee pools their investment dollars and uses them to buy stock in other firms.

business trust

Cooperative Associations

A cooperative association (or, simply, a co-op) is a group of persons who act together to accomplish some purpose. They are incorporated and the members elect a board of directors. Each member has only one vote. Co-ops do not seek to earn a profit in the usual sense of the term. They are set up to help their members. Any revenues that they earn in excess of their cost of doing business are returned to the owners. Examples of co-ops include

cooperative association

- employee credit unions—accept savings deposits from members who own shares in the co-op. Members can borrow from the co-op. Savers receive interest and borrowers pay interest to the credit union.

- agricultural co-ops—help member farmers to market their products. The Florida Orange Growers Association is an example.

- buying co-ops—help members to buy their products at lower prices. Farmers may get together and set up a co-op to buy seed, fertilizer, and so on.

- consumer co-ops—customer-owned retail facilities. Consumers get together and form a buying pool in order to get quantity discounts and to eliminate independently owned intermediaries like wholesalers and retailers. Owner-members in many rural areas also set up consumer co-ops for selling electricity.

Mutual Companies

mutual company

A mutual company is similar to a cooperative because the users are the owners. They have a board of directors like a corporation, but the vast majority of members typically do not vote. Many life insurance companies and savings and loan associations (S&LAs) are mutual companies. When you buy an insurance policy from Massachusetts Mutual, you become an owner and you receive a "dividend" on your policy. Unlike a dividend from a corporation, it is not taxable. When you deposit savings in a mutual S&LA, you also become an owner. You receive "dividends" on your savings, but the "dividends" are considered as interest for income tax purposes, and you pay income tax on them.

SUMMARY AND LOOK AHEAD

The three major forms of business ownership are the sole proprietorship, the partnership, and the corporation. These are all forms of private ownership in contrast to public ownership. Private ownership is the most common form of ownership in the United States. But there is more public ownership today than there was fifty years ago.

Most privately owned firms are sole proprietorships. Most of these are small and employ only a handful of people. In many, the owner is the only employee.

A partnership is a firm owned by two or more persons who voluntarily go into business together. There are several different kinds of partnerships.

A corporation is a creation of government authority, separate and distinct from its owners. It comes into existence when its owners are granted a corporate charter by the state in which it is formed. Ownership is gained by the purchase of shares of stock.

What form of ownership is "best" depends on the circumstances in each situation. In no sense is one form of ownership always better than another.

In the next section, we look at management and organization of the firm. Chapter 4 focuses on the management functions and decicion making; Chapter 5 examines the firm as an organization.

FOR REVIEW . . .

1. List and discuss four reasons for public ownership of the means of production in our economic system.

2. List, define, and discuss the relative advantages and disadvantages of the three most common forms of ownership of business firms.

3. Is there any necessary relationship between a firm's size and its form of ownership? Discuss.

4. What are the relative advantages and disadvantages of large-scale operation to a firm?

5. Contrast "owner-managers" and "professional managers."

6. Compare the three forms of ownership of business firms in terms of (a) numbers, (b) revenues received, and (c) profit earned.

7. Define (a) domestic corporation, (b) foreign corporation, (c) alien corporation, (d) public corporation, (e) private corporation, (f) close corporation, and (g) open corporation.

8. Discuss the corporate structure in terms of stockholders, the board of directors, and the corporate officers.

9. List and discuss five modifications of the three major forms of ownership of business firms.

. . . FOR DISCUSSION

1. Does the president of a big corporation get less personal satisfaction from his or her job than the proprietor of a small business?

2. What is the most serious disadvantage of the partnership form of ownership?

3. Which form of business ownership is "best"?

4. Who or what really controls a corporation?

5. Are the professional managers in a large corporation more likely to assume more social responsibility than a sole proprietor or partners in a small firm?

6. Is the profit incentive that we discussed in Chapter 2 as important to professional managers in a large corporation as it is to the sole proprietor of a small business?

7. Do owners of small businesses have any "countervailing power"?

INCIDENTS

Game-a-Tron Goes Public

One of the many firms that went public in recent years is Game-a-Tron Corporation, a firm that makes electronic video games for arcades. It raised $2.5 million by selling 10 million shares of stock at 25 cents each. This money helped finance the firm's expansion plans. For example, it has applied for a Nevada gambling license. If the license is granted, Game-a-Tron plans to develop video slot machines.

QUESTIONS

1. What are the potential advantages to the owners of a firm in going public?

2. Why might investors buy stock in a firm that has decided to go public?

3. Why do you think this particular firm went public?

The U.S. Postal Service versus Private Competitors

The U.S. government has operated mail service since colonial times. In 1970 Congress created the U.S. Postal Service in part to take politics out of the operation of the old Post Office Department and to make it operate more like a business. Recently, however, the Postal Service has been criticized by people complaining about rising postage rates, budget deficits, and allegedly deteriorating service. Between 1976 and 1981, the Postal Service incurred a deficit in every year except 1979 despite several postage hikes.

Some privately owned companies are trying to make a profit by offering their customers better service at lower prices. United Parcel Service (UPS) was one of the first private firms to offer package delivery. Newer entrants include firms that pick up mail from big volume mailers, combine and presort it by Zip codes, and take it to post offices for mailing. The postage on such mail is lower than if each mailer had dropped it off at the post office. The difference is enough to save big volume mailers (such as utility companies) money plus provide a profit to the firms that perform some of the Postal Service's functions.

QUESTIONS

1. Why have private businesses begun to offer some services that used to be offered only by the Postal Service?

2. The federal government has historically subsidized the Postal Service's operations. As those subsidies are phased out, the Postal Service's operating costs will have to be paid out of the revenues it collects. What do you think that means as far as the operation of the Postal Service is concerned?

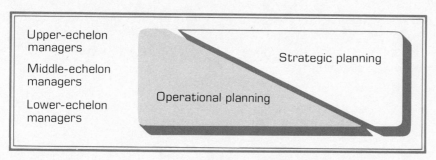

Upper-echelon managers

Middle-echelon managers

Lower-echelon managers

Strategic planning

Operational planning

FIGURE 4-3

The relative importance of strategic and operational planning at the various levels of the management hierarchy

planning for a small apparel store may cover a period of six months to one year. How far ahead a firm plans (its planning horizon) depends on the particular industry a firm is in, its technology, and its products.

Long-range planning makes it easier for a firm to adapt to a changing environment. The purpose is not to show how well the firm can predict the future but to gain insight into the actions the firm has to take in the present to help ensure that it will, in fact, have a future.

There are basically two different types of planning: strategic planning and operational planning. (See Figure 4-3.)

Strategic planning is concerned with a firm's long-range future and its overall strategy of growth. This is the type of planning for which top-level managers are responsible. For example, RCA Corporation's decision to introduce SelectaVision was a result of top management's strategic planning.

strategic planning

Operational planning is planning for the day-to-day survival of the firm. Middle and lower-level managers engage mainly in this type of planning. For example, middle and lower-level managers planned the sales training program that RCA's SelectaVision distributors used to train their dealers' salespeople.

operational planning

Regardless of the time frame for a particular objective, it is generally accepted that sound objectives should

- be specific
- be measurable
- identify expected results
- be reachable with reasonable effort
- be expressed within a time frame for accomplishing them

The person or department responsible for accomplishing objectives should have the necessary authority to accomplish them in order to prevent buck passing.

Recently, many managers have been adopting the management by objectives (MBO), or managing by results, approach. The manager

management by objectives (MBO)

meets with each subordinate to set his or her objectives. The subordinate participates in goal setting and, if the objectives are accomplished, the subordinate is considered to have performed well. It's the result that counts!

MBO offers the following advantages:

- subordinates know at the beginning of a planning period what is expected of them, thereby reducing their uncertainty about what they are supposed to accomplish

- subordinates often enjoy participating with superiors in determining a method for measuring their performance, which increases their motivation to reach the objective

- subordinates are given more opportunity to use new approaches to reaching their objectives since MBO does not predetermine the means for reaching objectives

- managers have more confidence in future planning and predicting results

Managers who use the MBO approach assume that their subordinates (1) have higher-level needs which they desire to satisfy through their work, (2) are creative and have ideas and knowledge to bring to the job, and (3) will work harder to accomplish goals which they help to set.

Among the potential problems in implementing the MBO approach are (1) subordinate suspicion that the real purpose of MBO is to get more work out of them, (2) desire to "beat the system" by setting very minimal objectives to make their performance look good, (3) desire to "please management" by setting unrealistically high objectives, and (4) desire to avoid spending time with the boss discussing and writing objectives. Other problems may arise in integrating the various individuals' goals with those of the organization, setting a priority of objectives, and time-scheduling to accommodate them.

Deciding How to Reach Objectives

In planning, managers rely on knowledge of past and present conditions in their environment. They use this to forecast probable future developments and to plan a course of action in accordance with this forecast. Because no one knows for sure what the future holds, managers operate under conditions of uncertainty. The future, however, is not completely uncertain. Some conditions can be more or less taken for granted and projected into the future, thereby reducing the number of planning "unknowns."

For example, there is no doubt that 76 million Americans were born during the baby boom years 1946–1964. They now account for about one-third of our population. Firms that sell houses, home appliances, and furniture knew years ago that when these people reached their twenties and thirties they would be good prospects as buyers. But those firms could not have predicted as easily the high interest rates, high inflation, and high unemployment of the early 1980s that prevented many of them from buying new houses.

Planners, therefore, plan in the face of something more than complete uncertainty and something less than complete certainty. They plan under conditions of risk; they have knowledge (or a good guess) about the likelihood of occurrence of some factors, but not all.

Planning and decision making are bound up in a future filled with risk. This is why some managers avoid planning. They argue that it takes them away from "doing" and accomplishing results. They do not try to foresee problems; they "cross those bridges when they come to them." This, of course, is very shortsighted.

Usually there is more than one way to reach an objective, but there is no sure way of identifying the "best" way. Most managers will choose the approach they predict will yield the highest return relative to cost. This type of analysis is called *cost-benefit analysis.*

In other words, we set out the various plans that could be used to reach an objective. Underlying each plan is a set of planning premises, or assumptions about the future. Probabilities, or odds, are assigned to each set of premises to indicate our "best guess" as to which ones will become reality. Each plan's expected profit along with its probability of success also are estimated. The plan most likely to be chosen is based on the most realistic planning premises and offers the highest return, given the estimated probability of success in carrying out the plan.

"I have the result of your cost-benefit analysis. You should have retired four years ago."

Organizing

A firm becomes a structured organization through the process of organizing. **Organizing is the management function of relating people, tasks (or activities), and resources to each other so that an organization can accomplish its objectives.** Plans are carried out by the organizing process. Like planning, organizing also is a dynamic process. This means that changes in objectives and plans usually lead to changes in the organization's structure. We will discuss organizing in greater detail in Chapter 5.

organizing

The Systems Concept

According to the systems concept, a firm is not the accounting department or the marketing department. It consists of a network of interrelationships among the various departments and their environ-

systems concept

ment. The marketing research department is a *subsystem* of the firm. However, the firm is a subsystem of its industry, and the industry is a subsystem of the total economic system, and so on. Top management must integrate the various subsystems so that overall system performance can be improved. Top management also must work for acceptance of this view by others in the firm.

The systems view underscores the need for top management to set clearly defined goals and to communicate them to lower-level managers and workers. In judging their effectiveness, credit managers tend to think in terms of reducing bad debts, while sales managers tend to think in terms of annual dollar sales increases. They often view the firm from different perspectives, but they should be striving to accomplish common goals.

The more that company personnel view the firm as a system, the less their actions will conflict and the more efficient the firm will become. The credit manager recognizes that some bad debts are acceptable in order to increase sales. The sales manager recognizes the need to deny credit to customers with poor credit ratings in order to keep bad-debt losses down. This is the essence of the systems view. Another indicator of systems thinking is a firm's responsiveness to social problems. When a firm accepts social responsibility, it is viewing itself as a subsystem of the larger socioeconomic system.

Staffing

staffing

An organization is meaningless without people. The quality of its managers and workers probably is a firm's single most important asset. **Staffing includes the recruitment, selection, training, and promotion of personnel to fill both managerial and nonmanagerial positions in a company.** Because staffing is so important, we will study it in detail in Chapter 6.

Directing

directing

Assume that we have developed plans, created an organization structure, and staffed it. It now must be stimulated to action through the management function of directing. **Directing means encouraging subordinates to work toward achieving company objectives. It sometimes is called leading, guiding, motivating, or actuating.**

A manager's opinion of subordinates affects how they will be directed. Managers who think subordinates are lazy, irresponsible, and immature rely on rewards and punishments and use formal authority to get things done. Managers who think subordinates are responsible and are striving to achieve goals will likely "let them work." The amount and type of directing that are needed depend largely on the manager's view of his or her subordinates.

The discussion that follows focuses on four basic concepts that relate to the directing function:

- participation
- communication
- motivation
- leadership

Participation

Managers who practice participative management do not rely only on their formal authority to issue orders to subordinates. **Participative management means that the manager encourages and allows his or her subordinates to involve themselves directly in the decision making that will affect them.**

participative management

Douglas McGregor has suggested that there are two types of managers, *Theory X managers* and *Theory Y managers.*[2] Theory X managers assume that the average person

- inherently dislikes work
- is, by nature, lazy, irresponsible, and self-centered
- is security oriented and indifferent to the needs of the organization
- wants to avoid responsibility and has little ambition

Because they make these assumptions, Theory X managers believe that the average person must be threatened, coerced, and controlled in order to motivate him or her to work toward company goals.

Theory Y managers make the opposite assumptions about the average person. Theory Y managers assume that the average person is capable of

More and more women are moving into managerial jobs in all types of business and industry

- developing interest in his or her work
- committing himself or herself to working to reach company goals
- working productively with a minimum of control and threat of punishment

According to McGregor, workers who fit the Theory X manager's set of assumptions do so because of the nature of their work and the supervision they receive. In other words, their jobs and the supervision they receive tend to make the workers dislike their work, become irresponsible, and so on.

Many managers believe that participative management is the key to building *employee morale,* the worker's attitudes about the job and employer. The more that workers view the firm as the source of their need satisfaction, the higher their morale is likely to be.

Some workers, however, *do* fit the Theory X assumptions. A manager who assumes they fit Theory Y assumptions probably will fail to motivate them. Furthermore, good employee morale is no guarantee of high employee productivity. Employees could be very happy on the job and still produce very little. They also could be very unhappy and have low morale and yet be very productive because they are afraid to be fired!

For participative management to work effectively

- there must be adequate time to anticipate problems and make plans because participation requires more time than authoritarian decision making
- subordinates must be assured that their participation is genuine or else they will not see any personal benefit from participating
- managers must believe in it and trust their subordinates
- managers must understand that it involves accountability to subordinates as well as superiors because they no longer merely pass "orders" down the chain of command

Communication

communication

Communication is a transfer of information between people that results in a common understanding between them. When workers believe that they are not only "talked down to" but can also talk up to their supervisors, two-way communication exists. Workers feel more important when their voice is heard.

Modern managers recognize the advantages of two-way communication. Communication of orders may by initiated at the top. But feedback (the receiver's response) from people lower in the firm is critical to the planning and control functions because these people are closer to the situation than upper-level managers. A production manager who recently installed new machinery on the assembly line wants feedback from foremen regarding the machinery's performance. Foremen, in turn, want feedback from assembly-line workers.

Motivation

motivation

Motivation is the result of the drive to satisfy an internal urge. Managers must structure jobs so that they provide incentives that

will satisfy workers' needs if those workers apply effort on the job. By doing this, managers can motivate their subordinates to work toward company objectives. The more effectively organizational and personal objectives are integrated, the more motivated workers are to achieve the organizational objectives.

For many years, money has been used as the "carrot" (incentive) to motivate workers. Money is an effective motivator as long as most workers are focusing on satisfying their lower-level needs, such as the needs for food, clothing, and shelter. But for many workers today, money no longer is the all-powerful motivator.

The Hawthorne Experiments mark the beginning of modern research into employee motivation and the human relations movement in management. These experiments were conducted between 1927 and 1932 at Western Electric's Hawthorne plant near Chicago. The researchers were studying the effects of the physical work environment on worker productivity. For example, it seemed reasonable to assume that better lighting would lead to greater employee productivity. The researchers found, however, that production increased when the lighting level was raised *or* lowered. The apparent explanation for this surprising result was the importance the workers felt because they were being studied by management.

The human relations movement brought new approaches to motivating and leading employees. Managers have come to understand that people are people, on and off the job. Workers are not machines. As we will see in Chapter 5, if their higher-level needs are not satisfied by the formal organization, workers will create an informal organization to satisfy them.

All managers are responsible for motivating their subordinates, but managers are limited in what they can do. Foremen are limited by company policies on wage scales and fringe benefits, and the company's president may be limited by policies set by the board of directors. Because the typical employee is said to work at about 30 percent of capacity, however, motivating them to become more productive is a big challenge for all managers

An interesting view of motivation has given managers added insight into how to motivate employees.[3] Frederick Herzberg's research led him to conclude that many factors managers often rely on to motivate workers are not true motivators. He divides job factors that generally are considered to be motivators into two groups:

- maintenance factors (hygiene factors), such as pay, working conditions, job security, and the nature of supervision
- motivational factors (motivators), such as achievement, recognition, responsibility, advancement, and growth potential

Maintenance factors occur as part of the work environment. They are job context, or extrinsic, factors that are not part of the work itself. If they are absent or inadequate, they tend to be *dissatisfiers*. Their presence, however, helps to avoid worker dissatisfaction. Thus poor pay and poor working conditions are dissatisfiers but improving them will *not* provide true motivation.

Motivational factors occur as part of the work itself. They are job content, or intrinsic, factors. Motivational factors make work rewarding in and of itself—they are *satisfiers*.

Herzberg's motivation-hygiene theory has helped in focusing management attention on job content factors in motivating workers. **Job enrichment is the process of redesigning jobs to satisfy higher-level needs and organizational needs by improving worker satisfaction and task efficiency. It gives workers more responsibility, authority, and autonomy in planning and doing their work.**

job enrichment

Some managers believe that job enlargement and job rotation can help in providing more satisfying work for subordinates. *Job enlargement* involves adding new tasks to a job in order to make it less boring and more challenging. It is especially useful for assembly-line jobs that are repetitive and monotonous and do not involve the worker's mental processes.

Job rotation among management trainees has been practiced for many years to give them an overall view of the firm's operations and to prepare them for promotion. This practice has been used at the operative level in recent years. Workers periodically are assigned to new jobs in order to reduce boredom. The new job usually does not require the worker to learn a major new skill; but it does, for example, give assembly-line workers a better understanding of the total production process. They can relate their specialized jobs to the creation of a finished product.

Quite recently, a lot of attention has focused on quality-of-work-life programs. As we will see in Chapter 5, the goals are to increase job satisfaction and to improve productivity.

Leadership

leadership

Leadership is a manager's ability to get subordinates to develop their capabilities by inspiring them to achieve. It is a means of motivating them to accomplish goals. Leadership is practiced in different degrees by the people in a firm. The president is ultimately responsible for directing the entire firm. He or she sets the style of leadership in the firm. If the president is a dictator, other managers are likely to be dictators, too.

One of the earliest leadership theories was the "great person" theory. It assumed that certain persons were gifted with leadership talent and that they would arise as great leaders in any situation. Examples of these "born leaders" are Alexander the Great, Napoleon, Abraham Lincoln, and Queen Elizabeth I.

Another theory is the "traitist" theory. The "traitists" believe that leadership traits don't have to be inborn. They feel that leadership ability can be acquired through experience and learning. For years, the "traitists" have been searching for common traits among leaders, but there are striking differences among the lists compiled by various researchers. Some of the more common leadership traits, however, are intelligence, dependability, high tolerance for frustration, persistence, imagination, and cooperativeness.

Most of the newer research on leadership has focused on leadership styles. Figure 4-4, for example, presents a continuum of possible leadership styles. At the left is the boss-centered leader and at the right is the subordinate-centered leader. Most managers feel that the more subordinate-centered leadership styles are more effective than the more boss-centered styles.

Other commonly used terms to describe leadership styles are

- autocratic, dictatorial, or authoritarian
- democratic, or participative
- laissez-faire, or free rein

Autocratic leaders keep all decision-making authority to themselves, while democratic leaders share it with their subordinates.

FIGURE 4-4

A continuum of leadership behavior

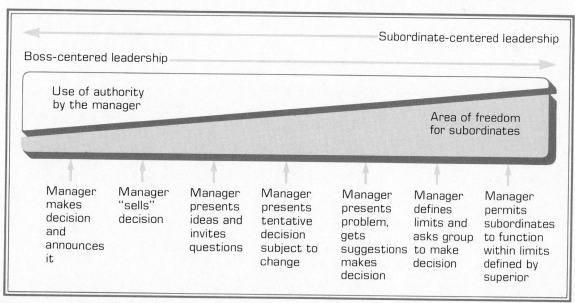

Boss-centered leadership

Subordinate-centered leadership

Use of authority by the manager

Area of freedom for subordinates

| Manager makes decision and announces it | Manager "sells" decision | Manager presents ideas and invites questions | Manager presents tentative decision subject to change | Manager presents problem, gets suggestions makes decision | Manager defines limits and asks group to make decision | Manager permits subordinates to function within limits defined by superior |

**What Is
Management?**

POINT OF VIEW

A lower-level manager
"I'm a supervisor on a production line. To me, management means attending to detail—making sure that my subordinates do exactly as they are told. The really important work that can't be left up to somebody else to do is what it's all about. I spend a lot of time working right along with my subordinates. I'm not afraid to get my hands dirty!

"As far as management functions go, and I'll admit I never thought of management in those exact terms, most of my time is spent on directing. Controlling would come in second. My job is to get production out of my workers and that means getting them to do a good job and making sure that they do it."

A top-level manager
"I'm president of a large firm that manufactures sporting goods. To me, management means keeping yourself free of detail work so that you can concentrate on thinking about your company's future—where your company will be 10 to 15 years from now. Of course, thinking by itself won't accomplish the job. That's why I've spent several years bringing together the best possible group of executives to carry out my plans for the future.

"Undoubtedly, my most important function is planning."

Laissez-faire leaders try to delegate total responsibility for decision making to their subordinates. They do not want to share their decision-making authority; they want to join the group for decision-making purposes.

As we suggested earlier, many modern managers regard the more participative styles of leadership as desirable because participative leadership

- permits subordinates to satisfy their higher-level needs (competence, knowledge, self-confidence, feelings of achievement, esteem) through the job
- is an approach to motivating subordinates
- permits managers to receive feedback from operatives at the lowest levels in the firm

In the final analysis, the "best" style of leadership depends on the three elements in the leadership environment:

- the leader
- the followers
- the situation

Participation will not work if the leader cannot inspire subordinates to participate or if the subordinates do not want to participate. Situations that call for quick decisions limit the time available for true participation of subordinates.

Fred Fiedler has developed a *contingency theory of leadership,* which makes it clear that there is no one "best" leadership style.[4] For example, situations that are either very easy or very difficult are handled best by task-oriented leaders. Situations that are only moderately difficult are handled best by subordinate-oriented leaders.

Controlling

Managers must always monitor operations (evaluate performance) to see if the firm is achieving its goals. This is the management function of controlling. **Controlling involves**

controlling

- **setting standards of performance**
- **measuring actual performance and comparing it to performance standards to detect deviations from standards**
- **taking corrective action when significant deviations exist**

As we suggested in our discussion of MBO, planning and controlling are closely related. When spouses prepare a budget, they are planning *and* setting up a control device. Suppose the budget plan is to save $1,000 by the end of the year. If their savings account shows a balance of $200 on July 1, the standard is not being met. Awareness of this should lead to corrective action. The earlier they discover the deviation from their saving standard, the quicker they can take corrective action.

Examples of controlling are an office manager's efforts to keep expenditures for typing paper in line with the budget or a plant manager's efforts to keep the number of rejects down to an acceptable minimum. First there must be a definite idea of what we want to accomplish (a standard). The office manager, for example, cannot exceed the budget for paper. In practice, setting standards is not always simple. How should management evaluate the production department's performance? On the basis of the number of rejects? On the basis of the average time required to produce an average unit of output? On the basis of the average cost of producing an average unit of output? Actually, all are important. A 3 percent reduction in

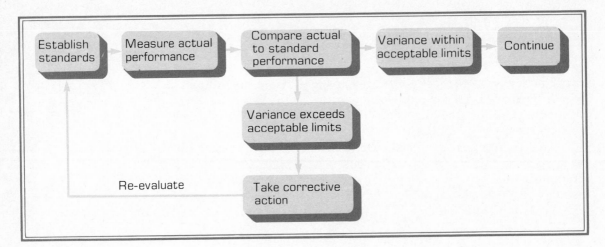

FIGURE 4-5
The control process

rejects along with tripled production costs probably is not desirable. But whether it is or is not depends on the relative importance of avoiding rejects and avoiding cost increases.

Second, a manager measures actual performance and compares it to the established standard. Measurement is not so simple either. There are many problems in measuring employee performance. In some jobs only quantitative results (number of units produced) are important. In other jobs qualitative results (quality of the units produced) are the crucial basis for comparison.

The final element of control is taking corrective action. It is desirable to detect deviations from standards quickly. The longer that corrective action takes, the more it will cost. (See Figure 4-5.)

THE DECISION-MAKING PROCESS

Everything a firm does is the result of decisions made by managers. Examples are deciding on the firm's goals, what products to make, what equipment to buy, what advertising appeals to use, where to get funds, and where to sell its products. Decision making is a very complex process. The management functions are involved at each stage.

Stages in the Decision-Making Process

decision-making
process

The stages in the decision-making process are as follows:

· **recognizing an opportunity or a problem**
· **gathering information**

- **developing alternatives**
- **analyzing alternatives**
- **choosing the best alternative**
- **implementing the decision**
- **evaluating the decision**

Recognizing an Opportunity or a Problem

A business opportunity must be recognized before it can be exploited. Because a firm's resources are limited, management must decide what types of opportunity can be exploited. Exploiting the opportunity also requires decision making.

Decision making also is needed when management recognizes a problem. Often this is little more than a feeling that "something is not right." Decisions must be made regarding a clear definition of the problem and whether or not anything will be done about it.

Gathering Information

After recognizing the opportunity or problem, the decision maker's next step is to gather information about it. This involves talks with company personnel and outsiders who might provide greater insight. Company records and secondary sources of information such as libraries also might be investigated.

Because of the tremendous capacity of computers to store data, many firms now have *management information systems.* These systems are made up of people and machines. People feed in the data needed for decision-making purposes, and these data are processed, summarized, and reported to decision makers who need it.

Developing Alternatives

After developing a good "feel" for the opportunity or problem and its setting, the decision maker begins to formulate alternative courses of action. The support of others might be sought in brainstorming sessions in which the participants offer ways to deal with the opportunity or problem. Freewheeling creativity is important here, so no evaluation is made of the alternatives offered at this stage. The goal is to stimulate new ways of looking at the opportunity or problem and to develop alternative ways of dealing with it. If there is only one alternative, there is no decision to make!

"Go on in, Harry—what are you waiting for?"

Analyzing Alternatives

After making a list of alternatives, the decision maker begins to analyze them critically. Alternatives that are unlikely to pay off are eliminated along with those that involve high risk in comparison to

"INFORMANIA"

It's having weekly reports in a business that changes minute to minute.

You're responsible.

You decide, make the policy, spend the money, and reap the rewards.

Or suffer the consequences.

Yours is not a leisurely business, either. Markets change almost as fast as minds can think.

So when you're told "we sold 40,000," but nobody can tell you if that's units or dollars, it isn't surprising that there's a sudden ringing in your ears.

That's "Informania."

The solution is information. The right information. In the right form. For the right people in the right place and time.

Burroughs can help. Because we know how to manage information. We've put 95 years of thought and experience into it. We offer a comprehensive solution to the problem of "Informania."

Our computers and office automation systems can help you collect, compose, analyze, store, recall, reformulate and distribute information.

So that you will know. Minute by minute.

When "Informania" strikes, the answer is Burroughs. Write for our brochure: Burroughs Corporation, Dept. FT-18, Burroughs Place, Detroit, Michigan 48232.

Burroughs
Building on strength

expected payoff. Those that remain often are ranked in terms of their expected payoff. The payoff could be stated in terms such as least cost, maximum profit, or maximum customer service.

This process might involve analyzing the projected consequences of each of the remaining alternatives, which is always tough because it involves forecasting the future. Nevertheless, the thought process required here helps to ensure that the decision maker considers the future consequences of present decisions.

Choosing the Best Alternative

In choosing the best alternative, a decision maker establishes a decision criterion and a decision rule. If the goal is to improve delivery service to customers, the decision criterion might be "fastest delivery." The decision rule would be to choose the transportation method that provides the fastest delivery to customers. The decision criterion, however, could have been "lowest cost." Choosing decision criteria requires good judgment concerning the firm's goals and an understanding of the risks involved.

AUTHORS' COMMENTARY

Japanese and American Management Styles Will Become More Similar

Japanese managers are more likely than American managers to practice participative management; they seek to manage by consensus. The goal of consensus management is to encourage subordinates to participate in the decision making that will affect them in order to get their commitment to the decision. There is more stress in Japan on "group think." Thus performance in Japanese firms tends to be evaluated more on group, or team, accomplishments than in American firms, where performance tends to be evaluated more on the individual's accomplishments.

Although it ordinarily takes Japanese managers longer than American managers to make decisions, the Japanese can usually implement their decisions more quickly because most of the opposition to a decision will have been eliminated before it is made. American managers make decisions more quickly but typically spend more time implementing them.

It is likely that Japanese and American styles of management will become more similar as firms in these two nations compete more aggressively for sales in the global business environment. Productivity will play a major role in determining which features of Japanese and American management styles will remain and which ones will be modified or discarded.

Implementing the Decision

Once the decision has been made (the best alternative or a combination of several of the initial alternatives has been selected), the decision maker must move toward implementing it. Implementation, of course, also requires decision making in performing the management functions.

Evaluating the Decision

After implementing the decision, the decision maker must evaluate it. Operations must be monitored, or checked, to see whether the decision is being implemented properly. Monitoring also gives the decision maker feedback that helps in assessing whether the "right decision" was made and if corrective actions are needed.

Types of Decisions

There are two basic types of decisions, routine decisions and nonroutine decisions.

routine decision

A routine decision is a decision that must be faced over and over. The set of circumstances that call for the decision recurs. Managers often set up policies and standard operating procedures to handle routine decisions. An office manager who sets up a policy of "no smoking in the office" does away with the need to make a decision each time an office worker asks if it's all right to smoke in the office.

nonroutine decision

A nonroutine decision is a nonrecurring decision. The set of circumstances that call for this type of decision does not occur regularly. There are two types of nonroutine decisions, strategic and tactical. Strategic decisions are made by top-level management.

One example of strategic nonroutine decisions is decision making about the types of opportunity that a firm will attempt to exploit—what business the firm will be in. Examples include The Coca-Cola Company's decision to buy Columbia Pictures in order to enter the entertainment business and Avon Products, Inc.'s decision to buy Mallinckrodt, Inc. in order to enter the health-care business.

Another variety of strategic nonroutine decisions is whether or not a company should buy out a competing firm. In 1981, G. Heileman Brewing Company's top management decided it wanted to buy Jos. Schlitz Brewing Company. The Justice Department, however, opposed the deal because it felt competition would be reduced in the brewing industry. This example underscores an important point. Managerial decision making is subject to constraints. Forces beyond the control of management can and do affect their decisions. In this case, Heileman decided to abandon its effort to buy Schlitz.

Whereas strategic nonroutine decisions have an important long-run effect, tactical nonroutine decisions have less long-run effect. For example, in an attempt to stimulate car sales, an auto maker may decide to offer cash rebates to new car buyers. This may result in an immediate sales increase but will have little or no long-term effect.

The dividing line between strategic and tactical decisions is often an arbitrary one. Philip Morris Inc. bought the Seven-Up Company in 1978. That strategic nonroutine decision was in line with Philip Morris's effort to diversify. The firm then had to develop an advertising program for 7-UP. Some people consider this a nonroutine tactical decision. If you think about it, however, decisions about 7-UP's advertising could also have strategic implications. Should 7-UP be advertised only against other lemon-lime drinks like Sprite and Mountain Dew? Or should it attempt to take on *all* soft drinks, including colas?

One important reason for distinguishing between routine and nonroutine decisions involves the concept of management by exception. **According to the concept of management by exception (or the exception principle), routine decisions should be pushed as far down in the firm as possible. By granting authority to lower-level managers to make routine decisions, higher-level managers can devote more time to nonroutine decisions.**

management by
exception

Management by exception is related to the control function. It requires a well-developed system for monitoring operations. It also requires setting standards of performance, measuring actual performance, and comparing actual to standard performance. The idea is to allow subordinates to review performance against set standards and bring to the manager's attention only those cases that involve exceptions to normal or acceptable performance. This frees the manager from reviewing performance in situations where performance is in line with standards. He or she can concentrate on cases of exceptionally good performance and exceptionally poor performance. By studying these cases, he or she can develop ideas for improvement.

There are several potential drawbacks to management by exception. For example, advancing technology may make old standards obsolete. Unless they are re-evaluated from time to time, managers may assume incorrectly that performance is acceptable and operations are going along as planned when, in fact, they are not. If some aspects of operations that are critical to success are not identified in advance, they will go unmeasured by the subordinate. There also is a measurement problem, especially for factors such as human behavior. It may be next to impossible for such a system to call attention, for example, to a situation where employee morale is on the decline.

SUMMARY AND LOOK AHEAD

Businesses are living things that seek to accomplish objectives. Through the performance of nonmanagerial work and managerial functions a firm moves toward the realization of its objectives. The three managerial skills required for effective performance of these functions are conceptual, people, and technical skills.

Managerial and nonmanagerial work can cause stress on the job. Firms do what they can to help control stress, but how a person deals with it is basically a personal decision.

The functions of management—planning, organizing, staffing, directing, and controlling—are performed by managers in the process of achieving goals by bringing together people and other resources. Management is necessary whenever results depend on group effort. There are different echelons (levels) of management in a firm. A firm's success or failure is traceable to the effectiveness of its managers. Likewise, there are different styles of management. For example, some managers practice participative management to a greater extent than others.

In reality, management cannot be broken down into a series of separate functions. It is a process. This becomes clear when we think of the firm as a system.

We can also view the management task in terms of decision making. Managers make decisions in performing their functions. There are seven stages in the decision-making process: (1) recognizing an opportunity or a problem, (2) gathering information, (3) developing alternatives, (4) analyzing alternatives, (5) choosing the best alternative, (6) implementing the decision, and (7) evaluating the decision.

Decisions can be routine or nonroutine. Nonroutine decisions can be either strategic or tactical. Truly strategic decisions are made by top management. Management by exception helps to ensure that upper-level managers will have adequate time to devote to strategic decisions.

The next chapter looks at the firm as an organization. We will see how management goes about organizing a business.

FOR REVIEW . . .

1. Do lower-echelon managers spend more time performing nonmanagerial work than upper-echelon managers? Explain.

2. Why are people skills important at all echelons of management?

3. Should management strive to eliminate all conflict in the firm? Explain.

4. List and describe the five major functions of management.

5. Discuss the similarities and differences between operational and strategic planning. Which one is more important? Why?

6. What is meant by management by objectives (MBO)? What are its advantages? What are some of the potential problems in implementing the MBO approach?

7. What is the "systems concept"?

8. Discuss the relationship between Herzberg's motivation-hygiene theory and job enrichment.

9. What is the "best" style of leadership? Explain.

10. List and describe the seven stages in the decision-making process.

. . . FOR DISCUSSION

1. Why do managers encounter stress on the job?

2. "All managers should practice MBO and be Theory Y managers." Do you agree?

3. It has been said that the president of a company need not be a good manager. All the president need do is possess an ability to select well-qualified subordinates. Do you agree?

4. Do you think that a company president should direct subordinates in the same way that the boss of a work crew would direct subordinates?

5. "The major difference between workers and managers is that workers work and managers think." Do you agree?

INCIDENTS

A Middle Manager Squeeze

The low birthrate during the Great Depression created a big need for management trainees during the 1960s and 1970s. Promotions from trainee to lower-level manager and from lower-level manager to middle-level manager were typically rather rapid for good performers during those two decades.

The earliest arrivals in the baby boom years of 1946–64 were 34 years of age in 1980. The latest arrivals were 16 years of age in 1980. By 1990, they will be 44 and 26 years of age, respectively.

People in middle management positions tend to come from the 35 to 44 year old age bracket. As shown in the graph, the number of people aged 35 to 44 will increase from 25.4 million to 36.1 million between 1980 and 1990. That represents an increase of 42 percent.

The graph also shows that the Bureau of Labor Statistics projects that the number of middle manager jobs will increase from 8.8 million in 1980 to 10.5 million in 1990. That represents an increase of only 19.1 percent. The result could very easily be a middle manager squeeze.[5]

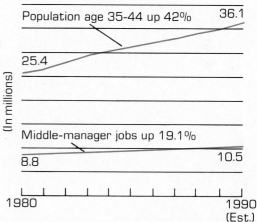

The middle-manager squeeze

Population age 35-44 up 42%   36.1

25.4

(In millions)

Middle-manager jobs up 19.1%

8.8   10.5

1980   1990
                                 (Est.)

QUESTIONS

1. What do these facts and projections suggest about the rate of speed with which lower-level managers will be promoted into the ranks of middle management during the 1980s?

2. What do these facts and projections sug-

gest about the nature of competition among lower-level managers for promotions to middle management?

Motivating Employees

In carrying out the directing function, American managers focus a lot of effort on motivating their subordinates to perform well. Japanese managers, however, focus less attention on motivating their subordinates. One reason is that larger firms in Japan and their employees tend to look at their employer-employee relationship as extending over a lifetime. A newly hired worker in such a firm tends to expect that he or she will be working for that employer until retirement. As a result, employees view their future well-being as directly tied to that of their employers. They reason that the more productive they are, the more the employer and the employees benefit.

Japanese firms like Nissan, Honda, Toyota, Hitachi, Sanyo, and Sharp with plants in the United States sometimes have management problems related to employee motivation. Japanese managers in those plants sometimes find American employees less dedicated to the company than Japanese employees. Thus these managers begin to focus more attention on motivating their workers.

QUESTIONS

1. Which of the three basic managerial skills are most needed when a manager seeks to motivate workers? Explain.

2. Would a Japanese manager more likely be a Theory X or a Theory Y manager? Explain.

3. Do you think the concept of lifetime employment is beneficial to employers and employees? Why or why not?

3. Do you think that job stress among lower-level managers will increase during the 1980s? Why or why not?

CHAPTER 5

Organizing The Firm

OBJECTIVES

After reading this chapter, you should be able to

1. Tell the difference between personal and organizational objectives and explain how they are integrated.
2. Draw a figure that illustrates the hierarchy of organizational objectives.
3. List and give an example of the different bases for departmentation.
4. List and explain the factors that affect a manager's optimum span of management.
5. List and explain the three actions involved in the delegation process.
6. Relate the delegation process to the degree to which a firm is centralized or decentralized.
7. Compare the line, line and staff, and committee organization structures and discuss the matrix organization and quality-of-work-life programs.
8. Tell the difference between line function and staff function and line managers and staff people.
9. Draw an organization chart and tell what it indicates and does not indicate.
10. Discuss the hierarchy of human needs.
11. Compare formal and informal organizations.

KEY CONCEPTS

Look for these terms as you read the chapter

organization

hierarchy of organizational objectives

departmentation

span of management

delegation

responsibility

authority

accountability

centralization

decentralization

organization chart

line authority

line functions

staff functions

staff

functional authority

matrix organization

quality-of-work-life (QWL) programs

hierarchy of needs

informal groups

informal organization

The Coca-Cola Company has had a long history as a rather conservatively and closely managed company in which authority was largely centralized at company headquarters. In 1980 Mr. Roberto Goizueta took over as chairman and chief executive officer and things started to change.

One of Mr. Goizueta's first actions as chief executive officer was to issue a corporate "vision" statement in which he outlined Coke's plans to remain the "dominant force in the soft-drink industry" around the world.

According to Mr. Goizueta, "The day of the one-man band is gone. . . . My job is to pick the people, then give them the responsibility and authority to get the job done."

Mr. Don Keough, Coke's president, echoes the same philosophy. "We're giving our division managers around the world a lot of authority, and we're holding them responsible."

The Coca-Cola Company, a very large organization that is over one hundred years old, has been undergoing some organizational changes since Mr. Goizueta took over. It has become a much more decentralized organization.

A business is a logical combination of human, financial, and physical resources put together by management so that certain goals can be accomplished. Individuals can accomplish their personal objectives and help to achieve company objectives if both types of objectives are carefully integrated. The formal organization, therefore, is the structure that helps a firm and its employees to achieve their goals.

A manager's span of management refers to the number of subordinates he or she supervises. How wide or narrow the span is depends in part on the type of organizational structure the firm has.

A firm, or any other type of organization, contains a collection of smaller, informal groups. They are not created by management but by the group members themselves. The entire set of these small groups is the informal organization. It is separate and distinct from the informal organization.

WHAT IS AN ORGANIZATION?

Imagine two cars traveling in opposite directions on the same street. They approach an intersection with four stop signs. Both cars stop. No other cars are present. Suppose driver A signals for a turn that will put his car in the path of driver B. Both drivers must interact to avoid a wreck. Avoiding a wreck is an objective of both drivers. Traffic signals and rules lend structure so that one driver will always let the other pass first.

Now consider a business firm whose objective is to make a profit by providing want-satisfying products to customers. The employees' objective is to earn a living. Workers interact with one another and with the tools of production. They perform those tasks necessary for the firm to make a profit and for the employees to earn a living. People, tasks, and physical resources must be combined into a structure that enables the firm and its employees to achieve their goals.

We have seen two examples of organization. They are very different types because they vary in size, length of life, complexity, and formality. The two drivers interact briefly and informally. The greater number of employees interact over a longer period of time on the basis of work rules and procedures. There is more formal structuring of the relationships among people, activities, and physical resources than there is between the two drivers.

Both, however, are examples of organization. Notice that three key elements of organization are present:

. human interaction

- actions toward an objective (goal-directed activity)
- structure

An organization, therefore, is something that is structured so that   organization
human activity can be coordinated to accomplish objectives.

Why Do People Join Organizations?

People belong to organizations because they believe that they
can achieve their goals better within them than they could outside.
You might join a fraternity or a sorority because you might figure
that you would have more social functions to attend than if you were
not a member. Most of us belong to many organizations because we
have so many different goals. No one organization could satisfy
them all.

In a business firm people's needs are similar enough to enable
them to satisfy some of their needs through the firm. Employees can
earn a living and perhaps receive bonuses for doing exceptionally
good work. But, as we'll see, people on the job have other social
needs that may not be satisfied by the firm. A worker may be earning
a living by doing the tasks assigned to him or her by the boss. But this
person also may want to "feel important" and be well liked by
coworkers. As a result people on the job often form informal groups
that help them to satisfy wants that may not be satisfied by the
formal structure of the firm. People tend to remain in an organization only if it helps them to satisfy their goals.

Involving workers in
decision making can
often help them satisfy
their goals

Personal and Organizational Objectives

People contribute to an organization if they think it helps to
satisfy their personal objectives. Integrating various personal objectives into a unified statement of the firm's objectives is not easy. For
example, an employee may easily accept a company's objective "to
make a profit." Doing so may provide money to be shared in the
firm's profit-sharing plan. But that same employee may not accept a
company objective "to be a good community citizen." Doing so, for
example, could cause the firm to invest in pollution control equipment and to make contributions to the local symphony orchestra.
These "extra costs" might leave less money for pay raises.

Ideally an organization would meet all the personal objectives
of all the people associated with it. Personal goals, however, often
conflict. As a result a firm's objectives usually are something other
than the sum of the personal objectives of its different publics (employees, suppliers, owners, creditors, customers, etc.).

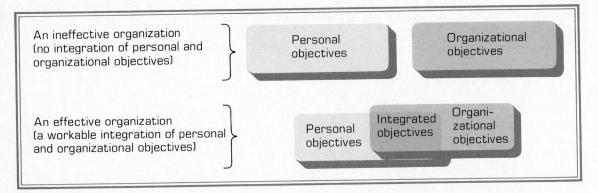

FIGURE 5-1

Personal objectives, organizational objectives, and organizational effectiveness

Formal organizations like business firms *suboptimize* objectives. This means they settle for less than the total achievement of all the objectives of their publics. Not all the personal goals of all of a firm's publics will be fully satisfied. Nor will company goals be completely achieved. For example, an employee may want to grow on the job—to be given the opportunity to learn new skills and be promoted to a higher-level job. But the firm may need his or her services in a very specialized job. The worker's desire for more varied tasks conflicts with the firm's objectives. The reason that every employee is never totally satisfied with his or her employer is that the personal and organizational objectives never are in total harmony. There always is some degree of conflict. (See Figure 5-1.)

A *tradeoff* is necessary. Neither the worker's objective nor the firm's objective will be achieved 100 percent. A compromise is worked out whereby the firm and the worker each get something, but not all that each might want. The employee's job might be broadened to include a greater variety of tasks. This increases his or her job satisfaction and the employee may become more productive; and the firm, of course, benefits. The management by objectives approach discussed in Chapter 4 can help in integrating personal and organizational objectives.

ORGANIZATION AS STRUCTURE

All firms are structured to help achieve company and personal goals. How complex and formal this structure is depends on many things. Firms with only a handful of employees, for example, require less formal structure than firms with many employees. Large firms require more attention to structure because there are more workers, greater specialization of labor, and a greater number of levels of managers.

For example, an owner-manager of a women's dress shop selects and orders merchandise from dress manufacturers, determines prices, and sets credit policies. He or she may have several salespeople, a bookkeeper, and perhaps a credit manager and a delivery driver. These people are in face-to-face contact, and the owner personally runs the business. But in a large department store, there are many more salespeople, several delivery drivers, an entire credit department, an accounting department, and managers (buyers) for each separate department. It's almost impossible for one person to run such a large business alone.

What Is Being Structured?

An organizational structure is created to help achieve goals. Within that structure, activities are performed to help achieve those goals. Organizational "structuring," therefore, focuses first on those activities.

For example, a primary goal of your school is to educate students. One of your goals is a good education. Relationships among the activities needed to reach these goals must be structured. The two essential activities here are teaching and learning; and they require people, books, and classrooms for their performance.

Teachers must be assigned to courses, textbooks must be related to courses, and classrooms must be assigned. Of course, students also must be assigned to teachers and courses. In other words, three basic components must be related to each other through the process of organizing:

- people
- activities
- physical resources

Organizing to Reach Objectives

Objectives are the ends that we want to accomplish in an organization. In order to accomplish them, certain activities must be performed by people working with other resources. These activities are the means for accomplishing the organization's objectives. Activities are the connecting link between an organization's objectives and its structure. It is through the organizational structure that management coordinates the activities of workers that are required to reach the organization's objectives.

But what objective tells Harry the janitor to sweep the floor? The overall company objective "to supply customers with a quality

**Work Groups and
the Organizational
Structure**

POINT OF
VIEW

The concept of the hierarchy of organizational objectives says that individual workers, work groups, departments, divisions, and the company itself have objectives. An organizational structure is needed to help the business firm and its employees accomplish their objectives. But, as we have seen, some conflict always exists between the organization's objectives and those of its employees. Conflict also often exists among individual employees.

Many experts on organization are now focusing on work groups in their efforts to build effective organizations. The idea is to build work groups that are made up of individuals who see their personal goals as being essentially the same as those of the group as a whole. For this approach to organizing to be effective, however, management must be willing and able to allow work groups to participate in the decision making that will affect them. It cannot succeed if managers insist upon practicing Theory X management.

product at a reasonable price" does not tell Harry what he should do to help the firm reach its goals. The company objective is too broad to provide a specific objective for Harry.

hierarchy of
organizational
objectives

The concept of the hierarchy of organizational objectives involves breaking down broad company goals into specific goals for each person in the organization. Broad organizational goals are broken down successively into goals for company divisions, departments, work-groups, and individual workers. This process tells Harry that his job (activity) is sweeping the floor. The number of levels of objectives depends on the firm's size and complexity. There are fewer levels in very small firms than in very large ones.

Identifying, Grouping, and Assigning Activities

The first step in building an organizational structure is to analyze the major activities that must be performed to help the organization reach its objectives. For a manufacturer these activities usually are production, marketing, and finance. Each activity is assigned to a separate department within the firm.

departmentation

Firms are broken down into departments through the process of departmentation. **Departmentation means identifying, grouping, and assigning activities to specialized departments within an organization.**

There are two basic approaches to identifying activities. First, we could observe workers and classify their activities such as assembling parts, buying raw materials, and pricing products. The other approach is to start with company goals and determine which activities are needed to reach those goals. This method is the only one available to a brand-new firm.

Next, activities are grouped and assigned. There are six major bases upon which an organization could be departmented:

- function
- geography
- product
- customer
- process
- time

These bases are discussed in Table 5-1.

Many firms use several bases for departmentation. A firm might be divided by function into production, marketing, and finance departments. The marketing department could be divided into a domestic sales organization and a foreign sales organization (geography). Decisions of this type are influenced by the relative advantages of the different approaches and the experience, preferences, and judgment of top management.

Many factors can affect departmentation decisions. One is technology. For example, the increasing importance of computer technology in business has led many firms to create specialized data processing departments. The faster pace of technological change also

TABLE 5-1

Six major bases upon which an organization can be departmented

Base	Examples
1. Function	1. Many oil companies are departmented by functions: exploration, production, refining, marketing, and finance.
2. Geography	2. The U.S. Internal Revenue Service is departmented partly on a geographical basis. Where you live determines where you send your tax return and where your refund will be mailed from.
3. Product	3. General Motors has separate divisions for Pontiac, Oldsmobile, Chevrolet, Buick, and Cadillac.
4. Customer	4. McDonnell Douglas has a commercial aviation division and a defense production division.
5. Process	5. A brewery has a cooking and an aging department.
6. Time	6. Some colleges operate regular day classes and also have an evening division.

has led many firms to create specialized research and development departments.

Top management's decisions about the types of business opportunity the firm will seek to exploit also affect how a firm is departmented. When Texaco's top management decided to diversify its operations outside the energy business, it set up a new division to search for new types of business opportunity.

Recently, the federal government has begun to reduce the number of government departments. Many business firms are doing likewise. Managers are seeking to delete departments that are no longer necessary and to consolidate necessary and closely related activities spread among several departments into one department. Too much departmentation raises costs, reduces productivity and ability to compete, and slows the decision-making process.

Departmentation is not intended to create "walls" around departments. For example, when problems arise that involve two or more departments, personnel from the departments involved work together to solve them. Engineering, production, finance, and marketing personnel, for example, might try to modify a product that, due to faulty design, is causing customer complaints. After the problem is solved, the work group is dissolved.

Activities are departmented to make work more efficient and to provide a means for controlling operations. Sometimes a firm will change the manner in which it is departmented to increase efficiency. IBM, for example, used to have three major sales divisions: data processing, general systems, and office products. As a result, some customers were called upon by three different IBM salespeople, each of whom was selling different IBM products. IBM now has two divisions, each of which sells all of IBM's products. The national accounts division sells to large accounts and the national marketing division sells to intermediate, small, and new accounts.

An obvious reason for departmentation is the simple fact that the number of subordinates a manager can manage is limited. Without departmentation a firm's size would be limited to the number of persons the top manager could supervise directly. Let's discuss this concept of the span of management.

THE SPAN OF MANAGEMENT

span of management

Span of management refers to the number of persons an individual manager supervises. The nature of the work that a manager's subordinates perform is a basic factor that affects the span of management. If those subordinates perform very similar and routine tasks, the manager's span of management is likely to be wide. Thus many lower-level managers, such as assembly-line foremen, have wide spans of management because they do not spend much time supervising any one subordinate.

On the other hand, a manager whose subordinates perform very different, nonroutine types of work will likely have a narrow span of management. Thus top-level managers have narrow spans of management because they must spend considerable time supervising each subordinate. This is why large firms usually have several echelons of management.

The personal characteristics of managers and their subordinates can also play a role in determining a manager's span of management. We discussed Theory X and Theory Y managers in Chapter 4. Theory X managers tend to have narrower spans of management than Theory Y managers because Theory X managers do not trust their subordinates and will supervise them more closely than Theory Y managers.

As we saw earlier in this chapter, technology can affect the departmentation process. It can also affect a manager's span of management. For example, big retail chains like Kmart and Woolco are using computers to record sales of various products in each outlet. The computer simplifies store managers' decisions about what to buy for their stores and enables a district manager to supervise a greater number of store managers.

In their efforts to increase productivity, many American firms have turned to automation, especially in production work, as we will see in Chapter 8. This has helped many firms trim their labor costs. Recently there has been growing interest in cutting management costs. Firms try to have fewer echelons of management and to increase the managers' spans of management.

Although there is no single generally accepted formula for determining the optimum span of management, there are several factors that managers should consider in determining what their optimum span of management is. These include

- how well-defined the subordinates' jobs are and the complexity of their work
- the subordinates' training and ability to work with others
- the subordinates' motivation
- the pace of technological change in the industry
- the ability of the manager and subordinate to communicate effectively with each other
- the manager's capability
- the manager's willingness and ability to plan, to delegate, and to evaluate subordinates' job performance

THE KIND OF SERVICE
WE DON'T PROVIDE

Layers. Some big banks weight the client-banker relationship with an army of assistant loan officers. Post Oak Bank provides you with one, very good, very capable banker *team. Two people who work with you.*

Post Oak Bank puts this team right in your office, too. Where else can we learn how you do and what you do best? It also helps because you only need to explain your operation once. You don't have to worry about educating this week's trainee. You get *two bankers.* Their experience and education will match or surpass those of the downtown bankers. If one isn't available when you need him, the other is always ready and willing to get you the answers you need.

QUICK DECISIONS

We also respect your time schedules. You won't grow old waiting to hear the outcome of your loan requests. Your bankers get things moving, quickly. That's because there's no bureaucracy to muddle through, no fancy footwork or committees to placate and no big bank red tape. Post Oak Bank believes a bank should be run simply and efficiently. It works out better for both of us.

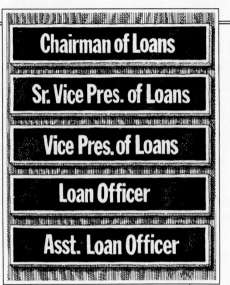

Chairman of Loans
Sr. Vice Pres. of Loans
Vice Pres. of Loans
Loan Officer
Asst. Loan Officer

CAPABILITY COUNTS

Post Oak Bank's building doesn't dominate the Houston skyline. It doesn't have to. It does stand proudly in the dynamic Post Oak area — Houston's other downtown — fast becoming the 8th largest business district in the country. And inside the bank are bankers who have the knowledge, the ability and the intellect to understand you — coupled with the financial resources to back your ventures.

Our commercial lending

officers are prepared to help you with working capital, fixed asset or equipment financing, acquisitions, real estate, construction, and stock loans. The bank also has special expertise in the areas of foreign services and professional and executive lending.

INDIVIDUAL ACCOUNTS

The bank can service your personal needs as well. Our innovative Personal Banking Package includes 24-hour MPACT automatic tellers, 19 drive-thru lanes, American Express Gold Card, convenient pre-arranged Check Credit and our exclusive BonusChek NOW account which requires only a $500 minimum balance.

THE POST OAK COMMITMENT

Our commitment to our clients is more than lip service and smiles. It's dedication to getting the job done right, the first time.

Consider the service your present bank is giving you. If it doesn't measure up, call us or stop by. You'll very happily discover that there's one other thing Post Oak Bank doesn't share with the old downtown — parking problems.

POST OAK BANK

Located between Westheimer and San Felipe on Post Oak Boulevard – in the heart of the other downtown. Nineteen drive-through lanes. Very convenient parking. 24-hour MPACT automated teller. Call (713) 966-2200. or write Box 22716. Houston. Texas 77227-9976.

THE LEADING BANK IN HOUSTON'S OTHER DOWNTOWN™

Member FDIC

An ad that suggests that too many layers of management can reduce the service a firm provides to its customers

The Delegation Process

Without delegation, a firm could not be departmented. **Delegation means entrusting part of a superior's job (or activities) to a subordinate. Three actions are involved in the delegation process:**

- **assigning responsibility**
- **granting authority**
- **establishing accountability**

Responsibility is the obligation of a subordinate to perform an assigned task. In delegating activities the superior assigns a responsibility to subordinates to carry out their assigned tasks.

Authority is the counterpart of responsibility. **Authority is the right to take the action necessary to accomplish an assigned task.** Authority and responsibility must be balanced to enable subordinates to perform their assigned tasks.

Accountability is the act of holding subordinates, who have been delegated adequate authority to fulfill their responsibilities, liable for performing their assigned tasks and for reporting results to their superiors. The subordinates are accountable to their superiors.

Roy manages a car tire shop. Sam removes old tires, Tom switches them on the rims, and Bill balances and remounts them. Roy assigned responsibility to them for performing these tasks and he also granted authority to them to use the necessary tools to accomplish their tasks. Roy also established accountability because the subordinates are answerable to him for results.

Delegation, however, does *not* relieve Roy of the responsibility for seeing to it that his subordinates do their jobs. If a customer's tires wear out because of faulty balancing, it is Roy's responsibility. In other words, the final responsibility rests with the person who is delegating.

The fact that delegation does not relieve a manager of responsibility makes some managers afraid to delegate. Theory X managers are especially unlikely to delegate. To delegate effectively managers must have faith in their subordinates' abilities, be willing to let them learn by their mistakes, and be willing to follow up on how well they are doing their jobs. Managers, therefore, should select qualified subordinates who are capable of performing their assigned tasks.

Span of management and delegation are closely related. Except for very small firms, no firm could function effectively without some delegation. Managers who are afraid to delegate do everything themselves. Their span of management is likely to be very narrow. A sole proprietor, for example, who refuses to delegate limits the size

Margin glossary terms: delegation · responsibility · authority · accountability of his or her firm. It cannot expand beyond what the proprietor is capable of doing alone.

Centralization versus Decentralization of Authority

centralization

The amount of delegation in a firm determines how much the power to decide (authority) is concentrated. **Centralization of authority means that decision-making authority is concentrated in the hands of a few people at the top level of a firm. Such a firm is said to be relatively centralized.** Its managers believe that this centralization makes it easier to coordinate and control the firm's activities.

decentralization

Decentralization of authority means that decision-making authority is spread throughout the firm. Such a firm is said to be relatively decentralized. Middle- and lower-level managers have more decision-making authority than in more centralized firms. This frees top-level managers to devote more time and effort to long-range planning.

As we saw in Chapter 4, participative management means the manager encourages and allows subordinates to involve themselves directly in the decision making that will affect them. Firms that encourage participative management are less centralized than those which do not. So are firms that practice management by exception and management by objectives.

Centralization and decentralization of authority have nothing necessarily to do with geography. A firm with plants in many cities is not decentralized if decision-making power is concentrated at headquarters. But the degree to which a firm is centralized or decentralized does affect its organizational structure.

TYPES OF ORGANIZATIONAL STRUCTURES

organization chart

A firm's structure can be quite complex. **An organization chart graphically depicts a firm's formal structure at a given point in time.** It indicates

- the functions (production, marketing, etc.) that must be performed if the firm is to achieve its goals
- the lines of authority (chain of command)
- how the firm is departmented

- how the departments relate to each other
- the various positions and standing committees in the firm
- the titles of those positions

How complex these charts are depends on what management wants them to show. Generally, the larger the firm, the more complex the chart will be. There are three basic types of organizational structures:

- the line organization
- the line and staff organization
- the committee organization

"You're right, Perkins. Our corporate structure does look like the New York Giants' offense."

The Line Organization

The line organization is the oldest and simplest type of organizational structure. It has been used by military organizations and the Roman Catholic Church and by business firms. In the army the general gives orders to the colonel, the colonel gives orders to the major, the major gives orders to the captain, the captain gives orders to the lieutenant, the lieutenant gives orders to the sergeant, the sergeant gives orders to the corporal, and the corporal gives orders to the private. The Pope is the head of the Roman Catholic Church and the chain of command extends downward through cardinals, archbishops, bishops, and priests.

From one point of view, line authority is the authority relationship that exists between superiors and subordinates. **Line authority is the right to direct subordinates' work.** The chain of command extends from the top to the bottom of the organization. At any given position in the chain, a person takes orders from people higher in the chain and gives orders to people lower in the chain.

line authority

Each superior has direct line authority over his or her subordinates, and each person in the organization reports directly to one boss. Each superior also has total authority over his or her assigned tasks. Figure 5-2 shows a simplified line organization in a business firm. Line authority extends from the stockholders to the individual salespeople.

The major advantages of the line organization are

- the organizational structure is easy to understand
- each person has only one direct supervisor
- decisions may be made faster because each supervisor is accountable to only one immediate supervisor
- authority, responsibility, and accountability are defined clearly

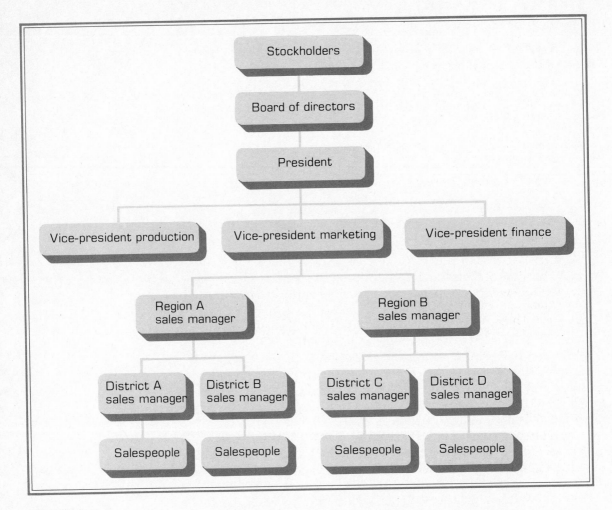

FIGURE 5-2

A simplified line organization

and exactly, which makes it hard to "pass the buck" to someone else

Despite its advantages the line organization suffers from some disadvantages that restrict its use in modern business to very small firms. The major disadvantages are

- each supervisor must be an expert in all aspects of his or her subordinates' work because there are no "specialists" or advisors to turn to

- the paperwork required in directly supervising each subordinate is a burden on each supervisor's time

- the organization has the potential of becoming too inflexible and too bureaucratic

The Line and Staff Organization

Another view of authority involves the distinction between line functions and staff functions. **Line functions contribute directly to reaching primary firm goals.** For example, consider the case of a manufacturing firm whose primary goal is "to make a quality product and sell it at a fair price." The line functions are "production" and "marketing." For a retailer, "purchasing" and "selling" are the line functions. In a personal finance company, "lending" and "collecting" are the line functions.

line functions

Staff functions help the line to achieve primary firm goals. In the manufacturing firm above, "quality control" and "marketing research" are staff functions. Quality control helps the production manager to produce a quality product. Marketing research helps the marketing manager to sell it.

staff functions

The use of staff is one way to divide up the work of line managers. **Staff are people who advise and assist line managers to achieve company objectives.**

staff

The *personal staff* perform duties at the request of his or her line boss. The duties can range from opening the line manager's mail to representing the line manager at company meetings. Personal staff usually have the title of "assistant to."

Specialized staff serve the entire firm, not just one line manager. They have a high degree of expertise in their area of specialization. Thus the personnel manager in a firm usually serves all managers in the firm.

Staff people primarily serve and advise line managers. They usually do not have the authority to issue orders to line managers. The head of a staff department, such as the director of marketing research, however, does have the necessary line authority to run the marketing research department.

There is a lot of potential for line-staff conflict. For example, the director of marketing research is a specialist who knows more about research techniques than the vice-president of marketing. Thus if the vice-president of marketing frequently rejects the research director's advice, conflict between the two of them is likely to arise.

In order to reduce the potential for line-staff conflict, the line manager may be encouraged to *discuss* problems with staff but is not required to follow their advice. Some firms require line managers to *consult* staff people before making decisions on matters in the staff's area of expertise. Going a bit further, some firms require line managers to get the *approval* of the staff before making certain types of decisions. Thus a production manager has to clear new recruits with the personnel department before they are hired.

functional authority

In still other cases the staff have authority to issue orders directly to line personnel. This is functional authority. It is granted only in the staff's area of expertise and only if it will benefit the firm. Thus a plant manager's authority over safety matters may be removed by superiors and given to a safety inspector who has the authority to shut down the plant if dangerous working conditions exist.

Automation and computers enable some firms to eliminate some lower-level management jobs. Suppose a computer can do the same tasks as a lower-level manager at a lower cost. Chances are that

FIGURE 5-3

The line and staff organization

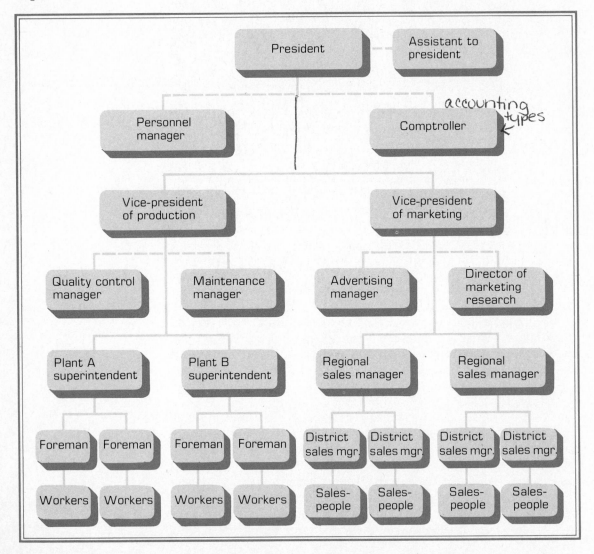

Equal Pay for Similar Work?

AUTHORS' COMMENTARY

As indicated in Table 6-1, the Equal Pay Act of 1963 requires that employers pay men and women equal pay for equal work. Jobs must be *substantially* the same for the law to apply. In 1981, the U.S. Supreme Court ruled that a woman can file a suit for equal pay if her job is *similar* to one held by a man; she receives less pay than the man; and there is intent to discriminate on the employer's part. Thus it is likely that wage and salary administrators will be looking at the issue of unequal pay for similar work much more closely in their efforts to eliminate discriminatory pay practices.

mative action plans must be implemented to eliminate that adverse effect.

SELECTING APPLICANTS FOR EMPLOYMENT

Firms that seek to find the best person for the job will undertake intensive recruiting and be quite careful in selecting applicants. Employers often use job application forms, employment interviews, selection tests, and background investigations in selecting applicants for employment.

The Job Application Form

The job application form (application blank or biographical inventory) is prepared by an employer and filled in by a job applicant. The applicant provides job-related information that helps the employer to determine if the applicant has the needed education, experience, training, etc., for the job. The care with which an applicant fills out this form can be very revealing. (See Figure 6-3.)

job application form

Antidiscrimination laws make it illegal to require an applicant to supply data regarding religious preference, color, race, sex, or nationality. Many firms that formerly required applicants to attach photos to the job application form have dropped the practice. This helps assure the applicants that race will not be considered in the employee selection process. A job application form that asks for "wife's name" instead of "spouse's name" makes it rather obvious that the firm assumes all applicants will be men.

FIGURE 6-3

A job application form

APPLICATION FOR EMPLOYMENT AS FIELD REPRESENTATIVE

ALLYN AND BACON, INC. — 7 WELLS AVENUE — NEWTON, MA 02159

Return to: _____ ( ) ELHI   ( ) COLLEGE

PLEASE FURNISH COMPLETE ANSWERS TO ALL THE QUESTIONS. WRITE NEATLY IN INK (OR USE TYPEWRITER)

DATE _____   Social Security No. _____

NAME _____   U.S. Citizen: Yes_____ No_____
     Last   First   Middle

HOME ADDRESS _____   Tel. No. _____
     Street   City   State   Zip Code

Is any additional information relative to a change of name, use of an assumed name or nickname necessary to enable a check on your work record? Yes___ No___.
If "Yes", please identify name or names used and the period of time in which they were used on page three.

Present condition of health_____ Are you willing to have a physical examination by our doctor? _____

Number of days ill during last two years and types of illness _____

Have you ever applied for a position with Allyn and Bacon before? _____ When? _____ Where? _____

Have you any friends or relatives with Allyn and Bacon? _____ Who? _____ Relationship _____

Draft Classification _____ If deferred, state basis _____

U.S. Military Service _____
     Branch   Date Entered – Discharged   Nature of Discharge   Rank

Member of Reserves? _____ Active? _____ Inactive? _____ Date Active Reserve Duty Completed? _____

List all military, business and social organizations to which you belong (Note A) EXCEPT organizations of a religious or racial character or that indicate national

origin of its members: _____

In order to have a complete overview of your qualifications, please complete the following sections in conjunction with your employment history.

Education	Name of School	Where Located	FROM Mo. Yr.	TO Mo. Yr.	Course of Study	Graduate?	Degree
Prep or High							
College							
Other Education							

What was your standing and average in H.S.? _____ In College? _____

What was your college major? _____ Extra curricular activities? _____

To what undergraduate clubs or organizations did you belong? (See Note A above) _____

Are you studying now? _____ What and where? _____

What further courses do you expect to take? _____ Where? _____

Referred to Allyn and Bacon, Inc. by _____

Toward what type position do you want to work? _____

When can you start work? _____ Minimum income requirement: _____

The Preliminary Employment Interview

preliminary
employment interview

The preliminary employment interview is the first time that the employer and the applicant meet face-to-face. The employer is usually represented by an interviewer who informs the applicant of job openings and the applicant has an opportunity to ask questions and to discuss skills, job interests, and so on.

Great care also is needed to avoid discrimination in conducting these interviews. For example, questions such as "Do you plan to have children?" or "What does your husband think of your going to work?" should be avoided. Otherwise, the firm may be subject to lawsuits or to government action. Job interviews are discussed more fully in Chapter 21.

Selection Tests

Selection tests are used to measure an applicant's potential to perform the job for which he or she is being considered. These tests include intelligence tests, aptitude tests, performance tests, interest tests, and personality tests. Of course, not all firms will use all of the selection tests we will discuss. The size of the firm and the type of job, for example, influence the types of selection tests that will be used, if any. Selection tests should supplement (not substitute for) judgment and other information that is available about an applicant.

selection tests

Intelligence tests measure general verbal ability and specific abilities such as reasoning. Aptitude tests measure ability, such as mechanical aptitude or clerical aptitude. Performance tests measure skill in a given type of work, such as typing. Interest tests (inventories), such as the Kuder Preference Record, are designed to predict whether a person will like to perform a particular task. Personality tests (inventories), such as the California Psychological Inventory, measure some aspect (or aspects) of a person's total personality. They are designed to predict whether a person will be able to accept a lot of stress on the job, work well with other people, and so on.

The use of selection tests is controversial. Some people believe that the tests are biased. Intelligence tests, for example, have been attacked because of their alleged white, middle-class cultural bias. To stay within the law, selection tests should be carefully designed to measure ability to do the specific job for which an applicant is being considered.

The In-depth Interview

An applicant who passes the selection tests may be scheduled for an in-depth interview, especially if he or she is applying for a higher-level job. **An in-depth interview is one conducted by trained specialists to shed light on the applicant's motivation, ability to work with others, ability to communicate, etc.**

in-depth interview

The Background Investigation

After in-depth interviewing, an applicant's references are checked. **In a background investigation, the applicant's past employers (if any), neighbors, former teachers, etc. are questioned about**

background investigation

their knowledge of the applicant's job performance, character, and background.

There is a lot of controversy here, also. An employer has the right to look into an applicant's suitability for a job, but it is easy to go overboard and invade the applicant's privacy. Employers often use reference letters to obtain information about job applicants. Because reference letters are now open for review by the person about whom they are written, former employers tend to say only complimentary things in writing. A growing number of employers are refusing to provide reference letters other than those that state the person's period and status of employment. Although job applicants cannot be forced to do so, they sometimes are asked to sign a release stating that they are volunteering to take a polygraph (lie detector) test.

The Final Selection Interview

final selection
interview

If the results of the background investigation are satisfactory, the applicant may be called in for a final selection interview, especially when the applicant is applying for a higher-level job. **In the final selection interview, all company personnel who have interviewed the prospect are present, along with the manager under whom the applicant will work.** The manager is the person who makes the decision whether or not to hire the applicant. Any hiring decision, however, is contingent on passing the company's physical (and perhaps, psychological) exam.

Physical and psychological exams that are not job-related are illegal. Weight and height requirements, for example, have often been used to discriminate against women. It is also illegal to deny physically or mentally handicapped people a job if the handicap cannot hurt job performance. The same is true for people with hidden handicaps such as a history of epilepsy.

bona fide occupational
qualification (BFOQ)

The concept of the bona fide occupational qualification (BFOQ) is important in preparing job specifications and in the employee selection process. **A BFOQ is an occupational qualification based on sex, age, religion, or national origin that is justified and legal as a basis for discrimination in selecting job applicants.** The EEOC allows employers to set BFOQs if they can be justified. For example, airlines can use age as a BFOQ to screen out applicants for pilot positions if the applicants are over a certain age, provided the employer can prove that age is related to job performance (safety).

BFOQs always must be related to the job being filled. Thus a coal mining company cannot refuse to hire a woman simply because male miners believe an old superstition that women underground are bad luck. Male applicants for jobs as flight attendants or women applicants for sales jobs that require travel with men cannot be rejected because of their sex.

Selecting Managers

Applicants for management positions are screened in somewhat the same way as other employees. But job requirements and criteria for success are much harder to define for managers and managerial skills are harder to test. This is why many firms rely very heavily on interviews in selecting managers.

In recent years the use of assessment centers has become popular in selecting managers. Graduating college seniors who are applying for a management trainee position may be given the standard personality, interest, and intelligence tests, but these are supplemented by a series of typical management problems to be solved as a group. For example, a group may be set up as a "company" to manufacture and market a product. The members are observed by experienced managers who get together to make an overall evaluation of each candidate's performance. Their judgments are passed on to the persons who are making the selection decision.

TRAINING AND DEVELOPING EMPLOYEES

Up to the point of hiring, the main goal of personnel activities is to accept or reject the applicant. After the employer tells the applicant that he or she is hired, the "point of hire" has been passed. The employer can then ask for personal information that it may have been illegal to request earlier. For example, medical insurance inquiry cards legally can require age and sex data. Of course, it still is illegal to engage in discriminatory practices after the person is hired.

Employee Orientation

Employee orientation (induction or indoctrination) involves introducing the new employee to the job and to the firm. It is the first, and probably most critical, phase of the employee's training. An applicant gets some orientation to the firm and the job during the selection process, but it only touches the surface. For an employee, the orientation should be much more formal and complete. Serious-minded employees always want to know what is expected of them on the job.

employee orientation

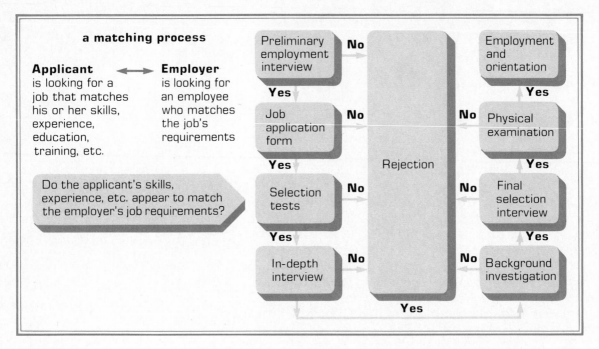

FIGURE 6-4

The sequence of steps an applicant may go through in the employee selection process

A good orientation program helps to relieve the new employee's feelings of insecurity in a new environment. He or she is told about the firm's history, its products, and its operation. Company policies and rules are explained as are company-sponsored employee services. These often are spelled out in a personnel manual, or employee handbook. To acquaint the new employee with the firm, a tour of the plant often is made, coworkers are introduced, and the new employee's questions are answered.

The personnel department coordinates the orientation program, but the new employee's supervisor plays the major role. Effective supervisors know that the time they devote to orientation can save them "headaches" later in disciplining and answering questions from new employees who received a poor introduction to the job.

Figure 6-4 shows the sequence of steps an applicant may go through in the employee selection process. It is basically a matching process in which the employer seeks to hire applicants whose skills, experience, and so on match the employer's job requirements.

Employee Training

job-skill training

Job-skill training teaches employees specific job skills. It can be done on the job or away from the job.

On-the-job training (OJT) can be used to teach new employees their jobs or to teach new skills to experienced employees. OJT is best suited to teaching simple jobs. The trainee works under the guidance of an experienced worker who advises and shows the trainee how to do the job.

Away-from-the-job training is used when a higher level of skill is required and when OJT is too dangerous, or causes too much interruption of the workflow in the plant. The trainee may go to a company-sponsored training program either at the plant or in the company's training school. He or she is trained on the same machines that are used in the plant, but the training is done in a classroom. This often is called *vestibule training*.

Training is a continuous process because new employees must be trained and those with longer service must be retrained. The rapid pace of technological change means that employee skills become obsolete much faster. Thus techniques of in-company training also are changing. Computers, closed-circuit TV, programmed text materials, video-cassettes, and other technical aids are being used. As factories and offices become more automated during the 1980s, firms will be investing huge sums of money to retrain displaced workers for new jobs. This type of investment in the human resource pays off in improved morale and productivity.

Management Development

Management development refers to efforts to prepare people for managerial positions and to improve the managerial skills of present managers. Among the techniques of management development that are used, especially in larger firms, are lecture, case method, simulation, laboratory training, and transfer.

management development

The *lecture method* is good for presenting facts. It is a good way of informing managers of the meaning of new laws that regulate business activity. In the *case method*, participants are given a problem situation to analyze and solve as if the case situation were real. Examples of *simulation* are management games and role-playing. Simulation techniques force trainees to act out real business behavior that is supposed to give them practice in decision making. In a management game, for example, several teams compete against each other. Each team is a separate "company." Role-playing emphasizes the human aspects of management. A trainee might play the role of a supervisor who is disciplining a subordinate or evaluating the performance of a subordinate.

In T-group training (also called sensitivity training, *laboratory training*, or encounter groups), small discussion groups become involved with real (not simulated) problems that exist within the

"This job will give you a lot of independence—because no one will have time to train you."

training group itself. The purpose is to help trainees learn about their individual weaknesses, how groups work, and how to behave more effectively in interpersonal relations.

Transfers involve rotating a manager among different plants or offices, often in different geographical locations, to broaden their exposure to the firm's operations. Transfers can help both new recruits and more experienced managers to develop their managerial abilities.

Organization Development

organization
development

Management development is concerned mainly with the manager as an individual. **Organization development (OD) is a re-education process that is used to change the values and behavior of the entire organization in order to improve its effectiveness in reaching its objectives and in solving problems.** OD uses knowledge in the fields of psychology and sociology to improve organizations. OD programs are based on the systems view of management and can lead to organizational changes, such as redesigned jobs and participative work groups.

OD programs can be successful only if the chief executive officer is convinced that change is necessary, is willing to accept it, and can inspire all lower-level managers and workers to want and accept change. The quality-of-work-life programs we have discussed require a great deal of change in an organization as it moves away from traditional patterns of behavior. The concept of participative management must be translated into the creation of work teams made up of members who are committed to the belief that it can work and are dedicated to making it work. A major focus is getting supervisors to recognize the need to change their management styles—for example, to become more like Theory Y managers and less like Theory X managers. Personnel departments can help provide the type of training necessary to make an OD program work.

APPRAISING EMPLOYEE PERFORMANCE

performance appraisal
system

The personnel department often helps to develop a formal performance appraisal system to enable supervisors to rate their subordinates' job performance. A good performance appraisal system provides a basis for measuring an employee's contribution to the firm. It reduces employee suspicion that promotions and pay raises are based on favoritism rather than performance. It is important for supervisors and subordinates to understand the system that is used by the firm because there are several types of performance appraisal systems.

Traditional performance appraisal systems require a manager to appraise a subordinate's work habits and personal traits. In the merit rating system, each employee's job performance is appraised every six months or every year. Initiative, ability to work with others, dependability, etc., are appraised. There is, of course, a lot of room for error in rating these personal traits and work habits objectively.

Because of these problems, some firms rely mainly on an employee's seniority as a basis for granting pay raises and promotions. **Seniority refers to an employee's length of service. The longer that service, the more seniority an employee has.** It is a lot easier to be objective in measuring seniority than in measuring initiative or ability to work with others. This is why labor unions favor the seniority system. By and large, however, this approach dodges the issue of appraising employee performance.

merit rating system

seniority

POINT OF VIEW

Supervisor A:
"As a supervisor, I have to evaluate my subordinates every six months. The people over in the personnel department keep tabs on these evaluations for use when promotions open up and for granting pay raises. Honestly, I think it's a lot of bull. If I rate any of my subordinates low, it's a bad reflection on me. After all, my job is to inspire them to good performance. For example, if I check the box that says 'poor attitude toward job,' in effect I'm admitting that I'm failing as a manager.

"On the other hand, if I give 'top grades' to my subordinates, I look good to them and to my boss. It sort of reminds me of school and the lousy grading system. You can bet that all of my subordinates always get good marks."

Supervisor B:
"As a supervisor, I want to evaluate my subordinates every six months. I have an obligation to my subordinates to rate their performances realistically and objectively. They want to know where they stand and how well they are progressing on the job. I also have an obligation to my superiors to make the best use of my subordinates.

"As a manager, I must work through others. The more that I can help them develop into good employees, the more valuable they are to me, to the company, and to themselves."

Employee Evaluation

As we saw in Chapter 4, the management by objectives (MBO) approach can be used in rating employee performance. It does away with some of the subjective elements in a merit rating system. But it requires mutual trust and respect between boss and subordinate, ability to communicate effectively with each other, and faith in each other's abilities.

COMPENSATING EMPLOYEES

wage and salary
administration

Wage and salary administration is the process of developing and implementing a sound and fair method of compensating employees. It involves setting pay ranges for all jobs in the firm and setting a specific amount of pay for each employee.

Compensation is important to employees because pay is the main factor that determines the standard of living for most American families. It is the major source of buying power. Pay is also important in a psychological sense. Many workers, for example, measure their importance to their employers in terms of their pay.

To an employer, employee pay is a cost of doing business. Although wage and salary administrators want to hold this cost down, they know that low pay usually leads to low employee morale. Low pay does not always mean more profit to the firm. We must consider labor productivity. It is better to pay a worker $10 per hour for producing 100 units of output than it is to pay a worker $5 per hour for producing 30 units.

Determining the Basis for Payment

A worker's pay can be based on

- output produced
- time spent on the job
- a combination of output produced and time spent on the job

piece rate

Some workers are paid a piece rate. Each worker is paid a certain rate for each acceptable unit of output produced. A worker who sews together a pair of overalls could be paid a piece rate. This method, of course, can be used only when each worker's labor can be identified with specific units of output.

incentive pay

To encourge greater worker productivity, some firms offer incentive pay. For those units produced by a worker above the normal output per day (the quota), the piece rate is increased. Suppose the quota is 100 pair of overalls per day. A worker gets $.50 for each pair sewed together. Meeting quota means a daily payment of $50. If a bonus (incentive payment) of $.05 were paid for each pair produced above quota, a worker who produced 120 pairs would receive $61 for that day's work (100 pairs × 50 cents + 20 pairs × 55 cents, or $50 + $11 = $61).

A worker paid on the basis of time spent on the job gets paid by the hour, week, or month. **A worker paid on an hourly rated basis receives a wage.** Thus a worker who gets $8 per hour and works 40 hours a week gets $320 in wages for that week. Hourly workers can get overtime pay by working extra hours.

wage

A worker paid a fixed amount on a weekly, biweekly, or monthly basis receives a salary. Salaried workers usually work for a fixed amount of pay per year. Most white-collar jobs are salaried jobs. Salaried workers usually do not get overtime pay.

salary

A salesperson might be paid a base salary plus a commission for sales made. This is a combination of time spent on the job and output produced. If a salesperson gets a bonus for selling more than the quota, the pay plan provides incentive.

Features of Wage and Salary Administration

There are four main features of wage and salary administration:

- wage and salary surveys
- job evaluation
- performance rating
- incentive plans

Wage and salary surveys are conducted to determine the general pay level in the firm's community and industry. The firm can pay above, at, or below the prevailing pay level in the industry or community. If it wants to recruit the best talent available, the firm may pay "above-market" rates. If there are many unemployed people who have the skills the firm needs, the pay level may be set at or below the prevailing level. Of course, other factors, such as minimum wage laws and unions must be considered. After determining the general pay level, the focus shifts to finding what other firms are paying for comparable jobs.

Job evaluation is a method for determining the relationship between pay rates for particular job classifications. For example, how much pay should typists, accountants, and salespeople receive? Important factors here are the prestige and status attached to different jobs, the desirability of the work, and the amount of skill, experience, or education needed to perform a given job.

A series of rates (steps, or pay ranges) are set for each job. New employees usually start at the base rate for the job, and workers advance to higher rates as they gain experience, proficiency, and seniority. This is called *performance rating.* Some firms set pay ranges on a strictly judgment basis; others develop detailed rating systems, or point systems. Under "the relative desirability of the type of work," for example, the firm might set point values for such things as danger and exposure to pollution. Regardless of approach, the goal is to come up with a pay range that is fair for each job in the company.

Finally, wage and salary administrators must decide how much each individual worker should receive. Firms with *incentive plans* pay the base rate only for a "normal amount of production," as determined, for example, through a time study. Employees who produce more than the normal amount get an extra incentive bonus.

The Equity Theory of Compensation

Equity is the *perceived* fairness of what a worker does compared to what he or she receives from the employer. The worker exchanges inputs (such as skills) for outputs (tangible and intangible rewards from the employer) and compares the inputs and outputs to those of other workers doing the same job. Inequity results when there is an imbalance between the inputs and outputs as a result of the comparison process. Pay inequity has been a major issue in the women's movement. Many women argue that they do the same work as men (equivalent inputs) but receive lower pay (unequal outputs).

Workers who feel that their inputs are greater than their outputs might try to get a pay raise, reduce their inputs, quit the job for a more equitable job, or learn to live with dissatisfaction. On the other hand, workers who feel their inputs are less than their outputs may put forth more effort on the job or re-evaluate their inputs to "prove" to themselves that they actually are not being overpaid.

Compensating Managers

An owner-manager's compensation is tied to the firm's profit. With professional managers, however, this is not always the case. Many of the same factors that determine a worker's pay affect how much a manager will receive. But there are no union wage scales to serve as guidelines.

Employee benefits in addition to salary are very important to managers in high income-tax brackets. Deferred income plans enable them to receive part of their compensation after retirement. Income deferral shelters some earnings from the high tax rates they pay in their working years. A firm tries to "lock in" good executives

WHAT DO YOU THINK?

Some firms pay their employees year-end bonuses that are tied to profit growth. Thus a firm that increased its profit by a larger percentage in the current year than in the previous year will share some of that profit with its employees. The underlying belief is that this gives workers an incentive to increase their productivity.

As long as a firm is increasing its profit growth year after year, employees go along with the bonus plan. If a firm's rate of profit growth declines, there may be no bonuses. In recent years many firms have experienced little or no profit improvement and their workers have become upset when there were no bonuses. These workers often say that they have little or no direct impact on a firm's profitability. They prefer bonus plans that are not tied to profitability. Should employee bonus plans be tied to profitability? WHAT DO YOU THINK?

Should Employee Bonus Plans Be Tied to Profitability?

by offering many benefits that hinge on their staying with the firm. Liberal retirement benefits are an example.

PROMOTING EMPLOYEES

A promotion means moving up to a higher position in the firm, usually one that involves more pay and more challenge. It is a way of compensating an employee for good performance in the previous job.

promotion

Firms set up promotion programs to decide which employees are promotable. The personnel department can help by developing "career ladders" that will encourage promising employees to take the risks involved in being promoted. The important thing is that the system used is fair, is understood by employees, and is consistently and objectively used. Performance in the present job should be the basic factor in determining an employee's promotability to a higher job.

PROVIDING PERSONNEL SERVICES

Personnel departments are called on to provide a variety of services for the firm and its employees. The personnel manual which we mentioned earlier is usually prepared by the personnel department in conjunction with upper-level managers. Other examples of personnel services include putting together employee benefits packages; establishing employee safety and health programs; and formulating employee discipline policy.

Employee Benefits

Employee benefits are compensation other than wages or salaries—cafeterias, credit unions, group life and medical insurance, paid vacations, and retirement programs. Employee benefits account for about 35 percent of the typical worker's compensation and their cost is growing about twice as fast as wages and salaries.

A recent innovation is flexible benefit plans, or "cafeteria plans." The employer offers a basic core of benefits to all employees and individual employees are allowed to "buy" additional benefits to suit their own needs. Employees "buy" these benefits with their benefit credits, based on, for example, salary or length of service. Thus a single male employee fifty years of age might choose to pass up maternity coverage for additional pension contributions.

"I'm hoping to find something in a meaningful, humanist, outreach kind of bag, with flexible hours, nonsexist bosses, and fabulous fringes."

Employee Safety and Health

Employee safety and health programs help to reduce absenteeism and labor turnover. The personnel department creates and implements the company-wide safety and health program. This program raises productivity and boosts morale by making jobs safer and more healthful.

Occupational Safety and Health Act (OSHA)

In 1970, the Occupational Safety and Health Act (OSHA) was passed to help ensure that every working man and woman in the nation has a safe and healthful work environment. This law is enforced by the Occupational Safety and Health Review Commission.

Employee Discipline Policy

The personnel department also plays a major role in formulating employee discipline policy and in explaining it to workers. Although most workers abide by the rules, some workers do break them. Disciplinary action is administered by the worker's supervisor, but usually only when other approaches to correct employee performance problems have failed. For first offenses, employee disciplinary action usually means an oral reprimand in private. The more serious the offense and the greater the number of prior offenses, the stiffer the penalty. After oral warnings, there are written warnings, disciplinary layoffs, and discharge from the company.

Miscellaneous Services

Personnel departments also provide many other types of services, which vary widely among firms. These include such services as setting up policies to cope with allegations of sexual harassment on the job and helping employees arrange car pools.

Time and circumstances greatly affect the nature of personnel work. For example, a firm may experience a big decrease in one department's work load and a big increase in another department's work load. The personnel department might help the two department managers to shift workers between departments, help in a retraining effort if that is needed, or help to develop a plan for sharing the available work among employees—shorter work weeks for all workers or layoffs in order of seniority.

Personnel departments in many firms help in developing flexible working hours schedules. "Flex time," as opposed to fixed working hours, makes it easier for many workers, especially working mothers, to enter the labor force. The concept of flex time is built around a core of working hours, for example, 10 a.m. to 2 p.m. All employees are required to work between those hours. Each individual employee, however, is given the opportunity to select other hours of work to make up a full work week. Although it presents scheduling problems, flex time also makes it possible for some employees to work full-time instead of having to settle for part-time work.

TERMINATING EMPLOYEES

Eventually every employee will leave the company's service. This may come about by death, retirement, voluntary resignation, dismissal, or discharge.

Retirement

Many firms have retirement plans as one of their employee benefits. Employees who have had continuous service for a number of years get compensation from the firm during their nonworking, or retirement, years. It is a type of deferred compensation. Most retirement plans are based on the employee's age. The Age Discrimination in Employment Act has been extended to cover workers up to age 70. In most cases, forced retirement at age 65 no longer is legal if the employee wants to stay on the job and is mentally and physically able to do so.

The Employee Retirement Income Security Act of 1974 (the "Pension Reform" act) protects the pension rights of workers if the employer goes out of business or if the worker quits or is dismissed after a certain period of employment. The term *vesting* means that the worker's right to his or her accumulated pension benefits is guaranteed to the worker if he or she has stayed with the firm for a specified number of years. The law does not require an employer to set up a pension plan but it does set up regulations for company or union plans. A Pension Benefit Guaranty Corporation was created to pay workers whose pension plans fail because of employer bankruptcy or union corruption.

Since January 1, 1982, any employed person can establish an Individual Retirement Account (IRA) at various types of financial institutions. Money in an IRA—and the interest it earns—is tax-free until the person begins to withdraw it after age $59\frac{1}{2}$. People who set up IRAs reduce their dependence on Social Security and company pension plans for retirement income.

Voluntary Resignation

resignation

Resignation occurs when an employee voluntarily leaves the employer's service. There are many reasons for employee resignation. Some employees want to leave to take a job with another employer. In fact, a lot of firms try to hire away good employees from other firms. Some employees quit in order to dramatize a point of difference with the firm or their supervisors.

exit interview

Because of the poor effect on morale, a wise employer does not want to hold on to an employee who can improve his or her position at another firm. **But it is a good practice to conduct an exit interview with an employee who is quitting the firm. The purpose of an exit interview is to determine the reasons why an employee is leaving.** Perhaps the work environment could be changed to discourage others from leaving.

Dismissal

dismissal

Dismissal is an involuntary temporary or permanent separation of the employee. Some workers are laid off temporarily when business is slack. Of course, a layoff can become permanent if laid-off workers are not called back.

Union contracts usually specify that a laid-off worker's right to be recalled, based on his or her seniority, will not continue beyond a certain period of time, usually one or two years. This means that a layoff which lasts longer than that period of time results in the loss of the worker's claim to other employee benefits that are based on seniority. In other words, a rehired worker comes back as a new employee.

Discharge

Discharge is a permanent involuntary separation due to a permanent layoff or outright firing of an employee. It sometimes is called "industrial capital punishment." A firm might permanently lay off workers in a plant when it is closed down. An employee might be discharged because of an inability to do the job or serious violations of work rules. Some or all employees of a firm that is bought by another firm may also be discharged.

discharge

SUMMARY AND LOOK AHEAD

A firm's most important resource is its human resource, its personnel. Top management is responsible for putting together and keeping intact a productive work force that includes managers and workers.

Top management delegates to the personnel manager the task of carrying out its human resource philosophy at the firm's operations level. Usually, this means setting up a personnel department headed by a personnel manager. This is a staff position created to advise and assist line managers in managing their personnel.

The main activities of personnel management are (1) determining human resource needs, (2) searching for and recruiting applicants to fill those needs, (3) selecting applicants for employment, (4) training and developing personnel, (5) appraising employee performance, (6) compensating employees, (7) promoting employees, (8) providing personnel services, and (9) terminating employees. All of these activities are interrelated and are vital aspects of human resource management. It is crucial that all these activities be conducted with awareness of antidiscrimination laws.

In the next chapter, we look at labor relations. The viewpoint for personnel management is the employer-individual employee relationship. In labor relations, the viewpoint is the employer-union relationship. The focus is on the employees as a group, as members of one or more labor unions. Labor relations activities often are referred to as "industrial relations." Even when line managers handle negotiations with labor unions, the personnel department is responsible for providing advisory services through its labor-relations specialists.

FOR REVIEW . . .

1. Do all managers participate in managing the human resource? Explain.

2. Why might a firm create a personnel department?

3. What are the two basic approaches to determining a firm's human resource needs?

4. What are three techniques a firm might use to specify its human resource needs? Discuss each.

5. Why is recruiting for the long range beneficial to a firm?

6. Give two examples of sources of recruits and two examples of recruitment methods.

7. Distinguish among a) a preliminary employment interview; b) an in-depth interview; and c) a final selection interview.

8. Explain how the use of assessment centers can help in selecting managers.

9. What should be covered in an employee orientation program?

10. List and discuss five techniques of management development.

11. Why is it important to have a good performance appraisal system?

12. List and discuss the four main features of wage and salary administration.

. . . FOR DISCUSSION

1. When a firm buys a new typewriter, it expects that its value will diminish with the passage of time. The typewriter becomes "used up." Is the same true of a new management trainee who recently began working for the firm?

2. Applicants for managerial positions are usually given more "subjective" tests than are applicants for nonmanagerial jobs. Why is this?

3. Should a firm retrain employees whose skills have become obsolete if it can hire persons already possessing the needed skills?

4. Do you think that it is fair for a firm to have a policy of not promoting from within?

5. Do you think that it is proper for a retailing firm to ask job applicants to submit to a polygraph (lie-detector) test? Is it fair to ask salespeople to take a polygraph test every six months?

INCIDENTS

Coping with Job Erosion

Job erosion has been a big problem in a variety of industries during recent years. American auto manufacturers, for example, have laid off thousands of blue-collar and white-collar workers and some airlines have furloughed pilots. To reduce their managerial ranks, some firms have encouraged some of their managers to take early retirement. The underlying causes of these dismissals, discharges, and early retirements vary by industry but include such factors as automation reducing the need for some employees; falling sales and a resultant need for less personnel; and a general effort by firms to cut their operating costs.

The federal government has also laid off or demoted thousands of government employees because of budget cutbacks. The process is called "rif"—reduction in force. Employees who are "riffed" are either discharged or are demoted to lower-paying jobs. The government's Office of Personnel Management has set up programs to help riffed personnel find other government or nongovernment jobs. Many firms have also turned to their personnel departments for help in finding other jobs for employees who are being discharged.

Referrals as a Recruitment Technique

In their efforts to attract recruits, firms in many high technology industries are turning to their current employees for help in attracting genetic engineers and other hard-to-find, highly specialized technicians and engineers. Thus instead of relying only on outside search firms to locate recruits, these companies are also offering their employees expense-paid vacations and cash awards for referrals of recruits whose scarce talents and skills are needed to fill job openings.

QUESTIONS

1. Can the fear of being laid off or demoted create morale problems and lower the productivity of an employer's work force? Explain.

2. Should an employer assist employees who are being discharged in dealing with their job loss and in finding jobs elsewhere? Why or why not?

QUESTIONS

1. What are some of the potential benefits to an employer who uses referrals as a recruitment technique?

2. Should firms in high technology industries engage in continuous recruiting? Why or why not?

CHAPTER 7

Labor Relations

OBJECTIVES:

After reading this chapter, you should be able to

1. Outline the history of unionism in the United States.
2. List the major federal labor laws and discuss the major provisions of each.
3. Identify the general reasons workers join unions and explain how unions are organized.
4. Discuss the National Labor Relations Board's role in certifying a union as the exclusive bargaining agent for a firm's employees.
5. Give examples of union objectives.
6. Cite specific issues that might lead to labor-management conflict.
7. Explain how employees and employers bargain collectively through union and management representatives.
8. List and discuss labor and management's "weapons" in dealing with conflict.
9. Appraise the future prospects for the union movement in the United States.

KEY CONCEPTS:

Look for these terms as you read the chapter

labor union

collective bargaining

collective bargaining agreement

blacklists

unfair lists

injunction

Norris-LaGuardia Act

Wagner Act

Fair Labor Standards Act

Taft-Hartley Act

National Labor Relations Board (NLRB)

Landrum-Griffin Act

craft unions

industrial unions

local union

national union

union federation

lobbying

guaranteed annual wage

closed shop

union shop

right-to-work laws

agency shop

open shop

supplemental unemployment benefits (SUB)

bargainable issues

escalator clause

conciliation

mediation

voluntary arbitration

compulsory arbitration

grievance procedures

strike

picketing

boycott

lockout

Perhaps one of the most dramatic confrontations between labor and management in recent years was the walkout of 11,500 members of the Professional Air Traffic Controllers Organization (PATCO) on August 3, 1981. They walked off the job because PATCO was unable to negotiate a new labor contract covering wages and working conditions with management of the Federal Aviation Administration, the controller's employer. Several days after the walkout, the striking workers were fired and told they could not get their old jobs back. They were also banned from working for the federal government in any capacity for three years. (This ban, however, was lifted in December, 1981.)

Federal government employees can belong to labor unions such as PATCO, but the government does not recognize its employees' right to strike. Thus in October, 1981, PATCO was decertified as the exclusive bargaining agent for the controllers. This meant it could no longer legally represent them in collective bargaining and the Federal Aviation Administration stopped collecting union dues from the 2,000 PATCO members who stayed on the job rather than participate in the strike. In November, 1981, PATCO filed for protection from its creditors under the Federal Bankruptcy Act. In January, 1982, its president resigned and a replacement was elected.

The PATCO case vividly depicts the importance of good employer-employee relations. The relationship between employer and employees is crucial whoever the employer may be.

When the employer-employee relationship is between the employer and employees as individuals, it is called employee relations or personnel relations. When the employees belong to labor unions, the relationship between the employer and the employees' union(s) is called labor relations.

In labor relations, management representatives bargain with union representatives over wages and working conditions for unionized employees. In some firms the personnel manager does the bargaining for the employer. But as unions have become more powerful, labor relations specialists are increasingly found in unionized firms.

We begin this chapter with a brief look at the history of unionization in the United States and the major federal laws that deal with unions. We will also look at why workers join unions, the nature of labor-management relations, and the future of unions in the United States.

WHY UNIONS BEGAN

labor union

A labor union is an organization of employees formed for the purpose of dealing collectively with their employers in order to further the interests of those employees.

The dealing that occurs between the employer and the union is called collective bargaining. **Collective bargaining is the process of negotiating a labor agreement between union representatives and employer representatives and also involves the ongoing process of administering an existing labor agreement.**

collective bargaining

collective bargaining agreement

The contract negotiated between employer and union representatives is called the collective bargaining agreement. **A collective bargaining agreement sets forth the terms and conditions under which union members will offer their labor services to an employer.**

To explain the apparent conflict between capitalism's emphasis on individualism and unionism's emphasis on collective action, let's briefly study the history of unionism in the United States.

A BRIEF HISTORY OF UNIONISM IN THE UNITED STATES

American workers' earliest attempts to organize for collective action occurred at the time of the American Revolution. These were very small local groups of workers who joined together in what essentially were benevolent societies. For example, if a member became ill and was unable to work, the other members would help to care for that member's family. The nearest thing to a modern labor union was formed by shoemakers in Philadelphia in 1792.

The Industrial Revolution of the 1800s brought great changes in the world of work. Many workers saw the growth of big factories and mechanization (substituting machines for human labor) as a threat. Small-scale production was largely replaced with large-scale production. To deal with those and other threats to their security, workers turned more and more to unionization. Thus unions began to focus their efforts more on higher wages and better working conditions rather than on purely benevolent activities.

As we saw earlier in this book, however, the economic philosophy of laissez-faire was at the heart of our economic system until the 1930s. Most Americans rejected government interference in business and economic affairs and unions generally did not have widespread public support. In many cases efforts to organize workers were violent. For example, the Haymarket Riot in Chicago in 1886 resulted in the death of 7 police officers and 4 workers and injury to 66 people who were protesting the use of police to break up employee efforts to strike. The rights of private property and freedom of individual contract were used to justify antiunion moves by employers. Courts held that unions were criminal or civil conspiracies against trade and property. The employment contract was between the individual worker and the employer, not between the employer and employees as a group.

The employer-employee relationship also became much less direct as firms grew in size. Managers who were themselves employees dealt with other employees. Communication among owners, managers, and workers became more formalized through the chain of command. Because courts tended to side with employers, big business had the upper hand.

In the absence of adequate legislation, even young children worked in factories and mills at the turn of the century

For many years, employers battled with workers sympathetic to unions. **Employers circulated blacklists which contained the names of workers who were known to be in favor of unions.** These blacklisted workers were refused employment.

blacklists

Labor unions circulated their lists also—"unfair lists." **Unfair lists contained the names of employers whom unions considered unfair to workers because these employers would not hire union members.** Furthermore, violent strikes and riots were much in evidence during the nineteenth and early twentieth centuries.

unfair lists

During the early 1930s, things began to change. As much as 25 percent of the American labor force was out of work during the Great Depression. Laissez-faire economics began to lose public support and government turned its attention to getting workers back to work. Laws were passed to guarantee workers the right to form and join unions.

Labor Legislation

Individual states take various positions on labor law in intrastate commerce (commerce within a given state). Following is a brief summary of the major *federal* labor laws.

The Norris-LaGuardia Act of 1932

Congress passed the Sherman Antitrust Act in 1890. This act prohibits "every contract . . . or conspiracy in restraint of trade or commerce among the several states, or with foreign nations. . . ." The Sherman Act was the first of several acts passed by Congress to prevent monopolies, but it was not clear whether the Sherman Act applied to labor unions. The courts, however, generally held that it did. This is why unions were considered conspiracies against trade and property by the courts.

Under the Sherman Act, employers frequently were granted injunctions to prevent their workers from forming unions or engaging in strike activity. **An injunction is issued by a court. A mandatory injunction requires performance of a specific act. A prohibitory injunction orders the defendant to refrain from certain acts.** In addition to holding that unions were not subject to the Sherman Act, the Clayton Act of 1914 sought to prohibit the use of an injunction in labor disputes unless the employer could prove that irreparable injury to property or property rights was threatened. The Clayton Act, however, was narrowly interpreted by the courts and the use of injunctions actually increased.

The use of injunctions in labor disputes was greatly reduced after passage of the Norris-LaGuardia Act. **The Norris-LaGuardia Act prohibits employers from using an injunction unless they can meet the strong requirements set out in the act. It also outlaws the yellow-dog contract.** (This contract required an employee to agree, as a condition of employment, not to join a union.)

The Wagner Act of 1935

Three years after passage of the Norris-LaGuardia Act, the Wagner Act (the National Labor Relations Act, NLRA) was passed. This prolabor law showed that Congress wanted to equalize the bargaining power of labor and management. **The Wagner Act, often called labor's "Magna Charta," strengthened the workers' right to form unions without fear of employer reprisal. It lists several em-**

injunction

Norris-LaGuardia Act

Wagner Act

Norris-LaGuardia Act (1932)
1. Greatly limits the use of the injunction by employers engaged in a labor dispute
2. Outlaws the yellow-dog contract

National Labor Relations Act (NLRA), or Wagner Act (1935)
1. Makes it illegal for employers to
    a. interfere with the rights given workers under the act
    b. interfere in the organization or operation of a union
    c. discriminate against workers who file charges or testify under the act
    d. discriminate in hiring and firing because of union affiliation
    e. refuse to bargain collectively with unions
2. Created the National Labor Relations Board (NLRB)

Fair Labor Standards Act (1938)
1. Defines the normal work week (40 hours)
2. Requires time-and-a-half pay for overtime
3. Established a federal minimum wage

Labor-Management Relations Act, or Taft-Hartley Act (1947)
1. Makes it illegal for unions to
    a. coerce workers to join unions
    b. coerce employers to discriminate against workers who do not join unions
    c. refuse to bargain collectively with employers
    d. set excessive or discriminatory union dues
    e. force an employer to pay for services which were not performed or offered to be performed
2. Outlaws the closed shop
3. Permits states to pass right-to-work laws
4. Provides for injunctive processes in national emergency strikes and in certain types of illegal strikes

Labor-Management Reporting and Disclosure Act, or Landrum-Griffin Act (1959)
1. Requires unions and employers to file reports with the Secretary of Labor
2. Sets up rules for election of union officers
3. Guarantees each union member the right to
    a. attend and vote in union meetings and elections
    b. vote on proposals to increase union dues
    c. testify and bring suit against the union for violations of the act and for discriminatory treatment
    d. receive a hearing before the union can take disciplinary action against the member

TABLE 7-1

Major federal labor laws

ployer practices that are unfair to labor. (See Table 7-1.) The Wagner Act also created the National Labor Relations Board (NLRB) to administer the act. We will discuss this more fully later.

The Fair Labor Standards Act of 1938

The Fair Labor Standards Act of 1938 defined the normal working week, required time-and-a-half pay for all hours over forty worked by an employee during a week, and established a federal minimum wage. It set the stage for later congressional action relating to discrimination on the basis of age, sex, race, color, and national origin.

Fair Labor Standards Act

The Taft-Hartley Act of 1947

Between 1935 and 1947, employers tried to curb legislative and judicial actions, which they claimed had placed them at a disadvantage in collective bargaining. The Wagner Act, for example, listed unfair practices of management, but not of unions. Because of this and a rash of major strikes and clashes among unions over the right to organize workers, Congress passed the Labor-Management Relations Act, or Taft-Hartley Act, in 1947. **The Taft-Hartley Act is a "promanagement" act that lists several practices that are unfair for unions to commit.** These and other provisions are also listed in Table 7-1.

Taft-Hartley Act

Thus today the National Labor Relations Board investigates cases of alleged unfair labor practices committed by employers and unions and issues orders to prevent them. It also holds representation elections to determine whether or not a firm's employees want a union and, if so, which one. If a union wins a representation election, it is certified by the NLRB as the employees' exclusive bargaining agent.

National Labor Relations Board (NLRB)

The Landrum-Griffin Act of 1959

The Labor-Management Reporting and Disclosure Act is also known as the Landrum-Griffin Act. **The Landrum-Griffin Act is a labor reform amendment to the Taft-Hartley Act intended to ensure democratic operation of unions and to give employers added protection from unscrupulous union practices and leaders.** (See Table 7-1.)

Landrum-Griffin Act

Passage of this law was aided by the McClellan Senate committee's investigation of labor racketeering. In their investigation, committee members had uncovered cases in which some union leaders were engaged in blackmail, arson, and other practices such as embezzling union funds for personal use and accepting bribes and payoffs from employers for protection. The Wagner, Taft-Hartley, and Landrum-Griffin Acts are the pillars of American labor law.

Figure 7-1 reflects how some observers view the balance of labor-management bargaining power before and after the passage of the major labor laws we have discussed. These laws have a major impact on the way unions go about the process of organizing workers.

WHY DO WORKERS JOIN UNIONS?

The answers to this question are as varied as the people who are members of labor unions. For example, maintenance crew workers

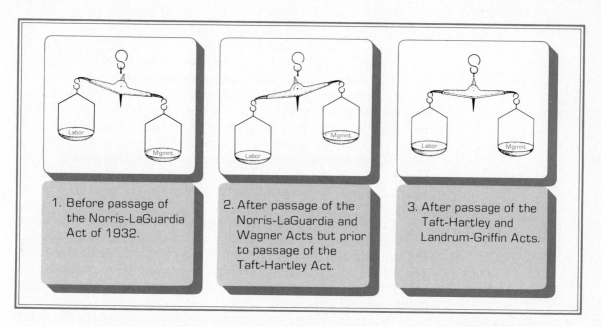

1. Before passage of the Norris-LaGuardia Act of 1932.

2. After passage of the Norris-LaGuardia and Wagner Acts but prior to passage of the Taft-Hartley Act.

3. After passage of the Taft-Hartley and Landrum-Griffin Acts.

FIGURE 7-1

How some observers view the balance of labor-management bargaining power

at a big sports arena might join the International Brotherhood of Teamsters or some other union mainly because they think that membership will bring higher pay. A professional baseball player, on the other hand, may join the Major League Baseball Players Association for other reasons. That union does not negotiate players' salaries, but it did represent them in their 1981 strike against club owners. The union demanded increased compensation for players lost to a rival team as free agents. Let's consider a few general reasons workers join unions

First, there is strength in numbers. The individual worker's threat to strike would cause little interruption of the workflow. A collective strike, however, could easily cripple the workflow.

Second, union members are represented in collective bargaining by professional negotiators. The employer is also represented by professional negotiators. The outcome is likely to be better for each worker than if each negotiated individually.

A third reason is the feeling of power that workers get from union membership. Although the employer-employee negotiations are handled by professionals, the workers at least have a chance to vote for union officers and also have veto power over any "settlement" that is reached regarding wages, fringe benefits, and working conditions.

Finally, many workers believe that union membership is necessary to keep employers interested in and concerned with their well-being. We will discuss this in greater detail later in the chapter.

HOW ARE UNIONS ORGANIZED?

Like business firms, unions have organized structures. The two basic types of union are craft and industrial unions.

craft unions

Craft unions are organized by crafts or trades—plumbers, barbers, airline pilots, etc. Craft unions restrict membership to workers with specific skills. In many cases members of craft unions work for several different employers during the course of a year. For example, many construction workers are hired by their employers at union hiring halls. When the particular job for which they are hired is finished, these workers return to the hall to be hired by another employer.

Craft unions have a lot of power over the supply of skilled workers. This is because they have apprenticeship programs. A person who wants to become a member of a plumber's union, for example, will have to go through a training program. He or she starts out as an apprentice. After the training, the person is qualified as a "journeyman" plumber.

industrial unions

Industrial unions are organized according to industries—steel, auto, clothing, etc. Industrial unions include semiskilled and unskilled workers. Industrial union members typically work for a particular employer for a much longer period of time than craft union members. But an industrial union does have a lot of "say" regarding pay and personnel practices within unionized firms.

local union

The local union (or local) is the basic unit of union organization. A local of a craft union is made up of artisans in the same craft in a relatively small geographical area. A local of an industrial union is made up of workers in a given industry in a relatively small geographical area. Thus plumbers in a local labor market may be members of the local plumbers union. Truckdrivers and warehouse workers in that same area may be members of a Teamsters local.

national union

Many local unions are affiliated with a national union. **A national union is the organization set up to bring all the member local unions together for bargaining purposes.** Each local union sends delegates to its national union meetings. There are close to 200 national unions in the United States. Some, however, are called international unions. These are unions that have members in other countries. The United Automobile Workers (UAW), for example, is made up of local unions in the United States and Canada. Table 7-2 lists the twenty largest unions in the United States.

union federation

A union federation represents the unions that comprise it in presenting labor's views on political and social issues, and it helps to resolve conflicts among its affiliated unions. The AFL-CIO is a national federation of roughly 15 million members in over 100 affiliated unions. Prior to 1955 the American Federation of Labor (AFL)

Union	Number of members (in thousands)
Teamsters	1,891
National Education Association	1,684
Automobile workers	1,357
Food and commercial	1,300
Steelworkers	1,238
State, County (AFSCME)	1,098
Electrical (IBEW)	1.041
Carpenters	784
Machinists	754
Service employees (SEIU)	650
Laborers (LIUNA)	608
Communications workers	551
Teachers (AFT)	551
Clothing and textile workers	455
Operating engineers	423
Hotel and restaurant	400
Plumbers	352
Ladies' garment workers (ILGWU)	323
Musicians	299
Paperworkers	275

TABLE 7-2

The twenty largest unions in the United States

housed craft unions. The Congress of Industrial Organizations (CIO) contained industrial unions. In 1955 the two merged to become the AFL-CIO. The AFL-CIO is made up of many, but not all, national unions. For example, the International Brotherhood of Electrical Workers is affiliated with the AFL-CIO, whereas the International Brotherhood of Teamsters is not.

HOW DO UNIONS GET NEW MEMBERS?

Skilled craft workers in a given area often seek membership in their respective local unions. People who wish to learn a particular craft also may seek to join as apprentices. Industrial unions, however, devote more effort to recruiting members.

Suppose an industrial union is seeking to organize workers at a local plant. If the union secures signed authorization cards from at least 30 percent of the employees, it can ask the NLRB to hold a representation election to see if a majority of employees want the union. If the union wins the election, it is certified by the NLRB as the employees' exclusive bargaining agent. If rival unions are trying

"Are you calling me a liar? Are you telling me that last night I didn't dream that you were skulking around the plant asking people to join a union?!!"

FIGURE 7-2
Proportion of
representation
elections won by unions

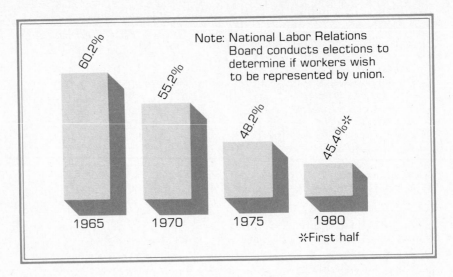

Note: National Labor Relations Board conducts elections to determine if workers wish to be represented by union.

60.2% — 1965
55.2% — 1970
48.2% — 1975
45.4%※ — 1980
※First half

to organize the workers, the NLRB will conduct an election to see which one will be certified as the workers' exclusive bargaining agent.

During the union's organizing drive, employers can exercise the right of free speech to dissuade their employees from voting for the union. They cannot, however, coerce their employees to vote against unionization. In recent years some employers have hired consultants who specialize in helping employers to win NLRB representation elections. As you can see in Figure 7-2, the proportion of these elections won by unions has been declining.

UNION OBJECTIVES

Unions today have a broad range of objectives. Let's take a brief look at these objectives.

Representing Labor's Views

Unlike union movements in most Western-European nations, the union movement in the United States is a minority movement. Only about 24 percent of our nonfarm workers are unionized. (See Table 7-3.) Furthermore, there has been a decline in the proportion of our labor force that is unionized over recent years. (See Figure 7-3.) We have no separate labor party in the United States, but organized labor does try to speak for the labor force.

Unions and business both engage in lobbying. **Lobbying is efforts by a group of people who have the same special interest. These**

lobbying

Total union membership (thousands)	21,784
Percentage in AFL-CIO	78.1
Percentage in independent or unaffiliated unions	21.9
Percentage males	76.5
Percentage females	23.5
Percentage white-collar	18.7
Percentage blue-collar	81.3
Percentage of nonagricultural workers in unions	~~23.6~~
	19%

declining

TABLE 7-3

Characteristics of national and international union membership

people, called lobbyists, seek to influence the passage of laws or to influence their administration or enforcement.

The labor lobby is powerful and well organized, and it often participates in coalition groups to make its lobbying efforts more effective. The AFL-CIO's Committee on Political Education (COPE) lobbies for passage of prolabor laws and helps prolabor candidates get elected. Among recent legislative goals of unions are: restricting imports of foreign-made products, restricting American firms from setting up plants in low-wage countries overseas, and raising the federal minimum wage.

Improving Members' Standard of Living

Unions seek to improve their members' standard of living. In the past this meant getting higher wages. The pay envelope, how-

FIGURE 7-3

Union members as proportion of total work force

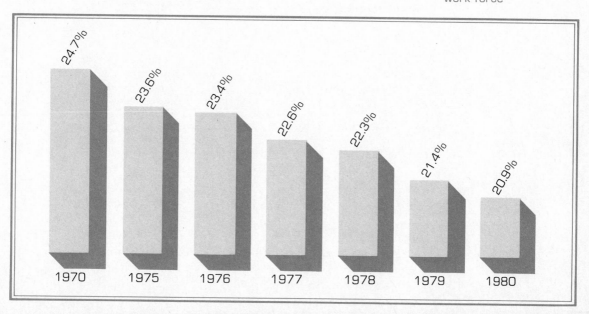

| 24.7% | 23.6% | 23.4% | 22.6% | 22.3% | 21.4% | 20.9% |
| 1970 | 1975 | 1976 | 1977 | 1978 | 1979 | 1980 |

ever, is no longer the only concern of union members. The entire benefits package—working conditions, pensions, paid vacations, and so on—is an important bargaining issue.

Although the average working conditions in business today are much better than those during the "sweat-shop" days of the Industrial Revolution, dirty and dangerous jobs still exist. Brown lung, black lung, lead poisoning, and asbestosis are some examples of dangerous industrial diseases. As we saw in the previous chapter, the Occupational Safety and Health Act was passed, with major support from unions, to help improve the situation. Interestingly, robots are taking over some of the dullest and most dangerous jobs in many plants.

Improving Job Security

Job security is reflected in union goals. The seniority provision in most contracts spells out the workers' rights when layoffs, transfers, and promotions occur. Employees are ranked in terms of length of service. Those with longer service get better treatment.

FIGURE 7-4

The percentage of the nonagricultural labor force that is unionized in each state (shaded states have right-to-work laws)

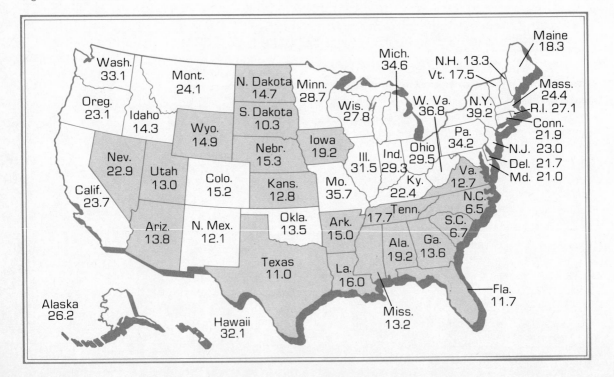

seniority. A history of discrimi-
resulted in less seniority for
workers are the first to be laid
er jobs; they tend to oppose the

reflects the worker's concern
annual wage is a provision in a
workers' income level during a
inimum amount of work during
ts provide for early retirement,
eaves for employees.

guaranteed annual wage

e. The three major forms of union

security is the closed shop. **In a**
only union members. The Taft-
p. Some states, however, do allow
only if the employer is not engaged
in interstate commerce.

closed shop

The Taft-Hartley Act permits the union shop. **In a union shop**
an employer may hire nonunion workers even if the employer's
present employees are unionized. New workers, however, must join
the union within 30 days of being hired or else be fired. Roughly 90
percent of all unionized blue-collar workers work under a union
shop agreement.

union shop

The Taft-Hartley Act permits individual states to pass right-to-
work laws. **Right-to-work laws outlaw the union shop.** (See Figure
7-4.) They weaken union bargaining strength and make organizing
efforts more difficult. A firm's unionized and nonunionized employees are paid the same wage for the same work. Union members
believe that nonunion employees take advantage of union-won
benefits without paying union dues. Unions have been lobbying for
years to repeal that section of the Taft-Hartley Act which allows
states to pass right-to-work laws. On the other hand, the National
Right to Work Committee opposes compulsory unionism and supports right-to-work legislation.

right-to-work laws

Some states permit an agency shop. **In an agency shop all em-**
ployees for whom the union bargains must pay dues but need not

agency shop

Handwritten note:

for Friday
Quiz 6,7,8

For Mon.
1 page paper)

what are the pros
and con's of right
to work laws?
pg. 205

I am not proud of used most Moss strategy

open shop

join. This is a compromise between the union shop and the open shop.

In an open shop an employer may hire union and/or nonunion labor. Employees need not join or pay dues to a union in an open shop.

A relatively recent development in some industries, notably the construction industry, is the trend toward going "double-breasted." Many unionized contractors who have lost business to nonunion contractors have reacted by setting up nonunion subsidiaries. Such a firm is called a "double-breasted" company. This arrangement has also become more common in the airline and trucking industries, especially after they were deregulated by the government. This trend, of course, has become a major concern of unions. They view the growth of "double-breasted" arrangements with alarm.

SOURCES OF LABOR-MANAGEMENT CONFLICT

In the United States today the vast majority of unions accept the capitalist system while the vast majority of employers accept the right of workers to form and join unions. Top leaders of the AFL-CIO and chief executives of several major firms have set up a Labor-Management Group to seek solutions to the economic problems confronting our economy and to improve labor-management relations in the United States. In their statement of purpose, the union leaders acknowledge the need for a free, capitalistic economy while the industry leaders express support of the right of a free labor movement to exist. It is within this framework that labor and management bargain.

There are, of course, some basic differences in outlook between labor and management. We will look at several sources of conflict and discuss each from a "labor viewpoint" and a "management viewpoint."

The Loyalty Issue

Some employers think that the presence of a union reduces employee loyalty to the firm. When the collective bargaining process results in a pay raise, for example, the employees may think that the union "won" the raise—it was not "granted" by management. Union people, of course, question whether the raise would have been granted in the absence of the union.

Employee Loyalty

POINT OF VIEW

Roughly one-third of Japanese workers enjoy lifetime employment with their employers— typically the largest firms in Japan. These workers ordinarily start working for their employers as soon as they finish trade school or graduate from college. When they reach the typical retirement age of 55, they receive a handsome bonus payment for their years of service. Many of these retirees are then rehired by smaller firms. These are often the firms that supply the products the larger firms need in their operations. In the case of workers whose skills have become obsolete, employers and the government sponsor retraining programs. This type of employer-employee relationship helps to build strong worker loyalty.

Many employers and unions in the United States think this type of employer-employee relationship is too paternalistic. They tend to view unions and management as adversaries. Furthermore, most unions in Japan are organized along company lines. Thus there is closer cooperation between unions and management than in the United States, where most unions are organized by crafts and along industry lines— not company lines. In general, therefore, American workers do not have as strong feelings of loyalty to their employers as Japanese workers.

The Jobs Issue

Many workers and their unions think that a firm's major goal should be to provide jobs for workers. Several approaches to dealing with unemployment have been tried over the years. Thus some labor contracts provide for supplemental unemployment benefits. **Supplemental unemployment benefits (SUB) are payments made by employers to the workers they have laid off.** The concept developed in the auto industry in 1955. The idea is to deal with the problem of short-term joblessness among auto workers during yearly model changeovers. The employer pays a certain amount of money into a fund for each hour an employee works. The accumulated funds are used to make payments to workers who are laid off. The problem is that the SUB concept is not designed to deal with longer-term unemployment.

supplemental unemployment benefits (SUB)

Union people's fear that automation will reduce jobs has also been addressed in contract negotiations. Automation has made some jobs obsolete but unions often try to protect the members' whose jobs are taken over by machines. Some employers, in order to maintain labor peace, have been willing to keep these people on the payroll even if their services are not needed. The Taft-Hartley Act makes it illegal for unions to force an employer to pay for services which are not performed *or offered to be performed.* (See Table 7-1.) The term *featherbedding* is often interpreted to mean paying workers for work they do not do. Actually, this is featherbedding only if the workers also do not offer to perform the work. In practice, however, workers are sometimes paid for doing work that could be done faster and more efficiently by a machine. The result, of course, is higher costs for the firm and higher costs to consumers for its products. Competitive inroads into American markets by foreign-based firms are making featherbedding even more distasteful to employers.

Recent widespread unemployment in such industries as autos, airlines, steel, and rubber has focused unions' attention more on job security than on big pay hikes and more fringe benefits. In some cases, employers and unions in those industries have made concessions to existing contracts. The concessions employers sought involved such elements as wage and benefit cuts, wage freezes, and work rule changes that would help increase productivity. In return for those "givebacks" unions sought greater job security for their members.

The "Right to Manage" Issue

An employer must bargain with a union that is certified by the NLRB. The employer does not have to grant the union everything it wants, but both parties must bargain in good faith on bargainable
bargainable issues   issues. **Bargainable issues are aspects of the work or job environment that are subject to collective bargaining between union and management representatives.** Examples include vacations, holidays, rest periods, wages, seniority regulations, transfers, promotions, layoffs, and size of work crews.

Some unionized companies favor including a very specific statement of management rights in their contracts with unions. An example is a statement that management retains the right to institute technological changes. Other firms believe that a specific listing of management rights can become too restrictive. The union could contend that anything that is omitted from the list is outside the exclusive domain of management. These companies tend to include only a very general statement of management rights in their contracts.

When employees are unionized, personnel policies on pay, job transfers, promotions, discipline, fringe benefits, etc., are written into the collective bargaining agreement. Unionization also often results in more centralization of decision-making authority over personnel matters. Decisions on discipline, job transfers, etc., may

---

WHAT DO YOU THINK?

Many firms are facing tough decisions today in trying to increase productivity, remain competitive, and increase profitability. In order to accomplish this, suppose a firm's management wants to close an obsolete plant in the Northeastern United States and build a new plant in the Southeast. Assume also that the workers at the older plant are unionized.

Who Should Make Plant Relocation Decisions?

While management may say the relocation decision was made to accomplish the above results, unions tend to believe that the real reasons for "runaway plants" are to avoid the union and to pay lower wages. Thus firms that have closed older plants in heavily industrialized areas and have built new ones in the less unionized Sunbelt states are often accused of "running to avoid the union." Unions want plant relocation to be a bargainable issue.

Unions are not the only group with a stake in relocation decisions, however. In recent years relocation bills have been passed in a few states and have been introduced in others. The purpose is to require firms that shut down plants to compensate both the affected community and employees—for example, by giving the local government and employees a year's advance notice of the intention to close a plant; by making a compensatory payment to the government for the loss in tax revenues it will suffer from the closure; and by continuing to provide employee benefits for a specified period of time after the plant closes. Who should make plant relocation decisions? WHAT DO YOU THINK?

---

be removed from lower-level managers in order to exercise more control over these aspects of the collective bargaining agreement.

The quality-of-work-life programs we discussed in Chapter 5 can produce desirable results in unionized plants only if the unions support the programs. Involving workers in plant-floor level decisions about redesigning jobs to make them more satisfying and productive will lead to changes—new job classifications, modified work rules, changes in job assignments, and so on. These are already issues for collective bargaining in most unionized firms. Thus the management rights clause in some labor contracts may have to be narrowed to gain union support of these programs.

The Seniority Issue

Unions often are critical of wage and salary plans that are not based on seniority. Labor argues that any other system is subjective and/or interferes with the collective bargaining process. Union work rules, for example, may limit the use of the MBO method of employee performance appraisal. But management resists basing all pay and promotion decisions on seniority alone, on the grounds that it ignores employee productivity.

The Productivity Issue

Productivity has become a major issue in recent years. American labor's productivity has not been increasing as rapidly as that of workers in some other countries. This is a serious problem when American firms must compete for customers with foreign-based firms whose workers are increasing their productivity at a higher rate. It helps to explain why both union leaders and top managers in some of our largest corporations are members of the President's national productivity committee.

Management often blames declining productivity on restrictive union work rules, a decline of the work ethic, taxes and inflation that reduce their incentive to invest in new machines, and government regulations, such as the Environmental Protection Act, which require firms to invest in financially nonproductive areas.

Unions, however, argue that management too often is unwilling to invest in training programs to upgrade labor skills. Other criticisms include underspending on research and development, poor product engineering, poor communication between workers and managers, too much red tape in big firms, a dehumanized work environment, and lack of effective cooperation with unions in trying to improve workers' standard of living.

When increases in productivity do occur, management and labor often disagree over how much of the increase in output is due to labor and how much is due to capital. Workers who double their output per hour will want more pay. Management argues that at least part of the increase is due to the fact that workers work with newer and better machines. At any rate, if all the increase in output is paid to the worker in higher wages, management would have little or no incentive to invest money in new plants and equipment. The result, according to management, is rising costs, less profit, and eventually, a business failure because of inability to compete.

The Inflation Issue

escalator clause

Many recent labor contracts have included cost-of-living escalator clauses. **An escalator clause means that, during the period of time covered by a labor contract, wage hikes will be granted on the**

basis of changes in the cost of living. These hikes are called cost-of-living adjustments (COLA).

Management has tended to accept COLA on the grounds that it helps to avoid demands for big "catch up wage hikes" when a current contract expires and a new one is negotiated. It also makes unions less likely to want to bargain for shorter pacts and to reopen negotiations when their contracts do not have COLA provisions. A major conflict issue, however, has been whether there should be an upper limit on the COLA employers might have to pay during a contract period—whether COLA should be capped or uncapped. In fact, bargaining over the formula to be used for making the adjustments can be tough. The COLA provision has been one of the items many employers have sought as a "giveback" in negotiating contract concessions with unions during recent years.

THE NATURE OF COLLECTIVE BARGAINING

In preparing to bargain on a new contract, the union sets up a negotiating team long before the current contract will expire. This team develops a list of demands that will satisfy the union membership. It also is common for the union members to vote a strike authorization that will go into effect if the current contract expires and a new one has not been negotiated.

The management negotiating team tries to anticipate the union's demands and prepares for them. For example, if management expects the union to bargain for a large wage hike, management negotiators will enter the bargaining sessions armed with forecasts concerning the impact of the higher wages on the firm's ability to compete against other firms in the industry.

During the early bargaining sessions, the union presents its demands first and the management proposes changes in the old contract that it would like to include in the new contract. Any issues brought up for discussion can be objected to by either labor or management, but as we have seen, the law requires both to bargain in good faith on bargainable issues. Suppose management believes that one of the union's demands infringes on the employer's area of managerial discretion and refuses to bargain on this point. The union might file a complaint with the NLRB which will decide if the issue is bargainable.

By now, both sides have their demands on the table and it may look as if there is little chance of coming to an agreement. The bargaining process then focuses on concessions. Each team is authorized to make concessions in order to narrow the gap between labor's demands and management's offers.

The closer the bargainers get to the expiration date of the current contract, the harder they work to hammer out a new contract. Around-the-clock bargaining sessions may be held to come up with a contract. The union negotiators, however, are not authorized to accept the contract they eventually work out with management. They can recommend it to the membership but rank-and-file union members must vote on it before it can be binding. If they ratify (accept) it, a formal and binding contract is prepared and signed by labor and management.

A national contract covers major issues like wage rates and fringe benefits. But while the national contract is being negotiated, local unions and plant managements work out specific provisions on rest periods, sanitary facilities, washup periods, and so on. These can vary from plant to plant but local negotiations are, in general, consistent with the national contract. If an agreement cannot be worked out on an issue at the local level, the plant may be struck by the local union.

In heavily unionized industries like steel, autos, trucking, and rubber, national contracts tend to set a pattern. Thus the national contract hammered out between the United Steelworkers and US Steel may set a pattern for the other steelmakers. Even in less unionized industries, national contracts worked out between major firms and their unions often affect the wages and fringe benefits nonunionized employers pay their workers. These employers want their pay and benefits packages to be at least comparable to those of unionized workers in order to remain nonunionized.

Recently there has been a tendency, especially in troubled industries, to allow local plant managers and local unions to negotiate concessions to national contracts. For the most part, these concessions have involved work rules. In some cases, however, they have involved concessions on wage and fringe benefits that are part of the national contract. Quite often these concessions are agreed to in order to prevent a plant from being closed due to inability to compete.

During the collective bargaining process, labor and management sometimes get deadlocked in their negotiations. They can call in a neutral third party to help break the deadlock. **In conciliation the neutral third party's task is to prevent negotiations from breaking down. If negotiations break off, the conciliator tries to get the two parties back to the bargaining table.** The conciliator, however, has no authority over either party.

Mediation goes a step further. **In mediation, the neutral third**

Kenneth Moffett, acting director of the Federal Mediation and Conciliation Service, was involved in negotiations during the PATCO and baseball strikes

conciliation

mediation

party's task is to suggest a possible compromise. The mediator tries to persuade the parties to settle the dispute. Like the conciliator, the mediator has no authority over either party.

Some states have mediation services but most mediators are provided by the Federal Mediation and Conciliation Service. This agency was set up by the Taft-Hartley Act.

Arbitration is another process that may be used in settling labor-management conflict. Very few labor contracts, however, provide for arbitration as an approach to negotiating a labor contract. **In voluntary arbitration a neutral third party hears both sides of the dispute and settles the issue. The two parties decide voluntarily to submit the dispute to arbitration and both parties are usually bound by the settlement.**

voluntary arbitration

Compulsory arbitration is compelled by federal or state law. The arbitrator's settlement is binding. Compulsory arbitration is used only when essential public services are involved. An increasing number of states are turning to this method of settling strikes by government workers.

compulsory arbitration

The President of the United States can use an injunction to stop strikes if they "imperil the national health or safety." President Carter used an injunction to force striking coal miners back to the mines in 1978. That strike was held to be a national emergency strike. If the miners had refused to obey the back-to-work order and violence had broken out, the President could have called out federal troops to help prevent any further violence. The President also could have sought congressional action to authorize seizure of the mines. The miners, however, did obey the back-to-work order.

Grievance Machinery

If given a choice, most employers probably would prefer that their workers be nonunionized. But a firm may, in fact, benefit from the presence of a union. Unions can help manage employee discontent by bringing problems to the surface where they can be dealt with through collective bargaining. Workers may express their individual discontent through work slowdowns or quitting. A union, however, provides a mechanism for channeling this discontent to management while, at the same time, keeping the work force intact. Thus employer-employee communication improves. Supervisors who want to initiate changes in work procedures will often discuss it with union representatives before they "announce" the changes. This gives the supervisor the chance to "sell" the proposed changes to the union representative who, in turn, may help "sell" them to the union members.

The collective bargaining agreement enables management and labor to coexist. The rights of each are stated. But no such contract could cover every situation in which trouble might occur. Also, problems sometimes arise over the interpretation of the contract.

grievance procedures

A grievance is something that causes a worker to complain. Not all complaints, however, are grievances—only those complaints that relate to alleged violations of the labor contract or the law are grievances. To deal with grievances, labor contracts include grievance procedures. **Grievance procedures spell out the sequence of steps a grieved employee should follow in seeking to correct the cause of the grievance.** These procedures are set up to reduce the chance that employee gripes will cause a breakdown in labor-management relations.

A worker who is told by a supervisor to do a task the worker does not think is part of his or her job may want to file a grievance. The worker might discuss this with the shop steward (a union representative in the plant) who might then take it to the worker's boss. If the issue is not settled at this stage, the grievance may be presented in writing to the union grievance committee and the plant manager. If the issue is still unresolved, it may be presented in writing to still higher union and company officials. Ultimately, the issue may be submitted to binding arbitration. Although, as we said earlier, contract arbitration is very rare, grievance arbitration is common in administering a collective bargaining agreement. It helps reduce the chances that grievances will lead to work stoppages.

WEAPONS OF LABOR AND MANAGEMENT

Most grievances are settled through grievance procedures. Sometimes, however, issues divide labor and management so much that they resort to certain weapons. This is likely to happen when employee discontent is widespread, the parties are unable to agree on a new contract, or there is a dispute over contract terms.

Labor's Weapons

Labor's main weapons are

- the strike
- the picket
- the boycott

A strike is a temporary withdrawal of all or some employees from the employer's service. The presumption is that they will return when their demands are met or a compromise is worked out. The strike is the union's ultimate weapon. It ordinarily will not be used, however, unless the union has the financial resources to ride it out.

strike

Picketing means that people (pickets) form a picket line and walk around a plant or office building with placards (signs) informing other workers and the general public that the employer is held unfair to labor. Strikes are usually accompanied by picketing, but picketing may take place without a strike.

picketing

In general, picketing is protected under the right of free speech as long as it does not include any fraud, violence, and/or intimidation. An effective picket may keep other employees who belong to different unions from entering a plant. If a picket line around a plant is honored by truck drivers, the picketed firm finds itself without deliveries.

In a boycott a union tries to get people to refuse to deal with the boycotted firm. There are *primary* and *secondary boycotts.* Suppose that the employees of Company Y are involved in a dispute. They might send circulars to Y's customers and suppliers asking them not to do business with Y. This is a secondary boycott.

boycott

Secondary strikes are generally legal. *Secondary pickets* enjoy some protection as an exercise of free speech. The legality of a secondary boycott depends on its purpose, the means used to carry it out (degree of coercion, etc.), and the remoteness of the third party to whom pressure is applied. The Taft-Hartley Act allows the NLRB to secure a federal court injunction against unions that engage in illegal strike, picket, and/or boycott activity. These tools of labor power are also used by nonunionized labor and minority groups—especially the boycott and the picket.

The "corporate campaign" is a new and controversial approach to organizing workers whose employers strongly resist unionization. It involves the use of picketing to inform the target firm's customers and others that the firm is nonunionized. It also involves an attempt to induce the target firm's workers and customers to stop buying the firm's products—a boycott. A third element is directed at the outside directors on the target firm's board of directors. These board members are not officers of the corporation, but they are often executives of firms that buy from the target firm or executives of banks that lend money to it. The goal is to encourage them to pressure the target firm's management to cease its interference or resistance to the organizing effort. Otherwise, the outside directors' firms might be targeted for picketing and/or boycotting.

In recent years, municipal employees in many cities have gone on strike

Management's Weapons

Management's main weapons are

- the lockout
- the layoff
- the injunction
- the employers' association

For many years management used the lockout to counter labor's threat to strike or to organize. **In a lockout employees are denied access to the plant until they accept the employer's terms of employment.** This weapon is now used mainly as a defensive weapon once a strike is called.

lockout

Today the layoff is more effective. A general strike against steel makers that lasts long enough to deplete their inventories leads to layoffs in steel-using industries. Although autoworkers who are laid off claim they are "behind" the steelworkers, a lengthy steel strike brings hardship to the autoworkers. This may lead to indirect pressure by the autoworkers on the steelworkers to reach an agreement.

The Norris-LaGuardia Act greatly limited the use of the labor injunction. But employers who can prove that unions are engaging in unlawful practices can seek injunctive relief in the courts.

Employers' associations are important in industries with many small firms and one large union that represents all workers. Member firms in an industry sometimes contribute to a strike insurance fund. Such a fund could be used to help members who are struck. They are similar in purpose to strike insurance funds built up by unions.

Firms or industries with labor problems often publicize their side in newspapers and other media to gain public support. Unions also do this. The strength of public opinion sometimes leads to new laws.

THE FUTURE OF UNIONISM

As we have seen, the percentage of our labor force that is unionized has declined over recent years. The future of unions in the United States will depend largely on the success with which they can organize people in geographic areas, industries, and occupations that traditionally have not been unionized.

During recent years there has been some movement of people and industry from the older industrialized Northeastern states to the Sunbelt states of the South and Southwest. Some of the Sunbelt

AUTHORS' COMMENTARY

Union Participation in Pension Fund Investment Decisions

Hundreds of billions of dollars are tied up in pension programs that individual employers negotiate with their employees' unions. A federal law prohibits unions from exclusive control over decisions about how these funds are invested, but it does not prohibit them from participating in these decisions. Because the law holds employers ultimately liable for investing these funds prudently in the best interests of the workers, employers have been reluctant to share control with the unions. With some exceptions, employers decide how the funds will be invested—often with some help by big insurance companies and trust companies.

Some of this money is loaned to businesses and some is used to buy stock in corporations. Union leaders would like to have more say in how the money is used. For example, they might want to invest more of it in rebuilding decaying inner cities. That might help them satisfy both an economic objective of creating jobs for union members and a social objective of aiding the community.

It is very likely that unions will push for more participation in decisions about how these pension funds are invested. That would give unions more economic power.

states are highly nonunionized and unions will have to step up their organizing efforts to increase membership in these states.

In Chapter 1 we said that our service industries are growing more rapidly than manufacturing industries. Workers in the service industries traditionally have not been highly unionized. Many work part-time and the typical firm is small. This makes it harder and more costly for unions to organize these workers than it is to organize full-time workers in large factories. Unions will have to intensify their organizational efforts in the service industries.

White-collar workers now account for more than half of our labor force. In the past some union leaders assumed that these workers were hard to unionize because of their tendency to identify more closely with their employers than with unions and blue-collar workers. But during recent years many white-collar workers have been experiencing many of the same problems blue-collar workers have faced. Mechanization and automation in factories gave rise to fears about job scarcity and stimulated unionization. More recently the effects of automation are being felt in white-collar occupations. Some clerical workers, for example, are facing loss of jobs and rapidly changing job requirements as employers use computers to automate office operations. Unions are appealing to these and other white-collar workers, including professionals such as librarians, teachers, nurses, and interns in hospitals. We can expect even greater effort by unions in the future to organize these workers.

For many women work has become an important aspect of their lives. As a result, the percentage of our labor force accounted for by women is increasing and unions will have to make even stronger efforts to appeal to them.

Federal labor laws exclude federal, state, and local governments in defining the term "employer," and the Wagner Act does not recognize the right of government workers to strike. Although unions for federal government workers are now similar to unions for workers in private industry, there are some differences. The U.S. Office of Personnel Management, for example, still has a great deal of control over personnel policies and regulations. Most government jobs are white-collar jobs and, therefore, most unionized federal government workers are white-collar workers. This is the segment of white-collar workers that unions have been most successful in organizing.

The overall health of the economy will play a major role in the future of unionism. If labor and management negotiators continue to focus heavily on "givebacks," more employers may find themselves setting up profit-sharing plans so that unions will feel they are getting something in return. "Givebacks" may also reduce the impact of national contracts as they are amended by concessions at local levels. Greater worker participation in quality-of-work-life programs also may mean that unions will push for greater participation in the sharing of profit and a narrowing of management rights clauses in labor contracts.

SUMMARY AND LOOK AHEAD

A labor union is an organization of employees formed for the purpose of collective bargaining with the employer. Union and employer representatives negotiate a collective bargaining agreement—a contract that sets forth the terms and conditions under which union members will offer their labor services to an employer.

The earliest attempts of workers to form unions were frustrated by court rulings which held that unions were criminal or civil conspiracies against trade and property. Gradually, as public sympathy shifted in favor of unions, laws were passed to guarantee the worker the right to join a union.

The National Labor Relations Board (NLRB) holds elections and certifies unions as bargaining agents. Once a union is certified, union and management must bargain in good faith on bargainable issues.

The two basic types of unions are craft and industrial unions. Craft unions are organized by crafts or trades and restrict membership to workers with certain specific skills. Industrial unions are organized according to industries and include semiskilled and unskilled workers. The union organizational structure includes local unions, national unions, and union federations.

Unions have a broad range of objectives. These include representing labor's views of major issues, improving their members' standard of living and job security, and improving union security.

The three major forms of union security are: (1) the closed shop; (2) the union shop; and (3) the agency shop. Some states have right-to-work laws which outlaw the union shop. This is permitted under the Taft-Hartley Act and unions have been fighting for repeal of this provision in the Act.

Many factors can lead to labor-management conflict. These include seniority rights, working conditions, the scope of bargainable issues, labor productivity, and management's right to manage.

Collective bargaining sessions between union and management are conducted by professional negotiators. If they become deadlocked in their negotiations, the bargaining representatives can resort to conciliation, mediation, and arbitration. Grievance procedures spell out the sequence of steps a grieved employee should follow in seeking to correct the cause of the grievance.

When labor-management conflict results in a standoff, labor uses its weapons—the strike, the picket, and the boycott. Among management's weapons are the lockout, the layoff, the injunction, and the employer's association.

The union movement has always been a minority movement in the United States. Recently unions have sought to increase their membership by growing in new directions, such as organizing white-collar workers. This is necessary because of the declining percentage of the labor force that is in blue-collar jobs.

In the next chapter, we look at how firms produce goods and services and how this production effort is managed.

FOR REVIEW . . .

1. List the major federal labor laws and discuss their main provisions.

2. Why is the Wagner Act referred to as labor's "Magna Charta"?

3. Why do many consider the Taft-Hartley Act "promanagement"?

4. Discuss the role of the National Labor Relations Board (NLRB) in labor-management relations.

5. Is the scope of "managerial discretion" narrowed when a firm's workers form a union? Explain.

6. Distinguish between a craft union and an industrial union.

7. List and discuss the major objectives of modern unions.

8. In light of the declining proportion of our labor force that is engaged in blue-collar jobs, what are unions doing to increase their membership?

9. List and discuss four issues that might lead to labor-management conflict.

10. List and discuss the "weapons" of labor and management.

11. Why do some employers want "give-backs" from unions?

12. What is a national contract? Are concessions ever made to such contracts? Why or why not?

. . . FOR DISCUSSION

1. Is a union responsible to persons or groups other than its members?

2. Do the employees of a firm whose management is "employee-oriented" need a union?

3. How would you explain the fact that most American workers do not belong to a union?

4. Suppose you are in charge of selecting a location for a new plant to be built next year by your firm. Would the absence or presence of state right-to-work laws influence your decision?

5. What should business, government, and unions do to increase the productivity of American workers?

INCIDENTS

Growth in the Number of Employee-owned Plants

In recent years a growing number of firms like Ford, General Motors, Rath Packing Company, and Sperry Rand have offered their employees the opportunity to buy plants that the companies had decided to close. The decision to close the plants was usually based on the fact that the plants were either marginally profitable or unprofitable.

In some cases, the employees decided to buy the plants. Under various types of financing arrangements, the workers wind up as part owners of the plants with their employers. In other cases, the workers end up owning the entire plant. Sometimes the employees get financial help from local residents and government agencies in buying the plants.

The basic incentive for employees to become full or partial owners is to preserve their jobs. Thus they may be willing to work for lower wages and benefits and to accept a lower rate of return on their investment than their employers were willing to accept. The basic incentive for local residents and governments to lend financial support to the employees is the desire to prevent a plant from closing—a move that would reduce the affected communities' tax bases.

QUESTIONS

1. Do you think employees are likely to be more productive in employee-owned plants than in employer-owned plants? Explain.

2. Suppose a company operates a plant that manufactures products that compete for customers with an employee-owned plant. How do you think that company would feel about competing with an employee-owned plant?

3. Do you think that the workers in a plant that is partially owned by those workers would want a union? Explain.

4. Do you think that the workers in a plant that is entirely owned by those workers would want a union? Explain.

Labor and Management—Adversaries or What?

As we saw in Chapter 1, one of Solidarity's goals was to win the right for Polish workers to choose their own managers instead of having them appointed by the government. In Chapter 3, we saw that Germany's "codetermination" law enables workers to sit on boards of directors as well as on work councils at the plant level.

In the United States, labor and management have traditionally had an adversarial relationship in collective bargaining. Many people believe that boards of directors, composed of management people, should decide major policy issues, and that unions should be in a position to criticize those decisions from the worker's point of view.

There have been some exceptions, however. For example, the president of the United Auto Workers sits on Chrysler's board and unions at Pan American World Airways nominated a director to sit on its board. In both cases, this was largely in return for union givebacks in collective bargaining.

QUESTIONS

1. What are the relative advantages and disadvantages of an adversarial relationship between labor and management in collective bargaining?

2. As we saw in this chapter, givebacks and contract concessions have become more common in recent years. What are the implications of that as far as corporate governance is concerned?

3. Do you think it is possible for labor and management to remain adversaries at the bargaining table while also working together in quality-of-work-life programs at the plant-floor level? Explain.

CHAPTER 8

Production Management

OBJECTIVES:

After reading this chapter, you should be able to

1. Illustrate the nature and growth of production.
2. Illustrate the inputs, processes, and outputs of production.
3. Show how production processes may be classified.
4. Review the management functions and give an example of each as applied to production.
5. Develop a checklist for plant location decisions.
6. Evaluate the dangers of loss of human motivation in a big factory.
7. Explain the process of control as it applies to product quality.
8. Distinguish between value analysis and vendor analysis.
9. Distinguish between a production management view and an operations management view of problem solving.

KEY CONCEPTS:

Look for these terms as you read the chapter

production
combination
breaking down
treatment
intermittent production
continuous production
automation
labor-intensive
capital-intensive
production management
make-or-buy decision
plant capacity

plant layout
control chart
PERT
CPM
quality control
preventive maintenance
obsolescence
reciprocity
value analysis
vendor analysis
operations management

It is really very difficult to turn a business on and off like a faucet," observed Richard M. Smith, vice chairman at the Bethlehem Steel Corporation in Pittsburgh, which is operating at about 60 percent of capacity. "We can't just turn the taps on our steel blast furnaces."

Downturns in production plagued most U.S. industry in 1982. The layoffs of workers were huge and the problems faced by plant managers because of the downturns were staggering as well.

Cutbacks may save money, but they can also mean laying off trained employees, postponing research and development, and halting recruiting efforts. The cuts not only affect a company's current profitability and its ability to survive a downturn, but they may also affect its ability to compete and grow when the economy recovers. Managers must try to make the cuts that will be most feasible and most effective, while causing the least damage.[1]

Adjusting to reduced demand is only one of the challenges a production manager must meet. In this chapter we examine the functional area of production and the management techniques applied to it. We approach production management by applying the traditional management functions of planning, organizing, staffing, directing, and controlling to the production function. Special emphasis is given to planning and control. The logical place to start is with a definition of production.

WHAT IS PRODUCTION?

production

Production activity creates goods and services. Because of production more wants can be satisfied. Production can also be viewed as a sequence. **It starts with the *input* of resources which are fed into one of several kinds of production *processes*. Finally an *output* of goods or services results for use or sale.** Figure 8-1 illustrates this view and makes it easier for us to explain the elements of production management.

The Inputs to Production

To produce something, the following set of resources is usually needed as input:

- materials
- capital goods
- the human input

Materials include raw materials such as raw cotton, corn, and crude oil; semimanufactured products such as sheet steel and unfinished lumber; and manufactured parts such as spark plugs, bolts, and tires. Electric power and other energy sources are usually included. Capital goods include the plant investment, which can range from a huge refinery to a barber shop, and equipment such as a lathe or a typewriter.

One of the greatest problems facing producers today is the fact that one of the critical inputs, raw materials, is often scarce. As the world's resources are used up, producers are turning to chemical research to find new materials for industry. 3M Company, for example, recently developed its Silverlook film for making duplicate negatives as a part of the offset printing process. The film is made from a metal that is more plentiful and cheaper than silver. This kind of

FIGURE 8-1

The production process

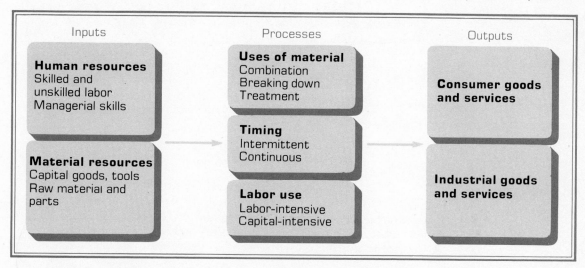

research can reduce the problems created by increasing scarcity of certain raw materials.

The human input includes

- unskilled labor
- skilled labor
- supervisory skills
- managerial skills

The main distinction between skilled and unskilled labor is ability to perform a special task that cannot be performed by all employees. Examples of skilled workers include carpenters, pipefitters, and technicians. Supervisors and managers, of course, are responsible for directing the activities of others.

Processes

There are several ways of classifying production processes. The first depends on the way that material inputs are dealt with. The second relates to the timing of the process. The third depends on the degree of use of labor.

Uses of Material Inputs

A process may combine two or more material inputs, break down an input, or treat an input.

U.S. Production Will Continue to Rise

Below is a short table providing an index* of the growth of U.S. production since 1950:

	1950	1960	1970	1983†
Total Production	45	66	107	149
Manufacturing	45	65	105	149
Mining	66	83	110	116
Utilities	27	62	128	173

*1967 = 100

†Represents first half of year

The serious challenge to U.S. production, especially by Japan and the Common Market countries as well as by low-wage emerging nations, has forced U.S. firms to apply more and more ingenuity and technical means of efficiency improvement so as to multiply productivity. We have more than tripled total production in three decades. The challenge of other nations and our technological response will likely lead to even more dramatic production gains. Some of the new technology that helps to suggest this additional leap forward in total production will be described in Chapter 20.

combination

Combination means putting parts together. It is the most common process. Cars, pumps, and pencils must go through the process of combination. For example, side panels on new cars are traditionally made by combining six or more pieces of steel. This, of course, requires welding to combine the pieces.

breaking down

Breaking down means removing or at least separating some of the original input, usually a raw material. When a log is cut into two-by-fours or when juice is taken from oranges, the process, which is also very common, is one of breaking down.

treatment

Treatment is doing something to an input without adding or subtracting from it. It may involve hardening or softening or cooling or reshaping an input. Smoking a ham or molding a plastic toothbrush handle is a treatment process. Forming a part out of a basic material is often called *fabrication*.

Tropicana Products, Inc. makes orange juice at its plant in Bradenton, Florida. The plant operations are highly integrated and all the three preceding production processes are performed. Juice is taken from oranges by breaking down. The plant also produces glass bottles and corrugated shipping boxes, largely through combination processes. Finally, treatment (refrigerating the juice) is necessary while the product is being transported by rail to market.

Timing

We can also classify production processes according to a time dimension. They can be intermittent or continuous, and also either for stock or to order.

An intermittent production process starts and stops and starts again, maybe several times. Intermittent production may occur only when stocks fall below a critical level. It may also occur to build up stocks when machines and workers would otherwise be idle. A specialty toolmaker, for example, may nickel plate certain batches of output and not others. Some products may require special heat treatments. The nickel plating and heat treating departments of the firm are used intermittently.

intermittent production

A continuous production process, as the name implies, goes on and on. A cola bottling plant repeats the same process countless thousands of times without interruption. The demand for this product is large and easy to predict. **The process, as in the case of most continuous processes, is highly automated. This means that little human supervision is needed because computers and machines can deal with nearly everything that could happen to interrupt operation.** Automation is discussed more fully in Chapter 13.

continuous production

automation

Most continuous processes produce products *for stock.* This means that output is kept in inventory in anticipation of demand. This could not be done without losing money if the firm did not have good reason to expect a fairly steady demand. The reason is that keeping inventories costs money in several ways. They take up valuable space, they require financing, and they may be damaged or stolen or become obsolete. Manufacturers of cigarettes and beer use a continuous production process. Demand is fairly predictable and manufacturers can afford to produce in anticipation of actual demand. Electric generating plants and oil refineries also engage in continuous production. Their operations go on around the clock because demand is even more predictable.

The alternative to producing for stock is producing *to order.* This means that the firm waits until there is a specific order in hand before starting to produce. Such production is also called *jobbing.* This kind of production usually uses general-purpose machines and tools—those which can do a variety of jobs. Often production to order is "custom" production in which a specific design or feature is provided for the customer. Boeing and McDonnell Douglas, for example, produce airplanes only upon receipt of orders.

Wine-making involves the processes of combination, breaking down, and treatment

Labor Use

labor-intensive

Processes also vary in the amount of human input they need. **Labor-intensive processes depend more on people than on machines.** Some parts of the apparel trade are like this. Labor-intensive processes are most likely to be used when labor is cheap or when there is an artistic element in the work. There are some kinds of jobs, too, in which it is really hard to apply machines because the process varies a lot. Many kinds of farming are still highly labor-intensive as is the making of high-quality jewelry. Today many items of clothing for U.S. markets are made or are partly made by U.S. firms with low-cost labor in less-developed nations.

capital-intensive

The opposite situation exists when machines can do the job better than people. **This calls for capital-intensive processes in which people may have little to do with production. Instead, investment in machinery is great.** The huge petroleum refinery is a classic example of a capital-intensive process. A refinery that may cost hundreds of millions of dollars to build and equip may operate with fewer than 100 employees.

How Will Modern Technology Affect the World of Work?

POINT OF VIEW

An Optimistic View

As far as I'm concerned, I can't wait to work less. They say that the thirty hour week is just around the corner. The computers and robots that are taking over much of the busywork of offices and factories will enable us to produce all our nation needs with fewer hours of work. Certainly the physical effort part of work will be all but eliminated. We'll spend more of our work time planning and making sure that things are done right. And don't forget the leisure time we'll have. I'm already getting into continuing education courses and I've put a down payment on a fishing boat.

A Pessimistic View

I look at it differently. It seems to me that those guys who own the plants and big businesses are out to protect themselves, period! They want to install more and more labor-saving machines and computers so that they can avoid the trouble of dealing with workers and unions. These machines make us less important and that means less power for the worker. They talk about retraining programs and higher-skill jobs for us, but you can't fool me. New machines mean less work and less work means lower income for the average person.

Coal mining used to be highly labor-intensive. Since the energy crisis began, however, oil, steel, and utility companies have been investing in the coal industry. They are buying expensive equipment to mechanize and automate coal mining operations. Thus their operations are becoming more capital-intensive. To make such heavy investment in equipment pay off, the equipment has to be operated nonstop. Thus their operations more closely resemble continuous production than intermittent production.

Likewise, computers used to be custom-built and their manufacturing processes were highly labor-intensive. In recent years computer manufacturers have turned to high-volume, mass production operations and manufacturing processes have become more capital-intensive. Strong price competition has driven computer prices down and computer makers have had to focus on lower-cost production. Thus they too have invested billions of dollars to automate their manufacturing operations.

Shortages of skilled workers can also be a problem. For example, some machine tool makers in recent years have been advising their customers that they will experience increasing difficulty in hiring skilled machinists. Thus the machine tool makers are moving into electronic technology and are offering computer-controlled machines that require less-skilled machine operators.

Outputs of Production

The outputs of production are divided into consumer goods and services—those things that are purchased and used by individuals

Programmable industrial robots are becoming familiar sights along the production line.

and households—and industrial goods and services—those things purchased and used by businesses and institutions. A full explanation of this classification scheme is provided in the following chapter. At this point, we will offer a few examples of each.

Consumer Goods

Consumer goods surround us. They are produced by every kind of process. If you had Kellogg's Corn Flakes for breakfast this morning you were consuming a consumer good that was produced by a process that included mixing ingredients (assembly) and cooking (treatment). This process is also continuous and capital-intensive. All of the inputs shown in Figure 8-1 were used, including various forms of human input and material input.

Consumer Services

Consumer services also abound. A good example is hairstyling. The process in this case is primarily treatment with perhaps a bit of assembly and/or breaking down. The process is intermittent and labor-intensive. Services are by their nature labor-intensive. The inputs are primarily the skilled labor of the stylist, accompanied by some materials.

Industrial Goods

Industrial goods production can be demonstrated by the case of building construction. To erect a skyscraper in a major city requires a variety of processes, but it is predominantly assembly. It has become more and more capital-intensive, but still requires substantial skilled and unskilled labor input. Construction could also be characterized as intermittent processing, although some parts of the process are continuous, particularly when deadlines for completion are approaching. The material inputs of steel, glass, and insulating materials are assembled by skilled and unskilled workers and supervised by skilled managerial people.

Industrial Services

A good example of an industrial service output might be security services offered to a bank by Pinkerton, a firm specializing in protecting people and property. Bank security services might, for example, include some assembly of alarm components and locks, but it is also a labor-intensive service involving the human input of around-the-clock security guards (continuous process).

WHAT IS PRODUCTION MANAGEMENT?

Production management is the application of managerial functions to production. The inputs, processes, and outputs we have just described require planning, organizing, staffing, directing, and controlling. As we will see near the end of this chapter, this topic is often viewed in a broader way. This broader view, known as *operations management*, is more "systems"- or "process"-oriented than the traditional approach taken here. Meanwhile, we will examine the managerial functions in a production context.

production management

Production Planning

Planning is concerned with the future. It is a mapping out of how things are going to be done. It has short-run and long-run dimensions and requires a forecast of demand.

Planning for production is no exception. It includes planning the product (outputs) and planning for capital, labor, and material needs (inputs). We will emphasize strategic, long-run planning with an emphasis on capital-goods planning and planning for the product itself.

Planning the Product

The logical time to start planning for production is when planning the product. This type of planning really involves both production and marketing functions of the firm and is discussed more fully in our chapters on marketing. At this point we will describe just a few features of the product-planning process.

Product planning amounts to answering the following questions:

- What kind of products can be sold at a profit?
- How much can be sold?
- What styles and sizes should be produced?
- What special features should the product have?

The answers to these questions require study in the laboratory to determine the best inputs of raw materials and component parts. In many firms this kind of thinking is done on a continuous basis by a product development department. The basic questions are always "will it sell?" and "can it be produced at a profit?"

The product mix of a firm—that is, the combination of products that it produces—has both market and cost effects. Producing a line of related products has certain advantages from the selling standpoint. Producing several products, whether they are related or not, may affect the unit cost. A local Coca-Cola bottling company could begin to bottle other soft drinks in the Coca-Cola Company's line. This would probably increase its total production volume without adding much cost for plant or equipment. Thus fixed costs (such as plant and equipment) would be spread over more units, and the cost per bottle would be reduced.

make-or-buy decision

One question that often arises in planning the product is the decision whether to make a product or a component part or to buy it—the "make-or-buy" decision. If we are talking about a firm that makes only one product, buying it rather than making it would take the firm out of the production business entirely. This could be the right decision if the firm could make more money by buying a product and reselling it than by making it and then selling it.

Other factors are involved in the "make-or-buy" question. If it is to be a question at all, there must be a reliable source from which to buy the product or part. There must be a supplier who is willing to meet the buyer's needs in terms of quality, quantity, and delivery schedules. A decision to buy rather than to make is often made for the component parts of an assembled product. The major auto makers, for example, buy many of the component parts of the cars they make. In the construction industry, a contractor often uses one or more subcontractors to produce various parts of the project.

Once a firm reaches a certain size, it might stop buying one or more component parts and begin to make them. This may reduce total costs of production and make the producer more secure about sources of inputs. It may also make the firm less flexible. In recent years, for example, some brewing companies have stopped buying cans from can makers and have started making their own. This, of course, means that the "buyer" has one supplier—itself.

Planning the Plant

There are several important questions that relate to planning for the plant itself. These include the decisions of

- where to locate the plant
- how large a plant to build
- how to arrange the plant internally

Plant location can affect overall cost, employee morale, and many other elements of a firm's operation. A manager should carefully weigh any location decision. A checklist such as the one pro-

Area Selection
1. Cost of materials and parts transportation
2. Cost of transportation of finished products to customers
3. Location inducements and deterrents by city and state
   governments
4. Quality and quantity of appropriate labor supply
5. Adequacy of power and water supply
6. Attractiveness as a place to live—climate, schools, safety, etc.

Specific site selection
1. Size
2. Accessibility to highways, railways, or water transport
3. Restrictions on land use, waste disposal, etc.
4. Land costs
5. Availability of leased facilities, such as public warehouses

TABLE 8-1

Factors in plant location

vided in Table 8-1 could be a great help. The first question is "in what area do we wish to locate?" This refers to a city or county or, perhaps, metropolitan area, but an even broader geographic location decision may be needed first. The factors to consider in selecting an area include input transportation, output transportation, and city and state inducements (such as tax exemptions) and deterrents (such as high property taxes). These should be estimated well in advance of making a decision.

Input transportation cost depends on the distance of raw material and parts suppliers from the proposed area and the kind of transportation facilities connecting them. Output transportation cost depends on the expected location and density of customers in the proposed area. Sometimes these cost factors make it hard to meet competitors' prices.

Local labor, water, and power supplies are sometimes crucial. Southern California, with its large supply of skilled aircraft workers, would have to be a major contender for a new aircraft production plant. Chemical plants, which require large water supplies for processing, cannot ignore sites along the Mississippi River. Especially in times of tight energy supplies, any plant that will use large amounts of energy must consider if there is enough natural gas, petroleum, or coal at the proposed site.

A less tangible factor is the attractiveness of the area as a place to live. Important items here are climate, schools, housing, public parks, police protection, and taxes. A firm trying to decide between two possible locations might make estimates of their comparative profitability, taking into account the expected effects of each location on sales and on the various cost components—especially taxes, transportation, and labor. The state of Maryland advertises its attractions in the ad on the following page.

Maryland advertises for industrial development

Once an area is selected, the next problem is to choose a specific site. The firm surveys available parcels of land that are suitable in terms of size, zoning restrictions, drainage, and access by highway, railway, and water. If several sites are satisfactory, the decision might depend on cost. There is the added possibility of finding a suitable existing plant available for sale or lease, which could mean an earlier date for plant opening.

Specific site selection calls for compromise among the items on the checklist. A specific firm's choice may be determined by the emphasis placed on access to a river or on distance from population centers. The site may be selected because it is close to a large university or to a major industrial customer.

Railroads help manufacturers find industrial sites. One major railroad operates a briefing center at which it presents complete descriptions of all available spots to prospective plant builders. This saves firms a lot of legwork and searching costs.

Plant location decisions are becoming more difficult as land in and near major population centers becomes scarce. Also, traffic congestion, crime, pollution control, and plant obsolescence are forcing many plants to leave urban centers. These moves often involve heavy losses in moving or abandoning heavy machinery and equipment.

Once a site is chosen, the next step in planning is to design the building itself. With the help of production experts and architects, the firm must plan plant capacity. **Plant capacity is the limit of the production output of the facility.** A pocket calculator assembly plant, for example, may require 10,000 square feet of space to produce an expected maximum output of 2,000 units a day.

plant capacity

Plant layout describes the relative location of the different parts of the production process in the building or buildings. The planner of a new calculator assembly plant might plan capacity and layout with the following factors in mind:

plant layout

- expected output level
- possibility of 24-hour operation
- demand variation by month
- inventory storage needs
- expansion needs
- limits imposed by financing

How much weight is placed on each of these factors might vary according to the type of production process. Most calculator assembly plants involve a continuous, for-stock, labor-intensive process. It might well be laid out on one floor in a straight line. The parts could be stocked at one end, the several-step assembly process could occur in the center and the inspection, testing, packaging, and shipping could be done at the other end.

Organizing for Production

Some of the departmentation process (referred to earlier in Chapter 5) depends on the type of plant layout. A plant may be arranged according to process or according to product, depending on the number of products being produced and the volume of production. A *process-organized* plant, for example, might have a grinding department, buffing department, stamping department, etc. A *product-organized* plant might have a pocket calculator department and a desk calculator department, each of which is arranged on an assembly-line basis. How machines are related to each other often determines the organizational structure, including the number of persons in each department.

Production Organization Structure

Sometimes a firm's organization may have the structural features of both product and process. The organizational chart for the Punch Products Corporation in Figure 8-2 shows such a case in which there are two products, each run by a superintendent. Each product group has two or more processes, each of which is in a separate department. This firm is decentralized in that each product organization has

FIGURE 8-2

Punch Products Corporation— organization for production

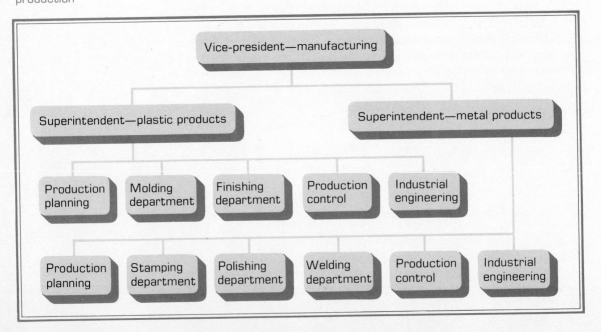

production planning, production control, and industrial engineering departments.

The specific organization for production in a firm may be heavily influenced by the nature of the production process as well as by the number and variety of products made. The Switzer Company produces small amounts of twenty different products at different times of the year. This is the reason that production planning, control, and engineering will be centralized. If the twenty products go through many of the same processes, including processes A, B, C, and D, the organization may appear as in Figure 8-3.

Many new restaurant chains provide interesting examples of a trend toward centralization. The Joshua Tree restaurants and others operated by Marriot Corporation in the Northeast have centralized the food preparation function so that most of the outlets do no cooking on the premises. The large, centralized kitchens serve restaurants over 150 miles away and cut operating costs down and keep more uniform food quality standards at the same time.

Other special organization problems are forced on a firm when it grows and acquires competing or unrelated manufacturing firms. Deciding what can be combined, whether to remain decentralized, and other related problems call for careful study.

Production management often faces a tough challenge in maintaining employees' enthusiasm for work, especially when production operations are highly automated. As we saw in the previous chapter, management and labor unions are cooperating in many ways to humanize the workplace by improving the quality of work life.

A related problem is conflict in assigning activities among work groups. Introduction of new technology in the plant may cause work to be distributed in a new way. What the new machines require

FIGURE 8-3
Switzer Company—
organization for
production

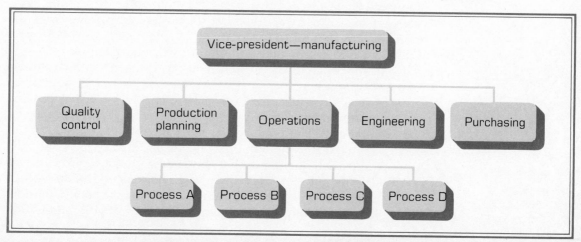

in the way of work assignment and departmentation may not be accepted by workers or by their unions. In organizing a factory, traditional union definitions of job responsibility—what kind of work a worker can or cannot do in the production process—cannot be ignored by a manager. Nor can a manager ignore regulations by the Occupational Safety and Health Review Commission designed to protect workers. These regulations can affect factory design and layout. (See Chapter 19.)

Staffing and Directing for Production

Staffing and directing together represent the application of the human resource to the production process. Staffing for production is often complicated by the need for highly specialized personnel. Such needs demand highly developed search techniques. The alternative is a long and expensive training program. Another complicating factor is the large role played by unions in manufacturing industries. As we saw in the preceding chapter, labor contracts often restrict or limit managers in the process of hiring, transferring, and promotion, as well as in making job assignments and in setting up working conditions.

A production manager must cope with the fact that machines, their timing, their coordination, and their very high costs determine how the production process is carried out. This includes determining the relationships among jobs, the span of management of supervisors, and other factors that must influence the kind of direction a supervisor can give.

The Human Dimension in Production

It is easier to motivate workers to outproduce coworkers than to motivate them to operate at the pace dictated by a machine. How does a manager set a wage rate that all workers think is fair when the principal contributor to productivity is a machine? Also, many production workers fear that automation will put them out of work. This makes it hard to motivate them, especially when their unions oppose automation.

In such situations, harmony is hard to achieve. It may be done by means of cooperation between labor and management. Both sides can agree that greater productivity is good for all. If automation can bring about greater productivity and management can assure the unions and their members that workers will share fairly in this increased productivity, a good working relationship can be built. It takes planning to prepare for the period of change to automation. This planning includes worker retraining and relocation and other guarantees of security for those workers most affected. Wage rates will rise because workers expect to share in the benefits of increased productivity.

Controlling Production

Controlling production involves setting production standards and developing systems for comparing production performance to those standards. There are several different types of production control. They include

- order control
- product quality control
- plant maintenance control
- inventory control

Order Control and Scheduling

When a plant is engaged in continuous, high-volume production of standard products, close control of individual orders is not very important. But in those plants using intermittent production, it is vital to create systems to control the flow of orders. New orders that have never been processed before must be checked to see what operations must be performed. They must be checked for correct sequence and to see that the right tools are on hand. This may require use of a control chart. **A control chart is a device which shows the standard set of steps to be taken in the performance of a procedure.** It ensures that things will be done as planned. Control charts were first conceived by Henry Gantt in the early 1900s, and today a wide variety of commercial variations of Gantt Charts is available. (See Figure 8-4.)

control chart

Plants that produce a variety of products on an intermittent basis establish a system of *decision rules* to guide the movement of orders through various manufacturing processes. Suppose there is a question: Which of two orders should be processed first by a given machine? It is not always logical to say that the order with the earliest due date should be processed first. Some firms use a simple "first-come, first-served" rule; others use a "first-come, first-served within priority class" rule for making these decisions. Which rule is best depends on the kind of processing going on in the plant. Regardless, some form of decision rule is necessary in intermittent-process production to guarantee a smooth flow. In recent years, computer simulation techniques have been used to speed up production.

Important tools used in order to assure a smooth scheduling of operations include PERT (Program Evaluation and Review Tech-

FIGURE 8-4
A Gantt chart

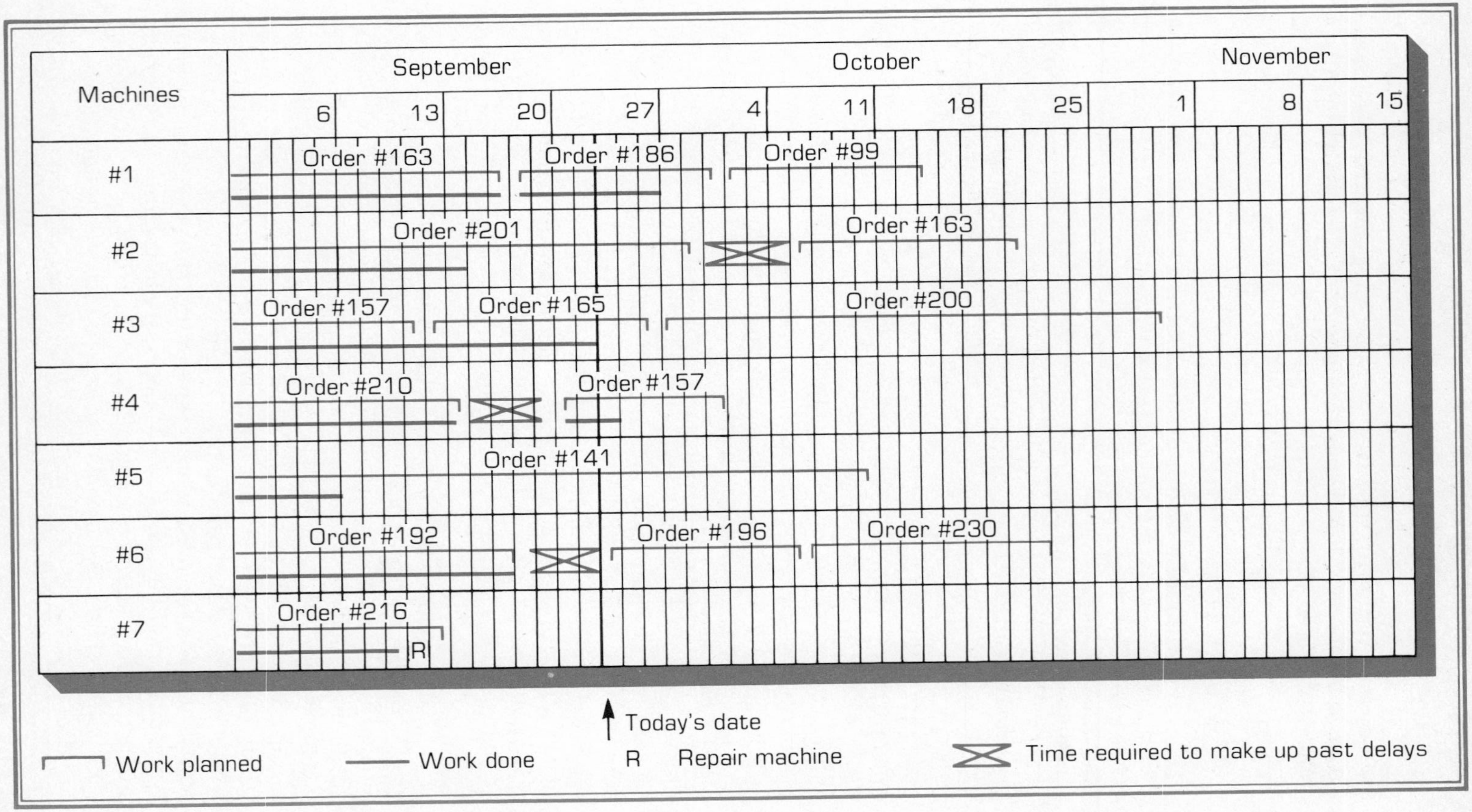

Machines	September		October			November	
	6	13	20	27	4	11	18	25	1	8	15
#1	Order #163		Order #186		Order #99		Order #163				
#2		Order #201									
#3	Order #157		Order #165			Order #200					
#4	Order #210			Order #157							
#5			Order #141								
#6	Order #192		Order #196			Order #230					
#7	Order #216	R									

⎣ Work planned   ─── Work done   ← Today's date   ⊠ Time required to make up past delays   R Repair machine

nique) and CPM (Critical Path Method). **PERT is a planning and control tool focusing on the timing of the occurrence of many operations included in a project.** It helps identify and remove bottlenecks. This tool was first applied by the government to speed up completion of vital weapons systems.

    A CPM diagram is illustrated in Figure 8-5. **CPM is much like PERT except that specific estimates rather than variable estimates of elapsed time in operations are used.** Wetherall Utility Buildings plans construction of a standard 20,000-square-foot warehouse by listing the major stages of construction, the time needed for each, and the sequence in which they occur. The letters in parentheses are events. The order of events is indicated by arrows. *Branching* occurs whenever two events can be worked on at the same time. The numbers next to arrow-segments show how many days are needed. A manager can follow a "path" to completion and can tell which chain of events is the longest or "critical" path (ABDF in our example). It is this chain of events that the manager must focus on to cut production time or to avoid delays.

PERT

CPM

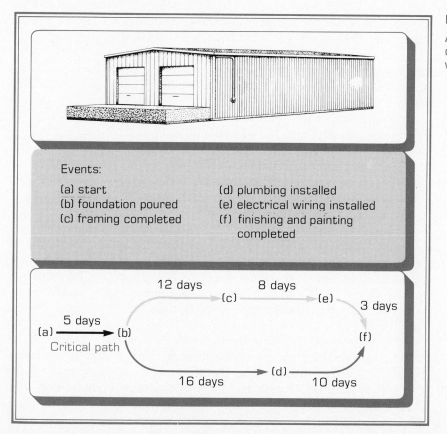

FIGURE 8-5
A CPM diagram for constructing a small warehouse

Events:

(a) start
(b) foundation poured
(c) framing completed

(d) plumbing installed
(e) electrical wiring installed
(f) finishing and painting completed

Order control systems must include rapid communication systems, such as special mail service or teletypes or even direct feedback to a central computer. They help management to take action quickly enough to correct flaws in the operation. This is the essence of control.

Product Quality Control

quality control

Clearly, there is a need to control the movement of orders through a production process. There is also a need for quality control. **A quality control system sets up a standard for an input or output and makes comparisons against this standard to prevent nonstandard items from going into or coming out of the production process.** This, however, does not necessarily mean that quality must be kept high. It means that the level of quality must be known and checked so that it can be kept within a certain *range of acceptable quality standards.* Of course, a manufacturer does not always seek to avoid high quality. Lower quality, however, may be acceptable when higher quality control would be too costly.

What constitutes a range of acceptable quality standards? The range is very narrow for firms in the pharmaceutical, nuclear, aircraft, and genetic engineering industries. Rockwell International, the prime contractor for the space shuttle, also uses extremely tight quality control standards. The range of acceptable product quality is much broader for firms that make nails, garbage cans, and household furniture.

BFGoodrich's new noise and vibration laboratory will ensure high-quality, quieter tires

Some firms traditionally insist on buying the highest quality materials available and tell us about it in their advertising. Owens sausage, for example, advertises that it could reduce its costs by using cheaper ingredients but says that would hurt its reputation for quality. There is little doubt that a lot of the success of Japanese car makers in the United States is due to the image they have created for using strict quality control standards.

Quality standards may also vary within a firm. A manufacturer of canned foods is likely to exercise great care to ensure the highest quality for products it sells under its own brand. For those it sells as unbranded or generic products, meeting the minimum government standards for quality may be enough. Kitchenaid sets higher standards for its top-of-the-line dishwasher than for its bottom-of-the-line model.

It is almost impossible to guarantee 100 percent quality of all inputs and finished products. Ordinarily, this would be too expensive. Most manufacturers, therefore, use sampling in quality control inspection. Thus a bicycle manufacturer's purchasing department may require that a sample of fifty twenty-foot sections be examined whenever a shipment of steel tubing arrives. Instructions might require that a shipment be accepted if no more than one defective section is found in the sample. This is called *acceptance sampling*. In certain types of production, of course, a 100 percent inspection is necessary because the sale of even one faulty unit could have very serious results.

The basis for classifying a unit as defective depends on what features of the unit are "critical." For steel tubing, perhaps hardness and strength are important. Applying these standards may require mechanical assistance or perhaps it can be done visually. Welds, for example, may be examined visually or by using x-rays, as was done for the Alaskan pipeline. A variety of measuring and testing machines exists in industry today. Often, however, a simple visual inspection is sufficient. A balance is needed between the cost of inspection and the cost of failure to meet standards.

Plant Maintenance Control

In a manufacturing plant—particularly a continuous process, assembly-line plant—one critical machine breakdown means high costs. During this "downtime" most of the other machinery is idled, and all the workers on the line are being paid even though their machines are idle.

This points up the need for maintenance. **Many firms practice preventive maintenance. This means that they inspect and/or replace certain critical machines and parts on a regular basis to avoid downtime.** Not all firms practice this, however. It may cost more than a firm is willing to pay. The units may be very expensive to replace. Also the cost of interrupting the production process for maintenance work may be too high. Some production managers prefer to "leave well enough alone." They install the highest-quality equipment to start with. This decision is a matter of balancing costs.

preventive maintenance

Control of Inventory Levels

A fourth area of production control is the control of inventory levels. This includes inventories of raw materials, parts, and finished and partly finished goods.

There are some good reasons for keeping high levels of inventory. A firm using assembly-line production is less likely to "run out" of parts and partly finished products. Running out of inventory can mean expensive downtime. This also applies to finished products. Big orders (and possibly big customers) can be lost if deliveries cannot be made as promised. Large stocks protect against this.

There are some equally good reasons for keeping inventories low, however. First, inventories require an investment of funds. A

obsolescence

factory that operates with a lower inventory is operating more efficiently—that is, it is producing profits with a smaller investment than a factory with a large inventory. Second, inventories take up scarce space. Third, products in inventory may decrease in value because of deterioration, theft, or damage. **Inventory items also may be subject to obsolescence—become out of date or not as efficient as newer products.** New inputs or new finished products may be invented or found which would make existing inventories obsolete.

Some firms use mathematical formulas to determine the best inventory levels to maintain. These formulas include such things as order-loss risks, storage costs, interest, expected delivery time, and other factors. They also aid in determining the best quantity of inputs to order and the time interval between orders.

As we will see in our discussion of accounting in Chapter 12, there are other important control devices relating to production costs. These include cost systems and various budgeting devices.

PRODUCTION AND ECOLOGY

Many production processes cause problems of ecological balance in the areas where a product is produced and consumed. Extracting coal by strip mining has sometimes caused long-lasting environmental damage. The use of aluminum and glass containers for certain consumer products has contributed to a solid-waste disposal problem. It has brought unsightly litter to our cities and countryside. The manufacturing process itself has poured smoke into our air and poisonous wastes into our waters. Nuclear energy plants, especially since the Three-Mile Island accident, have represented an ecological threat in the minds of many citizens.

For years our factories have made only limited use of waste materials and by-products. They have used these materials only when there was obvious profit in it. There are many recyclable inputs that have little dollar value, but that should be recycled for the sake of our ecological balance. The government is setting new standards, and it is up to production management to do its work within the new limits at a cost that will permit the sale of products at competitive prices.

A growing number of firms are burning trash like pallets, crates, sawdust, and waste paper to heat buildings. After labor and raw materials, energy is the third largest cost of doing business for many firms, and energy costs have been rising much faster than labor and raw materials costs. Firms that burn waste products to generate energy not only reduce their energy costs—they also reduce their disposal costs.

MATERIALS MANAGEMENT

The variety of materials purchased by a firm—raw materials, partly finished products, finished products, supplies, and capital goods—requires a special managerial effort. These products must be purchased, physically handled, and stored. Capital goods also need to be maintained in working order.

The most highly developed managerial activity in dealing with materials—one that often requires setting up a special department—is purchasing.

The Purchasing Task

The purchasing task can have a critical effect on profits for manufacturers, retailers, and wholesalers. In manufacturing this is especially true when materials and parts are a major part of total manufacturing cost. Many firms establish a separate purchasing department with its own manager. Many large purchasing departments have divisions that specialize in specific types of purchases and divisions for records management and follow-up.

A typical large manufacturing firm must buy fuels, cleaning supplies, lumber, sheet steel, dyes, handtools, nails, electronic calculators, stationery, electrical equipment, paint, food for the company cafeteria, trucks, and many other items. They must prepare for fulfilling these needs by forecasting them and by locating adequate sources of supply. The sources must be adequate in terms of volume, delivery schedule, and quality levels. The purchasing department must be in constant contact with their suppliers' sales offices to keep up with their pricing policies, new product features, and delivery schedules.

Many firms, especially large ones, practice *centralized purchasing* rather than allow individual departments and divisions to make their own purchases. This can result in cost savings from large-volume buying, greater coordination of purchasing and receiving functions, and a more uniform application of standard purchase specifications.

Depending on the nature of the product or service, the purchasing department may provide different types of advice and perform different types of functions. When specialized and expensive machinery is needed, the purchasing department must work closely with the production manager whose department will use it.

Often, finance, purchasing, production, and engineering people work together to develop a list of specifications for the equipment and to plan for its financing and procurement. This team approach is helpful in "make-or-buy" decisions, and it helps to ensure that the right machine will be bought. The production manager alone might specify higher quality than is actually needed. If the finance manager were to make the decision alone, perhaps quality would be compromised in order to save money. The team objective is to get the level of quality needed by the using department at the best price. This requires a systems approach to decision making in which the "net" welfare of the firm is the guiding principle.

For less expensive items the purchasing department assumes a larger role. The purchasing department makes its own price and quality decisions for items such as paper clips. Most routine purchases are handled in this way.

Purchasing Policies

Over time, firms usually develop *standard purchasing policies.* For example, some follow a policy of building up inventories when prices are right. The purchasing agent is a "professional purchaser," who generally has a very good idea of when prices are right.

Some purchasing agents follow a policy of concentrating all their purchases for a specific good or service with one supplier. This is often because that supplier's past performance has been excellent. Other purchasing agents avoid this for fear of "being taken for granted" or "putting all their eggs in one basket." A strike, for example, at a supplier's plant may place the buyer firm in a bad position.

Other purchasing policies involve such matters as taking discounts offered by suppliers. Discount practices are discussed in Chapter 11. If a supplier offers a *cumulative quantity discount,* all purchases made during a certain period are subject to a discount based on the total volume purchased during that period. This policy builds buyer loyalty but probably reduces the average size of orders. A *noncumulative quantity discount* probably leads to larger orders but may not do much to develop customer loyalty.

Should Purchasing Agents Accept Favors?

WHAT DO YOU THINK?

The purchasing agent is the firm's professional buyer. He or she is a very important person as far as salespeople are concerned. That is why purchasing agents often receive "special favors" from salespeople who want to sell to them. Christmas gifts, free "samples" for the purchasing agent's personal use, and other "favors" are not uncommon.

Is it unethical for purchasing agents to accept "favors" and for salespersons to offer them? WHAT DO YOU THINK?

Some firms follow a policy of leasing equipment rather than purchasing it whenever possible. Leasing often offers a tax advantage because lease payments are deductible business expenses. It also shifts part of the risk of equipment obsolescence to the lessor and ties up less of the lessee's capital. Just as firms face "make-or-buy" decisions, they also face "buy-or-lease" decisions. You could lease a truck from Ryder Truck Rental, for example, rather than buy it.

A common purchasing policy involves reciprocity—"you buy from me and I'll buy from you." Reciprocity is widely practiced by industrial marketers and buyers. It makes buyer and seller interdependent and it guarantees the seller a customer but limits the sources of supply. It may also cause buyers to become too lazy in their search for "the best quality at the lowest price."

    reciprocity

The purchasing function is being handled increasingly by professionals. Two tools that are receiving growing attention are value analysis and vendor analysis.

Value Analysis

Value analysis starts by reviewing existing product specifications as set by user departments. Attention then focuses on identifying and eliminating nonessential cost factors. This review may involve a committee including engineers, cost accountants, production representatives, and others. They review the specifications set by the user department. Wherever a specification is thought to add unnecessary cost, the function of that "spec" is examined to see if it can be eliminated or if a cheaper way of doing it can be found. Such a review requires close contact with potential vendors to verify cost.

    value analysis

Value analysis has played a big role in the auto industry, especially after the federal government imposed mandatory miles-per-gallon requirements. Cars sold by a certain date had to meet certain mileage standards. One thing that value analysis showed was that parts made from fiberglass-reinforced plastic can be substituted for steel parts in many cases. This helps to reduce a car's weight and fuel consumption.

Careful investigation of the costs of alternative input components can lead to significant savings. However, a value-analysis decision of this type cannot omit consideration of whether the product will significantly lose quality.

Vendor Analysis

Vendor analysis evaluates and rates the technical, financial, and managerial abilities of potential suppliers in terms of their past performance. It is a method of substituting facts for feelings in the selection of suppliers.

    vendor analysis

After a purchasing department has analyzed possible suppliers, it is in a position to decide. It makes the decision and sends a purchase order to the supplier. Some purchasing departments, however, invite sellers to submit bids. In some cases, the buyer elects to award the purchase contract to the lowest bidder. This *competitive bidding* requires that the buyer specify in detail what it is that he or she wants to purchase. In other cases, specifications are not so exact, and bids received are subject to further *buyer-seller negotiation* over price and quality. Bids, however, are not used in all cases. The buyer might contact and deal with only one supplier.

A purchasing department is also accountable for following up on purchases already made. Elaborate file systems are used to ensure that deliveries are made on time. This permits quick follow-up on transportation details and expected delivery dates. A final responsibility is for the physical receipt of shipments. This involves checking contents against invoices before giving approval to the accounting department to make payment.

OPERATIONS MANAGEMENT— A BROADER VIEW

Up to now we have emphasized the use of management techniques for the production of goods—production as opposed to marketing or finance, and physical goods as opposed to services. This approach is justified on two grounds. First, scientific management was developed in factories, not in retail stores; and second, the next few chapters will be devoted to marketing and finance.

Most of the techniques discussed so far in this chapter can be made to work quite well outside the factory. These methods work in service firms like beauty parlors or repair shops; they also work in distribution firms like wholesalers or truckers.

operations
management

Operations management is an expanded version of the idea of production management. It represents a systems approach to all business functions with an emphasis on current operations and control rather than on long-range planning.

An operations management view is likely to conceive of a business, or a part of a business, as a productive system. Such a system normally involves making a series of key decisions within a system, such as are outlined in Table 8-2.

Consider the World Trade Center in New York City, a twin-tower, 110-story complex. As you might suspect, cleaning such a huge building is a massive job. It requires a well designed system to direct the efforts of a cleaning crew of 800 people working over such a large area.

BIRTH *of the System*	What are the goals of the firm? What products or services will be offered?
PRODUCT DESIGN *and* PROCESS SELECTION	What are the form and appearance of the product? Technologically, how should the product be made?
DESIGN *of the System*	Where should the facility be located? What physical arrangement is best to use? How do you maintain desired quality? How do you determine demand for the product or service?
STAFFING *the System*	What job is each worker to perform? How will the job be performed, measured; how will the workers be compensated?
STARTUP *of the System*	How do you get the system into operation? How long will it take to reach desired rate of output?
The System in STEADY STATE	How do you run the system? How can you improve the system? How do you deal with day-to-day problems?
REVISION *of the System*	How do you revise the system in light of external changes?
TERMINATION *of the System*	How does a system die? What can be done to salvage resources?

TABLE 8-2

An operations management view of key decisions in the life of a productive system

If all 50,000 wastebaskets are to be emptied and 50,000 desks are to be dusted and 3,600 toilets are to be checked and cleaned, each of the 800 workers must know and understand his or her task. They must perform it in a coordinated way so that, for example, the elevators are used efficiently, so that energy is not wasted, and so that the predetermined time schedule is adhered to.[2]

For all of this to happen there must be a central control post. The superintendent of operations has an office in the basement. The huge building is divided into cleaning zones, each with a supervisor who keeps in regular touch with the superintendent by walkie-talkie. Each zone supervisor must know the specific cleaning task assigned to each of the workers under his or her control and must see to it that it is done on time and in the manner specified by the cleaning standards. If modern operations management techniques were not employed, and if the best concepts of organizing, planning, staffing, directing, and controlling were not employed, it would be impossible to keep the World Trade Center clean.

Operations management techniques also played a role in the decisions by big retailers like J. C. Penney and Sears to adopt area cashiering. Studies indicated that management could reduce the number of salesclerks by placing cash registers in a few locations in a store rather than placing them in each department.

SUMMARY AND LOOK AHEAD

Production creates goods and services by a variety of processes out of human and material inputs. The management of such a process begins with planning the product, the plant, and its location. Production includes special organizational and staffing problems related to the impact of technology. It requires the application of a variety of control devices to assure uniform quality of output and efficient production scheduling.

Purchasing has evolved into a science in itself. Centralized purchasing departments develop purchasing policies and procedures to help ensure that the firm gets goods and services at required quality at a minimum price. Operations management brings some of the systems concepts and scientific approaches to decision making to bear upon production and nonproduction activity.

The mountain of products generated by a giant production system demands an ingenious marketing effort to move them into American markets. Financing a manufacturing plant and its related facilities is also a complex undertaking that requires up-to-date accounting methods. Computers are needed to support production, finance, accounting, and marketing. All of these topics will be examined in the next few chapters. Marketing is the first to be examined. It is such a large subject that we will devote three chapters to it. The first chapter presents an overview of the marketing task and introduces some of the basic concepts of modern marketing.

FOR REVIEW . . .

1. Distinguish between production management and operations management.

2. Does continuous production or intermittent production justify larger capital expenditure? Why?

3. Locating a plant near suppliers but far away from customers implies what about the nature of inputs and outputs and their transportation costs?

4. Distinguish between production organization along product lines and production organization along process lines.

5. Does production management have human-relations problems not found in other management? Explain.

6. What is reciprocity? Is it a sound basis for purchasing decisions? Why or why not?

7. What are the pros and cons of centralized purchasing?

8. What is the essential idea of value analysis?

. . . FOR DISCUSSION

1. Develop a detailed example of the inputs, process(es), and output(s) of a plant in your town. What would happen to the process and output if one input were not available?

2. Draw a simple CPM chart, modifying the example in your text. Identify the critical path. In what sense is it critical?

3. Find a real-life example of buying on a bidding basis and discuss the advantages of this to the buyer.

4. Give an example of the use of operations management in the control of the quality of hamburgers at a McDonald's restaurant. Identify the standard employed.

INCIDENTS

The Boxwood Company

The Boxwood Company is about to choose a location for its new box factory. With help from the accounting, production, and marketing experts, Ned Rink, head of the expansion committee, has come up with cost comparisons. They have narrowed the choice down to the cities of Memphis and St. Louis because they are nearest to the market that is not presently being served. The sales and cost estimates are below.

QUESTIONS

1. Which city is the better choice? Why?

2. What assumptions are necessary to reach a conclusion in Question 1?

3. How would you answer if estimated sales in Memphis were $60,000? How would you answer if taxes in St. Louis were $.30 per unit and sales remained as shown below?

		Memphis		St. Louis
Estimated annual sales in units		80,000		120,000
Selling price		$5.00		$5.00
Cost of materials	$1.10		$1.20	
Labor	1.20		1.40	
Average transportation to market	1.30		1.10	
Taxes	.60		.80	
Other costs	.20		.20	
Total costs per unit		4.40		4.70
Net profit per unit		.60		.30
Expected total annual profit		$48,000		$36,000

The Parkins Corporation

The offer came from Lister Industrial Supplies and was being discussed by top management at the Parkins Corporation. Lister's offer was as follows: To provide the requirements of Parkins' plant for tools, cleaning supplies, and lubricants. (These represented 6 percent of Parkins' total annual costs.) They offered a 10 percent discount for an exclusive one-year arrangement.

With costs in general rising rapidly, and profits slipping, Parkins' management is seriously considering the offer. Recent purchasing history showed that the service and quality of products provided by five suppliers (including Lister) to Parkins was quite satifactory.

QUESTIONS

1. What are the principal advantages and disadvantages of the Lister offer?

2. How would you advise Parkins' management in this case? Should they make a counteroffer to Lister? Discuss.

CASE STUDY

CONSENSUS IN SAN DIEGO

Time clocks are banned from the premises. Managers and workers converse on a first-name basis and eat lunch together in the company cafeteria. Employees are briefed once a month by a top executive on sales and production goals and are encouraged to air their complaints. Four times a year, workers attend company-paid parties. Says Betty Price, 54, an assembly-line person: "Working for Sony is like working for your family."

Her expression, echoed by dozens of other American Sony workers in San Diego, is a measure of the success achieved at the sprawling, two-story plant, where both the Stars and Stripes and the Rising Sun fly in front of the factory's glistening white exterior. In 1981 the San Diego plant turned out 700,000 color television sets, one-third of Sony's total world production. More significantly, company officials now proudly say that the plant's productivity approaches that of its Japanese facilities.

Plant manager Shiro Yamada, 58, insists that there are few differences between workers in the U.S. and Japan. Says he: "Americans are as quality conscious as the Japanese. But the question has been how to motivate them." Yamada's way is to bathe his U.S. employees in personal attention. Workers with perfect attendance records are treated to dinner once a year at a posh restaurant downtown. When one employee complained that a refrigerator for storing lunches was too small, it was replaced a few days later with a larger one. Vice President Masayoshi Morimoto, known as Mike around the plant, has mastered Spanish so he can talk with his many Hispanic workers. The company has installed telephone hot lines on which workers can anonymously register suggestions or complaints.

The firm strives to build strong ties with its employees in the belief that the workers will then show loyalty to the company in return. It carefully promotes from within, and most of the assembly-line supervisors are high school graduates who rose through the ranks because of their hard work and dedication to the company. During the 1973-75 recession, when TV sales dropped and production slowed drastically, no one was fired. Instead, workers were kept busy with plant maintenance and other chores. In fact, Sony has not laid off a single employee since 1972, when the plant was opened. The Japanese managers were stunned when the first employee actually quit within just one year. Says Richard Crossman, the plant's human relations expert: "They came to me and wanted to know what they had done wrong. I had to explain that quitting is just the way it is sometimes in Southern California."

This personnel policy has clearly been a success. Several attempts to unionize the work force have been defeated by margins as high as 3 to 1. Says Jan Timmerman, 22, a parts dispatcher and former member of the Retail Clerks Union: "Union pay was better, and the benefits were probably better. But basically I'm more satisfied here."

Sony has not forced Japanese customs on American workers. Though the company provides lemon-colored smocks for assembly-line workers, most prefer to wear jeans and running shoes. The firm does not demand that anyone put on the uniforms. A brief attempt to establish a general exercise period for San Diego workers, similar to the kind Sony's Japanese employees perform, was dropped when managers saw it was not wanted.

Inevitably, there have been minor misunderstandings because of the differences in language and customs. One worker sandblasted the numbers 1 2 6 4 on a series of parts she was testing before she realized that her Japanese supervisor meant that she was to label them "one to 64." Mark Dempsey, 23, the plant's youngest supervisor, admits that there is still a vast cultural gap between the Japanese and Americans. Says he: "They do not realize that some of us live for the weekend, while lots of them live for the week—just so they can begin to work again." Some workers grumble about the delays caused by the Japanese system of managing by consensus, seeing it instead as an inability to make decisions. Complains one American: "There is a lot of indecision. No manager will ever say do this or do that."

Most American workers, though, like the Japanese management style, and some do not find it all that foreign. Says Supervisor Robert Williams: "A long time ago, Americans used to be more people-oriented, the way the Japanese are. It just got lost somewhere along the way." The Sony experience in San Diego might show Americans how to regain some of their lost skills at employee relations.

Questions

1. Why do you think time clocks are banned from the Sony plant?

2. Do you agree with Mr. Yamada that giving workers a lot of personal attention will help to motivate them? Why or why not?

3. What are the relative advantages and disadvantages of promoting from within?

4. How do you think the plant's human relations expert, Mr. Crossman, helps the plant's operations?

5. Why do you think the plant's workers voted not to unionize?

6. What is your opinion of the desirability of consensus management in a production facility?

CAREERS IN HUMAN RESOURCES AND PRODUCTION MANAGEMENT

Career opportunities are expanding rapidly in human resources and production management. Jobs in these areas require a high degree of human relations skills. People with this type of job often work in various industries in the course of their careers.

Personnel recruiters (or employment interviewers) generally travel widely to search for promising job applicants. They talk to applicants, conduct preliminary interviews, and select and recommend those who appear qualified to fill vacancies.

Job analysts collect and examine detailed information on jobs, including job qualifications and worker characteristics, in order to prepare job descriptions.

Wage and salary administrators establish and maintain pay systems. They devise ways to ensure that pay rates within the firm are fair and equitable, and conduct surveys to see how their pay rates compare with others. They must ensure that the firm's pay system complies with applicable laws and regulations.

Training specialists supervise or conduct training sessions, prepare manuals and other materials for these courses, and look into new methods of training. They also counsel employees on training opportunities, which may include on-the-job, apprentice, supervisory, or management training.

Employee-benefit supervisors handle the employer's benefits program, which usually includes health insurance, life insurance, disability insurance, and pension plans. They coordinate a wide range of employee services, and counsel employees who are approaching retirement.

Labor relations specialists advise management on all aspects of union-management relations. They provide background information and technical support before and during negotiations. These specialists must be well versed in economics, labor law, and collective bargaining methods and trends.

Most beginning positions in personnel and labor relations are filled with college graduates. Interestingly, some personnel and labor relations workers are self-employed as management consultants or labor-management relations experts.

Many jobs in production also require college degrees. *Industrial engineers* determine the most effective ways for an organization to use the basic factors of production—people, machines, and materials. They are more concerned with people and methods of business organization than are engineers in other specialties. To solve organizational, production, and related problems, industrial engineers design data processing systems and apply mathematical concepts (operations research techniques). They develop and conduct plant location surveys; design production planning and control systems; and design or improve systems for the physical distribution of goods and services. Automation is one factor operating to increase the demand for industrial engineers.

Purchasing agents, also called *industrial buyers,* are responsible for maintaining an adequate supply of materials, supplies, or equipment. Their work includes buying goods and services, market forecasting, production planning, and inventory control. In a large firm or government agency, purchasing agents usually specialize in one or more specific commodities. There are no universal educational requirements for entry-level purchasing jobs. Most big organizations, however, require a college degree, especially for promotion into a managerial position.

CAREER PROFILE

My name is Celeste Foster-O'Keefe. I am a systems analyst with Amoco Production Company, an oil exploration and drilling firm.

When I graduated from college in 1981, I began my career with Amoco as an assistant administrative analyst. For the first five weeks, I worked in the oil fields—doing assorted jobs and learning about petroleum exploration and drilling at the operations level. I was then transferred to the financial records section, where my responsibilities included determining charges and analyzing and coding invoices. Eight months later I joined the Production Systems Group in our regional office as a systems analyst.

In this position I help engineers to relate the needs of their jobs to the information stored in our computer system, and to select appropriate types of computer applications. I am responsible for solving problems in the way computer programs run, and for updating and maintaining the computers which store company information. I participate in training programs and seminars for less experienced system users.

I chose to work for Amoco because of its concern for its employees and the exciting and challenging career opportunities the company offers.

MARKETING MANAGEMENT

Section 3 described human resources and the production process. Firms are guided in their production activities by what they perceive to be the demands of the marketplace. The process of marketing matches these demands with the firm's production capabilities. The use of resources to produce goods and services depends greatly on marketing.

In Chapter 9 we show how production and marketing are interdependent and how rising income levels affect marketing. We introduce the marketing concept and some basic marketing strategies, and also examine the role of

marketing research and the challenge of consumerism.

In Chapter 10 attention is turned to the marketing mix, with special emphasis on the role of the product and its distribution. The different means of bringing products to their point of consumption are described.

Promotion and price are the primary subjects of Chapter 11. We discuss the complementary relationship between advertising and personal selling. We also examine basic price-setting and its place in the marketing mix. Special attention is given to the marketing of services.

CHAPTER 9

The Marketing Concept

OBJECTIVES:

After reading this chapter you should be able to

1. Discuss the nature of marketing.
2. Demonstrate the relationship between income level and discretionary income.
3. Explain the consumer's role in the marketing concept.
4. Give examples of industrial and household target markets.
5. Compare the strategies of differentiation and segmentation.
6. Name and explain two different approaches to marketing research.
7. Distinguish among four kinds of utility in a product.
8. Discuss the history and effects of consumerism.

Consider the car rental business. Hertz dominated the market when Avis entered, but Avis differentiated itself through its advertising slogan—*We're number two. We try harder.*

Hertz, Avis, and National are the "big three" in the car rental business. Other firms have managed to make a profit in this business by catering to selected market segments. Budget Rent-A-Car's market research helped it target a segment of customers—the professional care segment—that the big three had not identified. This segment consists of people who consider travel directions an important part of the service they are buying. Budget, therefore, developed a program to supply its customers with specific preprinted travel directions.

Rent-A-Wreck, Lease-A-Lemon, and Ugly Duckling Rent-A-Car also went into business by appealing to specific market segments with special products. They rent and lease used cars to people who want to pay lower rates than those charged by firms renting and leasing new cars.

In this first chapter about marketing we will define what it is, show how it has become a central concept in business planning, and explain how it is practiced somewhat differently to reach different markets. We will see how Avis's and Rent-a-Wreck's strategies fit in with other marketing strategies practiced today.

We will also describe the vital activity called marketing research and show how it guides marketing decisions. This chapter develops an economic justification for marketing activity by showing how marketing creates utility and then closes with a discussion of consumerism. Let's begin our study of marketing with a working definition.

WHAT IS MARKETING?

marketing

Marketing is the whole set of activities undertaken to find, influence, and serve customers for products and services. It often means finding out what products and services people already need or want. Sometimes it involves creating or stimulating new wants. These wants, once established, must be satisfied. Marketing activities include such things as marketing research, retailing, salesforce management, advertising, and transportation. These activities will be examined in the pages to follow.

The greater the production ability of a nation or firm, the more important it becomes to improve its marketing ability. The benefits of production technology are wasted in a free economy if the wrong things are produced or if the people don't know about the product.

Should Marie, a hairdresser from Louisiana, open a shop in Chicago she would face a serious problem despite her ten years experience in Louisiana. The problem is essentially a lack of understanding of the Chicago-area market for hairstyling. She could overcome this problem, however, with the right kind of marketing. To succeed in Chicago, Marie would certainly have to learn a lot about her new market. She would have to find out as much as possible about hairstyle fashions in Chicago and something about techniques and supplies used there which might differ from what she had used in Louisiana. This might require a period of apprenticeship under a Chicago-area stylist. When she opens her shop she will have to look carefully at the competition to decide such things as the right location, hours of operation, shop atmosphere, and promotion techniques. All of these have to be considered in a complete marketing plan.

Marketing and Discretionary Income in Advanced Economies

In a rich nation like the United States or Canada, there are many choices available to consumers. The more income a family or individual has, the smaller is the proportion of income required for absolute necessities. Wealthy buyers can shift their spending patterns around. As we have seen in Chapter 2, what a buyer has to spend on things other than necessities is called *discretionary income*. Figure 9-1 shows that one family, the Collinses, has 33 per-

The Browns and the Collinses are each four-member families of two adults and two children. The Brown's income after taxes is $30,000. After spending $28,000 on necessities, they have only $2,000 to spend or save as they like. The Collinses, with $40,000 income, spend $34,000 on necessities and have three times as much as the Browns ($6,000) left over. As income increases, discretionary income increases at a greater rate.

FIGURE 9-1

Discretionary income of two families

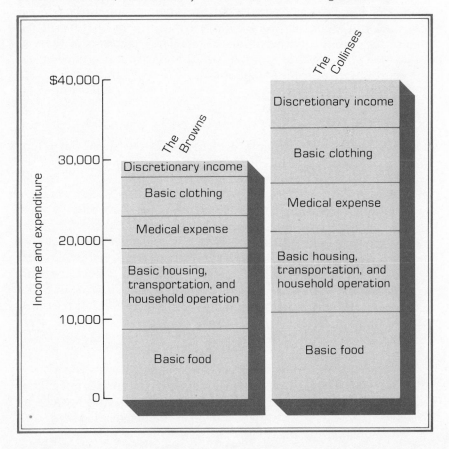

cent more after-tax income ($40,000 versus $30,000) than another family, the Browns. However, it also demonstrates that the discretionary part of the Collins's income is 200 percent greater than that of the Browns ($6,000 versus $2,000). Rising income, then, means businesses find it harder to predict what will be bought. This complicates the marketing task and makes it even more important to watch the consumer closely. The consumer's tastes and preferences can change quickly.

In recent years there has been a big increase in the number of *multiearner families*—families with more than one earner. The rise in job opportunities for women together with the rising number of working wives means a big jump in discretionary income for many families. These multiearner families are reputed to spend more on household help and dining out and less on child-related goods and services. They represent a market for luxury goods and services.

The marketing process must also cope with risks related to technology. A firm never really knows when a competitor will devise a new product that outdates the firm's present product or that makes its present product unnecessary. The invention of the versatile food processor, for example, has led to a decline in the demand for many single-purpose kitchen tools.

The Marketing Concept

marketing concept

We have seen in Chapter 8 that the United States has a long history of advances in production. In recent decades this has been matched by equally impressive advances in marketing. With the growth of discretionary income, stiffer competition, and the maze of government regulation, a new concept has been adopted by most of the leading firms in the country. **This new concept is called the marketing concept. It means that the whole firm is coordinated to achieve one goal—to serve its present and potential customers and to do so at a profit.** This means getting to understand what customers really want and to follow closely the changes in tastes that occur. If the firm is to follow up on this awareness of customer wants in a profitable way it must operate as a system, well-coordinated and unified in the pursuit of the common goal—customer satisfaction.

Adopting the marketing concept means that financial, production, and marketing components of the firm must *all* be guided by the common goal. The need for such an orientation throughout the firm has led many businesses to select their leadership from their marketing departments.

THE TARGET MARKET

If a firm is to adopt the marketing concept, it must define the characteristics of its customers. This set of customers is called the target market. Aiming at this target guides the firm in designing its marketing program. Often there are certain factors, such as existing investment in production facilities or experience of personnel, that restrict the kind of target at which the firm "aims." In other words, there may be a compromise between the resources already available for marketing and the selection of target markets. Thus RCA, after having started marketing computers, decided to withdraw from that line of business. It discovered that its resources and capabilities were better suited to marketing other products. The same was true of General Motors when it decided to sell its Frigidaire home appliances division to White Consolidated Industries.

target market

When choosing a target, one thing is usually easy—deciding whether the item produced will be used for its own sake or whether it will be used to make something else or to help provide a service. This is an important distinction.

Industrial goods are goods or services that will be used by a firm or an institution to make another product or to provide a service. For example, tractor tires sold to Caterpillar Tractor or an examining table sold to a doctor is an industrial good. Manufacturers, hospitals, and lawyers buy goods and services for reasons that are different from those of ordinary consumers. These buyers are *industrial buyers*.

industrial goods

Consumer goods are goods and services that people buy for their own use—to wear, to eat, to look at, or to live in. We usually call these buyers *ultimate consumers*. Their motives and buying behavior are quite different from those of industrial buyers.

consumer goods

Besides industrial buyers and ultimate consumers, firms must also consider a third kind of customer. These are called middlemen because they usually hold products briefly during the process of bringing them from their producer to their user. Retailers and wholesalers are examples of middlemen.

middlemen

Let's clarify the importance of defining the target market by comparing the industrial goods market with the consumer goods market and with other distinctive markets.

The Industrial Market

What are the features of the industrial market? First of all, the target market is generally *smaller* than it is for consumer products. The Boeing Company and McDonnell Douglas build planes for sale to airlines and the military. They have a much smaller number of potential customers than, for example, a single McDonald's restaurant in a large city.

Industrial customers are often *more concentrated geographically* than are household or ultimate consumers. Many industries that are the sole users of certain products are centered in one or a few areas. The aircraft industry on the West Coast, the auto industry in Detroit, and the steel industry in the Great Lakes area are only a few examples. A firm selling electronic parts for aircraft is likely to locate in California where many of its customers are.

Industrial buyers are also different from household or ultimate consumers because they have *more formal systems for buying*. They set up purchasing departments to handle procurement. For example, DuPont's Energy and Materials Department buys all raw materials, supplies, and equipment for all the firm's domestic and foreign branches and subsidiaries, in addition to planning for long-range energy procurement. Purchasing departments in large firms may buy thousands of products from hundreds of sellers.

A firm also has *more clearly defined* and *profit-oriented purchase motives*. Industrial markets can be especially risky because of the dynamic nature of technology. One change in technology can cause the sudden death of many industrial products (parts, supplies, etc.) that go into the production of one newly obsolete major product. Conversion from the older type of electron tube to solid state parts in TVs and radios hurt many small producers of the older tubes.

Trade shows are an important means of reaching the industrial market

Industrial goods include:

- *installations,* such as plants, office buildings, land, and very expensive assets like cranes
- *raw materials,* such as cotton, iron ore, and lumber
- *accessory equipment,* such as typewriters, accounting machines, and small fork lift trucks
- *supplies,* such as maintenance items (brooms and light bulbs); repair items (nuts and bolts to repair equipment); and operating supplies (lubricating oil and typewriter ribbons)
- *component parts and materials,* such as tires, batteries, and steel beams
- *business services,* such as uniform rental, security services, and cargo transportation

These goods and services have either narrow or broad target markets. The target depends on how widely the goods or services are used in industry. Many types of supplies (stationery and fuel), accessory equipment (typewriters), and services (legal assistance) are used by nearly all firms. On the other hand, most types of major equipment or installations, raw materials, and parts have a much narrower market. It is common practice in marketing some installations, for example, to build the product to the buyer's exact specifications.

The breadth of a market for an industrial product is limited by the product's nature. Who the customers of a given firm are also depends on its location, its experience and good name, its financial strength, and the size and strength of its distribution system.

Governmental and Institutional Markets

Goods and services sold to nonprofit institutions, such as federal, state, and local governments, nonprofit hospitals, and schools, are also industrial products. Many of the same products that are sold to businesses are also sold to nonprofit institutions. These are often like industrial firms because they use a formal purchasing system. They often draw up product specifications and request bids from several suppliers.

Marketing to the federal government is a special case because of the complex purchasing system it uses. Many firms sell only to the government. Large defense purchases may involve years of congressional debate and lobbying. Furthermore, it may take a long time after a contract is awarded for the government to receive the finished product. For example, developmental work on the Army's XM1 tank began in 1973 but the tanks were not delivered until 1980.

Government, in fact, is the biggest customer in the United States. There are one federal government, fifty state governments, over three thousand county governments, and more than eighteen thousand city governments. Roughly 20 percent of our Gross National Product is bought by government agencies. The products range from spacecraft to floor polish.

There are two types of federal government buying—civilian and military. Each government agency buys some products on its own, but the General Services Administration does a lot of centralized buying of standard products for the civilian sector. The Department of Defense handles military buying. The Defense Supply Agency buys products that the various branches of the military use in common. Many state and local governments have an agency similar to the General Services Administration. Independent agencies like state highway departments are also often large buyers.

The Consumer Market

Manufacturers that produce goods for ultimate consumers often face a huge, tricky market. The "household" buyer is not as professional or as formal as the industrial firm. However, the high

"HERE'S SOUTHERN RAILWAY'S FOR THE LUMBER INDUSTRY."

"THE LONG AND...

The simple fact is, that the way the energy situation is today and, undoubtedly, will be tomorrow, railroads make more sense for long hauls than trucks do.

Because railroads are a lot more energy-efficient than trucks.

But does that mean trucks will soon be a thing of the past for the lumber industry? No. We think trucks have a very definite place in the future of transportation.

As long as trucks are used in the right place.

Harold H. Hall, President
Southern Railway System
Washington, D.C. 20013

An ad for a business service

NSWER TO THE ENERGY SHORTAGE

...THE SHORT OF IT"

The right job for trucks is the short haul
where the railroad begins and ends.

We believe so much in this concept, and its
important implications for the future of this
country, that we've set up a system to capitalize
on our advantage for long hauls and trucks'
advantage for short hauls. We've made inter-
change agreements with over 180 trucking firms
all over our route to give you dock to dock
service even when your dock isn't on our railroad.

We think the wave of the future is to have
each mode of transportation do what it does
best.

We have the energy for the long haul.

SOUTHERN
THE RAILWAY SYSTEM THAT GIVES A GREEN LIGHT TO INNOVATIONS

level of income among American consumers leads to the purchase of a fantastic number of different goods and services. This affluence also makes possible frequent changes in taste.

These changes, with the amazing rate of technological progress, cause a rapid "turnover" of consumer products. New products and new brands of products appear daily on retail shelves. Nearly as many soon disappear.

Consider a few examples from recent years. Per capita beef consumption has been decreasing while per capita chicken consumption has been increasing. A major reason for these changes is that many Americans want to reduce their cholesterol and fat intake. Another change results from the aging of the "baby boom" generation. This has meant reduced sales of soft drinks and increased sales of wine, a fact that may help explain why the Coca-Cola Company acquired Taylor Wine Company.

Perhaps the most obvious adaptation to taste and technological change has been the U.S. car buyer's abandonment of traditional full-size cars in favor of sub-compacts. Not many years ago owners of imported sub-compacts were considered a little offbeat.

Tougher competition for the consumer dollar represents the main challenge in marketing consumer goods and services. A number of different marketing strategies are used to meet the challenge, as we will see later in this chapter and in the following two chapters.

Classes of Consumer Goods

Although many specific products are hard to classify, it is useful to distinguish three kinds:

- convenience goods
- shopping goods
- specialty goods

This classification depends on frequency of purchase, the product's significance to the buyer, and the buyer's preselection of a specific product brand.

convenience goods

Convenience goods are items bought frequently, demanded on short notice, and often purchased by habit. Cigarettes and many foods and drugs are examples. These are usually low-priced products that people don't think much about when buying. They don't make very careful price and quality comparisons.

shopping goods

Shopping goods are items which are taken seriously enough to require comparison and study. Most clothing, appliances, and cars fall into this category. Gifts are almost always shopping goods. Stores that sell shopping goods are frequently grouped together, of-

Selling convenience goods   Selling shopping goods

ten in planned shopping centers, to help customers make price and
quality comparisons.

Specialty goods are those for which strong conviction as to   **specialty goods**
brand, style, or type already exists in the buyer's mind. The buyer
will make a great effort to locate and purchase the specific brand.
Usually, such products are high in value and aren't purchased frequently. Examples are Leica cameras and Steinway pianos. For some
customers, however, a can of soup could be a specialty product. The
class depends on the individual consumer's buying behavior. A certain item (a shirt, for example) could be classed in three different
ways by three different people. However, there is enough agreement
among consumers on most products to make this product-class
scheme useful to firms in decision making. Marketers judge the way
that most customers will behave toward the product and classify it
accordingly.

How a firm classifies a product greatly influences the way it is
sold. A manufacturer who considers a product a convenience good
will want it to be sold in as many places as possible. Coke, Wrigley's
gum, and Marlboro cigarettes are available in countless supermarkets, drugstores, and vending machines. If, however, the product
is viewed as a shopping good, it is likely to be placed in stores that
are near stores selling similar shopping items. A typical consumer
shopping for a new TV wants to be able to compare Zenith, Sony,
RCA, and so on. A specialty good manufacturer needs to worry less
about retail location. There are relatively few Rolls Royce dealerships. A consumer who wants to buy one is willing to make a
special effort to find a dealer—even if the dealer is a few hundred
miles away. Since such buyers will go out of their way to locate the

	Convenience	Shopping	Specialty
How far will a buyer travel?	Short distance	Reasonable distance	Long distance
How much does it cost?	Usually low-priced	Usually middle-to-high priced	Usually high-priced
How often purchased?	Frequently	Occasionally	Infrequently
Emphasis on comparison?	No	Yes	No
Purchased habitually?	Often	Not usually	Not Usually
Which advertising media?	Television, news-papers, and general magazines	Television, news-papers, and general magazines	Special-interest magazines and catalogues

TABLE 9-1

Classes of consumer goods

product, the firm's distribution channel problem is simplified. These are only a few examples of how the way that consumers classify products may affect the way that they are marketed. Table 9-1 summarizes the features of the three classes of goods.

In summary, consumer goods producers must put themselves in the shoes of the buyer to figure out the probable class in which most buyers will place a given product. This is an application of the marketing concept and makes it more likely that the marketing effort will be truly matched to what consumers want.

To get a better definition of a consumer target market, Batton, Barton, Durstine, and Osborne, a large advertising agency, has developed a "problem tracking" system that shows the process a consumer follows in selecting a product. This "problem tracking" system helps to group people with common problems and then suggest specific products and services which can serve such a group or target market. Full-scale marketing, of course, requires other marketing activities to go along with the product or service. The set of activities which marketers use is often called the *marketing mix*.

PRODUCT DIFFERENTIATION

The way in which a firm approaches and defines its target market or markets may include a strategy of product differentiation. This strategy requires a good understanding of the target customer, whether that customer be a household, an individual, or a business firm.

Product differentiation is a process of convincing target customers that one brand is different from, and better than, the competition's. It can be done by stressing distinctive product features or the product's guarantee, service, or availability. Peugeot cars have silver-tipped spark plugs that last longer than ordinary spark plugs. Curtis-Mathes televisions come with a four-year limited warranty, and Sears' Craftsman hand tools are replaced free if they break. As you can see from the following ad, American Express stresses the utility and unique financial services of its Gold Card.

Product differentiation can also be achieved by an advertising campaign that emphasizes product features or creates the impression of special product advantages. Morton salt is differentiated by its shaker spout, the "Umbrella girl," and the slogan "When it rains, it pours." Wisk's "Ring around the collar" and Crest's "Look Ma, no cavities" are well known advertising phrases that help set these brands apart from their rivals. When Procter & Gamble introduced Crest in 1960, ads stressed the fact that it contained Fluoristan. When Advanced Formula Crest was introduced in 1981, the ads stressed that it contained Fluoristat. No other brands can claim to have that ingredient because Fluoristat is a trademark registered by Procter & Gamble.

product differentiation

MARKET SEGMENTATION

A strategy of product differentiation may treat customers as one general target group to be aimed at with one common marketing mix. **A strategy of market segmentation, however, calls for making a special marketing mix for a special segment of the market or several different mixes for several different segments.** The idea is that there is really more than one set of needs to be satisfied within the general market for a product. If a firm believes it will improve its market position, it might make a different version of the product to satisfy the special needs of each group, or market segment.

market segmentation

In some cases, market planners focus on only one segment of a market. Bobbie Brooks, for example, focuses on sportswear for junior sized women. Napoleon's Closet, The Short Shop, and Short Sizes Inc. are clothing stores that cater to small-sized men who formerly had to have their clothes custom tailored or had to buy them in boy's departments. At one time, Xerox focused its effort on marketing its copiers only to big-volume users.

A marketer's success in serving one segment may lead it to expand its marketing effort to other segments. For example, Volkswagen used to focus only on economy-minded car buyers with its Beetle. Recently it has been marketing several models, including the

Speak softly and carry a big stick.

There is a charge card that says more about you than anything you can possibly buy with it. The Gold Card® from American Express.® To qualify for the Card and all its services,* you have to be accepted by both American Express <u>and</u> a major bank.

And once accepted, it means you are part of a group whose finances and credit rating are among the top five percent of the nation.

Those who like to speak softly. And carry a big stick.

*In addition to worldwide charge privileges, financial services include a substantial independent line of credit, check-cashing privileges around the world, and access to a bank cash machine network in major cities around the country. For more information and an application, see your participating bank, savings institution, and finer places where the Card is welcomed. Or write American Express Company, Gold Card, American Express Plaza, New York, N.Y. 10004. (800) 528-8000.

The *Gold Card* is designed to differentiate the credit standing of its owner

This store's personal shopping consultant is part of a marketing strategy targeted at affluent professional women

Quantum which is targeted to more affluent buyers. Hart Schaffner & Marx for many years focused on the top-of-the-line segment in men's clothing by making and selling such brands as Hickey-Freeman and Christian Dior. It recently expanded into other segments of the clothing market by acquiring Country Miss Inc., a manufacturer of medium-priced women's clothing.

A firm might use the demographic characteristics of its customers to construct a grid such as Figure 9-2 to decide on two profitable segments towards which to focus its efforts in marketing sportswear.

Consider the case of a producer of wristwatches. Such a firm might design one marketing mix to satisfy the "jewelry" watch market and another to satisfy the "time-telling" watch market. There might be important differences in product design, perhaps gold cases with gems for one and waterproof steel cases for the other. Advertising themes for one would emphasize romance or prestige, while the other might emphasize accuracy, durability, and price. They might even use two different sets of retail stores. The expensive ones might be sold in jewelry stores and the cheaper ones in drug and variety stores. Deciding which of these means of segmentation to use requires a study of the market and the cost of segmenting.

Other bases for segmenting markets for certain products might be

- age of customers
- sex of customers
- income level
- personality traits
- educational level
- lifestyles

Some marketers target their effort to many segments based on combinations of such factors. Profitable segmentation always requires knowledge about potential customer wants and behavior, changes in the makeup of the market, and an awareness of competitors' product offerings.

Burger King and McDonald's used to focus mainly on children but broadened their menus to compete in the family fast food market. A declining birthrate led Hasbro Industries to start marketing family games and arts and crafts sets in addition to children's toys. Homelite, a manufacturer of chain saws, learned through research that a fourth of its customers are women who buy chain saws for gift-giving and adjusted its marketing accordingly.

		MALES			FEMALES		
		Age			Age		
		Under 26	26-45	46 or over	Under 26	26-45	46 or over
Small towns and rural areas	Non-white						
	White						
Metropolitan areas	Non-white	X					
	White		X				

FIGURE 9-2

Selecting two market segments for sportswear

AUTHORS' COMMENTARY

The Ultimate Segmentation

Rapid development in computer-controlled factories will permit easier gratification of the individual tastes of every buyer of cars and appliances. These kinds of products were among the first to benefit from cost-cutting mass production of assembly lines. At that time, however, the consumer had to pay a large price in the form of a very standardized product. Henry Ford said "Give them any color they want as long as it is black." Today, the firm that bears his name is able to produce such an astounding combination of features, styles, colors, and accessories that it is possible to produce a unique car for every car buyer in America.

There may be some exaggeration in this kind of claim, but with the advent of computer-based rapid communication, and the robot precision of the assembly plant, the day may have arrived when car dealers will be able to order and deliver such customized cars on very short notice. The computer will have successfully combined the advantages of mass production with the ultimate capacity to segment the market—a unique car for every buyer.

MARKETING RESEARCH

Intelligent decisions about marketing strategies require a clear understanding of those who are or who might become customers. This kind of decision calls for marketing research. **Marketing research means applying the scientific method of problem solving to marketing problems. It usually involves getting information from the people who make up the market.**

Two general approaches to the study of the market are the demographic approach and the behavioral approach. The former collects facts about individuals, families, or firms who are thought likely to become customers. It concentrates on counting and tabulating. The behavioral approach uses ideas from psychology about human behavior and attitudes. It seeks to understand why buyers feel and behave the way they do. An effective new technique in both approaches is focus group interviewing, which is discussed later in this chapter.

Demographic Approach

The demographic features of a market of ultimate consumers are such things as the age, sex, race, occupation, education, and income of its members. Often, a firm makes assumptions about the relationship between these characteristics and the likelihood of a person buying a product. These assumptions may be based on past knowledge about customers. For example, brewing companies know that the heaviest consumers of beer are males with blue-collar jobs. Advertisers know that college graduates are more likely to buy *The New Yorker* than those who have not attended college.

Assume that a firm decided which characteristics are related to consumption of its product. Now it seeks information about the number of prospects in the area to be served. It may find this information in U.S. Census publications or other government or private sources. **Looking things up in already-available materials is called secondary research.** On a local basis, a census tract map, accompanied by important facts about people in each tract, can be very valuable to a marketer. (See Figure 9-3.) In each of the numbered sections of the map is a tract. The Bureau of the Census reports income, age, and other important market data for each tract in metropolitan areas. Just think what a manager planning to locate a shopping center could do with this kind of information!

Westerhaus Associates, Inc., a midwestern shopping center developer, simplified choice of location in the Akron area by using this tract map and the facts provided with it by the Census Bureau. This

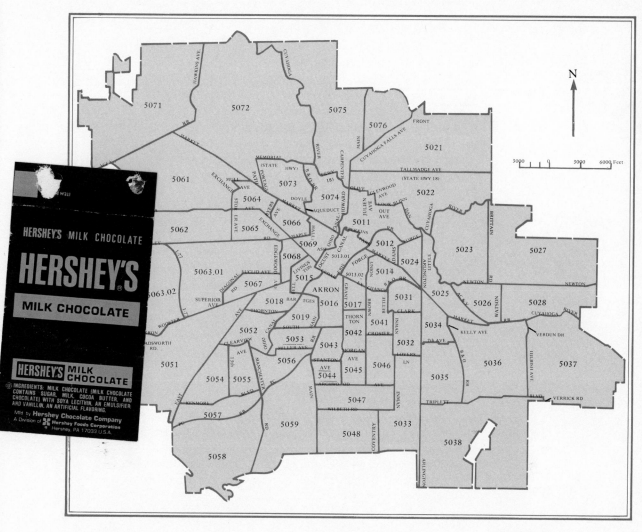

FIGURE 9-3

Census tracts in the
Akron, Ohio standard
metropolitan statistical
area

data, along with estimates by the U.S. Department of Labor of the
amounts spent by different types of households on food, clothing,
and other items, gave the planners a pretty good basis for projecting
the center's sales volume.

Marketing planners may also benefit from primary research.
Primary research is getting new facts for a specific purpose. For
example, Konica cameras come packaged with a registration card
requesting the buyer to fill in facts about herself or himself and mail
it in to the company. These cards tell the firm about the people who
buy their cameras.

primary research

Behavioral Approach

Instead of finding out who the customers are, what they buy, when they buy, etc., the behavioral approach asks the question "why do they buy?" This approach assumes that what people buy often depends on complex motives that can only be understood by psychological probing. Experts in human motivation test a sample of people to find out the basis for their product choice. The researcher might try to find, for example, what a particular brand name "means" to certain people. These researchers often use techniques borrowed from psychologists to discover motives and/or attitudes that customers might ordinarily try to hide.

The firm of McCollum, Spielman and Company, specialists in advertising research, has developed a new way of testing consumer awareness and recall of TV ads. The new system tests three groups of 100 to 120 people in three parts of the country at the same time. A videotaped interviewer asks the people questions about commercials after they have seen them, along with entertainment programs. These tests help tell how much repeating a commercial improves the chance that a viewer will remember it. It is a specialized and advanced type of marketing research.

Will Modern Marketing Techniques Become Widely Applied to Solving Social Problems?

WHAT DO YOU THINK?

When the National Heart, Lung, and Blood Institute (NHLBI) launched its high-blood-pressure control campaign in 1972, it had two major objectives: make the public aware of the danger of high blood pressure and educate hypertension sufferers and their families about the variety of treatments available to control the condition.

NHLBI called in Porter, Norvelli & Associates Inc. to design a media campaign for the National High Blood Pressure Program. The Washington, D.C.-based social marketing firm specializes in applying marketing and communications techniques to social issues.

Social marketing combines marketing research, advertising, and public relations strategies to educate the public on social issues. The principles behind social and commercial marketing are basically the same—both disciplines are concerned with changing human behavior. The difference is that social marketers design, implement, control, and evaluate "social programs."

The practice of social marketing is relatively new, but it has become widely-enough accepted to justify social marketing specialist firms like Porter, Norvelli. Will marketing continue to grow outside of the business world? WHAT DO YOU THINK?

Focus Group Interviewing

Another important marketing research technique that helps firms to understand consumer attitudes and behavior towards their products and services is called focus group interviewing. **A focus group interview entails listening to eight to twelve people at one time with very little formal questioning by the interviewer. The idea is to provide a natural conversational setting in which a group of similar people frankly exchange opinions and attitudes toward a product, store, or idea.** Focus groups provide stimulating ideas for further research. For example, a firm that developed a new filter for air-conditioning systems used a focus group to help identify target markets for the product. It singled out families in which one or more members had allergies or respiratory problems and persons seriously concerned about air pollution as good potential targets.[1]

Regardless of the approach, marketing research must be undertaken on a continuous basis. You need only look at the changes in products for sale in the last few years to see how dynamic the market is. How long ago was it that we had never heard of home smoke detectors, food processors, video games, and household computers? Consumer tastes and values change so fast that a firm must keep its eyes open to the future. This requires marketing research.

focus group interview

MARKETING AND UTILITY

The utility of products and services is at the heart of the marketing problem. We can distinguish the following kinds of utility

- form utility
- place utility
- time utility
- ownership utility

We will show how these four aspects of utility relate to the household purchase of sugar.

Form utility is utility resulting from a change in form. It is produced by treatment or breaking-down processes such as those described in Chapter 8. Sugar, for example, becomes more useful after the juice is extracted from the sugar cane or sugar beets and is cooked and refined. The sugar refineries of Louisiana create form utility.

form utility

Form utility, unfortunately, is not enough to satisfy the millions of people who want this sugar for use in their homes. Place utility is needed, too. **Place utility is that aspect of usefulness deter-**

place utility

mined by location. Refined sugar on a loading dock in Louisiana must be moved to Chicago before its usefulness to a Chicago household can be realized. The train or truck that transports the sugar "up North" creates, in the process, *place utility* for people in Chicago.

time utility

Time utility is somewhat harder to explain. It is that aspect of utility determined by the passage of time as it relates to consumption. It depends on an idea we explored in the early chapters, the principle of *diminishing marginal utility*. Let's take the case of the Jones family in Chicago. They have a pound of sugar in a bowl on the kitchen table. A five-pound bag on the shelf of the Jewel supermarket down the street is not yet fully useful to the Joneses for several reasons. One, as we have seen, is that it needs more place utility. Another is that more time must pass until the present stock of sugar is used up and they "need" more sugar enough to go to the store to buy it. That bag on the Jewel shelf is gaining *time* utility as the bowl of sugar at home is used up. In other words, the sugar must be available to the Joneses at the time and in the place that they consume it.

Finally, full usefulness of the five-pound bag on the supermarket shelf, as far as the Jones family is concerned, can't be reached until they own it. Because of the concept of private property, this sugar must be *bought*. **Ownership utility is that aspect of the usefulness of a product related to the passage of legal title to the final user.** When Mr. or Mrs. Jones goes to the store, pays for the sugar, and brings it home to fill the sugar bowl, the *full utility* of the sugar is realized. Marketing activities have been directly involved in the creation of place, time, and ownership utility. How firms do this is the main topic of this section of the textbook.

ownership utility

The question of how well the marketing system creates these utilities and whether the marketing concept is really working is continually being raised. This brings us into the realm of consumerism.

CONSUMERISM

As we have seen earlier, *consumerism* is a movement to strengthen the power of users in relation to the power of suppliers. Throughout the 1960s and 1970s, the consumer movement grew and began to include an ever-larger list of objectives. Leadership in the movement has been provided primarily by Ralph Nader, who first became well known when he wrote a book critical of General Motors and the Corvair in 1966. By pointing out the defects in the Corvair, Nader succeeded in gathering support throughout the country. With a broad base of support in the Congress and good press

POINT OF VIEW

The Firm:

Consumer Protection

This consumer movement is going to ruin us! We just get our new model on the market and bang! The self-appointed guardians of the people are starting a campaign against us. They're writing to the Federal Trade Commission and the State Products Safety Board and they're even giving TV interviews saying that the ZINGER is a death trap and that it has a faulty braking system.

We market researched that car and know we've built in the features that customers said they wanted—super styling, bucket seats, stereo system—the works. It's got all the latest accessories, too. I call that real consumer responsiveness! We have been pioneers in applying the marketing concept.

The Consumer Advocate:

The marketplace does not provide consumers with guarantees to protect them from unscrupulous manufacturers like the ZINGER Company. The average consumer doesn't know enough about technical products like cars to know if he or she is getting gypped. All it takes is a high-pressure ad campaign and a lot of superficial gadgets to convince him or her to buy.

Consumers need protection. They need product safety codes with heavy penalties for those firms who don't follow them. At present, only the consumer movement—people like Ralph Nader—are around to prevent consumers from making dumb mistakes. Without us they are almost helpless against the marketing skills of the giant corporations. Corporations don't care who gets hurt as long as they make their profit.

coverage, the consumer movement got several important laws passed. The new laws gave consumers more protection in the areas of packaging, product safety, and information on consumer financing plans. Much of the "grass roots" support came from young people. Many young lawyers on the local and national level worked to draw up and pass consumer laws and to put public pressure on businesses to become more consumer-conscious.

Although the era of intense consumerism has passed, the spirit of consumerism is still alive in the form of improved safety and more consumer information. Marketing today is still influenced by the consumer movement.

A quick check of J.C. Penney's catalogue will reveal several pages of consumer information. Among the subjects covered are credit and financing plans, product warranties, how to save money on shipping costs, product service, how to return merchandise, and facts about the care and use of products. Many manufacturers and retailers also have a consumer affairs department to help improve communication between marketers and consumers. Quite often, the heads of these departments report directly to the presidents of their companies. Whirlpool Corporation has a toll-free "Cool-Line" that consumers can call for information or to register complaints about Whirlpool products.

SUMMARY AND LOOK AHEAD

Marketing complements production by focusing on the customer's needs and wants. Firms that adopt the marketing concept agree that such a focus is necessary to make a profit. They take steps to build all of their efforts around meeting the customer's needs. In so doing firms define their target market, which can consist of individuals, households, firms, or combinations of these. The goods produced are classified as industrial goods or consumer goods. The latter are either convenience, shopping, or specialty goods. Firms often adopt strategies of product differentiation or market segmentation. The latter involves special ways of meeting the needs of special sets of customers.

Effective marketers realize that marketing research can help them to identify and satisfy target customers' needs and wants and to understand their market. Such research is of either a primary or secondary variety, and usually concentrates on demographic or behavioral aspects of the market.

The process of marketing is related to utility because marketing activity adds different kinds of utility to goods: time, place, and ownership utility. Consumerism is a social movement to protect rights of consumers. It is part of the environment in which marketers must make decisions.

In the following two chapters we will examine in detail the kinds of marketing decisions that firms must make. These include decisions about products, distribution, promotion, and price. Chapter 10 concentrates on products and their distribution.

FOR REVIEW . . .

1. Why is the marketing task more complex in an economy where there are high levels of discretionary income than in one where the people live at the subsistence level?

2. Why is there a demand for industrial goods?

3. Contrast the demographic and behavioral approaches to marketing research.

4. What is product differentiation? Give an example.

5. Market segmentation can be accomplished on several bases. Name three of these and give an example of each.

6. If a product possesses only form utility, is it useful to a customer? Why or why not?

. . . FOR DISCUSSION

1. How is the marketing concept related to the economic problem we discussed in Section One?

2. If a firm adopts and implements the marketing concept, all of its actions are oriented to the satisfaction of its target market. Is that desirable?

3. Why is marketing research necessary?

4. Two divergent views of the proper relationship between buyer and seller are "let the buyer beware" and "let the seller beware." Which is the "proper" view? Why?

INCIDENTS

Discretionary Income and the Growth of New Products

In an affluent country like the United States a large part of the spending is discretionary. It is discretionary spending power that prompts the continued growth of new products appearing on the market.

In a study by the firm of Booz, Allen and Hamilton of product development practices at seven hundred major companies, it was found that the average company expected to bring out ten new products over the following five years. These firms expected new products to represent 37 percent of their sales growth during that period.

QUESTIONS

1. If you were marketing manager for a large kitchen tool manufacturer and you found out from a census report that buying power in your market area had dropped 20 percent in the past ten years, how would this affect your new product planning?

2. Suppose you were marketing manager for a vegetable cannery and you found out that your market had gained 20 percent in family income, how would your planning be affected?

Will Snyder

Will Snyder, a marketing research professor at a southern university, was approached by the local Chamber of Commerce to find out why the area was not attracting new industry. Snyder had been observing the economic conditions of the area for ten years. He was provided with a substantial budget and had the services of five experienced student workers.

The city in question had a population of 150,000 and, besides the university, its major source of employment was a steel fabrication plant specializing in trailer bodies and a variety of specialty vehicle bodies. The newest major industrial plant had arrived six years before the study. It was a fruit and vegetable canning operation servicing area growers. The Chamber of Commerce knew very little about the cause of the problem of attracting new industry. They wanted Snyder to make no easy assumptions in getting at the answer.

QUESTIONS

1. If you were Snyder, would you start with primary or with secondary sources of information? Explain.

2. Would you recommend using focus group interviews at any point in this study? Why or why not?

CHAPTER 10

The Product and Its Distribution

OBJECTIVES:

After reading this chapter, you should be able to

1. Describe the components of a firm's marketing mix.
2. Construct a chart showing how the four "Ps" relate to the target market and to the environment.
3. Identify the bundle of satisfactions offered by a product to its user.
4. Draw a chart illustrating the life cycle of a product.
5. Present arguments for and against a broad product mix.
6. Explain the functions that a package performs.
7. Distinguish among brands, patents, and labels.
8. Illustrate how a middleman may bring about economies in distribution.
9. Provide an illustration of the total cost concept.
10. Compare the major modes of transportation.

KEY CONCEPTS:

Look for these terms as you read the chapter

marketing mix

product

product life cycle

planned obsolescence

new product committee

product mix

brand

patent

trademark

informative labeling

place (or distribution)

channel of distribution

manufacturers' agent

franchised retailer

physical distribution

total cost concept

common carrier

contract carrier

private carrier

containerization

Videotex—is it a bigger phenomenon than printing and TV? Press a button and watch your TV screen for any of the following:

all types of news and
feature stories

detailed weather reports

sports scores and other
statistics

price and product information

restaurant menus

stock market and other
financial information

your bank statement

games and quizzes

TV and radio program schedules

telephone directories

movie theater and other
entertainment listings

road conditions

real estate, classified, and help
wanted advertising

educational materials and
curriculum lists

If you want a printed copy and your set has facsimile capability, press another button. This viewer-controlled information revolution is a reality. Like TV itself forty years earlier, it is viewed by some as just a toy. Yet the *Financial Times* of London predicts "By the end of this century it is quite possible that videotex will be so enmeshed with everyday living that people will wonder innocently how we ever did without it."[1]

It is revolutionary new ideas like Videotex and thousands of not so revolutionary product ideas that form the base of marketing plans. This chapter will show how elements in a marketing plan are organized to meet a firm's marketing objectives. The principal elements to be examined in this chapter are the product itself and the way that the product is distributed. We will consider such questions as how a product's life can be extended and how the package and brand can affect marketing success. We will also show how products get to their customers. This includes a description of the kinds of firms that participate in their distribution and the services that they contribute to the overall marketing operation.

THE MARKETING MIX

marketing mix

To apply the marketing concept effectively, a firm must understand the major factors or tools it may use to meet (and to influence) target customers' wants. These factors are called the marketing mix. (See Figure 10-1.) The marketing mix includes four elements, often referred to as the "four p's."[2] They are

- **product**
- **place**
- **promotion**
- **price**

All four elements of the marketing mix are focused on present and potential customers and are influenced by factors in the environment such as the society, technology, the economy, and the law.

There are many possible combinations of these four major elements and the relative importance of each one may vary. The product element is the key element in the marketing mix for cars. When General Motors decided to go after a new target market with its Cadillac, it knew that it had to design a new type of Cadillac. It wanted a car that would appeal to high-income people in their thirties. These people, for the most part, were buying imports like BMW and Audi. Thus GM decided to start from scratch and designed the Cimarron. This Cadillac is smaller than traditional Cadillacs and is equipped with features, such as leather seats and steering wheel, that appeal to people in the target market.

On the other hand, place may be the most important element in the marketing mix for snacks. A potential Cimarron buyer may be willing to seek out a Cadillac dealer miles away. But a potential buyer of snacks wants them readily available nearby. Several years

FIGURE 10-1
The marketing mix

ago Anheuser-Busch decided to test market several snacks and it knew that the products had to be available in many outlets. The same wholesalers that distributed its brands of beer, therefore, were used to distribute the snacks to taverns and supermarkets in the test markets.

For other firms, price and promotion are the most important elements in the marketing mix. We will postpone further discussion of these elements until Chapter 11.

As we have seen, marketers must consider the political, economic, technological, and social environment in developing their marketing mixes. Increased defense spending in recent years has created market opportunity for the defense industry and profit potential for firms like Raytheon and General Dynamics. The economic recession of the early 1980s convinced many consumer products marketers to increase the use of coupons and cash rebates in their marketing mixes.

Technological advances led Sears to test market a home video catalogue that enables shoppers to view the products on specially designed TVs that were placed in their homes. Several years ago the Coalition for Better Television threatened to start a boycott of products whose marketers sponsored TV programs that the group thought contained too much sex and violence. This led some marketers to drop sponsorship of these TV programs. Thus changes in the marketing environment can create opportunities and/or problems for firms in developing their marketing mixes. Let's look at the product element of this mix in greater detail.

PRODUCT

Decisons about what and how much to produce represent the first step in the product planning process. Good product planning requires coordination with other marketing mix elements and strong customer orientation.

product

The relationship between a firm and its customers focuses mainly on the product. It should be viewed as a "bundle of satisfactions," which might include a variety of things, such as the guarantee, the brand, the package, and the services that go with it. For example, what is the buyer of a new General Electric trash compactor buying? The product item consists of a motor and other component parts enclosed in a steel casing. This product item will perform the function of compacting trash, but the total product is much more than the product item. What about the benefits and satisfactions the buyer is getting? The product will reduce the number of trips the buyer must make to take out the trash, thereby providing convenience and more time to spend on more enjoyable activities. The retailer who sells the compactor is also a critical factor in the "bundle of satisfactions" the buyer receives. This includes such aspects as the convenience of the location, the parking facilities, credit, assortment, skill of the salespeople, returned merchandise policy, and all those things that may attract customers. The enjoyment of shopping itself is for many customers a very important part of the "bundle of satisfactions."

"Want something that projects reason and reciprocity, quiet, confident leadership, and understated yet unmistakable power."

The Product Life Cycle

product life cycle

The life history of a product is called the product life cycle. The cycle has four phases: introduction, growth, maturity, and decline. Figure 10-2 shows a typical life cycle for a product. Both product classes and individual brands of products have life cycles. The

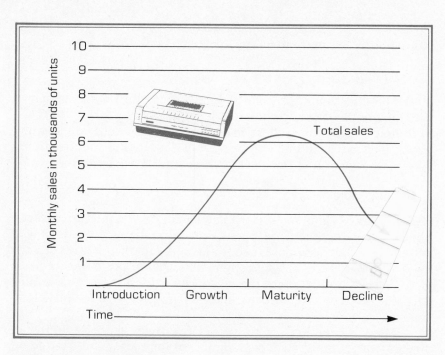

FIGURE 10-2
The product life cycle

brand's lifetime is shorter than that of the product class. People still drive cars (product class) but they no longer can buy Edsels, DeSotos, and Packards (brands).

Introduction

A new product is introduced to the market during the introduction stage of its life cycle. Because the marketer's basic goals are to gain initial acceptance and distribution of the new product, he or she will invest heavily in promotion to create awareness and interest among potential customers. Nevertheless, sales volume is very low during the introductory stage.

One of the most critical and delicate marketing tasks occurs when a firm introduces a new product. Because only one out of perhaps twenty new products is successful, most firms try to avoid expensive failures by using marketing research. This reduces, but doesn't by any means prevent, the chance of loss. Success depends on the new product's ability to perform a service customers will buy at a price that more than covers the firm's cost of making and selling it. It also depends on good introductory promotion and strong distribution.

Services also require innovation to succeed. Examples from recent years include automated bank tellers, Home Box Office, drive-in claims adjustments by auto insurance companies, rental clubs for movies to be shown on videotape cassettes, and the addition of breakfast to Burger King's menu.

Growth

A new product that has been introduced successfully will experience rapidly growing sales in the growth stage. Many of the customers who first bought the product in the introduction stage are making repeat purchases, and new customers are buying for the first time. Notice in Figure 10-2 the steep increase in the sales curve.

Maturity

Sales volume begins to level off and decline in the maturity stage, the longest part of the cycle. By the time the product enters this stage of its life cycle, many rival brands are on the market. Because rivals tend to copy features of successful brands, the various brands tend to become very similar. Once the market for a product becomes saturated, the profit potential for marketers of brands in that product class declines.

Many marketers try to extend the lives of their profitable brands. For example, Arm & Hammer baking soda's sales started to decline when homemakers decreased their use of the product for baking. The brand's life cycle was extended, however, by developing new uses for the product. These include using the product as a deodorant for kitty litter boxes, refrigerators, and kitchen drains.

Decline

Marketers usually cut back on promoting their brands near the end of the maturity phase. This phase ends when a better product appears or a need disappears and the old product enters the decline

Church & Dwight Co. made a concerted effort to develop new uses for its Arm & Hammer baking soda

<table>
<tr><td>

POINT OF VIEW

Shopper A:
    "After my recent trip to several Soviet Bloc countries and to several of the less-affluent Western European nations, I realized what an incredible selection U.S. supermarkets provide for their patrons. It really was a treat after my return from abroad to wander slowly through the endless rows of products. There must have been over a hundred choices of brands, types, and sizes of cleaning products alone. And the variety of meats, fruits, vegetables, and frozen foods was astounding. There was nothing like it in East Germany or in Bulgaria."

Shopper B:
    "It really drives me crazy to find my way through the maze of aisles and displays past the needless duplication of brands and minor product variations in the supermarket. I wish the government would *do* something about this waste. If advertising were reduced and the markets required to stock no more than three brands and two sizes of each basic product, we'd all save time and money."

</td><td>

Are There Too Many Products on the Supermarket Shelf?

</td></tr>
</table>

stage. Examples of products that have entered the decline stage of the life cycle include CB radios, mechanical bulls, eight-track tape players, four-barrel carburetors, and black-and-white TVs.

Some marketers will stop marketing their brands during the decline stage while others will try to recycle theirs. For example, sales of home smoke detectors skyrocketed during the mid 1970s and entered a serious decline by the early 1980s. Honeywell, Inc., once one of the biggest suppliers, stopped making the product. Pittway extended the life of its First Alert brand by adding an escape light to the smoke detector.

When a firm intends to replace a product, it is called planned obsolescence. Business has been criticized for this practice on the grounds that it is wasteful and somewhat deceptive. Many people feel that they are not getting a full lifetime out of the appliances and other durable goods they buy. When obsolescence occurs because of new technical features, it is called *technological obsolescence.* Invention of the electric typewriter made the manual typewriter technologically obsolete. As the Olympia ad shows, the electronic typewriter now has begun to make the electric typewriter technologically obsolete. We will discuss the technological environment of business in more detail in Chapter 20. When only appearance or style is changed, it is called *fashion obsolescence.* Promotional ac-

planned obsolescence

Goodbye, old friend.

Olympia® Electronics are to the future what IBM Selectrics® were to the past.

OLYMPIA

Electronic typewriters are rapidly making traditional electric typewriters obsolete.

tivities help to create this type of obsolescence by making customers dissatisfied with the "old" product.

Regardless of the type of obsolescence—technological or
fashion—a product that is no longer purchased is obsolete. As we
have seen, a firm spends money on research and development (R&D)
to improve its product so that it won't become obsolete. Sometimes
R&D leads to an entirely new product that takes the place of the old
product, making the old product obsolete. Polaroid spent many years
and millions of dollars to develop Polavision—a product that enabled
people to take home movies and show them without having to send
the film away for processing. It extended the idea of instant photography to home movies. The product was on the market only a short
time when it was made obsolete by the introduction of video cassette and disc recorders. Polaroid, therefore, dropped the product.

New Product Committee

**In many larger firms the task of developing new products is
performed by a new product committee. This committee, an example of the matrix form of organization which we discussed in Chapter 5, consists of personnel from several different departments, such
as production, marketing, finance, and R&D.** Such a committee
brings together different kinds of expertise to review and act on new
product ideas generated by the firm.

new product committee

The Product Mix—Broad or Narrow?

**A manufacturer's or a retailer's product mix is the combination
of products it produces or sells.** General Mills produces hundreds,
while Coca-Cola produces a much smaller number. The size of the
product mix affects marketing policy.

product mix

First of all, there is safety in numbers. A firm with a broad
product mix has a kind of insurance against the dangers of obsolescence. Also, economies of scale (lower costs per unit as volume
rises) often make the difference between success and failure. A firm
with many products can spread its overhead cost over the entire
product mix. This means savings in production costs if the products
are manufactured in the same factory. It also cuts unit distribution
cost. A firm can save on distribution costs by using the same salespeople or transportation system for all the products in its mix. Thus
General Mills' salespersons can represent many products when they
call on customers, and can ship in larger, more economical quantities.

At the retail level and, to some extent, at the wholesale level, firms with many products (a broad product mix) have an advantage in the form of product exposure. When a shopper goes to Montgomery Ward to buy toys, he or she will see children's clothing and may buy some along with the planned purchases. This couldn't happen in a single product store like Toys R Us. A single product store may enjoy some advantages, however. A firm that has a narrow product mix also tends to have a lot of depth to its product mix. Although a shopper can only buy toys at Toys R Us, there is a much greater variety of toys at Toys R Us than at Montgomery Ward. Toys R Us can promote itself as a specialist in toys. This projects an image of knowledgeability and credibility to customers. A department store, on the other hand, is a generalist.

Packaging

All the elements that constitute the broad concept of "product" must be considered in developing the product mix. Among these is the *package*. In recent years, packaging has become a more important part of product policy. Packaging does several things:

- protects the product
- divides the product into convenient units
- becomes part of the product
- helps with promotion

Think of what polyethylene packaging has done to protect thousands of food and clothing items sold in self-service stores! The egg carton and the plastic or cardboard six-pack or twelve-pack beverage container illustrate the importance of convenient unitizing. For many cleaning and polishing products, the can or bottle also serves as the dispenser or applicator for the product. In countless consumer products advertised on TV the package and the brand are displayed together prominently so that they will be remembered when the shopper sees them on the supermarket or other self-service store shelf. Brands are an important part of marketing all by themselves.

Branding

brand

A brand is "a name, term, symbol, or design, or a combination of them, which is intended to identify the goods or services of one seller or group of sellers and to differentiate them from those of competitors."[3] Brands usually include both a *name* and a *symbol*. The key to successful branding is making a lasting impression in customers' minds. A good brand name such as *Charmin* or *Seven-Up* is distinctive and easy to remember.

Brand names like Coke, Jell-O, Jeep, Scotch Tape, Styrofoam, Vaseline, Formica, and Xerox are so widely known that many people think they are dictionary words that describe a product category. They are actually brand names whose owners go to great lengths to protect them from becoming dictionary words. Thus we see Xerox ads reminding us that Xerox is not a synonym for photocopying, and ads for Sanka that stress the fact that Sanka is a brand of coffee owned and manufactured by General Foods.

Brands that are owned by manufacturers are called *manufacturer brands*, or *national brands*. All of the preceding are exam-

WHAT DO YOU THINK?

Are Better Marketing, Ad Spending Needed if National Brands Are to Maintain Market Share?

National brands are entering a turbulent period, and marketing dollars will have to be spent more efficiently if those brands are to avoid serious market share erosion, according to Pillsbury Company's vice president-marketing services, Don A. Osell.

"The competition from private label brands will certainly not decrease, even if generics fade as they likely will. Unless national brands as a category address the price differential between many national brands and private labels, the private label growth could be even greater than we expect."

"The reason for being for national brands is quite simple: to develop products with unique differences, to deliver consistently high quality at a good value to the consumer, to advertise these products in a way that builds consumer confidence and loyalty to the brand."

To do this, marketers must concentrate on: closer scrutiny of how marketing budgets are developed and how spending is allocated against product lines; the issue of improving product productivity, particularly projects which address product cost without eroding quality; the issue of "price value" between national brands and private label products; and the need for placing a premium on advertising creativity.

Will the trend toward private brands and away from national brands continue? Or will national brand marketers rise to the challenge as Pillsbury's Mr. Osell suggests? WHAT DO YOU THINK?

ples of manufacturer brands. Brands also play a role in the marketing strategy of wholesalers and retailers. Brands developed by such middlemen are called *distributor's brands,* or *private brands.* Sears' Kenmore appliances and Craftsman tools are examples. They are produced by other firms for Sears. Large grocery chains do the same thing. They generally make a larger profit per unit on private brands. Montgomery Ward & Co. operates Montgomery Ward stores, which sell mostly private-label merchandise, and Jefferson Ward stores, which are discount stores that sell mostly manufacturer-branded merchandise. Kmart for many years sold mostly manufacturer brands but recently began adding its own private-label products with an economy appeal.

Patents and Labels

patent

Legal protection is available for products and brands. **A patent protects an invention, a chemical formula, or a new way of doing something from imitation. It makes it very hard for a competitor to copy this new product or new idea for a period of 17 years.** The United States Patent Office supervises this activity. It accepts applications for patents and, if an idea is "patentable," it is registered and protected. The Polaroid Land Camera is a good example.

trademark

The patent office also protects a name printed a certain way or a symbol which, when registered, is called a trademark. Once the trademark is accepted by the patent office, it is protected for a period of 20 years and can be extended for a like period indefinitely. Miller's Lite beer and the Ford Escort are examples of trademarks. They are also, of course, brands.

informative labeling

One of consumerism's goals is informative labeling of products. Such labeling helps a buyer to make a more informed choice among products, particularly when self-service is involved. The label describes in simple terms the content, nutrition, durability, precautions, or other special features of a product. It might also indicate the grade or standard of quality of the item as established by industrywide agreement or by law.

Marketers can use nutritional labeling to improve their products' images. For example, many consumers are concerned about the nutritional content of snack foods, which some people think of as "junk food." Frito-Lay, a snack foods marketer, decided to do something about this. It added nutritional information to its labels to show that its products contain nutritious ingredients.

Informative labeling can lead to better purchase decisions *only* if the labels are read. How many people today even understand the long-standing meat and milk quality standards? Some consumers

Labels must meet government standards. They are a good means of educating the consumer

want a massive consumer education program to teach buyers the benefits of using label information.

Much of a firm's policy regarding products is governed by its decision whether or not to segment the market. As we saw in Chapter 9 it is often wise to segment a market. This requires a different marketing mix for each segment, but the product is usually the main marketing mix element in a segmentation strategy. Topol, the smokers' toothpaste, is an example of such a strategy.

However well designed a product may be, it will not sell unless it is distributed effectively. This brings us to a discussion of the place element of the marketing mix.

PLACE

Both time and space separate a manufacturer from its customers, as we have 'seen in the previous chapter's discussion of the various forms of utility. Such time and space "gaps" occur as a result of differences between the production rate and the consumption rate and because the final users of products are more widely scattered than the producers.

Place (or distribution) is an element of the marketing mix concerned with the movement of products through a channel from producer to consumer or industrial user. This movement is accompanied by the performance of a wide range of functions which are essential to marketing, including storage, breaking bulk, and cre-

place (or distribution)

ating new assortments. Marketers set up channels of distribution to perform these functions.

Channels of Distribution

channel of distribution

A channel of distribution is the firm, or usually the set of firms, directly involved in selling a product. Channels also make up for the difference between one manufacturer's product mix and the product mix a consumer wants. Since these two mixes rarely match, other firms are often needed to complete the marketing process. For example, General Foods and General Mills each produce many consumer products. But a grocery shopper wants their products *and* the products of other firms such as Procter & Gamble, Campbell, Heinz, Armour, Borden, and so on. Wholesalers bring these products together and make them available to retailers, such as grocery stores. This enables the grocery shopper to buy, in one place, a broad assortment of products. These firms, except for the producer, are usually called *middlemen*. The type and number of such middlemen describe the distribution channel.

Some consumer products manufacturers sell directly to consumers. Examples of products that are distributed this way are Electrolux and Kirby vacuum cleaners and World Book Encyclopedias. This type of direct distribution is much more common in industrial marketing because a typical manufacturer of industrial products sells to a much smaller number of customers than a typical consumer products manufacturer. Thus Xerox can afford to send salespersons directly to its customers. This would be too costly for Procter & Gamble or Pillsbury because their customers number in the millions. The final decision about how to get products to customers requires a compromise between cost control and providing the best service and convenience. This means that the final development of a channel depends on

- the number of customers
- the functions which the channel is expected to perform
- the costs of alternative channels
- the importance of controlling the marketing process

Thus a maker of lathes selling to a handful of industrial firms may sell directly to customers. A maker of toothbrushes selling to millions of customers, by contrast, will need a long (several levels of middlemen) channel. A firm making several different appliances with high unit profit margins, like Singer, can operate its own retail stores because the overhead cost is spread over several products. A manufacturer of blankets could never afford to do so.

It is important to understand that marketers are always trying to develop new and better channels to reach their customers. Xerox, for example, decided recently to begin producing and marketing copiers for small-volume users to compete with copiers by Savin and other rival firms. Xerox knew that to call on small users, such as doctors, lawyers, accountants, and small business firms would require too large a salesforce so it began opening its own retail stores to reach them. Meanwhile, Xerox continued to use its direct salesforce to call individually on large-volume users. This is an example of the use of multiple channels to reach a firm's customers.

The Principal Middlemen

There are three basic types of middlemen:

- merchant middlemen
- agent middlemen
- facilitating middlemen

Merchant middlemen actually take title to the products they offer for sale, while *agent middlemen* do not. *Facilitating middlemen*, like transportation firms, participate in the transportation and storage of the product, without actually buying and selling it.

Examples of merchant middlemen include *wholesalers* and *retailers*. These firms regularly buy stocks of products and resell them. Retailers are involved in selling a wide variety of consumer products. Food, for example, is sold mostly through food and grocery retailers known as supermarkets, some of which are parts of large chains (Kroger, Safeway, A&P) and some of which are independent. Independent supermarkets usually buy from independent wholesalers, while chain stores receive products from their own firm's central distribution points, which perform the wholesaling function.

The top part of Figure 10-3 shows a typical channel of distribution used by a processor of a food product. This firm sells to a central buying office of a large food chain which, in turn, distributes to its retail stores. These, of course, sell to households. Other important retailer types include department stores, drug stores, variety stores, discount houses, and vending machine operators.

Agent middlemen include manufacturers' agents, brokers, and selling agents. These firms are involved in selling a wide variety of products, including consumer products and industrial products. **Manufacturers' agents are paid a commission to represent manufacturers of several noncompetitive lines in a limited geographic territory. Without taking possession of products, such agents aggressively seek to establish these products in this territory.**

manufacturers' agent

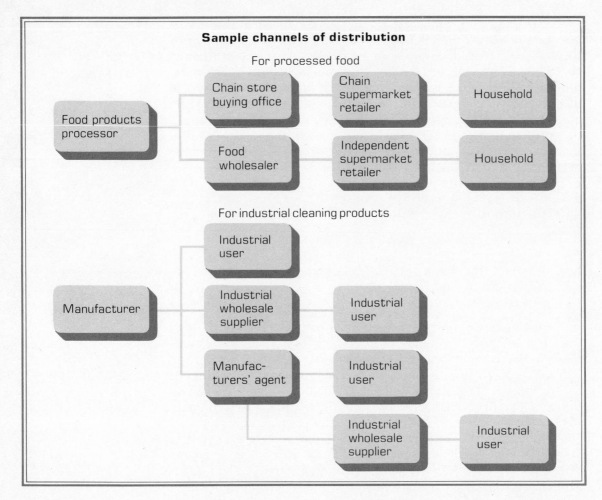

Sample channels of distribution

For processed food

FIGURE 10-3

Typical channels of
distribution

A manufacturers' agent may help a producer of industrial cleaning products to introduce the line in California. Because the agent gets paid a commission only for the actual sales made, this can be a more efficient way of distributing in a new territory than dealing directly or exclusively through wholesale industrial suppliers. The bottom part of Figure 10-3 shows the "set" of channels that a manufacturer of industrial cleaners might use. In some cases, this firm sells directly to large industrial users, using its own salesforce. In other cases, the producer sells to industrial suppliers (wholesalers) who sell to industrial users (usually the smaller customers). Another method is to use a manufacturers' agent to reach either users or wholesale industrial suppliers. It is common for a national manufacturer to use different channels of distribution in different parts of the country.

The more direct (shorter) a channel is, the more control a manufacturer has over distribution, because there are fewer middlemen to coordinate. Control is improved by means of franchising. **A franchised retailer is tied closely by contract to a manufacturer and its operations are strictly supervised.** Examples of franchised outlets include McDonald's and other fast-food firms, as well as auto dealers and many gas stations. Franchising is discussed in detail in Chapter 17.

franchised retailer

Facilitating middlemen are not pictured in Figure 10-3 although they may be involved in each case. These are railroads, warehouse companies, insurers, and other firms who facilitate or assist in distribution but are not directly engaged in buying or selling.

Are Middlemen Necessary?

At some time you might have heard a friend say that she got a great bargain from a store because it bought "direct from the factory," or "eliminated the middleman." Your friend assumed that the price was reduced by the profit that would have gone to the middleman. Such a claim would lead you to believe that middlemen are unnecessary and expensive and should be abolished. Let's examine this claim.

Super Valu Stores is a giant grocery products wholesaler based in Minnesota. It buys a great variety of grocery products from a large number of manufacturers. It buys in huge volume and resells these products in smaller volume to nearly 2,000 independent food retailers.

Why don't the retailers buy all the items they carry direct from the manufacturers? The answer is clear—they save money by buying through the wholesaler. Super Valu simplifies the number of purchases and sales and reduces unit purchasing costs and record keeping. It provides quicker delivery to the retailers than they could get

Some fabric mills sell directly to consumers

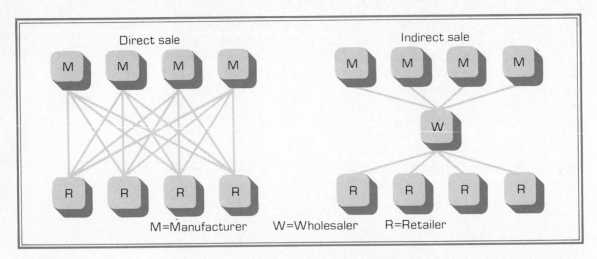

FIGURE 10-4

Direct versus indirect sale

Without the wholesaler, each retailer would have to deal with all four manufacturers. Each manufacturer would also have to deal with all four retailers. With the wholesaler, each retailer and each manufacturer need deal only with one intermediary—the wholesaler. Thus, the wholesaler reduces the number of transactions (represented by the connecting lines) and makes it possible to increase the average size of transactions. This increase brings about economies of scale and thereby justifies the existence and the profit margin of the middleman.

by dealing directly with the manufacturers. Figure 10-4 illustrates this principle. Each connecting line represents a transaction. Clearly, shipping in carload lots is much cheaper than the many small shipments which would be needed for direct sales from manufacturers to retailers.

There are great economic advantages in a system of distribution that uses a wholesaler. This middleman

- buys in large quantities and sells in small quantities
- makes it possible for the retailer to simplify its buying process by carring a broad line of items
- often takes credit risks which manufacturers might not accept
- guarantees delivery on short notice so that retailers need not keep large stocks

In most cases, wholesalers and their margins (the difference between the costs of products to them and what they sell them for) are justified. If the wholesaler did not exist, all of these activities could not be conducted without raising prices.

If your friend got a real bargain from the retailer who "eliminated the middleman," she probably made the purchase under very special circumstances.

Facilitating middlemen are important to many channels of distribution, even though they are not included in a description of those channels. They often help marketers to perform the physical distribution function. Florida oranges, for example, could not be marketed in New York without the services of trucking companies and railroads.

Physical Distribution

The growth in volume and variety of products sold, together with new transport technology, have turned marketers' attention toward the problem of physical distribution, or *logistics*. **Physical distribution is concerned with the physical movement of raw materials and semimanufactured products into and through the plant, and the movement of finished products out of the plant to middlemen and on to the ultimate consumer or industrial user.**

physical distribution

The Total Cost Concept

At one time physical distribution management was mainly concerned with minimizing the cost of transportation. This is a narrow view because the transportation cost may be less than half the total cost of physical distribution. **Modern firms apply the total cost concept, which considers all costs related to a particular means of physical distribution. Their goal is to minimize their total costs without sacrificing their desired level of customer service.** In addition to transportation, there are storage costs and "out-of-stock" costs. Concentrating only on transportation rates is shortsighted.

total cost concept

Many firms have developed distribution systems that depend on computers to schedule the flow of products from manufacturer to consumer or industrial user. They select the best location for intermediate storage points and the best means of transportation. These computer-based systems take into account the costs of transporting and storing as well as the cost of "running out" of merchandise. Such accurate cost systems are common where the channel is under the control of a retailer or manufacturer. The objective of modern physical distribution management is to achieve a *balance* between costs and service.

The Modes of Transportation

Firms have a choice among railroads, motor trucks, air freight, and, in some cases, ships and barges or pipelines to move their pro-

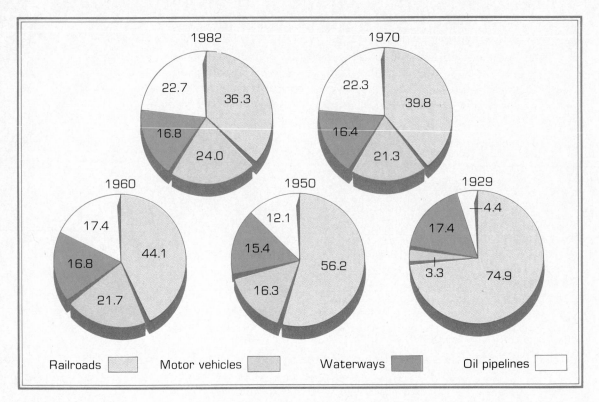

FIGURE 10-5

Percent distribution of
ton-miles of domestic
intercity freight traffic,
by mode of
transportation: 1982

ducts. Decisions like this are in the hands of the *traffic manager*. This important decision maker keeps track of the in-and-out flow of materials, delivery dates, and storage space with the goal of coordinating all aspects of physical distribution and thereby ensuring customer satisfaction at the lowest cost. Recent history, as can be seen in Figure 10-5, has seen some dramatic shifts in the relative importance of the various modes of transportation.

There is a legal relationship between a firm that wants to move freight (the shipper) and the transportation firm (the carrier) that will handle the actual transport. Carriers (railroads, truckers, shipping companies, etc.) can be

- common carriers
- contract carriers
- private carriers

common carrier

A common carrier offers its services to the general public at uniform, published rates. These carriers' rates and services are supervised by public agencies. Railroad rates, for example, are regulated by the Interstate Commerce Commission (ICC). In recent years, however, there has been a lot of deregulation in the transportation industry. It started with the airlines and spread to the railroad and trucking industries. Thus our transportation system is more competitive now than it was in the past. Price competition is much more common now, both among the various modes of transportation and among different firms within a given mode. This is important to physical distribution managers who are searching for ways to reduce their costs while maintaining the level of service their customers desire.

When a firm needs to move freight that can't be moved by a common carrier, it may call on a contract carrier. **A contract carrier is a firm, such as a trucking company, that negotiates long- or short-term contracts with shippers to handle their freight.** It is a private contract between the shipper and the carrier. The shipper may want *customized service* and may want a guarantee of availability without investing in its own truck or barge fleet.

If a manufacturer or middleman owns and operates its own transportation, it is called a private carrier. This kind of operation is justified when a large, predictable volume exists and common or contract carriers are not as economical or can't do exactly what the shipper needs. Many oil companies, for example, own fleets of ships to transport their oil.

Railroads. Each of the major modes of transportation has its good and bad points. The railroad's major advantage has alway been low cost, long haul transportation for heavy and bulky commodities that have a low value in relation to weight. Coal, sand, gravel, steel, lumber, and grain are examples of products hauled by railroads. The railroad also provides reliable service, because varying weather conditions do not often affect it. Economies of scale are evident in railroading because one diesel engine can pull one or many loaded cars. This enables the railroad to spread the cost of the motive power over a large number of shipments.

The major limitations, however, also relate to *economies of scale.* Less-than-carload lots (l.c.l.) are not well-suited to rail movement. Modern railroads use mechanized loading and unloading equipment that is designed to handle single, large units. Small shipments require very costly manual handling. Furthermore, the more cars that can be moved with one engine, the lower the cost to move each car. Therefore, the small shipper may find its shipment waiting on the siding while a large train is being made up.

Recent deregulation, however, along with new types of equipment and operating procedures are helping railroads to increase their traffic in farm products other than grain, manufactured products, as well as bulk commodities. Snowy freight cars, for example, have a two-inch coating of foam insulation to keep pre-cooled perishable products like fruits and vegetables at the desired temperature en-

contract carrier

private carrier

route without ice or mechanical refrigeration devices. Aerated cars haul dry bulk cargoes like flour and cement. They operate on the vacuum cleaner principle and "inhale" their cargo when loading and "exhale" it when unloading. This reduces the need for packaging. Hot slab gondola cars haul hot slabs of steel from steel plants to rolling mills. This, in effect, makes rail service a part of the steel industry's production line.

Trucking. The major advantage of motor truck transport is flexibility. Trucks can go anywhere there is a road. Thus by truck the shipper can reach many more potential customers than by other modes.

As in the case of the rails, there are many different types of trucks, some of which are highly specialized. Because the required investment is rather small, many shippers own and operate their own trucks. Door-to-door service is possible with trucks, and service is speedy.

A major problem facing highway carriers today is the high cost of fuel. In their efforts to reduce fuel consumption, many truck lines are placing air deflector shields on top of their long-haul tractors, switching to more fuel efficient radial tires, and installing devices that disconnect the cooling fans on big truck engines when not needed. Studies have shown that such fans are needed only five percent of the time the motor is running.

Waterways. Water transport is important in both domestic and foreign commerce. The major advantage is low cost transport for low-value, bulky products. As bulk goes up and value goes down, the advantage of water transport increases. On the other hand, as delivery time becomes more important, barges become less attractive. Accessibility to waterways and ports is, of course, necessary.

Pipelines. Pipelines are the most "invisible" of the modes, although they move many millions of tons of goods over many miles. Thousands of miles of pipelines move crude and refined petroleum, chemicals, and natural gas from major production points and ports of entry to cities all over the nation. A process called batch processing permits several different products to be moved at the same time. Lines are also now built for the movement of pulverized coal in slurry form (suspended in water) but, as the demand for coal rises, problems arise due to the increasing water shortage in major coal producing areas.

Pipelines are almost completely unaffected by weather and, once they are installed, the cost of operation is very low. Very little labor is involved in operating them.

Water is the oldest mode of transportation and still offers cost savings for bulk commodities

Airlines. In the not too distant past, airplanes were considered basically "people carriers." At best, they could move only very high-value, low-bulk cargo. The arrival of the jet age and jumbo jets, the increased number of airports, and sophisticated materials-handling techniques have changed many of these ideas. Air transport is speedy, safe, and can help the shipper in reducing other elements of total distribution costs. Many airlines appeal to the shipper on the basis that if it is willing to spend a little more money on transportation, its other distribution costs can be reduced. One major problem is that higher fuel costs have led some airlines to discontinue service to smaller cities.

Containerization

Our discussion of physical distribution would be incomplete without some discussion of containerization. **Containerization is the**

containerization

AUTHORS' COMMENTARY

Containerization on a giant scale is changing the face of ocean-going commerce. One variety of containerization is RO/RO, or roll-on, roll-off. Loaded trailers are trucked to a port where they are wheeled aboard the ship for the ocean voyage. When the ship arrives at the overseas port, the trailers are wheeled off and trucked to their final destinations.

On an even greater scale, an increasing variety of industrial and consumer products are being loaded aboard barges that serve as containers. These barges are then loaded aboard specially designed ships (Seabee or LASH vessels) for transport overseas. For example, the barges can be loaded upstream on the Mississippi River and its connecting waterways at shippers' plants, then pushed or pulled by tugboats to New Orleans where they are floated onto or lifted aboard ocean-going ships. Thus a ship may carry seventy barges loaded with cargo from New Orleans to Rotterdam where they are off-loaded and pushed or pulled by tugboats on the inland waterways to their final destinations. The time needed to unload these vessels is only a fraction of the time conventional ships require to load and unload one pallet at a time by crane. This means the vessels can spend more time at sea and less time in port. Quick, and therefore economical, use of capital equipment, together with less pilferage and wear-and-tear, are the reasons that containers will continue to change the decisions physical distribution managers make.

Containerization Will Continue to Change Water Transport

practice of using standard large containers, preloaded by the seller, to move freight.

Modern containers move many types of freight. They are loaded at the shipper's plant, sealed, and moved to the receiver's plant. Instead of many individual items being individually handled, the entire container is mechanically handled. They move with great efficiency from truck to train (piggyback), from train to ship (fishyback), and from truck to plane (birdyback). This is called *intermodal transportation*. The savings in distribution cost can be great because of reduced theft and damage as well as lower transportation rates on intermodal movements.

SUMMARY AND LOOK AHEAD

The kind of product and the target market help to define the "marketing mix" or combination of product, place, promotion, and price that a firm will use. Product policy is the focal point of the marketing mix of many firms, who keep a close eye on the product life cycle and try to keep products alive and profitable. Research and development help to keep old products alive and to replace them with new products. Packaging and branding are also vital parts of the product element in the marketing mix.

Marketers create channels of distribution to reach their customers. In some cases manufacturers sell directly to consumers and industrial users. In other cases they use middlemen such as retailers, wholesalers, and agent middlemen. Facilitating middlemen such as railroads and warehousing companies may also participate in distributing products. Thus marketers face decisions about physical distribution. The overall goal of distribution activities is to provide the level of service customers want at the lowest cost.

In Chapter 11 we go on to complete our examination of the marketing mix. Special attention will be given to methods of promotion and pricing techniques. We will also look at the strategies used in advertising and in personal selling as well as the ways that firms adjust to market conditions and cost structures in setting prices.

FOR REVIEW . . .

1. Name the four "Ps". To whom should they be directed? Why?

2. When you purchase a new toaster, what "bundle of satisfactions" are you buying? How about a tube of toothpaste?

3. How long does a product "live"? Why does a fashion product "live" a shorter time than a hardware item like a wrench? Explain the concept of "life cycle" as applied to these two types of products.

4. Has packaging become more important or

less important in selling consumer products in recent years? Discuss.

5. Why does the distribution channel for an industrial product differ from a convenience consumer product channel? How does it differ?

6. How is it that middlemen exist even though they must cover their cost of operation and make a profit? Are their functions necessary? Why or why not?

7. Draw a chart illustrating four different channels of distribution that a manufacturer of toys might use. Could these be shortened? Explain.

8. What are the main advantages of rail transportation over water transportation?

. . . FOR DISCUSSION

1. How could the manufacturer lengthen the life cycle of your favorite brand of toothpaste?

2. What packaging functions does a six-pack of Coke perform?

3. Name six brand names that you think have good "memory value." Name six that you think are poor. What makes the difference?

4. Discuss the application of the total cost concept to the distribution of expensive flowers from farms in California to florists in the New York City area.

5. Why would a manufacturer operate its own private carrier?

INCIDENTS

De Seviny Ski Fashions, Inc.

De Seviny Ski Fashions, Inc. is an American subsidiary of a large French manufacturer of clothing. De Seviny produces a line of high-fashion winter sportswear at its plant in Phoenix, Arizona. Its product design policy has been to produce and market products (ski jackets, scarves, and gloves) identical to those made and marketed by its parent company in France.

For several years after entering the American market, De Seviny held a substantial market share in the Rocky Mountain area because of the unique French design of its products. In 1982, Hubert Delon, the marketing manager, is aware of the declining sales in the major ski resorts in Colorado. He feels sure that the taste of cus-

tomers in this area is moving away from the sophisticated styles still popular in European ski areas toward simpler, "Western" styles. Delon is seriously considering a radical change in product design for next Fall's line.

QUESTIONS

1. What are De Seviny products experiencing at this time?

2. What factors must Delon consider in making the decision he faces?

3. How can Delon get the facts he needs to make the right decision?

Spaghetti Pot

One of the outgrowths of the changing lifestyles in the nation is the growing takeout food market. Many believe that during the 1980s the rise of dual-income households and the increase in one-person households will cause Americans to turn to takeout food such as that offered by the small California chain, Spaghetti Pot. This food is designed to be a cut above standard fast-food fare and to appeal to those who want to eat at home without cooking. Takeout is nothing new, but the owners of Spaghetti Pot are banking on a strong increase in reliance on this kind of food

delivery system as the "baby-boomers" begin to set up households and time for cooking is at a premium.

QUESTIONS

1. Define the product here in the sense of an element in the marketing mix.

2. What is the channel of distribution in this case?

3. Will this kind of operation compete with McDonald's? Why or why not?

CHAPTER 11

Promotion and Pricing

OBJECTIVES:

After reading this chapter, you should be able to

1. Explain the role of promotion.
2. Describe the activities of an advertising agency, including media selection and printed ad composition.
3. Summarize public complaints against and regulation of advertising in the United States in recent years.
4. Give a brief description of the functions of selling and sales management.
5. Differentiate among publicity, public relations, and sales promotion.
6. Distinguish between two approaches to basic price and illustrate how market conditions influence pricing.
7. Describe two possible pricing strategies for introducing a new product.
8. Provide an illustration of price lining in a retail store.
9. Show how a marketing mix might be developed for marketing the services of a banker or a lawyer.

KEY CONCEPTS:

Look for these terms as you read the chapter

promotion

advertising

advertising agency

account executive

advertising media

AIDA process

personal selling

publicity

public relations

sales promotion

price

oligopoly

price leadership

monopolistic competition

markup

pricing model

cash discount

trade position discount

functional discount

quantity discount

market penetration
      pricing

market skimming pricing

inventory turnover rate

price lining

Are all fresh, dressed chickens the same? Or is a yellow chicken a better chicken? As we have seen in Chapter 9 many marketers use a strategy of product differentiation. In the case of fresh, dressed chickens, however, this is a difficult strategy to use. Poultry wholesalers, butchers, and supermarket managers ordinarily stocked whatever chickens were available at the lowest price, and many still do this. The lack of differentiation makes it difficult for the chicken grower to control price or distribution of the product. Perdue Farms, Inc. has found a way—their chicken is "yellower" than other chickens.

Many people believe that a yellow chicken is tastier and more tender than other chickens. Perdue Farms chickens are yellower and this fact has given them something to crow about. They have tied this into their advertising and have strengthened the already strong preference among East Coast customers for yellow chickens. Now many poultry wholesalers and grocers in the East must stock Perdue Farms products which are easily sold at a higher price than unbranded chickens.

The Perdue Farms experience illustrates the importance of attention to promotion and pricing policies. It also shows how these two aspects of the marketing mix are interdependent.

In this chapter we will introduce the subject of advertising, the roles of various advertising institutions, and the complementary relationship between personal selling and advertising. The problems involved in setting basic price will be examined. Special features of the practice of new product pricing and retail pricing will also be discussed. We begin with the subject of promotion.

PROMOTION

promotion

Promotion is probably the most dynamic, aggressive, and persuasive element of the marketing mix. Promotion includes all communication by a firm with its customers or potential customers for the purpose of expanding sales, directly or indirectly. Promotion is communication that

- gains attention
- teaches
- reminds
- persuades
- reassures

At any point in a product's life cycle, promotional communication can be used to do any of these things. For example, the Brown & Williamson Company spent roughly $150 million to launch Barclay cigarettes. This included spending on magazine, newspaper, radio, and TV ads and free sample packages of Barclay cigarettes. The goal of promotion during the introductory phase of Barclay's life cycle was to gain the attention of target customers and to inform them of its existence.

Savin, IBM, and Xerox also spend a lot of money on promotion. Some of it focuses on gaining attention and informing target customers of their new products. But a lot of money is also spent to teach present and potential customers the benefits of their products. This is common during the growth phase of a product's life cycle. In many cases, this type of promotion facilitates the personal selling efforts of salespeople when they call on prospective customers.

The Coca-Cola Company spends millions of dollars every year to promote its products. Some of this money is spent to promote its new products. But because Coke has been on the market for decades, the main goal of promotion is to *remind* consumers of the product's availability and good qualities. "Coke adds life," "The real thing," "Things go better with Coke," "A Coke and a smile," and "Coke is it!," are examples of reminder themes from recent years. This type of promotion is most common during the maturity phase of a product's life cycle.

Creative promotion has helped Perdue Farms to differentiate its product

AUTHORS' COMMENTARY

Teenage Daughters Assume New Marketing Role

Working mothers view their teen daughters as "partners" in the household decision-making process, according to a new survey sponsored by *Seventeen* magazine.

The study, which was conducted by Yankelovich, Skelly and White, Inc., New York, found that teenage girls not only significantly influence the purchase of a wide variety of household goods, but also the specific brands.

Either by providing her mother with opinions or information or by actually buying the product herself, the teen daughter had been influential in the family's purchase of all fourteen items studied.

Marketing planners, especially those engaged in promoting household goods, would be wise to take note of this finding. Their advertising and other promotional efforts ought to take this new role for teenagers into account and appropriately integrate it into promotional programs.

A major goal of most promotional effort, however, is to *persuade* target customers to do something. Usually, of course, this means persuading target customers to buy the product. Quite often target customers are persuaded to respond very quickly. Ads on TV that feature record albums and tapes, for example, often include a toll-free number that viewers can call to place their orders immediately after seeing the ad.

Finally, considerable promotional effort is devoted to *reassuring* present customers that they made the right decision in buying the firm's product. Auto dealers and auto manufacturers, for example, often send letters to their new car buyers congratulating them on their purchase decision. The purpose is to help reassure these buyers that they made the right decision—they bought the "right" car. This can help to dispel any second thoughts they may be having about the new car they just bought.

Because of the dynamic nature of competition, promotion must be viewed as a communication process. It is the process of sending messages through a variety of media. Figure 11-1 illustrates the communication process. It shows that a message must be encoded (expressed in a particular way), sent through a particular medium (such as television, word-of-mouth, or billboards), and decoded (interpreted by the target market). This must occur despite noise (distractions) which might interfere with the communication such as competing commercials, traffic sounds, or rock music. A complete communication process also involves some kind of feedback. This is another way of saying that when a message is sent out there is

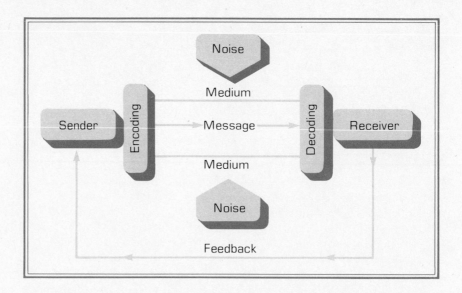

usually a response of some kind. In most cases, the desired response is purchase of the product or service by target customers. The choice of a medium can influence the way that the message is received. For example, it would probably be a mistake to promote burial insurance during a TV situation comedy program.

The principal methods of promotion are advertising and personal selling. Of somewhat less importance are the methods of sales promotion, publicity, and public relations. Let's discuss these methods and how they relate to one another.

Advertising

Modern Americans are familiar with the process of advertising. They are subjected to it during a large part of every day of their lives, much of it through TV. **Advertising includes all nonpersonal promotional activity for which a fee is paid.** The special feature of advertising is its ability to reach large numbers of people at the same time and at a moderate cost per contact. It is done through the principal advertising media of television, consumer magazines, newspapers, business publications, radio, direct mail, and billboards. It is carried on by such institutions as advertising departments of firms or advertising agencies.

advertising

The volume of advertising in each of the major media is shown in Figure 11-2. The use of TV continues to grow at the expense of newspapers and magazines.

Individual firms spend most of their advertising budgets on *brand,* or *selective, advertising.* This means that the purpose is to promote the particular brand of product sold by that firm. Sometimes firms also engage in *institutional advertising,* which promotes the good name of the firm as a whole. When a group of firms advertise a general class of product without mentioning brands, this is called *primary demand advertising.* You have probably seen ads urging you to drink more milk or eat more beef. Let's turn now to a discussion of the principal institutions that are involved in advertising and examine the functions of each institution.

Advertising Institutions

The principal institutions involved in making advertising decisions are

- advertising departments of firms
- advertising agencies
- advertising media—newspapers, television stations, magazines, and so on

Advertising Departments. Most large- and medium-sized firms have a separate department to oversee advertising activities. If a firm has adopted the marketing concept, its advertising department is under the authority of the top marketing executive. This provides for coordination of advertising with other promotional activities and with the rest of the marketing mix. Advertising departments serve as communicators between the firm and the advertising agency.

FIGURE 11-2

Share of total advertising volume by media: 1968 and 1981

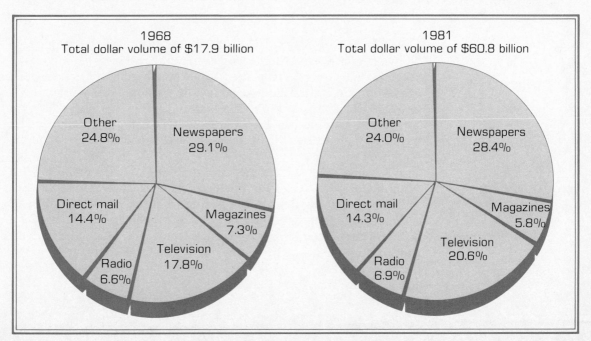

1968
Total dollar volume of $17.9 billion

Other 24.8%
Newspapers 29.1%
Direct mail 14.4%
Magazines 7.3%
Radio 6.6%
Television 17.8%

1981
Total dollar volume of $60.8 billion

Other 24.0%
Newspapers 28.4%
Direct mail 14.3%
Magazines 5.8%
Radio 6.9%
Television 20.6%

Small firms, on the other hand, generally do not have an advertising department. One or two people usually handle the firm's advertising. When they have ideas for an ad campaign they go to the local newspaper, radio, or TV station and present those ideas. If the small firm buys a certain minimum amount of newspaper space or radio or TV time, the medium will handle the production of the ad at no cost to the client. The client pays only for the space or time. Local, independent grocery stores often take this approach in running their weekly ads.

advertising agency

Advertising Agencies. **The principal creative centers for advertising for most medium-sized and large firms are their advertising agencies. An advertising agency specializes in performing advertising functions for other firms.** It serves its clients by planning advertising campaigns, by buying time and space in the broadcast (radio and TV) and print (newspapers and magazines) media, and by checking that ads appear as agreed. Sometimes ad agencies perform additional marketing functions, such as marketing research and public relations. Agencies are normally paid a 15 percent commission based on the dollar amount of advertising placed in the media. They also charge additional fees if they perform marketing research or other special services for their clients.

account executive

A key role in the advertising agency is played by the account executive. **An account executive is in charge of the entire relationship between the agency and a particular client (account) and coordinates the work of the group of professionals involved in the client's ad program.**

advertising media

Advertising Media. **The advertising media carry the message designed by firms and their agencies to many receivers (customers or potential customers). The most important media are newspapers, television, direct mail, and magazines, in that order.** As we have seen in Figure 11-2, since 1968, the largest gain in the share of total advertising volume has been made by TV. The other major media have lost share except for radio. Newspapers and magazines were the big losers.

An advertiser selects media (often with an agency's help) with a number of factors in mind. The marketing executive must first ask "Which medium will reach the people I want to reach?" If a firm is selling turkey breeding equipment, it might select *Turkey World,* a business paper read mostly by turkey breeders. If it is selling silverware, it might choose a magazine for brides. If it is selling toothpaste, the choice might be a general audience television program or a general audience magazine like *Reader's Digest.*

Another important factor in media choice is the medium's ability to deliver a message effectively. Some messages need visual

Is it Desirable for
Professionals to
Advertise?

**WHAT DO
YOU THINK?**

Until a few years ago, professionals like certified public accountants, physicians, dentists, and
lawyers were prohibited by their
ethical codes from advertising their services. They essentially
were limited to listing their phone numbers in the phone book
and putting their names on their doors.

But things have changed in recent years. The Federal
Trade Commission (FTC) finally won its long battle with
several professional organizations that prohibited their members from advertising. Thus we now see some professionals
advertising on TV, radio, and in newspapers. In fact, the
American Bar Association's commission on advertising publishes a how-to manual on advertising for lawyers.

In your opinion, is it proper for professionals to advertise? What about a certified public accountant who advertises
a price for preparing a client's tax return? A physician who
advertises a price for an appendectomy, or a dentist who advertises a price for extracting a wisdom tooth? What about a
lawyer who advertises a price for handling an uncontested
divorce? Does this benefit the professional? Does it benefit
the client? Is it desirable for professionals to advertise? WHAT
DO YOU THINK?

communication and some need the added dimension of color. Foo
are an example of products that benefit from color in communication. Selling an electric organ requires a sound-oriented medium. Some messages need color, sound, and motion. This is only
available in color television, the medium with the greatest set of
"communicating tools."

There are other special considerations in media selection. For
example, print media are more permanent. They can communicate
several times or be taken to the store as a shopping aid. Some media
(radio, television, and daily newspaper) provide frequent communication and relatively short "lag" time before the ad will appear.
Finally, there is the cost per contact with a customer or prospect.
This will vary greatly, but the one-dimensional media, such as radio
and newspapers, are usually inexpensive per contact. TV costs more.
The cost of a one-minute commercial during the 1981 Super Bowl on
CBS was $468,000, or $7,804.03 per second. Over 100 million people,
however, watched the game on TV.

How an Advertisement Works

Much of what advertising can do can be shown by careful examination of a particular advertisement. **A promotional process can be**

AIDA process

thought of in terms of how it works on a particular receiver or prospective customer, leading him or her through the stages of attention, interest, desire, and action—the AIDA process.

Headlines are usually attention-getters and interest-builders. Sometimes they go a long way toward building desire, too. Copy, in many ads, is the desire-builder or convincer because it gives facts and anticipates objections by the reader. The signature is usually the familiar company trademark or brand name. It says who is sending the message. Sometimes it is accompanied by a coupon or an action-inducing offer.

The color ads shown in this chapter display a variety of appeals or themes used to "reach" customers. The advertiser uses an appeal, such as sex or prestige, that fits the product and the target customer.

The arrangement of parts in a print ad—illustration, headline, and copy—is called the *layout*. Ideally, the layout makes it easy to "carry the reader through" the phases of attention, interest, desire, and action. The first color ad in this chapter is an example of this. A similar AIDA "game plan" can also be used in personal selling.

The magazines and newspapers that you read every day can provide you with many examples of the AIDA process. Examples of different advertisements appear on the following pages. Consider the format of each advertisement. What different appeals does each use to attract its particular audience? Are they effective?

Advertising Complaints and Regulation

Because advertising is such an obvious part of the lives of Americans, it is not surprising that it is subject to much criticism and government regulation. Complaints come from consumer groups, conservationists, sociologists, and economists about the effects and some of the methods of advertising.

Some complaints relate to *truth in advertising*. Some exaggeration about the quality of products has always been permitted, but there are limits to the degree of exaggeration permitted. The Federal Trade Commission has, in recent years, imposed stiffer penalties for false and misleading advertising. Its ground rules provide that all statements of fact be supported by evidence. In some cases, the FTC has required that the advertisers run corrective advertising. The makers of Listerine mouthwash, for example, were required in their advertising to correct the impression which they had created in earlier advertising that Listerine is effective in controlling colds or sore throats. The Food and Drug Administration and the Federal Communications Commission have also increased their efforts to control advertising abuses. Most states have passed laws to control deceptive advertising. These laws are called "Printer's Ink" statutes and their level of enforcement varies greatly from state to state.

Other questions that could be raised about advertising are:

- Are we being brainwashed?
- Is much of competitive advertising wasteful?
- Does advertising lead to monopoly and high prices?
- What effect is advertising having on the values of our people?

While some of these questions have merit, it is hard to imagine how our economy could have achieved its great productivity and wealth without the stimulating effect of modern advertising.

Personal Selling and Sales Management

In some situations there is no substitute for one-to-one human persuasion. All of us experience it nearly every day. There is a lot that one person can do to convince another of a point of view. This could mean one's willingness to try a new brand of beer or to change an attitude toward a politician. However, persuasive talent cannot serve a business effectively unless it is properly managed.

Personal selling includes any direct human communication for the purpose of increasing, directly or indirectly, a firm's sales. The special quality of personal selling is its individuality—the one-to-one relationship between the seller and the buyer—and the fact that the seller may give very special attention to the buyer's needs. The tone of personal selling can vary widely. It can be like that of a sideshow barker or of a skilled computer salesperson. The style is different, but the goal is quite similar—to sell. Both hope to guide the receiver through the AIDA process. See Table 11-1 for a typical example of how a salesperson might follow this process. Advertising and personal selling are complementary; they work well together. Avon, for example, advertises on TV to stimulate interest in its products. It also has a door-to-door salesforce of nearly one million people to make personal calls on its target customers.

The modern view of personal selling is that salespeople are expected to help their prospects identify and solve problems. An Avon salesperson, for example, may demonstrate to a woman with very sensitive skin how a particular type of makeup can help her to deal with the problem. In many cases industrial salespeople require training in engineering, chemistry, data processing, or other scientific and technical areas in order to deal effectively with their

personal selling

Salesperson (S)	*Prospect (P)*
Enters situation with thorough knowledge of product, incomplete knowledge of prospect's needs. Is confident.	Enters situation with a poorly formed idea of need, very little information about salesperson or product. Some distrust and hostility toward salesperson.
1. Attracts attention of P by setting up appointment and, perhaps, by indicating some awareness of the needs of P.	2. Greets S, attitude improved by the pleasant, interested manner of S.
3. Begins to show how product can solve a problem that P has.	4. Becomes more deeply interested, but brings up certain objections regarding price and quality.
5. Answers P's objections by describing credit plan and explaining how the service department of S's firm can overcome the problems in (4). Asks for the order.	6. Finds another reason to object to signing order, but the objection is mild.
7. Answers last objection and closes with "If you'll just give me your O.K. on this, we can make delivery on the first of the month."	8. Agrees to buy on a trial basis.
9. Thanks P, checks over details of order. Later, checks on P's satisfaction.	10. May experience some post-sale doubt, but reassures self of wise decision.

TABLE 11-1

A typical personal selling sequence

prospects' problems. Thus a salesperson who sells oil field equipment must know a lot about petroleum engineering. Many firms staff their sales organizations with sales specialists. NCR (National Cash Register) Corporation, for example, has sales specialists who call on prospects in particular types of markets. Thus some sales representatives may call on banks, others may call on hospitals, and others may call on schools. Because these prospects' data processing problems often vary, NCR thinks the sales reps who call on them should be trained to handle their specialized data processing problems.

Selling and sales management both require the development of a wide variety of skills and techniques. The nature of the sales task will determine which kinds of skills and techniques are needed. Retail selling, for example, requires quite a different kind of preparation and ability than selling technical equipment, such as computers, to industrial buyers.

Salespeople operate in many different ways, but most of them

- do some "prospecting" and/or "qualifying." This involves developing lists of prospective customers and screening them for likelihood of purchase and profitability as customers
- get to know their products and services in every way possible, including strong points and weak points
- formulate sales strategies that best suit their product and their customer as well as their own personal talents
- learn to answer customers' objections
- learn to be persistent, positive, and confident enough to close the sale
- follow up to ensure customer satisfaction

A salesperson who sells vacuum cleaners door-to-door would probably have to do all the things listed above, although all those activities may not be necessary in every selling situation. For example, when Del Monte decided to introduce a new line of Mexican foods in American grocery stores its salespeople had to win the support of Del Monte's wholesalers and retailers in stocking the new products. Salespeople who called on Del Monte's wholesalers did not have to engage in prospecting or qualifying but they did have to perform the other activities in the list. They had to learn about these products and develop sales strategies to encourage the wholesalers to stock the products and encourage the wholesalers' salespeople to push their sale. Meanwhile, other Del Monte salespeople were calling on grocery stores. Their job was to inform retail grocers about details like package sizes, merchandise return policy, introductory pricing details, sharing introductory advertising costs for the new product line between Del Monte and grocers (cooperative advertising), and so on. This helped convince grocers to allocate some of their valuable space to the new line of products.

There are special problems in managing a salesforce that are not usually as serious in managing other personnel. To be successful, salespeople must be confident in themselves and in their product. Their morale must be kept high. Sales managers are often handicapped in trying to maintain high morale because they usually lack continuous personal contact with sales personnel.

The sales manager's responsibilities include

- building an effective salesforce
- directing the salesforce
- monitoring the sales effort

WATS Line Usage and Promotion Policy

POINT OF VIEW

One of the best ways to reach more customers and prospective customers and to have them reach you is through a WATS line. Wide Area Telephone Service (WATS) has become especially important as a means of following up on national advertising. More and more national ads contain a toll-free 1-800 number for customers whose interest has been caught by the ad but who still need more information. Sometimes ad readers or viewers call to place an order.

WATS lines are also important for sales manager-salesforce communication and for salesforce-customer follow-up. All in all, WATS has been a real boon to contemporary sales techniques.

A recent change in the rate structure for WATS lines, which provides for charges by the minute instead of a monthly flat rate, is giving some marketers second thoughts about WATS. Marriot Hotels, Holiday Inn, and Hertz, for example, have experienced significant reservations cost increases. Some large firms are considering changes in WATS use strategy.

The change may actually increase use of WATS by smaller firms, for whom charges by the minute may result in lower WATS cost per sales contact. This is a case in which a pricing change by one firm may mean significant changes in promotional methods by thousands of others. Whether a firm is a large or a small WATS user will make a difference in its point of view.

To build a salesforce, the sales manager must develop recruiting sources and techniques, devise methods of selecting from the recruits, and maintain an effective sales training program for those selected. Directing the salespeople includes developing workable pay plans, which might include salaries, commissions and/or bonuses, and programs for appealing to higher-order motivations such as those discussed in Chapter 5. The third task, that of monitoring sales effort, is a special form of control. The sales manager must, therefore, set up standards, such as sales quotas and sales expense budgets for sales territories, products, and individual salespeople. He or she must also make regular comparisons of actual sales results to such standards and make the necessary corrections. Corrective action may range from redefining sales territories to dismissal of ineffective sales employees.

Other Promotional Methods

Promotional activities other than advertising sometimes play a major role in the marketing mix of business firms. These include publicity, public relations, and sales promotion.

Publicity

Publicity is a communication through the news media as a legitimate part of the news. It is usually an inexpensive means of promotion, because its only cost is preparing the news story or press release. But only items considered "newsworthy" by the press are used and, very often, carefully prepared items are never printed or broadcast. Often, news stories (like the announcement of the new models of Ford Motor Company) may be cut down by newspapers for lack of space. Thus publicity is a promotional method over which the firm has little control. Also it is limited to reporting facts.

publicity

Firms sometimes receive negative publicity. The marketer of a product that the Consumer Product Safety Commission orders recalled from the market will receive some negative publicity. Firms, of course, try to avoid this by, for example, following quality control procedures in manufacturing their products. But sometimes things go wrong. The question is how to deal with this negative publicity? The consensus appears to favor cooperating with regulatory agencies and the news media in providing relevant facts rather than attempting to cover them up. Thus a firm that is either ordered to recall a product or that does so voluntarily would want to provide the media with information for consumers concerning how to get the product repaired or replaced.

Public Relations

Public relations is harder to define. **Public relations includes any personal communication with the public or with government (lobbying) that seeks to create goodwill for the firm. Its effect on sales is usually indirect and long-run.** Recently, for example, some people have been strongly critical of the use of nuclear reactors to generate electricity. To help dispel this criticism and to give the public an opportunity to see the safety features built into such plants, some companies conduct guided tours of their facilities. Your college probably also has a public relations department. One of its activities might include sending representatives to talk to seniors at nearby high schools to point out the advantages of attending the college.

public relations

Sales Promotion

sales promotion

Sales promotion includes special events directed at increasing sales. Special sales, coupon offers, contests, games, entertainment features, and trading stamps are examples. Some would include specialty advertising devices such as matches, calendars, and ballpoint pens. Others might add "PMs" or "spiffs," which are cash payments to retailers and their employees to promote a manufacturer's products.

Sales promotion is often directed at consumers. Marketers of food products are major users of cents-off coupons. *Reader's Digest* sponsors frequent consumer sweepstakes, Kool cigarettes sponsors hot air balloon races, and Eckerd drug stores give two prints on film developing for the price of one.

Sales promotions can also be directed to a manufacturer's salesforce, middlemen, and middlemen's salesforces. Examples include a manufacturer offering an all expenses paid vacation for the top salesperson in each sales territory, and Miller Brewing Company supplying its retailers with point-of-purchase displays.

PRICE

price

In a competitive world dominated by advertising, price still plays a part. **The price element in the marketing mix includes the dollar cost to customers as well as the conditions of sale.** Most firms still concentrate much of their effort on the problem of setting price. How this process fits into the firm's planning is different for almost every firm.

Market Conditions and Pricing

The concepts of price, market, supply, and demand were introduced in Chapter 2. This early introduction to price did not, however, fully explain the impact of market conditions. For the market to work perfectly, certain conditions must be met. These conditions include: a large number of buyers and sellers, a homogeneous product, easy entry into the market, and market information in the hands of buyers and sellers. A homogeneous product in a market means that the buyers do not perceive any difference among the brands of competing firms. Easy market entry occurs when no large capital investment is needed for new sellers to enter the industry. The necessary market information includes facts about the numbers of competitors and supply and demand conditions.

As consumers we know that all these conditions rarely exist. The more common kinds of market conditions are oligopoly and monopolistic competition. **An oligopoly means there are only a few sellers of the same or slightly different products.** The market for automatic washing machines, for example, might be classified as oligopolistic. There are few sellers and price competition is rare.

oligopoly

In oligopoly one of the stronger competitors may sometimes raise price, and it is likely that others will follow suit. This is called price leadership. Traditionally General Motors has set pricing patterns in the domestic auto industry.

price leadership

Monopolistic competition occurs in a market with many sellers, each of whom sells a somewhat differentiated product. This is most common in the retail and service markets. Location and quality of service are the differentiating factors. New competitors can easily enter the market. This prevents the typical competitor from making large profits.

monopolistic competition

Monopsony, a situation in which there is one large buyer in the market, often occurs also. Large manufacturers, for example, are often the only buyers of a wide range of component parts. This gives them market power over several or many small suppliers of these parts. Large auto manufacturers, for example, buy such a high percentage of the output of a small producer of electrical system fuse assemblies that they have the upper hand in setting the price of this item.

There is such a great array of markets and products in the developed Western nations that labels such as *oligopoly* and *monopolistic competition* are not adequate. They help us understand some of the price behavior, but they are not enough to guide price decisions. Such theoretical market concepts don't account for the use of the marketing mix elements other than price. Price is *only one* of the competitive tools.

Setting Basic Price

Under the guidelines of pricing objectives, firms must set basic prices. We will examine two different approaches to the problem of setting basic price: the cost approach and the demand approach (see Figure 11-3) and then we will see how some firms combine these two approaches. First, let's look at the cost approach.

The Cost Approach

The cost approach to setting basic price involves "building" unit selling prices on the basis of cost. This approach is simple when the cost of one unit is easy to identify. **A markup is an addition to cost**

markup

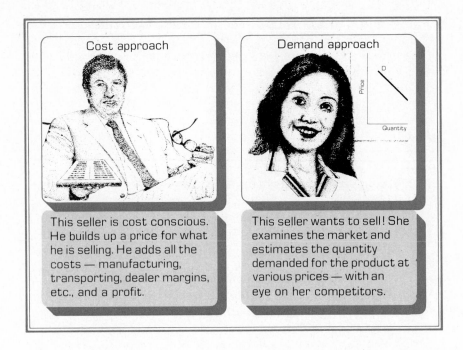

Cost approach

This seller is cost conscious. He builds up a price for what he is selling. He adds all the costs — manufacturing, transporting, dealer margins, etc., and a profit.

Demand approach

This seller wants to sell! She examines the market and estimates the quantity demanded for the product at various prices — with an eye on her competitors.

to reach a selling price. It is usually expressed as a percentage. Mr. Schultz, who operates a men's clothing store, uses a percentage markup applied to his unit costs for an item or group of items. Thus he might buy 100 suits at $80 apiece and apply a 50 percent markup on cost, resulting in prices of $120 per item for his customers (150 percent of $80). Schultz might use this same percentage markup on all items in his store. If so, his basic price policy is a very simple one with a cost basis. He probably has allowed demand factors to influence his markups only in an indirect way.

Mr. Schultz probably knows from past experience about how much his customers are willing to pay. But he does not look at consumer price attitudes very closely because cost-plus pricing is so easy for him. He also knows that, over the years, the policy has allowed him enough gross margin (the difference between total dollar sales and costs of goods sold) to pay his rent, his clerk's salary, and other costs of operation, and to leave him a fair profit. These calculations will be covered more completely in the next chapter when we discuss the income statement in accounting.

Manufacturers may also use a cost approach to pricing. However, it is not always easy for them to identify costs attached to a given unit of output. It becomes more difficult as the number of units produced increases. Cost accounting systems have been developed to aid in this task. Manufacturers who sell to governments often use cost-based pricing because government buyers frequently specify such pricing, sometimes called *cost-plus*. In some cases the federal government is a firm's *only* customer. The government often requires cost-plus pricing which allows the contractor to cover cost and to make a certain profit.

The Demand Approach

In its most extreme form, the demand approach to pricing neglects the cost side. It is more in tune with the marketing concept than the extreme cost approach because it considers possible customer reaction. More precisely, it estimates the amounts which are likely to be sold at different prices (the slope of the demand curve). The most extreme form of demand-approach pricing would set prices very low to sell the greatest number of units.

The concept of a *customary price* is important in understanding the demand approach to pricing. The classic example of a customary price was the nickel candy bar. Candy makers resisted raising this price for many years despite increases in their production costs. Of course, the cost increases eventually became too great and the nickel price had to be increased.

In 1981 Hershey Foods Corporation ran an ad with the headline "No news is good news. Hershey is holding the line on candy bar prices." Hershey pointed out in the ad that some competitors had recently raised the wholesale price of some of their candy bars. Thus Hershey appeared to be following the demand approach to pricing more closely than its competitors who had raised their prices.

Combined Approaches

Many firms set prices by making both cost and demand estimates. These are translated into profit estimates at various unit price and sales levels. Breakeven charts, which are explained in Chapter 13, may be used to help in such analysis. Some firms use a technique borrowed from economic theory called *marginal analysis* which helps to estimate the "best" price and quantity produced in terms of greatest profit.

Pricing models might be developed in firms that have trained economists and computers at their disposal. **A pricing model is an equation or set of equations that represents all the important things in a pricing situation to help decide on the "best" price.** Past experience in pricing and knowledge of the market conditions help to determine the equation that best predicts pricing results. This process is known as *model building*. No matter how carefully it is done, it still requires judgment about what other human beings will do and what their tastes and needs will be.

pricing model

Cash Discount	The Smith Insurance Agency receives a bill for $1,000 from Walter Stationery Supplies, Inc. with payment terms of 2/10, net /30. A cash discount of 2/10, net /30 means that the full price is due within 30 days of the invoice date. But Smith Insurance is entitled to a 2 percent discount if payment is received within 10 days, which is 20 days earlier than the due date. If Smith pays the bill in 30 days, it is like paying 36 percent interest per year, because there are 18 twenty day periods in a year. (18 × 2 percent = 36 percent). Even if Smith has to borrow money at 20%, it will pay them to take the cash discount.
Quantity Discount	A quantity discount is based on the quantity of merchandise a buyer buys from a seller. There are two types: noncumulative and cumulative.
Noncumulative quantity discount	Suppose a wine bottler offers the following discounts on cases of wine:

Cases purchased on individual order	*Discount percentage*
1–10	0.0
11–25	2.0
26–50	3.5
over 50	5.0

	If Johnny's Liquor Store ordered 12 cases at a base price of $50 a case, the store would pay the bottler $600 less 2 percent, or $588.
Cumulative quantity discount	When purchases are totaled during a year and the discount percentage depends on the total volume of purchases made during that year, this is a cumulative quantity discount. If Johnny purchases 210 cases during the year and the bottler's discount schedule is as shown below, Johnny will get a check for $315 from the bottler at the end of the year. (210 × $50) × 3 percent = $315.

Total cases purchased in 1983	*Discount percentage*
1–100	2.0
101–500	3.0
over 500	4.0

Trade position discount	A manufacturer receives two orders for small appliances. One comes from a wholesaler and the other from a retailer. The wholesaler gets a discount of 50 percent off the suggested price to ultimate consumers. The retailer gets a discount of 30 percent from the same suggested price to ultimate consumers.
Functional discount	A processor of frozen turkeys grants a special discount of 2 percent to a supermarket chain in return for featuring the product in the chain's weekly ad in Chicago papers the week before Thanksgiving.

TABLE 11-2

Examples of discounts

Discounts

Specific prices actually charged by a manufacturing firm often vary from the basic price. Such variations generally result from an established discount policy. Discounts from "list" prices are granted **cash discount** for a number of reasons. **For instance, it is common for a firm to offer small discounts for prompt payment of bills. These are called *cash***

". . .Second tire at half-price when you buy the first tire at double-price. . . .!!"

discounts. Another typical discount is the *trade position discount.* A wholesaler who normally sells to retailers, for example, may make a special sale to another wholesaler at a discount from the regular price to retailers. **Any discount granted because of a difference of position in the distribution channel is called a trade position discount.**

trade position discount

Sometimes a functional discount is granted to a customer in return for services rendered. A retail grocer, for example, may receive a discount or allowance from a detergent manufacturer if the grocer features the manufacturer's brand in local newspaper ads. Some would argue that this practice is not really a discount but rather a simple purchase of a service. Such a discount could also be called a promotional allowance.

functional discount

Still another common discount is the *quantity discount* which involves reduced unit prices as the size of the order increases. A firm's discount policy makes its pricing more flexible in special competitive situations. However, it is often also the cause of serious legal problems concerning price discrimination laws. Table 11-2 shows how some of these discounts are computed.

quantity discount

Pricing New Products

Some special considerations arise in pricing a new product. There are two opposite approaches: market penetration pricing and skimming pricing.

To feature low price when introducing a new product is called market penetration pricing. The firm's goal is to build a large initial market share and to build brand loyalty before competitors can enter the market. The initial low price discourages some competitors who foresee smaller profit at such a low price.

market penetration pricing

Texas Instruments, Inc. has often used market penetration pricing in introducing its various models of pocket calculators. It wants to build a large market share and discourage the entry of rivals, especially Japanese producers. By capturing a large market share, the firm is able to produce in large volume and, it is hoped, reduce per-unit costs because of the economies of large scale production.

market skimming pricing

To feature a high price when introducing a new product is called market skimming pricing. The goal is to get the greatest early revenue from sales to recover product development costs before competitors enter the market. This approach is often used by small firms, by firms with large development costs, and by firms that are not well protected by patents and good reputations. This policy amounts to "getting it while the getting's good." For example, SmithKline Corporation, a pharmaceutical firm that is research and development oriented, invested millions of dollars to develop Tagamet, a drug used in the treatment of ulcers. The firm practiced skimming pricing in this case in order to recoup its development costs as soon as possible.

Retail Pricing

As we saw earlier, most prices charged in retail stores are determined by a markup mechanism. Ms. Jill Gladney runs a jewelry store. She knows that, on the average, her costs of doing business—including salaries, rent, and desired profit—have amounted to about 50 percent of sales revenue. She also knows that the cost of goods she buys for resale accounts for the other 50 percent. She might plan prices so that, considering special "sales" to sell slow-moving items, she would realize a 50 percent gross margin. Thus her average initial prices might need to be more than double the cost of goods. A shipment of rings costing her $100 apiece might be marked up to $250 and finally sold at $200, just enough to provide a gross margin of 50 percent of sales.

Jill Gladney's initial markup could be expressed two ways: it represents $150/$250 or 60 percent of the originally established sales price and $150/$100 or 150 percent of the original cost price. It should always be made clear whether a percentage markup is expressed in terms of cost or in terms of expected selling price. Of course, Ms. Gladney may assign different markups to different classes of items in her inventory, depending on competitors' practices and her experience in the turnover rate of various items.

inventory turnover rate

The inventory turnover rate in a particular period of time is determined by dividing cost of goods sold by the average inventory value. If Ms. Gladney's inventory value on January 1 is $50,000 and on December 31 it is $70,000, the average inventory is $60,000. If cost of goods sold was $600,000 the turnover rate is $600,000/$60,000 which equals 10 "turns" per year.

If Ms. Gladney uses different markups on different items, she will try to average them out to provide her desired *gross margin.* Sometimes retailers use very low markups on certain items to attract customers. This is known as a *leader item.* The goal is to increase sales of items carrying higher margins. Such practices may be illegal if it is shown that the item is sold below cost. Some firms use illegal "bait and switch" schemes. This means advertising one inexpensive item that is really not available and then convincing people to buy a more expensive substitute when they arrive. Such schemes are illegal in interstate commerce and many states outlaw them in intrastate commerce (within their own borders).

An apparel retailer may make ten purchases of men's sport coats in a season. Marking up each of these by the same percentage might result in ten different prices for sport coats. **Partly to simplify** **choices for customers and partly to simplify the job of the sales-** **people, the retailer may use price lining—grouping the products at** **three or four sales price levels.** Thus Bill's Men's Wear might make ten purchases of coats in a cost range from $51.00 to $78.50 per unit and present them to customers in the $69.95, $89.95 and $109.95 price range. This makes it easier for the salesperson to get the customer to "trade up." He comes into the store expecting to buy the $69.95 sport coat he saw in the newspaper ad and finally buys the $89.95 or $109.95 coat, after comparing quality and listening to the salesperson's advice.

price lining

The prices selected by Bill's Men's Wear are "odd" amounts and they were close to the next "$10 break." Partly out of tradition and partly because of a slight psychological effect, retailers tend to set prices at $69.95 rather than $70. A price starting with sixty "sounds" like more of a bargain than one starting with seventy. Prestige stores, such as Neiman-Marcus, however, often use "even prices" to bolster their status.

Special promotions such as "one-cent sales" and "two-for-one sales" are also a part of the art of pricing. They require careful estimation and experience in order to result in overall profits for the retailer. Marketers must consider the entire marketing mix whenever planning a change in price or any other one element in the mix.

We turn now to the general problem of designing a marketing mix for a growing segment of the economy—services. We will explore the fact that the nature of services dictates a somewhat different mix than that which we have described for traditional products.

MARKETING OF SERVICES

Sales of services have been growing at a rapid rate in recent years. (See Table 11-3.) A service is like a product in that it provides

Kind of Business	1974	1980[1]
Business services	$42,364	$111,160
Advertising	11,564	25,517
Advertising agencies	9,448	N. A.
Automobile services	15,187	32,117
Automobile repair shops	9,455	18,706
Motion pictures, amusement and recreation services	14,161	28,327
Personal services	13,785	23,587
Laundries, laundry services, cleaning and dyeing plants	4,886	8,819
Beauty shops	2,964	5,443
Barber shops	927	1,232
Hotels, motels, tourist courts, trailer parks, camps	10,236	25,102
Hotels, motels, tourist courts	9,314	23,038
Miscellaneous repair services	8,465	17,168

NA: not available
[1]unadjusted figures

TABLE 11-3

Selected service industries—receipts, by kind of business, 1974 and 1980 (in millions of dollars)

a benefit, but it is unlike a product in that it is not a concrete, physical object. More than 40 percent of what consumers spend is for services. Services represent a big part of what firms buy, too. A service may be quite personal, such as the service provided by a physician or beautician. It can be impersonal as well. Banks, insurance agents, and people who do repair work provide impersonal services in the sense that the human tie between the producer and consumer is not close. In any case, it is usually hard to separate the service from the person who provides it. It almost always requires that the producer be a specialist. Julius Irving and Larry Byrd provide the service of entertainment on the basketball court. They are highly paid because they are specialists. The same is true of a heart surgeon or an actress. Insurance agents are specialists, too, as are plumbers and electricians.

Because we have defined the product part of a marketing mix in terms of the "bundle of satisfactions" it provides, it follows that marketing services is not very different from marketing products. There are a few differences, though. Perhaps the biggest difference is the simple fact that most service producers have not paid as much attention to marketing as they should. Only recently have public accounting firms and commuter airlines, for example, realized the importance of the marketing concept. They have begun to think in terms of attracting and pleasing customers and of differentiating their services.

Despite recent changes in professional practice and the laws and rules applying to it, there still remains in medicine a tradition which inhibits the use of ordinary promotion. In medicine and other professions, however, the concept of marketing and the use of a full marketing mix are applicable. The "product" could be enhanced, for example, by "humanizing" medical services. "Distribution" could be improved by paying more attention to hospital location and parking. There are already signs of change in pricing policies of professionals, too, despite traditional ethical restraints. Evidence of increased recognition of the importance of marketing in medicine is the publication of a new journal in 1981—*The Journal of Health Care Marketing.*

For most services all four parts of the marketing mix—product, place, promotion, and price—should be developed. Success in marketing services, even more than in marketing tangible products, depends upon knowing the buyer well and serving his or her needs. This is especially true for personal services where success requires treating each client as an individual market segment.

For many services the distribution part of marketing is a little different. Usually the producer and distributor are the same. In most cases there is no "channel" of distribution as we normally think of it. Yet, the location of the bank branch or the watch repair shop or even the doctor's office must be considered carefully. A successful TV repair shop often provides home pickup and delivery. A marketer of rented apartments in a distant suburb might offer private commuter bus service to tenants. This is another way of distributing.

The marketing of services has a long way to go, however. The sooner service producers realize that the marketing concept applies to their "product," the better off the consumer will be.

SUMMARY AND LOOK AHEAD

Promotion is the most creative and aggressive part of the marketing mix. Its two main components are advertising and personal selling. These parts complement each other in that advertising deals best with mass markets through one-way communication and personal selling provides direct, two-way communication with individuals or small groups. Both can be analyzed in terms of the AIDA process. The main advertising institutions are the advertising departments of firms, advertising agencies, and the media. They cooperate in the creation and execution of advertising programs. These efforts must be coordinated with the personal selling effort which is directed and monitored by the sales manager.

Price is one of management's decision areas. It is an element in the marketing mix because, in most situations today, competition is not perfect and markets don't dictate prices. When setting basic price, a marketing manager must consider costs of production, expected demand, and competition. Breakeven charts and marginal analysis play a role in the pricing decision. Discounts from basic price also enter into the competitive scheme. These include cash discounts, quantity discounts, trade position discounts, and functional discounts. Retail pricing centers around the question of appropriate markups. New product pricing must choose between market penetration and skimming.

All four parts of the marketing mix, to a greater or lesser degree, enter into the marketing of services. The same general rules and concepts apply, except that the product and distribution elements are significantly different.

In Section 5 we turn to accounting, computers, and information management. We will see how firms keep financial and managerial records, the systems they employ, and the extent to which they depend on electronic data processing and mathematical and statistical devices in order to understand financial and managerial data better.

FOR REVIEW . . .

1. What are the various functions of promotion?

2. Name the important advertising media in the order of their volume in the United States.

3. What is the AIDA process? How does it apply to personal selling?

4. What are the broad responsibilities of a sales manager?

5. Compare the two approaches to setting basic price.

6. What is the difference between cash discounts and trade position discounts?

7. Contrast the policies of "skimming" and "penetration" pricing.

8. How does a marketing mix for a service differ from one for a product?

. . . FOR DISCUSSION

1. Write a brief piece of copy for a television commercial announcing a new chain of sandwich shops called "Margy's" to be introduced in your city next month.

2. Write a paragraph giving advice to a salesperson for a hardware wholesaler going out on his or her route for the first time.

3. Is advertising brainwashing? Does it lead to waste?

4. Why is a retailer likely to take the cost approach to pricing?

INCIDENTS

IBM Sells Computers on TV

Did you know that a computer is a warm and personal thing? IBM says so. In going after the

huge new market for personal computers, IBM made the big break and resorted to TV ads. For example, they ran ads during the telecast of the U.S. Open Tennis Tournament. The ads themselves are full of words like "warmth" and "creativity" and "OK to touch". Many of the ads feature warm, domestic scenes in which the computer is surrounded by happy people.

QUESTIONS

1. In your opinion, why is IBM turning to TV as a medium for this advertising?

2. Explain how this communication technique fits in with Figure 11-1.

3. What kinds of limits does TV advertising impose on the total selling process for personal computers?

Pricing Used Subcompact Cars

Sandy's Used Cars in Miami used to follow a simple pricing strategy. If a used car cost them $800 they would advertise it for twice that amount. Faced with a recession and a general upheaval in public attitudes toward U.S. and foreign cars, Sandy's manager is considering using different markups for domestic and foreign cars.

QUESTIONS

1. Should Sandy's use two different markups for domestic and foreign cars? For full-sized and subcompact cars?

2. Describe the markup policy you would like to see employed.

CASE STUDY

SPECIALTY-MAGAZINE PUBLISHER SUCCEEDING WITH A DIFFERENCE

John Tillotson publishes three little-known but profitable magazines: *The Workbasket, Flower and Garden,* and *Workbench.* He made his fortune doing things differently than most publishers. The success of his Kansas City company, Modern Handcraft Inc., suggests that small-business owners shouldn't necessarily rush to copy bigger rivals.

"To make a living with these types of magazines," says David Z. Orlow, a New York marketing consultant specializing in periodicals, "you have to be a really good manager. You have to run a tight ship."

Profiting in special-interest magazines that appeal to people who garden or knit, crochet and sew, and to the do-it-yourself carpenter and home handyman is no mean trick. "Big publishers," says an industry specialist, "enter the field thinking they can spend more on promotion and get more readers to attract more advertising. Then they don't get it. There is no more littered road in publishing."

Mr. Tillotson's tight operation is apparent from the mastheads of his magazines. Two list only three editorial employees. Another masthead lists more, but several, he says, are part-timers. Many magazines employ scores of writers and editors. Mr. Tillotson relies heavily on outside contributors, paying them $300 to $1,000 an article.

Most magazines depend heavily on advertising. But Modern Handcraft publications get as much as 75 percent of their revenue from subscriptions. The three magazines had combined revenue of $14.3 million in 1980. While most publishers use outside companies to maintain subscriber records, the Tillotson magazines do it themselves with an efficient computer system using an optical scanner that can "read" typewritten words.

In their battle for readers and advertisers, big magazines such as *Time* and *Newsweek* spend heavily for circulation. Advertisers buy space in these publications based on the number of readers the magazines deliver. A drop in circulation could be interpreted as a loss in popularity.

"*Newsweek* has to replace thousands of subscribers every week just to stay even," says Charles I. Tannen, an editor at *Folio,* a publication for magazine management. So big-circulation magazines must promote extensively to keep up.

But circulation at the Tillotson magazines has been allowed to drop at times without great harm. In fact, it can be better strategy to absorb a circulation decline, Mr. Tillotson says, than to spend more money trying to prevent a slide.

Promotion decisions, nevertheless, are a crucial aspect of the business. Direct mail sent third-class is the main promotional tool. Responses to previous mailings indicate how many pieces of mail must be sent to produce a certain number of new readers. Mr. Tillotson explains the process: "We look at the subscription expirations coming in the next 24 months, calculate what the renewals will be (based on past renewal rates) and then figure how much promotion is needed to maintain the same circulation."

If the cost seems too high, circulation is allowed to drop. Between 1978 and 1980, *Flower and Garden's* circulation shrank to 500,000, a decline of 100,000 subscribers.

Appeals go to subscribers when they don't renew. "We keep mailing to them until the cost exceeds our cost of signing up a new subscriber," Mr. Tillotson says. That can mean as many as eight mailings to those whose subscriptions have lapsed. However, higher postal rates have forced the company to cut the number of renewal mailings in recent years, he says.

Modern Handcraft doesn't solicit pay-later subscriptions. "Every collection letter means an additional expense," Mr. Tillotson says. A subscription to *The Workbasket* is only $4, he notes, and the cost of a few dunning letters to a subscriber can eat up 10% of the subscription price.

Postal rates have become a significant cost for all publishers. But the new rates penalize smaller publications, Mr. Tillotson says, because to qualify for the lowest piece rate, six pieces of mail must be sent to the same postal zone. His magazines don't have six or more subscribers in many zones. The company's average mail rate is 23.6 cents a pound. An average issue weighs two ounces to $2\frac{1}{2}$ ounces, he says. So postage runs three cents to 3.7 cents a copy. "One cent on a million copies is $10,000," he says to emphasize the effect of a seemingly small rate increase.

Questions

1. Contrast the characteristics of the target markets of the publisher of *Reader's Digest* and the publisher of *Flower and Garden.*

2. How would you classify Modern Handcraft's magazines—as convenience, shopping, or specialty goods? Explain.

3. Does Mr. Tillotson practice market segmentation? Explain.

4. Why is a magazine's circulation so important to potential advertisers in that magazine?

5. *Sports Illustrated* is often promoted by direct response commercials on TV. Viewers are invited to call a toll-free telephone number, give the operator their VISA or MasterCard numbers, and subscribe to the magazine. Would you advise Mr. Tillotson to do this? Why or why not?

CAREERS IN MARKETING

Careers in marketing are about as varied as are to be found in any field. However, the nature of this field is such that it depends heavily on people who are creative and who have communications skills. Two of the largest areas of opportunity are advertising and personal selling.

In advertising there are jobs in ad agencies, in magazines, newspapers, and television as well as in the marketing or advertising departments of manufacturing and service firms. Some of the most interesting jobs are with ad agencies, including jobs as account executives, media buyers, graphic artists, and copywriters. Besides creativity, an *account executive* needs business training and understanding of accounting and statistics in order to provide the client with an effective advertising program. Usually, this job requires a college degree, either in business or in communications. *Media buyers* need business training too, so they can purchase the "best" time and space in the media within the budget agreed to by the advertiser. A college degree (four years) is preferred, but not always necessary. *Graphic artists* and *copywriters* need training in their respective crafts so they can design attractive layouts and filmstrips and write exciting copy. Usually, these workers have some college training, although a four-year degree is not always required. Except for the account executive, who may do a fair amount of traveling to confer with clients and prospective clients, these are desk jobs. Pay is high for account executives, especially in large agencies. Those representing major national accounts often earn between $50,000 and $100,000 a year. Account executives in smaller agencies have a less stable income, which depends on the success of their ad programs. The other agency-related jobs usually pay somewhat less.

Jobs related to selling are also many and varied. *Retail selling* usually requires the least education and training and pays less than jobs in industrial or wholesale selling or specialized selling such as insurance or real estate. Retail selling is mostly in-store and often amounts to little more than "finding what the customer wants." The exception here is in the case of shopping goods retailing which often requires skills in customer relations and detailed knowledge of the product. Higher level retailing careers, however, such as *merchandising manager* and *buyer*, often require college degrees.

Personal selling of technical products such as computers or pharmaceuticals often requires a business degree in addition to courses and training in, for example, engineering or biological sciences. Personal selling of simpler products, such as some types of building materials or office supplies, does not usually require a college degree, although some college work is helpful. *Outside*

1978 and Projected 1990 employment in selected
marketing-related occupations*

Occupation	1978 Actual	Employment** 1990 Projected***	Percent Change 1978-1990
Commercial artists	100	126	26
Pub. Relations Specialists	81	104	29
Buyers, Retail and Wholesale	238	298	25
Sales Managers, Retail Trade	261	323	24
Store Managers	926	1107	20
Wholesalers	234	284	21
Real Estate Brokers	34	49	44
Sales Agents, Representatives, Real Estate	255	400	57
Sales Clerks	2771	3362	21
Survey Workers	40	49	21

*based on 1981 BLS data
**thousands
***moderate high trend

selling jobs require exceptional human relations skills and great self
confidence. Often, much travel is involved. Pay is usually at least
partly on commission and can range very widely, depending on the
competitive position of the product or service and on the energy
and skill of the salesperson. Some salespeople earn well over
$100,000 in a year.

Marketing jobs are also available in retail and wholesale
activities. *Sales management* and *purchasing* are closely related
fields which may interest you. The table above shows the Bureau of
Labor Statistics' (BLS) 1981 estimates of job growth. For each
occupation we include the intermediate estimate made by BLS for
1990 as well as the actual count in 1978.

In sales, opportunities are especially bright; this includes *real
estate brokers* and *sales representatives*. Real estate brokerage and
sales jobs are expected to grow 44 and 57 percent respectively—well
above the national average for employment opportunity growth.

The demand for *sales clerks*, however, will not keep pace
with the national average (up 21 percent), but the absolute number
of sales clerk openings is huge—almost 600,000 from 1978 to 1990.

The survey from which this table was drawn did not include
jobs held by fewer than 25,000 persons in 1978. This means that
some of the higher-paying marketing jobs such as advertising

account executive and market research analyst are not analyzed for future demand. The most recent estimates suggest that demand is above average in these occupations. The educational requirements are high, however. In market research, statistics, psychology, and math majors as well as four-year degree holders in marketing are in demand. In jobs as account executives, backgrounds in English, psychology, and marketing, with either a bachelor's or master's degree, are in great demand.

CAREER PROFILE

My name is James L. Matthis III. I am currently the Area Manager in St. Louis, Missouri for Miller Brewing Company.

When I graduated from college in 1977 with a bachelor's degree in Business Administration, I began my career with Miller as a merchandiser. In this position I was responsible for point-of-purchase displays and related promotional activities. After one year I advanced to an Area Manager position in a secondary market where I remained for three years before being promoted to my current job.

Miller Brewing Company sells its products through a network of over 800 distributors. These independent businesses, in turn, serve the retail outlets where beer is purchased. As Area Manager for a primary market, I am the company's representative to the distributors and am responsible for ensuring that their operations conform to our policies and procedures. This entails explaining company marketing and sales programs and providing guidance on effective means of implementing these programs. I work continuously with the distributors to develop local advertising, merchandising, and promotional campaigns, and call on retailers to advise the distributors of problems and opportunities. In addition I monitor market conditions and their relationship to sales and inventory levels.

Miller's number two position in the brewing industry, together with its innovative marketing program, make it an exciting company to belong to.

SECTION 5

Accounting, Computers, and Information Management

This section introduces you to two funda-mental tools for managing business information. One is very old and the other is very new. Chapter 12 describes the role of accounting—a very old tool of business—in making information avail-able and useful to managers, creditors, and in-vestors. The principal emphasis is on financial accounting and preparing and interpreting a firm's financial statements.

Section 5 also presents an overview of computers—the dynamic new partner of ac-counting in managing information for decision making. In Chapter 13 we will discuss computer-related concepts, major uses of computers by business, and some of the problems encountered in introducing computers to a firm's operations. Basic concepts of hardware and software are explained.

This section is closely related to the next in that it sets the stage for understanding financial management and the many institutions related to today's world of finance.

CHAPTER 12

Accounting

OBJECTIVES:

After reading this chapter, you should be able to

1. Distinguish between financial and managerial accounting processes.
2. Identify the three principal tasks of accounting.
3. Describe what a CPA does.
4. Prepare a chart showing the major information flows of accounting.
5. Explain the relationship between transactions and accounts.
6. Complete both of the principal accounting equations.
7. Draw up a simple example of the two principal financial statements.
8. Explain the purpose of the two principal financial statements.
9. Demonstrate how an investor might use the statements of a firm he or she may wish to invest in.
10. Explain and use at least one of the "key" ratios.
11. Illustrate the managerial accounting concepts of budgeting and cost accounting.

KEY CONCEPTS:
Look for these terms as you read the chapter

accounting

financial accounting

managerial accounting

Certified Public Accountant (CPA)

account

asset

equity

liability

owners' equity

revenue

expense

transaction

basic accounting equations

net profit

balance sheet

current asset

fixed asset

depreciation

current liability

accrued expense

income statement

gross profit

key ratio

current ratio

budget

sales forecast

responsibility accounting

product cost accounting

Mobil Corporation has been looking for a large corporation to buy. It lost out on its recent bids for Conoco and Marathon Oil. Mobil's lawyers and accountants carefully examined the accounting statements of these giants before offering to buy them. The purchase had to be examined in terms of its effect on the liquid assets of the combined firms and on the corporate income tax liability of the firms. They asked themselves questions about the value of Conoco's and Marathon's oil and gas leases and about the revenues that might come from their current exploration and drilling activities. They also examined these firms' financial records to determine which parts of these firms were efficient and which were not. They looked for other features of the buildings and operations of these corporations that might affect Mobil's tax burden and antitrust status.

In this chapter, we will find out what accounting is all about. We will illustrate the reasons that firms need accounting. The traditional financial accounting records and statements will be explained as will the managerial accounting tools—budgeting and cost accounting. By the time you have studied this chapter you should know why Mobil Corporation lawyers and accountants depended so heavily on accounting records in deciding which firms to bid on and how much to bid.

WHAT IS ACCOUNTING?

accounting

Accounting has been defined in many ways. We will define it as a process of recording, gathering, manipulating, auditing, and interpreting information that describes the assets and operation of a firm and aids in decision making.

This process is guided by certain widely accepted principles and rules. These principles are especially important when a manager must reach people outside of the firm. They play a smaller role when accounting is for internal use. We call the internal processes *managerial accounting* and the external process *financial accounting*. Both financial and managerial accounting are useful to managers.

financial accounting

Financial accounting helps the manager to "keep score" for the firm. It watches the flow of resources and lets those who have an interest in them know where they stand.

managerial accounting

Managerial accounting calls attention to problems and the need for action. It also aids in planning and decision making. It is aimed more at *control* and less at *valuation* than financial accounting. It is also less traditional.

Like any tool, accounting must be designed to do its various jobs (scorekeeping, calling attention, and helping in decision making) quickly and at a fair cost. The accounting system must provide clear and efficient estimates of financial facts. What it produces must be, above all, *relevant*. Accounting is relevant when it is useful to managers, creditors, investors, or government agencies in doing their jobs. Accounting is a much broader activity than simple bookkeeping. Bookkeeping is simply the mechanics of accounting—the recording of financial data.

What Is an Accountant?

An accountant is much more than a person who keeps the books. Accountants know basic procedures for recording transactions quickly, accurately, and with maximum security. They know enough about the law to build a system of accounts that reflects those laws, especially tax laws. They know where to find specialized information about laws and the answers to other tough questions, especially as they relate to the firm they serve. For example, an accountant for the International Paper Company might keep a library relating to land valuation and the use of natural resources. He or she must also be aware of the history and policies of the firm.

Certified Public Accountants (CPAs) are accountants who have fulfilled the legal requirements of their states for knowledge in accounting theory, practice, auditing, and law and who are licensed to sign legally required financial reports. Often their knowledge must be quite broad because they deal with the accounting processes of many different firms. Their duty to report the financial positions of firms extends to the general public as well as to the firm that hires them. Much of the independent CPA's work is classified as auditing (checking the accuracy of records). Some accountants serve a government directly and develop a much more specialized skill in reporting and checking the spending of public funds. Careers in accounting, then, are usually classified as in private, public, or governmental accounting.

Certified Public Accountant (CPA)

In the last three decades the process of increasing specialization in the accounting profession has been made evident by the introduction of the following financial certification programs:

- CDP or Certificate in Data Processing
- CFA or Chartered Financial Analyst
- CBA or Chartered Bank Auditor
- CMA or Certificate in Management Accounting
- CIA or Certified Internal Auditor

In the ad on the following page, one of the major accounting firms describes what it has to offer to prospective clients. Although the language of the ad may be somewhat sophisticated for you at this point, after you have completed this chapter, it should make a lot of sense to you. To understand some of the more technical terms used by Deloitte Haskins & Sells it might be helpful to discuss the ad with your instructor or with a CPA of your acquaintance. This will help you to decide whether a career in accounting is something that might interest you.

Accounting to Whom and for What?

Accounting traces a sequence of information flows. Figure 12-1 indicates something about who is "accounted to." Employees at the operating level use accounting to "account to" managers (A) who

An ad describing the range of information services a large public accounting firm offers its clients

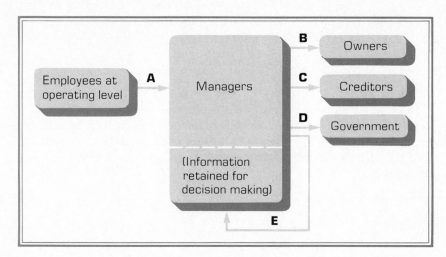

FIGURE 12-1

The flow of accounting
information

must use accounting to "account to" owners (B). The firm's managers must also "account to" creditors and future creditors (C) and to government agencies (D).

The flow of information is quite varied—and some of the bits of information reaching managers do not go any further, but are retained for internal purposes (E). Much of the same information is contained in flows, B, C, D, and E, although it takes different forms and emphasizes different kinds of facts, depending on who is to read it. Firms have many uses of their own for this information, as we will see when we discuss managerial accounting.

What are "accounted for" are the firm's resources, expressed in dollars and cents (usually cost) terms. In some cases units other than money are accounted for, but the units are usually money. Non-monetary units, such as products made in a factory or coupons received by a retailer are related to managerial accounting. First, we will consider financial accounting.

FINANCIAL ACCOUNTING

Financial accounting is an old and traditional practice designed to "keep tabs" on what a firm owns and to protect its owners' property rights. It also has many built-in safeguards for outsiders who want to know about the firm's financial condition. Financial accounting is a scorekeeping process.

Financial accounting is a general system because it includes the entire firm (or entity). Managerial accounting, on the other hand, usually focuses on one activity within the firm. We will discuss this in a later section of this chapter.

Transactions and Accounts

account

A basic idea in accounting is that of an account. This is a register of financial value. The set of accounts kept by a firm represents all those separate classes of values, both positive and negative, and the changes in value that occur. There are four principal kinds of accounts:

- asset
- equity
- revenue
- expense

asset

An asset is something of a positive dollar value to a firm. Asset values are registered in asset accounts. Usually a firm keeps a large number of asset accounts. Examples are Land, Cash, and Accounts Receivable (money owed to the firm by customers).

equity

An equity account is a register of claims or rights of different groups to a firm's assets. These include the claims of outsiders and the claims of owners. The sum of all equity accounts, as we shall see, always equals the sum of all asset accounts.

liability

The claims of outsiders are called a firm's liabilities. An example of such an account is Notes Payable, which shows what a firm owes in the form of promises or orders to pay. Another example is

"I can explain my excessive and unexplainable deductions. When I made out the return, I was at the lowest point in my biorythm chart."

the account designated Wages Payable, which indicates how much pay is due to the firm's employees.

The claims of insiders, or owners, are kept in owners' equity or capital accounts. Examples of these are Retained Earnings and Common Stock. Retained Earnings represents additions to the owners' equity attributable to profits.

owners' equity

A revenue account is a register of gross earnings or inflows of value to a firm during a given time period. The most important revenue account is Sales. It includes the total selling price of all goods or services sold during a given time period.

revenue

Expense accounts are measures of the using up of resources in the normal course of business in a given time period. Typical examples are Wages Paid, Utilities Paid, Rent Paid, Interest Expense, and Supplies Used. Expenses are deducted from revenues to calculate profit or loss.

expense

AUTHORS' COMMENTARY

Inflation Will Require Major Changes in Accounting

The method most firms traditionally use to value inventories of raw materials or component parts or goods purchased for resale is known as FIFO (first in-first out). This means, for example, that if a new shipment of 1,000 units of steel plate costing $20 per unit is received by a fabricator who already has 500 units in stock costing $15 per unit, the fabricator will charge out all of the $15 units to the production cost of finished products before charging any of the $20 units.

LIFO (last in-first out) works the opposite way, so that the fabricator would charge the more recently purchased units to production costs first. In this period of rapid inflation there has been a shift from FIFO to LIFO among American firms. This has the effect of increasing costs of production and reducing profit (and income tax) as reported by the firm. There has been no real loss in such a case, but rather an indefinite postponement of profit-reporting and of the accompanying income tax.

Should substantial inflation continue to plague our business environment, the acceptance of LIFO inventory valuation and other methods which distort reported results could make much traditional financial accounting meaningless. The profession is already taking steps to require firms to account for inflation in such a way as to portray a true financial picture to all interested parties.

It is likely that many accepted accounting reporting practices, especially those relating to inventory valuation, will be revised unless inflation is controlled.

transaction

The term *transaction* is used to describe any change in an asset or an equity. If we buy raw material for cash, we must reduce the Cash account balance and increase the Raw Material account balance. If the firm sells an order of merchandise on credit, it must increase the Sales Revenue account and the Accounts Receivable account by the amount of the sale.

For a better idea about how the basic types of accounts are related, we will study some basic accounting equations that underlie the financial statements.

Important Accounting Equations

An equation represents the fact that two expressions are equal. One expression is placed on the left side of the equal sign, and the other expression is placed on the right. For example, $12 + 4 = 16$. **Basic accounting equations are equations that explain the basic system of relationships in financial accounting.**

basic accounting
equations

The first basic accounting equation represents the fact that the sum of the assets equals the sum of the equities (claims on assets) and that these equities include liabilities and owners' equity. This basic accounting equation, then, is

$$\text{Assets} = \text{Liabilities} + \text{Owners' Equity}$$

or

$$\text{Assets} = \text{Equities}$$

If one side of the equation (assets) is increased or reduced, then the other side must be increased or reduced by exactly the same amount, just as in algebra. Some transactions, of course, affect only two individual assets or only two equity accounts. They do not affect the totals on either side of the equation, as in our earlier example concerning the cash purchase of raw materials.

A second equation reflects current operations. It is as follows:

$$\text{Revenues} - \text{Expenses} = \text{Net Profit}$$

net profit

Current revenue minus the expenses incurred in gaining that revenue equals *net profit*. Net profit measures the success of the firm's current operations during the period. When expenses exceed revenues, there is a net loss for the period. Net profit is also an index of the change in the owner's equity that occurs during the period. The capital account, Retained Earnings, is increased by profitable operations and reduced by payments to owners. Net profit is added to or net loss is deducted from retained earnings. The basic equations are illustrated in Figure 12-2.

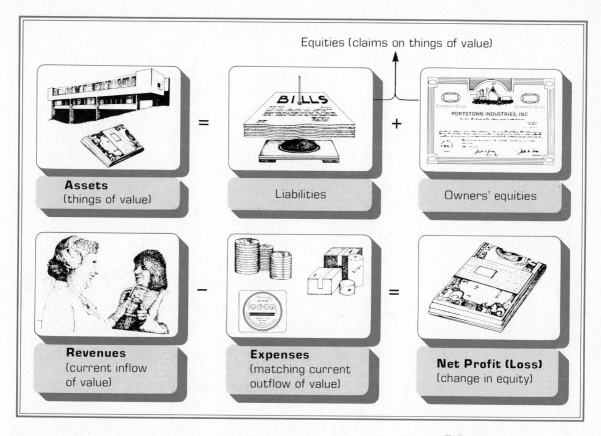

Equities (claims on things of value)

Assets (things of value)	= Liabilities	+ Owners' equities

Revenues (current inflow of value)	− **Expenses** (matching current outflow of value)	= **Net Profit (Loss)** (change in equity)

FIGURE 12-2

Two basic equations that sum up financial accounting

FINANCIAL STATEMENTS

You have probably seen financial statements in a newspaper or in a firm's annual report. Two of them, the balance sheet and the income statement, have been widely used for more than a century. These statements are useful for managers, investors, and creditors. They are central to financial accounting.

The Balance Sheet

A business is a living, functioning entity. **A balance sheet (also known as a statement of financial position) presents a financial picture of a firm at one point in time.** Family albums filled with snapshots of children as they grow represent a record of that growth for their parents. A file of x rays kept by a doctor records the progress a fractured bone makes in healing. Likewise, a set of balance sheets

balance sheet

Current assets:			Current liabilities:		
Cash	$ 6,000		Accounts payable	$10,000	
Accounts receivable	18,000		Accrued expenses payable	1,000	
Merchandise inventories	10,000		Estimated tax liability	7,000	
Prepaid expenses	2,000		Total current liabilities		$18,000
Total current assets		$36,000			
Fixed assets:			Other liabilities		
Land		4,000	Bonds payable		10,000
Building	$ 8,000		Owners' equity:		
Less depreciation	4,000	4,000	Common stock	$25,000	
			Retained earnings	1,000	26,000
Other assets:					
Goodwill		10,000			
Total assets		$54,000	Total equities		$54,000

FIGURE 12-3

Gloria's Dress Shop,
Inc. Balance Sheet
(December 31, 19*3)

drawn at the end of each year, over a period of years, depicts the rate
of growth and nature of the growth of that firm.

Figure 12-3 is a balance sheet for Gloria's Dress Shop as of
December 31, 19*3. This is a more detailed way of expressing the
first basic accounting equation: Assets = Equities. The firm's assets
are divided into three major classes: current assets, fixed assets, and
other assets.

Current Assets

current asset

**A current asset is one that the firm normally expects to hold no
longer than a year.** Examples are *cash* (currency and checking account), accounts receivable, merchandise inventories, and prepaid
expenses. *Accounts receivable* are amounts owed to the firm from
its normal operations. In this case, they are amounts owed by customers for dresses purchased from the firm recently. As of December
31, 19*3, 43 different customers owed the firm the total sum of
$18,000 "on account."

Merchandise inventory consists of all goods purchased for resale but not yet sold. Most retailers must take an inventory of stock
at the end of the year to determine the value of their goods for
balance sheet purposes. At the end of the year, Gloria's counted
$10,000 worth of goods for sale.

Prepaid expenses might include prepaid insurance premiums
which have not yet been used by the firm. Gloria's purchased a fire
insurance policy on July 1, 19*3, and the premiums were paid one

year in advance. Thus the firm now owns something of value—that is, a prepaid insurance policy, only half of which has been "used."

Two current assets not shown in Figure 12-3 are *marketable securities* and *notes receivable*. The former are short-term investments a firm holds, such as stocks and bonds of other firms and government bonds. The latter represent short-term loans to customers or others.

Fixed Assets

A fixed asset is a tangible resource that is expected to remain useful for more than a year. Such an asset is valued at its cost to the firm. When a firm buys a building, it is listed among the firm's fixed asset accounts at a value equal to its purchase price.

fixed asset

As an asset loses value, it suffers depreciation. This loss of value is charged off as an expense and the stated value of the fixed asset is reduced on the balance sheet. In Figure 12-3 $4,000 has been deducted from the value of the building because of depreciation. This means that this fixed asset is "half used up."

depreciation

There are many acceptable methods of figuring depreciation in traditional accounting. The simplest is called *straight line depreciation*. It provides for charging equal parts of the original cost of an asset in each year of its expected life. Thus Gloria's firm is using straight line depreciation on the building which was purchased four years before the date of the balance sheet. This building, the only *depreciable* asset Gloria has, will be fully depreciated four years after the date of this balance sheet.

One other general class of assets is included in Figure 12-3. It is an intangible asset known as *goodwill*, which results from years of good business reputation. According to accepted accounting principles, goodwill is assigned a dollar value only when it is bought by the firm. In other words, when the corporation bought the assets of the previous sole proprietorship, it was estimated that the corporation paid $10,000 more than the tangible net worth of the proprietorship (the difference between the value of tangible assets and the liabilities).

Current Liabilities

Under the liabilities section of Figure 12-3, the current liabilities total $18,000. This figure includes the $10,000 due to suppliers, $1,000 of accrued expenses, and $7,000 in estimated taxes owed. **These are current liabilities because they will be paid off within a year.**

current liability

Accrual is a major accounting principle. Expenses are charged against revenue in the period in which the firm benefits from them. An accrued expense is used up but not paid for yet. Gloria's accrued

accrued expense

expenses are the result of some work performed by several sales-clerks during the Christmas season who had not yet been paid as of the end of the year.

Long-term Liability and Owners' Equity

Gloria's owes bondholders $10,000. This is a long-term liability because it won't be paid off within a year. Owners' equity is listed at $26,000 including the original "stated value" of the stock when it was issued and $1,000 in retained earnings (earnings of previous years which have been put back into the firm). Together these add up to what the owners' claims on assets are—*owners' equity*. If the firm were still a proprietorship, the owners' equity would simply be listed on the balance sheet as "Gloria Smith, Capital." The owners' equity, then, is the owners' claim against the firm's resources.

In any case, the sum of the equities is always equal to the sum of the assets. The basic accounting equation always holds. The $54,000 in current, fixed, and other assets have claims upon them (equities) in the amounts of $18,000 (current liabilities), $10,000 (bondholders), and $26,000 (owners).

The Income Statement

The balance sheet, or statement of financial position, shows a "cross section" of a firm's resources and equities at one point in

FIGURE 12-4

Gloria's Dress Shop, Inc. Income Statement (year ending December 31, 19*4)

Net sales	$267,000	(100.0%)
Less cost of goods sold	152,000	(56.9%)
Gross profit	$115,000	(43.1%)
Less expenses:		
Wages and salaries paid	$68,200 (25.5%)	
General and administrative expenses	38,000 (14.2%)	
Interest expenses	1,500 (0.6%) 107,700	(40.4%)
Net profit before taxes	$ 7,300	(2.7%)
Taxes (paid and accrued)	2,000	(0.7%)
Net profit after taxes	$ 5,300	(2.0%)

time. **The income statement, on the other hand, shows what actu-** income statement
ally happened over a period of time to explain some of the differences
between successive balance sheets. It summarizes the revenue and
expense accounts, just as the balance sheet summarizes the asset
and equity accounts. Figure 12-4 illustrates Gloria's income statement for the period ending December 31, 19*4, one year after the
statement in Figure 12-3.

Revenues

Gloria's sold $267,000 worth of dresses this year. The selling price of
the dresses is used in this valuation rather than the original cost.
Sales are *net* because any discounts or returns and allowances
granted to customers have been subtracted from the gross sales.

From net sales is deducted the actual cost of goods sold. The
cost of goods sold is calculated as follows. First, a physical inventory
of goods in stock at the end of the year is taken. The cost of these
goods is then subtracted from the sum of the cost values of (a) the
inventory a year earlier and (b) purchases made during the year.
Gloria's had $10,000 in inventory at the beginning of the year,
bought $180,000 more during the year, and had $38,000 remaining
when the closing inventory was taken ($10,000 + $180,000 −
$38,000 = $152,000).

Expenses

The difference between net sales and cost of goods sold is gross gross profit
profit. Figure 12-4 shows a few expense accounts, including wages
and salaries, general and administrative expenses, and interest
expenses. Wages and salaries include Gloria's salary, wages of a
bookkeeper and a janitor, and wages and commissions paid to salespersons. General and Administrative Expense includes depreciation,
office expenses, utilities, and insurance. Interest Expense includes
interest paid to the Second National Bank for a loan made and repaid
during the year. The difference between gross profit and expenses is
$7,300—Net Profit Before Taxes. From this amount taxes paid or
accrued are deducted in the amount of $2,000. Notice the taxes that
apply to this year's operations—whether paid or not—are rightfully
deducted from this year's revenue. This is another example of the
principle of accrual. Net profit after taxes is $5,300, or 2 percent of
sales. Of this, the board of directors can allocate a part to dividends,
and the rest goes to owners' equity as retained earnings.

The usefulness of the income statement, especially for internal
purposes, is increased when it includes a "percentage of net sales"
column as does Figure 12-4. This feature makes the income state-

ment easier to compare to those of earlier years, to those of other firms, and to industry averages.

Financial Accounting—Users and Uses

Before we begin a discussion of key ratios, we will describe two specific cases tying in accounting processes and their use. These examples will show how financial accounting serves the interests of investors as well as credit users and givers. We will start with the case of Dr. William Franklin.

William Franklin is a retired doctor who has invested a large part of his savings in the common stock of the Marshall Corporation, a producer of steel tubing. He owns 2,000 shares, which represent about three percent of Marshall's outstanding stock. Dr. Franklin is interested in getting a reasonable return on his investment in the form of common stock dividends.

This investor does not know any of the corporation's officers or managers personally, and he lives in a town in which none of the firm's plants is located. He needs information, so he must rely on the firm's financial statements to judge the quality of his investment.

Let's review how these statements came to be. Dr. Franklin could not have made a wise decision about his investment if someone (probably Marshall's treasurer or comptroller) had not set up an information collecting, processing, and reporting system (see Figure 12-5) that did the following things:

- retained facts about financially significant events on a variety of source documents
- classified these into accounts
- summarized accounts in financial statements
- distributed statements to stockholders

First, the firm's operations were scanned to identify financially significant events (those having a bearing on the firm's profit), and these were entered on some kind of source document. For example, when the office manager bought an order of stationery, he or she signed a purchase order describing the items to be purchased and the amount to be spent. The purchase order, or perhaps a copy of the

FIGURE 12-5

How the Marshall Corporation generated its financial statements

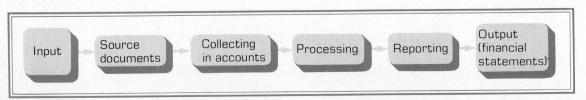

invoice (list of items shipped) made out by the stationery store, is a source document for the purchase event.

The second step involved recording the dollar amount and the nature of the event in some form of register (account) set up in advance by the comptroller. This is the classifying function. The basic facts found in the purchase order were entered into the firm's computer and stored for later use.

At the end of the quarter, Marshall's accounting department took all the stored bits of data, such as the stationery purchase record, and processed them. The department also added up all company expenditures by type and constructed Marshall's quarterly financial statements.

The reporting function has also been fulfilled. The statements, first printed by the firm's computer, were checked by the accounting staff and published for distribution to stockholders. This is how Dr. Franklin got the financial statement he needed to evaluate his investment. He can calculate earnings per share (total profit divided by the number of outstanding shares of common stock) and other financial ratios from these statements. He can, of course, get similar earnings-per-share and dividend data about other firms from his stockbroker.

Financial accounting can also help make credit decisions. Suppose Hydraspace Company wishes to sign a long-term contract with the Marshall Company that will make Hydraspace the supplier of an

Should Auditors be Responsible for Uncovering Fraud?

WHAT DO YOU THINK?

Auditors are responsible for checking to see if a client has followed accepted accounting principles in reporting its results of operations. Recent discovery of fraud in the financial reporting of major firms has led to some serious questioning by the Congress, by regulatory agencies, and even by the accounting profession itself of the adequacy of present auditing practices. The possibility of suing auditing firms for not uncovering fraud has also been raised.

A large CPA firm, Peat, Marwick, Mitchell & Co., has pointed out that traditional auditing practices are not enough to detect management fraud in world-wide businesses tied together by computer. New tools quite different from ordinary auditing are needed. Some believe lawyers should accompany CPAs; others recommend that auditors should automatically "blow the whistle" to government when suspicions arise instead of bringing discoveries to the firm's management. Should auditors be responsible for uncovering fraud? WHAT DO YOU THINK?

important part for Marshall's major product. It's important for Hydraspace to know about Marshall's financial condition so that it can be sure that Marshall can pay on time. Hydraspace will use a number of sources of information for this purpose. They will depend a lot on Marshall's past financial statements, especially those statements that indicate Marshall's ability to pay its current bills.

Marshall's accounting system should be able to provide a summary of its past payment behavior if the firm wishes to give this information to Hydraspace. In practice, this kind of information is accumulated by independent credit reporting services, such as Dun & Bradstreet, and sold to their customers.

Once the contract is negotiated and the first shipment of parts has been made, Hydraspace becomes a trade creditor of Marshall. For further insight about how a creditor might interpret financial statements, we now turn to the subject of ratio analysis.

Important Financial Ratios

The numbers on the financial statements take on more meaning when they are related to each other. For instance, the net profit of a firm is more meaningful when it is mathematically related to that firm's sales or to the owners' equity. Such relationships are usually expressed as financial ratios or "key" ratios.

key ratio

A key ratio is a value obtained by dividing one value on a financial statement by another value. A particular firm's financial condition can be judged by comparing several important key ratios of items from its financial statements to typical key ratios of similar types of firms. Dun & Bradstreet publishes typical key ratios for a variety of types of firms. Such typical ratios are presented in Table 12-1 on page 360.

Let's look at several of these ratios and see how Gloria's Dress Shop compares with other women's ready-to-wear stores as reported by Dun & Bradstreet. First, let's look at a ratio that measures overall performance—return on net worth—which is net profit divided by owners' equity.

From Figure 12-6 we see that Gloria's net worth (owners' equity) equals $71,300. From Figure 12-4 we see that net profit after taxes is $5,300. The ratio, then, is $\frac{5,300}{71,300} = .0743$ or 7.43 percent.

Now, turn to the typical ratio of net profit to net worth in women's ready-to-wear stores as found in Table 12-1 on page 360. The last item in the table pertains to women's ready-to-wear stores. The circled figure in the last column represents the median (typical) return on net worth for such stores in that year as reported by Dun

Current assets:			Current liabilities:		
Cash	$17,000		Accounts payable	$10,700	
Accounts receivable	22,000		Accrued expenses payable	1,000	
Merchandise inventories	38,000		Estimated tax liability	1,000	
Total current assets		$77,000	Total current liabilities		$12,700
Fixed assets:			Other liabilities:		
Land		4,000	Bonds payable		10,000
Building	$ 8,000				
Less depreciation	5,000	3,000			
Other assets:			Owners' equity:		
Goodwill		10,000	Common stock	$69,000	
			Retained earnings	2,300	71,300
Total assets:		$94,000	Total equities		$94,000

FIGURE 12-6

Gloria's Dress Shop, Inc. Balance Sheet (December 31, 19*4)

& Bradstreet. Gloria's ratio is somewhat below average (7.43 percent versus 10.1 percent). This suggests that Gloria's is somewhat less profitable than the average store of its type.

Gloria's will compute this ratio and others each year to measure its financial strength. Banks or investors will compute such ratios to see whether they should lend money to Gloria's when the firm requests it. Let's look at some other ratios which measure specific things about a firm.

A short-term key credit ratio which is widely used is the current ratio. It is computed by dividing current assets by current liabilities. The result indicates how easily current debt could be paid off with current assets. On December 31, 19*4 (Figure 12-6) Gloria's current ratio was $\frac{77,000}{12,700} = 6.06$. This is excellent and it means that Gloria's is quite solvent; it can easily pay off the current debt. Compare this ratio to the typical one in the second column (circled) of Table 12-1. The average women's ready-to-wear store had a current ratio of only 3.4.

<u>current ratio</u>

The sales-to-inventory ratio can be used to point out problems related to product design, performance by the salesforce, and buying policies. Gloria's sales-to-inventory ratio is computed from Figures 12-3, 12-4, and 12-6:

$$\frac{\$267,000 \text{ (sales)}}{\frac{1}{2} (\$10,000 + \$38,000) \text{ (average inventory)}} = \frac{267}{24} = 11.1$$

TABLE 12-1
Selected Dun & Bradstreet key ratios—retailing.

Line of Business (and number of concerns reporting)	Quick Ratio	Current Ratio	Current liabilities to net worth	Current liabilities to inventory	Total liabilities to net worth	Fixed assets to net worth	Collection period	Net sales to inventory	Total assets to net sales	Net sales to net working capital	Accounts payable to net sales	Return on net sales	Return on total assets	Return on net worth
	Times	Times	Percent	Percent	Percent	Percent	Days	Times	Percent	Times	Percent	Percent	Percent	Percent
5251 Hardware Stores (109)	2.8	8.4	9.7	19.6	14.3	6.5	—	5.7	39.6	5.0	2.7	7.6	11.6	17.2
	1.4	5.1	20.5	30.6	38.0	16.6	—	4.0	54.0	3.2	4.8	4.2	7.5	12.0
	0.6	2.7	45.2	54.2	82.6	34.4	—	2.6	67.9	2.3	6.7	2.0	4.8	7.2
5311 Department Stores (102)	2.2	5.1	20.0	34.4	33.3	8.3	—	6.9	35.7	7.9	1.8	5.7	11.8	21.4
	1.0	3.1	45.0	60.3	61.5	20.6	—	4.7	44.4	4.6	4.3	2.6	5.9	11.2
	0.5	2.1	79.5	87.7	137.0	48.3	—	3.8	59.6	3.0	6.4	1.0	2.9	5.0
5411 Grocery Stores (105)	1.3	3.9	21.0	44.7	27.9	33.5	—	25.8	12.6	31.0	1.3	3.6	15.1	20.6
	0.7	2.3	36.1	73.9	61.4	55.2	—	17.7	16.8	18.0	2.1	1.8	8.8	17.6
	0.4	1.5	84.6	116.9	124.0	99.9	—	12.4	25.3	10.2	3.5	1.0	6.1	10.7
5531 Auto & Home Supply Stores (105)	2.5	7.2	12.7	22.1	25.7	13.1	—	7.9	35.2	8.6	3.0	8.7	11.2	21.5
	1.4	3.1	33.6	55.7	57.2	28.4	—	4.9	49.1	4.4	5.9	4.9	4.6	10.7
	0.6	1.9	102.6	93.7	123.1	49.1	—	3.6	82.1	2.2	10.5	1.3	1.8	3.6
5611 Men's & Boys' Clothing & Furnishing Stores (105)	2.5	11.4	7.0	15.7	8.6	5.4	—	5.6	49.6	5.4	3.1	15.6	14.0	24.9
	1.1	4.8	20.3	38.7	30.7	19.7	—	3.4	67.4	2.6	5.3	7.1	6.6	8.1
	0.3	2.2	61.0	73.1	93.3	58.3	—	2.2	120.4	1.8	10.9	1.6	2.7	3.5
5621 Women's Ready-to-Wear Stores (105)	2.3	6.0	7.3	30.9	15.2	11.4	—	7.8	40.5	6.3	3.3	11.2	11.5	17.9
	1.2	(3.4)	25.5	60.6	32.9	25.8	—	(5.0)	69.0	3.7	5.2	5.2	6.4	(10.1)
	0.6	2.1	58.2	95.7	74.0	48.0	—	3.5	135.8	2.0	8.2	1.4	2.4	3.6

TABLE 12-1 (continued)
Interpreting the ratios

In the various ratio tables three figures appear under each ratio heading. The center figure is the **median:** the figures immediately above and below the median are, respectively, the **upper** and **lower quartiles.** To understand their use, the reader should also know how they are calculated.

First, year-end financial statements almost exclusively from corporations with a tangible net worth of over $100,000 are drawn from Dun & Bradstreet's computerized financial-statement file and categorized by their primary industry or line of business. Then each of the fourteen ratios is calculated individually for every concern in the statement file.

These individual ratio figures are then arranged in order of size— the best ratio at the top, the weakest at the bottom—within each size group. The figure that falls in the middle of this series becomes the *median* for that ratio in that line of business. The figure halfway between the median and the top of the series is the *upper quartile;* the number halfway between the median and the bottom of the series is the *lower quartile.*

In a statistical sense, each median is the *typical ratio figure* for all concerns in a given category. The upper and lower quartile figures typify the experience of firms in the top and bottom halves of the sample, respectively.

Upper quartile figures are not always the highest numerical value, nor are lower quartile figures always the lowest numerical value. The quartile listings reflect *judgemental ranking,* thus the upper quartile represents the best condition in any given ratio and is not necessarily the highest numerical value.

The fourteen Key Business Ratios are categorized into three major groups

Solvency, or liquidity, measurements are significant in evaluating a company's ability to meet short- and long-term obligations. These figures are of prime interest to credit managers of commercial companies and financial institutions.

Efficiency ratios indicate how effectively a company uses and controls its assets. This is crucial information for evaluating how a company is managed. Studying these ratios is useful for credit, marketing and investment purposes.

Profitability ratios show how successfully a business is earning a return to its owners. Those interested in mergers and acquisitions consider this key data for selecting candidates.

This is better than the average ratio of 5.0 shown in column 8 of Table 12-1.

Dun & Bradstreet has been a pioneer in the development and analysis of key ratios. For many years it has published "industry average" ratios for many kinds of firms. This provides benchmarks by which the financial status of similar firms may be evaluated.

An overview of modern accounting must also include discussion of some of the internal management tools. Although financial accounting helps, a good manager needs some managerial accounting tools, too.

MANAGERIAL ACCOUNTING

Accountants gather and report the financial information that aids managers and investors in decision making

Managerial accounting provides information for a manager's own use. It helps management to plan, to measure and control performance, to set prices, and to analyze situations. The biggest difference between managerial and financial accounting is the lack of traditional rules and principles in managerial accounting. Management is free to make up its own systems.

Because managerial accounting practices are less rigid, different systems will be found in every firm. The idea is to keep any kind of record or summary of costs and revenues that managers need for planning or control purposes. They might want to evaluate other managers or to judge the success of new products or a new piece of equipment.

Such special accounting is needed because regular financial accounts aren't enough to measure the performance of departments or products or managers within the firm as a whole. They focus, rather, on overall firm profit.

If the Norton Sales Company wishes to evaluate the performance of its salesforce, it must maintain adequate records of the salesforce's activities. Suppose those records show that the average travel expenditure per salesperson has been 20.2 cents per month per square mile of sales territory. After analysis, the sales manager decides to adopt this average amount as a standard. Any salesperson whose expenses exceed the average would be checked out. This shows how accounting can be used to control selling costs.

Managerial accounting can be used to set minimum order sizes, to decide whether to shut down a production line, to help a manager allocate funds for growth among territories, or to set standards for entertaining customers. Such managerial accounting activities fall under one of two headings: budgeting or cost accounting.

Budgeting

By tradition, financial accounting is not expected to provide predictions of a firm's condition. Predicting is a risky business, but it must be done. Managers use special managerial accounting tools to help them make predictions. One such device is the budget.

A budget is a formal dollar-and-cents statement of expected performance. It is a means of (1) requiring managers to plan carefully for the future; (2) causing managers to examine present and past performance critically; and (3) helping to coordinate the plans made by different parts of the firm. A budget may be very specialized, or it may be general. It may be a short-term (one year or less) or a long-term budget.

budget

The marketing manager, for example, is expected to prepare an advertising budget for the coming year. In consultation with the advertising agency and the comptroller, the marketing manager will specify how the money he or she needs to accomplish advertising objectives will be spent. This includes the amount designated for each product to be marketed, the amounts earmarked for each advertising medium, and a month-by-month schedule for the year's spending.

POINT OF VIEW

Fluctuating Exchange Rates and Accounting for Foreign Subsidiaries

U.S.-based business firms operating abroad were obligated by a regulation set by the Financial Accounting Standards Board (FASB) to include any change in valuation of monetary assets arising from fluctuations in the exchange rate between the currency of the host nation and the dollar in the earnings from foreign subsidiaries. Thus the FASB—the accounting profession's rule-making organization—was, in effect, causing an exaggeration of the earnings of, for example, U.S. firms' British subsidiaries during the time that the value of the dollar increased in relation to the British pound.

Many U.S. firms operating abroad complained to the FASB that these distortions in earnings were misleading investors concerning the firms' true profitability picture. Late in 1981, the FASB reversed the earlier rule and permitted such gains or losses to be excluded from the income statement. Instead, they will be placed directly into stockholders' equity on the balance sheet.

This new rule represents a change in the FASB's point of view and, we hope, a change in the point of view of prospective investors in the multinational firms affected by the rule.

sales forecast

The sales forecast is the starting point for a general (master) budget. It predicts what sales will be over a certain period of time. This forecast depends on what effect the marketing manager thinks the planned changes in the marketing mix will have on sales. Sometimes the sales forecast is tied to a projection of Gross National Product or to industry sales forecasts. Larger firms, employing a staff of economists and computer facilities, often construct models to predict sales. Whether it be made by such a method or by a simple assumption of a 5 percent increase over the current year, the sales forecast is a keystone for planning.

Cost Accounting

Cost accounting includes responsibility accounting and product cost accounting. **Responsibility accounting involves setting up responsibility centers in a firm. These are used to classify cost information so as to evaluate the performance of various parts of the firm and their managers.** The costs of operating the shipping department, for example, may be collected in a shipping department responsibility center. Figure 12-7 shows how responsibility accounting works.

Suppose that a plant has set up responsibility centers to control its costs, and that one such center is the plant loading dock. The dock superintendent buys an insect fogger to reduce the problem of mosquitoes on the dock. The accounting system assigns this cost to the loading dock responsibility center. Company accounting policy classifies such an expenditure as *controllable* and further classifies it as a "miscellaneous operating expense." During the month this responsibility center incurs thirty-seven other cost items. Six of these were required by general company policy and so were deter-

responsibility
accounting

FIGURE 12-7

The responsibility
accounting process

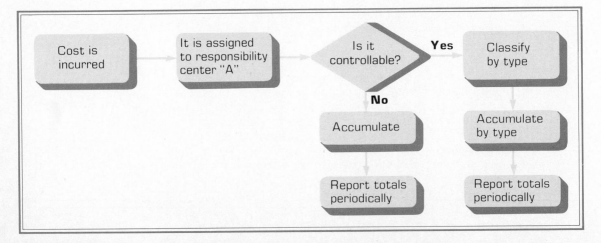

mined to be *uncontrollable* by this responsibility center. The other items, including purchase of paint for the dock floor and parts for the dock scale, are accumulated by type. The paint is classified as a maintenance expense and the scale parts as a mechanical repair cost. At the end of the month all controllable expenses are totaled by type and reported to the plant manager. The manager now has a monthly measure of the controllable costs incurred by this responsibility center. This helps the manager evaluate the dock's efficiency for the month.

Product cost accounting systems also use cost centers to allocate all costs to the various products made by a firm. This gives a firm a better idea about which products are profitable and which are not. Some firms use *standard* product cost accounting systems. Standard costs assigned in such a system are those that should have been incurred, not those actually incurred. Differences between actual and standard costs are called *variances* and are charged to *variance accounts*.

product cost accounting

MANUAL VERSUS COMPUTER-BASED ACCOUNTING SYSTEMS

For many years accounting activities were restricted in what they could do because they were manual. They started with a handwritten record of a transaction that was later copied by hand into a summary book of some kind for monthly or weekly tallying purposes.

Such simplified manual systems still exist in small businesses, but they are gradually being replaced by machine- or computer-based systems. Some of these systems depend on modern cash register equipment, and some depend on punched cards. Although every accounting system is a data processing system, we now restrict the use of the term *data processing* to machine- or computer-based systems.

A data processing system must do the following:

- select relevant data describing the business transaction and prepare a document containing such a description
- classify and store these input items in appropriate places and summarize them for future use
- convert such information into proper form for use by decision makers
- prepare reports, such as financial statements

A computer-based accounting system requires still another step to convert the source document to a form that can be handled by the system. In the typical case the original document is converted to machine-readable form and stored either in the computer's own memory, as punched cards, or on magnetic disk or tape. In Chapter 13 we will see how such computer storage makes it easier to classify, summarize, and report.

SUMMARY AND LOOK AHEAD

Accounting's task is threefold: (1) to "keep score" of the use of financial resources; (2) to draw attention to problems; and (3) to assist in decision making. Financial accounting does the first task and managerial accounting does the second and third.

Accounting principles guide managers in making and interpreting financial statements. Two principal financial statements represent the focus of the financial accounting process: (1) the balance sheet, and (2) the income statement. Key financial ratios are applied to values reported on the financial statements to help make comparisons of the performance of a single firm over time, or to make comparisons among firms in the same year.

Managerial accounting is internally oriented. Planning for financial (and other) resources can be greatly assisted by a variety of budgeting techniques. Cost accounting is another broad component of managerial accounting. It usually takes the form of responsibility accounting or product cost accounting. In either case, costs must be identified and assigned so as to improve internal managerial control of operations.

What we have learned about financial and managerial accounting also helps to explain the need for computers in business. This is the subject of our next chapter. With a basic knowledge of accounting and computers we will be able to proceed with the next section of the text—financial management.

FOR REVIEW . . .

1. What kinds of information are communicated by means of accounting? Give two examples.

2. To whom is the accounting process directed? What are its three principal tasks?

3. Must all accountants be CPAs? Discuss.

4. What are the basic accounting equations? Show how a change in one side must result in a change in the other.

5. What are the major classes of accounts on a balance sheet?

6. What is meant by the principle of accrual? Explain by giving an example involving rental expense.

7. Construct a simple budget of your own weekly expenses.

8. In what way could an accounting system help to control salespeople's entertainment expenses? Explain.

9. What is product cost accounting? What is a variance? How are these two concepts related?

10. What must a good data processing system do?

. . . FOR DISCUSSION

1. What do we mean when we say that financial accounting is relevant?

2. Is it possible for a transaction to occur without affecting the balance of any account?

3. What is the functional relationship between a balance sheet and an income statement?

4. What kind of business is Dun & Bradstreet in? Ask any manager what his or her relationship with this firm is, if any.

5. What is the relationship between managerial accounting and the management function of controlling as discussed in Chapter 4?

INCIDENTS

Carson's Hardware Store

The Williams family had inherited a large sum of money and was looking for a good investment. They were approached through a mutual friend by Samuel Carson, the owner-manager of Carson's Hardware Store concerning the purchase of a half-interest in the store. With the help of an accountant they examined Carson's audited financial statements and computed some of the key ratios. They discovered that the current ratio for the most recent full year of operation was 2.0 and that the return on net worth was 6 percent in that same year. Ratios for the two previous years were very similar.

Despite Carson's assurance that the stable ratios over the three years were evidence of consistent, stable management, the Williams family remained apprehensive.

QUESTIONS

1. How would you advise the Williams family regarding the proposed investment?

2. Is the fact that the statements were audited important to the Williams family? Why or why not?

3. How would you evaluate Carson's Hardware Store's credit standing? Which ratio measures this? What other information would you like to have?

Understanding Financial Reports

The following table contains some financial facts about the Armstrong Rubber Company that were reported in a feature story on this firm in *The New York Times*.[1] The amounts are in $1000s.

For the 3 months ended June 30:

	1981	1980
Revenues	144,900	95,400
Net Income (loss)	4,094	(1,390)

For the year ended December 31:

	1980	1979
Revenues	401,000	394,000
Net Income (loss)	(16,400)	8,500

On December 31, 1980, total assets were valued at $394 million and current assets, at $156 million. On that same date current liabilities were $61.5 million.

QUESTIONS

1. What was profit (loss) as a percent of revenues in the year 1979? In 1980? In the second quarter of 1981?

2. What was the current ratio for Armstrong on 12-31-80? How does it compare with that of Gloria's Dress Shop as shown in the text?

3. Are things improving for Armstrong as indicated by the most recent financial data given here? Explain.

CHAPTER 13

Computers and Basic Quantitative Tools

OBJECTIVES:

After reading this chapter, you should be able to

1. Describe one important way that a computer enters your life.
2. Give some examples of common business applications of computers.
3. Distinguish among automation, data processing, and word processing.
4. Draw a diagram of a computer system.
5. Recognize common input-output devices for computers.
6. Explain the function of software.
7. Explain the impact of microcomputers on business.
8. Contrast several ways that people react to computers.
9. Compute an arithmetic mean and median.
10. Prepare a breakeven chart.

KEY CONCEPTS:
Look for these terms as you read the chapter

computer

data processing

word processing system

computer program

hardware

central processing unit (CPU)

outside data storage systems

input-output (I-O) devices

modem

distributed data processing

software

time sharing

controllers

online real-time system

assembly language

machine language

FORTRAN

COBOL

BASIC

Pascal

Ada

documentation

quantitative tools

statistics

arithmetic mean

median

mode

frequency distribution

histogram

sample

breakeven analysis

operations research (OR)

linear programming

Some people call it the "paperless office of the future." With that goal in mind, big electronics firms like Texas Instruments, Inc. are developing strategies to capture a big piece of the market for desk-top computer terminals. Such terminals are used in many ways by more than two million white-collar workers in businesses all over the U.S. in a variety of industries. It has been predicted that this number will exceed 12 million by 1990. Today these terminals, hooked up with computer-stored data inside or outside the firm, are proving to be a mainstay of business communication. They may indeed lead to the "paperless office."

These terminals look like a typewriter with a TV screen attached and they are used by stockbrokers, airline reservation clerks, bank tellers, and typists. The latter, as we will see later in this chapter, are fast becoming known as word-processor operators. The terminals are often sold in combination with telephone-connection devices and are used to tie together widespread operations of large corporations.

Although the new terminals, selling for little more than the price of a top-quality electric typewriter, are mainly used to communicate with large centralized sets of information stored in distant computers, they have other uses, too. They can provide intercompany electronic mail service, routing and storing memos and messages electronically.

What we have just described is only one part of the dramatic story of the arrival of the computer age in the business arena. This chapter will explain the basic concepts related to business use of computer systems. We will discuss the components of such a system and the many uses to which they are put. We will also introduce some mathematical tools which, with accounting systems and computers, make up a powerful array of tools for data gathering, analysis, and retrieval for business.

WHAT IS A COMPUTER?

computer

A computer or, more exactly, a computer system is an electronic machine capable of storing and retrieving huge amounts of data and performing mathematical calculations very quickly. It is also called an electronic data processing (EDP) system. Computers are an important part of many thousands of business firms and non-business organizations.

The Wide Range of Computer Applications

Computers play a big role in your everyday life. Stop and think about it! They do some of the little everyday things like figuring your bank balance or the size of your family's bill at J. C. Penney. A computer might even prepare your quarter or semester grade report. Computers do thousands of repetitive operations like these. They perform very efficiently for a big institution like a corporation or a university. They store a huge mass of information and make thousands of routine calculations. They allow large or small firms to communicate with all their customers, employees, or suppliers quickly and accurately.

Firms and people at home are finding all kinds of new uses for small computers. Income tax preparers are using them to figure out and print income tax returns. Garages and service stations are using specialized computers to find out what is wrong with your car. In fact, small special-purpose computers called *microprocessors* are being built into cars and appliances to improve their performance. High technology firms like United Technologies are pouring hundreds of millions of dollars into research for new ways to apply these electronic marvels. Perhaps at Christmas time you noticed the flood of electronic games. Each of these games is controlled by a special purpose computer. Special purpose computers even control those electronic video games you see in amusement centers and other public places.

AUTHORS' COMMENTARY

Two decades ago the idea that a six-mile footrace "for women only" would lure more than a handful of entrants was as far-fetched as the idea of a portable computer.

But wasn't that a Honeywell Level 6 minicomputer scoring Boston's fourth annual Bonne Belle 10-kilometer race last October?

In crowded races like the Bonne Belle, where over 5,000 lady runners crossed the finish line, a computer makes it possible to record times when there's a jam-up at the end. When the runners cross the line a time is noted and special codes on their running numbers are scanned like items at supermarket checkouts. The computer then matches times and order of finish to particular runners. The computer also provides a printout, within hours of the race, that breaks down results by age, level of experience, size, etc.

Scoring sports events may not seem a serious function, but it illustrates how the computer is invading every aspect of modern life. And Honeywell minis have been used to provide current scores and in-play standings at golf tournaments—surely a business application.[1]

As the figure suggests, computer applications to sports will multiply rapidly. Computers will be especially important in sports where precise timing, complex calculations, and scoring are necessary—in a hurry.

Computer Application to Sports Events

Suppose you use your VISA card to buy gas at a service station. The attendant uses it to print your account number before you sign the charge slip. This slip ends up being processed by a computer. The amount of your purchase is added to your VISA bill. Because of the great speed and accuracy of computers, thousands of transactions, like your gasoline purchase, can be quickly and accurately processed.

But a computer can do a lot more than routine data processing or controlling an electronic game. Think of its role in our space program! Without computers, space shuttle flights would have been impossible. In fact, much of the progress in science and technology has depended on computers. Computers touch your life in at least these two ways—as a go-between for large institutions and the people they deal with and as an instrument that speeds up technological and economic progress.

Common Business Applications

It is obvious from what we have seen in our earlier chapters about production, marketing, and accounting that much of the success or failure of a firm depends upon its ability to *collect, process, organize,* and *retrieve* information. The accounting department needs to collect data concerning transactions and periodically produce financial statements. The production department needs to keep records of inventories and costs of production and to estimate production schedules. Financial managers need to measure cash flows and construct capital budgets. All of these and many additional jobs in all but the smallest firms require the speed, accuracy, and data-handling capacity of the computer. A successful firm needs to be able to gather, store, combine, and use this mass of data at a cost which is lower than the benefit it brings. If a computer is well designed and well used, it can do this.

Businesses use computers to

- prepare payrolls
- analyze past-due accounts receivable
- prepare and mail out bills
- keep social security and tax records
- keep track of inventories
- simplify reordering of goods
- control production costs

There are thousands of other specific jobs a computer can do for a business. The previous chapter outlined some of the financial and

Wholesalers and distributors are being supplied with more accurate data.

NCR computers are making it happen.

Wholesaling and distribution demand constant attention to details. There are physical details like inventory counts, sizes and quantities, stock levels, and item locations. Order and accounting details like markups, discounts, and pricing exceptions. And, of course, "bottom-line" details like item, class, and salesperson profitability. The list is practically endless, and as a company becomes more successful and diversified, it only gets longer.

That's why more and more wholesalers and distributors of every size are turning to NCR systems for help. These systems provide all the benefits of real-time information processing at a readily affordable cost. They automate order processing, inventory control, purchasing, sales reporting and accounting to create a single, integrated package of management tools. And they make critical operating data accessible wherever and whenever it's needed. Data

that can often mean the difference between marginal operation and real profitability. Thanks to innovative NCR technology, the cost-per-day of operating these systems is surprisingly low.

Wholesalers and distributors aren't the only ones turning to NCR computer systems for help in these inflationary times. Executives in major industries around the world are finding new ways to hold down operating costs and increase productivity. And NCR computers are making it happen.

NCR can make it happen for you, too. Learn more about the system that's just right for your business. Talk to your local NCR representative now.

This NCR ad describes the benefits of a computerized inventory system

managerial accounting functions that are often computer-aided. Some more detailed examples follow.

Some Specific Examples

A company that uses a combination of ingredients to make syrups and beverages needs to keep track of all the formulas the company uses. It also needs to print the batch tickets that are sent to the production facility. In addition, the company needs to know the costs of any quantity of the formula for the various container sizes. Such an application is called a *formula costing* system and is ideally suited to a computer. The NCR ad on the previous page illustrates inventory applications.

Professional firms (lawyers, accountants, engineers) need to account for and bill their time and expenses. A *professional time analysis and billing* system on a computer will allow a data entry person to set up a master file containing the names, addresses, and other important information about the professionals and their clients. The system allows timely entry of the time and expenses of the professionals as they relate to their clients. Using this system, the firm can get accurate analysis reports and bill their clients.

An architectural firm needs to know direct labor costs, indirect miscellaneous expenses, and outside consultant costs for each project. The firm must have up-to-date information regarding a project's budget and the actual costs for any given period of time. A *job costing* system allows original entry of personnel and client information as well as constant updating. The system calculates labor costs by multiplying hours worked by the billing rate per hour. Some job costing systems can also be used by the firm to calculate a bid on a contract.

Many businesses need to send out marketing-oriented messages, letters, or perhaps, Christmas cards to all their customers. In order to get a cheaper mailing rate, bulk mail must be sorted in zip code order. A computer can perform a sorting job like this in minutes, thereby saving time and money. The business can use the computer to print the sorted customer mailing list.

BASIC COMPUTER-RELATED CONCEPTS

Before discussing how a computer works, let's discuss three important ideas related to the use of computers. These are data processing, word processing, and automation.

Computers and Data Processing

As we saw in Chapter 12, all businesses need to collect, store, manipulate, interpret, and report data. This is called data processing. It includes financial and nonfinancial data. Governments and other nonbusiness institutions need to process data too. These data processing needs vary a lot because of the great differences in the type and the size of data flows among these institutions. In all cases, however, there is a need to keep accurate tallies of all those numbers that are important to these institutions—counting hospital admissions or adding cash collected by a grocery store or figuring the net profit of Gulf Oil Corporation.

The size of the data flow (need) and the financial resources of the institution (ability to pay) determine the scale and complexity of its data processing system. Not all firms need, nor can they afford, computers.

On a very small scale, such as would be found in a small rural gasoline service station, no machines at all may be involved. Keller's Service Station in Bush, Texas, uses only a pencil and a loose-leaf notebook to record sales and expenses.

data processing

Word processing systems can simplify the flow of information in many types of industry

Computers and Word Processing

It is midnight and a paper that you were assigned six weeks earlier is due tomorrow morning. As usual, you waited until the last minute to type it. Now, after it is typed and you are reading the copy, you realize that it needs major reorganization and that much of the material must be moved around. Because a good grade is important, you lose some sleep and stay up to retype the whole paper. The next morning, when you are about to turn it in, you notice that you spelled two words incorrectly throughout. There goes your "A"!

A word processing system would have greatly simplified your problem. **A word processing system is a computer that is programmed to manipulate letters, words, and paragraphs. It is a text-editing computer.** This means that you can type your paper (text) as you normally would, but instead of the characters appearing on paper as you type, the characters are displayed on a television-like screen (CRT terminal) and at the same time are stored on a floppy disk—a soft plastic disk similar to a record. Once you have typed your text, you can re-display it on the screen at a later date and, with simple key strokes, make changes. You don't have to retype your paper. All you need to do to make changes is to indicate where you want to move the text. The word processor can also be used to correct spelling errors by simply keying in the correct letters in place of the incorrect ones. The word processor will repage the text and

word processing system

type the revised paper on a printer that looks like a typewriter. Deleting, adding, or otherwise editing your paper is very easy with a word processor. This makes it one of the most useful applications of computers for the business community. It is one feature of the "office of the future" that is here now!

Computers and Automation

In an earlier section of the book we used the term *automation*. An activity or process is automated when it is possible to set its controls in advance so that it can work a long time without human attention.

Some automated processes are fairly simple and don't require computers. An example is a household heating and air-conditioning system. The thermostat permits the system to operate without much human interference.

A petroleum refinery is a more complex system. There are many points in the refining process at which information must be fed continuously into a computer. The information relates to such things as the rate of flow, temperature, and so on. The refinery's central computer has been programmed so that it uses this information to control the refining process.

The computer automatically makes certain computations and relays instructions to machinery in the factory. It does this in accordance with the program fed into it at an earlier time. Thus valves are opened and closed and temperatures are raised and lowered automatically.

computer program

Programming, as we will see in greater detail later in this chapter, is the process of telling a computer what to do. **A computer program is a detailed set of instructions in a special computer language.**

COMPUTER HARDWARE

hardware

Any discussion of computers usually falls under two headings: the *hardware* and the *software*. **The hardware consists of the machinery and electronic components.** Let's examine the various parts of the hardware and what they can do.

The tasks performed by the hardware, in logical order, are

- input
- storage and/or manipulation
- output

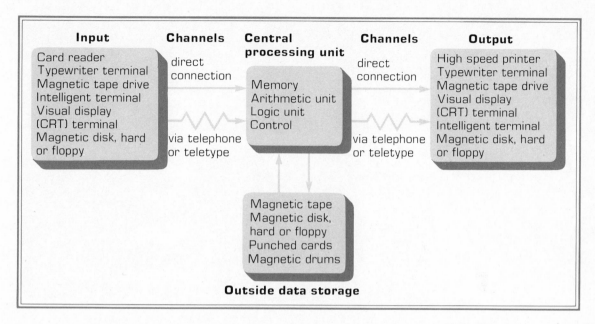

Input	Channels	Central processing unit	Channels	Output
Card reader Typewriter terminal Magnetic tape drive Intelligent terminal Visual display (CRT) terminal Magnetic disk, hard or floppy	direct connection via telephone or teletype	Memory Arithmetic unit Logic unit Control	direct connection via telephone or teletype	High speed printer Typewriter terminal Magnetic tape drive Visual display (CRT) terminal Intelligent terminal Magnetic disk, hard or floppy

Magnetic tape
Magnetic disk, hard or floppy
Punched cards
Magnetic drums

Outside data storage

FIGURE 13-1

Hardware components of a computer system

The tasks of inputting, storing, manipulating, and outputting are performed by four kinds of parts or components: (1) input devices; (2) central processing units; (3) outside data storage systems; and (4) output devices. (See Figure 13-1.)

The heart of any computer is its central processing unit (CPU). The CPU includes an internal memory for storing data, an arithmetic unit for performing calculations, a logic unit for comparing values and helping to "make decisions," and a control unit that actually operates the computer and sends instructions for controlling all of the other components.

A computer's internal memory can be added to by means of outside data storage systems. These are separate systems for storing information, such as magnetic disks, floppy disks, cassette tape, magnetic tape, and decks of punched cards. (See Figures 13-1 and

central processing unit (CPU)

outside data storage systems

The IBM 3033 is a large, mainframe computer system

Datamaster is IBM's
new, low-cost, small
business micro-
computer system

13-2.) Information can be recorded on any of these devices and read
into the computer at any time. Internal memory is used when response speed is important, such as during a sorting operation. Outside memory devices are usually used for information that is not in
constant use by the computer system.

Input and Output Devices

input-output (I-O)
devices

**Input and output (I-O) devices are the hardware used in getting
information in and out of the computer.** These pieces of hardware,
as a group, are also called *peripheral* equipment.

Magnetic disk and magnetic tape units are commonly used as
both input and output units. They are usually wired in directly to the
central computer. As noted above, the data they contain may be

FIGURE 13-2

Some of the devices
used to store, enter,
and retrieve data from
computer systems

Magnetic disk   Magnetic tape

Computer Age Quickens Pace of Salespeople

> ### POINT OF VIEW
>
> Bedford, Ohio—Mary Ellen Parulis, a saleswoman for Seaway Foods Inc., sweeps down the supermarket aisle carrying a calculator-like device in her left hand.
>
> Standing on tiptoe, she feels behind the bottles of generic shampoo on a top shelf. "That will take at least six more," she says of the empty space.
>
> Then she punches the five digit product identification code and—because the shampoo is sold in three-bottle lots—a "2" into her machine.
>
> Like a growing number of salespeople, Mrs. Parulis has adopted the portable data-entry terminal for recording sales. The terminals allow salespeople to enter information in their companies' computers directly, eliminating the need for key punchers. In addition, they increase the salespeople's productivity. According to Richard L. Nichta, Seaway's director of data processing, the average salesperson at Seaway, a food and drug wholesaler, gains two to three hours a day for selling by using the terminals.
>
> On this particular day, Mrs. Parulis records orders for 504 items in the drug section of Reider's Stop & Shop. Then she attaches the bell-shaped end of a rubber tube to the receiver of a pay telephone and plugs the other end into her terminal. About thirty seconds later, the orders arrive in Seaway's computer center for billing and shipping. . . .

stored outside the system itself. Still in use, but becoming obsolete, are card readers for input and card punch units for output. The punched card, pictured in Figure 13-2, was once the principal medium for data storage in computer systems.

An important output device is the high-speed printer. This unit is especially important for creating long lists of data such as in

FIGURE 13-2
(continued)

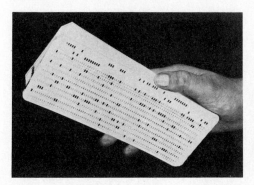

Punched cards

Floppy disk

TABLE 13-1

Special purpose input
and output devices

COM (computer output microfilm)	Displays data on a CRT screen from microfilm. Example: parts specifications at a large warehouse
OMR (optical mark recognition) reader	Device that reads data recorded in pencil on documents. Example: computer-graded test answer sheets
MICR (magnetic ink character recognition) reader	Device that reads characters written on documents with magnetic ink. Example: account number and amount on check
UPC (universal product code) reader	Device that reads the special product code identification bars on grocery items as they pass over the checkout counter at the supermarket
Voice digitizer	Device that translates voice input into digital form for processing in the computer

payrolls, invoices, and summary reports for accounting purposes. Some line printers can produce hundreds of lines of data per minute.

One of the most important input and output units in use today is the typewriter terminal, often accompanied by a visual display screen (cathode ray tube, or CRT). **Such terminals are often connected to the central processing unit by means of telephone lines. The device used to make this possible is called a modem. A modem modulates or converts direct current (DC) signals to tones and demodulates or converts tones back to DC signals.** These remote units may have computing power themselves and perform some data accumulation and processing functions independent of the central computer as well as feed information to the central computer. These are called *intelligent terminals* and may be programmed to "converse" with the central computer.

modem

Today there is a wide variety of special purpose input and output devices you will come across in your business career. Some of these are described briefly in Table 13-1. The first item listed is an output device and the remainder are input devices.

The Boom in Microcomputers

The recent invention of very tiny but powerful electronic components has led to the development of a new set of business and individual "microcomputers." Microcomputers, which cost only one-fiftieth as much as a large computer, can do much more than one-fiftieth of the work. The low cost of models made by many vendors has made the computer available to hundreds of thousands of small firms and private households. More than half a million "home" microcomputers had been sold by the end of 1981. Home-makers all over America are now using APPLE, PET, or TRS-80 microcomputers for a variety of purposes: to teach math or grammar to their children; to learn to speak German or to play bridge; to

FIGURE 13-3

Microcomputers and their applications

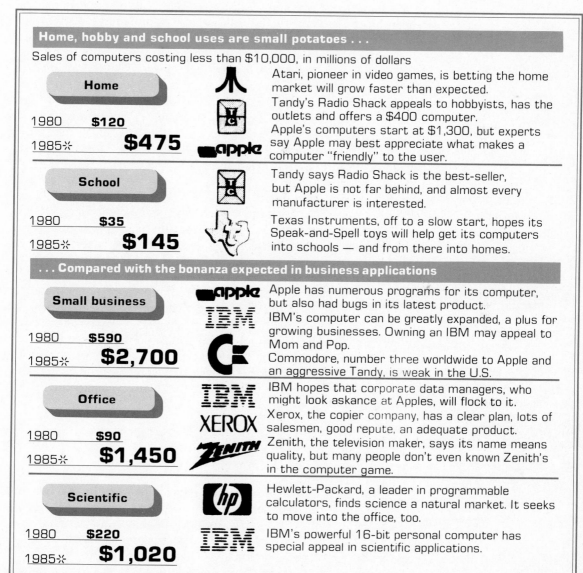

Home, hobby and school uses are small potatoes . . .

Sales of computers costing less than $10,000, in millions of dollars

Home

1980   **$120**
1985☀   **$475**

Atari, pioneer in video games, is betting the home market will grow faster than expected.

Tandy's Radio Shack appeals to hobbyists, has the outlets and offers a $400 computer.

Apple's computers start at $1,300, but experts say Apple may best appreciate what makes a computer "friendly" to the user.

School

1980   **$35**
1985☀   **$145**

Tandy says Radio Shack is the best-seller, but Apple is not far behind, and almost every manufacturer is interested.

Texas Instruments, off to a slow start, hopes its Speak-and-Spell toys will help get its computers into schools — and from there into homes.

. . . Compared with the bonanza expected in business applications

Small business

1980   **$590**
1985☀   **$2,700**

Apple has numerous programs for its computer, but also had bugs in its latest product.

IBM's computer can be greatly expanded, a plus for growing businesses. Owning an IBM may appeal to Mom and Pop.

Commodore, number three worldwide to Apple and an aggressive Tandy, is weak in the U.S.

Office

1980   **$90**
1985☀   **$1,450**

IBM hopes that corporate data managers, who might look askance at Apples, will flock to it.

Xerox, the copier company, has a clear plan, lots of salesmen, good repute, an adequate product.

Zenith, the television maker, says its name means quality, but many people don't even known Zenith's in the computer game.

Scientific

1980   **$220**
1985☀   **$1,020**

Hewlett-Packard, a leader in programmable calculators, finds science a natural market. It seeks to move into the office, too.

IBM's powerful 16-bit personal computer has special appeal in scientific applications.

balance their checkbooks; to keep an inventory of their household possessions; or to manage their personal finances.

The potential volume of microcomputer sales to small businesses appears to be even greater than the home computer market (See Figure 13-3). Although many managers of smaller firms might still be skeptical about having their own system, the financial reasons for not doing so are rapidly disappearing. These small systems have been marketed with broad accounting packages and specialized programs tailored for many industries. They can do payroll, general ledger, billing, inventory, and sales analysis; and clerks, secretaries, and floor salespeople can use them after a short training program.

In the larger firm, microcomputers may have a similar impact. Larger firms, in recent years, have felt the pressure of mounting data processing loads and a shortage of trained computer operating staff. This problem has caused them to centralize data processing in larger, more powerful computers. It seems, however, that centralization, in turn, has often led to conflict between those actually using the systems and those controlling them at data centers. The falling costs of microcomputers has started to reverse the trend toward centralized data processing.

distributed data processing

Firms that implement distributed data processing (DDP) can avoid the frustration created by large centralized computers. **DDP is a multiple systems approach to information handling. It puts computer power in many different places.** Microcomputers enhance large-scale computers by placing additional computing power throughout the organization. Such linkages are called *networks*. When the Vitalite Corporation discovered that the recently-installed central computer at its head office was causing some slowdowns in decision making at remote distribution points, management installed microcomputers (Apple IIs) at these points. These low cost systems easily handled the everyday load of inventory and other problems at these locations. Linkage between these units and the main computer also provided the necessary central control and information.

COMPUTER SOFTWARE

software

Computer software complements hardware by giving instructions and setting hardware into motion. It includes system software and application software, both of which are written in a computer language and require a kind of interpretation called documentation. All of these topics are discussed below.

Software is just as important as hardware. In fact, it is reported that software now costs more than hardware and that the proportion of computer system dollars spent for software will increase greatly in the future.

System Software

System software consists of internal instructions which tell the computer system how to manage the various tasks assigned to it. **System software may enable a computer to permit many users to interact with the computer at the same time. Such a process is called time sharing.** The internal speed of the computer, together with the relative slowness of the several remote input-output devices, makes such time sharing possible. Thus the inventory clerk in a warehouse can be typing in data on a newly arrived shipment of bolts while the payroll department is feeding in a magnetic tape containing information needed to print this week's paychecks. There is no noticeable interruption of either input. **Devices known as controllers regulate the "traffic" of peripheral hardware into the CPU.**

When those using the system are in direct communication with the computer, either by telephone or directly wired in, the system is called an online system. When such a system can respond immediately it is called a real-time system. A large proportion of the computers in use today are online real-time systems. Such a system may, for example, be used for constant energy management.

With such a system, thousands of employees can use a modern building like the World Trade Center in New York with a minimum of heating, cooling, and lighting. Thermostats and other monitoring devices send information to the computer. The computer is programmed to digest this information and to make a variety of computations and "decisions" that will keep energy consumption to a minimum.

Instead of online real-time systems, some firms use *batch processing*. Batch processing is data processing in which data are collected for a period of time before being entered into the computer system. Batch processing is used where there is a large amount of input, but no need for immediate output. For example, the University of New Orleans library accumulates records of books checked out by students, faculty, and the general public. These records are periodically entered into the university computer and summaries of outstanding books are printed by the computer and sent out at the end of each semester.

System software and, as we will see in the next section, application software require programming. Programming, in turn, requires a computer language.

Systems software programs are usually written in assembly language. This is called an intermediate level language because it

Margin terms: time sharing · controllers · online real-time system · assembly language

machine language

lies between machine language and the higher-level (English-like) languages used in writing applications programs. These are discussed in the next section. **Machine language consists of binary (1 and 0 digits only) code and relates to a specific computer or set of computers.** It is used because the CPU only understands the fact that its tiny memory cells are either on or off. A cell turned on is recognized as a 1 and a cell turned off is recognized as a 0.

Application Software and Programming

Application software means programs that are designed to do a variety of jobs for users, such as the financial accounting functions described in Chapter 12 or market research tabulations discussed in Chapter 9. These programs are likely to be written in one of the major languages described below—FORTRAN, COBOL, BASIC, Pascal, and Ada.

FORTRAN

FORTRAN has for years been the most widely-used language for scientific and engineering programming applications. FORTRAN is short for FORmula TRANslator.

COBOL

COBOL (Common Business Oriented Language) is specially designed for conventional commercial applications. COBOL is especially good for handling large files of alphabetic and numerical data such as payrolls.

BASIC

BASIC was originally designed to teach students how to program. Because it is easy to use, it has become the most widely implemented language for microcomputers. Recent enhancements have made it useful in both business and scientific applications.

Pascal

Pascal is a relatively new language that uses most of the modern techniques of good programming design. It features an important software design technique called *structured programming*. It is powerful in its data description and in its ability to process that data. It is also used in microcomputers.

Ada

Ada is a programming language recently developed by the U.S. military in an attempt to design a more efficient language than any of the above. It is suited to both scientific and business applications. Because it is the language of the Department of Defense (DOD), it could make a large impact on the computer industry, as computer manufacturers compete for large DOD contracts.

The BASIC program in Figure 13-4 is explained below. The computer responds to input from the operator. It performs a series of steps in the order of the program line number at the left of each line. Lines 10 and 20 are directions to the operator. Line 30 sets the counter for the sum, T, at zero. Line 40 allows the operator to enter a number. Line 50, in effect, tells the program when to stop adding.

FIGURE 13-4

A BASIC program for finding a sum

```
10   PRINT ''EACH TIME YOU SEE '?'TYPE IN A
     NUMBER. WHEN YOU HAVE NO MORE NUMBERS TYPE
     -99.99 AS YOUR FINAL NUMBER.''
20   PRINT ''I WILL TELL YOU THE SUM OF THE
     NUMBERS THAT YOU TYPED.''
30   LET T = 0
40   INPUT X
50   IF X = -99.99 THEN 80
60   LET T = T + X
70   GO TO 40
80   PRINT ''THE SUM IS ''; T
90   END
```

It does this by checking for a "dummy" number, -99.99. Line 50 says: "When you come to the dummy number (-99.99), skip to line 80." Line 60 is the actual adding process. It tells the computer to set up a counter, T, and to add the next value of X, to the counter, T. Line 70 says to start the cycle at line 40 again. The computer continues the cycle of lines 40 to 70 until the dummy number, -99.99, is typed in. Line 80 says to print the words "The sum is" and the value of T. Line 90 tells the computer to stop the program.

This may seem like an awful lot of trouble for a simple addition. It is. But if there were hundreds of numbers and much more complex mathematics than addition, it would be worth the trouble.

Documentation

An important part of software is known as documentation. This means an explanation either in English (or other spoken languages) or in diagram form of what a program does, how it is used, and how it works.

documentation

Documentation is important to both those who write and those who use programs. Programmers are interested in the documentation that concerns the design, logic, function, and utility of the program. Users are interested in the purpose of the program, when to use it, and what preparations are necessary to run it successfully. Documentation for the user is written in the ordinary spoken language of the nation in which it is used, and is usually given to the user in the form of operator instructions.

In developing programs for most businesses today, the traditional method of flowcharting is used as documentation for pro-

FIGURE 13-5

A flowchart (block diagram) for a payroll

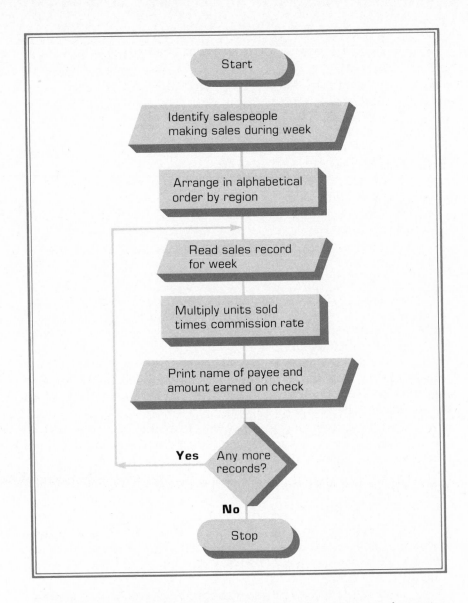

grammers. Flowcharts, or block diagrams such as the one shown in Figure 13-5, give the nontechnical person a graphic illustration of the logical steps in a program. This particular illustration describes the steps taken to produce a weekly payroll for a salesforce whose income depends on their commission on sales. The flowchart shows that the computer: (1) searches files for all salespeople who have made sales during the last weekly payroll period; (2) arranges these in alphabetical order by sales region; (3) reads from sales records the amount sold and the commission rate; (4) multiplies units sold times commission rate; (5) prints the check; (6) goes to the next sales record, etc. until all checks are written; and (7) stops processing. This is a bit simpler than a real-life computation which might include different commission rates on different products and various tax deductions from the total pay due.

Flowcharts are still widely used for both whole system design and individual program design, but there is a big change in documentation taking place today. The change stems from the rise in the use of structured programming, mentioned earlier in the description of Pascal. The concept is a complex one and would take a chapter of its own to explain fully. The general idea, however, is to simplify the process of program development and then, at a later time, to simplify program modification.

HOW ARE COMPUTER SYSTEMS SELECTED AND INSTALLED IN A FIRM?

A sad fact about the typical use of computers in businesses is the poor planning that often occurs. This is caused by a variety of things. Consider this typical sequence of events leading up to the installation of a computer system at the Ajax Bolt Company.

Selecting a System

Ajax is a middle-sized manufacturer which once had an outdated, partially manual system of processing data. The information systems in the production, marketing, and finance departments were all somewhat different. There was a serious need for a modern computer-based information system.

The subject of computers came up at a board of directors meeting after Ajax's president, Sam Black, visited a competitor's plant. He saw the fancy computer room there, with all the blinking lights and spinning reels of tape. Sam also noticed the lower volume of paper work and learned that the competitor's profits had improved since the system was installed.

The next time the computer firm's sales representative visited Ajax, Sam listened carefully to the sales pitch. The salesperson outlined what seemed to be a very good application of the computer company's hardware and software to Ajax's needs.

The proposed system provided for more integration of all the marketing, production, and financial data gathering, sorting, anal-

"Just listen to all that whirring and buzzing and clicking, and not a single demand for a raise!"

ysis, and reporting. It seemed to provide an improved basis for making decisions in these three functional areas and for top management planning.

Being a smart businessman, Sam arranged for three computer firms to make presentations to his staff. After study and comparison of the proposals (which were all similar), Ajax picked a medium-priced computer made by the firm with the best service reputation of the three.

Ajax's need for a computer system was clear, but Sam Black did not take the best approach. Ideally, Ajax should have started by hiring an independent systems consultant or a permanent systems analyst. This person would have talked to all department heads to develop a complete set of concepts of the firm's needs. Next, with the analyst's help, Ajax would have examined the computers made by several manufacturers, including a variety of components that best fitted Ajax's needs. Finally, the necessary programming, testing, and installation would have been done.

Under this plan, Ajax would have had a better understanding of its needs. This understanding would not have been limited by the readymade systems of a given manufacturer and by such a firm's "outsider's view" of Ajax's problems and operations. In other words, it's wise to define your true computer needs first. The following guidelines can help a lot.

Hardware evaluation:

- What are the costs involved? The rent, lease, or purchase price as well as the costs of operation and maintenance must be considered.
- Can it perform to your satisfaction? This includes adequate work volume capacity and speed.
- Is it compatible with the system already in operation?
- Is it expandable to meet your growth expectations?
- Can your staff be trained to run it?

Software evaluation:

- Do packaged programs fit your needs and staff expertise?
- Are programs documented adequately?
- Are the operating system, compilers, etc. reliable?

Vendor evaluation:

- What are the maintenance capabilities of the vendor?
- Does the local office of the vendor provide programming and systems support?
- What support will the vendor provide during conversion?

- What is the record of the vendor as to past performance, consistency during negotiations, etc.?

Other Options

Firms that are thinking about a new computer, of course, have other options open to them besides the choice from among hardware manufacturers. First of all, they now have the choice of leasing from manufacturers or of leasing from computer leasing firms. The latter are independent middlemen who can often provide combinations of various manufacturers' hardware components which might more closely meet the user's needs than can the products of one manufacturer. Often, a user can save money by using a middleman's services.

Another option available is to lease a line connected into an existing large system with time-sharing capabilities. Such an arrangement can be made with a large user such as a bank or with a leasing firm. This option, of course, is not feasible for a firm that needs a large, complex data processing capacity. Another option for the small firm is to let a computer service firm take over its data processing needs entirely.

How People React to Computers

Human reactions to the computer range from worship to outright fear. Most people who know computers reject these extremes. Rather, they learn that the computer is a marvelous tool. They find that people and computers can bring their different abilities together and that this combined power can be used very effectively.

Fear of the computer takes different forms. Some fear that people will become so dependent on complex control systems that a small human error in programming or data entry could produce chaos. The Three Mile Island near-disaster is a reminder of the basis for such fears. Some people fear the computer because they feel it can bring about mass unemployment. Others fear it because it brings change in the firm—new ways of doing things. Still others fear the computer for another reason. They know that the government and many private agencies have stored huge quantities of personal data about private citizens and feel that this is a violation of their right to privacy. This is a special problem because of the prevalence of electronic spying.

Closely related to the question of privacy is the fear of loss through "computer crime." Clever thieves have, in many cases, discovered ways to abuse computer systems, often in bank accounts or in payroll systems, for their personal gain. This is a growing

Computers,
Mailing Lists, and
Politics:
Is privacy
threatened by
mailing list
data bases?

WHAT DO YOU THINK?

The PBS program, NOVA, recently looked at some of the more sensitive public issues related to the growth of computer technology. One part of this TV show was an interview with Richard Viguerie. Mr. Viguerie heads a direct mail company which, according to NOVA, raises 30 million dollars a year for conservative clients.

Mr. Viguerie is quoted as follows:

"I used to say that this room was probably the most important room in America to conservatives, but now that we have Mr. Reagan in the Oval Office, I no longer can say that. We have about three, maybe four files of these magnetic tapes here in this room. Each one can hold about 650,000 names and addresses. I guess if you unduplicated all the names here, we'd probably have about 25 million separate names and addresses. Of those 25 million, maybe about 4½ million we've identified are conservative on one or more issues. We get the names from hundreds and hundreds of mailings that we do each year. We mail about 70 or more million letters each year; and we will mail to gun lists for gun clients, we'll mail to religious-type lists for our, say, pro-life clients."

The issue raised by NOVA with respect to this huge direct mail operation is not the political view of the operation—similar operations are conducted for quite different political causes. Rather, the issue is one of invasion of privacy involved in mailing millions of unsolicited letters to American households, many of whose names and addresses (with other information suggesting income or political leanings) are stored, categorized, bought, and sold without their knowledge or consent. None of this would be possible without modern computer capability. Is our privacy being threatened? WHAT DO YOU THINK?

problem which computer system designers are working on. Naturally, not much is publicized about techniques being used to combat such theft. Space-age thieves are too clever.

One measure which is being tested specifically to avoid the theft of private information is coding, not unlike the coding used in military and CIA communications. Such codes are being developed by specialized computer consulting firms for use by all kinds of businesses. All messages on SWIFT, a computer network linking 500 international banks, are being sent in coded form. Bank customers who use automatic tellers to transact business are being issued "secret passwords" to help protect against electronic thievery.

Sometimes people (even managers) feel that a computer will magically solve all their problems. This can cause as many problems for a firm as fear of the computer. The truth is that managers must plan very carefully. They must get accurate data and a "debugged" program (one in which all the problems have been worked out) before they can count on using a computer's output. Someone invented the phrase GIGO (garbage in—garbage out) to describe how much the computer depends on reliable human input. A chimpanzee is unlikely to be able to count his toes even with a computer's help!

WHAT FUTURE APPLICATIONS ARE POSSIBLE FOR BUSINESS?

If you hate the thought of data entry on a keyboard, perhaps by the time you graduate, you will not need to know how to type. Research is already well under way on designing electronic hearing devices to decode human speech, regardless of accent. At the same time, work is continuing on electronic voice output. Texas Instruments' *Speak and Spell* toy has already demonstrated low cost electronic speech.

Alvin Toffler, in his book, *The Third Wave*, introduced the concept of the "electronic cottage." By the time you graduate, you may not need to commute to work daily. With the use of a microcomputer, a phone, and a modem at home, and a large-scale or minicomputer at work, you may be able to work at home. Only an occasional visit to your employer's office will be necessary. The electronic cottage will be made possible by the explosion in data communications—with distributed data processing and advanced telecommunications.

As the designers of computers become more sensitive to human needs, the distinction between data processing and word processing will decrease. We will also see extensive use of color graphics in both business and scientific applications. A picture is worth a thousand words!

Eventually, programming that you may have seen in offices will become obsolete. Computer systems themselves will be able to write the programs for particular office needs.

While computers have grown to be a vital part of business activity, a parallel growth has occurred in the use of mathematics and statistical tools. That these two things have grown at the same

Computer graphics offers enormous possibilities for marketing and other business applications

quantitative tools

time is not coincidence. **Many of the mathematical and statistical tools depend on computers for their practical application. We refer to this whole set of mathematical and statistical applications to business as quantitative tools.**

SOME QUANTITATIVE TOOLS FOR MANAGEMENT DECISIONS

The use of quantitative tools by managers is increasing. Whereas managers in the past often relied only on their own judgment, modern managers strengthen their judgment by collecting and organizing data to support it. We will examine some basic statistical concepts and some examples of quantitative tools used today.

Statistics for Business

statistics

Managers have dealt with numerical data in their decision making for many years. These numerical data and methods of summarizing them are called statistics. Data may represent internal facts, such as number of units sold, or external facts, such as the population of the states in which a firm does business.

It is often helpful to summarize numerical data by using special kinds of averages. For example, we may wish to refer to average family income in the United States or to the average number of years of school completed. An average is a summary figure that describes the facts we are studying. There are three principal types of averages:

- the arithmetic mean
- the median
- the mode

arithmetic mean

The arithmetic mean is an average computed by first adding numbers, finding the total, and then dividing that total by the number of numbers that were added together. Look at Table 13-2. It is a list, or array, of the ages of seven employees in the receiving department of a factory. It also shows that the sum of their ages is 210 years. We can compute the arithmetic mean of their ages, their average age, by simply dividing 210 years by 7. The answer, of course, is 30 years. This is the most common form of average.

median

Another measure of an average is called a median. It means the middle number when numbers are listed in rank—from smallest to largest or vice versa. To find the median of the ages of the employees in Table 13-2 we first rank ages in an array, starting with the youn-

Employee	Age
Harold	30
Janet	28
Gordon	38
Clyde	27
Susan	27
Richard	34
Thomas	<u>26</u>
Total	210

TABLE 13-2

Ages of employees in the receiving department

gest. The list becomes 26, 27, 27, 28, 30, 34, 38. The middle number is 28 years (Janet's age). There are three people older than Janet and three who are younger.

To find a median of an even number of numbers, we still rank the numbers and then take an arithmetic mean of the two "middle" numbers only. If we added Paul, aged 29, to our list the median would be 28.5, which is the arithmetic mean of the two middle numbers, 28 and 29.

A third average is called a mode. It is the most common or frequent number in a list. In our example, only two people are the same age. Clyde and Susan are both 27, so this is the mode. Their age, 27, is the modal age.

mode

These types of "averages" are different ways of making a summary measurement of a characteristic of a group. Which one is best depends on the use to which the measurement is put and how the raw data are distributed.

Suppose we collected statistics on family incomes in your home county and organized them into five groups. The statistics might appear in grouped form as shown in Table 13-3. This is called a frequency distribution.

A frequency distribution is a table that shows how many members of a larger group fall within various classes or subgroups. In this case it shows how family incomes are distributed among five income intervals or ranges. There are, for example, 180 families who received less than $6,000, and 752 who received at least $6,000 but less than $12,000. Of course, the same information could have been provided by giving a whole list or array of all families and their incomes. The frequency distribution gives a clear summary of what family incomes are in the county without the extreme detail of such a list. It also tells us more than a single average of incomes could tell. It shows

frequency distribution

TABLE 13-3

Frequency distribution
of family incomes

Annual family income	Number of families
$ 0– 5,999.99	180
6,000–11,999.99	752
12,000–18,999.99	957
19,000–25,999.99	702
26,000 and over	140
Total	2,731

something about how incomes are dispersed or scattered around the average income. Figure 13-6 shows the same information in the form

histogram

of a histogram. **The histogram, or bar chart, portrays a frequency distribution in vertical or horizontal columns whose length, measured on an accompanying scale, indicates the number or percent in each class.** The average, frequency distribution, and histogram are examples of *descriptive statistics*. Managers use them in preparing reports that describe their business operations or marketing data.

Sampling

sample

Another widely used tool is the *statistics of sampling.* **A sample is a part of a larger group called a universe or population. It is in-**

FIGURE 13-6

Histogram of data in
Table 13-3

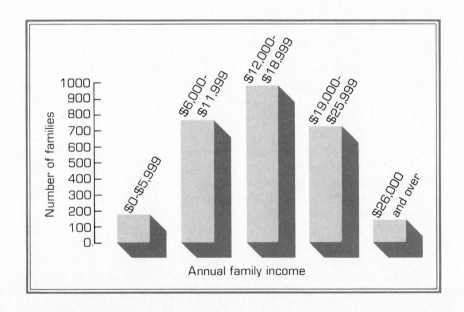

tended to take the place of the larger group and to convey some information about that larger group. Political analysts, for example, base their projections of winners in elections by studying a relatively small number of voters (the sample). The time, costs, and effort involved in interviewing every voter (the universe) would be too great. By interviewing a sample of voters, a pollster can make a good estimate of the election results.

Businesses also use sampling. Suppose a manufacturer of light bulbs wishes to guarantee that its bulbs will last a certain number of hours. The company might find, based on a study of a sample, that the average bulb life is two hundred hours. It would be unrealistic to base the guarantee on a study of all the light bulbs it produces. Its entire inventory would have to be "burned out." So it tests a sample of these bulbs.

A TV program sponsor uses a rating to decide whether to keep a particular program. A TV rating firm such as A. C. Nielsen cannot check all viewers in the country. Think of the cost! Nielsen conducts a sample drawn from all viewers and then estimates the national audience from the sample.

Some samples are selected in a such a way that certain things can be estimated about the larger group with a given degree of confidence. Other samples are not drawn according to strict mathematical rules but still try to approximate the characteristics of the larger groups. They don't provide a measurable degree of confidence in their accuracy, but they are cheaper to get and are more often used than the other (random) kind because of the lower cost.

Breakeven Analysis

A useful management tool in both production planning and pricing of products is breakeven analysis. Breakeven analysis demonstrates the profitability of various levels of production. The breakeven point shows at which level total costs are exactly equal to total sales revenue. As you can see in Figure 13-7, the number of units produced is measured on the horizontal scale and dollar costs and revenues are measured on the vertical scale. The sales revenue line starts at the zero point (lower left corner). Because the product sells for $100, this line moves up $1,000 each time it moves to the right by 10 units. If we make and sell 20 units, we get $2,000 in revenue.

Costs are of two kinds: fixed and variable. *Fixed costs* occur whether we produce zero or 20 or 1,000 units. These costs are often called *overhead costs.* They include depreciation on plant, insurance, and other costs that do not vary with the level of production. In this case fixed costs are $1,000.

breakeven analysis

FIGURE 13-7

A breakeven chart

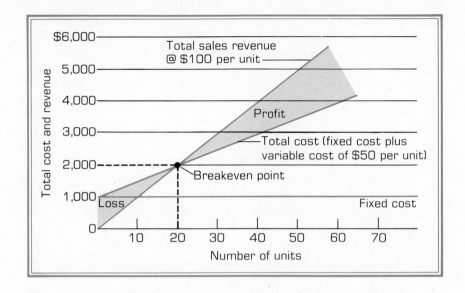

Variable costs depend on the number of units produced and sold. These might include raw materials, labor, and other costs that go into each unit produced. For each unit we produce and sell, it costs us $50 more—in addition to fixed costs. The effect of variable cost is represented by another line sloping up from the $1,000 mark on the left vertical axis. This line, because it starts from the $1,000 fixed-cost level, also measures total cost at various levels of production. If 20 units are made, the total cost is $2,000, consisting of $1,000 in fixed costs and $1,000 (20 × $50) in variable costs. If 25 are made, the total cost is $2,250.

At the level of 20 units of production, the cost and revenue lines cross. This is the *breakeven point,* the production level beyond which the firm begins to make a profit. For each additional unit made and sold the firm realizes an increase of $50 in profits. This is so because unit revenue minus unit variable cost ($100 − $50) equals $50.

A breakeven chart can help a plant manager decide several things. It can help a manager decide whether to install expensive new machines that would change the production cost structure. It can help to set prices or help to decide whether to buy or to lease a plant. A retailer could also use a breakeven chart to make similar decisions. Without the use of a breakeven chart the breakeven point (BP) can be computed by dividing total fixed cost (TFC) by the difference between unit revenue or price (P) and unit variable cost (VC):

$$BP = \frac{TFC}{(P\text{-}VC)}.$$

Operations Research

Many new mathematical tools have been developed to solve business problems. For example, determining how many units of a product to keep in its warehouses is a tough problem for a firm selling hundreds of products around the world. Mathematical tools are available to help solve this and other problems. **The various quantitative techniques used to solve problems of scheduling or allocation are called operations research (OR).** Without computers, however, the mathematical calculations needed to apply these techniques could take years to perform. Linear programming is one of the techniques of operations research.

Linear programming is a mathematical tool used to allocate resources in the "best way" so as to maximize or minimize a desired objective. This desired objective may be the greatest profit, the least cost, or another "best" result for the firm. For example, this technique could allow a firm that is selecting a location for a new plant to minimize the total cost of getting raw materials into the plant, getting finished goods to warehouses, and moving them to customers. It would consider these and the many other variables that influence plant location and determine the "best" location. Linear programming is widely used in situations in which there are limited resources (time and money) and a value (profit or cost) that is to be maximized or minimized. The limitations are called constraints.

operations research (OR)

linear programming

SUMMARY AND LOOK AHEAD

How the special talents of computers fit in with unique human talents is gradually being learned as people and computers work together solving business problems. Computer hardware and software together comprise a computer system that can serve a firm in many ways.

Computers are used in information storage and retrieval tasks. They simplify the manipulation and organization of data. Computers, together with people who know how to use mathematical tools, expand the power of managers and help them solve problems quicker and with less chance for error. The mathematical tools include statistics, sampling, and breakeven analysis.

In the next chapter we begin our survey of the world of finance. The main subject is banking, but we will look at many other financial institutions, too. We will see how they fit in the scheme of business decision making.

FOR REVIEW . . .

1. Name the three major hardware components of a computer. How are they interrelated?

2. What is a computer language? Name and describe two common ones.

3. What kinds of business processes make good use of the rapid repetitive capabilities of a computer?

4. What is a computer program?

5. Explain what is meant by documentation. Draw a simple block diagram.

6. Contrast the alternatives of computer leasing and time sharing.

7. Fixed costs are $100 and variable costs are $1 per unit. How many units must be sold at $2 to break even?

8. Identify two probable future applications of computers to business.

. . . FOR DISCUSSION

1. Besides the space shuttle, what startling modern accomplishments do you think never could have happened without computers?

2. Review the experiences you had yesterday and try to determine which of these were in some way influenced by the existence of computers.

3. Will the growth of microcomputers in small business widen the use of various quantitative tools?

4. What happens to the breakeven point when the sales price goes up?

INCIDENTS

Office Automation

Just over half the 100 million workers in the U.S. are now considered "white-collar," with service workers bringing the total to almost two-thirds. Blue-collar and farm workers comprise only 35 percent of the labor force and, in number, are growing at half the white-collar rate.

Although there are numerous computer applications in industrial or environmental control, real-time process monitoring, and now robotics, most computer power is aimed at clerical tasks. Since these are the tasks associated with the largest, fastest growing, and most expensive sector of the workforce, there should be no shortage of incentive to automate.

In fact, an army of devices is about to descend on the white-collar workplace.

In 1981 there were about 15 million computers, word processors, telecopiers, and switchboards compared to 52 million white-collar workers. Within just five years, when the white-collar workforce will be 57 million strong, the installed base of those devices will grow to 38 million. At those rates there will be more than one intelligent office gadget for every white-collar worker—not even counting new systems, like intelligent TVs or voice-mail boxes—by the end of the decade.[2]

QUESTIONS

1. How can you explain the tremendous growth in the number of white-collar and service workers in the United States? (Hint: You may want to review the discussion of the post-industrial service economy in Chapter 1.)

2. What incentives can you cite for firms to automate their clerical tasks?

3. What are the problems and opportunities that firms will face as they seek to automate their clerical tasks?

Hardware or Service—Which to Buy

In a recent magazine ad, Automated Data Processing, Inc. (ADP) stated "A computer, expertly used, will eventually pay for itself. But certainly not the first week. Computing, on the other hand, pays for itself almost at once. Mainly because you buy only what you need . . . With computing you avoid not only the cost of the hardware, but also the inevitable add-ons: installation, programming, maintenance, re-programming, maintenance, re-programming, and re-programming."

An ad for a computer hardware manu-facturer would make a different argument. It might say that its product, once installed and doing a high volume of work, would be more effi-cient than the services of a firm like ADP.[3]

QUESTIONS

1. How can you tell whether it is wiser for you to hire a computer service company or to buy a computer?

2. In what way might you use a breakeven chart to make this decision?

CASE STUDY

Accountants are in a position to see the results of good and bad management. Many advise clients how to improve their businesses. So it's ironic that some of them don't manage their own practices very well.

Any accountant worth his certification would caution a small-business owner to set aside time for managing and planning. Yet accountants often don't take their own advice.

"It's difficult to properly manage your practice when you haven't allocated time for it," says Jake L. Netterville, chairman of the American Institute of Certified Public Accountants' committee on management of an accounting practice. The fortunes of small practices tend to be limited by the amount of work the principals can do. Most small-practice CPAs, Mr. Netterville says, "are always overworked." They're busy doing financial statements, tax forms and other client work, but seldom managing their own practices.

When Seymour Siegel and Edward Mendlowitz formed a partnership in 1974, they were concerned with survival, not managing a practice. "We didn't know if we were going to make a living," says Mr. Siegel, who concentrates on client and banking relations for Siegel & Mendlowitz. But the New York CPA firm has prospered because its principals realized they needed to devote time to building the practice.

They resigned from another firm because it wasn't growing. "We did a lot of one-shot things," recalls Mr. Mendlowitz, a tax specialist. "We weren't building clients."

Although they had been in accounting more than 10 years at that point, it was like starting over. "We did everything ourselves," Mr. Siegel says. Even so, they took in $138,000 in fees the first year. Clients referred them to prospective clients, and Mr. Siegel's extensive social and political activities brought in business, too. Soon they had too much work to do themselves.

A decision to hire help started them toward a prospering practice. "Profits are made from those who work for you," Mr. Netterville notes. Many CPAs practicing alone ignore this obvious business tenet because they are accustomed to "working and not managing other people."

The first year of their partnership Messrs. Siegel and Mendlowitz made more than in the second year, when they had 30% more revenue and four employees. It was four years until they earned as much as in their first year together. But they continued to add staff, which they value.

"We do everything we can to make them happy," Mr. Siegel

says. "We don't want them to leave." They give raises every six months. Most have stayed. In 1975, they lured a friend, Paul Rich, from Laventhol & Horwath, a large CPA firm. A year later, he became an equal partner.

The partners decided about three years ago that their own firm had to be put in order. "We were growing too rapidly and were scattered all over the field" in types of clients, Mr. Rich says. They dropped clients who weren't worth keeping. Some had marginal businesses, others were so demanding that "we knew they wouldn't let us make any money from them," Mr. Siegel says.

They also raised their fees. "Those were scary days," Mr. Siegel says. "We didn't know how our clients would react. But the first few said 'Yes,' and we got the courage to ask the others. I don't know what we would have done if they'd said, 'No.'" After dropping 15% of its clients and raising fees, the partnership increased its revenue 30%.

The firm has about 150 clients today and revenues that exceed $1 million, which suggests that each partner earns more than $133,000 a year. The partners could make more by adding new clients, though they're selective nowadays. Says Mr. Mendlowitz, "Implicit in a good client is someone with a financial awareness and a desire to get good advice."

Finding good staff has slowed expansion, not a lack of prospective clients. "Our biggest problem is getting people with good solid accounting knowledge," says Mr. Rich, who oversees personnel. "We advertise almost every week for accountants." Starting pay for an experienced person is $30,000 to $40,000 a year.

New rules permit CPAs to raid each other's clients. A Big Eight firm quoted a low fee to one of Siegel & Mendlowitz's clients recently, but the firm withdrew its bid after seeing the problems Siegel & Mendlowitz had detailed in work papers made during the annual audit. Says Mr. Siegel with a smile, "The big guys backed out after they saw how much work we were doing."

Questions:

1. Explain why "accountants are in a position to see the results of good and bad management."

2. Is a CPA firm a business? Explain.

3. Are the firms described in this case engaged in financial accounting or managerial accounting? Discuss.

4. In addition to auditing accounting records, what else might a CPA do for a client firm?

5. If you were in charge of personnel at a big CPA firm, how would you go about recruiting new accountants?

6. Is the firm of Siegel & Mendlowitz more likely to use computers today than they might have when they first started? Why or why not?

CAREERS IN ACCOUNTING AND COMPUTERS

If you are considering a career in either accounting or computers, there is good news and bad news. The good news is that there are more opportunities in these fields than almost any other. The bad news is that you'd better get down to serious business if you want to succeed in them. These are among the most challenging of all occupational paths.

In nearly all of the accounting-related jobs—*auditing, tax accounting, budgeting, managerial accounting,* and *public accounting*—you must have completed at least several semesters or

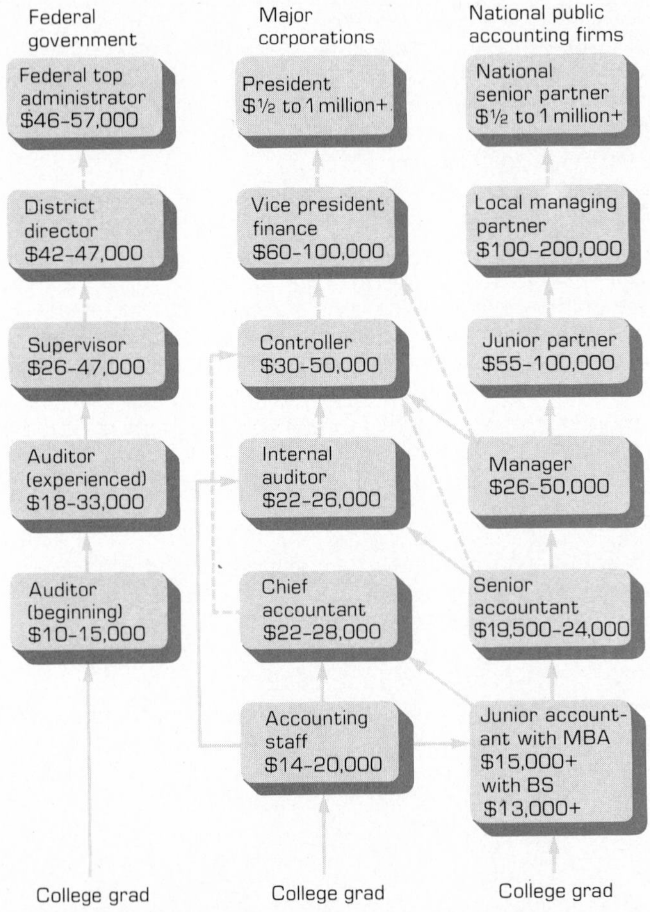

FIGURE V-1

Accounting positions, salaries, and mobility

Federal government	Major corporations	National public accounting firms
Federal top administrator $46-57,000	President $½ to 1 million+	National senior partner $½ to 1 million+
District director $42-47,000	Vice president finance $60-100,000	Local managing partner $100-200,000
Supervisor $26-47,000	Controller $30-50,000	Junior partner $55-100,000
Auditor (experienced) $18-33,000	Internal auditor $22-26,000	Manager $26-50,000
Auditor (beginning) $10-15,000	Chief accountant $22-28,000	Senior accountant $19,500-24,000
	Accounting staff $14-20,000	Junior accountant with MBA $15,000+ with BS $13,000+
College grad	College grad	College grad

quarters of college-level accounting courses. About the only accounting-related jobs that don't require a college degree are simple *bookkeeping* and *personal tax preparation* jobs. If you want to be a *CPA*, of course, you must also pass a very difficult state examination. The rewards are great, however. Figure V-1 shows some of the paths of advancement in accounting careers. These data, of course, are for 1980.

In computers, opportunities are also quite attractive and the educational requirements are great for most of these jobs. *Data entry positions*—keypunch and peripheral equipment operators—are the exception in that they require relatively short training periods and do not call for a college degree. *Programmers* usually require some college training, sometimes two-year college diplomas. *Computer operators* require similar training and education. If you are thinking of a position as a *systems analyst*, the four-year degree is necessary, usually with a major in computer science or mathematics. Such higher-level jobs require attention to detail and the application of logic and mathematical concepts.

Nearly all of the computer and accounting jobs are "inside"—office-bound jobs with regular hours. When auditing or systems analysis is performed for clients, travel is required for such consultation. Working conditions for all of these jobs, which are found wherever large to medium sized businesses are found, are quite comfortable. For a prediction of the level of opportunity in these fields, please examine the table below.

Among the strongest growth rates are those for jobs in accounting and computers. Accountants and auditors are still in demand. The number of new positions by 1990 is projected at

1980 and projected 1990 employment in selected accounting and computer occupations

| | Employment* | | Percent Change |
	1980 Actual	1990 Projected**	1980-1990
Accountants and Auditors	833	1107	32.9
Computer Programmers	228	381	67.1
Computer Systems Analysts	205	412	101.0
Computer Operators	184	338	83.7
Peripheral EDP Equipment Operators	49	76	55.1
Keypunch Operators	325	341	4.9
Accounting Clerks, and Bookkeepers	1715	2131	24.3

*thousands
**moderate high trend

330,000—32.9 percent more jobs than in 1980. Somewhat smaller percentage increases are expected in jobs as accounting clerks and as bookkeepers. These lower-paying jobs will grow by 24.3 percent.

In the computer field, as the table shows, the rates of growth are expected to be even greater by 1990. The number of jobs as programmers will grow from 228,000 in 1980 to 381,000 in 1990—a 67.1 percent increase in ten years. Systems analyst positions and computer operator positions will increase at even greater rates, namely 101 percent and 83.7 percent, respectively. The need for peripheral equipment operators will also grow rapidly. Only keypunch operator jobs will grow below the national job growth average. This is because of a shift to other forms of data entry.

CAREER PROFILE

My name is Louise Schreiner. I graduated with a bachelor of science degree in accounting. Along with many accounting courses, I took courses in Business Law and Computer Science which complement the knowledge gained through my accounting studies. I am now a staff accountant with approximately two and one-half years' experience with Arthur Young & Company (AY), an international public accounting firm. Shortly after joining AY, I took and passed the Certified Public Accountant (CPA) examination. Obtaining the CPA certificate is necessary to advance in a public accounting firm.

ARTHUR YOUNG

I obtained my job with AY after numerous interviews, group discussions, and field trips. My college's Career Planning and Placement Office was a tremendous help. This office organized interviewing schedules so that prospective employers and employees could meet. I interviewed with ten firms and eventually began working at AY.

The one area for which my accounting and other business courses did not prepare me was the tremendous people contact involved in performing an audit. The stereotyped concept of the accountant who deals only with numbers is false! An audit is a service performed for a business which is managed and/or owned by people. Meeting our clients' needs is our job. It is my responsibility to keep the manager and partner on the job informed at all times and to be AY's day-to-day representative to the client. Another area of responsibility for me is training assistants; that is, explaining to them the how's and why's of an audit, as well as being on hand to answer their questions and review their work.

I chose a career at AY for three main reasons. First, I decided that I wanted the opportunities a large international public accounting firm can offer, such as a widely diversified client base and good education and training programs. Second, the people were friendly and interesting, and seemed to be the type of people with whom I would work well. Third, I thought that there were opportunities available for career advancement. The first "promotion" to the level of senior accountant would take approximately two years. A senior accountant runs the audit on a day-to-day basis, and supervises and trains the less experienced staff people. After the senior level, the next advancement is to manager, and finally, to partner. The usual timetable starting from the first day of work to becoming a partner is approximately twelve years.

My short time with AY has been just about what I expected it to be. I have met new people and developed many friendships. Although I often work long hours, the work has been challenging and I have learned a great deal about the business community. I have been given more responsibility and now supervise several people during an audit.

I believe that I made the right decision to join AY two and one-half years ago. I am looking forward to many more years with the firm. In ten years, perhaps I'll even be a partner.

Financial Management

This section surveys the major financial institutions and their use by business managers in pursuit of profit objectives. Chapter 14 concentrates on commercial banks and the commercial banking system. It also describes briefly the nature and functions of savings banks, savings and loan associations, trust companies, and several other financial institutions. In addition, it explains the operation of the Federal Reserve System.

Chapter 15 turns to the role of the financial manager. It explains the general sources of funds for business and the criteria for their selection. The uses and sources of short-term financing are then discussed, including various forms of loans and the use of commercial paper.

Risk management is the second major topic of Chapter 15. The basic concepts of risk and risk-shifting by means of insurance are discussed. The underlying principles of insurance and the major types of insurance are described.

Chapter 16 describes the securities (stock and bond) market and the major institutions involved in it. A detailed explanation of the "securities" pages of the newspaper is provided as well. The securities market is tied to the financial manager's job in that it is the major source of long-term capital. The sources of such capital for noncorporate businesses are also discussed as are the uses to which long-term funds are put. Chapter 16 closes with a discussion of extraordinary financial arrangements, with special emphasis on mergers and acquisitions.

CHAPTER 14

Banks and Other Financial Institutions

OBJECTIVES:

After reading this chapter, you should be able to

1. Describe the commercial bank and its services.
2. Explain the functions of the FDIC.
3. Discuss the future of Electronic Funds Transfer.
4. Compare and contrast the operations of savings banks, savings and loan associations, and credit unions.
5. Outline the functions of commercial finance companies, sales finance companies, and factoring companies.
6. Explain the roles of trust companies, consumer finance companies, and commercial paper houses.
7. Explain the recent growth of money market mutual funds and "all-in-one" financial institutions.
8. Discuss the various forms of commercial bank deposits.
9. Describe the loan function of the commercial bank and the role of the prime rate.
10. Develop an example showing how the commercial banking system creates money.
11. Describe the structure of the Federal Reserve System.
12. Outline the operations of the Fed.

KEY CONCEPTS:

Look for these terms as you read the chapter

money
commercial bank
Federal Deposit Insurance Corporation (FDIC)
savings bank
negotiable order of withdrawal (NOW)
savings and loan association
trust company
credit union
life insurance company
factoring company

commercial finance company
sales finance company
consumer finance company
commercial paper house
demand deposit
time deposit
money market mutual fund
prime rate of interest
Federal Reserve System
reserve requirement
margin requirement

Welcome to the era of "all-in-one" money institutions! Big things are happening in the money business. The largest insurance company, retailer, and credit-card company in the nation have all gotten involved in the stock market by buying up some of the biggest stock-and-bond firms. Wall Street—the financial center of New York—will never be the same. The buyers are Prudential Insurance, Sears, and American Express and the firms acquired are, respectively, the Bache Group, Dean Witter Reynolds, and Shearson Loeb Rhoades. The price tags ranged up to a billion dollars. Sears also bought a big real estate and mortgage firm, Coldwell Banker.

This list of mergers and acquisitions in the world of finance signals a dramatic change in the nature of competition among financial institutions and the scope of services they offer. In this chapter we will find out more about these changes and the special impact they will be having on banks, savings and loan institutions, and the distribution of functions among financial institutions in America.

In this first of three chapters about finance we will describe many of the financial institutions that serve industry and commerce. These include commercial banks, savings and loan associations, commercial finance companies, and credit unions, to name only a few. Because of its central role, we will give most attention to the commercial bank and to the commercial banking system. Because of the general state of experimentation and rapid evolution in current financial circles we will try to avoid detailed description of regulations and financial practices.

Another important institution that we will study is the Federal Reserve System, one of the chief influences on the money and banking activity of the United States. The descriptions in this chapter will serve as an introduction to subsequent discussions of short, intermediate, and long term financial decision making.

TYPES OF FINANCIAL INSTITUTIONS

Without money, business as we know it could not exist. Money is anything that people generally will accept in payment of debts. Paper currency and coins issued by a recognized government are legal tender in that nation. If you owe a debt that is stated in money terms, your creditor must accept your payment in legal tender.

money

But that is not all there is to money. Most American workers, for example, are paid with checks. Many workers deposit their checks in their checking accounts and pay their bills with checks. This is possible because of our modern banking system. **Money, therefore, means paper currency, coins, checkable deposits at banks and other financial institutions, as well as travelers' checks of nonbank issuers.**

There are many different types of financial institutions. Their customers include consumers, businesses, and nonbusiness organizations. As the nature of these customers' needs changes and as the laws that regulate financial institutions change, new types of financial institutions appear and old ones may disappear. The same, of course, is true of the types of services they offer. The following discussion focuses on the major types of financial institutions in our business system:

- commercial banks
- savings banks
- savings and loan associations
- trust companies
- credit unions

- life insurance companies
- factoring companies
- commercial finance companies
- sales finance companies
- consumer finance companies
- commercial paper houses

Commercial Banks

The heart of our banking system is the commercial bank. **A commercial bank is a privately owned, profit-seeking firm that serves individuals, nonbusiness organizations, and businesses. Commercial banks offer checking accounts and savings accounts, make loans, and offer many other services to their customers. They are the main source of short-term loans for business firms.**

Table 14-1 lists several types of services offered by many commercial banks. Commercial banks chartered by the federal government are national banks. Those chartered by state governments are state banks. Both types are closely regulated.

Perhaps you have read about "banking panics" or "runs on banks" that occurred in the history of banking in the United States. The last series of major panics occurred during the Great Depression. Depositors lost faith in the economy and wanted to withdraw their funds from banks. A typical bank could not possibly pay off all its depositors if they wanted to withdraw on the same day, because it

commercial bank

1. Checking accounts
2. Safe deposit boxes
3. Storage of idle cash in certificates of deposit
4. Short-term loans (1—6 months)
5. Long-term loans
6. Loans to a firm's customers
7. Exchange of U.S. dollars for foreign currencies
8. Exchange of foreign currencies for U.S. dollars
9. Advice to business people on financial matters
10. Registration of corporations' stocks
11. Transferring ownership of corporations' stocks
12. Safeguarding property entrusted to them

TABLE 14-1

Some important services provided by commercial banks

**What Is the Future
of Electronic
Funds Transfer?**

```
╭──────────────────╮
│  WHAT DO YOU     │
│     THINK?       │
╰──────────────────╯
```

Electronic Funds Transfer (EFT)
is one of the remarkable new
ways in which commercial
banks serve their customers.

It now takes many forms:

- *Automated Teller Machines* or *24-Hour Tellers* are electronic terminals that permit you to bank at almost any
time of day or night. Generally, you insert a special EFT
card and enter your own secret identification number
(PIN) to withdraw cash, make deposits, or transfer funds
between accounts.

- *Pay-by-Phone Systems* permit you to telephone your
bank (or other financial institution) and instruct it to pay
certain bills or to transfer funds between accounts.

- *Direct Deposits or Withdrawals* allow you to authorize
specific deposits such as paychecks and social security
checks to your account on a regular basis. You can also
arrange to have recurring bills such as insurance premiums and utility bills paid automatically. You must
authorize such arrangements in advance.

- *Point-of-Sale Transfers* let you pay for retail purchases

kept only a small percentage of its customers' deposits in cash. Thus
many banks failed. They simply could not call in all their outstanding loans that fast.

**Federal Deposit
Insurance Corporation
(FDIC)**

**Congress created the Federal Deposit Insurance Corporation
(FDIC) in 1933. All national banks must carry deposit insurance and
most state banks voluntarily do so. Each insured bank pays a fee
(based on its total deposits) for this insurance. The FDIC uses these**

24-hour tellers allow a
bank's customers to
bank when it's
convenient

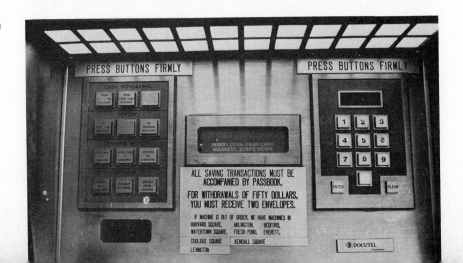

with your EFT card. This is similar to using a credit card with one important exception: the money for the purchase is immediately transferred from your bank account to the store's account.[1]

These new banking services do carry with them, however, certain pitfalls or drawbacks. For instance, under the new EFT law once you make a transfer you have no right to stop payment except in very special circumstances. It is also possible to lose up to $500 if you lose your EFT card and do not notify the bank within two business days. If there is an error in your account you have sixty days to notify the bank, otherwise you may be out of luck.

For bank customers who are not careful about checking their monthly statements or who lose things like their EFT cards, the opportunities for loss are significant. These pitfalls may be serious enough to discourage many bank customers from using such banking features. If the usage rate of EFT privileges is low, such costly bank services may not pay for themselves and will lower bank profits. In times of tight money, especially, the future of EFT may be in jeopardy. What is the future of electronic funds transfer? WHAT DO YOU THINK?

funds to pay off depositors (up to $100,000 per account) who have accounts in banks that fail. The FDIC has authority to examine all insured banks.

Nationally chartered banks are audited by the comptroller of the currency and state banks are audited by state banking authorities. Day-to-day operations of banks are regulated with respect to the *maximum* interest rate they can pay on deposits and the types of investments they can make. Their lending policies are also subject to review.

There has been some deregulation of banks and savings and loan associations in recent years and further deregulation is being considered. For example, prior to January 1, 1980, banks could not pay interest on their customers' checking account balances and savings and loan associations could not offer checking accounts. Now banks can pay interest on checking accounts and savings and loan associations can offer checking accounts. Under consideration are other moves toward deregulation, including removal of the ceiling on the interest rate that banks can pay on their customers' regular savings accounts. Deregulation has made banks and savings and loan associations more competitive.

Savings Banks

savings bank

Savings banks are not as numerous as commercial banks. **A savings bank serves small savers by accepting their deposits and paying them interest on their savings. Savings banks invest the funds mainly in real estate mortgages and government securities.**

There are two types of savings banks. Stock companies are owned by stockholders who earn dividends from net profit. Mutual companies are owned by the depositors. Most savings banks are mutual companies. Stock savings banks, for the most part, have developed into commercial banks.

negotiable order of
withdrawal (NOW)

Mutual savings banks in the New England states and New York were the first to offer "negotiable order of withdrawal" (NOW) accounts. These accounts enable depositors to write checks on their interest-bearing savings accounts to pay their bills. Many require a minimum balance. Today, many commercial banks and other savings institutions offer NOW accounts. A mid-1981 report showed that 85 percent of NOW money had been placed in commercial banks and only 5.6 percent in mutual savings banks. Savings banks were especially hurt recently by rising interest rates and the deregulation of competing institutions. The problem has been so serious as to require a substantial number of mergers of savings banks so they could survive. Federal subsidy programs have also been under consideration. The problems many savings banks have stem from the heavy proportion of low-interest loans still held by such banks since the era of abundant housing credit.

Savings and Loan Associations

savings and loan
association

Another financial institution is the savings and loan association (S&LA). **A savings and loan association accepts deposits from the general public. It lends funds mainly for mortgages on homes and other real estate.** Recent changes in the law permit them to buy corporate debt instruments and otherwise broaden their lending capability. Further legal changes that might help make S&LAs roughly competitive with commercial banks are being considered so as to increase their (S&LAs) earning power.

An S&LA can be a mutual company (owned by depositors) or a stock company (owned by stockholders). S&LAs also help businesses to finance the purchase of real estate. The Federal Savings and Loan Insurance Corporation (FSLIC) insures each account in member S&LAs up to $100,000.

Newer S&LAs are thriving compared to older, well-established ones. This is because they are receiving the income benefits of dereg-

SAVE AT GREAT RATES
From SOUTH BOSTON SAVINGS BANK

We offer a wide range of savings accounts to choose from. Call or stop by any of our convenient offices and start earning these high rates from the highest earning savings bank in Massachusetts.

ALL DEPOSITS INSURED IN FULL

6 MONTHS
$10,000 Minimum Deposit
9.50%

1-YEAR
$1000 Minimum Deposit
10.00%

2 YEARS
$1000 Minimum Deposit
10.50%

3 YEARS
$1000 Minimum Deposit
11.00%

MONEY MARKET DEPOSIT ACCOUNT
$2500 Minimum Deposit
9.50%

Federal Regulations require a penalty for early withdrawal.

MAIN OFFICE:
460 West Broadway, South Boston
9 a.m. to 3:30 p.m.— Monday thru Friday
Saturday — 10:00 a.m. to 1 p.m. Call: 268-2500

NEPONSET CIRCLE OFFICE:
740 Gallivan Boulevard
8:30 a.m. to 5:30 p.m.— Monday, Tuesday,
Wednesday & Friday
Thursday — 8:30 a.m. to 7:30 p.m.
Saturday — 8:30 a.m. to 12 Noon

QUINCY OFFICE:
690 Adams Street, Lakin Square
Monday, Tuesday, Wednesday, Thursday
8:30 a.m. to 5 p.m.
Friday 8:30 a.m. to 7 p.m.
Saturday — 8:30 a.m. to 12 Noon

South Boston Savings Bank
"ALWAYS THE LEADER"

Savings banks have begun to offer high-interest accounts in an attempt to compete with money market funds

ulation without suffering from the burden of past housing loans at very low interest rates.

The Federal Home Loan Bank Board, which oversees operations of S&LAs, has taken action to aid financially troubled institutions. This includes lifting the former limit on borrowing from firms outside the system and making available emergency loans from FSLIC. S&LAs have also been helped by the lifting of interest limits from retirement accounts and the creation of new tax free certificates, called "All Savers" certificates, made available through S&LAs, credit unions, and commercial banks as an experiment in 1981–1982.

To compete with other institutions, some S&LAs offer a special investment opportunity for individuals and businesses—repurchase agreements. The S&LA buys large-denomination government agency obligations and sells "pieces" of them to investors along with agreements to buy them back at the option of the investor. The investor will then be paid the original investment plus total interest earned to date. The minimum investment is $1,000 and there are no penalties for early redemption. The total investment plus all interest earned will be returned at any time, even before the end of the eighty-nine day term, with no penalty. The interest rate is fixed for eighty-nine days. The greater the amount of the repurchase agreement, the higher the interest rate. Repurchase agreements, however, are not savings accounts or deposits and are not insured by the FSLIC. They enable S&LAs to compete for customers who want to earn interest rates higher than those offered on passbook savings.

Trust Companies

trust company

Another financial institution that serves individuals and businesses is the trust company. **A trust company safeguards property— funds and estates—entrusted to it. It also may serve as trustee, transfer agent, and registrar for corporations and provide other services.**

A corporation selling bonds to many investors appoints a trustee, usually a trust company, to protect the bondholders' interests. A trust company can also serve as a transfer agent and registrar for corporations. A transfer agent records changes in ownership of a corporation's stock. A registrar certifies to the investing public that stock issues are correctly stated and in compliance with the corporate charter. Other services include preparing and issuing dividend checks to stockholders and serving as trustee for employee profit-sharing funds. Commercial banks in many states also provide trust services.

Credit Unions

Credit unions are important to business because they lend money to consumers to buy durable goods like cars and furniture. **A credit union is a cooperative savings association formed by the employees of a company or nonbusiness organization.** Members (owners) can add to their savings accounts (share accounts) by authorizing deductions from their paychecks or by making direct deposits. Members can also borrow from the credit union. The cost of borrowing is usually lower than that from other lenders because the credit union is owned and operated by its members. The National Credit Union Administration (NCUA) insures each account in member credit unions up to $100,000.

Some credit unions are state chartered and others are federally chartered. Both can now offer thirty-year residential loans and can participate in tax-sheltered retirement accounts and NOW accounts. In 1981 they were authorized to issue All-Savers certificates as well.

credit union

Life Insurance Companies

An important source of funds for individuals, nonbusiness organizations, and businesses is the life insurance company. **A life insurance company is a mutual or stock company that shares risk with its policyholders for payment of a premium.** Some of the money it collects as premiums is loaned to borrowers. We discuss life insurance companies in greater detail in our next chapter, where we will see that their scope of activities is also changing.

life insurance company

Factoring Companies

An important source of short-term funds for many firms is the factoring company. **A factoring company (or factor) buys accounts receivable (amounts due from credit customers) from a firm. It pays less than the face value of the accounts but collects the face value of the accounts. The difference, minus the cost of doing business, is the factor's profit.**

A firm that sells its accounts receivable to a factor "without recourse" shifts the risk of credit loss to the factor. If an account turns out to be uncollectible, the factor suffers the loss. However, a factor is a specialist in credit and collection activities. Using a factor may enable a firm to expand its sales. The firm does not have to tie up as much of its own money in accounts receivable financing when it uses a factor. In effect, the firm trades accounts receivable for cash. The factor notifies the firm's customers to make their payments to

factoring company

the factor. This also often reduces the firm's collection costs. In periods of relatively tight money supplies many firms need to rely heavily on factors.

Commercial Finance Companies

A commercial finance company is similar to a factor. **A commercial finance company makes loans to firms with accounts receivable, inventories, or equipment used as security (collateral) for the loans. Unlike a factoring company, it does not collect the accounts or share the credit risk.** Ordinarily the client's customers do not know that their accounts have been pledged as security for a loan. They continue to make payments to the client. This is called a nonnotification plan.

Commercial finance companies borrow from commercial banks to increase their lending ability. Sometimes clients use commercial finance companies rather than commercial banks if their credit positions are too weak to satisfy a bank.

commercial finance company

Sales Finance Companies

A major source of credit for many firms and their customers is the sales finance company. **A sales finance company specializes in financing installment purchases made by individuals and firms.**

When you buy a durable good from a retailer who is on an installment plan with a sales finance company, the loan is made directly to you. The item bought serves as security for the loan. Sales finance companies enable many firms to sell on credit, even though the firms could not afford to finance credit sales on their own.

General Motors Acceptance Corporation (GMAC) and General Electric Credit Corporation are sales finance companies. These are "captive" companies because they exist to finance installment contracts resulting from sales made by their parent companies. During the "credit crunch" of 1981–1982 such firms offered below-market-rate interest on loans for the purchase of cars and appliances to stimulate the sagging sales of their parent manufacturing companies.

sales finance company

Consumer Finance Companies

An important source of credit for many consumers is the consumer finance company. **A consumer finance company makes personal loans to consumers. Often these loans are made on a "signa-**

consumer finance company

ture basis," and the borrower pledges no security for the loan. For larger loans, collateral may be required, such as a car or furniture.

These companies do not make loans to businesses. But they do provide the financing that turns many "would-be" customers into "paying" customers. Blazer, Dial, or Beneficial Finance offer such personal loans in cities throughout the United States.

Commercial Paper Houses

Large corporations often borrow money by issuing *commercial paper*. Commercial paper is an unsecured promise to pay back a set amount of money at a stated date in the future, usually within 3 to 180 days. It is a type of promissory note, which we will discuss later in this chapter. Promissory notes are one of the most widely used credit instruments for getting short-term funds. The good faith of the issuing corporation is the backing for commercial paper. The interest rate on this paper is usually lower than that on loans from commercial banks.

A commercial paper house is a financial institution that buys commercial paper directly from issuing corporations and resells it to buyers such as pension funds, trust departments in commercial banks, and other corporations with extra temporary cash on hand. In some cases a commercial paper house acts as a middleman who charges a commission for bringing the issuing company and a buyer together.

commercial paper house

The "All-in-One" Financial Institutions

The newest development in the history of financial institutions is the "all-in-one" institution or "super" institution which was described at the very beginning of this chapter. As a result of a rapid series of large-scale mergers involving brokerage houses, realty firms, retail store chains, and an unbelievable variety of other firms, there has arisen what may be the financial institutions of the future. These may in many ways supplant most existing institutions. Sears, for example, has a brokerage firm, a real estate firm, a savings and loan association (in California), Allstate Insurance, and other financial capabilities. These capabilities, combined with its established reputation and network of locations throughout the nation, can make it a chain of "one-stop" financial centers as well as America's biggest retailer. To what extent these all-in-one institutions like Sears and Merrill Lynch will take the place of traditional commercial banks, S&LAs, and so forth, remains to be seen. Their success will be largely a function of further changes in financial

IF YOUR INVESTMENTS ARE
THEY AREN'T DOING

PRESENTING
THE MERRILL LYNCH CASH

Until quite recently, the traditional role for an investment portfolio was rather strictly defined: To grow in worth. To provide income. Basically, to earn money.

But, no matter whether it was stocks, bonds, money market instruments or simply certificates of deposit, the net result was that earning money was all that your investments could do for you.

Then a few years ago, Merrill Lynch invented the Cash Management Account* financial service. A revolutionary new kind of brokerage account that not only earns money for you, but also manages it at the same time.

In effect, CMA™ allows your money to work continually at its maximum potential, without relinquishing the least amount of liquidity, flexibility and convenience that you demand.

Today, there is no question about CMA's proven abilities and potential for the sophisticated investor. In fact, more than 450,000 investors with over 25 billion dollars invested now rely on its many features.

The only question remaining should be how the Cash Management Account program can begin working for you, immediately.

QUALIFICATION. To open a CMA account requires that you place a minimum of $20,000 in cash or securities, or a combination of both, in a Merrill Lynch brokerage account.

This obviously affords you a safe and convenient place to hold your securities.

And, importantly, it entitles you to the services of an experienced Merrill Lynch Account Executive whom you can rely upon for sound advice, counsel and an immediate conduit to our number-one research department.

But, much more, this is just the beginning your assets need to give them the special qualities that make the CMA service so unique.

MAXIMIZATION. There is virtually no such thing as idle cash in a CMA account. On opening your account, any cash you originally place there is automatically invested in your choice of three professionally managed money market funds. The choice of which fund is best for your particular investment strategy is, of course, your decision. But the CMA Money Fund, Tax-Exempt Fund or the new Government Securities Fund can provide definite advantages for any portfolio.

Daily, the dividend on your money market fund is reinvested for you. And any cash that is generated on your securities (i.e. dividends, interest, proceeds from sales) is also automatically invested in your money fund. Without you, your

Merrill Lynch, a well-known securities brokerage house, is now offering a variety of checking, loan, and investment services

ONLY EARNING YOU MONEY, NEARLY ENOUGH.

MANAGEMENT ACCOUNT.®

broker or the postman ever getting involved. So, your money continually works earning more money, without your having to work at doing anything.

LIQUIDITY. Now, let's assume that while your money is busy working for you, it's necessary to take an important business trip. Or, on vacation in Mexico City, you spot a rare antique.

With the CMA service, you have instant access to your assets, anywhere in the world, at any time. You can make purchases. And although Merrill Lynch is not a bank, you can get cash advances when you need to.

CMA's special checking and VISA® card (provided by Bank One of Columbus, Ohio,

N.A.) are all the credentials you'll need to use your money when you want to. If there is not enough cash to cover your purchases from the balance in your money market fund, you are entitled to borrow up to the full margin value of your securities, instantly. This constitutes an automatic loan on *our* part. With no time limit of repayment on *your* part.

CONVENIENCE. At the end of each month, you'll receive CMA's comprehensive computerized statement. It lists all your

transactions, and a daily reconciliation of your account. You'll have a record of everything from the market value of your security positions, including annual percent yield and estimated income, as well as all your VISA and checking activities, on one convenient form.

And, if on any business day during the month, you want to know exactly how much money is available to you, you only have to call a special toll-free 800 number.

So, there you have it. The Merrill Lynch Cash Management Account. A unique service that keeps your money working productively, while giving you immediate access to your assets.

For more complete information, including a prospectus containing all sales charges and expenses, call 800-526-3030 (in New Jersey, call 800-742-2900). Read the prospectus carefully before you invest or forward funds. We're convinced that once you realize all that your investments can do for you, you won't want to be without it.

THE MORE YOU DEMAND OF YOUR MONEY, THE MORE YOU NEED CMA.™

Merrill Lynch
Merrill Lynch, Pierce, Fenner & Smith Inc
A breed apart.

There are Serious
Grounds for
Criticizing the Role
of Money Brokers

POINT OF VIEW

At first blush, Sparta Sanders State Bank in Kentucky seemed a vital, growing concern. In just two years its deposits had doubled, to $16.5 million.

But when regulators closed the bank in April of 1983, they found a nearly worthless concern. All but about $4 million of the bank's deposits, it turned out, had been raised from around the country through money brokers. Local deposits had actually been shrinking. Officials quickly realized they wouldn't be able to find a stronger bank to take over the failing one. Sparta Sanders was a shell with little local deposit base.

Sparta Sanders would probably have failed months earlier if not for the money brokers, a growing corps of financiers who direct deposits to institutions. Money brokers are a powerful tool—they let banks and savings and loan associations break the shackles binding them to their local service areas and tap an increasingly national market for large deposits.

But regulators complain that brokers may harm more than they help. They worry that brokers seek only the highest rates, regardless of an institution's reliability or financial strength. As a result, they warn, brokers could give ailing little banks the means to finance dubious activities and become big problems. And, critics say, brokers enable banks to raise money for reckless investing much faster than the government can keep track.

"The brokers are removing all the discipline that now exists from the deposit-taking process," says Raymond Garea, executive vice president of Cates Consulting Analysts Inc. in New York.

One now-closed bank, Western National of Lovell, Wyoming, raised more than $10 million by offering 11 percent on $100,000 "jumbo" certificates of deposit. The going rate at the time was about 9 percent. The bank used the funds to buy insurance annuities that turned out to be worthless.

That isn't an isolated case. Penn Square Bank of Oklahoma City, which failed in 1982, helped finance a spree of dubious energy lending by using brokers to raise more than $120 million of its $473 million in deposits. Similarly, $82.2 million of the $259.7 million in deposits at American City Bank in Los Angeles, which failed in February 1983, were placed by brokers.

While it is easy to sympathize with small banks that see their local deposits shriveling, the final result of money brokerage has often been bank failure, not to mention significant losses to the Federal Deposit Insurance Corporation.

regulation and of the way that the new "supers" stand up under political and economic strain.

In the long run there is the possibility that only a few such institutions will dominate the whole financial picture. At that point, and maybe before it, there is a chance that antitrust forces will block their growth for fear of monopolies in the money market. Certainly, the powerful banking community will not go down without a fight.

THE COMMERCIAL BANKING SYSTEM

Of all the financial institutions we have discussed, the commercial bank is the most important to businesses. As you can see from Table 14-2, many commercial banks hold assets well in excess of $10 billion.

Commercial Bank Deposits

For many years there was a careful distinction between two types of deposits in commercial banks: (1) demand deposits and (2) time deposits.

A demand deposit is a checking account. Customers who deposit coins, currency, or other checks in their checking accounts can write checks against the balances in their accounts. Their banks must honor these checks immediately. That is why checking accounts are called demand deposits. Demand deposits are the most important type of money in our economic system. They account for about 80 percent of the total money supply.

demand deposit

A time deposit is one that is to remain with the bank for a period of time. Interest is paid to depositors during the time their money is on deposit in the bank. The bank, of course, uses this money to make loans to its customers. The bank pays interest to its depositors and it charges interest to its borrowers. Table 14-2 illustrates the deposits held by the largest U.S. banks.

time deposit

The distinction between these kinds of deposits has become blurred by the introduction of NOW accounts in commercial banks as well as in other financial institutions. The NOW account, as we have seen, permits check writing and pays interest but requires a minimum balance.

There are two basic types of time deposits: (1) regular passbook accounts and (2) certificates of deposit (CDs). Passbook accounts are intended mainly for small individual savers and nonprofit organizations. Depositors put their savings in these accounts and, for all practical purposes, there is no required amount of time that they

Bank	Assets $ Thousands	Deposits $ Thousands
1. Citicorp (New York)	129,997,000	76,538,000
2. BankAmerica Corp. (San Francisco)	122,220,806	94,341,795
3. Chase Manhattan Corp. (New York)	80,862,903	56,857,847
4. Manufacturers Hanover Corp. (New York)	64,040,552	43,824,670
5. J. P. Morgan & Co. (New York)	58,597,000	37,910,000
6. Chemical New York Corp.	48,274,842	27,998,414
7. Continental Illinois Corp. (Chicago)	42,899,424	28,175,021
8. First Interstate Bancorp. (Los Angeles)	40,884,296	30,542,067
9. Bankers Trust New York Corp.	40,427,059	24,492,559
10. Security Pacific Corp. (Los Angeles)	36,991,034	25,848,489
11. First Chicago Corp.	35,876,372	27,418,645
12. Crocker National Corp. (San Francisco)	24,938,759	18,194,526
13. Wells Fargo & Co. (San Francisco)	24,814,047	18,179,790
14. InterFirst Corp. (Dallas)	21,030,000	14,405,000
15. Mellon National Corp. (Pittsburgh)	20,294,405	12,328,322
16. Marine Midland Banks (Buffalo)[3]	20,238,764	15,056,936
17. Irving Bank Corp. (New York)	19,514,285	14,152,624
18. First National Boston Corp.	18,267,397	11,674,496
19. Texas Commerce Bancshares (Houston)	18,217,000	13,212,000
20. Northwest Bancorp. (Minneapolis)	17,584,679	11,971,229

TABLE 14-2

The twenty largest banks in the United States, 1982 (ranked by assets)

must be left on deposit. Although a bank can require 30-days notice before withdrawals can be made, this is seldom done.

NOW account customers earn interest on what used to be noninterest-paying checking accounts. This represents a cost to financial institutions but many of them are finding record keeping easier for NOW accounts, thereby saving them money. The traditional passbook cannot be handled as readily with modern electronic data processing equipment. Many commercial banks, as well as S&LAs and credit unions, have encouraged their depositors to convert their passbook savings accounts to statement accounts. The depositor who converts receives a monthly or quarterly computer-prepared statement summarizing his or her account's activity during the period. There is no need for a passbook.

The certificate of deposit (CD) is a deposit made for a certain period of time at a fixed rate of interest. The time period can range from thirty days for large amounts of money (usually $100,000 or more) to several years for smaller amounts (usually $500 or more). CDs are available to all and are insured up to $100,000. The interest rate paid is higher than that paid on regular passbook savings and withdrawal prior to the date of maturity results in a penalty. If you

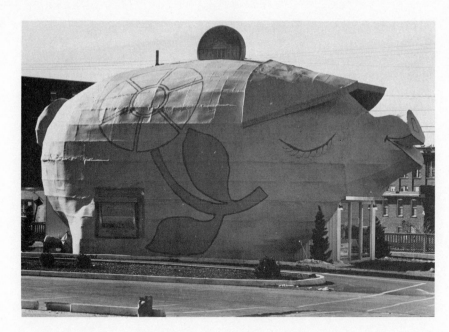

Commercial banks offer a full range of services to businesses and consumers

expect interest rates to rise you might hesitate to buy a CD, especially one with a distant maturity date.

The inconvenience and cost involved in premature withdrawal from a CD have contributed to the popularity and growth of the money market mutual fund. **Money market mutual funds are pools of funds invested in Treasury bills, commercial paper, and "jumbo" ($100,000 or more) CDs.** The interest rate returned to investors varies with the return received from the average of the funds' various investments. Because there are many investors in the money market mutual fund it is possible for them to enter or withdraw at any time and to add to their accounts or withdraw a part of their investment without penalty. Some permit check writing against the balance.

money market mutual fund

Money market CDs are not to be confused with the money market mutual fund. Money market CDs are sold by commercial banks, S&LAs, credit unions, and savings banks. The interest rate paid is tied to the interest rate paid on six-month U.S. Treasury Bills. Every week, the interest rate for certificates bought during the week is announced. The rate, once established, remains effective for the certificate until its maturity.

Commercial Bank Loans

As we will see in the next chapter, commercial banks are the major source of short-term (one year or less) loans for businesses.

Although they make long-term loans to some firms, commercial banks prefer to specialize in providing short-term funds.

Borrowers pay interest on their loans. Large firms with excellent credit records pay the prime rate of interest. **The prime rate of interest is the lowest rate charged to major business customers by a specific large bank. It often differs from one bank to another and from one region to another. It is most important as a general indicator of the availability of loanable funds.** Securities dealers, for example, keep a close eye on the movement of the "prime" at major banks to get an idea of the direction in which interest rates may be going. Sometimes there is no connection at all between changes in the "prime" and changes in the "going rate" for home mortgages. The former is a short-term money rate and the latter is a rate for long-term lending. Commercial banks offer both secured and unsecured loans.

A secured loan is backed by collateral such as accounts receivable or a life insurance policy. If the borrower cannot repay the loan, the bank sells the collateral. An unsecured loan is backed only by the borrower's promise to repay it. Only the most creditworthy borrowers can get unsecured loans.

prime rate of interest

Deposit Expansion

Suppose you save $100 in 50-cent pieces, take them to a commercial bank, and open a checking account. Some portion of your $100 is likely to stay in your account. Your bank can earn interest by lending some of it to borrowers.

Banks subject to federal regulation must keep some portion of their demand deposits in vault cash or as deposits with a Federal Reserve Bank. These are legal reserves. Let's assume that the reserve requirement is 10 percent. Your bank, then, must keep $10 of your $100 deposit in legal reserves. It has $90 to lend.

Now suppose Tom Powers borrows that $90 from your bank. Tom has $90 added to his checking account. Assume that Tom writes a check for $90 payable to the Acme Store. Acme's bank ends up with a $90 deposit. But Acme's bank only has to keep 10 percent of $90 ($9.00) in legal reserves. Acme's bank, therefore, can lend out $81.00.

This is the process of *deposit expansion*. It can continue as shown in Table 14-3. The commercial banking system does create money in the form of demand deposits. Of course, the process of deposit expansion is much more complex in practice. General economic conditions, for example, influence the willingness of bankers to make loans and the willingness of borrowers to borrow.

". . . and we give you $9\frac{1}{2}$% if you never withdraw it."

FIRST LOCAL S&L

6% INTEREST - 90 DAY ACCT.

6¾% INTEREST - 3 YR. ACCT.

7¾% INTEREST - 6 YR. ACCT.

Bank	New deposit	New loan	Legal reserve
Your bank	$100.00	$90.00	$10.00
Bank 2	90.00	81.00	9.00
Bank 3	81.00	72.90	8.10
Bank 4	72.90	65.61	7.29
Bank 5	65.61	59.05	6.56
Bank 6	59.05	53.14	5.91
Bank 7	53.14	47.83	5.31
Bank 8	47.83	43.05	4.78
Bank 9	43.05	38.74	4.31
Total for first nine banks	$612.58	$551.32	$61.26
Expansion limit for entire banking system	$1,000.00	$900.00	$100.00

Note: Assume a reserve requirement of 10 percent.

But as you can see from Table 14-3 your original deposit of $100 in coins could result in an increase of $1,000 in new deposits for all banks in the commercial banking system. Remember, we are assuming a reserve requirement of 10 percent. Thus your original deposit of $100 in coins could expand by 10 times (the reciprocal of the reserve requirement, $\frac{100}{10}$). If the reserve requirement were 20 percent, your original deposit could expand by only 5 times ($\frac{100}{20}$) or to $500. Our example in Table 14-3 assumes that no borrower takes part of his or her loan in cash and that the banks want to lend as much as they legally can. Otherwise, the increase would be less than $1,000.

TABLE 14-3

How the commercial banking system creates money

THE FEDERAL RESERVE SYSTEM

To understand how commercial banking works, we must discuss the Federal Reserve System. **The Federal Reserve System (the Fed) was created by the Federal Reserve Act of 1913. The Fed is the central bank of the United States. Its main purpose is to control the nation's money supply.**

Federal Reserve System

The Board of Governors

The board of governors of the Federal Reserve System is composed of seven members who are appointed by the President of the United States with the advice and consent of the Senate. Each member is appointed to a 14-year term. The board of governors provides

There are Limits to Automated Banking

"Automated teller machines have extended banking hours by dispensing cash and making other transactions 24 hours a day. Now U.S. banks are exploring ways to use the same 22,000 machines to expand their geographic reach.

"Within a few years, credit card and bank-card holders may be able to withdraw cash at machines from Portland, Maine to Portland, Oregon."

The authors wonder whether there aren't some basic conservative human instincts when it comes to money-handling that will prevent large-scale application and use of automated tellers and other consumer-level electronic banking devices. Maybe it's old-fashioned, but we feel that most bank customers—even those who hold electronic banking cards or compatible American Express Gold Cards—will be reluctant to use them extensively, partly because of a low level of trust in electronic gadgetry and partly because of security problems (real or imagined) surrounding their use.

Retailers are painfully aware of the repeated failures of attempts to automate grocery shopping. The resistance was at the consumer level. There is reason to believe that much the same psychological barrier applies to banking.

general direction to the twelve Federal Reserve Banks. It can audit their books, and it coordinates their operations in the public interest.

Federal Reserve Banks

The United States is divided into twelve districts, each of which has a Federal Reserve Bank (FRB). (See Figure 14-1.) Each district is composed of several zones, each containing a branch of the District Federal Reserve Bank. Each FRB is owned by member commercial banks in its district. How many shares a member bank has in the FRB in its district depends on the member bank's size. But the board of directors of an FRB are not elected like board members in a business corporation. If this were permitted, the large commercial banks in a given FRB district would control the election of its board of directors.

Of the nine directors of an FRB, a maximum of three can be bankers, three must be business people, and three are appointed by the board of governors of the Fed to represent the general public.

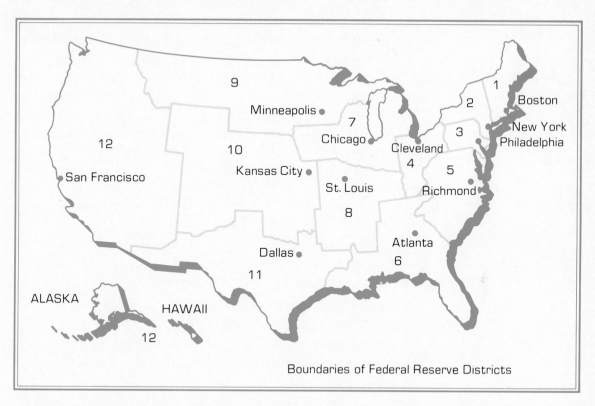

Boundaries of Federal Reserve Districts

FIGURE 14-1
Federal Reserve
Districts

Member commercial banks in each FRB district elect the directors who represent banking and business. These member banks are divided into three classes—large, medium, and small banks. Each group elects one director to represent banking and one member to represent business.

The Federal Open Market Committee (FOMC)

The Federal Open Market Committee (FOMC) is composed of twelve members (the seven members of the board of governors and five FRB representatives). The FOMC sets the Fed's open market policy by directing the FRBs either to buy or to sell government securities. This is explained below.

The Federal Advisory Council

Another important part of the Fed is the Federal Advisory Council. The Federal Advisory Council is composed of twelve members, one from each Federal Reserve Bank. The council's task is to advise the board of governors and to make recommendations to it.

Member Banks

Of the roughly 15,000 commercial banks in the United States, only about 5,500 are members of the Federal Reserve System. But all national banks must be members. State-chartered banks may join if they meet the Fed's requirements. Actually, all of our major commercial banks are members of the Federal Reserve System.

Operations of the Fed

The following activities of the Fed are important to member banks, businesses, investors, and consumers:

- controlling the money supply
- setting the margin requirement
- setting interest ceilings
- using other credit controls
- clearing checks

Controlling the Money Supply

The central Federal Reserve Bank is in Washington, D.C.

The major tool the Fed uses to control the money supply is its open market operations. If the FOMC wants to increase the money supply, it directs FRBs to buy government securities. The FRB pays for these securities by crediting the reserve accounts of the member banks that sell the securities. This increases member bank reserves at the FRB and, therefore, increases member banks' lending ability.

If the FOMC wants to decrease the money supply, it directs FRBs to sell government securities. Purchases by member banks reduce their reserve accounts at their FRBs. This reduces member banks' lending ability.

The unusually high rate of inflation, often combined with unemployment in recent years, has put these tools for controlling the money supply to the harshest test. It is likely, however, that inflation would have been even more severe if the Fed's controls had not been put to use. A member bank that wants to borrow at its FRB may present commercial paper to the FRB. The FRB will discount this paper—give the member bank less than the face value of the commercial paper. The *discount rate*, in effect, is the FRB's interest rate on member bank borrowing.

To **stimulate** business activity and increase the money supply	To **slow down** business activity and decrease the money supply
1. Buy government securities: These purchases by FRBs increase member bank reserves and their ability to make loans to businesses and consumers.	1. Sell government securities: These sales by FRBs decrease member bank reserves and their ability to make loans to businesses and consumers.
2. Lower the discount rate: By increasing the willingness of member banks to borrow at their FRBs, more loans to businesses and consumers can be made.	2. Raise the discount rate: By decreasing the willingness of member banks to borrow at their FRBs, fewer loans to businesses and consumers can be made.
3. Lower the reserve requirement: Member banks are required to keep less cash in their vaults or on deposit with their FRBs.	3. Raise the reserve requirement: Member banks are required to keep more cash in their vaults or on deposit with their FRBs.

TABLE 14-4

Federal Reserve System actions to stimulate or slow down the level of business activity

Each FRB sets its own discount rate subject to approval by the board of governors. Raising the discount rate makes member banks less willing to borrow, tends to raise the interest rate member banks charge their borrowers, and reduces the money supply. Lowering the discount rate has the opposite effects. It encourages member banks to borrow, tends to lower the interest rate member banks charge their borrowers, and increases the money supply.

The board of governors sets the reserve requirement. **The reserve requirement is the percentage of their deposits that member banks have to keep in vault cash or as deposits with their FRBs.** Lowering the reserve requirement increases the money supply. Raising it decreases the money supply. Table 14-4 summarizes these money supply controls.

reserve requirement

Setting the Margin Requirement

The margin requirement is the percentage that buyers of corporate securities must pay in cash when they buy securities. The remainder of the purchase price is borrowed from the broker. Raising the margin requirement discourages investors from buying securities. Lowering it has the opposite effect.

margin requirement

Setting Interest Ceilings

By raising the maximum rate of interest that commercial banks can pay on savings accounts, the Fed seeks to increase people's willingness to save. This brings in deposits to member banks and increases their ability to lend. Lowering the maximum rate, of course, has the opposite effect.

Using Other Credit Controls

The Fed can also use consumer credit controls and real estate credit controls to regulate the volume of credit. For example, in an effort to reduce inflation by holding down the growth of credit, the Fed on March 14, 1980, announced new rules that were to remain in effect for several months. One required money market mutual funds to deposit 15 percent of all new money they received from investors after that date in a non-interest-bearing reserve account with the Fed. This served to moderate the high interest rates the funds were paying to their investors.

FIGURE 14-2

How a check is cleared through the Federal Reserve System

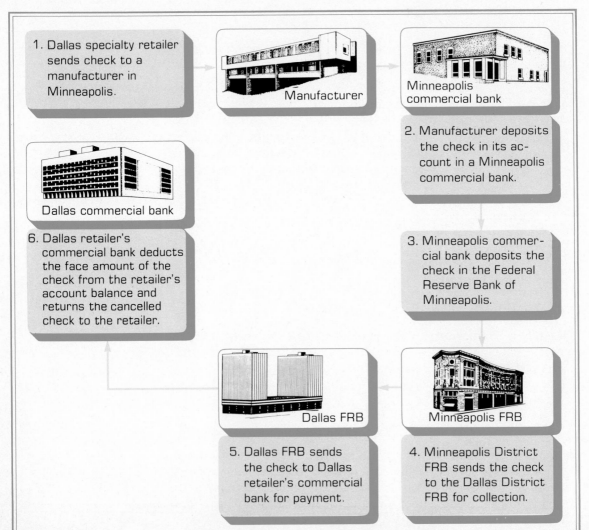

1. Dallas specialty retailer sends check to a manufacturer in Minneapolis.

Manufacturer

Minneapolis commercial bank

2. Manufacturer deposits the check in its account in a Minneapolis commercial bank.

Dallas commercial bank

6. Dallas retailer's commercial bank deducts the face amount of the check from the retailer's account balance and returns the cancelled check to the retailer.

3. Minneapolis commercial bank deposits the check in the Federal Reserve Bank of Minneapolis.

Dallas FRB

Minneapolis FRB

5. Dallas FRB sends the check to Dallas retailer's commercial bank for payment.

4. Minneapolis District FRB sends the check to the Dallas District FRB for collection.

The Fed sometimes uses "moral suasion" when it tries to influence bankers to do what it believes is in the economy's best interest. The Credit Control Act of 1969 allows the Fed, at the request of the President of the United States, to impose a broad range of credit controls, including regulation of minimum down payments and maximum maturities on consumer loans. Thus, in 1980 the President announced that, as part of his program to restrain credit card use, credit card issuers also had to set aside 15 percent of any new credit in a non-interest-bearing account with the Fed. This lasted for several months. As a result, some bank affiliates of VISA and MasterCard that previously did not charge annual fees for their cards started doing so.

Clearing Checks

The Fed also helps in clearing bank checks. Suppose Aaron draws a check on his account in bank A and mails it to Bob who deposits it in bank B. If both banks are in the same city, the clearing process is handled through the local bank clearing house association.

If Aaron's bank were in Jacksonville and Bob's were in Tampa—both cities in the Jacksonville zone of the Atlanta district FRB—the Jacksonville branch of the Atlanta FRB would clear the check. If the two commercial banks were located in two different zones of the same district or in two different districts, it would require the cooperation of the two branches or district FRBs to negotiate the clearance. Large commercial banks have direct clearance arrangements when volume between them is large, but notification of all such transactions must be made to the appropriate district or branch FRB. Figure 14-2 illustrates the various stages a check goes through to be cleared through the Federal Reserve System.

SUMMARY AND LOOK AHEAD

The commercial bank is at the heart of our banking system. It is the most important source of short-term funds for business firms. Our commercial banking system creates money in the form of demand deposits. The Federal Reserve System (the Fed) is the central bank of the United States. Its main job is to control the nation's money supply.

In addition to commercial banks, there are many other financial institutions—savings banks, savings and loan associations, trust companies, credit unions, life insurance companies, factoring companies, commercial finance companies, sales finance companies, consumer finance companies, and commercial paper houses. A new breed of "super" or "all-in-one" institutions, combining the functions of many traditional institutions, has begun to emerge.

All these institutions serve the financial needs of the business community. Business managers use them to meet the short-term, intermediate-term, and long-term capital requirements of their firms. In Chapter 15 we will discuss the short-term financing decisions of the firm and introduce the concept of risk management. Longer-term financing and the securities market will be covered in Chapter 16.

FOR REVIEW . . .

1. Contrast the new "all-in-one" financial institutions with the traditional commercial bank.

2. What are the major sources and uses of funds from a commercial bank's point of view?

3. What is a NOW account and where did it originate?

4. Explain what an Electronic Funds Transfer (EFT) system can do for a bank customer.

5. What is the role of the FDIC?

6. Contrast: (a) a factoring company and a commercial finance company and (b) a sales finance company and a consumer finance company.

7. Explain how the commercial banking system creates money.

8. Suppose the Fed wants to stimulate business activity. What should it do regarding: (a) the purchase or sale of government securities; (b) the discount rate; and (c) the reserve requirement?

. . . FOR DISCUSSION

1. How will traditional banks combat the growing strength of "all-in-one" financial institutions?

2. What can the government do to ensure the survival of savings banks and S&LAs?

3. Why might a small retailer sell its accounts receivable to a factoring company?

4. How do commercial paper houses help to increase the efficiency of short-term financing by large firms?

5. Federal Reserve Banks often are referred to as "banker's banks." Why?

INCIDENTS

Go for the NOW Accounts?

The First National Bank of Anywhere, USA has a problem since the new NOW accounts became available to them as well as to the aggressive savings and loan associations and credit unions in their city. It has become apparent that a strong marketing effort by S&LAs has brought in thousands of household consumer accounts. About 300 of these consumers deserted First National by dropping their checking accounts. Manny Clark, president of First National, and Bill Janes, his legal counsel, have decided, for the moment, not to seek NOWs for First National. There were three chief arguments against the use of NOWs: first, that the customers lost were small-balance, relatively low profit accounts; second, that the cost of installing the NOW accounts—including a promotional campaign—would be significant; and, third, that the profitability of many current regular checking accounts would be reduced significantly if their owners converted to NOW.

QUESTIONS

1. Do you agree with the bank president? Why or why not?

2. If the bank installed NOW accounts, how would you recommend they promote the new accounts in the face of S&LA competition?

Merger as a Result of the Savings Squeeze

The New York Bank for Savings, the state's oldest savings bank, the nation's second oldest, and the creator of the passbook savings account, was forced by the pressure of interest rates to merge with the Buffalo Savings Bank early in 1982. A week or so before the merger, Federal Deposit Insurance Corporation officials met with the N.Y.B.S. board to advise that a number of banks had been asked to submit merger bids. The banks had been asked to base their bids on the amount of FDIC subsidy they would require to take N.Y.B.S. over.

QUESTIONS

1. Why is it that the N.Y.B.S. could not continue to make a profit by the usual practice of paying savers a fair rate of return and receiving a somewhat higher rate of return from its lending activities? Does the rise in interest rates in the last 5–10 years have anything to do with it? Discuss.

2. Would a new savings bank or savings and loan association be less likely to suffer from the interest squeeze? Explain.

CHAPTER 15

Short-Term Financing and Risk Management

OBJECTIVES:

After reading this chapter, you should be able to

1. Identify a financial manager's three principal duties.
2. Outline the general sources of funds and the criteria for evaluating them.
3. Draw a chart showing the normal flows of working capital in a manufacturing firm.
4. Illustrate the use of two major sources of short-term credit—trade credit and commercial bank loans.
5. Distinguish between promissory notes and drafts.
6. Explain the relationship among risk avoidance, self insurance, and risk management.
7. Distinguish between pure and speculative risk.
8. Show how the law of large numbers is used to figure insurance premiums.
9. Provide a brief explanation of the major types of insurance.

Sir Freddie Laker started Laker Airways in 1978, when his standby fare, no-frills budget Skytrain service made air travel between Europe and the United States suddenly affordable for thousands of tourists. Early in 1982, however, Laker Airways collapsed because of both long- and short-term financing problems.

The company had millions of dollars of outstanding long-term loans that were made to finance its purchases of planes. It also had millions of dollars of outstanding short-term debts to suppliers of fuel and other items.

What had started as a unique no-frills airline in 1978 had become only one of several airlines offering this type of service in the early 1980s. Laker's success led other airlines to offer similar service and the competition for passengers heated up. In a last ditch effort to avoid collapse and to raise cash, Laker attempted to sell several of its planes in early 1982. The company intended to use the proceeds to help offset its negative cash flow, which was caused by the company spending more cash than it was taking in. But it could not find buyers for the planes in what, at the time, was a depressed aircraft market.

The pressures of difficult financial times have forced business firms to improvise in order to meet their financial needs. This is especially true in the case of short-term capital needs. We will examine the demands for working capital and the various alternative sources of such capital for business. The questions of maturity, claims on assets and income, tax effects, and management influences will be examined.

Managing risk is another important topic in this chapter. Risk management includes risk reduction and avoidance as well as the use of various kinds of insurance. We will examine two insurance options: self-insuring against risk and shifting the risk to insurance companies by purchasing insurance policies to protect against various forms of loss. These include property, casualty, and life insurance.

THE FINANCIAL MANAGER AND FINANCIAL PLANNING

Financial decisions are made by the financial manager (who may be called the comptroller or the vice-president for finance). This executive projects the firm's long- and short-term financial needs and meets them with the help of banks and others. As the chief guardian of the owners' equity, the financial manager is required to get the best return on the owners' investment without taking unnecessary risks.

Company presidents may include noneconomic or social objectives in their decision making, but financial managers must think of dollars and profit. Financial managers specialize in funds and their allocation. They help to provide the president of a firm with a purely economic, profit-maximizing point of view.

A financial manager's responsibilities are

- to evaluate and select from alternative sources of funds
- to identify and satisfy the firm's short-term (working) capital and long-term capital needs in the face of risk
- to manage risk while maximizing the firm's return on assets

General Sources of Funds

Where do business funds come from? For some firms there is little choice. For most, however, there is some choice of sources of funds. The basic choice is between debt financing and equity financing.

debt financing   **Debt financing is the use of borrowed funds.** This could mean a major corporation issuing bonds or it could mean a barber shop borrowing $1,000 for sixty days from a local bank.

Equity financing means the provision of funds by the owners themselves. This could involve issuing stock or using retained profits or funds available through depreciation (deducted from revenue but not actually spent). U.S. nonfinancial corporations since 1970 have used somewhat more equity financing than debt financing.

equity financing

Criteria for Evaluation of Sources

There are several important features of financing that help a firm decide between the use of debt and equity. These are shown in

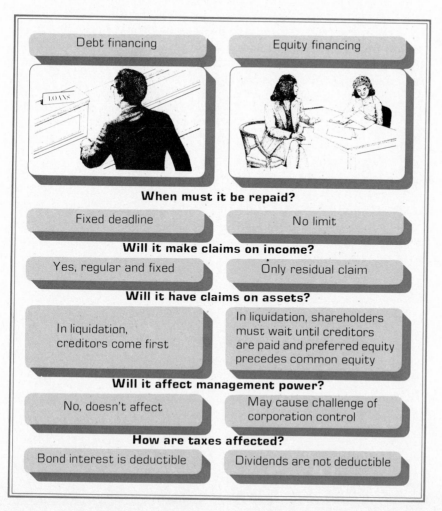

FIGURE 15-1

Comparing debt and equity financing

Debt financing	Equity financing
When must it be repaid?	
Fixed deadline	No limit
Will it make claims on income?	
Yes, regular and fixed	Only residual claim
Will it have claims on assets?	
In liquidation, creditors come first	In liquidation, shareholders must wait until creditors are paid and preferred equity precedes common equity
Will it affect management power?	
No, doesn't affect	May cause challenge of corporation control
How are taxes affected?	
Bond interest is deductible	Dividends are not deductible

Figure 15-1. **Maturity is the factor of time of repayment. When a debt matures, it must be paid.** If funds are internal, they need not be repaid at all. If they are borrowed, the date of maturity (due date) may vary.

Equity and debt financing also differ in the way they affect the claims on assets and earnings. To issue bonds means that the new bondholders will get the designated interest payment before stockholders get any dividends. They have a prior claim on income. Bondholders also come first in the event that the firm goes out of business. They are paid off out of the proceeds of the sale of the firm's assets before stockholders receive anything.

Still another factor in the choice of debt or equity capital relates to control of the corporation. If a firm issues more common stock and this stock is bought by newcomers to the firm, the original common stockholders may lose control over the election of the firm's board of directors. They might lose some influence over policy decisions. A bond sale would not run such a risk for the controlling shareholders.

Of course, the main reason businesses borrow in the first place is that they feel they can earn a higher return on borrowed dollars than the cost or interest they must pay to their lenders. Using borrowed funds in this way is called leverage.

Financial markets also play a role when a firm seeks new sources of capital. Sometimes there is a lot of money available to lend and sometimes there is not. The final selection is often a compromise between what management would like most and what suppliers of capital are willing to give.

A large firm that pays its bills on time and has a high current ratio (see Chapter 12) is in the best position to select from several financing sources. Small firms may overcome the advantage of larger firms by building a good credit record and practicing good money management.

SHORT-TERM FINANCING

As we have seen, there are two basic financial needs, each with its special characteristics. These needs are for short-term, working capital and for intermediate and long-term capital. We need to understand the uses of such funds and will concentrate in this chapter on the uses of working capital.

Working Capital and its Uses

Working capital is a term applied to a firm's investment in short-term assets, the current assets we discussed in Chapter 12. It

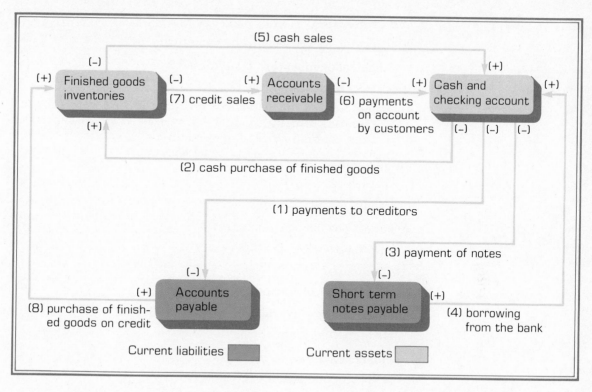

FIGURE 15-2

Flows of working capital. Notice that decreases in liabilities (−) are accompanied by decreases in assets (−) and increases in liabilities (+) are accompanied by increases in assets (+).

includes those assets that flow regularly in the day-to-day operations of a firm—cash, accounts receivable, and inventories (see Figure 15-2, where flows are identified by the numbers in parentheses). The complete flow pattern of working capital includes two current liabilities: accounts payable and short-term notes payable (usually payable to a commercial bank).

Cash and checking accounts *are reduced by*

(1) payments to creditors
(2) cash purchase of finished goods
(3) payments of notes to bank

and increased by

(4) borrowing from the bank
(5) cash sales
(6) payments on account by customers

Accounts receivable *are increased by*

(7) credit sales

and decreased by

(6) payments on account by customers

Finished goods inventory *is increased by*

(2) cash purchase of finished goods

(8) purchase of finished goods on credit (if this were a manu-facturing firm, finished goods inventory would also increase from internal processing of materials)

and decreased by

(5) cash sales

(7) credit sales

Accounts payable *are decreased by*

(1) payments to creditors

and increased by

(8) purchase of finished goods on credit

Short-term notes payable *are increased by*

(4) borrowing from the bank

and decreased by

(3) payments of notes to bank

This is a simplified version of the working capital flow because there are other inventories besides finished goods, especially when manu-facturing processes are involved.

To compute net working capital we deduct total current liabil-ities from the gross working capital (total current assets). Working capital must be handled carefully by the financial manager so as not to interrupt or slow the regular operations of the business. **The firm needs to have enough cash coming in to meet bills, wages, and other current payments. This ability to make payments that are due is the test of a firm's liquidity.** If the Mangham Feed Store has a payroll of $800 due next Monday as well as a repair bill of $500 due on the same day, the manager must examine Mangham's liquidity. If the firm has only $200 in its checking account and expects no significant cash inflow before Monday, some borrowing may be in order, maybe from the bank. If Mangham borrows $1,300 from the bank, the firm in-creases its gross working capital, but its net working capital stays the same because it has created a new current debt, a note payable to the bank. The firm could have found some temporary cash in other ways, as we will see.

The financial manager seeks to balance liquidity with profit. The goal is to minimize idle cash balances by keeping "near cash"

liquidity

Better cash management for middle sized companies.
So you won't get stuck in the middle.

Often firms your size get stuck—stuck between idle cash in one bank and overworked accounts in others. Stuck between the time a check is received and the time it's processed. Stuck in the middle of a cash management bind. Enter the Park.

Our systems for cash collection, disbursement, control and short term investments are outstanding, and flexible enough to match your unique day-to-day needs.

Our Cash Management people are ready to handle your needs promptly, professionally. To make sure you get the systems and service

you need when you need them.

More efficient cash management means reduced borrowing needs and more liquidity opportunities. Find out. Ask the Park. Write or call:

PARK
Park National Bank

Park National Bank
Corporate Services Department
505 South Gay Street
Knoxville, TN 37902
Phone: (615) 521-5160 or
(615) 521-5163

Member F.D.I.C.

This ad illustrates what a bank can do to help firms deal with working capital problems

on hand. This means "earning assets" or investments that pay interest to the firm, but that are also easy to "cash in" when needed. Examples are certificates of deposit (CDs) in banks or short-term government securities such as Treasury bills. Tying up cash in long-term investments such as bonds of another firm does not meet the goal of balancing liquidity with profit because these bonds might not be convertible into cash quickly. They could also involve some loss owing to changes in their market value.

Credit sales represent another use of short-term funds. A firm that sells "on credit" uses its funds to finance its customers' operations. The credit manager and the sales manager often disagree on credit policies. The sales manager sees this as a means of increasing sales. The credit manager sees it as a waste of working capital and maybe as a source of losses if credit customers fail to pay debts.

Notice in the above paragraph that credit sales represent a *use* of short-term funds. To the customers who buy on credit, however, credit is a *source* of short-term funds. In recent years many firms have been slow to pay their bills. They, in effect, are using their suppliers as a source of working capital. By stretching out payments to their suppliers, the buying firms conserve their working capital and may avoid the need to borrow money at high interest rates to pay their bills. Thus in periods of high interest rates, many suppliers will tighten up on their credit policies in an attempt to get their customers to pay their bills on time.

The financial manager seeks to achieve a balance between risk-taking and current return on assets. The firm wants profits to increase if more working capital must be tied up in accounts receivable. If the increase in receivables results from purchases by proven paying customers, profits will increase. The Mangham Feed Store may be wise to avoid selling on credit to a young farmer whose farm is poorly managed. Even if the debt will be repaid, it might take a long time to collect—tying up valuable working capital. The financial manager uses Dun & Bradstreet or other credit reporting services to judge possible credit customers. An example of a credit report is presented in Figure 15-3. It provides many financial facts about the customer to help measure the risk of selling to Rettinger Paint Corporation.

Another current asset, which was shown in Figure 15-2, is the inventory of finished goods. Raw materials are changed into finished goods through the production process. Between these two stages, they are called goods in process. The financial manager seeks to reduce excess inventories at all three stages. There may be a conflict with the production manager, who wants to keep large inventories of inputs so as to keep the production line running smoothly.

Suppose the sales manager at Monsanto Company forecasts a 10 percent increase in sales of plastic during the next year. The

©Dun & Bradstreet, Inc.

This report has been prepared for:

BE SURE NAME, BUSINESS AND ADDRESS MATCH YOUR FILE | ANSWERING INQUIRY | SUBSCRIBER: 008-001042

THIS REPORT MAY NOT BE REPRODUCED IN WHOLE OR IN PART IN ANY MANNER WHATEVER

CONSOLIDATED REPORT | {FULL REVISION}

DUNS: 06-647-3261
RETTINGER PAINT CORP.

727 WHITMAN WAY
BENSON, MI 48232
TEL 313 961-0720

CARL RETTINGER, PRES.

DATE PRINTED
AUG 13, 198-

WHOL PAINTS & VARNISHES

SIC NO.
51 98

SUMMARY

RATING	CC2
STARTED	1950
PAYMENTS	DISC-PPT
SALES	$ 424,612
WORTH	$ 101,867
EMPLOYS	5
HISTORY	CLEAR
CONDITION	GOOD
TREND	STEADY

SPECIAL EVENTS Business burglarized July 3 but $18,000 loss is fully insured.

PAYMENTS {Amounts may be rounded to nearest figure in prescribed ranges}

REPORTED	PAYING RECORD	HIGH CREDIT	NOW OWES	PAST DUE	SELLING TERMS	LAST SALE WITHIN
07/8-	Disc	30000	17000	-0-	2 10 30	1-2 mos.
	Disc	27000	14000	-0-	1 10 30	2-3 mos.
	Disc-Ppt	12000	4400	200	2 10 30	1 mo.
	Ppt	9000	8000	-0-	30	1 mo.
06/8-	Disc	16000	7500	-0-	2 10 30	2-3 mos.
05/8-	Disc	9000	3800	-0-	2 10 30	1 mo.
	Ppt	1500	-0-	-0-	30	1-2 mos.

FINANCE
06/22/8- Fiscal statement dated May 31, 198-:

Cash	$ 20,623	Accts Payable	$ 47,246
Accts Rec	55,777	Owing Bank	34,000
Merchandise	92,103	Notes Pay {Trucks}	7,020
Current	168,503	Current	88,266
Fixts. & Equip.	13,630	Common Stock	35,000
Trucks	8,000	Earned Surplus	66,867
Total Assets	190,133	Total	190,133

SALES {Yr}: $424,612. Net profit $17,105. Fire ins. mdse $95,000; equipt $20,000. Mo. rent: $3500. Prepared by Steige Co., CPAs, Detroit, MI.

--0--

06/22/8 - Laswon defined monthly payments: $3000 to bank, $400 on notes. Admitted collections slow but losses insignificant. Said inventory will drop to $60,000 by December. Expects 5% sales increase this year.

PUBLIC FILINGS
03/25/8 - March 17, 198- financing statement #741170 named subject as debtor and NCR Corp., Dayton, O. as secured party. Collateral: equipment.
05/28/8- May 21, 198 - suit for $200 entered by Henry Assoc., Atlanta, Ga. Docket #27519. Involves merchandise which Lawson says was defective.

BANKING
06/25/8- Account, long maintained, carries average balances low to moderate five figures. Unsecured loans to moderate five extended and now open.

HISTORY
06/22/8- CARL RETTINGER, PRES. JOHN J. LAWSON, V PRES.
DIRECTORS: The Officers
Incorporated Michigan February 2, 1950. Authorized capital 3500 shares, no par common. Paid in capital $35,000, officers sharing equally.
RETTINGER, born 1920, married. Employed by E-Z Paints, Detroit 12 yrs, five as manager until starting subject early 1950.
LAWSON, born 1925, married. Obtained accounting degree 1946 and then employed by Union Carbide, Chicago until joining Rettinger at inception.

OPERATION
06/22/8- Wholesales paints and varnishes {85%}, wallpaper and supplies. 500 local accounts include retailers {75%} and contractors. Terms: 2 10 30. Peak season spring thru summer. EMPLOYEES: Officers active with three others.
LOCATION: Rents 7500 sq ft. one-story block structure, good repair.

THIS REPORT, FURNISHED PURSUANT TO CONTRACT FOR THE EXCLUSIVE USE OF THE SUBSCRIBER AS ONE FACTOR TO CONSIDER IN CONNECTION WITH CREDIT, INSURANCE, MARKETING OR OTHER BUSINESS DECISIONS, CONTAINS INFORMATION COMPILED FROM SOURCES WHICH DUN & BRADSTREET, INC. DOES NOT CONTROL AND WHOSE INFORMATION, UNLESS OTHERWISE INDICATED IN THE REPORT, HAS NOT BEEN VERIFIED. IN FURNISHING THIS REPORT, DUN & BRADSTREET, INC. IN NO WAY ASSUMES ANY PART OF THE USER'S BUSINESS RISK, DOES NOT GUARANTEE THE ACCURACY, COMPLETENESS, OR TIMELINESS OF THE INFORMATION PROVIDED, AND SHALL NOT BE LIABLE FOR ANY LOSS OR INJURY WHATEVER RESULTING FROM CONTINGENCIES BEYOND ITS CONTROL OR FROM NEGLIGENCE. 9 R2-25(750320)

FIGURE 15-3
A credit report

production manager bases estimates of raw materials needs—ethylene, propylene, benzene, etc.—on this sales forecast. Now, suppose further that Monsanto's purchasing agent can receive a big discount if the regular order of these raw materials is increased by 20 percent. Should Monsanto's financial manager approve this use of funds to earn the additional discount? The correct answer depends in part on whether Monsanto could use these additional funds spent for raw materials in some other, more profitable way, such as by allow-

Borrowing to Save Money

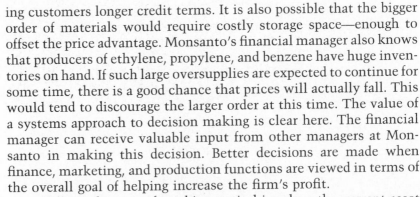

POINT OF VIEW

Dave Perry, business manager at Consolidated Supply, bought supplies from Acme Paper Company. Acme sent in a bill on June 1 for $1000 with terms of 2/10, net/30. Dave had the choice of paying $980 by June 10 or the full amount by July 1. By paying the bill within ten days—by June 10—Dave would receive a 2 percent discount.

Because he had no spare cash, Dave went to the Friendly National Bank and talked to the vice-president. She offered him a loan of $980 for twenty days at an annual interest rate of 10 percent. Total interest cost was only $5.44 ($\frac{20}{360} \times 10\% \times \$980 = \$5.44$). By borrowing from the bank to pay the bill early he saved $14.56 as follows:

Bill saving	$20.00
− Bank interest	5.44
Net saving	$14.56

Some managers take the point of view that "bills shouldn't be paid until the very last day that they'e due." This manager, however, correctly interpreted the options available to him and saved nearly $15. A good financial manager develops the habit of examining every opportunity to borrow in order to save.

ing customers longer credit terms. It is also possible that the bigger order of materials would require costly storage space—enough to offset the price advantage. Monsanto's financial manager also knows that producers of ethylene, propylene, and benzene have huge inventories on hand. If such large oversupplies are expected to continue for some time, there is a good chance that prices will actually fall. This would tend to discourage the larger order at this time. The value of a systems approach to decision making is clear here. The financial manager can receive valuable input from other managers at Monsanto in making this decision. Better decisions are made when finance, marketing, and production functions are viewed in terms of the overall goal of helping increase the firm's profit.

Still another use of working capital involves the current asset "prepaid expenses." You can buy a three-year fire insurance policy on your home, for example. Paying the three-year premium in one lump sum means that you are *prepaying* your insurance coverage. The same is true for a firm.

A financial manager carefully evaluates the option to pay insur-

"Harcourt, here, has a black belt in budget management!"

ance premiums in advance. The choice depends on the other uses that could be made of those funds. Prepaying expenses is wise when the savings exceed the opportunity costs. **Opportunity costs are costs of losing the option to use the funds in another way.** Suppose that the owner of a funeral home could save $100 by paying a fire insurance premium for three years coverage in advance instead of paying one-third each year. Suppose also that the owner could have earned $150 interest if he or she had invested the prepaid amount instead of buying two years of coverage in advance. If this were the case, prepayment would have been a mistake. The current (and expected) interest rate is a major factor in making all such financial decisions because it helps to determine what unused dollars can earn.

opportunity costs

A manager should have an overview of the flow of working capital such as we saw in Figure 15-2. He or she must understand this flow and the timing of it from one use to another. If the firm has a good sales forecast and a good collection policy, it can achieve the goal of providing *enough* working capital but *not too much*.

Specific Sources of Short-term Funds

Funds sources differ depending upon the length of time for which the funds are needed. When the need is for the short term, usually one year or less, it is generally in order to supply current asset needs such as cash, accounts receivable, and inventories. How-

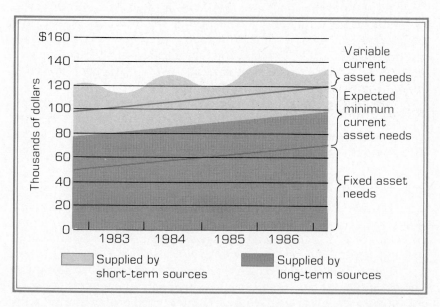

FIGURE 15-4

Asset needs and their financing by source

ever, some of these current asset needs represent a predictable minimum amount—what the firm *knows* it will always need. (See Figure 15-4.) This means that much of this part of current asset needs can be supplied from the same long-term sources that serve fixed asset needs. These sources will be discussed in the next chapter.

Variable current asset needs are partly of a seasonal nature and partly just plain unpredictable. All of these variable short-term needs and some of the "fixed" current assets needs can be met from three principal sources:

- trade credit
- commercial bank loans
- commercial paper

Trade Credit

trade credit

Trade credit, or "open book account," differs from other types of short-term credit because no financial institution is directly involved. It is simply credit extended by sellers to buyers. To the seller trade credit means accounts receivable. To the buyer it means accounts payable. When one firm (manufacturer, wholesaler, retailer) buys materials or merchandise from another, the transaction is handled in open book accounts with no complex credit papers. The buyer records a new account payable. The seller makes an entry showing a new account receivable. Nearly 90 percent of sales are handled that way.

In effect, the seller "lends" the buyer money for the time between receipt of the goods and payment for them. Without this type of credit, many firms could not survive. The same type of credit exists between the consumer and the retailer. When you "charge" the purchase of a TV on your account, the seller is really lending you money for a while. Instead of calling this an open book account, most people call it a charge account.

Most trade credit involves cash discounts for early payments, as we saw in Chapter 11. Firms who can borrow at market rates from banks will usually do so to take advantage of such discounts, the effective rate of which could be 36 percent per year.

Commercial Bank Loans

The commercial bank, as we saw in Chapter 14, accepts deposits and lends a part of these funds to businesses for their short-term commercial needs. Commercial banks are the most popular credit source among smaller business borrowers.

Depending on the current balance between the demand and supply of commercial credit, bankers will adjust standards for lending. When money is short, bankers are likely to become more careful about those to whom they lend money. In any case, a bank will always check a new borrower's past credit record and ability to manage. The banker will screen loan applications also on a basis of the current ratio of the firm as well as on the basis of some of the other key credit ratios. The bank loan officer may obtain a credit report such as the one presented in Figure 15-3.

A banker expects that the loan will be repaid normally out of seasonal declines of inventories and accounts receivable held by the borrower. The bank and borrower must agree on four principal terms of a commercial loan:

- the general nature of the arrangement
- the interest rate
- the quantity and type of security (if any)
- the repayment date

Unsecured Bank Loans. **For favored customers or customers with exceptionally good prospects for repayment, a bank will offer loans for short-term uses with no security or pledge of assets as guarantee of repayment. These are unsecured bank loans.** Such loans often take the form of a line of credit or revolving credit. **When a line of credit is set, the bank stands ready to lend up to this amount to the borrower with some restrictions.**

A revolving credit agreement, on the other hand, is a very formal and specific agreement that guarantees funds for a period of time with strict rules limiting the borrower.

Secured Loans. **Many commercial loans to smaller firms and to firms with lower credit ratings are "secured" loans. Here, the lender is protected by a pledge of the borrower's assets, or collateral.** Secured loans may also be arranged by firms that have reasonably good credit records and wish to borrow unusually large sums or want favorable interest rates. Items pledged as security for loans may include accounts receivable, inventories, equipment, stocks, or the cash value of life insurance policies.

A special kind of secured financing is called floor planning. An auto dealer who gets a shipment of new cars signs a note to a bank or other financing agency for the amount due. Title passes to the lender, who pays the bill. A trust receipt serves as a substitute for the actual asset. The bank holds the trust receipt for the cars until they are sold and the loans are paid.

Commercial banks are also the major institutions involved in the use of the other credit instruments described below—promissory notes, drafts, and acceptances.

Other lending institutions used by firms for short-term

Margin terms: unsecured bank loans · line of credit · revolving credit · secured loans · floor planning

financing include factors, commercial finance companies, and sales finance companies. The new all-in-one institutions are also an important source as are many large nonfinancial corporations.

promissory note

Promissory Notes.   A promissory note is a written promise by a customer (borrower or "maker") to pay a certain sum of money (principal and interest) to a supplier (payee) at a specified future date. (See Figure 15-5.) Although promissory notes are used in some industries in place of open-book accounts, they are used most often in credit sales to customers who have poor credit ratings or who are slow in making their payments on open-book accounts. The seller feels more secure in selling to such a buyer when the seller has a note signed by the buyer.

If a promissory note is negotiable, the supplier can sell it to another party. Suppose Supplier sells merchandise to Buyer. Supplier takes Buyer's promissory note for $1,000 to be paid in 180 days at 15 percent interest per year. If Supplier wanted to get the money sooner, Supplier could sell the note to the bank. Supplier gets $1,000 (the face value of the note) minus a fee for this service. Supplier might get less, however, if the bank wants to earn more than 15 percent per year on a loan. Buyer pays $1,000 plus interest to the bank on the due date. If Supplier sells the note *with recourse,* the bank can collect from Supplier if Buyer fails to make good on the note.

Usually, however, banks prefer to *discount* notes. Suppose Buyer B went directly to the bank to get a loan in order to pay cash for a purchase. The bank would draw up the note so that interest would be deducted from the face amount of the note in advance. Suppose the face value is $1,000, the interest rate is 15 percent (prior to discount), and the maturity is in 120 days. Buyer B gets $950 in

FIGURE 15-5
A promissory note

No. _777X_____   ___29 July_____ 19_8*__ $ _***00.00**_____

_____ after date the undersigned (jointly and severally if more than one) promise(s) to pay to the order of __John Doe_____

___***00.00**_____ Dollars

payable at _____11% per annum_____

Each and every party to this instrument, either as maker, endorser, surety or otherwise, hereby waives demand, notice, protest and all other demands and notices and assents to any extension of the time of payment or any other indulgence, to any substitution, exchange or release of collateral and/or to the release of any other party.

Address Only   275 Main Street   Signed By   Jane Doe   SAMPLE
                Clinton, Idaho

C 83

cash ($\frac{120}{360}$ or $\frac{1}{3}$ of a full year's interest charge of $150 has been deducted in advance from the face value). The effective annual interest rate is actually about 15.8 percent ($\frac{\$150}{\$950}$).

Drafts. There is a big difference between a promissory note and a draft. A promissory note is a *promise to pay* that is made by the maker, the person who promises to make the payment. A draft is an *order to pay* that is made by the drawer, the person who is to receive the payment.

When Supplier (drawer) ships merchandise to Buyer, Supplier sends two documents. One is the bill of lading. This is a written document from the carrier (transportation company) acknowledging receipt of the merchandise for delivery and setting out the terms of the shipping contract. The other document is a trade draft. **A trade draft is prepared by the supplier and it orders the buyer to pay a certain amount of money for the merchandise.**

trade draft

There are two types of drafts: (1) sight drafts and (2) time drafts. If Supplier sells to Buyer with a sight draft, Buyer must pay the sight draft as soon as Supplier presents it for payment. A time draft specifies a certain future date on which the draft must be paid.

A trade draft becomes a trade acceptance when the buyer signs it (accepts it). The buyer must sign it in order to get the merchandise from the carrier. The trade acceptance is returned to the supplier. (See Figure 15-6.) If it is a sight draft, Supplier (drawer) has the bank present it for immediate payment by Buyer (drawee). If it is a time draft, Supplier can hold it until the date specified on the trade acceptance and then send it to Supplier's bank, which will present it to Buyer for payment. If Supplier wants the money earlier, it can discount the trade acceptance at Supplier's bank.

trade acceptance

FIGURE 15-6
A trade acceptance

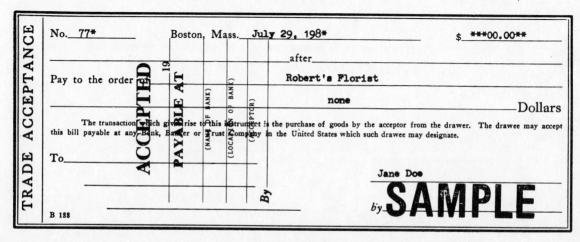

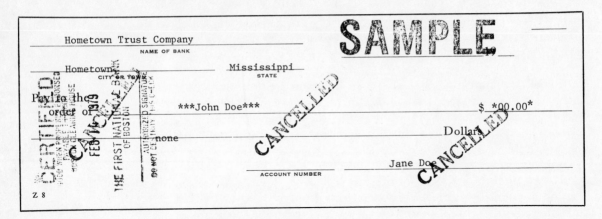

FIGURE 15-7

A certified check

Suppose Supplier does not want to use a trade draft but is unwilling to accept a check drawn on Buyer's account. Seller can require Buyer to pay with certified checks or cashier's checks. A certified check is a check stamped by the bank as certified. The bank immediately deducts the amount of the check from Buyer's account. This ensures that the check will not "bounce." The bank charges a small fee for this service. (See Figure 15-7.)

A cashier's check is a check written by the bank's cashier. The check is drawn on the bank itself (not on Buyer's account) and the payee is specified on the check. The bank collects the amount of the check from Buyer plus a small fee, or it charges Buyer's account. (See Figure 15-8.)

Commercial Paper

We saw in Chapter 14 that commercial paper houses are important financial institutions serving the short-term financial needs of businesses. The instruments they deal in—commercial paper—allow a

FIGURE 15-8

A cashier's check

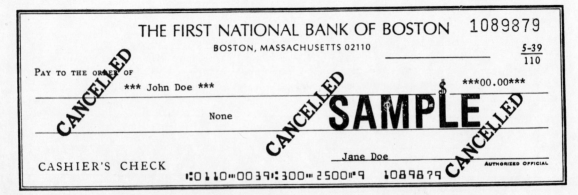

firm to borrow from another firm without collateral or security in the form of asset pledges. These loans depend on the good faith of the issuing firm and bear an interest rate below that available through commercial banks for unsecured loans.

Commercial paper houses act as middlemen, bringing lenders and borrowers together and operating on a relatively small interest margin. Insurance companies frequently make such loans. The amounts are usually large—from $25,000 to several hundred thousand dollars—and small or poorly financed firms would not ordinarily be able to get such funds. When interest rates for long-term loans and bonds are high, some large firms borrow and reborrow on commercial paper to avoid long-term financial commitments at high rates.

While the financial manager must be fully aware of these financial instruments in managing short-term funds, he or she must be equally aware of the risks that threaten profitability. Some of these risks are inevitable and demand constant efforts on the part of the financial manager. We turn now to the subject of risk management.

RISK MANAGEMENT

As we saw in Chapter 2, risk is the chance of loss. It cannot be avoided entirely when the complex process of business management is undertaken. All the firm's resources are subject to risk, and to protect them is a major task of the financial manager. Let us first describe the various kinds of risk that businesses face.

Kinds of Risks

There are risks in everything and the degree of risk may vary greatly. In lending money, we risk loss. In buying things, we risk the possibility of defective merchandise. In running a factory, we risk liability for accidents to employees or visitors. In owning buildings and cars, we run risks of fire, vandalism, and theft. We risk that secret processes or designs will be stolen, and we risk the death of corporate officers. All of these threaten the firm's resources and must be dealt with if the firm is to survive and prosper.

Self-insurance and Risk Avoidance

There are three basic approaches to dealing with risk. They can be used in combination. One is to assume risk yourself. The second

FIGURE 15-9

How a business
manages risk

1. Risk assumption: Self-insurance against fire, theft, etc.
2. Risk avoidance and/or reduction: Sound business management enables the firm to avoid unnecessary risk (i.e., credit policies that grant credit only to people with good credit records) and/or reduce risk (i.e., safety training to teach employees safe work habits).
3. Shifting risk: Shifting the risk to another party, such as an insurance company.

is to avoid or reduce it. The third approach is to shift the risk to others. (See Figure 15-9.)

self-insurance

Many firms practice self-insurance of certain types. This means assuming your own risk and preparing for loss. If, for example, a large chain of shoe stores regularly sets aside a certain amount to cover the possibility of fire in one of its outlets, it is practicing self-insurance. The idea is that, with a very large operation, some fire damage is bound to happen. Instead of paying insurance firms, the self-insurer pays itself.

Such a practice, of course, makes a firm very conscious of ways to avoid fires so as not to have to spend its reserved funds. It will install sprinklers, inspect heating systems, discourage smoking in the stores, and take other steps to minimize risk. There are many other types of operational precautions a firm can take to reduce or avoid risks in different phases of its business.

Mechanized cash control systems help to protect against theft, as do basic cash audit procedures and regulations for writing checks and making cash purchases. Related procedures provide for systematic purchasing (sometimes on a sealed-bid basis) to avoid losses because of favoritism in buying or commercial bribery. Usually, more than one signature is required for approval of purchases over a certain amount. Careful inspection of both quantity and quality of goods received also plays an important part in resource control.

Firms that deal in new ideas and processes must maintain secrecy. This includes careful personnel screening and constant development of employee loyalty. Also included are normal security precautions such as checking visitors to plants. Careful patent protection is another means of protecting this kind of resource from being copied by competitors.

There is always a danger that changes in market conditions will hurt a firm. A retailer may find some goods hard to move. To avoid losses, he or she may use one of several legal devices that allow the return of merchandise to the producer or wholesaler. When a wholesaler asks a neighborhood hardware store to stock a new line of expensive barbecue grills, the wholesaler may offer them *on consignment*. This means the retailer takes no risk that the grills won't sell. The retailer pays only for those sold at retail.

To protect against sudden rises in the cost of needed supplies, a firm might also have a policy of stocking up large quantities when the market is down. Such protective measures complement the role of insurance, which is our next topic.

Shifting Risk and the Use of Insurance

Insurance companies assume the risks of their policyholders for a price. A firm pays a premium for a *policy* that pays if the firm sustains certain types of losses. The policy specifies the types of risk that are covered, the amount of coverage, and the premium.

The insurance company is a professional risk taker, but it takes only certain types of risks. Insurance is available only for pure risks. **Pure risks are those that offer only a chance of loss. There is no chance of gain.** Examples are risk of fire and risk of death.

pure risk

Speculative risks are "gambles" in which there is possible gain as well as loss. Placing a bet at the race track is one obvious example. Going into business is another, because the quality of a new product or the quality of management may lead either to profit or to loss. Insurance is not available for such speculative risks.

speculative risk

State and federal governments are also in the insurance business. State governments operate unemployment and workers' compensation insurance programs. The federal government operates the social security program and other programs, such as savings account insurance on accounts in banks and mortgage insurance to lenders under VA and FHA programs.

Firms deal with insurance companies for the same reasons that individuals do. Most homeowners, for example, carry fire insurance rather than bear the entire burden of the risk themselves. The same is true of firms. Insurance companies combine or pool the risks of many policyholders (firms or individuals). To pool risks like this makes use of what is known as the law of large numbers.

Risk Management
Is the Trend

AUTHORS' COMMENTARY

The traditional role of a firm's insurance manager has been to buy the right insurance. As lawsuits and jury awards for damages rise and insurance rates go up, more and more firms are de-emphasizing insurance and emphasizing risk management. In other words, buying insurance is the "last step." If risk can be eliminated or greatly reduced or if self-insurance is feasible, "bought" insurance may not be necessary. This is in keeping with a systems concept of management.

Dealing with risk demands a person with a variety of skills and a broad perspective on a firm's resource conservation. This person is a professional risk manager and not merely an insurance buyer. We feel that the financial community will continue to expect more from risk managers and that the Risk Insurance Management Society will continue to grow at a rapid pace. Risk management will become one of the more demanding and richly rewarded professions serving America's firms.

The Law of Large Numbers

Insurance firms study past statistics about the number of deaths that have occurred in different age groups. These statistics are developed into mortality tables. (See Table 15-1.) Mortality tables are used to predict the number of policyholders who will die in a given year. **This prediction depends on the law of large numbers. In other words, if the insurance firm has a large number of policyholders, it can pretty well predict from the mortality tables how many of them will die in a year.**

law of large numbers

The same principle applies to other insured risks such as fire or theft. Past experience and the law of large numbers give insurance firms a fair idea of how much they will have to pay out in claims. They set their premiums at a level that will allow them to cover expected claims, operating costs, and a reasonable profit.

The loss-predicting experts (actuaries) of an insurance firm might know from historical records that in a year, on the average, 100 of the 5,000 buildings that they insure will actually suffer a fire loss. They also know that recent evidence shows that the average loss per fire is $40,000. Excluding an adjustment for inflation, the average premium must be $800 per year plus something extra to cover operating costs and profit. ($800 × 5,000 = $40,000 × 100.) If total operating cost and profit are $1,000,000 and the inflationary effect on payments to those suffering loss is expected to be 10 per-

Age	Deaths Per 1,000	Expectation of Life (Years)	Age	Deaths Per 1,000	Expectation of Life (Years)
0	20.02	70.75	50	7.38	25.93
1	1.25	71.19	51	8.04	25.12
2	.86	70.28	52	8.76	24.32
3	.69	69.34	53	9.57	23.53
4	.57	68.39	54	10.43	22.75
5	.51	67.43	55	11.36	21.99
6	.46	66.46	56	12.36	21.23
7	.43	65.49	57	13.41	20.49
8	.39	64.52	58	14.52	19.76
9	.34	63.54	59	15.70	19.05
10	.31	62.57	60	16.95	18.34
11	.30	61.58	61	18.29	17.65
12	.35	60.60	62	19.74	16.97
13	.46	59.62	63	21.33	16.30
14	.63	58.65	64	23.06	15.65
15	.82	57.69	65	24.95	15.00
16	1.01	56.73	66	26.99	14.38
17	1.17	55.79	67	29.18	13.76
18	1.28	54.86	68	31.52	13.16
19	1.34	53.93	69	34.00	12.57
20	1.40	53.00	70	36.61	12.00
21	1.47	52.07	71	39.43	11.43
22	1.52	51.15	72	42.66	10.88
23	1.53	50.22	73	46.44	10.34
24	1.51	49.30	74	50.75	9.82
25	1.47	48.37	75	55.52	9.32
26	1.43	47.44	76	60.60	8.84
27	1.42	46.51	77	65.96	8.38
28	1.44	45.58	78	71.53	7.93
29	1.49	44.64	79	77.41	7.51
30	1.55	43.71	80	83.94	7.10
31	1.63	42.77	81	91.22	6.70
32	1.72	41.84	82	98.92	6.32
33	1.83	40.92	83	106.95	5.96
34	1.95	39.99	84	115.48	5.62
35	2.09	39.07	85	125.61	5.28
36	2.25	38.15	86	137.48	4.97
37	2.44	37.23	87	149.79	4.68
38	2.66	36.32	88	161.58	4.42
39	2.90	35.42	89	172.92	4.18
40	3.14	34.52	90	185.02	3.94
41	3.41	33.63	91	198.88	3.73
42	3.70	32.74	92	213.63	3.53
43	4.04	31.86	93	228.70	3.35
44	4.43	30.99	94	243.36	3.19
45	4.84	30.12	95	257.45	3.06
46	5.28	29.27	96	269.59	2.95
47	5.74	28.42	97	280.24	2.85
48	6.24	27.58	98	289.77	2.76
49	6.78	26.75	99	298.69	2.69

TABLE 15-1

Sample mortality table for United States total population in 1980

cent, then the average premium will be $1,080 per building for the year $\left(\frac{\$5,400,000}{5,000} = \$1,080\right)$. Inflation has added $80 and operating costs and profit, $200 to the basic amount of $800.

Of course, an insurer attempts to avoid writing insurance for a group if the peril (danger) insured against would damage all members in the group at the same time. For example, a fire insurance firm would not concentrate all its coverage in one section of a city. A major fire there could affect too many policyholders and could ruin the insurance firm.

The risk from the insurance firm's point of view relates to how accurately it can predict total losses within a group of policyholders. If the probable range of losses is great, the risk is great.

What Is Insurable and Who Can Be Insured?

insurable risk

Insurance firms judge what kinds of dangers or perils they can insure against. These are what they consider to be insurable risks. An insurance company desires a reasonable amount of evidence dealing with the size and frequency of past losses. For the law of large numbers to work, a large number of objects must be insured. For a risk to be insurable, it must be measurable in dollars, too. Losses must also generally be unintentional to be insurable. A proprietor who is known to have burned his or her own store down may not recover the loss.

insurable interest

People or firms have an insurable interest when they can show that they would suffer a loss from the thing insured against. If the Ford Motor Company leases a building they can buy insurance protecting them against losses sustained by a fire in the building, even though they don't own it. They could suffer a great financial loss from such a fire. A corporation, because it has an insurable interest in the life of its president, can buy an insurance policy on his or her life.

Types of Insurance

We will discuss insurance under two principal headings—property and casualty insurance and life insurance. The subject is covered from the perspective of a business firm. Because most firms own a wide range of assets that need protection, we will begin with property and casualty insurance.

Property and Casualty Insurance

property and casualty insurance

Under the general heading of property and casualty insurance are traditionally included perils of fire, windstorm, flood, theft, burglary, accident, loss of health, and liability due to negligence. We will use fire insurance as a principal example of how property and casualty coverage works.

Fire. Firms and households insure buildings and homes against fire. Suppose a company's warehouse originally cost $200,000 and the current cost of rebuilding it is $400,000. The firm has a $500,000 fire insurance policy and it suffers a total loss by fire. **Under the principle of indemnity the insured cannot collect more than the actual cash value of the loss. In this case it can collect $400,000.**

principle of indemnity

Total destruction by fire is rare. Thus most business property is underinsured. Insurance companies use a *coinsurance clause* to induce firms to carry adequate coverage, usually 80 percent of the market value of the property. The policy with an 80 percent coin-surance clause works like this: Suppose Samantha Butte owns a motion picture theater that would cost $100,000 to rebuild. If she buys only a $50,000 fire insurance policy and suffers a $30,000 loss from fire, the insurer would pay only $18,750 of the loss. This is computed as follows. The insured gets paid a fraction of the loss equal to the amount of the policy divided by 80 percent of the cost to replace. In this case it was $\frac{50,000}{80,000}$ or $\frac{5}{8}$. Five-eighths of $30,000 = $18,750.

Fire insurance typically protects a building and its contents

Fire insurance protects against losses caused by fire or light-ning. Most firms buy added coverage (allied lines) against perils such as windstorm, riot, water, etc. Usually the contents are insured as well as the building. An accompanying policy is usually purchased to insure against losses due to interruption of business operations because of the fire or other catastrophe.

Auto. There are several different forms of auto insurance. Comprehensive auto insurance covers loss due to windstorm, fire, hail, theft, etc. Collision insurance covers damage from collision with another vehicle or a stationary object. Bodily injury liability insurance protects the insured against claims resulting from death or injury of another person due to the insured's negligent operation of a car. A medical payments feature pays hospital and doctor bills for persons injured in the insured's car. Property damage liability insur-ance pays for damage done by the insured to other cars, houses, or property. Uninsured motorist protection covers the policyholder for his or her bodily injury caused by an uninsured negligent driver. Some states have adopted "no-fault" insurance which allows the injured party to collect without requiring that fault be determined.

Burglary and Theft. Most firms carry protection against bur-glary. This covers losses resulting from break-ins which have left visible marks of entry. It does not cover shoplifting or employee theft. Insurance against loss due to employee embezzlement or theft

The cost of accident insurance depends on the hazards of the job

is available, too. Such coverage is known as fidelity bonding and can be purchased for individual employees, individual positions in the firm, or for all employees (blanket protection).

Accident and Health. Accident policies pay the insured for certain medical expenses due to accidents. Health policies pay expenses related to loss of health, whether due to an accident or sickness. Many firms provide group health insurance for their employees. Under a sick-leave plan, part of the worker's salary is paid when he or she cannot work due to sickness or accident. In the case of total disability, an income protection plan pays a certain percentage of the employee's salary while he or she is disabled. Major medical expense insurance provides coverage for long-term hospital stays and doctor bills. Many employees add to this coverage hospital money plans that pay a certain amount for each day the insured is in the hospital.

Liability. Public liability insurance is usually purchased to protect firms from losses stemming from claims by people who have used the firm's products or services or who have visited the firm's facilities. Thus a customer who slips on a newly-waxed department store floor or a buyer of a toy that breaks and injures a baby might seek damages against the store or the manufacturer. Product liability insurance has become very expensive lately as the number of claims has skyrocketed.

Will the Practice of Self-insurance Grow?

WHAT DO YOU THINK?

The option for businesses to insure themselves rather than to rely on insurance companies has not seemed a very practical one for most individual firms. The pressure of high rates, however, can lead to some inventive variations on the principle of self-insurance.

An important new development in self-insurance is the growth of plans shared by trade associations, especially in the field of product liability. The Chemical Specialties Manufacturers Association, for example, has responded to the steep rise in premiums for product liability insurance by offering its own plan to members.

Such initiative on the part of an industry group might point the way to major changes in the structure of insurance for business. It certainly demonstrates the adaptiveness of business when faced with a financial problem. With this kind of innovative thinking some forms of self-insurance could expand greatly. WHAT DO YOU THINK?

TABLE 15-2

Types of insurance
purchased by business
firms

Fire—Protects against fire damage, usually includes coinsurance provision. Building and contents usually covered, often accompanied by similar coverage against windstorms, earthquakes, and theft.

Auto—Firms purchase several coverages for company-owned vehicles, including property and bodily injury liability, collision (covering damage to own vehicle), and medical payments coverage relating to occupants of owned vehicle. Comprehensive coverage protects vehicles against fire, theft, windstorm, vandals, etc.

Burglary—Protects against loss from break-ins. Fidelity bonds protect against loss incurred through embezzlement and other theft by employees.

Accident and Health—Variety of coverages to protect employees against losses stemming from accidents and poor health. Usually the firm shares the cost with employees and deducts employee shares from paychecks. Sometimes includes sick pay in the event of loss of salary during illness.

Liability—Public liability protects against legal claims by nonemployees for damages stemming from firm's products or operations on or off firm premises. Workers' compensation insurance protects against workers' claims. In most states this is mandatory. It includes work-related accident or illness.

Marine—Ocean marine protects ships, cargoes against collision and other perils at sea. Inland marine protects against inland transportation losses.

Credit—Protects against losses stemming from nonpayment of accounts.

Title—Protects against losses due to defects in title to real property.

Surety—Protects against losses from nonperformance of contractual obligation.

Life—Businesses protect themselves against losses related to death of key personnel by insuring their lives. Firm is the beneficiary.

Business interruption—Protects firms against loss of business during time that premises are closed during repairs after a catastrophe.

Employees also make claims against their employers for accidents on the job or for illness induced by exposure to harmful substances in connection with employment. Such claims are covered in most states by mandatory workers' compensation laws. Employers with a minimum number of employees are required to purchase such insurance. The premiums vary with the degree of hazard involved in the work. Thus rates for miners would be much higher than for clerical personnel.

Other Property Coverage. Other important types of coverage include title, credit, and marine insurance and surety bonds. (See Table 15-2.) Title insurance protects the property owner against loss due to defects in title to real property. Credit insurance protects creditors against losses on uncollectible accounts receivable. Ocean marine insurance covers the ship and its cargo against theft, sinking, collision, etc. Inland marine insurance covers mainly land transportation modes. Surety bonds protect the insured against loss from nonperformance of a contractual obligation. A contractor might have to furnish a surety bond that a building will be completed by a certain date.

Life Insurance

life insurance

Life insurance provides a degree of financial security to the insured's family or firm. The insurer pays a cash benefit to a surviving person or firm upon the death of the person insured. Life insurance has grown rapidly in the last twenty years. (See Figure 15-10.)
Three major classes of life insurance policies are:

- term policies
- ordinary life policies
- limited payment policies

Term life insurance policies are issued for definite time spans such as 5–10–15 years. If the insured dies, the policy's face value is paid to his or her beneficiary. If the insured outlives the term of the policy, the insured receives nothing. Term insurance is pure protection.
Under ordinary life insurance, the insured pays premiums until death, at which time the beneficiary receives the policy's face value. If the insured person cancels the policy during his or her life, that person is paid the cash surrender value of the policy, which increases during the life of the policy. Thus a savings element is provided in addition to protection. The insured can also borrow money against the current cash value of the policy.

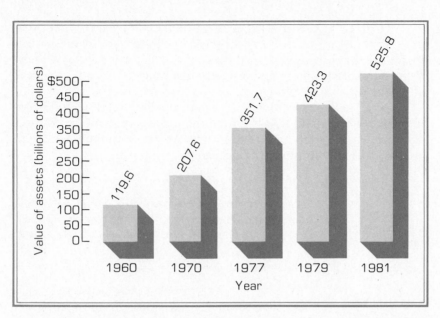

FIGURE 15-10
Assets of American life insurance companies

Under limited payment life insurance, premiums are paid for a stated number of years, usually in the 20–30 year range. At the end of the period, no further premiums are due. The policy is "paid up" but remains in force (that is, will pay the face value whenever the insured dies).

Many employers provide group life insurance plans for their employees. The premiums are lower than those on individually purchased policies. All told, the life insurance companies of the United States represent a huge part of the nation's assets (see Figure 15-10) and, as such, can have much influence over the financial climate of the country.

SUMMARY AND LOOK AHEAD

The financial manager's job is complex and requires a variety of talents. He or she must be aware of present and future needs for working capital and must also evaluate and select sources of funds. He or she thinks in terms of maturity, claims against assets and income, and control of the firm when deciding how to get funds. For short-term funds, trade credit, commercial banks, and commercial paper are the major sources. Executives who manage working capital must monitor its flow. To manage the flow they must often use financial instruments such as promissory notes, drafts, and trade acceptances.

To protect the firm's resources, a financial manager must think of ways to avoid, reduce, or shift risk. Insurance companies play a major role in shifting risk for firms as well as for individuals. Most firms purchase property and casualty insurance of several types and also take out life insurance on the lives of major officers.

In the next chapter we will turn to the long-term capital needs of business firms and will examine the process of planning to meet such needs. We will explore the major sources of long-term credit and the role the securities market plays in their use.

FOR REVIEW . . .

1. Briefly explain why it is important to distinguish short-term financing from long-term financing.

2. What specific uses are made of working capital?

3. How can short-term notes payable be increased and how can they be decreased?

4. What factors may affect the supply of credit to a small manufacturer?

5. How do debt and equity financing differ in terms of their maturity? Their claims on income?

6. Distinguish between a promissory note and a trade acceptance.

7. Describe two of the operational precautions that a firm might apply in order to protect its resources.

8. What is the law of large numbers? How does it relate to the size of insurance premiums?

9. Describe two types of property insurance.

. . . FOR DISCUSSION

1. How do investors' objectives influence their position on the question of adding to debt or equity capital?

2. What capital need is served by "open book account," or trade credit? Compare this source to the commercial bank.

3. Why can some firms use self-insurance while others cannot?

4. Explain how probability mathematics enters into premium setting in the insurance industry.

INCIDENTS

Texaco Hikes the Credit Charge

Texaco recently announced that they would demand of their dealers a 3 percent processing charge on all retail purchases made with Texaco credit cards. Considering the rise in credit card theft, and the growing rate of nonpayment by consumers, this action is not difficult to understand. The typical dealer is faced with the question of whether to pass this added cost on to the customer. The dealer must ask "is the luxury of credit purchasing worth this additional charge to my customers?" The dealer also must consider whether this added charge will go unnoticed in the face of past jumps in gas prices. The cost of credit is as real as the cost of gasoline and both of them are mounting.

QUESTIONS

1. If the average customer can delay paying for gas exactly one month because of the credit card and pays the added 3 percent for that delay, what effective annual rate of interest is the customer paying?

2. Suppose the dealer absorbs the charge instead of passing it on. What effect does this have on his or her short-term capital needs?

How Estate Tax Reduction Affects Life Insurance Sales

Starting in 1982, people who die and leave large estates will be able to leave more to their beneficiaries. The estate tax was lowered at that time and will continue to be reduced through the year 1987. By 1987 the tax-exempt amount will reach a maximum of $1.2 million, compared to the maximum of $350,000 which applied before 1982.

For people with large estates it becomes unnecessary to carry as much life insurance as was needed before the change in rates. The extra insurance was carried to "cover" a substantial tax bite. Certainly, this tax reduction will make it more difficult for life insurance salespeople to use the approaching estate tax burden as an argument for selling large policies to wealthy people in their later years. This larger exemption can be especially important to sole proprietors or partners, whose death might, because of estate taxes, force their businesses to close because of shortages of capital.

QUESTIONS

1. Discuss the impact of the changing estate tax exemption on the 65 year old owner of a retail store with an estate of $1,000,000, most of which is tied up in the store.

2. If you were an insurance salesperson, what arguments could you use to convince wealthy, elderly policyholders not to reduce their life insurance coverage?

CHAPTER 16

The Securities Market and Long-Term Financing

OBJECTIVES:

After reading this chapter, you should be able to

1. Name several components of the public securities market.
2. Distinguish among several types of preferred stock.
3. Explain what is meant by stock "value" and how this relates to stock dividends and stock splits.
4. Distinguish among several types of bonds.
5. Compare the services and functions of investment banks, brokerage houses, and securities exchanges.
6. Translate a quote for a stock or bond as reported in *The Wall Street Journal* into dollars-and-cents terms.
7. Compare speculating with investing.
8. Discuss the role of the Securities and Exchange Commission in the securities market.
9. Explain the uses of long-term capital and capital budgeting.
10. Show how the sources of long-term capital differ for corporate and noncorporate firms.
11. Present the advantages and possible disadvantages of leasing as an alternative to long-term financing of a purchase.
12. Explain the special need for intermediate-term financing.
13. Show the relationship among mergers, acquisitions, and asset redeployment.
14. Discuss the concepts of recapitalization, bankruptcy, and reorganization.

KEY CONCEPTS:

Look for these terms as you read the chapter

public securities market

bond

investment bank

brokerage house

securities exchange

over-the-counter market (OTC)

margin trading

short selling

mutual fund

blue-sky laws

prospectus

capital budget

sinking fund

lease

intermediate-term financing

equipment trust certificates

rolling over

merger

acquisition

asset redeployment

recapitalization

bankruptcy

reorganization

Traffic on the floor of the New York Stock Exchange is fast approaching gridlock.

As volume has crept upward, more traders and more machines have crowded the floor to handle it all. With space strained to capacity, executing a trade has become, as never before, a boisterous obstacle course.

"It's very crowded, and it's very hard to get around," complains the head of floor operations for one of the exchange's largest members.

Big Board officials are nervously scrambling to alleviate congestion and make the exchange ready for trading days when as many as 150 million shares could change hands (compared with the current daily average of 44 million).

But their planning is clouded by worries of another sort: that much of the anticipated volume will be handled away from the floor, and that the notion of a trading arena where brokers haggle face to face will gradually wither away. Such fears were given substance in 1981, when the Securities and Exchange Commission ruled that member firms could transact certain business from their offices rather than on the exchange's 80-year-old trading floor.

The crucial role played by the securities market in tending to the long-term financial needs of U.S. firms is the main topic of this chapter. We will describe the major institutions participating in the sale of securities and show how investors and speculators make use of the flow of information about securities markets. The kinds of financial needs that businesses fulfill through the securities market will be discussed, as will the alternative of leasing and special problems related to reorganization, bankruptcy, and merger. We begin with a discussion of the public securities market.

THE SECURITIES MARKET

Up to this point, our discussion of financial institutions has focused mainly on sources of short-term funds for businesses. The need for long-term funds has led to the creation of important financial institutions.

public securities market

With very few exceptions, most large- and medium-sized corporations use the public securities market as a source of long-term funds. **The public securities market is made up of millions of people who buy stocks and bonds and the business and nonbusiness organizations that also invest in corporate securities. Also included in the public market are the various securities "middlemen" who bring buyers and sellers of securities together.**

Types of Securities

The two major vehicles by which a firm gains access to the public market are stocks and bonds. As we saw in Chapter 3, only corporations issue stock. While a firm need not be a corporation to issue bonds, it usually must be a well-financed and sound firm if it is to attract any buyers of its bonds. You may want to review the discussion of common stock and preferred stock in Chapter 3. You should also examine Table 16-1, which outlines several types of preferred stock.

Stocks

Three different concepts of value associated with common stock are

- book value—the difference between the dollar values of what a company owns (its assets) and what it owes (its debts, or liabilities) divided by the number of shares of common stock.
- market value—the price the shares of stock are selling for on the market. This changes daily in response to supply and demand.

Type	Characteristics
1. Cumulative preferred	1. Dividends not paid in one year or more accumulate and must be paid before common stockholders receive dividends.
2. Noncumulative preferred	2. Dividends not paid in one year or more need not be paid in future years but, in a given year, must be paid before common stockholders receive any dividends.
3. Fully participating preferred	3. Once the dividend stated on the stock certificate is paid and the common stockholders receive the same sum, preferred shareholders share in any remaining dividends.
4. Nonparticipating preferred	4. Shareholders are entitled only to the dividend stated on the stock certificate.
5. Convertible preferred	5. Preferred shareholders can convert their preferred stock to common stock at their option.
6. Redeemable preferred	6. Preferred stock issued with a call price at which price the issuing corporation can legally require the holder to sell his or her shares back to the corporation.

TABLE 16-1

Types and characteristics of preferred stock

- par value—the value the corporation that originally issued the stock certificate may have printed on it. This is called par value stock. If no value is placed on the stock certificate, it is called no-par stock.

In most cases, the book value, market value, and par value of a corporation's stock are three different amounts.

Consider, for example, the giant corporate takeovers of recent years. Part of the explanation for them is that the stock market was depressed—the market value of many companies' stock was way down. Now consider the book value of the stock. Inflation drives up the cost of replacing assets like plants and equipment. As we saw in Chapter 12, these assets are carried on a firm's books at acquisition cost—not replacement cost. Thus many of the companies that are buying up other companies are, in effect, getting tremendous bargains.

Three other terms are also important:

- stock split
- cash dividend
- stock dividend

A stock split gives stockholders a greater number of shares but does not change the individual's proportionate ownership in the corporation. Sue Adams, for example, owns 100 shares of IBM common, which is selling at $100 per share. The market value of her shares is $10,000. If the directors vote for a 4-for-1 stock split, Sue will have 400 shares valued at $25 per share. The total market value of her shares right after the split is still $10,000. The purpose of the split is to reduce the selling price per share. This may make the stock attractive to more buyers, increase the demand for it, and raise its selling price.

A cash dividend is a payment of cash to stockholders. It rewards them for their investment in the corporation.

If a corporation wants to keep its cash, it might declare a stock dividend. This is a payment to stockholders in additional shares of stock rather than payment of cash. A 20 percent stock dividend means that each stockholder gets two new shares for each ten he or she already owns. A stock dividend is a way to reward stockholders when a firm wants to reinvest its earnings in the business. It conserves cash. Like a stock split, a stock dividend does not increase the stockholder's share of ownership in a corporation.

How Do You Go About Raising a Quick Billion?

WHAT DO YOU THINK?

Ma Bell (The American Telephone and Telegraph Company) raised $940,000,000 in one stock sale in June, 1981. At that time this was the largest sale of stock ever made in the history of U.S. business and, perhaps, in the history of world business. AT&T, the world's largest private firm in terms of assets, sold 16.5 million shares through underwriters. They were offered to the public at $57 a share. Only four years earlier the same firm sold 12 million shares in the same way at a somewhat higher price.

AT&T's management and board of directors, of course, had several options which might have been exercised to meet the huge growing capital needs of this far-flung corporation. They could have floated debenture bonds, for example (see Table 16-2). $940,000,000 worth of bonds might have required an annual interest payment of more than $110,000,000 to bondholders, but they would not, of course, have affected the voting power of existing stockholders. Bonds would eventually have to be paid off, too, whereas the common stock offering does not. Why did AT&T decide to sell the stock? WHAT DO YOU THINK?

Thank-you Carol
Carol + Brian!
Lisa + Gerry

Types	_Characteristics_
1. Secured bonds	1. Backed by security pledged by the issuing corporation. This can be sold by the trustee and the proceeds used to pay off the bondholders if the corporation fails to pay principal and/or interest.
(a) Real estate mortgage bonds	(a) Secured by real property.
(b) Chattel mortgage bonds	(b) Secured by movable property.
(c) Collateral trust bonds	(c) Secured by stocks and bonds in other corporations which are owned by the issuing corporation.
2. Debenture bonds	2. Not secured or backed by specific assets but by the general credit and strength of the issuing corporation.
3. Registered bonds	3. Owner's name is registered with the issuing corporation and is printed on the certificate. Interest is mailed to him or her by the corporation or its trustee.
4. Coupon bonds	4. Owner's name is not registered and does not appear on the certificate. Owner must clip coupons from the bond and present them to the corporation's bank.
5. Convertible bonds	5. Can be converted to common stock at the bondholder's option.
6. Serial bonds	6. The issuing corporation issues a large block of bonds which mature at different dates.
7. Sinking fund bonds	7. The issuing corporation makes annual deposits with the trustee so that those deposits, along with earned interest, will be available to redeem the bonds upon maturity.
8. Redeemable or callable bonds	8. Can be called in or redeemed prior to maturity.
9. Municipal bonds	9. Issued by cities or municipalities. Usually the interest income on such issues is not subject to federal income tax.

TABLE 16-2

Types and characteristics of bonds

Bonds

Although all corporations issue common stock, not all issue bonds. Stockholders provide equity (ownership) capital, while bondholders are lenders. Stock certificates indicate ownership, while bond certificates indicate indebtedness.

A bond is a written promise to pay. It indicates that the borrower will pay the lender, at some stated future date, a sum of money (the principal) and a stated rate of interest. Bondholders have a claim on a corporation's assets and earnings which comes before that of

bond

common and preferred stockholders. Federal, state, and city governments also issue bonds.

Most bond issues are sold to many individuals. The agreement under which they are issued (the indenture) names a trustee to represent the bondholders' interests. This trustee is usually a large bank or trust company. Table 16-2 describes several important types of bonds.

Investment Banks and Brokerage Houses

Two very important financial institutions are investment banks and brokerage houses. They are crucial to the purchase and sale of stocks and bonds.

The Role of Investment Banks

investment bank

An investment bank (or underwriting house) does not accept deposits from the general public. It helps corporations to sell new issues of stocks and bonds.

Suppose a major brewery decides to expand one of its plants and wishes to sell $25 million of bonds. It might contact an investment bank to assist in the sale. If the bank's study of the brewery's financial condition reports favorably on the issue, it would offer to buy the bonds. The brewery, if it accepts the offer, would receive the proceeds and the bank would offer the bonds for sale to investors. The bank earns a profit by charging a commission for its services or by selling the securities at a price higher than it paid for them.

If the risk of selling a large issue of stocks and bonds is too great for one investment bank, several may combine in a syndicate to underwrite the issue. Each bank in this underwriting syndicate agrees to take a portion of the securities offered for sale.

The Role of Brokerage Houses

brokerage house

A brokerage house is a firm that buys and sells securities that previously have been issued by businesses and governments. It buys and sells securities on behalf of its investor-clients.

Large brokerage houses perform many functions for corporations and investors:

- They engage in investment banking when they help corporations to sell new securities issues.
- They perform a brokerage function when they buy and sell previously issued securities on behalf of their investor-clients.
- They perform a credit function when they finance purchases made on credit by securities buyers (margin purchases).

A discount brokerage house advertises its services

"I would like to order a pair of overalls and 10 shares of AT&T!"

- They perform a research function when they compile information about firms.
- They perform an advisory function when they use the information gathered through research to advise their corporate clients on issuing new securities and when they advise their investor-clients on buying and selling securities.

Many changes have occurred recently in the way brokerage houses operate. Now it is common, for example, to distinguish between full-cost and discount brokerage houses. As you can see in the Kelly ad, discount brokerage houses charge lower commissions to their clients than full-cost brokerage houses. Another big change is the growth in acquisitions of brokerage houses. Thus, as we saw in Chapter 14, Sears acquired Dean Witter, a big brokerage house, as part of Sears' effort to become the nation's biggest financial services company.

Using Securities Exchanges

Securities exchanges are set up by brokerage houses to reduce the cost and increase the efficiency of financial investment. Buyers and sellers of securities can deal with each other through members of the exchanges. Members of an exchange own "seats" on that exchange. Only members can trade on an exchange.

securities exchange

Most large brokerage firms hold seats on most of the 17 exchanges in the United States. Of course, there are securities exchanges in other countries also, such as the London and the Tokyo Stock Exchanges.

A corporation does not receive money from the sale of its securities on stock exchanges. If an investor buys 100 shares of Abbot Laboratories common on an exchange, the money goes to the previous owner of the shares, not to Abbot Laboratories. Only when the stock was originally issued through a major brokerage house did Abbot Laboratories receive money. The stock exchange was not involved.

Listed Securities

Securities traded on organized stock exchanges such as the New York Stock Exchange (NYSE) and the American Stock Exchange (AMEX) are called listed securities.

The floor of the New York Stock Exchange, where purchase and sale orders are received and executed and where stock trading occurs

The NYSE is made up of roughly 1,400 individual members who hold seats on the exchange. Owning a seat enables a brokerage firm to buy and sell on the NYSE floor. The securities of most major corporations are listed here. Only those that have been traded for some time on other exchanges and are widely held can be listed on the NYSE. A fee must be paid before a security can be listed.

Buying a Listed Security. Suppose you want to buy a listed security. If you have never "dabbled" in the market, your first step is to go to a branch office of a brokerage house and open an account. A corporation has only a certain number of outstanding shares (issued by the corporation and owned by investors). If you want to buy some of those shares, you must deal with people who own them. The brokerage house brings you (the buyer) and someone else (the seller) together.

When you go to the brokerage house, you will be introduced to an account executive. This person is often called a stockbroker because he or she works for a brokerage house. If you are serious about becoming an investor, take the time to get to know your account executive. Be open about your investment goals and your financial situation. Because all of your dealings with the brokerage house will be handled by and through your account executive, you must know and understand each other.

After talking with your account executive, Ms. Perkins, you decide to buy some Westinghouse common stock. You ask her what the selling price is. Ms. Perkins uses an electronic device such as Quotron, which is linked to the stock exchange. It tells her the last price at which the stock sold. Now you must make a decision. If you tell Ms. Perkins to buy "at market," she will buy the number of shares you want at the lowest price offered. If that price is $80 per share, you would pay $8,000, plus commission, if you buy 100 shares.

But suppose you want to pay no more than $70 per share. You can place a "limit order" with Ms. Perkins. Your order would not be filled unless she could find someone willing to sell for $70 or less per share.

If you place an "at market" order, Ms. Perkins contacts her firm's New York office. That office contacts its representative on the New York Stock Exchange floor who goes to the "post" where Westinghouse stock is traded. That floor person buys the shares at the offering price. No delay is involved because someone is always willing to sell if a buyer is willing to pay the seller's asking price.

Within minutes, Ms. Perkins will get an electronic message direct from the exchange floor telling her that the transaction is complete. Meanwhile, the seller's account executive sends his or her client's stock certificate to Westinghouse's transfer agent, who cancels it and issues a new certificate in your name. This may be held by your account executive for safekeeping or sent to you.

A securities brokerage office where orders for stocks and bonds purchases and sales are received, usually via telephone, from investors and speculators

The Over-the-Counter Market

Most securities are unlisted. Unlisted securities are not listed on any of the organized securities exchanges. They are traded in the over-the-counter (OTC) market. **The over-the-counter market is a complex of dealers who are in constant touch with one another. Stocks and bonds of locally owned corporations are generally traded on the OTC market. All new issues of stocks and bonds, most government bonds, and the stocks of most banks, mutual funds, and insurance companies are traded here.**

Security dealers in the OTC market often buy securities in their own name. They expect to sell them at a higher price to their clients. These dealers also buy shares at the request of their clients. Dealers receive a commission for this. Dealers selling to one another charge a wholesale price and sell to their customers at a retail price.

The National Association of Securities Dealers, Inc. (NASD) is the self-regulatory organization for the OTC securities market. In 1971 it created a computerized communications system that collects, stores, and reports price quotations to brokers and dealers. This system is called NASDAQ—NASD Automated Quotations. Brokers and dealers are connected by this system, which enables them to get up-to-the-second price quotations. Thus a broker can get a price quote on a security that is quoted by NASDAQ merely by pushing a button. This makes possible more efficient trading of securities in the OTC market.

STOCK AND BOND PRICES

Stocks and bonds traded on the exchanges and the OTC market are listed and reported in the financial section of many daily newspapers. *The Wall Street Journal* gives more detailed coverage.

Stock Prices

Figure 16-1 explains the meaning of the various columns relating to the stock prices as reported in *The Wall Street Journal*. The corporation's name (in abbreviated form) is shown along with the number of shares sold (expressed in round lots of 100 shares). Prices are quoted in dollars and fractions of a dollar ranging from $\frac{1}{8}$ to $\frac{7}{8}$. A quote of $50\frac{5}{8}$ means that the price per share is $50.625. Follow the steps for the highlighted line in Figure 16-1 to understand each column.

Bond Prices and Bond Yields

Bond prices also change from day to day. These changes provide information for firms about the cost of borrowing funds.

Prices of domestic corporation bonds, U.S. government bonds,

1.   High   Low

32¼   23⅝

During the last 52 weeks the highest price was $32.25 and the lowest, $23.625

2.   Stock

AbtLb

Abbreviated company name — Abbot Laboratories.

3.   Div

$ .84

Total dividends issued in current year per share.

1		2	3	4	5	6	7	8	9	10
52 Weeks				Yld	P–E	Sales				Net
High	Low	Stock	Div	%	Ratio	100s	High	Low	Close	Chg
		— A – A – A –								
12 3/8	6	AAR	.44	6.5	15	4	6 3/4	6 3/4	6 3/4	– 1/4
50	31 1/2	ACF	2.76	7.9	7	276	35	34	34 3/4	+ 3/4
28 1/2	16 5/8	AMF	1.36	7.7	10	156	18 1/8	17 3/4	17 3/4	– 1/4
16 7/8	1 1/8	AM Intl		..	..	93	1 3/4	1 5/8	1 3/4	+ 1/8
7 3/8	3 3/4	APL		..	..	2	4	4	4	....
37 1/4	23 1/2	ARA	2	7.5	7	43	26 1/2	26 1/8	26 1/2	+ 1/4
56 7/8	26 3/4	ASA	4a	12	..	515	34 3/4	33 3/4	34 1/2	+ 1/4
36 5/8	11 1/2	AVX	.32	1.7	..	91	19	18 1/2	19	+ 1/2
32 1/4	23 5/8	AbtLb	s .84	2.9	14	1063	29 1/8	28 3/4	28 7/8	– 1/8
29 1/2	17 1/4	AcmeC	1.40	6.4	8	12	21 3/4	21 1/2	21 3/4	+ 1/4
9 5/8	7 1/2	AcmeE	n.32b	4.2	7	14	7 7/8	7 5/8	7 5/8	....
6 3/4	4	AdmDg	.04	.8	6	77	5	4 7/8	5	+ 1/8
15 5/8	12 3/4	AdaEx	2.25e	16	..	58	13 7/8	13 1/2	13 3/4	– 1/8
7 7/8	4	AdmMl	.20e	2.7	8	71	7 1/2	7 1/4	7 3/8	– 1/4

4.   Yld%

2.9

Dividends issued most recent year divided by current share price. (Col 3/Col 9)

5.   P–E Ratio

14

Price-earnings ratio, or current share price (col 9) divided by earnings per share in most recent year.

6.   Sales (in 100s)

1063

Total number of shares traded this date in round lots of 100. There were 106,300 shares sold.

7,8   High   Low

29⅛   28¾

On this date, the highest price paid was $29.125 and the lowest, $28.75 per share.

9.   Close

28⅞

At close of trading on this date the last price paid per share was $28.875.

10.   Net Chg

–⅛

Difference between today's closing price and previous day's closing price. Price decreased by $0.125.

FIGURE 16-1

How to read a stock quotation

and foreign bonds are reported separately. Bond prices are expressed in terms of 100 even though most have a face or par value of $1,000. Thus a quote of 85 means that the bond's price is 85 percent of par or $850.

A corporation bond selling at 155¼ would cost a buyer $1,552.50 ($1,000 par value times 1.5525) plus commission. U.S. government bonds, however, are quoted in $\frac{1}{32}$ points. A $1,000 par bond quoted at 101$\frac{8}{32}$ would cost $1,012.50 ($1,000 times 1.0125) plus commission. In the financial pages, the selling price would be shown as 101.8 rather than 101$\frac{8}{32}$. The interest rate on bonds is also quoted as a percentage of par. Thus "6½s" pay 6.5 percent of par value per year.

The market value (selling price) of a bond at any given time depends on (1) its stated interest rate; (2) the "going rate" of interest in the market; and (3) its redemption or maturity date.

If a bond carries a higher stated interest rate than the "going rate" on similar quality bonds, it will probably sell at a premium above its face value—its selling price will be above its redemption price. If a bond carries a lower stated interest rate than the "going rate" on similar quality bonds, it will probably sell at a discount—its selling price will be below its redemption price. How much the premium or discount is depends largely on how far off in the future the maturity date is. The maturity date is indicated after the interest rate. Figure 16-2 explains the various columns in a bond quotation.

Suppose you bought a $1,000 par value bond in 1977 for $650. Its stated interest rate is 6 percent and its maturity or redemption date is 1997. You paid $650 for the bond and its interest rate is 6 percent per year of par value. You get $60 per year in interest. Based on your actual investment of $650, your yield is 9.2 percent $(\frac{60}{650} = .092)$. If you hold it to maturity, you get $1,000 for a bond that originally cost you only $650. This "extra" $350, of course, increases your true, or effective, yield.

FIGURE 16-2

How to read a bond quotation

	Bonds	Cur Yld	Vol	High	Low	Close	Net Chg
		1 2 3	4	5	6	7	8	9
AMint	9 3/8 95	31.	103	30	29 1/8	30	+ 1
APL	10 3/4 97	20.	5	55 1/4	54 3/4	54 3/4	− 1/4
AlaP	7 3/4 s02	15.	12	50 3/4	49 3/8	50 3/4	+ 3/4
AlaP	8 7/8 s03	16.	10	55 1/2	55	55 1/2	− 3/4
AlaP	8 1/4 s03	16.	2	52 5/8	52 5/8	52 5/8	+ 5/8
AlaP	9 3/4 s04	16.	25	61	60 3/8	61	+1 1/8
AlaP	8 3/4 07	16.	23	54 5/8	54 1/2	54 1/2	−1 1/2
AlaP	8 5/8 87	12.	30	74 1/8	74 1/8	74 1/8	+ 3/8
AlaP	9 1/2 08	16.	11	59	59	59	− 1/2
AlaP	9 5/8 08	17.	5	58 1/4	58 1/4	58 1/4	− 5/8
AlaP	12 5/8 10	17.	3	75	75	75	+ 1/4
AlaP	15 1/4 10	17.	9	88	88	88	−1
AlaP	17 3/8 11	18.	155	99 1/2	98 3/4	99 1/4	+ 1/2
AlaP	18 1/4 89	17.	10	109	109	109	....
AlskH	16 1/4 94	17.	15	98	98	98	− 1/8
Alexn	5 1/2 96	cv	32	52 1/2	51	52 1/2	+2
Allgl	10 3/4 99	17.	13	62 1/4	61 3/4	61 1/4	− 3/4
AlldSt	4 1/2 92	cv	5	129	129	129	−1
Alcoa	9 s95	13.	3	67	67	67	−1
AluCa	9 1/2 95	14.	2	68 3/8	68 3/8	68 3/8	+3 1/8
AMAX	8 s86	10.	9	79 3/8	79 1/4	79 3/8	−1 5/8
Amax	8 5/8 01	15.	10	58	58	58	+ 1
Amerce	5 s92	cv	20	66	66	66	−2 1/2
AAirl	4 1/4 92	10.	17	42 1/2	40 1/4	42 1/2	+2 1/2

1.   Bond

Alcoa

Abbreviated company name—Aluminum Corporation of America.

2.

9

Annual interest rate paid on face, 9 percent.

3.

95

Maturity date, in this case, 1995

4.   Cur Yld

13

Annual interest paid divided by current market price.

5.   Vol

3

Volume traded this date in thousands of dollars.

6,7,8 High Low Close

67 67 67

On this date, high price paid, low price paid, and closing price paid were all the same — $670 for a $1000 face value bond.

9.   Net Chg

−1

Closing price paid on this date was $10 lower than the closing price paid on the preceding trading date.

Stock and Bond Averages

To give investors an overall idea of the behavior of security prices, several types of stock and bond averages are reported. The Dow Jones Averages and the Standard & Poor's Index are two such averages for stocks. The Dow Jones Averages include: (1) the average of 30 industrial stocks; (2) the average of 20 transportation stocks; (3) the average of 15 public utility stocks; and (4) a composite average of the preceding 65 stocks. Standard & Poor's Index covers 500 leading stocks.

Common stocks on the NYSE are averaged so that an investor can tell in dollars and cents how much an average share changed in price on a given day. The Dow Jones Bond Averages and several others provide information about the behavior of the bond market.

SPECULATING AND INVESTING

Speculating

Some people think that buying stocks and bonds is a way to get rich quick and buy on the basis of hot tips. This is called speculative trading, and means buying or selling securities in the hope of profiting from near-term future changes in their selling prices.

Sometimes amateur speculators do "strike it rich," but the losers far outnumber the winners. Speculating is most popular during a *bull market*, when stock prices as a whole are rising and there is a great deal of optimism among speculators. Speculating is less popular in a *bear market*, when stock prices as a whole are falling and there is a great deal of pessimism among speculators.

Margin Trading

A speculator has to pay cash for securities bought only when the margin requirement is 100 percent. Otherwise, the speculator buys partly on credit.

Margin trading enables speculators to buy more shares for a given amount of money because they are buying partly on credit. Brokers put up the shares they sell on margin as collateral for the loans they make from banks to finance their clients' margin purchases. As long as the price of a stock bought on margin rises, there is no problem. The banker's collateral increases in value. But if its price falls, the banker wants more cash from the broker or wants to sell the shares.

In the 1920s many speculators were buying on 10 percent margin. When stock prices began falling, bankers started selling, in large

margin trading

volume, the stocks they held as collateral. This helped to bring on the eventual collapse of the stock market. To protect against such collapse the Federal Reserve System now sets the margin requirement (see Chapter 14).

Short Selling

Speculators may also profit from selling stocks when prices are falling. Martha Todd, an established client of Broker B, believes that the selling price of GM common stock will fall in the next few weeks. It is now selling at 65. Martha does not own any GM stock but "borrows" several shares from her broker. Many investors do not take possession of the stock certificates they own but let their brokers keep them for them. Thus brokers can "lend" some of this stock to their other clients.

Martha tells her broker to sell 500 of these borrowed shares at 65. If the price subsequently falls, Martha buys the shares to "cover" her earlier sale. She buys in, say, at 55. She thus makes a $10 profit on each of the 500 shares (less commission). But if the price went up instead of down, Martha would incur a loss. This practice is called short selling. **Short selling means selling a security that you do not own by borrowing it from your broker. At some time in the future, you must buy the security to "cover" the short sale.**

short selling

Investing

Unlike a speculator, an investor buys securities for the longer haul. Before even considering investing, much less speculating, you should have a cushion of cash reserves and adequate insurance. You should be able to choose when you want to sell your shares and not be forced to sell them because you need cash for an emergency.

Your approach to buying and selling securities should be logical. Your investment goals should guide your buying and selling decisions. The kinds of goals may vary among investors but each investor should have definite goals.

An important goal for investors is to protect their invested dollars. You could do this by putting your money in a safe deposit box. But this earns nothing and, because of inflation, the buying power of those dollars declines. You would be wiser to place your funds in an insured savings account at a bank or S&LA, or in a NOW account. You might also buy U.S. Savings Bonds. These are safe and can easily be converted to cash. You could also earn more with a CD (as shown in Chapter 14)—especially a money market CD. A money market mutual fund, as we saw in Chapter 14, offers both high return and easy withdrawal. If you wish even higher returns you must increase the risk you take.

How Much Risk?

Of course, different investment strategies involve different degrees of risk. Investing in preferred stocks of established and profitable corporations is less risky, for example, than investing in common stocks of new ventures. In terms of return, however, the new venture might prove to be the better investment. In other words, risk and return tend to be directly related.

There is no one answer to the question of how much risk you should assume in your investment program. You have to consider your financial situation, age, investment goals, patience, self-discipline, etc. To put it simply, if your goal is to get rich quick, you will have to take a lot more risk than someone else whose goal is to get rich more slowly. Many recent savings and loan association and bank ads have featured tables dramatically illustrating this point. Suppose you start an Individual Retirement Account (IRA) at age 24 and deposit $2,000 each year. If you receive 12 percent interest compounded daily you will be a millionaire by age 60. You will have $1,311,254 in your IRA.

Balancing Objectives

The typical investor wants a safe investment that will return regular earnings and has a lot of potential for future growth. But it's hard to satisfy all three objectives.

Investing in securities involves keeping up with developments in the economy and in the industries and firms in which you invest. If you don't have the time or "know-how" to do this, you might invest in a mutual fund. **The owners of a mutual fund pool their investment dollars and buy securities in other businesses. Buying one share in a mutual fund makes you part owner of all the securities owned by the fund.** You spread your risk over a broad range of securities. Mutual funds are professionally managed. Before they were created, only people with large sums to invest could afford to hire professional managers to oversee their portfolios (the stocks and bonds that they own). The Scudder Fund Distributors brochure shown on the following page lists and discusses the types of mutual funds it offers to its investors.

mutual fund

SECURITIES REGULATION

Both the issuance of new securities and trading in previously issued securities are regulated by state and federal laws. **At the state level, blue-sky laws apply mainly to the sale of new securities. Their purpose is to prevent corporations from issuing securities that have**

blue-sky laws

THE SCUDDER FUNDS

The nine Scudder funds are all no-load. They may be purchased without any sales charge, commission or redemption fee. The investment objectives and minimum initial investment requirements for each fund are listed below. For a free prospectus containing information about management fees and expenses, return the attached card. Read it carefully before you invest or send money.

Money Market

Scudder Cash Investment Trust is a money market fund with a stable price and short-term portfolio. Initial investment: $1,000.

Scudder Government Money Fund is a money market fund that invests 100 percent in U.S. Government and U.S. Government guaranteed obligations. Initial investment: $1,000.

Scudder Tax Free Money Fund combines the advantage of tax free income* with money market fund convenience, liquidity, and relative stability of capital. Initial investment: $1,000.

Income

Scudder Income Fund seeks income from a managed portfolio of bonds and high-yielding common stocks. Initial investment: $500.

Scudder Managed Municipal Bonds seeks to provide tax-free income* from a diversified portfolio of high-quality municipal bonds. Initial investment: $1,000.

Growth

Scudder Common Stock Fund seeks long-term growth of capital through a diversified portfolio of common stocks, primarily seasoned and marketable securities of leading companies. Initial investment: $500.

Scudder Special Fund offers investors participation in special risks with the basic aim of capital appreciation. Initial investment: $500.

Scudder Development Fund invests for growth of capital through marketable common stocks of relatively small or little-known companies. Initial investment: $2,000.

International

Scudder International Fund provides diversification and appreciation potential through an actively managed portfolio of stocks and bonds denominated in foreign currencies. Initial investment: $1,000.

*Some income may be subject to state or local tax.

Various types of mutual funds are designed to meet the needs of investors with different investment objectives

nothing of value to offer the buyer. Issuing corporations must back up securities with something more than just "the blue sky." These laws also generally require the licensing of stockbrokers and the registration of securities before they can be sold.

At the federal level, the Securities Act of 1933 protects the public against interstate sales of fraudulent securities. It is a "truth in securities" law. Issuers of new securities are required to file a detailed registration statement with the Securities and Exchange Commission (SEC) before the securities are offered for sale to the public. This registration statement must disclose all information about the company that might affect the value of its securities, such as earnings, financial condition, and officers' salaries. In addition, every prospective buyer of the securities must be given a prospectus. **A prospectus is a summary of the registration statement that is filed with the SEC. It includes information about the firm, its operations, its management, the purpose of the proposed issue, and any other things that would be helpful to a potential buyer of those securities.**

prospectus

The Securities and Exchange Commission was established by the Securities Exchange Act of 1934. The SEC is a five-member commission appointed by the President with the consent of the Senate. The Securities Exchange Act requires *all* corporations whose securities are listed on national securities exchanges to file registration statements with the SEC and to file annual reports with the SEC to update their registration statements.

The Securities Exchange Act was amended in 1938 by the Maloney Act, which created a private trade organization, the National Association of Securities Dealers (NASD), to regulate the over-the-counter market. The SEC, however, retains final authority to regulate securities dealers in the over-the-counter market.

The Investment Company Act of 1940 brought the operations of mutual funds under the SEC's jurisdiction. The Securities Investor Protection Act of 1970 established the Securities Investor Protection Insurance Corporation to provide insurance protection to investors who buy securities but leave them with their brokerage houses for safekeeping. It also provides insurance protection to investors who leave cash with their brokerage houses.

The SEC licenses brokerage houses and establishes codes of conduct for them. A person who owns more than 10 percent of a firm's stock must register as an "insider" with the SEC. Such a person must file a report with the SEC if he or she does any trading in that stock. Insiders are not allowed to sell their firm's stock "short." The purpose is to prevent insider manipulation of the stock's selling price.

Although the SEC has broad regulatory powers, it does not judge the relative merits of individual securities. This position is reflected in the statement below, which appears in the prospectus accompanying many security issues:

These securities have not been approved or disapproved by the Securities and Exchange Commission nor has the commission passed upon the accuracy or adequacy of this prospectus. Any representation to the contrary is a criminal offense.

Security issues, we will see in the remainder of this chapter, play a major role in the long-term financing of most corporate and some noncorporate firms.

LONG-TERM FINANCING

In Chapter 12 we examined the financial statements of a business firm, and saw that firms usually need two kinds of assets—current assets and fixed assets. We also saw the other side of the accounting equation—claims on assets. These consist of current and long-term liabilities and owners' equity.

The basic choice in financing, as we saw in Chapter 15, is between debt and equity financing. Much of the short-term (working) capital is borrowed from banks or advanced from suppliers in the form of trade credit. To meet longer-term financial needs, we will see that firms use a combination of debt and equity sources. The securities market provides many of these sources.

Although the quality of management of production and marketing operations may be the principal determinants of a firm's sales and profitability, the final test of success from the owners' perspective depends equally on the skill and judgment of the financial manager. That final test is the return that owners get on their investment—profit as a percentage of the owners' equity. To the extent that the financial manager plans for and determines the firm's long-term capital needs, and to the extent that he or she minimizes the cost of such capital, that manager contributes in equal measure with operating managers to the firm's success or failure.

We will look at long-term capital from two perspectives—the uses to which it is put and the sources from which it comes. Long-term capital is at the same time a set of fixed assets that a firm uses in its operations and a long-term commitment of funds in exchange for a long-term claim against these assets.

USES OF LONG-TERM CAPITAL

Long-term capital is invested in land, buildings, heavy machinery, and other fixed assets that, to a large extent, determine the direction in which the firm is going. When RCA went into the computer business, it directed a large part of its long-term capital into assets that could not be sold without loss. RCA management assumed that such an investment would be profitable. This decision proved to be wrong, and RCA later sold its computer holdings at a loss of millions of dollars. More recently, several steel manufacturers in the U.S. have faced hard decisions concerning the amount and type of investment to make in modernizing their steel mills.

Financial managers must take a long-run view of the firm's operations. They do this with the help of some of the accounting devices we saw in Chapter 12. **One of these is the capital budget which is based on expected sales growth and technology changes and projects capital needs for from five to twenty years.** Such a projection requires that budget makers use every scrap of information about the long-range plans and expectations of the firm. They must take the environment into account, too. This includes technological events outside the firm and changes in consumer needs and tastes that might require changes in plant machinery and equipment. For example, financial managers in big manufacturing industries not only must help project the need for long-term capital for modernizing and automating many of their firms' production operations, but they also must help in securing that capital.

capital budget

Technological changes can be especially hard to predict. Consider the great technological change that has occurred in the airline industry. The propeller-driven airplane has long been replaced by jets. An airline must face the possibility that even recently bought planes will soon become obsolete. If they do, a decision must be made whether or not to replace them and, if so, with what.

Currently, aircraft manufacturers are spending large sums to develop more fuel-efficient planes. Consider the Boeing Company's schedule of new product introductions—the 767 in 1982, the 757 in 1983, and the 737–300 in 1984. Because of the tremendous financing requirements, however, Boeing is considering entering into a joint venture with another manufacturer, perhaps a foreign-based plane manufacturer, to help with the financing.

Planning for future capital needs is a lot easier for firms that sell products that are not subject to much in the way of technological change or fashion obsolescence. Compared to aircraft or electronics, the forecast of sales for a regional producer of kitchen cutlery is easy. Figure 16-3 illustrates such a forecast. The moderate growth trend projected here assumes roughly constant growth in the number of households formed in the market the firm is presently serving and a slight growth in income. It also presumes no major competitive changes in the market and no major technological changes. Faced with this kind of sales forecast, the plant expansion and the funding

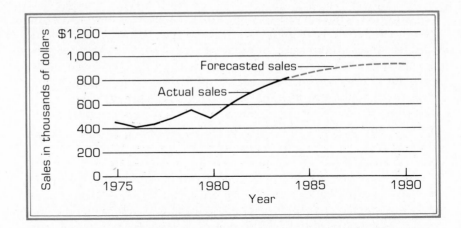

required over this time period can be planned with reasonable assurance.

Every capital investment decision requires a good estimate of the payoff of such investment. This, in turn, depends on good forecasting and expert analysis of capital needs and their costs over the planning period. In some cases firms will avoid the risk of long-term asset purchase by resorting to leasing.

SOURCES OF LONG-TERM CAPITAL

Corporations have wider access to long-term funds than do partnerships and sole proprietors. But in all cases, there is some choice between internal (equity) and external (debt) financing.

Sources for Corporations

Corporate long-term capital is available in the public securities market by means of stock issues and bond issues. As we have seen, there are several types of stock and several types of bonds. Issuing preferred stock is a source of growth funds for corporations with stable earnings. Common stock is more likely to be issued when good growth is expected but earnings are considered to be unpredictable. The "new" common stockholder, or shareholder, joins the "old" common stockholder on an equal footing. Depending on the relative size of "old" and "new" common stockholdings, the "old" shareholders may risk loss of or reduction in their control over the firm's affairs.

A corporation that needs additional debt financing for the long run may issue bonds. Firms have an implied right to borrow as long as it is done for the company's benefit.

A major decision in a bond issue is selecting a method to pay off bondholders. The most attractive way for a strong, growing firm is by debt replacement—relying on the ability of the firm to exchange maturing bonds for new bonds or for stock. **In other cases, firms set up a sinking fund to retire maturing bonds. This means putting aside money each year from profits to pay them off.** This is more likely to be done in a firm that is not expanding or that might find this investor protection feature the only way to attract bond investors. Also, using a sinking fund will bring the interest rate on the bonds down.

sinking fund

The convertibility feature is a tactic firms use to help float bonds in times of high interest rates. Convertible bonds can be swapped for common stock at a stated price. This tactic was used by MCI Communications Corp. and many other firms that issued bonds in 1981. MCI, a fast-growing rival of AT&T, sold $100 million in $10\frac{1}{4}$ percent bonds very easily in that year despite tight money conditions. These bonds could be converted into common stock two years after issue at a price 18 percent higher than the market price of the stock at the time of the bond issue. Soon after issue these bonds were selling on the open market at a price seven percent higher than par.

A profitable firm also has the option of using profits to pay dividends or to "plow back" into operations. Plowing it back permits fixed asset growth without the use of borrowed funds. It is a form of equity financing.

Common shareholders may or may not favor such financing, depending on their investment goals. Investors who view their shares as "growth stock" expect it to appreciate over the long run. They don't demand immediate dividends. Others invest for immediate income. They prefer to receive regular (and large) dividend checks rather than have profits stay in the business.

Conflict often exists among shareholders concerning the "dividend versus retained earnings" policy. Managers and shareholders may conflict on this point, too, unless managers are also shareholders. The availability of large amounts of capital is usually more attractive to managers than it is to shareholders. Retained earnings (a form of equity financing) have no maturity date and do not dilute managerial control as common stock does. Like common stock, retained earnings place no prior claim on income or assets. Financial managers are attracted to retained earnings as a source because they are not subject to the evaluation of the marketplace in their use of such funds.

Another outside source that has been available for long-term funds is insurance companies. Such companies have huge reserves to invest. They make these funds available, especially to large corporations, for long-term expansion at rates similar to or somewhat lower than those paid to bondholders.

Sources for Noncorporate Firms

Sole proprietorships depend on the personal funding of the owner-manager for equity financing. Partnerships have the same limitation except that there are two or more partners who may contribute fixed capital.

All forms of ownership may generate new funds internally if the firm succeeds. The amount available depends, in part, on the amount of retained earnings. In addition, the amount charged for depreciation of assets is "available" for current or long-term financing because, although depreciation reduces net profit, this value has not actually left the firm in the short run. Depreciation is not the same as a current expenditure.

Equity capital is available for an indefinite period of time and has a subordinate (after creditors) claim on the firm's earnings and assets. It can lead to dilution of the present owners' control if a new partner is added. The new partner may disagree with present partners in policy decisions.

The Alternative of Leasing

lease

One way to avoid the need for long- or intermediate-term financing for land, buildings, or equipment is to lease them. **A lease is an agreement to grant use of an asset for a period of time in return for stated regular payments.** Leasing such assets often has several advantages over borrowing funds for their purchase:

- It reduces the outstanding debt of the firm.
- Leased equipment may be replaced with more modern equipment without the losses that result from replacement of owned equipment.
- It is often a tax advantage to lease because the entire lease payment is tax deductible.
- A lease is usually a known, predictable cost factor, and, in a sense, is an aid in financial planning.

Many leasing arrangements provide the flexibility of a purchase option should changing circumstances favor purchase at a later date.

The decision to lease, however, is not always obvious. There are advantages to outright ownership. Often the cash payments on a lease are considerably higher than the equivalent financed purchase payments. Also there are often restrictions on the way a firm might use or modify leased assets. Such restrictions don't apply to owned equipment. Improved tax credits and depreciation systems in the income tax law have made purchase of capital equipment considerably more attractive in recent years, too.

A bank or a manufacturer often leases computer equipment instead of buying it. Such leasing can be viewed as a "source of long-term funds" rather than as an alternative to borrowing. In other words, what might have required a large part of a firm's long-term borrowing capacity is not needed, and other long-term projects can be considered.

A huge amount of leasing by major corporations occurred in 1981 upon passage of the Economic Recovery Tax Act of 1981. This kind of leasing is discussed in the Case Study at the end of this section.

INTERMEDIATE-TERM FINANCING

Between the short-term borrowing period (one year or less) and the long-term period (usually ten years or more) there is intermediate-term financing. To fill this kind of need firms have begun to turn to a variety of sources. One of the more traditional sources has been the term loan from a commercial bank or an insurance company, usually accompanied by a promissory note and secured by collateral to protect lenders in case of default.

intermediate-term financing

Some firms have issued equipment trust certificates of five to ten year maturity. These are like short term bonds backed by the equipment purchased with revenues from their sale. Such intermediate-term obligations have become a popular means of avoiding long-term bond issues at high fixed interest rates.

equipment trust certificates

Other firms have avoided long-term commitments at high interest rates by turning to the short-term market. They are borrowing by means of short-term commercial paper and "rolling over." **Rolling over means successive renewals of short-term notes as a substitute for longer-term financial commitments.** This kind of "invasion" of the short-term money market by the long-term market stems from unwillingness to obligate firms to high fixed interest payments. Some financial experts feel that this could bring serious troubles for the entire short-term money market. This added demand would drive up short-term interest rates.

rolling over

EXTRAORDINARY FINANCING ARRANGEMENTS

Financial managers are often called upon to assist in handling extraordinary financing arrangements. Consider, for example, the big job the finance people at U.S. Steel faced when the firm's top management decided it wanted to buy Marathon Oil Company. Carrying out the financing of such a venture goes beyond the ordinary conduct of the firm's operations. Such needs are extraordinary and call for very carefully planned and executed financing arrangements. We will look at five kinds of extraordinary financing arrangements:

- mergers
- acquisitions
- asset redeployment
- recapitalization
- reorganization

Mergers

Some firms seek growth by combining with other firms. The firms may or may not be in the same line of business. This combination can take the form of a merger or an acquisition.

Mergers are not a new device for growth, however. The Clayton Act of 1914 was passed in part to deal with the antitrust problem that some mergers raise. **In a merger, two firms join together, or combine, to create a new firm. The new firm is usually created under friendly terms and the stockholders of each merger partner usually get newly issued stock of the new firm.** Recent examples of mergers include Dart Industries, Inc. and Kraft, Inc. merging to become Dart & Kraft, Inc. and Nabisco, Inc. and Standard Brands, Inc. merging to become Nabisco Brands, Inc.

merger

Acquisitions

acquisition

An acquisition is the purchase by one firm of a controlling interest in another. To accomplish this, one firm bids for part or all of another firm's stock. The bid may involve a cash offer for 100 percent of the target firm's stock. Or it may involve a combination of a cash offer for part of the target firm's stock followed by an offer to exchange stock in the acquiring firm for the balance of the shares it wants. If an attempt at acquisition succeeds, the acquiring firm owns all or part of the acquired firm.

AUTHORS' COMMENTARY

The history of federal antitrust policy shows wide swings of attitude toward the accumulation of monopoly power by large firms and groups of large firms. This is so despite the Sherman Act of 1890 and the Clayton Act of 1914, both prohibiting contracts or conspiracies in restraint of trade. In the early days enforcement was lax. During Theodore Roosevelt's administration and several times since then, there have been waves of enforcement and strengthening of the basic antitrust laws. Most recently, the Reagan administration's appointments to the higher federal courts, including the Supreme Court, have indicated a more lenient policy toward mergers and other means of concentrating economic power.

The Justice Department has softened its guidelines for merger review as originally written in 1968 by an earlier Democratic appointee, Ramsey Clark. Among those changes are a more permissive definition of allowable power concentration in an industry. This swing is a clear reversal of Carter administration policies. This swing toward leniency in interpretation of antitrust laws is likely to continue. How far this swing will go will probably depend on general economic conditions. Historically the American people have clamped down on mergers and other concentrations of economic power whenever serious and sustained recession occurred.

In a hostile takeover attempt, the target firm's board of directors opposes the acquisition. In such a case, the firm that wants to acquire the target firm can bypass the target firm's board and try to convince individual stockholders to sell their shares to the would-be

acquiring firm. The target firm's board may respond, for example, by trying to convince stockholders not to sell their shares.

There are many recent examples of hostile takeover attempts: Conoco's board opposed Seagram's attempt to acquire it; Grumman Corporation's board opposed LTV Corporation's attempt to acquire it; and Marathon Oil Company's board opposed Mobil Oil Company's attempt to acquire it. When a target firm is the object of a hostile takeover attempt, another firm may try to enter the picture and acquire the same target firm. If that firm is more acceptable to the target firm's board of directors, it is called a "white knight." In many cases, the rivalry that results leads to a bidding war between the would-be acquiring firms. In other cases, the board of the target firm may try to start a long and costly court fight to stop the acquisition, or the government may step in to prevent it because of possible antitrust violations.

Asset Redeployment

Conglomerate mergers and acquisitions were extremely popular during the 1960s. A conglomerate is the result of a firm merging with, but more commonly, acquiring part or all the stock of different firms in very different lines of business. For example, during the 1960s W.R. Grace & Co. was a huge conglomerate. Its widely diversified operations included dressmaking, homebuilding, seafood processing, and much more.

asset redeployment

Recently, however, many conglomerates have been selling off some of the firms (divisions) they had previously acquired. **The action of selling company divisions is referred to as asset redeployment.** It is also called asset divestment, de-diversification, or deconglomeration. Whatever the process is called, the reasons for it include high interest rates, inflation, and economic slowdowns. Another reason is the desire by top managers to focus more specifically on those existing divisions that offer high profit potential and, perhaps, to acquire other firms that offer more profit potential than some of their existing divisions. Return on investment is the bottom line. They are no longer content with a rate of return percentage that, in fact, may be below the prime rate of interest. Financial managers, of course, play a key role in identifying which divisions or operations should be sold and in identifying potential candidates for acquisitions.

Bankruptcy is closely regulated by federal legislation

Recapitalization, Bankruptcy, and Reorganization

Recapitalization, bankruptcy, and reorganization are other extraordinary financial circumstances that require drastic financial action on the part of a firm and, in some cases, on the part of the courts.

Recapitalization occurs when a firm changes its capital structure to meet changing conditions. It does not raise more capital. It may involve replacing a high-yield preferred stock with a lower-yield preferred stock or floating a new bond issue to replace a maturing one. Sometimes a stock split is used to attract investors. Recapitalization often requires that the corporation amend its charter or receive permission of the Securities and Exchange Commission.

recapitalization

One well-known example of recapitalization occurred when Chrysler Corporation was in deep financial trouble in 1980. It tried a variety of solutions including loan guarantees from the federal government. As part of its effort to recapitalize, Chrysler also asked its lenders, mostly banks, to convert nearly $600 million in loans to preferred stock in Chrysler. At the time, that accounted for almost half of Chrysler's outstanding debt.

Firms go into debt (both long- and short-term) with the hope that they will be able to pay the interest and principal out of earnings. If this doesn't work out over the period of indebtedness, the firm is in trouble. **A firm that cannot meet its maturing financial obligations is insolvent. If, in addition, its liabilities are greater than its assets, the firm is bankrupt. Such a firm is said to be in bankruptcy.**

bankruptcy

Under voluntary bankruptcy, a person or firm files a petition in federal court claiming inability to pay debts because the debts exceed available assets. Once a firm files for bankruptcy under Chapter 11 of the Federal Bankruptcy Act, it has court protection from creditors while the firm tries to develop a reorganization plan to pay its debts.

Reorganization is an involuntary process. It occurs when a firm is in very serious financial trouble and the court steps in to protect creditors.

reorganization

Under involuntary bankruptcy, a person's or firm's creditors seek to have a debtor declared bankrupt by proving that the debtor committed one or more acts of bankruptcy as defined in the law. Once a defendant is declared bankrupt by the court, the procedure is the same as it is in voluntary bankruptcy.

SUMMARY AND LOOK AHEAD

The public securities market is made up of the millions of people who invest in corporate securities and the "middlemen" who bring them together for buying and selling. A corporation that issues new stock may use the services of an investment bank to help sell the securities. Brokerage houses buy and sell previously issued securities for their clients. Stock and bond prices and volume of sales are reported for every business day in *The Wall Street Journal* and other newspapers. Speculators and investors both depend on these reports.

A speculator looks mainly for short-term profits from buying and selling securities—in some cases by selling something he or she does not own (short selling). An investor takes a longer view. Speculating is very popular during bull markets and much less popular in bear markets.

Just as banks are regulated, so are the securities exchanges, brokerage houses, and stockbrokers. The Securities and Exchange Commission (SEC) has broad regulatory power, but it does not assure any investor of making a profit from trading in securities.

From the firm's point of view, long-term financing decisions are as crucial to success as production and marketing decisions. Long-term capital represents investment in fixed assets. It requires a commitment of funds for ten years or more. Capital budgets help the financial manager plan for capital needs, and the securities market provides the major source of such funds. Increasing use is being made of intermediate (one to ten year) financing. Leasing, as an alternative to intermediate- or long-term borrowing, is becoming increasingly common, especially for equipment needs.

Extraordinary financing situations include mergers, acquisitions, asset redeployment, recapitalization, bankruptcy, and reorganization. These occur in response to tax law changes, inflation, rising interest rates, and a variety of management shortcomings.

In the next chapter we focus on special problems and opportunities of the small business and on the government agencies and programs designed to assist them.

FOR REVIEW . . .

1. List and define three different concepts of "value" for common stock.

2. What is the purpose of (a) a stock split; (b) a stock dividend; and (c) a cash dividend?

3. What is a brokerage house?

4. What is the purpose of a stock exchange?

5. How do listed securities differ from unlisted securities?

6. What is a stockbroker?

7. Is speculation more likely to exist during a bear market or a bull market? Explain.

8. What is a mutual fund? Explain how it works.

9. Does the Securities and Exchange Commission guarantee the value of a corporation's stocks and bonds to investors? Explain.

10. Give several examples of uses of long-term financing.

11. Contrast the use of bonds and stocks for acquiring long-term funds. Refer to the preceding chapter if necessary.

12. Name two sources of intermediate-term financing.

13. What change in the tax law caused a flurry of leasing in 1981?

. . . FOR DISCUSSION

1. Why might a bond's market value (selling price) be above its face value (redemption price)?

2. Why do speculators engage in margin trading and short selling?

3. What factors might discourage firms from issuing long-term bonds?

4. What conditions might lead to voluntary bankruptcy?

INCIDENTS

Fighting a Takeover Attempt

If a corporation intends to buy up some of its own stock on the open market, it must notify the Securities and Exchange Commission (SEC). If the proposed purchase is made with the intention of opposing a takeover attempt, the firm must also disclose that to the SEC.

In 1981, LTV Corporation, a conglomerate, attempted to acquire Grumman Corporation. Because both firms had operations in the aerospace business, a federal appeals court barred LTV from acquiring more shares of Grumman's stock. LTV decided, therefore, to drop its takeover attempt.

Grumman had opposed the takeover bid from the start and tried to fight it. It notified the SEC that it planned to buy up some of its own stock but did not disclose that the purpose was to fight the takeover bid. Thus the SEC filed suit against Grumman.

QUESTIONS

1. Why do you think the SEC wants to be informed of a corporation's plans to fight a takeover attempt?

2. What factors should a firm that is the object of a takeover attempt consider in deciding whether or not to oppose it?

3. What role do you think a firm's financial manager plays in making decisions about potential candidates for a takeover?

A Boom in Mobile Home Financing

Manufactured housing, formerly known as the mobile home business, is expected to take a dramatic upward turn. This is because of changes in the status of the industry's product for financing purposes. Interest rate ceilings have been lifted; the Federal Home Loan Bank Board now permits lenders to treat such manufactured homes as real property when fixed permanently to a lot; and the Federal National Mortgage Association (FNMA), chief federal supporter of the mortgage market, now buys mortgages on such homes.

Most manufacturers of such homes view these developments as landmarks for the industry. The general level of interest rates could, of course, still slow the expected growth.

QUESTIONS

1. How should S&LAs react to these developments?

2. Which of the institutions described in this chapter might also be affected? Discuss.

CASE STUDY

When it comes to the leasing business, most people automatically think of companies like Hertz, Avis or Ryder System. In fact, much of the $30 billion-a-year leasing industry involves the back-and-forth renting between companies of everything from printing presses to jet planes. Certain provisions in the [1981] Reagan tax package now promise to shake up, and open up, the entire business.

Treasury officials say the changes are needed to boost business investment; critics complain that the provisions amount to little more than a multibillion-dollar federal giveaway.

Supporters of the measure contend that the changes will actually stimulate investment in new plant and equipment by companies that otherwise might not be able to take advantage of the new act's liberalized depreciation and investment tax credit provisions. For example, the investment tax credit lets a company reduce its yearly income taxes by either 6% or 10% of that year's capital investment. Unfortunately, such provisions are helpful only to those companies that are already profitable and actually paying taxes. Since low-profit and no-profit firms cannot make use of the benefits, they can find themselves at a disadvantage among healthy firms, which can.

To create what one Treasury official describes as a "level playing field" for business, the new provisions now let struggling companies sell their tax credits and depreciation opportunities to more profitable firms.

Take the hypothetical case of cash-starved Meager Motors, which is anxious to improve productivity at its auto assembly plant by buying $10 million worth of industrial robots. For help, M.M. turns to lucrative Moneytronics Corp. Once Meager Motors buys its robots, the high-tech firm agrees to step in and take them off the automaker's hands for a $2 million down payment, with the remaining $8 million to be paid out over five years.

Immediately upon buying the robots, Moneytronics turns around and leases them back to Meager Motors under a five-year deal in which the rental payments from the automaker exactly match, and cancel out, the loan payments by the high-tech firm. At the end of the lease, Meager Motors buys back the machines for $1. Result: Moneytronics not only receives a $1 million investment tax credit that offsets 50% of its down payment on the equipment, but the firm also gets to claim depreciation tax benefits. Thus it can effectively postpone paying taxes as well as enjoy interest-free use of substantial amounts of money over part of the lease. That makes the deal worthwhile. Meanwhile, M.M. benefits by getting $2 million in cash from Moneytronics, which amounts in effect to a 20% discount on the price of the equipment.

The losers are the nation's taxpayers. By fiscal 1986 the cumulative federal largesse could swell to $29 billion, making it one of the biggest business subsidies in the tax bill.

A growing list of companies in ailing industries like steel and autos have been hungrily eyeing the new regulations. But companies with poor credit ratings may not find the leasing razzmatazz so easy to arrange. Wary that the regulations could wind up leading to a wholesale corporate raid on the Treasury, officials in the department issued in October, 1981 temporary rules that could sharply restrict, if not actually prevent, a number of firms with low credit ratings from taking advantage of the leasing opportunities. That could prove bad news for companies like Chrysler, Ford and International Harvester, which have all been looking forward to raising cash by selling off investment tax credits. More financially sound companies should experience no such problems.

Questions

1. What is the investment tax credit described in this case designed to stimulate a firm to do?

2. Why is the investment tax credit helpful only to firms that make profits and pay taxes?

3. What does Maeger Motors gain from the leasing plan?

4. What does Moneytronics gain from the leasing plan?

5. In general, what are the relative advantages and disadvantages of leasing versus purchasing to the lessee and the lessor?

CAREERS IN FINANCE

Opportunities in finance include careers in banking, insurance, credit, corporate finance, and securities. Although these jobs all concern money and property value they have a personal, human dimension, too. They require a variety of skills and interests. On the whole, opportunities are quite good in finance, especially in bank and financial management and in claims adjustment and examination.

Jobs for college graduates include *trainee positions* which can lead to upper management responsibilities. There are over 400,000 bank officers and managers in the nation as a whole. Openings are growing rapidly, too. People in these jobs make decisions which require a broad business knowledge. This includes deciding whether loans will be granted to applicants and what kinds of investments will be made for trust department clients.

Operations officers of banks perform management tasks similar to those done by most business managers (see Section 2 careers discussion), namely, planning, coordination, and control of work. They must also develop the public acceptance and the efficiency of the bank. Working conditions for bank employees and managers alike are quite comfortable; hours are regular and clothing is somewhat formal.

Bank management trainees work in several departments before settling down into a specialty. Today, they are usually expected to have a four-year college degree. Some banks prefer MBAs. Starting salaries are about average for the amount of education expected, but the pay for senior officers is several times the starting pay.

Insurance-related opportunities include those in sales, claims, underwriting, and actuarial work. *Insurance salesworkers* are known as *agents* or *brokers.* They sell policies to businesses and to individuals. The agent works for an insurance company and the broker is an independent business person who may represent one or more insurance firms in a selling capacity. There were more than 325,000 agents and brokers in the United States in 1980. About half of these sold life insurance and half, property and liability insurance. Many of these jobs are part-time. Insurance selling requires flexibility in work hours and often a fair amount of travel to meet clients. College degrees are often preferred, but are not usually required. After a salesperson is hired, further training is encouraged. The Life Underwriters Training Council awards a diploma in life insurance marketing after a two-year training program. The outlook for employment growth is about average for all occupations, and earnings are dependent on sales success. Highly successful insurance salespeople may earn over $100,000 per year.

Insurance underwriters appraise and select the risks that their company will insure while *actuaries* analyze the probability of occurrence of various losses. Both work under normal, pleasant office conditions with regular hours. Both usually need a college degree. Underwriters are usually business or liberal arts graduates and actuaries, math or science graduates. There are about 76,000 underwriters and 8,000 actuaries working in this country and job growth is faster than average for all jobs. In 1980, the range of salaries for underwriters with varying degrees of experience and responsibility was from $14,000 (trainees) to $23,000 (supervisors). For actuaries, starting salaries are somewhat lower but top salaries are significantly higher.

Credit managers work for manufacturing, wholesale, and retail firms to supervise their credit activities. They make decisions about the granting of credit and base these decisions on financial evidence about the credit applicant. They must analyze financial information, including the financial statements in the case of credit to businesses. In larger firms they must supervise and train others in the performance of credit screening activities. They work in offices during regular working hours.

An important area of employment in the field of finance is in the securities market. About 63,000 people were employed in the sale of securities in 1980. The number of securities salespeople is expected to grow faster than the average for all occupations through the 1980s. Replacing people who retire or leave the field will also require recruiting thousands of workers each year. To enter this field, it is increasingly likely that a college degree will be required. Securities representatives must also pass qualifying exams given by the industry and their employers will provide training—usually four months—to qualify them for the exam.

Securities salesworkers are generally found in the office where they have immediate access to price quotations and other information related to the securities they sell. When the Department of Labor measured incomes in 1980, it was found that such occupations averaged $40,000 for sales to individuals and $88,000 for sales to institutions. The income is largely dependent on sales volume.

Opportunities for women in finance have been improving in recent years. In 1950, only 45 percent of bank tellers were women. By 1979, this had risen to almost 93 percent. More importantly, the number of women who are bank officials and financial managers is rising, from 13,000 in 1950 to 196,000 in 1979. The percentage has risen from 11.7 to 31.6.[1] In insurance sales, women hold only about 10 percent of the jobs and in actuarial work, only about 3 percent.[2] In insurance managerial positions, women represent more than 15 percent of the workforce. Opportunities for women in finance are improving, but there is room for many more in this growing field.

CAREER PROFILE

EF Hutton

My name is Geoff Rose. In May of 1979, I graduated from college with a Bachelor of Science degree in Management.

I began my job search by conducting a number of interviews with the help of the career placement staff at my university. Most of my interviews were with securities brokerage firms. After comparing opportunities carefully, I chose to go with E.F. Hutton. My reasons for selecting E.F. Hutton centered on the autonomous system of broker development which they offer. This system rewards brokers in proportion to their effort and motivation. I feel that I have fit well into such a system and that I am progressing well along my career path.

A good description of my function as a broker is to say that I help my clients by: 1) preserving their principal; 2) increasing their income; and 3) deferring their taxes when possible. In order to accomplish these goals I must be on top of the constantly changing economic environment. A successful broker must always be prepared to take advantage of special situations as they may arise. I must also continue my education in new products and find new applications for our established clients. I am also constantly developing my skills in serving and communicating with clients.

A good broker learns every day from co-workers—especially those brokers who have had years of experience in the field. I have gained familiarity with a wide range of investment alternatives and have, in the process, learned a lot about what factors influence stock performance. This kind of experience makes me and the thousands of securities brokers like me sensitive to news events—especially those that influence the quality of the investments for which we are responsible. This requires that I keep up with the business news every day and with the stream of reports made available to me by E.F. Hutton's research staff. Such reports supplement research that I must do on my own for my clients.

My long-range career goal is to become an increasingly valuable asset to my clients and to the financial community in general.

SECTION 7

Perspectives on the Scope of Business

You can lose your perspective by thinking of business firms only as large corporations. Firms come in all sizes and dimensions. For many firms there is a need to "think small" and for others a need to "think international."

We will adjust our sight in Chapter 17 to take a look at businesses that are quite small and that have many problems peculiar to small business.

We will also see that many opportunities exist for small business.

In Chapter 18 we will look at businesses that have an international perspective. There we examine the special challenges and opportunities involved in conducting business across national borders.

Small Business

OBJECTIVES:

After reading this chapter, you should be able to

1. Explain, in your own words, the meaning of a "small business firm" and discuss the economic importance of small business in our economic system.
2. List and discuss three ways by which a person might become a small business owner.
3. Discuss the nature of opportunity for small businesses.
4. Compare the benefits and burdens of entrepreneurship and assess your potential as a small business owner.
5. List and discuss the first steps in starting your own business.
6. List and discuss the benefits of franchising to the two parties to a franchising agreement.
7. Identify and describe the major types of programs sponsored by the Small Business Administration to aid small business.
8. Discuss minority-owned and women-owned small businesses.

KEY CONCEPTS:
Look for these terms as you read the chapter

small business

venture capitalists

Better Business Bureau (BBB)

economic development
council

franchiser

franchisee

franchising agreement

Small Business Administration (SBA)

SBA direct loans

SBA participating loans

SBA guaranteed loans

Small Business Investment Company
(SBIC)

Service Corps of Retired Executives
(SCORE)

Active Corps of Executives (ACE)

Small Business Institute (SBI)

Nolan Bushnell founded Atari in 1972 with an initial investment of $500 and sold the business four years later to Warner Communications for $15 million. John Z. De Lorean quit his executive job at General Motors in 1973 and founded De Lorean Motor Company, which manufactured cars in Ireland and exported them to the United States. Although the company declared bankruptcy in 1982, De Lorean was the first American to start a mass-production auto manufacturing company since Walter Chrysler started his business in the early 1920s.

Each year thousands of new businesses are started by people who want to go into business for themselves. Only a relatively small percentage of them turn out to be successful and profitable, however. Despite this fact, the challenge and potential rewards of starting one's own business attract many Americans.

Perhaps you have considered going into business for yourself, or have already done so. Most people who go into business for themselves start out in small businesses. Although our discussions on production, marketing, finance, personnel, and accounting in earlier chapters apply to all firms regardless of size, there are several aspects of small business that merit separate treatment.

In this chapter we discuss how and why a person might start a small business. Then we look at the pros and cons of going into business for yourself. After that, we take a close look at franchising. Franchising is a way of doing business that has enabled many people to go into business for themselves.

The Small Business Administration plays an important role in helping entrepreneurs to start and to keep their firms going. We will examine the nature of this assistance.

In the end, however, a small business owner's success (or lack of it) is the result of good (or poor) management. As you will see, it's still possible to make "big money" by going into business for yourself. On the other hand, it's just as possible to lose everything you have invested.

WHAT IS A SMALL BUSINESS?

Roughly 95 percent of American businesses are small businesses. They account for about 40 percent of our gross national product and employ about 58 percent of our labor force. Roughly eight out of every ten new jobs are provided by small business. But what is a small business?

small business

For business loan purposes, the Small Business Administration (SBA) defines a small business as one that is independently owned and operated for profit (except sheltered workshops), not dominant in its field, and that meets certain standards of size in terms of employees or annual receipts. The general size standards are as follows:

- *Manufacturing.* Maximum number of employees may range from 250 to 1,500, depending on the industry in which the applicant is primarily engaged.

- *Wholesaling.* Yearly sales must not be over $9.5 to $22 million, depending on the industry.

- *Services.* Annual receipts not exceeding $2 million to $8 million, depending on the industry in which the applicant is primarily engaged.

- *Retailing.* Annual sales or receipts not exceeding $2 to $7.5 million, depending on the industry.
- *Construction.* General construction: average annual receipts not exceeding $9.5 million for the three most recently completed fiscal years.
- *Special trade construction.* Average annual receipts not exceeding $1 or $2 million for three most recently completed fiscal years, depending on the industry.
- *Agriculture.* Annual receipts not exceeding $1 million.

A new standard definition of a small business is under consideration by the SBA. If the proposal is formally adopted, the definition of a small business will be based on a single measurement of size—total number of employees per firm. SBA field offices can advise firms which standard applies to them.

In addition to being small in size, a small business is usually localized in its operations. Its owner(s), employees, and customers often live in the same town in which the firm is located, although this is not always the case. As you can see by the ad on the following page, the Collin Street Bakery advertises in *The Wall Street Journal* and ships cakes to customers all over the world.

A small business is most likely to be a sole proprietorship, a partnership, or a family-owned corporation. Ownership and management are seldom separated; the owners usually run the business directly.

Becoming a Small Business Owner

A person becomes a small business owner in one of three ways:

- by taking over the family's business
- by buying out an existing firm
- by starting a new firm

Each way has its own set of problems and opportunities.

Every year many firms are taken over by relatives of the former owners who have either died, or who are no longer able to run the business, or who no longer desire to run the firm. This takeover is often not planned in advance and makes it very hard for the relative who is taking over, especially when the former owner is not there to help the new owner.

Many people go into business by buying out an existing firm. In many cases an agreement can be reached whereby the seller helps the new owner to learn the business from the ground up. It is good

practice to have a written contract outlining the duties of the former owner after the new owner takes over.

Sometimes, buying out an existing firm means buying it from a surviving spouse. This presents a different problem, because the owner is not there to help the new owner to get oriented to the firm. In many of these cases the surviving spouse has neither the desire nor the ability to continue the firm. This fact points out the need for a plan to continue the firm after the owner's death. However, many small business owners never prepare such a plan.

Starting a new firm has some advantages over buying an existing firm, but it also has some disadvantages. The new entrepreneur has the opportunity to build the firm from the ground up: there are no dissatisfied customers, no fixed plant or store location, and no bad debts. On the other hand, there is no established customer base to begin with.

Opportunities in Small Business

There are countless opportunities for small firms to serve ultimate consumers and industrial users. The big question is: "How does a would-be entrepreneur learn how to spot opportunity?" It is partly a matter of being sensitive to the environment. The highly

1. When a product does not lend itself to large-scale mass production, such as custom-tailored clothing and custom-made kitchen cabinets.
2. When customer convenience is more important than price and selection, such as in the case of small convenience food stores that offer late-night shopping and fast checkout to hurried shoppers.
3. When demand and/or supply fluctuates with seasons of the year, such as fresh produce that is harvested locally and sold at roadside markets by truck farmers.
4. When potential sales in a market are not large enough to attract a large firm, such as small communities that have many small retail shops rather than a major department store.
5. When large firms compete with each other for the big market segment and ignore one or more smaller segments, such as commuter airlines, which escape competition from major airlines.
6. When the product or service being offered requires a lot of personal attention to the customer by the seller, such as hair styling and funeral direction.

TABLE 17-1

Examples of situations that tend to favor small firms

successful Baskin-Robbins 31 Ice Cream Stores had its beginning back in 1945. Mr. Baskin and Mr. Robbins recognized an opportunity to sell hand-packed, quality ice cream in attractive stores. The trend at that time was toward sales of prepackaged ice cream through supermarkets. But they believed that customers would go out of their way to buy delicious ice cream that was sold in attractive specialty stores, even if it meant paying more for it. We could discuss many such success stories. What they teach is that opportunity always exists but hardly ever "knocks at your door." In a competitive economy you can be sure that it never knocks twice!

Some people say that opportunity has all but dried up for small businesses. They argue that only large corporations can afford to hire the talent needed to spot trends and to capitalize on them. But bigger does not necessarily mean better as far as business is concerned. A small firm is usually more adaptable than a large firm. It can often react to change a lot faster. Table 17-1 identifies several situations that tend to favor small firms.

SHOULD YOU GO INTO BUSINESS FOR YOURSELF?

Let's assume for a minute that you want to become your own boss. You have a rich relative who will lend you the money to get started. You also can assume that you have a product or service that will definitely lead to a good profit if you can succeed as a manager. Should you go into business for yourself?

Given these assumptions (and they may be very unrealistic), you still must evaluate a third vital input—you, the entrepreneur. Ask yourself the following questions:

1. Are you afraid of risk?
2. Are you unable to put off enjoying the "good life" today because you are afraid you won't be here tomorrow?
3. Are you overly security-conscious?
4. Do you have trouble getting along with people?
5. Do you lose interest in things that don't work out as quickly or as well as you think they should?
6. Are you a thinker and not a "doer"?
7. Are you a "doer" and not a thinker?
8. Are you easily frustrated?
9. Do you have trouble coping in situations that require quick judgments?

10. Do you "cave in" under stress?

11. Does your family make unreasonable demands on your time?

12. Are you emotionally unstable?

13. Are you unable to learn from your mistakes?

14. Are you "too good" to do manual labor?

If you answered "yes" to several of these questions, you probably are not ready to start your own business. If you do measure up, then you can begin to weigh the benefits and the burdens of starting your own firm.

The Benefits of Entrepreneurship

Perhaps the best thing about being your own boss is the sense of independence you feel. You get a great deal of personal satisfaction from being directly involved in guiding your firm's growth. It is also possible to make a sizable personal fortune. You not only draw a salary but you also own the firm, the value of which may increase manyfold over the years.

Owning your business also is good for your ego. The entrepreneur fulfills the "American dream." For many people, achieving their true potential means the same thing as becoming their own boss. Clearly, it gives you personal, economic, and social benefits.

Bouquets of balloons—what an opportunity! Started in 1979, Balloons over Boston averages 175 orders per week and has been imitated throughout the country

The Burdens of Entrepreneurship

Being in business for yourself, however, requires your full attention. You usually will not leave the office or shop at 5 P.M. Nor do you leave job problems at the office or shop. They follow you home as business homework. This means you have less time for your personal life.

A person with very limited abilities may be able to hold a job in a large company by doing just enough to get by. Maybe others will cover up for his or her shortcomings. There is, however, no one to "carry you" when you are in business for yourself. Incompetence is the major cause of business failures. (See Table 17-2.) Each year thousands of new and old firms go out of business because they cannot compete. (See Figure 17-1.) Most of these failures are small businesses.

TABLE 17-2

Causes of 7,564 business failures[1]

Underlying causes	% Manu- facturers	% Whole- salers	% Retailers	% Con- struction	% Commer- cial	% All
Neglect	0.3	1.6	1.4	0.9	1.1	1.1
Fraud	0.7	1.5	0.5	0.4	0.4	0.6
Lack of experience in the line	13.2	11.8	19.5	9.3	12.3	14.9
Lack of managerial experience	14.0	14.8	17.1	21.4	14.9	16.8
Unbalanced experience[2]	16.9	17.8	16.0	13.8	14.5	15.8
Incompetence	49.1	48.5	39.3	49.1	44.6	44.4
Disaster	0.9	0.4	0.9	0.1	0.1	0.6
Reason unknown	4.9	3.6	5.3	5.0	12.1	5.8
Total %	100.0	100.0	100.0	100.0	100.0	100.0
Number of failures	1,165	908	3,183	1.378	930	7,564
Average liabilities per failure	$832,771	$463,935	$200,081	$211,410	$373,924	$352,639

[1]Classification of failures based on opinion of informed creditors and information in Dun & Bradstreet reports.

[2]Experience not well rounded in sales, finance, purchasing, and production on the part of the individual in case of a proprietorship, or of two or more partners or officers constituting a management unit.

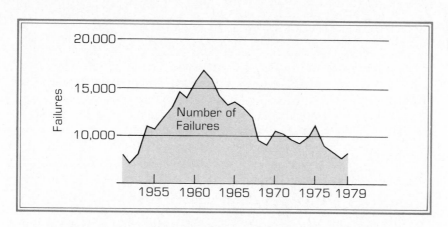

FIGURE 17-1

Business failures

While you may not have to report to a boss, you often have to bend over backwards for your customers. You have to contend with creditors, employees, suppliers, government, and others. In short, you are never completely independent.

As your own boss you might work for many months and not be able to take a penny out of the business. Your profits may have to be reinvested to meet short-term demands for cash or for long-term growth. Thus you may not be able to draw a salary during the period it takes to get the firm to become a truly going concern.

STARTING A SMALL BUSINESS— THE PRELIMINARIES

It's a sad fact that many people who want to start their own firms do not do so because they just don't know how to do it. Some people think that there is so much red tape involved that you need a team of lawyers to start a firm. At the other extreme, some people open shop without even checking to see if they need permits or licenses. Both views are wrong.

Starting a business always requires careful planning. In the following discussion, we will outline some of the steps in getting started.

Financing

Perhaps the most important step in starting a new business is estimating the amount of money needed to get started. Underestimating can result in failure to get the business off the ground. Start off with a ballpark estimate and refine it as you learn more about the business you are considering.

Projecting Your Financing Needs

A good starting place in estimating the amount of money needed is to draw up an overall business plan, setting your overall objectives and plans for accomplishing them. Focus on formulating specific plans for production, marketing, and personnel. For example, you should state the quantity and type of equipment you will need to manufacture your product, how the product will be sold, and how many employees you will need to get started.

The business plan is the basis for setting up a capital budget, which we discussed in Chapter 16. This will give you a good idea of how much money you will need to acquire buildings, equipment, and other fixed assets.

You should also prepare a month-by-month projected income statement in which you forecast your sales revenues and operating expenses during the start-up phase of your business. A review of Chapter 12 will help in preparing these projected income statements.

Next, you should focus on the need for cash in your month-by-month projected cash flow statements. This may help you to spot potential cash flow problems.

As we saw in Chapter 15, money will flow into and out of your business as you carry on your business activities. Cash inflow comes mainly from selling your product or service. Cash outflows are necessary to pay for supplies, salaries, telephone, etc. Some of these expenses are start-up expenses that have to be paid only once. For example, you do not have to pay a deposit to the telephone and electric company every month. Other expenses, such as wages and supplies, are recurring sources of cash outflows.

The main element in estimating cash inflows and cash outflows is timing. You must meet your bills as they come due. It's a good idea to seek help from an experienced accountant. He or she can help you learn to use leverage (see Chapter 15) to maximum advantage. Your accountant can show you that buying the equipment you need on time allows you to pay off the purchase price with cash inflow from your operations. Skillful use of trade credit also can help. If you are in a retail business, you may be able to buy merchandise from a wholesaler on credit and pay off the wholesaler with money you receive from sales of that merchandise to your customers. Your accountant will also point out the pros and cons of leasing equipment rather than buying it.

As a final planning tool, you should prepare a projected balance sheet to determine the projected net worth of your business at, for example, the end of the first year of operations. As we saw in Chapter 12, this will tell you what your firm owns and what it owes.

These projections of your financing needs will result in a ball-park estimate of the amount of money you will need to get started and survive the critical early years in business. It will also stimulate some serious thinking about the form of ownership.

Planning the Form of Ownership

We discussed forms of ownership in Chapter 3. Given the projected amount of money you will need to get started, can you realistically expect to be a sole proprietor or should you consider taking in a partner or partners? If you decide on a partnership, for example, you should set the minimum percentage of ownership in the firm that you are willing to settle for. What about incorporating? Is the Subchapter S form suitable?

In most cases it is not wise to put all your personal assets into the business. Financial reserves, such as a personal savings account, are needed to help you get your firm off to a good start. Don't count on quick profits to help finance operations in the beginning. The firm may be in operation for one or more years before it shows a profit. And even then you may be taking out little or no salary from the business. Beginning entrepreneurs tend to *over*estimate sales revenues and *under*estimate costs.

Planning for Debt versus Equity Capital

If you need more money to start up than you have available and what you can borrow, you will probably decide to form a partnership or a corporation. In other words, you will seek equity capital. We discussed the relative advantages and disadvantages of equity versus debt financing in Chapter 15.

Venture capitalists have become an important source of equity capital for many new firms. **Venture capitalists are individuals or businesses that are willing to provide equity capital to entrepreneurs who have new products or new product ideas that are as yet unproven on the market but that have a good chance of becoming successful.** Some venture capitalists will help to finance the start up of a new firm while others are interested only in firms that have been set up and need additional financing for rapid growth. Venture capitalists often acquire a controlling interest in the firms they help to finance.

venture capitalists

Debt financing may be available to you from the various types of financial institutions we discussed in Chapter 14. In general, you will find that commercial banks are more conservative about making loans to new businesses than are some other sources.

If you cannot get a bank loan, you may be able to get a personal loan from a consumer finance company. Or you might turn to the

More Venture Capitalists are Financing Entrepreneurs

AUTHORS' COMMENTARY

A venture capitalist may acquire stock in a firm it helps to finance and also provide management assistance over the years of initial rapid growth. Eventually, the firm may go public and the venture capitalist may sell its stock in the firm at a very attractive price. The recent lowering of the maximum tax rate on capital gains from 49 percent to 28 percent makes participation in such deals more attractive to venture capitalists. The change in the tax law permitting newly organized firms to write off their "startup" costs over a period of sixty months also produces tax advantages that increase the attractiveness of supplying venture capital to new entrepreneurs.

Venture capitalists helped to finance the growth of firms like Apple Computer, Federal Express, and Genentech. In our nation's efforts to increase productivity, to become more competitive in world markets, and to revitalize our economic system, we need people with ideas. We also need people who are willing to take the risk of helping to finance these ideas. Venture capitalists will become an even greater source of financing for new firms in "new industries" that are yet to be developed.

growing number of small-business money brokers who arrange loans for their clients through various types of financial institutions, such as commercial finance companies. Savings and loan associations can also help because they make loans on residential, commercial, and industrial property.

Some debt financing may also be possible through government agencies. The U.S. Department of Commerce's Economic Development Administration loans its own funds or guarantees bank loans to entrepreneurs who are setting up businesses in economically distressed areas—areas of high unemployment or low average household incomes. The U.S. Department of Agriculture's Farmers Home Administration does not loan its own funds but does guarantee bank loans to entrepreneurs who are setting up nonfarming businesses in rural areas. You should not overlook these as potential sources of help. We will discuss Small Business Administration loans later in this chapter.

Licenses and Permits

Before you start operations, you must have the required licenses and permits. Which ones you will need depends on state and local laws.

In many cities or counties you will need a certificate of occupancy from the city or county department of safety and permits. This certifies that your type of business is permitted in your location under local zoning codes.

In some states, cities, and counties you must get an occupational license to engage in any business activity or profession. These licenses are usually available from state and local departments of revenue. The cost depends on anticipated annual gross receipts and the type of business activity.

If your business deals with food, you will need a local food permit. These are usually issued by city or county health departments. If you plan to sell beer, liquor, wines, soft drinks, or tobacco, you will need a state beverage or tobacco permit. Requirements here vary a lot among the states.

Suppose you want to go into business for yourself by selling lamps door to door. You might find yourself in trouble if you don't have a local vendor's permit. The best advice on licenses and permits is to check with the local chamber of commerce, the local sheriff's office, or the state and local departments of revenue.

Food permits—and usually beverage/tobacco permits—are required for restaurants

Taxes

You will have to pay various types of taxes. Three common types are

- sales taxes
- self-employment tax
- employer taxes

Most states collect retail sales taxes. In these states, you must register with the state's department of revenue in order to comply with the law. This permits you to collect the tax for the state.

Many cities levy their own sales taxes. Again, you must register with the city revenue or finance department, tax collector, school board, etc.

If you hire employees, you must withhold federal (and perhaps state and city) income taxes as well as social security taxes from your employees' wages. You must also pay your own share of their social security taxes. You'll pay taxes for unemployment insurance. You'll have to get a federal tax number from the IRS.

Sales taxes collected and taxes withheld from employees' salaries and wages should be kept separate from the firm's other funds. The business owner is personally responsible for these funds and has to turn them over to the proper tax officials at set intervals of time.

Insurance

Selecting an insurance agent is an important step in starting your business. The agent can advise on the types of coverage you'll need in your line of business, but be sure to shop around for the best combination of price and coverage.

If you hire employees, you must carry workers' compensation insurance. This covers employees who are injured or killed on the job. The premium is based on your estimated payroll.

Information Sources

Better Business Bureau (BBB)

In starting your new firm, you will need information on many aspects of your business. **Many cities have a Better Business Bureau (BBB). A BBB is a nonprofit organization of business firms that join together to help protect consumers and businesses from unfair business practices. Businesses "police" themselves through the workings of the BBB.** Suppose you have doubts about buying from a particular supplier. You can call the local BBB to ask if any complaints have been filed against that supplier. If you have trouble with a supplier, you can file a complaint against that firm. It's a good idea to join the BBB.

Figure 17-2 shows the 10-point code of ethics that participants in the Greater New Orleans Better Business Bureau's Consumer Car Care Program follow. Notice in point 10 that subscribers agree to submit customer complaints to arbitration if they cannot be resolved between the customer and the company.

Many cities also have a Chamber of Commerce. A local chamber of commerce is a useful source of data on business conditions in that area. Active involvement in the local chamber can put you in contact with potential customers and suppliers.

economic development council

Some cities have an economic development council. **An economic development council is an organization of business firms and local government officials. It seeks to further the economic development of the area in which it is located.** It is a good source of data on the local economy. In many areas local governments cooperate with local action groups to aid small businesses.

Outside Assistance

Starting your own business takes a lot of planning. Running it also takes a lot of know-how. Unlike most larger firms, however,

SUBSCRIBER

BBB
Consumer
Car
Care
Program

THIS COMPANY HAS FULLY SUBSCRIBED TO THE FOLLOWING CODE DEVELOPED BY THE AUTO REPAIR INDUSTRY IN COOPERATION WITH THE BETTER BUSINESS BUREAU:

1. Perform high quality repair service at a fair and just price.

2. Use only proven parts and merchandise of high quality.

3. Perform only those repairs authorized by the customer. Obtain prior authorization in writing or by telephone for all work done. If by phone, record number, person called, time, and date.

4. Recommend and perform only those services necessary for vehicle safety, performance, comfort and convenience in the customer's best interest.

5. Upon request, furnish customer a price estimate for work to be performed.

6. Furnish an itemized invoice for all parts and services performed. Clearly identify any used or remanufactured parts.

7. Make available all replaced parts for customer inspection upon request.

8. Maintain customer's service records for one year.

9. Perform work required on comebacks on a preferential basis.

10. Maintain a system for fair settlement of customer complaints, which includes business-customer arbitration.

THIS COMPANY HAS A DESIGNATED REPRESENTATIVE _____, TEL: _____, WHO WILL BE GLAD TO ASSIST YOU WITH ANY COMPLAINT CONCERNING OUR SERVICE. IF THE COMPLAINT IS NOT RESOLVED TO YOUR SATISFACTION, CALL THE BETTER BUSINESS BUREAU OF GREATER NEW ORLEANS AREA, AT 581-6222.

FIGURE 17-2

A Better Business Bureau code of ethics for automobile-related businesses

you will not have a staff of experts to help solve tax problems, insurance problems, legal problems, and financial problems.

Remember, you cannot do it all without any outside help. At least you should know an accountant, a banker, an insurance agent, and a lawyer to whom you can turn for advice.

Anthony DiNovella, Owner, A-D Tile & Home Centers

STARTED FROM THE FLOOR UP

"I started my business in the recession of 1957 with $4000.00. Within a one year period I was in debt for $10,000.00.

"Having your own business sounds great to most people who have never had it. It certainly does have its good points, especially for a guy like me who has to go at things thoroughly and with a measure of tenacity. I'm sure I wouldn't be happy working for someone else. However, there are some tough things about it too, like long hours and pressure to keep generating new customers and improving things to keep customers satisfied. Another responsibility is getting reliable employees and keeping them happy at their job.

"But I wouldn't change too many things if I could start over again. My business has grown even though the industry has changed quite a lot. When I started, I would sell a job and then go out and install it myself. In those days most of the business was contract work for builders. Today the construction industry is off so that part of our business is down but on the other hand, people are improving and fixing up their present homes themselves, therefore the retail operation of our stores has taken up the slack.

"Today we sell a lot more than tile or vinyl floor coverings. In our stores you can find bathroom vanities, mirrors, wall coverings and most other home products. And today we have grown to three stores: 2641 W. 59th St., 14128 S. LaGrange Rd. in Orland Park and our newest store which just opened at 8320 S. Pulaski.

"Do I have any advice for the person going into their own business? First, I would tell them to forget about the forty-hour week. The more time you put into your business, the more you are assured of success, and you've got to enjoy what you are doing. And you have to satisfy your customers, a satisfied customer is repeat business and your best means of advertising.

"Marquette National Bank has helped me many times. Sure, they have supplied financing over the years, but if ever I had any other questions they were happy to help me too. When I started 24 years ago, I had some experience in tile and floor coverings but I didn't know much about running a business. It was trial and error. I believe there were fewer errors than things we did right because we have been fairly successful and I feel the help of Marquette National Bank has been a part of that success."

Marquette National Bank
"Good things are happening at Marquette National."
Main office, 63rd at Western; Pulaski office, 62nd at Pulaski; Member FDIC

This entrepreneur recognizes the important role a bank can play in a firm's success

FRANCHISING

During the 1960s franchising became a very popular way of going into business for many people. Familiar examples are Holiday Inn, Pizza Hut, Wendy's, Midas Muffler, and Baskin-Robbins outlets.

There are two parties in franchising. Each has certain duties or obligations and each receives certain benefits. **The franchiser is the firm that licenses other firms to sell its products or services.** The party that is licensed by the franchiser is called the franchisee. **A franchisee has an exclusive right to sell the franchiser's product or service in his or her specified territory. Each franchisee is an independent business owner.**

franchiser

franchisee

Wendy's International, Inc., for example, licenses independent franchisees to make and sell Wendy's hamburgers. Each franchisee pays an initial fee and yearly payments to Wendy's International, Inc., for the right to use the Wendy's trade name and to receive financial and managerial assistance from the franchiser.

The franchiser and the franchisees are related to each other through the franchising agreement. **A franchising agreement is a contract between a franchiser and its franchisees that spells out the rights and obligations of each party.**

franchising agreement

Many fast-food franchisers are owned by parent firms in the food and beverage industries. For example, PepsiCo owns Pizza Hut; Royal Crown Cola Company owns Arby's Inc.; Pillsbury owns Burger King; and Heublein owns Kentucky Fried Chicken.

Franchising and the Franchisee

Among the potential benefits of franchising to franchisees are:

- franchisee recognition
- management training and assistance
- economies in buying
- financial assistance
- promotional assistance

Franchisee Recognition

A franchiser enjoys widespread consumer recognition because the units are all basically alike. A Midas Muffler shop in Atlanta is very similar in appearance and operation to one in Los Angeles. The franchiser usually provides the franchisee with a blueprint for con-

FUNKY WINKERBEAN   **Tom Batiuk**

structing a building that will be just like all other franchised outlets.
The franchiser also insists on standardized operation of all outlets.
These are spelled out in the franchiser's operations manual and are
backed up with standardized forms and control procedures so that all
outlets look and operate alike.

Management Training and Assistance

Many franchisers operate training schools for their franchisees. They
learn business skills like record keeping, buying, selling, and how to
build good customer relations.

Ongoing training is also important. Many franchisers send representatives to give their franchisees advice and assistance. Franchisees with special problems can turn to the franchiser for help.

Economies in Buying

A franchiser either makes or buys ingredients, supplies, parts, and so
on in large volume. These are resold to franchisees at lower prices
than they would pay if each of them made or bought them on their
own.

Financial Assistance

A franchisee can get financial assistance from the franchiser to go
into business. Usually, a franchisee puts up a certain percentage of
the cost of land, building, equipment, and initial promotion. The rest
is financed by the franchiser, who is paid back out of revenues earned
by the franchisee. The franchiser also provides working capital by
selling to franchisees on account.

In some cases the two parties agree on a joint venture arrangement. The franchisee does not pay back the money put up by the
franchiser. Instead, the franchiser becomes a part owner of the franchisee's business.

Finally, franchisees may find local banks more willing to grant
loans than if they were completely on their own. Bankers know that

Franchising can be a
good alternative for
someone planning a
small business career

a reputable franchiser will license only dependable franchisees and will help them to be successful.

Promotional Assistance

Franchisers usually supply their franchisees with various types of promotional aids. These include in-store displays, radio scripts, and publicity releases. Franchisers also help them to develop their promotional programs.

Franchising and the Franchiser

Among the potential benefits of franchising to franchisers are:

- franchiser recognition
- promotional assistance
- franchisee payments
- franchisee motivation
- franchisee attention to detail

Franchiser Recognition

A franchisee benefits from being able to use the franchiser's name and products at his or her location. The franchiser benefits by expanding the area over which the trade name is known. A franchiser can achieve national and, perhaps, international recognition much faster by franchising than by any other form of expansion.

Promotional Assistance

A local franchisee pays a lower rate for newspaper advertising than a national franchiser. By sharing the cost of advertising, the franchiser and the franchisee both benefit. This is called cooperative advertising. Also, by using local radio and TV advertising in franchise areas rather than blanket network coverage, the franchiser may avoid wasted coverage—advertising in areas that don't have a franchisee. There are benefits from "localizing" promotion to suit customer tastes in a given area or to tie in with local events.

Franchisee Payments

The franchising agreement sets out the amount and type of payments that the franchisee will make to the franchiser. Sometimes the franchisee pays a royalty based on monthly or annual sales. In some cases the fee is fixed at a certain amount and is payable monthly or annually. Often the fee is determined on the basis of the

**How Independent
Is a Franchisee?**

WHAT DO YOU THINK?

David Darren has been a franchisee of a large franchiser in the fast-foods field for the past three years. David's business has been very successful. He has had a good working relationship with Rachel Petersen, the district representative of the franchiser. David always consulted Rachel on important business matters and followed her advice on running his business.

Last week David had lunch with his nephew, Sam. Sam is a college student majoring in business. He wants to go into business for himself after he finishes school.

When David told Sam about the terrific opportunities in franchising, Sam reacted rather negatively. "But, Dave, you're not your own boss. You're pretty much the same as a store manager—just like the person who manages a Safeway or Kmart store. The only differences are that franchisers make you think you're boss and make you risk your own money. You really work for them—you're an employee, not an independent businessman." How independent is a franchisee? WHAT DO YOU THINK?

market size in the franchisee's territory. In still other cases a combination of these methods is used. Less frequently, the franchiser gets only a one-time payment from the franchisee.

Franchisee Motivation

Some large chain stores have trouble recruiting and developing well-motivated store managers. These hired managers are not independent business owners. Franchisees are their own bosses. Their profits belong to them. A franchisee is, therefore, more likely to accept long hours and hard work than a hired manager.

Franchisee Attention to Detail

The headquarters of a chain store operation must keep payroll, tax, and other records on all of its units. It must be concerned with local laws regarding sales taxes, licenses, permits, and so on. Franchisees handle these details in franchise operations.

Franchising and You

Do you have a future in franchising? The answer depends on your willingness to work, your ability to find a good franchise oppor-

THE MOST IMPORTANT FACTS ABOUT ANY FRANCHISE ARE THE ONES ON PAPER.

THIS PAPER.

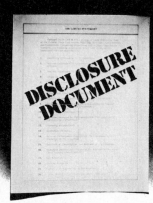

(ask for it)

Buying a franchise or business opportunity is a big decision. So use the disclosure document the seller must give you before you make up your mind. It's your legal right to receive it. Once you have the document, you must be given 10 business days to decide whether to sign.

The document must describe the costs of buying and running the business, the basis for any earnings claims, the seller's history and financial status—plus much more. Remember, don't make your decision based on oral promises. Only the contract and the disclosure document count. If you have questions about these, ask a lawyer or accountant.

The disclosure document will help you make an informed decision. Ask for it.

Federal Trade Commission

Atlanta Boston Chicago Cleveland Dallas Denver Los Angeles New York San Francisco Seattle Washington, D.C. 20580

The Federal Trade Commission requires franchisers to provide a disclosure document to potential franchisees

tunity, and your ability to buy into the operation. Many independent business owners have been very successful as franchisees. Keep in mind, however, that there are some possible drawbacks to franchising:

- unscrupulous franchise promotors may be selling franchises that have little merit
- monthly payments must be made to the franchiser, even if profits are low
- there is little room for creativity because of uniformity of product and operations
- there is less independence than you might expect
- other franchisees may start in nearby areas (oversaturation of the market)
- the franchiser may be unable to live up to commitments in the franchising agreement
- poor performance by some of the franchiser's franchisees may harm your business's image
- franchisers often make policy decisions without consulting their franchisees

THE SMALL BUSINESS ADMINISTRATION (SBA)

Small Business Administration (SBA)

The Small Business Administration (SBA) is an independent agency of the U.S. government. It was created in 1953 to promote and protect the interests of small business firms, and give substance to our national policy that small business should be encouraged and helped. It was intended to help ensure that competition would not lead to survival of only large firms.

SBA Financial Assistance

The SBA participates in and/or makes loans to qualified small businesses. All are term loans which means they must be paid back within a certain number of years. The proceeds can be used for almost any purpose, ranging from ordinary working capital needs to building a plant or store. Three basic types of SBA loans are

- direct loans
- participating loans
- guaranteed loans

SBA direct loans are made entirely with the SBA's own funds.
Usually these are made only for high-risk businesses. The SBA is
prohibited by law from making direct loans if the applicant can get
a loan from a private source. The interest rate typically is several
percentage points lower than comparable bank rates.

SBA direct loans

SBA participating loans supplement loans made from banks. In
these cases the proposed business activity and the entrepreneur's
talents are considered sound enough to merit some debt financing
from private lenders.

SBA participating loans

**In SBA guaranteed loans the money comes from a bank, but the
SBA guarantees 90 percent of the loan.** This helps many entrepreneurs to get loans who might otherwise be turned down. The interest rate banks charge on these loans cannot exceed the maximums
set by the SBA.

SBA guaranteed loans

Roughly 90 percent of the SBA's loans are guaranteed. These
enable private lenders to get in on the lending and reduce criticism
of government interference in business affairs. They also enable the
SBA to get more mileage out of the funds it has to lend.

In recent years the SBA has been encouraging private lenders to
participate more actively in aiding entrepreneurs to set up small
businesses. For example, it has arrangements with a growing number
of banks throughout the nation to reduce the red tape involved in
securing SBA guaranteed loans. Some companies also are being or-

---

POINT OF VIEW

Loan Approvals on SBA-Guaranteed Loans

Traditionally, SBA district offices handle credit analysis work
on applicants for SBA-guaranteed loans. Under the SBA's
certified-lenders program, however, banks and finance companies do the credit analysis and SBA officials simply review
the work. The program's major objective is to speed up the
processing of loan applications. Recently the SBA has decided
to try to divorce itself entirely from approving loans. The
SBA's preferred-lenders program, which was introduced for
testing in 1983, allows lenders to make SBA-guaranteed loans
without SBA approval. The SBA would only review the status
of those loans monthly. Thus the SBA is moving more in the
direction of delegating responsibility for approving loans to
lenders.

The General Accounting Office (GAO)—a watchdog
agency of Congress—opposes this move. In its review of the
certified-lenders program, the GAO found that lenders sometimes make loans too hastily on the basis of incomplete loan
applications. The GAO, therefore, is against the SBA's proceeding with the preferred lender's program.

**Small Business
Investment Company
(SBIC)**

ganized as SBA non-bank lenders to make loans that are guaranteed by the SBA.

The Small Business Investment Act of 1958 makes it easier for small firms to get long-term capital to finance their growth. **This act authorized the SBA to license Small Business Investment Companies (SBICs). An SBIC is a privately owned and privately operated company licensed by the SBA to help finance small firms for expansion and modernization.** Often an SBIC also will provide management assistance to small firms.

An SBIC finances small firms in two ways: (1) by straight loans and (2) by equity-type investments. In a straight loan the SBIC will take collateral that banks will not accept. The borrower and the SBIC negotiate the interest rate, subject to the laws in the state where the agreement is reached. An SBIC's transactions with small firms are private arrangements, but they must operate within SBA regulations.

An SBIC generally prefers, however, to participate as a venture capitalist in the growth of the small firms it finances. There are several ways to do this. First, the small firm can issue warrants to the SBIC in return for a loan. These warrants enable the SBIC to buy common stock in the firm, usually at a favorable price, during a specified period of time. Second, the small firm could give a debenture (a certificate indicating indebtedness) to the SBIC in return for a loan. The SBIC could either accept repayment of the loan, or it could convert the debenture into common stock in the small firm. Finally, the SBIC could receive common stock in the firm in return for advancing its funds for expansion.

In effect, SBICs give the small business owner access to equity capital without the need to make a public stock offering. SBICs range from the very small to the very large. Stock in some of them is publicly traded. Because of their key role in financing small business, Congress has authorized tax incentives to encourage investment in SBICs.

SBA Management Assistance

The SBA gives management help to small firms through its Office of Management Assistance. SBA loan approvals often require applicants to take positive steps to improve their management skills. Financial assistance has no lasting benefit to an owner who lacks basic management skills.

The SBA cosponsors management training courses with public and private educational institutions to instruct small business owners in the functions of management. It also sponsors management conferences and problem clinics. SBA field offices have professionals on their staffs to counsel small business owners.

The SBA's Service Corps of Retired Executives (SCORE) is a group of retired executives who volunteer their services to small firms that need management counseling. There is no charge to the firms except to pay the executives for out-of-pocket expenses they incur during their consultations.

Service Corps of Retired Executives (SCORE)

The SBA's Active Corps of Executives (ACE) is a group of active executives from all major industries, trade associations, educational institutions, and many of the professions, who volunteer their services to small firms that need management counseling. Like SCORE, there is no charge except for out-of-pocket expenses.

Active Corps of Executives (ACE)

In a typical case a SCORE or ACE volunteer is assigned to a firm that has requested help from the SBA. The volunteer visits the firm to analyze its problems and to make suggestions for solving them.

The SBA also sponsors the Small Business Institute (SBI). In the SBI program small business owners with problems are counseled free of charge by faculty members and senior and graduate students from collegiate business schools. The SBA contracts with the schools to provide this service. If you have the opportunity, enroll in such a course. You'll learn a lot about small business management.

Small Business Institute (SBI)

The SBA publishes a variety of booklets written by specialists in all areas of business. Any SBA field office can provide you with a list of free management-assistance publications and a list of booklets for sale.

MINORITIES, WOMEN, AND SMALL BUSINESS

In 1977, minorities owned 5.7 percent of all business firms in the United States. (See Table 17-3.) In that same year, women owned 7.1 percent of all business firms in the United States. (See Table 17-4.) A firm is considered women-owned if one-half or more of the partners are women. A corporation is classified as women-owned if 50 percent or more of its stock is owned by women. The same majority ownership criteria apply to minority-owned businesses. The vast majority of these are small firms.

Although small business provides numerous opportunities for minorities and women, their participation in ownership is relatively modest. A growing number of minorities and women are starting up their own firms. The failure rate among them, however, is typically high—mainly because of lack of experience and training in business.

TABLE 17-3

Minority-owned firms in
the United States

Industry	Percent of all firms owned by minorities	Percent of all receipts earned by minority-owned firms
Construction	4.7	2.9
Manufacturing	4.2	2.3
Transportation and public utilities	8.6	3.9
Wholesale and retail trade	6.0	3.7
Finance, insurance, and real estate	2.0	1.1
Selected services	6.5	4.9
Total for all industries	5.7	3.5

It is no coincidence that minority and female enrollment in business administration programs at two- and four-year colleges has dramatically increased in recent years. They are seeking to develop the skills needed to succeed in business.

The federal government, along with many state and local governments, also has programs to foster the formation and operation of minority-owned and women-owned businesses. For example, the SBA and the Minority Business Development Agency (MBDA) in the

TABLE 17-4

Women-owned firms in
the United States

Industry	Percent of all firms owned by women	Percent of all receipts earned by women-owned firms
Construction	1.9	4.0
Manufacturing	6.6	9.4
Transportation and public utilities	2.9	5.7
Wholesale and retail trade	8.8	8.0
Finance, insurance, and real estate	4.7	3.2
Selected services	8.7	5.9
Other industries	10.2	5.7
Total for all industries	7.1	6.6

Department of Commerce operate special programs to aid minority-owned small firms. Minority Enterprise Small Business Investment Companies (MESBICs) were authorized in 1969 to serve socially and economically disadvantaged American entrepreneurs. A MESBIC is similar to an SBIC, which we discussed earlier in this chapter. A growing share of the SBA's direct loans are being made to women and minorities. SBA-backed training programs also are serving the needs of these entrepreneurs.

One of the programs sponsored by the SBA and the MBDA is the set-aside program. Minority "set asides" are government contracts that are awarded to minority-owned firms without competitive bidding. Federal agencies remove contracts from competitive bidding and give them to the SBA to be awarded to minority-owned firms. The SBA and the MBDA are working to see that a greater number of minority-owned firms can survive under normal competitive conditions outside the program.

The SBA also operates various types of special programs that offer direct loans and loan guarantees to economically or socially disadvantaged applicants, the handicapped, and Vietnam veterans. Examples include the Minority Entrepreneur (ME) program and the Economic Opportunity Loan (EOL) program.

This record store owner started his business with an SBA loan

SUMMARY AND LOOK AHEAD

The entrepreneurial spirit is alive and well in modern America. Many Americans, including a growing number of young people, want to start their own firms. The opportunities are there for those who can spot opportunity and exploit it, but it takes work, know-how, and a determination to succeed in the face of chilling statistics on failures of new, small firms.

We presented a summary of the first steps in starting a firm. Local requirements may differ, so you must study them carefully.

Franchising is still a growth industry. It provides good opportunities for those who want to start their own business, but it is not without its drawbacks.

The SBA helps small business in many ways. It gives financial and managerial help, lobbies for small business interests, helps small firms get government contracts, and is committed to helping women and minority business enterprise. The SBA can help you to get started and to stay in business.

Small firms must face the challenges of survival and growth. To survive, an entrepreneur must be constantly alert to new opportunities and careful about spending. The keys to survival are creativity, determination, careful planning, and willingness to work.

Growth may enable a firm to achieve the benefits of specialization and economies of scale. A small firm that is growing may also provide greater motivation to employees. A rapidly growing small firm that needs more funding may attract the interest of a venture capitalist who will provide equity financing.

In our next chapter we will look at international business. Here there are challenges and opportunities for small, medium-sized, and large firms.

FOR REVIEW . . .

1. Discuss the three ways a person might become a small business owner.

2. Discuss the basic requirements for becoming a successful entrepreneur.

3. Discuss the benefits and burdens of entrepreneurship.

4. List and discuss the preliminaries of starting a small business.

5. Why is it important for an entrepreneur to consult an accountant, a banker, an insurance agent, and a lawyer?

6. Explain how a franchising agreement works.

7. Explain the advantages and disadvantages to the two parties in a franchising agreement.

8. What is the SBA? List and discuss the three basic types of SBA loans.

9. Explain how an SBIC can help finance a small firm.

10. Discuss small business ownership by minorities and women.

. . . FOR DISCUSSION

1. Why would a person who wants to go into business choose to become a franchisee?

2. Suppose you are a banker. A person comes to you and asks for a loan to help him or her get a new business started. What information would you want before acting on the loan request?

3. Why is the failure rate so high among small businesses?

4. How can small, independently owned grocery stores compete against giant chains such as Safeway?

INCIDENTS

Turning an Airy Pastime Into a Business

If you ever fantasize about leaving a job in the work-a-day world for the full-time pursuit of a favorite pastime, consider the success of the Bolands, who turned a passion for hot-air ballooning into a business.

The business, Boland Balloon, operates out of an expanded farmhouse in Burlington, Conn., west of Hartford. It is "fairly lucrative," Brian Boland says, declining to be any more specific about the couple's income than to say: "We're doing a whole lot better than the superintendent of schools." The superintendent topped the income ladder when Mr. Boland was a high school

teacher, a job he left five years ago for the balloon business.

"I think of myself as having retired at age 27," the 32-year-old entrepreneur says. His wife, Kathy, 30, left a job as a draftsman to fulfill what she calls "an obsession with getting into the air."

Both are licensed by the Federal Aviation Administration as balloon pilots, instructors, and repairers. They make money by taking people up at $150 an hour per rider. Repairing balloons and performing the annual inspections required for a balloon to retain an FAA license provide a steady stream of revenue, and the Bolands also sell a few balloons each year.

A basic craft with wicker basket and nylon "balloon," which is referred to as an envelope, costs $12,000. After 300 hours of use, the envelope needs to be replaced, something the Bolands do. A new one runs from $5,000 to $8,000.

Mr. and Mrs. Boland are the company's only full-time employees. Family and friends help out from time to time with cutting or sewing new envelopes.

The involvement in so many aspects of a pursuit both of them love pleases the Bolands and makes others envious, Mr. Boland says. "It never seems like work to us." Occasionally, well-heeled enthusiasts "offer to put up capital to have us grow," he says. "We're reluctant to do that. We have control over what we do, and we want to keep it that way."

QUESTIONS

1. Why do you think the Bolands turned their hobby into a business?

2. If the business were yours, would you have refused outside capital to help the firm grow? Why or why not?

Liz Claiborne Inc. Goes Public

For many companies, going public is a sign that they've finally arrived; they are ripe for expansion and are confident that outsiders will think them a good investment. For company owners, selling stock to the public for the first time can mean much more. It's an opportunity to pay themselves back for all the time and money they put into the business. If they've been doing a good job, the payoff can be substantial.

Consider Liz Claiborne Inc., the women's sportswear maker started in 1976 by Elisabeth Claiborne and her husband Arthur Ortenberg. The couple and two present officers of the New York company, Jerome Chazen and Leonard Boxer, put up about $165,000 of the original $250,000 in capital. A number of friends became minority shareholders by putting up the rest.

In retail jargon, the designer clothing "blew out of the stores." From $2 million in sales in 1976, Liz Claiborne grew to an $80 million business in 1980. Earnings in 1980 were $6.2 million.

In 1980 company executives began to think about going public. They wanted to cash in on their investment, and there were estate tax reasons for establishing a market for the company's stock. "If a shareholder passed away, it would have been up to the federal government to place a value on nonmarketable securities," says Mr. Chazen. "If the stock was valued at a high price, the family could have been stuck with a high inheritance tax." Among other considerations: Management wanted to establish stock bonuses to attract and stimulate good middle-level and top managers.

The stock offering included 345,000 shares sold by the company and 920,000 shares by its owners. The cost to go public was about $550,000. The company got a little over $6 million for its shares with the proceeds, most of which are earmarked for working capital. Each of the four original owners sold 153,689 shares, reducing their individual stakes in the company from about 16.7% to 10.7%. They each received checks for slightly more than $2.7 million. Miss Claiborne and her husband put their proceeds into Treasury bills.

QUESTIONS

1. Why do you think the Ortenbergs started their own business?

2. If you were one of the Ortenbergs, would you have favored going public? Why or why not?

3. Why were most of the company's proceeds from the sale of shares of stock earmarked for working capital?

CHAPTER 18

International Business

OBJECTIVES:

After reading this chapter, you should be able to

1. Explain why international trade is beneficial to the nations that trade.
2. Differentiate between state and private trading companies.
3. Identify and give examples of the various types of barriers to international trade.
4. Give examples of how the United States government aids American firms in conducting international business.
5. Distinguish between a country's balance of trade and its balance of payments.
6. Discuss the effects of fluctuating foreign exchange rates on international trade.
7. Give reasons why firms import and export products.
8. Identify and discuss the major tasks an exporter faces in exporting goods from the United States.
9. Compare exporting and foreign operations as strategies for entering foreign markets.
10. List and discuss several important environmental factors that affect multinational business.

KEY CONCEPTS:

Look for these terms as you read the chapter

international trade

absolute advantage

comparative advantage

exports

imports

state trading company

private trading company

trade barriers

tariffs

import quota

embargo

exchange control

tax control

dumping

General Agreement on Tariffs and Trade
(GATT)

balance of trade

balance of payments

foreign exchange rate

shipper's export declaration

combination export manager

foreign freight forwarder

piggyback exporting

multinational company (MNC)

cartel

regional trading bloc

expropriation

foreign licensing

joint venture

After having been almost completely devastated by World War II, Japan is today a major industrialized nation. Its economic rebirth has been described as a miracle by many people. But this miracle could not have occurred if Japan had been unable to trade with other nations. Japan has very few natural resources available domestically. If it could not obtain the oil, coal, iron ore, bauxite, and other raw materials it must import to supply its industries, Japan could not have become a major industrialized nation. Because of international trade, Japan can buy these resources from other nations and manufacture them into products. Some of these manufactured goods are consumed in Japan. Many, however, are exported to other nations, including many of the nations from whom it imports raw materials.

Up to now we have discussed business mainly in terms of U.S. firms operating in the United States. In this chapter we look at international business. Business activity is becoming more international in character. By and large, the days of political and economic noninvolvement with other nations are over.

International business creates new types of business opportunity, stimulates international contact, and leads to new business practices and new business challenges. Ours is truly an exciting age of international business. Let's begin with a discussion of the reasons why nations trade with each other.

WHY NATIONS TRADE

As we saw in Chapter 1, within rather broad limits greater specialization makes possible greater output. But specialization requires exchange, or trade. These processes do not have to be limited to the people within a country. Broadening the scope of the market makes greater exchange and specialization possible. This is one reason nations buy from and sell to each other. **International trade involves the exchange of goods and services between one country and other countries.** Let's examine some basic principles of trade that explain why nations specialize in certain kinds of products.

international trade

A country enjoys an absolute advantage in producing a product when either (1) it is the only country that can provide it, or (2) it can produce it at lower cost than any other country. If a product can be produced only in Switzerland, any other countries that want it must trade with Switzerland. If a product can be produced at a lower cost in France than in any other country, other countries must either trade with France to get it or pay the higher cost of producing it themselves. If all nations followed this principle, each would specialize in producing only those goods in which it enjoyed an absolute advantage, importing all other goods.

absolute advantage

Suppose a country can produce everything its people consume more efficiently than all other countries. It can still benefit from trade. Trade would enable that country to specialize in producing those products in which it is the most productive. **Comparative advantage means that a country should specialize in producing those products in which it has the greatest comparative advantage or the least comparative disadvantage in relation to other countries.** It should import the other products it needs.

comparative advantage

In the real world, the goods a given country will produce depend on many factors, such as presence of natural resources, cost of labor and capital, and nearness to markets. International trade enables each nation to use its scarce resources more economically.

Our foreign trade accounts for about 10 percent of our GNP. The foreign trade of some other countries accounts for half or more of their GNP. Some of our industries, such as chemical and agricultural industries, depend heavily on exports for sales revenues. **Exports are goods that go from one country to other countries.**

exports

Many of our industries also need imports. **Imports are goods that enter into a country from other countries.** American businesses import huge quantities of tin, nickel, natural rubber, chromium and petroleum.

imports

Table 18-1 lists the major exports and imports of the United States. Table 18-2 identifies our major trading partners. To restrict trade would hurt us. Our exports create jobs for the people who produce them and get them to overseas markets. This includes manufacturers, middlemen, transportation firms, banks, and insurance firms. Imports create jobs for people involved in importing products and place American dollars in the hands of citizens of the countries from which we import. They, in turn, can use those dollars to import other American products.

AUTHORS' COMMENTARY

More American Business People Will Be Working Abroad

Ours is the most highly developed service economy in the world. In addition to exporting goods, the United States exports a huge volume of services, such as those provided by banks, insurance companies, accounting firms, and engineering firms.

Americans who work in foreign countries used to pay income taxes to the U.S. Internal Revenue Service (IRS) on the income they earned there. The income was taxed at lower rates than if it had been earned in the United States, however.

Since 1982 Americans who work in foreign countries no longer have to pay income tax to the IRS if their *earned* incomes do not exceed the tax-free maximums. In 1982, that maximum amount was $75,000. The upper limit increases $5,000 a year until 1986, when it will reach $95,000. Thus an American who works abroad and whose earned income totals $95,000 in 1986 will pay no income tax on that money to the IRS. Much of the housing allowance is also tax-free.

This will become one more factor that will stimulate further growth in our exports of services. More Americans will be willing to work overseas in service-related jobs like construction, banking, engineering, and so on—particularly in countries that do not tax, or tax at low rates, the earned incomes of Americans working there.

Commodity	Exports in Billions of $	Imports in Billions of $
Food and live animals	24.0	14.5
Beverages and tobacco	3.0	3.4
Crude materials, inedible, except fuels	19.2	8.6
Mineral fuels, lubricants, etc.	12.7	65.4
Oils and fats, animal and vegetable	1.5	0.4
Chemicals	19.9	9.5
Manufactured goods	16.7	33.1
Machinery	59.3	39.5
Transport equipment	27.8	33.9

TABLE 18-1

Selected major exported and imported commodities of the United States, 1982

STATE AND PRIVATE TRADING COMPANIES

Although our main concern in this chapter is the international operations of business firms, we cannot ignore the fact that some foreign trading is handled by government agencies.

Because state-controlled economies like the Soviet Bloc countries view their foreign trade largely as an instrument of foreign policy, politics plays a large role in their trade with the noncommunist world. These countries conduct their international trade through state trading companies. **A state trading company is a government-owned operation that handles a country's trade with other governments or firms in other countries.** For example, an American firm selling to the People's Republic of China sells to one of seven state trading companies. These companies do the actual buying for the Chinese. The American firm does not deal directly with the people who will finally use the product.

On the other hand, the international trade of noncommunist countries is carried out primarily by private individuals and business firms. You should not confuse state trading companies with private trading companies. **A private trading company is a privately owned business that buys and sells goods in many different countries, either in its own name or as an agent for its buyer-seller clients.**

Perhaps the best known private trading companies in the world today are based in Japan. Such a company might buy iron ore and

state trading company

private trading company

Suppliers	Billions of $	Customers	Billions of $
Canada	46.5	Canada	33.7
Japan	37.7	Japan	21.0
Mexico	15.6	Mexico	11.8
United Kingdom	13.1	United Kingdom	10.6
West Germany	12.0	West Germany	9.3
France	5.5	France	7.1
Italy	5.3	Venezuela	5.2
Venezuela	4.8	Italy	4.6
Brazil	4.3	Brazil	3.4

TABLE 18-2
Major trading partners of the United States, 1982

coal in the United States and Australia as an agent for a Japanese steel mill and also sell the mill's steel products to buyers in other countries. Private trading companies provide many services for their clients. These services may include financing their sales, providing service on their products, storing and transporting their products, and getting the products distributed through retailers and whole-salers in many countries.

Japanese Mitsubishi Corporation, which is part of the Mit-subishi group (Japan's biggest trading, manufacturing, and banking coalition), is an example. New York-based Mitsubishi International Corporation is Mitsubishi Corporation's trading company sub-sidiary in the United States.

There are big obstacles to trade between communist and non-communist nations. There also are many types of barriers to trade between noncommunist nations. Let's look at these barriers.

BARRIERS TO INTERNATIONAL TRADE

Trade barriers are obstacles that restrict trade among countries.   trade barriers
They can be divided into three groups:

- **natural barriers**
- **tariff barriers**
- **other created barriers**

Natural Barriers

Even if a product can be produced more cheaply in country X than in country Y, the cost of shipping it to Y might wipe out the production cost advantage. Distance, therefore, is a major natural barrier to international trade. Technology has helped us to reduce many of the natural barriers. The jet airplane, for example, has helped to increase international trading of products that spoil rapidly. The big problems are the "created" barriers.

Tariff Barriers

tariffs

Tariffs are duties or taxes that a government puts on products imported into or exported from a country. Governments rarely impose tariffs on exports because they generally favor exporting products to other countries. Tariffs serve two main purposes:

- to generate tax revenue—revenue tariff
- to discourage imports—protective tariff

A revenue tariff raises money for the government that imposes it. Because the purpose is not to reduce imports of the product on which the tariff is imposed, revenue tariffs are usually rather low.

A protective tariff is set high enough to discourage imports of the product on which the tariff is imposed. They usually are levied on foreign products that are priced lower than comparable domestic products. Table 18-3 summarizes the major arguments used to justify tariffs.

There are three ways of setting tariffs: (1) ad valorem; (2) specific duty; and (3) combination ad valorem and specific duty.

An ad valorem tariff is one levied as a percentage of the imported product's value. It is used mainly for manufactured products. A specific duty is one levied on an imported product based on its weight and volume. It is used mainly for raw materials and bulk commodities. The duty is figured on the basis of pounds, gallons, tons, and so on. In a combination ad valorem and specific duty, both types of tariffs are imposed on an imported product.

Other Created Barriers

There are many other barriers to trade that are created by governments. They include

- import quotas
- embargoes

Argument	Reasoning
1. The infant industry argument	1. Tariffs are needed to protect new domestic industries from established foreign competitors. The industry that "grows up" under such a tariff tends to need it in adulthood.
2. The home industry argument	2. American markets should be reserved for American industries by building "tariff walls" around domestic industries regardless of their maturity levels. American consumers pay higher prices because the tariff is added to the selling price of the imported product or the lower-priced import is kept out of the American market.
3. The cheap wage argument	3. Keep "cheap foreign labor" from taking American jobs. When labor is a large cost of producing a product, firms in low-wage countries can sell it in America at lower prices than American manufacturers. Keeping such products out of the United States denies potential foreign buyers the American dollars with which to buy our products.
4. The defense preparedness argument	4. Certain skills, natural resources, and industries are vital to defense preparedness. They should be protected during peacetime in case of war. Many skills, resources, and industries far removed from defense preparedness are similarly protected because producers lobby for protection from foreign competition.

TABLE 18-3

Arguments for tariffs

- exchange control
- tax control
- government procurement policies
- government standards
- customs procedures
- subsidies and countervailing duties

Import Quotas

Most quotas apply to imports although some countries also impose quotas on exports. **An import quota places a limit on the amount of a product that can enter a country.** It may be an absolute limit, in which case all imports stop when the quota is filled. In some cases, a quota is combined with a tariff so that a limited amount can enter the country duty free. Additional imports carry a tariff.

import quota

Japan's Voluntary Export Quota

⬭ **POINT OF VIEW** ⬭

Because of the large and growing volume of Japanese-made cars imported by the United States, there was a lot of talk in 1980 and early 1981 about the need for the federal government to impose an import quota on these cars. Our government, however, supports the concept of free trade and prefers not to impose import quotas. The situation was diffused in the spring of 1981 when the Japanese government voluntarily placed a two-year export quota on shipments of cars to the United States. It also said it would consider extending it for a third year if conditions warranted it.

In the United States, supporters of the Japanese government's action said it would give the American auto industry time to adjust so that it could become more competitive with the Japanese auto makers. They believed this had been achieved without weakening our government's support of free trade.

Opponents, however, said that if demand for Japanese cars remained strong and there were fewer of them being imported, the result would be price increases on the cars. They also said that lessening the competitive pressure on American auto makers might encourage them to raise their prices and slow their efforts to become more competitive.

Still others in the United States wanted our government to impose an even lower quota on Japanese cars. Others felt a tariff should be imposed that would wipe out the Japanese exporters' price advantage in selling in the American market.

Embargoes

embargo

An embargo prohibits the import and/or export of certain products into or out of a country. This may be done for health purposes (the embargo on the import of certain kinds of animals), for military purposes (the embargo on the export of military equipment to certain countries), or for moral purposes (the embargo on the import of heroin). Embargoes also are used for political purposes; for example, the United Nations Security Council has placed an embargo on arms shipments to South Africa. Domestic industries that face stiff competition from imports sometimes lobby for embargoes for economic reasons.

Exchange Control

An American firm that opens a branch plant overseas wants the branch's profits to go to its American owners. If the branch is in West

Germany and West Germans buy products produced in that plant, they pay for the products with marks. But the American owners want dollars. If West Germany is short on dollars, it might stop the branch from sending the profit to America by limiting the amount of marks that can be converted to dollars. This is called exchange control. **Exchange control means government control over access to its country's currency by foreigners.**

exchange control

Tax Control

Foreign-based firms are reluctant to invest in countries that practice tax control. **A country's government practices tax control when it uses its authority to tax to control foreign investments in that country.** Underdeveloped countries, for example, need revenues but have no tax base at home. Taxing foreign-owned firms is an easy way out. In extreme cases tax control can lead to virtual control of these firms by the host country's government.

tax control

Government Procurement Policies

Most nations give some preference to domestic firms in government purchase contracts. The Buy American Act, for example, gives American firms preference over foreign firms in bidding for federal government contracts. Many states have similar laws that give preference to domestic firms when awarding state government contracts.

Government Standards

Government regulations concerning safety and health and other product standards also can serve as nontariff barriers. For example, the Japanese government requires foreign pharmaceutical firms to

"My BUY AMERICAN bumper sticker was 'made in Japan'!"

retest their drugs in Japan before they can be sold there. This can be very costly and time-consuming and may discourage some firms from selling in Japan.

Customs Procedures

All imports into the United States are subject to customs duties but exports are free of duty. Customshouse brokers help importers complete the documentation that is necessary to clear imports through customs.

Each nation has its own customs procedures. For example, each nation chooses its own method for valuing imported products for customs purposes. Some countries have objective criteria. Others leave it to the discretion of customs officials and this can discourage exporters from selling in those countries.

TABLE 18-4

Some examples of governmental assistance to international business

Institution	Purpose
1. Foreign Trade Zones	1. Areas into which goods can be imported without being subject to customs duties or quotas. Often, the imported materials are manufactured into finished products. If re-exported, they are not subject to any tariffs. If they enter into domestic commerce, they are subject to regular tariffs.
2. The Export-Import Bank (Eximbank)	2. Created by the U.S. government to reduce domestic unemployment. Makes loans to exporters who cannot secure financing through private sources and to foreign countries who use the funds to buy American-made goods.
3. The Foreign Credit Insurance Association (FCIA)	3. A firm can buy insurance from FCIA to cover political risk (such as expropriation and loss due to war). Comprehensive coverage can be bought to cover business risks (such as credit default). The exporter can also buy insurance coverage on credit sales to foreign customers.
4. The International Bank for Reconstruction and Development (World Bank)	4. Furthers the economic development of member nations by making loans to them, either directly by using its own funds, or indirectly by borrowing from member countries.
5. The International Monetary Fund (IMF)	5. Eliminates trade barriers and promotes financial cooperation among member countries. Enables them to cope better with balance of payments problems. Thus, if firms in Peru wish to buy from American firms but Peru lacks American dollars, Peru can

Subsidies and Countervailing Duties

Some governments subsidize some of their domestic industries. For example, unlike United States airlines, the majority of the world's airlines are either government-owned or are heavily subsidized by their governments. Some countries also use export subsidies to encourage exports. This can result in the product being sold at a lower price in a foreign market than comparable products made by domestic producers in that country. An importing country that finds its domestic industry being harmed by subsidized foreign competition can impose a countervailing duty on the product to offset the amount of the foreign government's subsidy.

Dumping means shipping substantial quantities of a product to a foreign country at prices that are below either the home-market   dumping

Institution	Purpose
	borrow American dollars from the IMF. It pays the loan back in gold or the currency it receives through its dealing with other countries.
6. The General Agreement on Tariffs and Trade (GATT)	6. Negotiated by member nations to improve trade relations through reductions and elimination of tariff and other barriers.
7. The International Development Association (IDA)	7. Affiliated with the World Bank. Makes loans to private businesses and to member countries of the World Bank. Similar organizations make loans to governments and firms in certain country groupings. The Inter-American Development Association, for example, is for countries belonging to the Organization of American States.
8. The International Finance Corporation (IFC)	8. Affiliated with the World Bank. Makes loans to private businesses when they cannot obtain loans from more conventional sources.
9. Domestic International Sales Corporation (DISC)	9. American firms can form tax-shelter subsidiaries (DISCs) to handle their export sales. The purpose is to spur exports and encourage American firms to enter the export market. A firm can defer some of its taxes on export earnings by establishing a DISC.
10. Overseas Private Investment Corporation (OPIC)	10. Offers insurance to American firms that operate overseas. Covers loss due to expropriation, damage caused by war, revolution, or insurrection, and inability to convert local currencies into U.S. dollars.

**price of the same product or the full cost (including profit) of produc-
ing it.** Under the United States Antidumping Act, American firms
that complain that foreign competitors are dumping in the United
States must show that the foreigners' prices are lower in the United
States than in their home countries and that the American producers
are being directly harmed by the alleged dumping. Only then will the
U.S. Department of Commerce investigate the situation. Some recent investigations include foreign-made steel, shoes, and TVs. If an
investigation shows that a foreign firm did engage in dumping, countervailing dumping duties will be assessed on the dumped products
to wipe out the foreign competitor's price advantage.

Removing Trade Barriers

Governments can help to promote trade by reducing or removing trade barriers. Agreements also have been made between
countries to relax trade barriers. Bilateral agreements are made between two countries. Multilateral agreements are made between
three or more countries. **One of the most important multilateral
agreements is the General Agreement on Tariffs and Trade (GATT).
It is a treaty that is administered by a permanent secretariat through
which member countries act jointly to reduce trade barriers.** In operation since January 1, 1948, GATT has resulted in tariff reductions
on thousands of products and has worked to eliminate nontariff
barriers to trade.

General Agreement on
Tariffs and Trade
(GATT)

The Bureau of International Commerce (BIC) in the U.S. Department of Commerce organizes trade missions, operates permanent trade centers in many foreign countries, and sponsors
district export expansion councils. The U.S. Department of State
provides information and promotion services to American firms interested in overseas business. Table 18-4 discusses several ways our
government aids international business. Many state and municipal
government programs also seek to boost exports. State industrial
development commissions, governors, and mayors often go overseas
to lure foreign firms to their areas.

Private efforts are also important. The Chamber of Commerce
of the United States and the National Foreign Trade Council provide
information and advice to firms interested in selling overseas. Members of world trade clubs in many American cities share their knowledge and experiences in overseas business. When banks, insurance
firms, transportation firms, ad agencies, accounting firms, and marketing research firms help and promote international business, they
bring new business to themselves.

THE BALANCE OF TRADE AND THE BALANCE OF PAYMENTS

In order to understand the importance of international trade to the United States, we should understand the concepts of the balance of trade and the balance of payments. An export from one nation is an import to another nation. International trade is a two-way street. Some governments, however, see it as a means of gaining an economic "edge" over other countries. National pride and mutual distrust cause many nations to view trade as desirable only if their exports are greater than their imports.

A nation's balance of trade is the difference between the money values of its exports and its imports. If it exports more than it imports, its balance of trade is favorable (surplus). If it imports more than it exports, its balance of trade is unfavorable (deficit). The United States enjoyed a favorable balance of trade for many decades prior to 1971. In that year, the value of our imports first exceeded the value of our exports.

balance of trade

A nation with a favorable balance of trade can have an unfavorable balance of payments. **A country's balance of payments is the difference between its receipts of foreign money and the outflows of its own money due to imports, exports, investments, government grants and aid, and military and tourist spending abroad.** For the United States to have a favorable balance of payments for a given year, the following would have to be true. Our exports, foreign tour-

balance of payments

TABLE 18-5

Typical movements in foreign exchange rates

Condition	Result
1. The U.S. balance of trade and balance of payments are unfavorable.	1. The supply of U.S. dollars overseas increases. This usually leads to a decline in the exchange rate of the dollar to foreign currencies.
2. Foreign demand for the dollar is strong and the Federal Reserve System wants to avoid a rise in the dollar to foreign currency exchange rate	2. The Federal Reserve System sells dollars to U.S. banks in exchange for foreign currency. This decreases the supply of foreign currency and increases the supply of dollars. This tends to reduce the dollar to foreign currency exchange rate.
3. The dollar to foreign currency rate declines.	3. American importers pay more dollars for imports. This raises domestic prices of imports in the U.S. and tends to reduce further U.S. imports. Because foreign buyers need less of their currency to pay for goods from the U.S., U.S. exports tend to increase.

Foreign competition could be the best thing that ever happened to your business.

Foreign competition has been blamed for many of the ills that affect America today. Everything from high unemployment to even higher inflation.

But there is something else foreign competition has done. It has forced all of us to take a long hard look into the way we do business.

And we're seeing a lot of things we don't like. We're no longer the leader in many of the industries that we created. A "Made in U.S.A." label doesn't have the appeal it used to have either domestically or internationally.

If we're going to regain our leadership position, we're going to have to make many significant changes. We're going to have to increase productivity and improve quality, for instance.

There are two groups that are vitally important in making these changes. They are America's small and medium-sized businesses. Together they make up 83.5 percent of American business. And they have the flexibility to change quickly.

The problem is, changing takes a great deal of capital. And this is where an independent business finance company like Westinghouse Credit Corporation can be very valuable.

For one thing, we will be there even when money is tight to help make businesses like yours more productive. And because we are a *business* finance company, our primary concern is financing businesses. That's why we can say that we really understand your problems. And this understanding has helped us develop some special services to fill some of your special needs.

There is hope, but one thing is very clear. We can't continue to do business the same old way.

We'd like to tell you more about us. Write: Westinghouse Credit Corporation, Three Gateway Center, Pittsburgh, PA 15222.

We can help you do

business a whole new way.

WCC Westinghouse Credit Corporation

ist spending in America, foreign investments in America, and earnings from overseas investments must be greater than our imports, American tourist spending overseas, our foreign aid grants, our military spending abroad, the investments made by American firms abroad, and earnings of foreigners from their investments in America.

In almost every year since 1950, America's balance of payments has been unfavorable. Although our balance of trade was favorable during the 1950s and 1960s, spending by American firms and tourists abroad, foreign aid, and military spending abroad more than offset the favorable balance of trade. Our unfavorable balance of payments position was made even worse by our unfavorable balance of trade during many recent years. Our huge oil imports and the tougher competition American-made goods have faced in international markets have been major factors.

Table 18-5 illustrates some of the common interrelationships among foreign trade activity, Federal Reserve System actions, and the foreign exchange rate of the dollar. **The foreign exchange rate is the ratio of one currency to another. It tells how much a unit of one currency is worth in terms of a unit of another.**

foreign exchange rate

Exchange rates can fluctuate from day to day. This adds an additional element of risk to international business, especially for small exporters. They generally are not as familiar as big corporations with the methods that may be used to help reduce the risk. These include engaging in currency speculation, a risky venture in itself. Although minor exchange rate fluctuations do not cause major problems, wide fluctuations do. They may be serious enough to discourage international business.

Let's turn now to a look at the reasons firms export and import products. Then we will focus on the different types of exporting and the general procedures a firm must follow in exporting goods from the United States.

Firms that engage in international business must watch foreign exchange rates closely

EXPORTING AND IMPORTING

Exporting and importing are types of involvment in international business. Firms engage in these activities for a variety of reasons.

Why Firms Export Products

Some mass production industries have to produce in large volumes to get the cost-per-unit down to a low level. If the home market is too small to absorb this output, these firms look overseas for additional customers.

Another reason to export relates to the product life cycle concept which we discussed in Chapter 10. Although the refrigerator is in the maturity stage in the United States, it is in the growth stage in some other countries. Without exports, General Electric's sales of refrigerators would be limited to new households and replacements in the United States.

Often, selling costs abroad are lower than selling costs in the home market. The American market is highly competitive. Many firms produce similar products and compete directly with one another. If there is less competition in a foreign country, the exporter might enjoy lower marketing costs there.

The demand for many products is seasonal. Many American firms shift their off-season production into foreign markets where the product is in season. This may lower production cost as a result of better production scheduling.

Finally, a firm might find it more profitable to expand its market coverage to foreign countries than to develop new products for sale at home. Its skills may be put to best use by producing and selling its traditional product rather than by taking on the risks of developing new products.

Why Firms Import Products

American firms import products such as chromium and coffee that are not available in the United States. Sometimes domestic sources must be supplemented by foreign sources, as in the case of oil. Our economy and lifestyles would be affected if products like these could not be imported.

Prices of foreign products are often lower than similar domestic products. Many American consumers want to buy lower-priced foreign-made products which they think are of equal or higher quality than American-made products. Examples include cars and cameras.

Importing products from foreign producers may lead to reciprocal exporting of products to them. This is true for nations and for individual firms.

Imported products may have prestige value. Some Americans, for example, are willing to pay extra for wine and cheese imported from France.

Types of Exporting

Firms have varying degrees of involvement in exporting. For example, a firm that supplies parts to Westinghouse may not know that some of Westinghouse's products are exported. This is a type of *unintentional* exporting as far as the supplier is concerned. Some firms engage in *unsolicited* exporting. Thus a firm may occasionally receive and fill an unsolicited order for its product from an overseas buyer. Although the firm is aware that the buyer is overseas, it did not solicit the order. Our main concern in this chapter is with exporters who *intentionally solicit* orders from foreign buyers.

Getting Involved in Exporting

Let's assume that you have uncovered an opportunity to make a profit by exporting goods to an overseas buyer. You are ready to begin exporting and must familiarize yourself with licensing requirements, shipping documents, international finance, collection documents, methods of payment, and export middlemen.

Licensing Requirements

As an exporter, you will need a license from the U.S. Department of Commerce. The goods you wish to export and the country to which you want to export them basically determine which type you need—a validated export license or a general export license.

To export goods that are either in short supply domestically or have potential application for military use, especially high technology products, you will need to apply for a validated export license. Each application is considered individually. If a license is granted it will set forth the conditions under which the goods may be exported. The government publishes a list of goods for which exporters must have validated licenses.

You will also need a validated export license to export goods to certain countries, mainly those deemed unfriendly to the United States. The government publishes a list of these countries.

If you want to export goods that have no potential military use, that are not in short supply domestically, and the destination is a friendly country, a general export license is sufficient. Our government classifies such goods as acceptable for export without the need to consider individual applications to export them.

Imports and exports must be cleared by a customs agent before they can enter or leave the country

Shipping Documents

shipper's export declaration

A shipper's export declaration is required for all goods exported from the United States. (See Figure 18-1.) **This document declares the quantity and dollar value of the goods and must be filed with the collector of customs at the port of exportation.**

Other important shipping documents include dock receipts, bills of lading, packing lists, and insurance certificates.

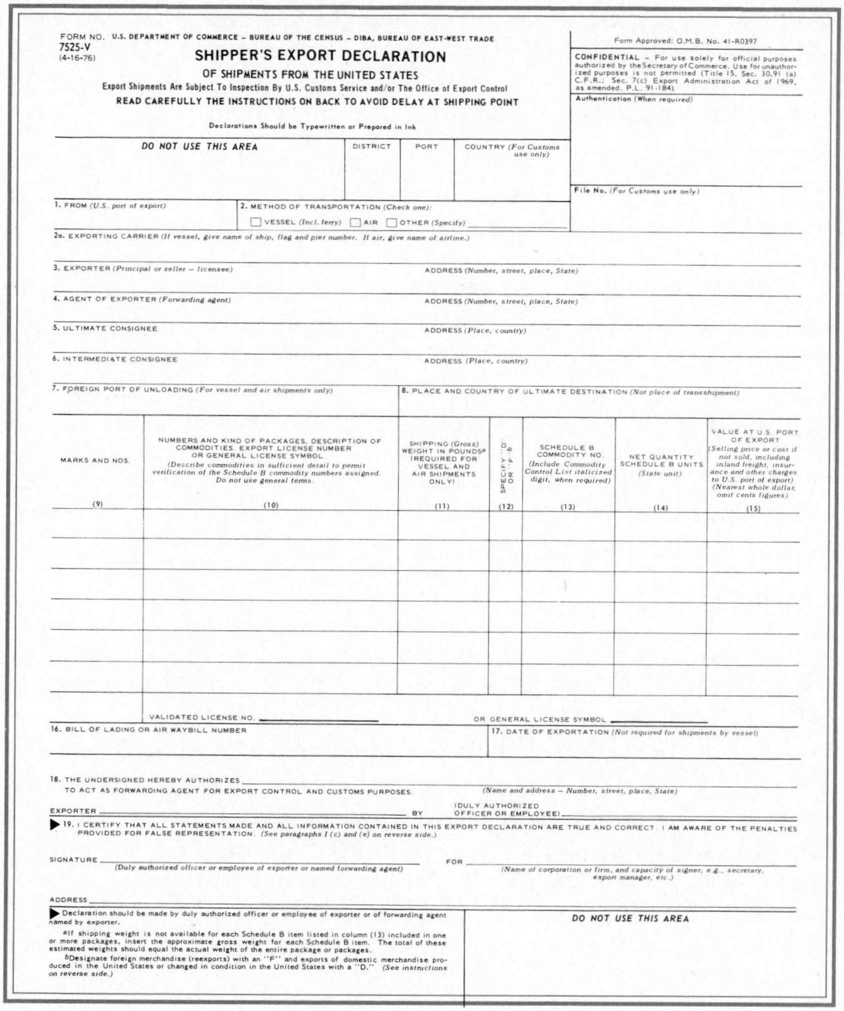

FORM NO. 7525-V (4-16-76) U.S. DEPARTMENT OF COMMERCE – BUREAU OF THE CENSUS – DIBA, BUREAU OF EAST-WEST TRADE

SHIPPER'S EXPORT DECLARATION

OF SHIPMENTS FROM THE UNITED STATES

Export Shipments Are Subject To Inspection By U.S. Customs Service and/or The Office of Export Control

READ CAREFULLY THE INSTRUCTIONS ON BACK TO AVOID DELAY AT SHIPPING POINT

Declarations Should be Typewritten or Prepared in Ink

Form Approved: O.M.B. No. 41-R0397

CONFIDENTIAL – For use solely for official purposes authorized by the Secretary of Commerce. Use for unauthorized purposes is not permitted (Title 15, Sec. 30.91 (a) C.F.R.; Sec. 7(c) Export Administration Act of 1969, as amended, P.L. 91-184)

Authentication (*When required*)

DO NOT USE THIS AREA | DISTRICT | PORT | COUNTRY (*For Customs use only*)

File No. (*For Customs use only*)

1. FROM (*U.S. port of export*)

2. METHOD OF TRANSPORTATION (*Check one*): ☐ VESSEL (*Incl. ferry*) ☐ AIR ☐ OTHER (*Specify*) ____

2a. EXPORTING CARRIER (*If vessel, give name of ship, flag and pier number. If air, give name of airline.*)

3. EXPORTER (*Principal or seller – licensee*) ADDRESS (*Number, street, place, State*)

4. AGENT OF EXPORTER (*Forwarding agent*) ADDRESS (*Number, street, place, State*)

5. ULTIMATE CONSIGNEE ADDRESS (*Place, country*)

6. INTERMEDIATE CONSIGNEE ADDRESS (*Place, country*)

7. FOREIGN PORT OF UNLOADING (*For vessel and air shipments only*)

8. PLACE AND COUNTRY OF ULTIMATE DESTINATION (*Not place of transshipment*)

MARKS AND NOS. (9)	NUMBERS AND KIND OF PACKAGES, DESCRIPTION OF COMMODITIES, EXPORT LICENSE NUMBER OR GENERAL LICENSE SYMBOL (*Describe commodities in sufficient detail to permit verification of the Schedule B commodity numbers assigned. Do not use general terms.*) (10)	SHIPPING (*Gross*) WEIGHT IN POUNDS[a] (REQUIRED FOR VESSEL AND AIR SHIPMENTS ONLY) (11)	SPECIFY "D" OR "F"[b] (12)	SCHEDULE B COMMODITY NO. (*Include Commodity Control List italicized digit, when required*) (13)	NET QUANTITY SCHEDULE B UNITS (*State unit*) (14)	VALUE AT U.S. PORT OF EXPORT (*Selling price or cost if not sold, including inland freight, insurance and other charges to U.S. port of export*) (*Nearest whole dollar, omit cents figures*) (15)

VALIDATED LICENSE NO. ____ OR GENERAL LICENSE SYMBOL ____

16. BILL OF LADING OR AIR WAYBILL NUMBER

17. DATE OF EXPORTATION (*Not required for shipments by vessel*)

18. THE UNDERSIGNED HEREBY AUTHORIZES ____ (*Name and address – Number, street, place, State*) TO ACT AS FORWARDING AGENT FOR EXPORT CONTROL AND CUSTOMS PURPOSES.

EXPORTER ____ BY (DULY AUTHORIZED OFFICER OR EMPLOYEE) ____

▶ 19. I CERTIFY THAT ALL STATEMENTS MADE AND ALL INFORMATION CONTAINED IN THIS EXPORT DECLARATION ARE TRUE AND CORRECT. I AM AWARE OF THE PENALTIES PROVIDED FOR FALSE REPRESENTATION. (*See paragraphs I (c) and (e) on reverse side.*)

SIGNATURE ____ (*Duly authorized officer or employee of exporter or named forwarding agent*) FOR ____ (*Name of corporation or firm, and capacity of signer; e.g., secretary, export manager, etc.*)

ADDRESS ____

▶ Declaration should be made by duly authorized officer or employee of exporter or of forwarding agent named by exporter.

[a]If shipping weight is not available for each Schedule B item listed in column (13) included in one or more packages, insert the approximate gross weight for each Schedule B item. The total of these estimated weights should equal the actual weight of the entire package or packages.

[b]Designate foreign merchandise (reexports) with an "F" and exports of domestic merchandise produced in the United States or changed in condition in the United States with a "D." (*See instructions on reverse side.*)

DO NOT USE THIS AREA

FIGURE 18-1
A shipper's export declaration

A dock receipt shows that your goods have been received in good condition by the carrier (ship or plane) and in the stipulated quantity. It transfers accountability for the goods from the domestic carrier to the international carrier.

A bill of lading is: 1) a document of title that can be transferred after endorsement, 2) a contract between the shipper and the transportation company, and 3) a receipt for the goods the shipper has placed on the carrier.

A packing list is a complete, itemized description of your goods—weight, size, type of packing, and so on. An insurance certificate is a form certifying that freight insurance was obtained, the value insured, and the type of insurance coverage.

International Financing

The first thing to do when arranging for payment from the importer is to talk with the international department of your local bank. If your bank does not have such a department, it can put you in touch with a bank that does.

International banking departments of U.S. banks offer their exporter-clients many services. These include securing credit information about specific importers, collecting overseas accounts, providing information, giving assistance in planning trips overseas, exchanging currencies, and establishing credit guarantees.

An international banking department's overseas correspondent banks can also help you. They can get information on the importer's creditworthiness, help you collect payment, and help you schedule trips to foreign markets to search out potential customers.

Collection Documents

In order to receive payment for your exported products, you must complete several types of documents. These include commercial invoices, certificates of origin, and inspection certificates.

A commercial invoice is a bill for the goods from you to the buyer. It shows all the facts associated with the sale—descriptions, costs, measurements, the insurance carrier, delivery date, payment terms, and so on. A certificate of origin certifies that the goods were produced in the United States. An inspection certificate is a document importers often require. It states that the goods were inspected by a third party to ensure that they are as described by the exporter to the importer.

Method of Payment

The most common methods of handling payment by the importer to the exporter are cash in advance, open account, letter of credit, and drafts.

Cash in advance eliminates the risk that the buyer will not pay. The buyer, however, may look at it as suspicion of his or her creditworthiness. It also ties up the buyer's working capital if payment must be made before the receipt of goods.

With an open account arrangement, the seller ships the goods to the buyer and the seller's commercial invoice indicates the buyer's liability to pay. Open account is used only when the seller is sure of the buyer's willingness and ability to pay.

A letter of credit is a document from the buyer's bank to you. It guarantees the bank will pay you for the goods if you meet the conditions set out in the letter. Usually, the exporter and the importer agree on the terms of sale in advance and incorporate these terms in the letter of credit.

A draft, or bill of exchange, is a written demand for payment. You could, for example, draw a draft instructing the buyer to pay the invoice to the buyer's bank. Your bank would send the draft to the buyer's bank for collection. A sight draft requires the buyer to pay before taking possession of the goods. A time draft allows the buyer a period of time, usually one to six months, to pay the invoice. The buyer takes possession of the goods before paying for them but only after accepting the time draft.

Although most exporters prefer to be paid in their currency, they may permit their buyers to pay in their currency. Thus a German importer may pay you in marks and you will have to convert them to dollars. How many dollars those marks will buy can change from day to day, depending on the foreign exchange rate. Your banker can give you information about foreign exchange rates and help you protect yourself from extreme fluctuations.

Using Export Middlemen

What we have described are only some of the major tasks you would face as an exporter if you handled all the details yourself. If you are exporting for the first time, you may want to rely more on middlemen to help you.

Many foreign governments, manufacturers, wholesalers, and retailers have resident buying offices in the United States that buy American-made products for their overseas employers. Sales to them are similar to sales to domestic customers because they handle all the details of exporting.

If you believe your product might appeal to buyers in several different countries, you could use a combination export manager. **A combination export manager serves as the export department for several noncompeting manufacturers on a commission basis.** This middleman has a long-term relationship with his or her clients.

combination export manager

Foreign freight forwarders can also help. **A foreign freight forwarder consolidates small export shipments into large ones, arranges for transportation and insurance, and handles both export and import documentation for clients.** This middleman will often pick up the client's freight, move it to the port, arrange for overseas shipment, and move the goods from the foreign port to the buyer.

foreign freight forwarder

In piggyback exporting, a manufacturer (the carrier) uses its overseas distribution network to sell noncompetitive products of

piggyback exporting

one or more other firms (riders). The carrier may buy your products outright or sell them for you on a commission basis.

In the following section we look at a type of international business activity that goes far beyond exporting—foreign manufacturing operations.

FOREIGN MANUFACTURING OPERATIONS

In recent decades there has been a tremendous growth of foreign manufacturing operations. Since the end of World War II, American-based firms have invested heavily in building plants in foreign countries. In fact, a large proportion of our exports are accounted for by sales of American firms to their overseas subsidiaries.

Foreign manufacturing operations represent a much greater commitment to international business than exporting. Sales revenues of overseas subsidiaries in which American firms hold majority ownership add up to four or five times the annual dollar value of our exports.

Ford Motor Co. has plants in many countries. Its plants in West Germany and Spain make cars for sale in those countries and for export to other countries. Those sales do not show up as exports from the United States. A large proportion of our exports are accounted for by sales of American firms to their overseas subsidiaries. Thus any parts that Ford might export from the United States to its plants overseas are counted as exports from the United States.

Foreign-based firms have also built plants in the United States. We will discuss this later in this chapter.

The Multinational Company

multinational company (MNC)

A multinational company (MNC) is a firm based in one country (the parent country) and has production and marketing activities spread in one or more foreign (host) countries. We tend to think of firms such as IBM, Procter & Gamble, Coca-Cola, and General Electric as American firms. But they are actually global firms. Many such firms sell more products overseas than they sell in the United States.

Of course, the United States is not the parent country for all multinational firms. For example, Switzerland's Nestlé does more than 90 percent of its business outside of Switzerland. Royal Dutch Shell and Unilever Corporation do more than 80 percent of their

Rank	Company	Country	Industry	Sales ($000)
1	Royal Dutch/Shell Group	Neth.-Britain	Petroluem	$83,759,375
2	British Petroleum	Britain	Petroleum	51,322,452
3	ENI	Italy	Petroleum	27,505,858
4	IRI	Italy	Metal mfg.—steel; ship-building; food products	24,815,296
5	Unilever	Britain/Neth.	Food products; soaps, cosmetics	23,120,471
6	Francaise des Pétroles	France	Petroleum	20,029,197
7	Petrobrás (Petróleo Brasilerio)	Brazil	Petroleum	19,004,999
8	Elf-Aquitaine	France	Petroleum	17,785,313
9	Siemens	Germany	Electronics; computers	16,962,630
10	Nissan Motor	Japan	Motor vehicles	16,465,167

TABLE 18-6

The 10 largest industrial corporations outside the United States (ranked by sales), 1982

business in host countries. Table 18-6 identifies the ten largest industrial corporations outside the United States.

Why the Growth in Foreign Manufacturing Operations?

Several factors help to explain the growth in foreign manufacturing operations. One is the growth in buying power in some countries. This helps to create enough demand for some products so that it is more profitable for their producers to set up manufacturing operations there instead of exporting the finished products from the United States.

Another factor is the growing spirit of nationalism in many countries, especially in the underdeveloped countries that export raw materials. Nations that produce raw materials argue that foreign-based firms come in and "take" their natural resources and export them to the industrialized nations where they are manufactured into products. These countries argue that the foreigners get the high-paying manufacturing jobs, their governments gets taxes from the firms, and the workers spend their money at home.

Instead of exporting their raw materials to the more developed countries, less developed nations want firms to set up manufacturing plants in their countries to use the raw materials there. This creates local jobs, gives the government some control over the MNC's operations, and increases the tax base. They also believe that they are in a poor bargaining position against the big firms. This is **cartel** why some less developed nations have formed cartels. **A cartel is a group of business firms or nations that agree to operate as a monopoly. Thus they regulate prices and production.** Although cartels are illegal in the United States, they are legal in some other countries.

Consider another example of nationalism. In order to encourage local production, some governments erect barriers against importing selected products that MNCs wish to sell there. These barriers practically force these MNCs to set up local manufacturing and marketing operations instead. Local content laws, for example, require firms that make products like cars to buy a set percentage of the parts in the country where the car is to be sold. Such laws encourage car makers to set up assembly plants in these countries.

Still another factor is the lower cost of producing in some countries. This can be due to lower labor costs, lower interest rates, lower taxes, government subsidies, or more availability of raw materials.

regional trading bloc Finally, the formation of regional trading blocs in some areas of the world may favor foreign operations for some firms. **A regional trading bloc is a group of countries that agree to eliminate barriers to trade among member nations.** In 1958, for example, Belgium, France, Italy, Luxembourg, the Netherlands, and West Germany formed the European Economic Community (EEC), or the European Common Market. Since then, Denmark, Ireland, the United Kingdom, and Greece have joined. Spain and Portugal have also asked to join.

There are no tariffs on exports and imports among member countries. But all members apply a common external tariff on products entering from nonmember countries. Thus an American exporter is at a disadvantage in competing with a French firm to export products to other Common Market countries. Many American firms have set up subsidiaries in member countries to get behind this tariff wall.

There are, of course, several risks in engaging in foreign operations. Each nation has its own system of government, laws, and money. Sometimes, foreign-owned firms receive discriminatory treatment by host-country governments.

expropriation Perhaps the biggest political risk in setting up a plant overseas is the risk of expropriation. **Expropriation means that the government of a country takes over ownership of a foreign-owned firm located in its country.** In some cases the owner is paid part or all of the market value of that property. *Confiscation*, however, means that the government does not compensate the owner. When the expropriating government keeps ownership and runs the firm, it is called *nationalization.*

A firm that engages in foreign operations must also consider the attitude of its home-country government. The U.S. government's attitude toward American firms that invest abroad depends largely on the situation and the time. It involves foreign policy and the national interest. On balance, however, our government encourages and helps American firms to do business overseas.

As foreign investments in the United States increase, more and more foreign banks are opening branches in U.S. cities

Foreign Operations in the United States

In recent years there has been a tremendous increase in foreign investment in the United States. Some of it has been oil money from the Arab nations. Some of it has been due to fluctuations in foreign exchange rates. For example, if the U.S. dollar drops a great deal in value relative to the German mark, German firms can build plants in the United States, or buy up plants already built here, at what amounts to bargain prices. Our highly stable political system also attracts foreign investment, especially from countries where political terrorist groups are active or newly-elected government officials are perceived to be anti-business.

Foreign investment in the United States takes many forms.

WHAT DO YOU THINK?

Should Our Government Have Greater Control Over Foreign Investment in the United States?

Our government supports the concepts of free trade and investment. Because of the explosive growth of foreign investment in the United States in the past decade, our federal government set up the Committee on Foreign Investment in the United States in 1975. The Committee's purpose is to monitor, not prevent, foreign investment in the United States. It has no power to stop a foreign firm from investing here.

Some people, however, think we should exercise more control over foreign investment in the United States. Many favor an approach similar to that taken by Canada. Canada's Foreign Investment Review Agency carefully analyzes all proposed foreign investments in Canada. If a particular proposal does not appear to be in Canada's best interest, the agency can prevent it from becoming reality. It can also impose conditions and limitations on proposals that it approves. Should our government have greater control over foreign investment in the United States? WHAT DO YOU THINK?

Nissan Motor Company decided to build an assembly plant in Tennessee from the ground up. Volkswagen bought and modernized an already existing plant in Pennsylvania and remodeled it. Renault bought stock in AMC (American Motors Corporation). In addition, foreigners are buying U.S. government securities and securities of American corporations. They also are big buyers of real estate, like office buildings, hotels, and farm land.

Foreign Licensing

foreign licensing

In our discussion of franchising in Chapter 17, we saw that a franchising agreement involves a franchiser licensing franchisees to sell its products or services. This is a type of licensing agreement.

In a foreign licensing agreement a firm in one country (the licensor) gives a firm in another country (the licensee) the right to use the licensor's patent, trademark, copyright, technology, processes, and/or products in return for an agreed-upon percentage of the licensee's sales revenues or profits resulting from such use. It is a very popular way for firms to enter foreign countries without the need to export to those countries or set up operations there. For example, B. F. Goodrich licenses its process for making polyvinyl chloride suspension resin, which is used in making pipes and other products, to an Egyptian petrochemical firm. Foreign-based pharmaceutical firms license American pharmaceutical firms to produce and market their products and vice versa. The licensee gets the rights to make and sell a product on which it spent nothing for research and development. The licensor may get a big royalty on its product's sales without having to spend money entering the licensee's market. Of course, termination of licensing agreements by one party can cause big problems for the other party.

As this Dutch menu suggests, McDonald's restaurants are becoming increasingly popular abroad

joint venture

Ownership of Foreign Operations

An overseas operation can be a wholly owned subsidiary of the parent firm or a joint venture. There are no local part-owners when the parent owns the subsidiary outright. Outright ownership gives the parent firm maximum control and makes it easier to coordinate subsidiary operations with those of the parent.

In international business, a joint venture means a partnership of two or more partners that are based in different countries. They share ownership and control of the venture's operations and property rights. The partners can be two foreign firms that are doing business in a host country, a foreign firm and a government agency, or a foreign firm and a locally owned firm.

The majority of foreign subsidiaries of American-based MNCs are wholly owned. But there is a strong worldwide trend toward requiring joint ventures. For example, since 1973 Mexico has limited to 49 percent the proportion of a new investment that can be foreign-owned.

THE MULTINATIONAL BUSINESS ENVIRONMENT

People who conduct business across national borders must pay attention to differences in environment between or among countries. They must consider differences in the sociocultural, economic, technological, and political and legal environments.

The Sociocultural Environment

Social and cultural differences can have a big impact on international business. Language differences can be a big problem. Consider, for example, American Motors' dismay several years ago upon learning that its "Matador" car translated as "killer" car in Puerto Rico.

Ad campaigns built around the idea of moving up in the social ladder are not likely to be effective in very class-conscious social systems, such as in India, nor are personnel policies that encourage employees to move up the job ladder. In Oriental societies, extreme politeness and formality are part of doing business, unlike the more informal American way. An American who wants to get down to business without engaging in the proper social behavior is headed for trouble.

Campbell Soup Company had trouble with its canned soup in Brazil because Brazilians prefer to prepare their soups from scratch. They are more likely to use dehydrated products as a soup starter and add their own ingredients to suit their tastes. Unlike Americans and many other people, Japanese drink soup at breakfast.

The Economic Environment

Most of the world's trade is conducted between the economically advanced nations. Underdeveloped countries that are rich in natural resources, however, have the potential to develop faster, and thus attract more interest as potential markets and bases for setting up plants, than underdeveloped countries that are poor in natural resources.

A country's tax structure also affects its appeal to multi-national firms that are considering setting up operations there. Other elements of the economic environment that are important for business include inflation rates, employment levels, per capita GNP, the distribution of income among the people, and the stability of the economic system.

The Technological Environment

Not all countries have transportation and communication systems as advanced as those in the United States. Managers must evaluate the level of technology in those countries where they expect to operate. This may enable them to adapt their operations to the present technology or attempt to import new techniques. NCR (National Cash Register Company) developed crank-operated cash registers to market in some countries where the availability of electricity is limited.

The Political and Legal Environment

An American-based firm that deals with foreign governments and/or businesses gets involved in politics. It's hard to keep sharp dividing lines between politics, economics, business, and ethics. This often poses a dilemma for managers. What about an American-based firm that applies to the Overseas Private Investment Corporation (see Table 18-4) for insurance on a plant it wants to build in a country that some people believe violates human rights? Should the application be approved?

When a government owns the means of production, foreign firms doing business there must deal with that government. A firm may have to enter into a partnership arrangement with a government before the firm can begin operations there. For example, Dow Chemical Company had to enter into a joint venture with Yugoslavia as a condition of setting up a petrochemical plant in that country. When the Mitterrand government came to power in France in 1981, it started to nationalize many French firms—some of which had been involved in joint ventures with American-based firms. Thus the American-based firm found itself in a de facto joint venture with France's Socialist government.

A lot has been said about technology transfer over the years. Some people, for example, believe that the United States is transferring too much computer technology to the Soviet Union. Several proposed sales of computers by American firms to the Soviet Union have been help up by the government in recent years because of the military implications of the proposed sales. The technology transfer issue tends to arise more often whenever the "cold war" heats up between East and West.

Many laws restrict a parent firm's control of its overseas operations. These include laws that require a subsidiary to hire local nationals or restrict how much profit can flow out of the country. A multinational firm takes on a considerable risk, much of which is political. IBM several years ago was forced to leave India. The government wanted the firm to allow Indians to have partial ownership and control of IBM's plants in India. IBM refused to comply. Coca-Cola was willing to share ownership, but it refused the Indian government's request that the firm give it the secret formula for Coke.

A firm operating in different countries is subject to different political and legal systems. Quite often what is legal in one is illegal in another. The firm is caught in the middle but must be careful not to violate the laws in any country in which it operates.

SUMMARY AND LOOK AHEAD

Trade among countries broadens the market and permits greater exchange and specialization. International trade enables each country to use its limited resources to the best advantage.

In free economies international trade basically means international business—firms and individuals in different countries buying from and selling to each other. In state-controlled economies, trade is handled through state trading companies.

Despite the advantages of trade, there are many trade barriers. Distance is a natural barrier. But there also are tariff and other created barriers. Examples of nontariff created barriers are import quotas, embargoes, exchange control, tax control, government procurement policies, government standards, customs procedures, and subsidies and countervailing duties. As governments recognize the mutual benefits from trade, they want more trade and work to eliminate the tariff and nontariff barriers.

The balance of trade and balance of payments are very important to international business people. In recent years the United States has had trade and payments balance deficits. This has affected the foreign exchange rate of the dollar.

Getting involved in exporting requires familiarity with licensing requirements, shipping documents, international financing, collection documents, and methods of payment. Various types of middlemen can help exporters.

There are different types of international business involvement. An unintentional exporter is much less committed to international business than is a multinational company. A multinational company is based in a parent country and has production and marketing activities in one or more foreign (host) countries.

A basic understanding of the environments of international business is important to executives in global firms. The surest way to fail in any type of overseas business dealings is to assume that foreigners are all alike.

Just as environmental factors are crucial in international business, they can be crucial at home. In the next section we consider the many environmental factors affecting business decisions in the United States.

FOR REVIEW . . .

1. Explain how trade between two countries can benefit their citizens.

2. Do governments engage in international trade? Explain.

3. List the three general types of trade barriers and give an example of each.

4. Are the majority of tariffs on imports into the United States protective tariffs or revenue tariffs? Explain.

5. Does the General Agreement on Tariffs and Trade (GATT) help to restrict or to increase international trade? Explain.

6. Can a nation with a favorable balance of trade have an unfavorable balance of payments? Explain.

7. What effects do fluctuating exchange rates have on international trade?

8. Suppose a country has an unfavorable balance of trade and an unfavorable balance of payments. Will this tend to result in a rise or a decline in the foreign exchange rate of its currency? Explain.

9. Contrast unintentional exporting and intentional exporting.

10. Discuss the licensing requirements for a person or firm planning to export goods from the United States.

11. Identify and discuss the types of shipping documents required to export goods from the United States.

12. Contrast an exporting company and a multinational company in terms of their commitment to international business.

. . . FOR DISCUSSION

1. To which country does the management of a large multinational company owe its primary allegiance?

2. Is it ethical for an American-based company to open a plant in a low-wage country when unemployment in America is at a high level?

3. "Investments made by American-based multinational firms in foreign countries are good for both the United States and the foreign countries." Do you agree?

4. "It is easier for a firm to live up to its social responsibility when its operations are confined to one country than when it engages in international business." Do you agree?

5. Doing business in many countries exposes a firm to many risks that could be avoided by limiting its operations to its home country. What are these risks and how does a firm cope with them?

INCIDENTS

The Pickup Truck War

Compact pickup truck sales started to increase rapidly in the United States during the second half of the 1970s. Japanese-made Datsun and Toyota trucks were taking market share from Detroit's full-sized pickups. In response, American auto makers started selling compact pickups, such as Chevrolet's Luv and Ford's Courier, both of which were made in Japan.

To help slow the imports, the tariff on all pickup trucks imported into the United States was raised from 4 percent to 25 percent in September, 1980. This, of course, included Luvs and Couriers. The Japanese government's voluntary quota on exports of cars to the United States did not apply to pickups. (See POINT OF VIEW in this chapter.)

In 1982, Detroit's auto makers entered the subcompact pickup truck market with American-made products—GM's S-10 and S-15, Ford's Ranger, and Chrysler's Rampage.

QUESTIONS

1. Do you think the increase in the tariff was justified? Why or why not?

2. What effect do you think the tariff hike had on competition between Japanese and American makers of pickup trucks?

3. Suppose you were the president of Toyota Motor Company. Would you have changed your export strategy for the U.S. market in light of the tariff increase and the voluntary quota? Explain.

Foreign Trade Zones

In the United States, a foreign trade zone is an area established under a grant of authority from the U.S. Department of Commerce's Foreign-Trade Zones Board and operated under U.S. Customs Service supervision. The purpose is to keep business activity in the United States that, in the absence of the zones, might be conducted overseas.

As we saw in Table 18-4, imports can enter such a zone duty free and are not subject to customs entry requirements and quotas as long as they remain in the zone. Raw materials can be manufactured into finished products, products can be repaired, and other types of operations can be performed within the zone. Goods exported overseas from the zone are not subject to duty or taxes. Goods that leave the zone and enter domestic commerce in the United States are subject to duties and taxes.

The Foreign Trade Zones Act was passed in 1934. Until the past few years, however, relatively few cities in the United States had established them. Similar type zones are now multiplying rapidly in other countries, especially in less-developed countries.

QUESTIONS

1. How might an American-based firm use a foreign trade zone in the United States? Give an example.

2. How might a foreign-based firm use a foreign trade zone in the United States? Give an example.

3. In recent years there has been more interest among American cities in establishing foreign trade zones. Why?

CASE STUDY

The smiling American standing in Hall 4, Booth 622, is John Villano, doing for the first time what European traders and industrial giants have been doing for hundreds of years—selling goods at a European trade fair.

Mr. Villano, president of Cam-Apt Inc. of Waterbury, Conn., a maker of computer-aided design and manufacturing gear with sales of only $1 million a year, is one of a small band of American small businessmen to discover that gold lies in fairs. "The big American companies, the ones that have been exporting for a long time, have always been at the fairs," says William Lynch, director of the U.S.'s international marketing center in Bonn. "In terms of the small guy, there has been an increase. It's not a big wave, but it's growing."

The eighteen trade fairs held in 1981 in Cologne alone have attracted some 550 American exhibitors, up from 475 two years ago, and much of the increase is attributed to smaller companies. As a way of getting a toe-hold in European markets, the fairs are valuable but relatively inexpensive. "By going to fairs, U.S. companies can cut down their lead time in entering a foreign market from four or five years to four or five months," says Harrison B. Sherwood, a U.S. trade attache in Bonn. "If a company goes for nothing more than market research, it still pays to find out if you can't get into the market."

Sales and Contracts

The European fairs are true markets in which sales are closed and contracts signed. The fairs give some manufacturers their only real crack at customers in smaller or distant markets. "Here in Europe, fairs are really a prime source of getting information to the buyer, and it becomes more important the farther east you go," says William Fletcher, manager for European promotions for Cincinnati Milacron Inc., the diversified Ohio machine-tool company.

Mr. Villano set up shop at Hanover's European Machine Tool Fair (EMO), which attracted 35,000 visitors in its ten-day run. The 1,843 exhibitors came from thirty-four countries to show 28,000 tons of equipment in twenty-three halls covering half the 250 acres of the Hanover fairground.

Restraining Congeniality

It can also be forbidding. "We had someone ("–a visitor–") who didn't speak either English or German," Mr. Villano says.

"What are you going to do?" Americans must restrain their conventioneering congeniality. European buyers expect conservative dress, punctuality and at least the appearance of gravity in business matters. "There's very little convention aspect to these fairs," Mr. Lynch of the U.S. marketing service says.

U.S. officials tell American businessmen that they can mount a small fair exhibit for $2,500 or $3,000, although large companies spend much more. At EMO, space cost $12.50 a square foot. Larger exhibitors spent tens of thousands of dollars more on their exhibits, some with private rooms and bars for customers. Exhibitors usually hope to cover their costs in actual floor sales. In 1980, sixteen U.S. exhibitors testing export markets for the first time sold $200,000 worth of goods at a European auto supply fair, but another sixteen companies that already sold in Germany got $12 million in floor sales.

The fairs give businessmen a chance to check the competition, meet new prospects and find distributors and sales agents. Ralph Barton, president of Rico Machine Co., Bristol, R.I., came to EMO to talk with his European agents at the same place instead of traveling throughout the continent to meet them separately. "I've always been surprised that more American companies don't come to the fair," he says. "Some think that the U.S. is the whole world, and it isn't."

Japanese Competition

Japanese companies are tackling the fairs more aggressively. The number of Japanese firms at EMO in 1981 rose by 120 percent to fifty-five from the number that exhibited at the prior EMO fair in Hanover in 1977. The number of American exhibitors rose only 19 percent to fifty-two. "The Americans themselves are to blame when they take a ten-year beauty sleep and wake up to find the Japanese here," says Gotz Burkhardt of Stenzel & Co. Maschinehandelgeschaft G.m.b.H., a German trading firm.

Sometimes a simple lack of sophistication keeps Americans shy of the fairs, says Walter Stadtler, commercial counselor at the American embassy in Bonn. "Some Americans," he says, "walk into these huge halls, see all these crowds of people, hear them all talking foreign languages and say 'I'll hold off.' They don't want to look like idiots." But some American trade officials complain that their efforts to hand-hold U.S. businessmen and introduce them to Europe to increase U.S. exports get undercut by changes in administration and policy in Washington.

In Bonn, officials try to make up for the lack of consistency with a missionary fervor. "It's like black magic," Mr. Sherwood says of the fair ritual. "buyers can walk around the product, look at it, kick it, and it leads to new sales."

QUESTIONS

1. Why do you think that small business people are becoming more interested in exporting their products?

2. If an American small business owner attends a trade fair primarily to engage in market research, what do you think he or she would be seeking to learn?

3. Why do potential buyers attend trade fairs?

4. Is Mr. Villano an unintentional exporter? Why or why not?

CAREERS IN SPECIAL TYPES OF BUSINESS

The desire to become your own boss by starting up a business is still very much alive. You must stay alert to recognize opportunity. Carole Ely and Lore Harp gave up homemaking in favor of starting up Vector Graphics Inc., a rapidly growing manufacturer of desk-top computers. Carol Brothers noticed that many working women have trouble finding maids. So she started a franchise operation, Pop-Ins, a house cleaning service. You may be able to start on a very small scale, perhaps operating out of your house. Philip Knight and Bill Bowerman started out by importing running shoes from Japan, storing them in the basement, and selling them to nearby retailers. In time, they began to design and market their own running shoes—Nike.

A growing number of venture capitalists, experienced executives, and consultants are available to help would-be entrepreneurs to get started. Federal Express and Prime Computer are examples of young companies that received help from venture capitalists.

Entrepreneurship is becoming more accessible to women who want to start their own firms. For many years some people believed that women entrepreneurs were at a cultural disadvantage because their traditional upbringing stressed security, and going into business involves a great deal of risk. There is growing evidence, however, that this fear of risk, if it does in fact exist, is being overcome. Consider the fact that there is a growing number of women venture capitalists. Various types of assistance are finally becoming more available to women, including private, nonprofit training and management assistance programs, such as New York's American Woman's Economic Development Corp. and the National Association of Women Business Owners.

Perhaps a career in international business appeals to you? Remember that it is unlikely for an entry-level job to lead to an immediate assignment overseas. The majority of Americans who work overseas for American-based firms are people who gained experience in their firms' domestic operations.

If you are highly skilled in one or more foreign languages, you may find employment as an interpreter or a translator. *Interpreters* translate spoken passages from one language into another; *translators* translate documents and other material from one language into another.

Other entry-level jobs include *export and import clerks.* They compute duties, tariffs, and weight, volume, and price conversions of merchandise exported to or imported from foreign countries. They also examine documents, such as invoices, bills of lading, and shipping documents, to verify conversion of merchandise weights or volumes into the system used by the importing or exporting country.

Several career options are available with the Federal government. *Customs inspectors* inspect cargo, baggage, ships, and aircraft entering or leaving the United States to enforce customs and related laws. They also oversee cargo loading and unloading to ensure compliance with customs and commerce laws. *Foreign service officers* represent the interests of the U.S. government and American citizens to foreign nations and international organizations. They help protect and advance our political, economic, and commercial interests overseas. They also render personal services to Americans abroad and to foreign nationals traveling to the United States. An especially important part of their work is to alert business people in the United States to potential foreign trade and investment opportunities. Many foreign service officers serve in Washington, D.C. as counterparts to their colleagues who are assigned to overseas posts.

Customs-house brokers are licensed by our government to act as intermediaries between importers, steamship companies or airlines, and the Bureau of Customs. They prepare and compile documents required by our government for a ship or airplane of foreign origin to discharge its cargo in the United States. They prepare entry papers in accordance with Bureau of Customs regulations. They also file papers with the Bureau and arrange for payment of duties.

CAREER PROFILE

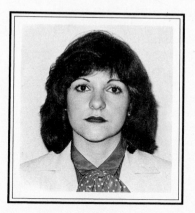

My name is Maria Leon Vallejo. I received a Bachelor of Science degree in marketing in 1980. The college courses I selected were in the various areas of marketing such as promotion and retailing, but I was always most interested in the distribution and logistics aspects. Upon evaluating the opportunities available in the job market, I decided to choose a career in logistics with emphasis on distribution.

During the second semester of my junior year, I spoke with the Career Planning Center at the University. They provided me with career counseling and information on many career opportunities. This was the only medium I used in searching for a job.

After interviewing with several companies, I decided to accept a job offer from Lykes Bros. Steamship Company in New Orleans. Although their salary offering was not the highest I received, I felt the position offered the best opportunity for professional growth. The position requires me to work with various departments within the company and allows me to gain a broad experience in all phases of the shipping industry.

I was recruited for a position in the Seabee Division, which deals with Lykes' United Kingdom and North European Continent trade routes served by the SEABEE ocean carriers. Developed exclusively by Lykes, SEABEE is a fully integrated shipping system which combines inland waterway barges, containers, and huge ocean carriers to provide maximum efficiency service to shippers.

One month after graduation I starting working at Lykes in the position of Westbound Cargo Coordinator. I went through a two-month initial training period. This consisted of rotating through the major departments within the company in order to learn their functions and interrelations.

I am responsible for coordinating the work of various departments, including Sales, Containers, Documentation, Marketing, Accounting, Operations, and Pricing to ensure the smooth physical movement of all East Gulf Containers and an effective customer service program. I am also responsible for gathering and analyzing marketing information. This includes analysis of competitors' rates. It also includes preparation of a quarterly Container Profit Analysis report which gathers customer and cargo information. The job requires an understanding of traffic priorities including reading and quoting tariffs, coordinating between inland cargo interests, and maintaining close contact with proper parties in the forwarding community. The job requires diplomacy in dealing with people inside and outside the company to solve logistical problems, often under extreme time pressures. I also have training and supervisory responsibilities for two clerks.

In the future I would like to strike a balance between family life and career. I would like to continue gaining experience and training in the shipping industry and gain successive promotions with increasing levels of responsibility. I hope to attain an upper management position and maybe tackle an overseas assignment.

SECTION 8

The Business Environment

Up to this point we have shown why economic systems exist and why the business firms within them come into being. We have also discussed the motivations of business people in a capitalistic system and have described the production, marketing, and financial functions of business. All of this takes place in an environment that can make the difference between success and failure.

Chapter 19 looks first at the environments related to business and how they change and interact. There follows, in the same chapter, a somewhat detailed examination of the various roles played by government as it relates to business. The active role of business in shaping government is discussed and basic business law concepts are introduced.

The more subtle effects of society itself on business are examined in Chapter 20. The effects of changing consumer tastes and evolving human values are included in the discussion. The role of technology is also treated in some detail. We will review the role of technological change in business competition and survival of the firm.

The subject of your career appears in the last chapter. Here we examine the job marketplace and the process of exploring it—selecting an industry and a geographic area as well as an occupation. There follows a discussion of how to evaluate yourself, and some detailed advice about how to conduct your job search. The chapter closes with some suggestions about how to make the final selection.

CHAPTER 19

Government and Business

OBJECTIVES:

After reading this chapter, you should be able to

1. Show how business creates part of the environment of society.
2. Explain how environmental influences are interdependent.
3. Give an example of at least three different roles played by government in the environment of business.
4. Name and describe the purpose of several federal administrative and regulatory agencies.
5. Explain the nature of antitrust activity.
6. Explain the concept of deregulation and its causes.
7. Differentiate between regressive and progressive taxes.
8. List and define the parts of a valid contract.
9. Discuss the basic ideas of agency and bailment.
10. Outline the main points of the laws of property.
11. Explain the significance of the Uniform Commercial Code to business.

KEY CONCEPTS:

Look for these terms as you read the chapter

environment

administrative law

voluntary compliance

consent order

antitrust laws

progressive tax

regressive tax

common law

statutory law

contract

agency-principal relationship

bailor-bailee relationship

real property

personal property

warranty

Uniform Commercial Code (UCC)

Supply side economics is one view of the way government relates to business and can affect the entire economic picture of a country. It has become associated with the Reagan presidency. What it means is that government should concentrate on encouraging business to grow and expand. It means reducing unnecessary restrictions on private decision makers by changing laws that restrict prices and that raise production costs. This applies particularly to some of those laws passed in the 1970s relating to ecology and safety. It also means reducing taxes in order to increase investment incentives. Government has the capacity to influence business in many ways.

The theory is that stimulating the supply side of the economy will create jobs and raise wages so that much of the direct benefits from government to the unemployed and the poor will become unnecessary. Whether this approach is working or not, the fact remains that government has a lot to do with the "climate" in which business operates. Decisions reached by Congress and the President at the national level, as well as those reached by state and local governments, can affect business profits.

Government laws, taxes, and regulations represent much of the environment in which business operates. Business itself, we will see, also represents much of the environment of society. Let's examine further this concept of environment.

WHAT IS AN ENVIRONMENT?

environment

The environment of something consists of all those things that come in contact with it and influence it. The influence can be direct or indirect. In some simple cases, such as that of the physical environment of a tree, the influences of soil, temperature, and moisture on tree growth are obvious. These environmental influences are independent of the quality of the seed from which the tree grows but they influence tree growth at least as much. Like trees, people depend greatly on their environment. The conditions under which you study for this course, especially for the fast-approaching final exam, will have much to do with your success. If you are disturbed by noise in the dorm, library, or home, or if lighting is poor, you may find it hard to review your notes or understand some of the reading. You may not be able to concentrate enough to accomplish your study goals.

The environment that helps determine success or failure of human activity is often much more complicated than the examples of tree growth or study efforts. Figure 19-1 indicates the complexity of the environment related to business success or failure.

Figure 19-1 suggests two important facts about environmental influences as they relate to business. The environments of business, government, society, and technology are dynamic and interdependent. They are dynamic in that change is continuous and, as modern experience proves, is occurring faster and faster as time goes by. They are interdependent in that a change in one environment usually results in a change in all of the others. There is a kind of chain reaction between and among them.

If we return to our introductory discussion of supply side economics, we can illustrate how the chain reaction might work. Suppose we start with government action—the relaxation of regulation of auto safety programs. This has an obvious first impact on the costs that car makers incur. This, in turn, has at least two effects on society. It may result in more car sales, which means more jobs for people in Michigan and other areas where cars are made, but it may also hurt society if car owners' safety is threatened and lives are lost. This original government action also reduces technological activity related to car safety and this, in turn, may lead to reduced employ-

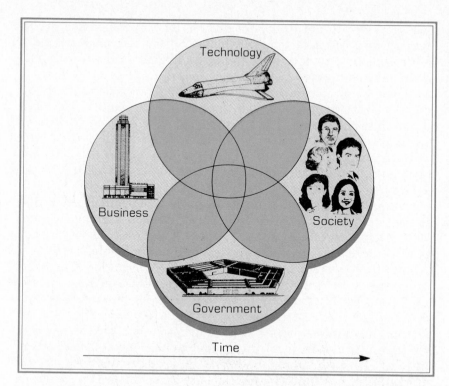

FIGURE 19-1

Interdependent and
dynamic environmental
factors: business,
government, society,
and technology

ment and social welfare among workers in the car safety equipment industries. The chain continues when injured drivers or displaced workers write their congressional representatives and (perhaps) the original laws are changed.

One of the wonderful things about environments which involve people is that people can fight back rather than remain passive victims of their environments. Business owners can react to high interest rates by writing their senators or even by supporting a presidential candidate's political campaign. Homemakers can lead boycotts against higher prices or unsafe products. Such environments are clearly *dynamic* and *interdependent*.

Business as Environment

How families and governments behave and whether they prosper are in part determined by the business environment. This means that millions of firms influence what people and governments do or don't do. If General Motors moves more of its engine manufacturing to Europe, U.S. unemployment rises and more households in this country must lower their spending levels. If the neighborhood phar-

Is the risk of unemployment too great to apply strict and costly pollution controls?

macy decides to open on Sunday, this increases shopping opportunities for customers. If a noisy foundry opens in a small town and nothing is done to control it, the quality of life of the town's residents may be lowered.

The Crown-Zellerbach Corporation, a large box and paper products manufacturer, decided to close two of its plants in the town of Bogalusa, Louisiana. The townspeople were very much affected when over 1,000 of the town's 18,000 citizens lost their jobs. Naturally, the workers' families, the grocery stores, the movie houses, the banks, the corner drug stores, and the schools—all aspects of the society—were affected by this business decision.

Why was the plant closed? The answer lies partly in the technological sphere and partly in the government sphere. Crown-Zellerbach management decided that the additional cost of meeting new air pollution standards set by the Environmental Protection Agency (EPA) would be too high for continued operation. Of course, other costs were rising too, including the cost of labor. Also, some of the plant's production equipment was becoming obsolete. The new EPA requirement was the "straw that broke the camel's back." All of this illustrates how business is an important part of society's environment, and how, in turn, the demands of the larger society (through the government framework) make up an important *societal* environment of business. More recent shutdowns led to the layoff of a substantial part of Bogalusa's city workforce including many police officers. Thus government—at the lower level—was seriously affected.

Government as Environment

Ours is one of the strongest and most flexible governmental systems ever created. Based on the Constitution, our federal government is divided into three branches—executive, legislative, and judicial. Laws are passed by the legislative branch—the Senate and House of Representatives. The judicial branch—headed by the Supreme Court and including lower federal courts—interprets the laws in light of the Constitution. It does this to decide whether an act performed by a business or citizen is lawful. The executive branch, headed by the President, provides leadership in government, including the national defense and enforcement of the law. It also introduces legislation to Congress. We call this threefold allocation of authority in government the "separation of powers." Similar separations exist at the state level.

Government serves two primary needs of society. First, it limits individual behavior that is thought to be contrary to the public interest. It does this by passing laws and setting up a system of justice and law enforcement. Second, it provides means of doing certain tasks that people could not perform very well alone or in small groups. These include military defense, basic health and sanitation services, water and recreation systems, schools, and a host of other services desired by the majority of citizens.

THE ROLES OF GOVERNMENT WITH RESPECT TO BUSINESS

The modern roles of government with respect to business are many. Among these are its roles as

- competitor
- economic stabilizer
- regulator
- supporter
- customer
- "housekeeper"

Government as Competitor

The two major political parties often differ on what government should do—how much it should regulate and how much it should compete with business. When a government "takes over" a service, it removes private business from that area of economic activity. The Tennessee Valley Authority (TVA), a major federal agency that produces electric power, is an example of this. When the TVA was established (during the depression of the 1930s), private industry was unwilling to risk the investment needed to provide electricity to some rural parts of the South.

Our railway system has changed from a strictly private system to one that is subject to substantial federal support and control because of the inability of private enterprise to operate the railroads (particularly passenger service) at a profitable level.

For some years now the system of the National Railroad Passenger Corporation (known as Amtrak) has operated most of the railroad passenger service in the United States. Lately it has been strongly criticized. Critics include Trailways and Greyhound, its private competitors, and the National Taxpayers Union, a private lobby against high government spending. The U.S. Department of Transportation has proposed large cutbacks in Amtrak trackage and service because of big deficits in its operation. There is also widespread criticism of the Postal Service; it is frequently compared unfavorably to its private competitors, such as United Parcel Service, Inc., Federal Express, and Purolator.

The government plays many roles with respect to business. As TVA or Amtrak, government is a competitor of private business. As the Small Business Administration, government is a supporter of private business. As a defense system, government is a customer of business. Government is also a regulator of business and a stabilizer of the economic environment of business.

Government as Economic Stabilizer

Ever since the Great Depression of the 1930s, our government has assumed increasing responsibility for the nation's economic welfare and stability. President Franklin D. Roosevelt's program of legislation, "the New Deal," reflected a new kind of economic theory developed by John Maynard Keynes, a theory that suggested a strong economic role for government.

Two laws which most clearly reflect the decision to have government play a strong role in the economy are the Employment Act of 1946 and the Humphrey-Hawkins Full Employment Act of 1978. The former declared federal responsibility to promote full employment, maximum economic growth, and price stability. It created the Council of Economic Advisers to help the President reach these goals. The council and the President are required to present an annual economic report to the nation, describing the state of the economy and current government programs to deal with it.

The Humphrey-Hawkins Act declared similar goals concerning employment, growth, and price stability and added goals concerning a balanced federal budget and an improved balance of trade. This act also differed from the 1946 act in terms of emphasis on economy in government and of primary reliance on the private sector. It also required the Federal Reserve Board (see Chapter 14) to report twice a year on its monetary policies and their relationship to the goals of the act.

Business people complain frequently about "undue government regulation and interference," but there is wide public support for a big economic role of the federal government in the business activity of the nation. No one really wants to risk another major depression. In fact, when a President has sponsored a bill to reduce government regulation, there is often as much opposition as support from business itself. The reason is that very often "one firm's regulation is another firm's protection." For example, strong opposition

Problems throughout the economy contributed to the Depression of the 1930s

by truckers and some unions arose following efforts to reduce regulation of the trucking industry.

Government as Regulator

Many kinds of business activities are affected by administrative law. Under this body of law, government officials—sometimes elected and sometimes appointed—act both as judges and as legislators. Some of the important administrative and regulatory agencies at the national level are described briefly in Table 19-1.

administrative law

The force of any agency is felt in several ways. Much is done by encouraging voluntary compliance to regulations. **Voluntary compliance means that the firm agrees to do what the agency advises without a hearing.** The Federal Trade Commission (FTC), for example, upon request of a firm, provides an advisory opinion on a particular practice. This clarifies for a business whether what it is doing is lawful.

voluntary compliance

The Federal Trade Commission also issues trade practice rules and trade regulation rules. The former are developed in conference with representatives of an industry and are purely advisory. The

---

POINT OF VIEW

Court Ruling Permits AT&T to Compete in Unregulated Market for Communications Services

In 1956 the American Telephone and Telegraph Company, the nation's largest corporation, signed a consent decree with the federal government. This decree barred AT&T from entering unregulated markets. In 1980 the Federal Communications Commission ruled that AT&T could compete in such areas as centralized answering services and national data-retrieval services.

The U.S. Department of Justice, chief guardian of U.S. antitrust laws, contested the FCC ruling in a federal district court and lost. The judge ruled in favor of AT&T, opening the way for their entry into these unregulated markets. The reasoning is that this operation will be quite separate from those operations of the giant firm which are protected from competition. Their actions in this new market will be regulated by the normal market force of competition.

The Justice Department and some small computer companies have argued that a regulated and protected "natural monopoly" like AT&T does not belong in the same competitive arena with the smaller firms. Smaller firms fear the possibility of abuse of monopoly power.

Agency	Major purpose
Interstate Commerce Commission (ICC), created in 1889	To regulate railroad rates. ICC jurisdiction extends to all forms of interstate public transportation with the exception of air carriers, pipelines for gas and water, and certain motor and water carriers operating in metropolitan areas.
Federal Trade Commission (FTC), created in 1914	To prevent unfair methods of competition and unfair or deceptive practices in interstate commerce, including false advertisements.
Federal Power Commission (FPC), created in 1920	To control the nation's water power resources and regulate interstate electric and natural gas utilities.
Securities and Exchange Commission (SEC), created in 1934	To oversee the operation of the securities exchanges and the issuance and sale of corporate securities.
Food and Drug Administration (FDA), created in 1938	To prohibit adulteration and misbranding of foods, drugs, devices, and cosmetics.
Federal Communications Commission (FCC), created in 1939	To regulate the broadcast media and communication carriers, including radio stations, telephone and telegraph companies, and, more recently, television broadcasting.
Equal Employment Opportunity Commission (EEOC), created in 1965	To settle complaints of discrimination in employment because of alleged bias in hiring, upgrading, salaries, and other conditions of employment.

TABLE 19-1

Some important administrative and regulatory agencies

consent order

latter can be used to bring a case against an alleged violator. The trade regulation rules are published and available to all competitors.

Once cases are instituted, the FTC will often settle informally if a firm agrees to discontinue a practice. If not, the FTC makes a formal complaint about the unfair method of competition or deceptive or monopolistic practice. **The firm may (this occurs in 80 percent of the cases) sign a consent order. This is an agreement to "cease and desist" a practice.** It avoids the need for further action by the commission. If the firm refuses to stop, a public hearing before an FTC examiner is held. The examiner reviews the facts and makes a decision which, in turn, may be reviewed by the full commission.

Whenever a firm has reason to believe that the agency has issued an erroneous order (one that does not accurately interpret the law under which the agency operates), that firm may bring the case before the appropriate Federal Circuit Court of Appeals and even to the U.S. Supreme Court.

Agency	Major purpose
Federal Aviation Administration (FAA), created in 1967	To regulate air commerce, to foster aviation safety; to promote civil aviation and a national system of airports; achieve efficient use of airspace and to develop a system of air traffic control and navigation.
Environmental Protection Agency (EPA), created in 1970	To set standards for and to enforce standards of quality in air, water, and other environmental elements.
National Highway Traffic Safety Administration (NHTSA), created in 1970	To improve the safety performance of motor vehicles, drivers and pedestrians. The Administration also publishes mandatory fuel economy standards for automobiles since the 1978 model year.
Occupational Safety and Health Regulatory Commission, created in 1971	To assure every working man and woman in the nation as safe and as healthful working conditions as possible.
Consumer Product Safety Commission (CPSC), created in 1972	To protect the public against unreasonable risks of injury from consumer products. It also helps consumers evaluate products for safety, develops uniform safety standards, and researches the causes and prevention of product-related deaths, illnesses, and injuries.
Nuclear Regulatory Commission (NRC), created in 1974	To assure that civilian use of nuclear materials and facilities is conducted in a manner consistent with public health and safety, environmental quality, national security, and the antitrust laws.

Some agencies have been attacked on the grounds that they are dominated by the industries they are supposed to regulate. The whole system of regulatory agencies has also been questioned. We are witnessing a strong trend toward deregulation.

The Deregulation Movement

According to testimony given at a U.S. Senate Hearing on Government Regulation (see Table 19-2) the typical corporation had to spend more than 238 hours each year filling out forms required by the federal government alone. State and local forms require many additional hours of paperwork. It has been estimated that the total cost of regulation to American business is over $65 billion each year.

The hearings from which Table 19-2 was drawn were part of a growing movement to do something about the heavy burden of government regulation, especially as it relates to business. In the Reagan

Agency	Form or Subdivision	Time to fill out form (hours)
Department of Commerce	Census of Manufactures	8.0
Office of Equal Employment Opportunity	Employer Information Report EEO-I	0.5
Federal Trade Commission	Division of Financial Statistics	0.8
Department of Labor	Log of Occupational Injuries and Illnesses	1.0
Department of Labor	Supplementary Record of Occupational Injuries and Illnesses	0.5
Department of Labor	Summary—Occupational Injuries and Illnesses	1.0
Department of Labor	Wage Developments in Manufacturing	0.5
Department of Labor	Employee Welfare or Pension Benefit Plan Description	1.0
Department of Labor	Employee Welfare or Pension Benefit Plan Description Amendment	1.0
Department of Labor	Employee Welfare or Pension Benefit Plan Annual Report	8.0
Department of Labor	Information on Employee Welfare or Pension Benefit Plan Covering Fewer than 100 Participants	—
Department of the Treasury	Federal Tax Deposits—Withheld Income and FICA Taxes	104.0
Department of the Treasury	Unemployment Taxes	12.0
Department of the Treasury	Employer's Annual Federal Unemployment Tax Return	3.0
Department of the Treasury	Employee's Withholding Exemption Certificate	—
Department of the Treasury	Reconciliation of Income Tax Withheld from Wages	24.0
Department of the Treasury	Report of Wages Payable under the Federal Insurance Contributions Act	64.0
Department of the Treasury	Return of Employee's Trust Exempt from Tax	1.0
Department of the Treasury	U.S. Information Return for the Calendar Year	3.0

TABLE 19-2

Federal government forms required of a typical corporation

administration, Vice-President Bush has headed a program aimed at furthering the progress of deregulation, a major campaign promise of the administration, and a key part of its economic strategy.

Deregulation has already made its mark on transportation—an

Subject	Description	Action
✓ Air bags and seat belts	To protect occupants in crashes, the air bag inflates on impact and the "passive" seat belts envelop passengers automatically on entering car. These devices were scheduled for 1983.	Rescinded
? Air pollution	Environmental Protection Agency seeks to soften emission standards. G.M. seeks a roll back to 1980 permissible emission levels.	Congress must act through revision of Clean Air Act
? Bumpers	Rules now require protection from damage at speeds up to 5 miles an hour. Proposal would lower speed to 2.5 m.p.h.	Safety agency considering 9 proposals
✓ Crash ratings	The results of crash tests at 35 miles an hour would have been required to be displayed on window price stickers on the various car models.	Rescinded
✓ Fuel economy	Federal standards on gas mileage expire in 1985. Officials were planning advance notice of proposed rule-making beyond that date.	Rescinded
✓ Speedometers	Proposed speedometer standards would have included calibration in miles per hour and kilometers. Measure also called for tamper-resistant odometers.	Rescinded
✓ Visibility	A ruling had been proposed to require minimum fields of direct view through the windshields of passenger cars and trucks.	Rescinded

FIGURE 19-2

The record: Major changes in auto deregulation

industry which for years was known as one of the most regulated of all industries. The first mode of transportation to be deregulated was the airlines. But what of the effects?

The price of air travel between some cities is lower than it was before deregulation because of fare wars (price competition) among the airlines. Although this benefits some passengers, there is another side. Some airlines have stopped serving the smaller communities they were required to serve under the old system of regulation. This complicates air travel for people in those communities who must now go to airports in larger cities. Other airlines have had serious financial problems, in part because of fare wars that reduced their revenues.

Lower profits disappoint both stockholders and employees. Stockholders get reduced (or no) dividends and employees' unions have agreed to wage freezes and/or cuts in order to help keep the airlines in business and to keep their members' jobs. Profitability problems have also contributed to mergers among some airlines while others have gone out of business.

After one year of the Reagan administration, the ailing auto industry hoped to derive significant economic benefits from deregulation. Removal of costly safety and anti-air pollution rules and standards seemed to promise the difference between profits and losses for the industry. As of the end of 1981, according to a General Motors executive, the efforts toward deregulation had not had much effect on cost reduction. Figure 19-2 summarizes the status of auto industry deregulation at that time. The most profit-sensitive issues—bumpers and air pollution—still required action by the regulatory agency or by Congress which was deliberating the Clean Air Act.

Government as Supporter

Whereas the government's roles as economic stabilizer and as regulator might be said to aid the economic system as a whole, some of its activities represent direct assistance to individual industries or firms.

Ever since the 1930s the American farmer has received direct aid from the federal government. Public funds administered by federal agencies are used to subsidize such crops as sugar cane, wheat, corn, cotton, peanuts, and oats. Annual payments to farmers, many of whom are large corporations, amounted to between one and four billion dollars annually in recent years. Public sympathy for this kind of subsidy depends in part upon the prices people have to pay for food at the supermarket. The most controversial of all such subsidies is the support program of the tobacco growers in the face of the health hazards associated with smoking.

Sometimes government support takes the form of a dramatic "bail out" of a large manufacturer that is in financial trouble. This occurred recently in the case of the Chrysler Corporation which was helped by a federal loan guarantee. Such aid was justified on the grounds that the failure of such a large firm would have had severe economic consequences including worse unemployment in an already troubled auto industry. Just a few years before, similar aid was given Lockheed Aircraft for much the same reason. These actions, in the form of loans or loan guarantees, were extraordinary and required special congressional action. Such actions represent a departure from the principle of free competition as originally conceived in capitalism (see Chapter 1).

As we saw in Chapter 17, the federal government supports business through the Small Business Administration in its various information, management assistance, and loan and loan-guarantee activities. These activities are justified on the grounds that small business is important to the American way of life and might not otherwise thrive or even survive the competition of big business. Special aid programs for minority enterprise were started in the 1960s. These were justified by the relative shortage of capital available to minorities and by the relative difficulty minority-owned firms were having in getting capital through normal financial market sources.

Government as Customer

The federal government is by far the single largest buyer of goods and services in the nation. Uncle Sam spends billions of dollars each year for everything from rockets to rubber bands. Naturally, almost every business in America wants a piece of this huge pie. As we have shown in Chapter 9 government purchasing systems are quite formal and carefully specified by law. These systems control roughly one fifth of all purchases in the country. It is important that businesses familiarize themselves with this huge market.

Big businesses, especially those firms that produce military hardware, have long been aware of the value of being sensitive to congressional debates over military budgets and have lobbied on a grand scale to influence their outcomes. Lobbying, as we saw in our discussion of labor activities in Chapter 7, is an accepted part of the legislative process, although it must be done according to the specifications of the Federal Regulation of Lobbying Act (1946). This law, among other things, requires that lobbyists be registered with Congress and sets limits on the favors they may offer lawmakers. Smaller businesses are protected against the power of big business lobbying by certain provisions of the public bidding laws. Business activities such as lobbying and attempts to influence regulatory agencies demonstrate the interactive nature of the government-business relationship.

Public bidding is a regular practice in government purchases of materials and services at the federal, state, and local levels. Figure 19-3 is a newspaper ad for a bid-invitation purchase process. Public bidding is designed to eliminate favoritism or political influence in the award of contracts. It also provides for economical use of public funds. For such a system to work well, widespread notice of the contract and bidding details must be given to as many prospective bidders as possible. In many cases, bidding systems provide "set aside" funds to guarantee participation by minority or small business competitors.

> THE Audubon Park Commission is accepting sealed bids for the construction of 3 carts to be used inside the Zoo to display Animal Artifacts. Bids will be opened on Friday, November 13, 1983 at 10 a.m. Detailed specifications can be obtained by calling Richard Roe at 555-6672.

FIGURE 19-3

A classified ad for bids on a construction contract for a local government agency

Should the Government Avoid the High Cost of Leasing?

WHAT DO YOU THINK?

The cost of leased office space used by the federal government has risen dramatically in recent years and opposition to this growth is rising. As shown in the figure below, it has risen from $459 million in 1977 to over $700 million in 1982. By 1985 the bill is expected to rise to $1 billion. U.S. Senate opposition to this rising trend has taken the form of a proposed law that will require that 60 percent of the federal work force occupy federally-owned buildings. In 1982 the percentage was only 52 percent, compared to 83 percent twenty years earlier.

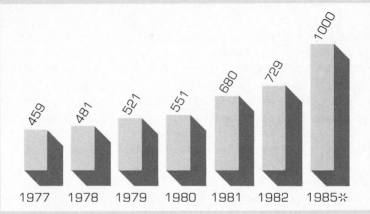

Supporting the Senate action is the General Services Administration (GSA), chief purchaser of non-defense material for the government. Studies by GSA indicate that federal construction is almost always cheaper than leasing. On the other side of the argument is the National Taxpayers Union, which feels that for the government to build rather than lease is wasteful and represents an admission that federal employment growth can't be avoided.

To place a limit on leasing would increase public ownership and diminish private ownership of the office building stock of the nation. At the same time, it might save the taxpayer money in the long run. Should the government avoid the high cost of leasing? WHAT DO YOU THINK?

Government as Housekeeper

Just as the government serves the average citizen it also serves the average business in the conduct of its everyday operations. Federal, state, and local governments provide a wide variety of services that make normal business operations possible. Cities and towns

Like many businesses, the government leases both office space and equipment

provide streets, lighting, sewers, sanitation and, most importantly, security for their grocery stores, insurance agencies, wholesalers, and factories. Cities or school districts provide educational opportunities for employees and their dependents. All of this, as we saw in Chapter 8, provides a climate which attracts or repels industry.

The federal government provides highways and postal services as well as a wealth of statistical data which helps business. The U.S. Censuses alone—including the *Census of Population*, the *Census of Housing*, the *Censuses of Retailing, Wholesaling and Selected Services*, the *Census of Manufactures*, and others—are of critical importance for planning and marketing research by businesses of all types.

Economic publications—including the *Annual Economic Report of the President* and the regular publications of the Federal Reserve system *(Federal Reserve Bulletin)* and the Department of Labor *(Monthly Labor Review)*—provide valuable insight into general economic conditions, financial summaries, and labor-related statistical information and commentary to thousands of businesses that could not otherwise afford it.

THE ROLES OF BUSINESS UNDER THE LAW

There are hundreds of ways in which the law affects today's businesses. We'll look at several such areas with an emphasis on law at the national level. We'll see that the law expects firms

- to compete
- to provide tax revenues
- to serve the consumer fairly

The Requirement of Competition

antitrust laws

Influenced by the economic theory of Adam Smith, the policy of our nation toward business for more than a century was one of laissez-faire, "hands off." Over time, it became obvious that laws were needed to keep businesses competing. Otherwise, one or several large businesses could take over and ruin competition in an industry. Such laws are called antitrust laws. (See Table 19-3.) **Antitrust laws are laws that try to get firms to compete against each other.** Unfortunately, there has never been a very clear agreement in Congress, in the courts, or among business people on how to define competition.

How well antitrust laws work is a tough question to answer. They place a big burden on many firms. This is because firms have to get involved in frequent legal battles. They also often lead to inefficiency. At the same time, however, many experts agree that they have helped to slow down or avoid the growth of monopoly power in some industries.

TABLE 19-3

Major antitrust laws

Legislation and date	Major purpose
Sherman Antitrust Act of 1890	The first of the general antitrust laws. It prohibits "every contract . . . or conspiracy in restraint of trade or commerce among the several states, or with foreign nations . . ." and names as illegal any act that monopolizes or attempts to monopolize any part of trade or commerce. The Antitrust Division of the U.S. Department of Justice enforces this act. Violation of the major provisions of the Sherman Act is subject to criminal penalties, including fines and prison terms. More common is the use of civil suits and "consent orders."
Clayton Act of 1914	Prohibits price discrimination, specific anticompetitive devices including tying contracts, interlocking directorates, and stock acquisitions that might substantially lessen competition.
Federal Trade Commission Act of 1914	Created a commission to consist of five members appointed by the President with the consent of the Senate. The commission was authorized to prevent persons and corporations, with the exception of banks and common carriers, "from using unfair methods of competition in commerce." If the commission finds after investigation that any person or corporation has engaged in any form of unfair competition prohibited by this act, the commission publishes a report of its

An experiment in improving antitrust enforcement has been tried in New England and in other areas. Under the New England program residents in five states can use a toll-free telephone number to let Justice Department attorneys know about suspected antitrust violations. Similar hotlines have also been established in Pittsburgh and Denver. The Pittsburgh hotline generated numerous antitrust complaints and led to several criminal and civil investigations into suspected antitrust violations.

Business as Taxpayer

Our Constitution gives the federal government taxing power in order to pay debts, provide for defense, and promote the general welfare. These three expense categories still dominate the budget. Figure 19-4 shows average income sources and outlays for the seven-year period from 1970 to 1976 and the estimates of the same data for 1984. National defense outlays dropped from 32 percent to 29 per-

Legislation and date	Major purpose
	findings and orders the offending party "to cease and desist from using such methods of competition."
Robinson-Patman Act of 1936: An Amendment to the Clayton Act	Updates and makes more explicit the price discrimination portion of the Clayton Act. Makes it illegal in interstate commerce to discriminate in price between different purchasers of commodities of like grade and quality or where the effect is to create a monopoly or injure competition for either the buyer or seller. This act also rules out certain specific forms of price discrimination such as disproportionate allowances for advertising and certain "commissions."
Wheeler-Lea Act of 1938: An Amendment to the FTC Act	Declares unlawful "unfair methods of competition in commerce, and unfair or deceptive acts or practices in commerce." False advertising is illegal if the article will injure the health when used as advertised or if the advertising was made with the intent to defraud or mislead the purchaser.
Celler-Kefauver Act of 1950: An Amendment to the Clayton Act	Substantially reduces the likelihood of monopoly in an industry by means of asset-acquisition merger. Since 1950, if the FTC thinks that the effect of acquisition of the stock or assets of one firm by another "may be substantially to lessen competition in any line of commerce in any section of the country," it may exercise its power to prevent it.

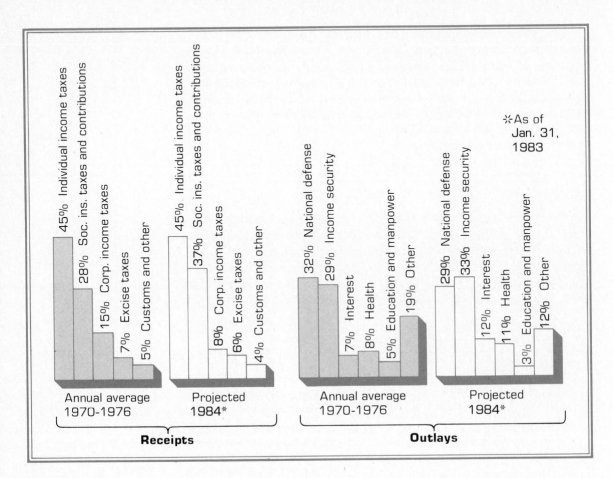

Federal receipts and outlays: 1970–1976 average and 1984 projection

cent of all outlays, despite a major upturn in defense spending in 1981. Income security programs rose from 29 percent to 33 percent and health programs from 8 percent to 11 percent. Education and manpower expenditures, however, are down from 5 percent to 3 percent of all outlays, while the rising interest rates and mounting public debt drove up the cost of interest on the national debt from 7 percent to 12 percent of all outlays.

In recent decades the major source of federal government revenue has been income tax. The federal income tax generated about 53 percent of the federal government's revenue in 1984, 45 percent from individuals and 8 percent from corporations. The current income tax law provides for progressive rates on the incomes of individuals and corporations. Corporations pay about one-fifth of all federal income tax. Additional income taxes are also levied by a majority of state governments and an increasing number of cities. **A progressive tax makes richer people pay a higher percent of their income than poorer people. The federal income tax is an example.**

progressive tax

AUTHORS' COMMENTARY

Value Added Tax as a Substitute for Income Tax

One of the simplest and fairest ways to tax people and business is a value added tax (VAT). This, in effect, is a national sales tax, and is used today in many nations all over the world. Compared to the present income tax with its complex deductions and depreciation provisions, VAT is very simple. Whenever something is sold, a certain percentage of the selling price is paid to the federal government.

It would require a fairly expensive organization and reporting system to see that it works—and works fairly. The odds are, however, that it would cost no more than the income tax to collect and administer. It would also be relatively "painless" in that millions of Americans would neither have to compute and pay income tax annually, nor see dollars withheld from their paychecks. Taxpayers would not have to worry about the threat of an audit of their returns, nor would they worry that wealthier people would find ways of avoiding taxation.

Some say that VAT is regressive and that it would be much too hard on the poor. This problem could be avoided by exempting basic commodities such as food and shelter from the VAT. Congress has strongly opposed the proposal for a value added tax, but unless the income tax is simplified and made more clearly equitable, more members of Congress may soon consider VAT a workable alternative.

Altogether, state governments rely most on sales taxes and next on gasoline and income taxes for their revenues. Cities most commonly use general property taxes and sales taxes. The latter are regressive. **A regressive tax means that poorer people pay a higher percent of their income than richer people.**

regressive tax

Businesses, labor unions, consumer groups, the poor, and many others demand government services. These services must be paid for with taxes. Taxes are compulsory payments. There is much controversy about their purposes and the best way to levy them.

Rarely does anyone feel happy about taxes. This is especially true of business owners. They spend large sums to find legal ways to avoid taxes and to influence the content and/or the final passage of new tax laws.

In the last few years we have witnessed in some states a large-scale taxpayers' revolt. The strength of the antitax movement was first made known in California with the passage of Proposition 13 in 1978. The proposition to cut back substantially on taxes in that state was overwhelmingly passed in a popular vote. The people were willing to cut back on state and local services in order to get tax relief. Since 1978, cutbacks in services have led to the return of some state taxes.

At the national level, Ronald Reagan's election in 1980 signaled that the average taxpayer was very unhappy. Sweeping tax reform was implemented with the Economic Recovery Tax Act of 1981. This law cut income taxes for all taxpayers starting with the 1981 tax liability and extending several years beyond. The tax cuts were viewed as an essential part of the supply side economic philosophy announced during Reagan's election campaign. The fact that the tax cuts passed the Congress reflected the continued mood of the general public in support of reductions in taxation and in federal spending. Since 1981, reversals of attitude toward taxation were considered when it became apparent that budget deficits were growing and strong resistance to cuts in Social Security and other domestic expenditures were being encountered. It is difficult to predict how successful or how durable the tax cuts of the early 1980s will be. Cuts in corporate taxes that encouraged businesses to expand are likely to continue to have public support only if the expansion (and the accompanying employment) actually come about.

Business as Servant of the Consumer

In Chapter 9 we introduced the marketing concept—the principle that business success is predicated upon satisfying the consumer. Many firms have adopted the marketing concept but there is ample evidence that not all consumers are satisfied. The formation of consumer groups like Ralph Nader's "raiders" and the passage of wide-ranging consumer-oriented laws such as the National Traffic and Motor Vehicle Safety Act and the Fair Packaging and Labeling Act during the 1960s and 1970s suggest that all consumers aren't satisfied with the goods and services they are getting. Further evidence lies in the dramatic shift away from some products made in the United States to competitive products from Japan, Germany, and other parts of the world. Domestic automobiles and television sets have been especially hard hit by rising acceptance of Japanese products.

If antitrust laws work reasonably well—that is, if reasonably effective competition exists, whether it comes from foreign or U.S.-based firms—the consumer will be better served. How well business serves the consumer will also be determined by the degree to which the consumer is informed. During the early 1960s President John F. Kennedy proclaimed "the basic rights of consumers" and these rights have been accepted as part of national policy since

Children's toys fall under the jurisdiction of the Consumer Product Safety Commission

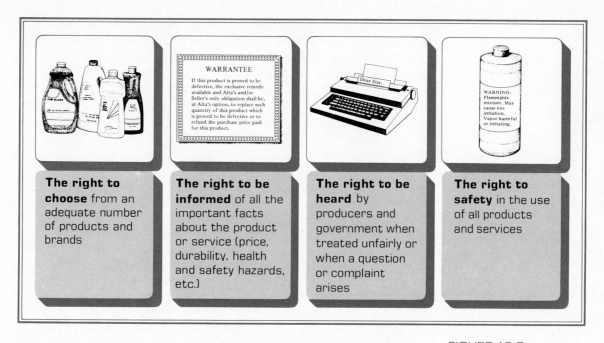

The right to choose from an adequate number of products and brands

The right to be informed of all the important facts about the product or service (price, durability, health and safety hazards, etc.)

The right to be heard by producers and government when treated unfairly or when a question or complaint arises

The right to safety in the use of all products and services

FIGURE 19-5
The basic rights of consumers

that time. These basic rights are the right to choose, the right to be informed, the right to be heard, and the right to safety. These rights are illustrated in Figure 19-5.

The rights of consumers are still recognized, but public enthusiasm for the consumer cause has waned somewhat in recent years. The philosophy of business freedom has, in some cases, prevailed over the philosophy of consumer rights. The 1980s marked the beginning of an era of belief in deregulation.

We have looked at a number of ways in which government and business interact. Our discussion would not be complete if we did not provide a brief overview of business law. This aspect of business has grown so important that many corporations have internal legal staffs the size of large law firms to advise them.

THE BROAD CLASSES OF LAW

There are two major broad classes of law, both of which form major parts of the environment of business. They are common law and statutory law. **Common law is built on precedents, or the previous opinions of judges.** These opinions are, in turn, developed from the customs and traditions of the people of the nation in which they develop. Where there is no explicit written law—statutory law—and

common law

where there has been an earlier case or earlier cases in which the point at issue has been decided by a court in the same legal jurisdiction, the decision (according to precedent) will be the same as that rendered in the previous case.

statutory law

The great majority of law today, however, is statutory law. This kind of law is written, or codified, by city councils, state legislatures, or the Congress of the United States. We have discussed many of the relevant federal laws earlier in this chapter.

BUSINESS LAW CONCEPTS AND INSTITUTIONS

An understanding of several basic legal concepts and institutions is important if we are to understand the judicial-legal aspects of government's impact on business. These concepts and institutions are:

- the law of contracts
- the law of agency and bailments
- the law of property
- the Uniform Commercial Code

The Law of Contracts

The interdependence of people in an advanced economy requires a great number of transactions and agreements among them. Sales transactions, for example, are often based on formal sales contracts. A partnership agreement is a contract that spells out responsibilities and rights of each of the partners. The law of contracts is basic to the right to own property.

contract

A contract is a mutual agreement between two or more people to perform or not perform certain acts. In order to be valid, a contract must include

- an agreement—an offer seriously and clearly made by one party (the offeror) to another party (the offeree) who must accept it seriously and clearly.
- consideration—the value that each party gets or gives. With few exceptions, it must be shown that both parties intended to bargain and have actually exchanged something for a contract to be enforceable by a court.
- competence—the ability to incur liability (debt) or to gain legal rights. A person who is insane or below a certain age (it varies

from state to state) may not be legally competent to make a contract.

- a legal objective—what a legal objective is depends on the law in the jurisdiction where the contract is made.

Businesses enter into contracts with suppliers for materials, customers for purchases, employees for employment, and with other persons and firms. A court will enforce a contract if it meets the requirements discussed above.

The Law of Agency and Bailments

An agency-principal relationship exists when one party (the agent) is authorized and consents to act on behalf of another (the principal). An agent must always act for the benefit of and under the control of the principal. The principal usually is liable for acts of the agent that come within the scope of the agent's authority.   agency-principal relationship

A common example of this relationship occurs when a firm sells some of its products through a manufacturers' agent. This person is not on the firm's payroll as a salesperson. He or she is an independent agent middleman. Suppose Paula Smith is a manufacturers' agent who sells $20,000 of auto parts to a garage on behalf of her principal, Acme Steel. Acme must deliver the parts as long as the contract between Smith and Acme is valid and it does not prohibit the action taken by Smith.

Another common business relationship is the bailor-bailee relationship. A bailor gives possession and control of his or her property to a bailee. The bailor, however, still owns the property. An   bailor-bailee relationship
example is a public warehouse that leases space to firms for storing their inventories. A bailment, therefore, is a transfer of possession without sale.

The Law of Property

In law, property means ownership of a thing, including the right to possess, use, or dispose of that thing. In one sense, it means the same thing as *title*. There are two main types of property:

- **real property—land and its permanent attachments, such as houses, garages, and office buildings.** Table 19-4 discusses several types of real property ownership.   real property

- **personal property—all property other than real property, such as furniture, clothing, cars, and bank accounts.**   personal property

In the sale of property, the question of warranty may become important. **A warranty is a representation, or a legal promise, made**   warranty

Joint tenancy	Two or more persons share title. Each has equal rights to use and enjoy the property during their lives. When one owner dies, the entire estate goes to the survivors, not to that owner's heirs. The last survivor is the full owner of the estate. Today, a joint tenancy also can be created in personal property. An example is a savings account in a bank.
Fee simple	A person is the owner in fee simple of real property when he or she owns the entire estate. The last survivor in joint tenancy has an estate in fee simple.
Tenancy in common	Two or more persons share title. Each tenant's share passes to his or her heirs at the tenant's death.
Community property	Property husbands and wives own together under the laws of community property states. In general, any property obtained through the efforts of both husband and wife becomes community property. Excluded are gifts and legacies to only one partner or property a husband or a wife owned before marriage. When a husband or wife dies, half of the property belongs to the survivor. Only the other half can be willed to others.
Life estate	An interest in property that is granted to or willed to a person that lasts only during the possessor's lifetime.
Future estate	Property owned but which cannot be enjoyed until some future time. Children own a future estate in property that their parents own but that will go to them upon their parents' death.

TABLE 19-4

Types of real property ownership

by the seller of a product that assures the buyer that the product is or shall be as represented by the seller.

There are two kinds of warranty: express warranty and implied warranty. An *express warranty* is a specific representation about the product that is made by the seller. For example, a label on a shirt that says "This garment is 50 percent cotton and 50 percent nylon" is an express warranty. An *implied warranty* does not state but suggests that all merchandise will perform satisfactorily. Suppose you buy a food blender and the motor burns out after one week's normal use. You could return the blender or keep it and sue for damages (legally demand payment for loss), even though no express warranty had been made.

In recent years, the Federal Trade Commission (FTC) has required sellers of products to provide clear and unambiguous warranties, for example, to specify the time period covered by the warranty and to spell out the meaning of the warranty. For most products you see today, the manufacturers offer limited warranties. Some guarantee their products against "defects of material or work-manship" for 30 or 90 days. Others go a lot further. Sears, for example, offers a one-year replacement guarantee (not just repair) on some of its appliances.

The Uniform Commercial Code

Many of the laws that pertain to business are state laws. A firm in interstate commerce must understand and conform to the laws of different states. If these laws were all uniform in content, coverage, enforcement, and so on, there would be little problem. But they are not uniform.

Efforts to bring some degree of uniformity to state business laws began in the 1890s. By the 1950s these efforts resulted in the establishment of uniform laws pertaining to such things as sales, bills of lading, partnerships, and negotiable instruments. Thus we had the Uniform Sales Act, the Uniform Bills of Lading Act, the Uniform Partnership Act, and the Uniform Negotiable Instruments Act. The problem was that not all states adopted all of these uniform statutes.

Effort, therefore, was directed to developing a uniform statute that would encompass all the various individual uniform acts. **The result was the Uniform Commercial Code (UCC). The UCC is a statute that combines and coordinates uniform acts into a single commercial code.** All states except Louisiana have adopted the UCC, which has reduced the problems firms face in interstate commerce.

Uniform Commercial Code (UCC)

The UCC, however, does not cover all areas of commercial law. The various states still do rely on precedent (common law) in solving some commercial disputes. For example, the code provides that it shall be supplemented by the principles of law that pertain to capacity to contract and fraud.

SUMMARY AND LOOK AHEAD

Environments of business are dynamic and interdependent. Government and business are especially interdependent. Government plays several roles in the life of business. Government is a competitor, an economic stabilizer, a regulator (sometimes a deregulator), a supporter, a customer, and a housekeeper for business. The government expects business to compete, to pay a large tax bill, and to serve the consumer. Its expectations in all three areas are changing. We have reviewed in this chapter the major concepts and institutions of business law, with particular reference to the law of contracts and the law of property.

In the following chapter, we turn our attention to the impacts of social change and technology on the sphere of business. We will see how changes in population characteristics, social values, and scientific discovery intrude on the decision-making process in business.

FOR REVIEW . . .

1. What is an environment? Give an example.
2. Give an example of the federal government's role as a competitor of business.
3. What did the Employment Act of 1946 do to the role of government in the economy?
4. Describe the way the FTC deals with an antitrust case.
5. What proportion of total federal income tax revenue is paid by corporations?
6. Give two examples of consumer impact on specific corporations in the last eight years.
7. List and discuss the requirements of a valid contract.
8. What is an agency-principal relationship?
9. Distinguish between real property and personal property.

. . . FOR DISCUSSION

1. How did the 1980 national elections affect the government-business relationship?
2. Give an example of how government can affect the success or failure of a neighborhood grocery. Discuss the chances that the grocer has to prevent this influence.
3. Discuss both sides of the argument regarding the regulation of business in regard to pollution control.
4. Why does consumerism exist at the same time that firms practice the marketing concept?

INCIDENTS

The Great Compute-off

Late in 1982 a decision was scheduled to be made in Montgomery, Alabama concerning a computer contract with the U.S. Air Force. Award of a contract worth about half a billion dollars was to be made based on a competition between Sperry Univac Division of Sperry Corporation and Burroughs Corporation. Ten years earlier the Air Force was embarrassed by the fact that it purchased a major computer system without sufficient advanced testing and later found that its technicians could not program it. As a result the Air Force has subjected Burroughs and Sperry to the same kind of trial as competing fighter plane contractors. In this case, they were to design and demonstrate their versions of the Air Force's "Phase IV" computer system.

Each of the two firms must rewrite 1.3 million lines of Air Force programs to make them compatible with their own systems. The winner will install computers at more than 100 bases all over the world. This constitutes a real innovation in government purchasing of capital equipment from private suppliers.

QUESTIONS

1. Does this procedure eliminate the problem of lobbying? Why or why not?
2. How do you suppose the contract decision would be made if the two systems were judged to be equally competent?
3. How does this role of government as customer conflict with the performance of any of its other roles?

The Audubon Society's Energy Plan

The National Audubon Society, long a defender of nature and ecology, has come up with a proposal for a major shift in energy dependency for the U.S. which could have significant impact on the way we do business.

The plan for the year 2000 calls for 28 percent of our energy to come from coal (20 percent in 1980) and 39 percent to come from oil and gas (69 percent in 1980). It also calls for substantial increases in the share of energy to be derived from solar renewables, such as biomass, solar collectors, and windpower.

QUESTIONS

1. Assuming the federal government accepted the Audubon Energy Plan in its entirety, what are some of the major ways that businesses would be affected?

2. How could the government implement such a plan?

3. If you were in the oil business, how would you react?

CHAPTER 20

Society, Technology, and Business

OBJECTIVES:

After reading this chapter, you should be able to

1. Show how businesses can deal with change.
2. Describe population growth and regional shifts from 1970 to 1980.
3. Describe the major projected changes in the United States' birthrate, income distribution, educational attainment, and sex composition of the workforce.
4. Give examples of the impact of the changing population on business planning.
5. Discuss changes which have occurred in American values since 1900.
6. Distinguish between the traditional business ethic and the professional-managerial ethic.
7. Evaluate the potential for public-private partnerships in solving social ills.
8. Show how our nation has adjusted to the energy shortage.
9. Show how changing technology affects the need for businesses to plan.
10. Define the military-industrial complex and show how it relates to research and development in the United States.

Mr. Yamazaki, senior executive managing director of the Yamazaki Machinery Works, Ltd., points toward a cavernous factory in which giant computerized machines—each with a pair of yellow tool drums that resemble enlarged roulette wheels—are grinding, boring, and fashioning parts for high-technology machines like themselves.

"Robots making robots" is the catch-phrase used to describe the process here. Only a few human workers are involved; they direct cranes that load metal castings onto fixtures that are then wheeled automatically to a storage area.

On the night shift, the machines work unassisted. The place is rather dimly lit. One solitary human sentinel—the night watchman—patrols the factory floor armed with a flashlight as the machines labor on, milling metal castings weighing several tons and moving them about the plant.

The startling leap forward in Japanese robot technology has given U.S. business leaders reason to reappraise their international competitive position in many markets. This same kind of concern exists in some U.S. industries when their domestic competitors make technological advances.

History shows that huge industries have collapsed because of failure to keep abreast of new ideas and inventions. What often causes this failure is a kind of "marketing myopia" among managers. They are overconfident about their products. This is compounded when they don't spend enough on research for new products.

In this chapter we discuss the fact that no business can afford to ignore its social and technological environments. We examine social changes and how they may affect a firm's ability to produce and sell at a profit. We also review the continuing technological revolution and what it implies for business planning, research, and development. We also examine the important area of social responsibility.

HOW BUSINESS DEALS WITH CHANGE

"blue skies" unit

Successful businesses recognize that they cannot survive if they take only a passive role with respect to their environments. Businesses develop many strategies to deal with social and technological change. Some establish "blue skies" units within the firm. **A "blue skies" unit is a special unit or committee responsible for bringing new ideas about the operations of a firm to its management.** This can include new products, policy or organizational changes, or anything new that is perceived to put the firm in touch with the future. Such a unit usually reports directly to the firm's president and is protected from retaliation by others within the firm who might be threatened by the suggestions for change. Many large firms use the services of "think tanks" such as the Rand Corporation for major future-oriented problem-solving. Still others depend upon management consulting firms or advertising agencies. It is expected that the unique position of such "blue skies" thinkers will give them an unbiased and fresh view of how to meet the changing demands of the public and the evolving faces of competition.

technology forecasting

A special technique used to deal with the dizzying rate of technological change—especially in high technology industries such as defense, electronics, energy, and medicine—is called technology forecasting. This involves gathering and interpreting all evidence of scientific advances in a field by reading scientific journals and attending scientific and technological conferences. Specially-trained experts interpret this evidence to diagnose the direction of technological change that will affect the future of the firm they work for.

Some scientific and fashion-related industries practice industrial espionage, some forms of which are unlawful. Security measures, often as elaborate as those practiced by the U.S. State and Defense Departments, are used to protect a private firm's trade secrets. Because new ideas are often the life's blood of a firm and because they are very expensive to develop, security programs are essential.

We turn now to a description of those characteristics of our society that business decision makers will be watching as signals of relevant change in the environment of business.

CHANGING CHARACTERISTICS, VALUES, AND LIFESTYLES

When Alvin Toffler wrote the book *Future Shock*,[1] he told Americans what they should have been aware of already—that our society is going through a process of change which is ever more rapid. Many of these changes affect even our most fundamental institutions—motherhood, education, the family, work, and religion. One way of measuring such changes is to examine reports of the changes in our population and its characteristics.

Changes in the Population and Population Characteristics

One central indicator of economic growth is the nation's population. As shown in Figure 20-1, the population grew from 152 mil-

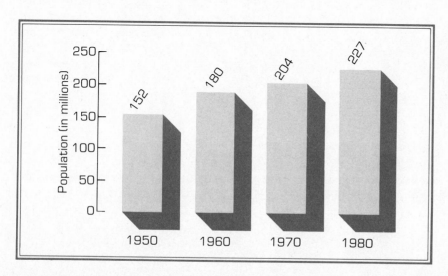

FIGURE 20-1

Total population of the United States, 1950–1980

Next time you're in the checkout line, look around. That's your intermarket.

Shoppers in today's marketplace don't sort out as neatly as they do in the marketing plan. Just look at all the different customers reaching for your products these days.

There's the traditional four-member, working-father family (although now only 7% of all households and not the market it used to be). And the growing number of working women. Men with major shopping responsibility (nearly one-fourth of all principal supermarket shoppers). Teenagers with family influence and buying power of their own. Two-paycheck couples. Students. Singles of all sorts.

It makes you wonder if the people who talk about narrow demographic targeting ever went through a checkout line. If you follow their thinking and narrow your sights, you'll probably limit your sales.

To compete in the '80s, you need to reach your intermarket: all those diverse but significant groups that make up your total market.

TV Guide will make intermarketing work for you. With TV Guide as a base, you'll cover your top priority audience. By the millions. And then go on to reach your next most important group in the checkout. And the next. And the next. All the groups that together could put a smile on just about any sales curve.

TV Guide's editorial pages attract nearly 38 million adult readers each week. Plus 8.8 million teenagers (12-17) with lots of buying power. And TV Guide reaches more audience at home than any other magazine, right where so many shopping decisions are discussed and made.

Intermarketing in TV Guide makes sense. See for yourself the next time you're in a checkout line.

TV GUIDE
TRIANGLE PUBLICATIONS, INC.

TV GUIDE: THE WAY TO REACH YOUR INTERMARKET.

TV Guide® and the TV Guide logo are registered trademarks of Triangle Publications, Inc.

Businesses must stay alert to changes in family makeup and characteristics

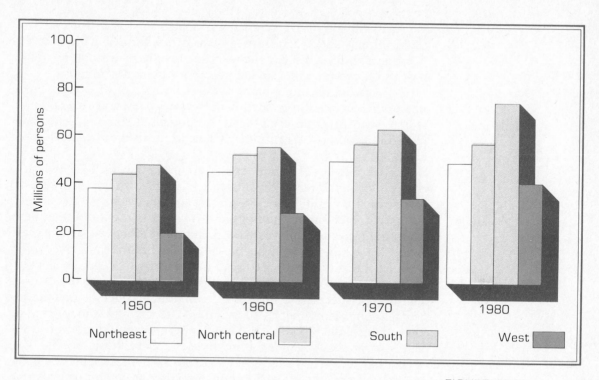

FIGURE 20-2

Population of the United States by region, 1950–1980

lion in 1950 to 227 million by 1980. The rate of growth since 1970 was 1.1 percent per year, far less than the 1.3 percent rate of the 1960s and the 1.7 rate of the 1950s. Decline in the growth rate generally means slower growth of the market for necessities, especially among basic goods and services for children, and it has important implications for the workforce. As we will see later, the effect of slower population growth on the demand for luxury products depends on income and its distribution.

On a geographic regional basis, the population changes are quite uneven. Figure 20-2 shows how the Sunbelt has grown consistently and rapidly, in contrast to the Northeast and the North Central regions. Since 1970, the North Central states gained only 4 percent and the Northeast less than 1 percent, while the South gained 20 percent and the West nearly 24 percent. States with huge gains include Florida and Texas, which gained 43 percent and 27 percent respectively. The State of New York and the District of Columbia lost population in the 1970s. New York lost nearly 4 percent of its population and the District lost nearly 16 percent in just 10 years!

The latest census data also show that rural and small town population grew during the preceding decade for the first time since 1950. Urban population grew from 149 to 166 million—about 11 percent—and rural and small town population grew from 53.9 to 59.5 million—about 10 percent—during the 1970s. The lower levels of crime, pollution, traffic, and taxation, together with simpler, more peaceful lifestyles, are drawing people to the nonurban areas.

These dramatic population shifts mean a great deal to businesses that are planning location of factories, warehouses, and retail stores. Such data can easily lead to removal of some facilities and addition of others by firms that think in terms of a national operation.

net annual household formation

For producers of durable goods (home appliances, TVs, and cars, for example), and marketers of services (homeowners' insurance or lawn care, for example) a crucial market guidepost is net household formation. **Net annual household formation is the number of new households formed in a year less the number dissolved in that year.** Figure 20-3 shows that, although the absolute number of households has continued to climb, the net annual formation began to slacken in recent years. This fact has deep meaning for thousands of business planners because the demand for household products is mainly dependent on the number of households. The size and composition of these households is also vital to planning for production of thousands of products ranging from houses to breakfast cereals. The formation rate is a function of marriages, divorces, and changing patterns of separate living for young unmarried and for widows and widowers.

Figure 20-4 portrays some of the trends that have altered the traditional concept of family household. Married couples represented a sharply declining proportion of all households from 1960 to 1980. At the same time, the number of divorced persons per 1000 married persons (with spouse present) rose from 35 to 100, and the number of unmarried couples living together rose from half a million in 1970 to over one and a half million in 1980.

FIGURE 20-3

Households and household formation

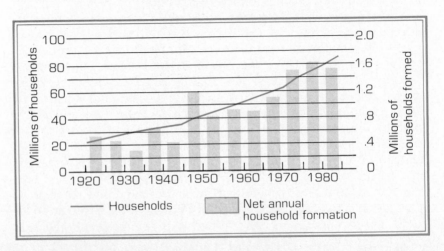

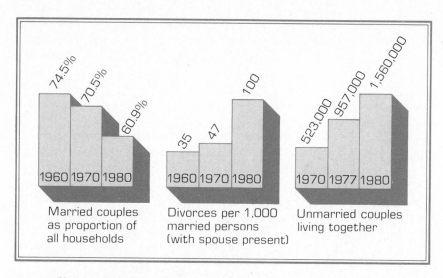

FIGURE 20-4
Changing patterns of
marriage and divorce

74.5% 70.5% 60.9%

1960 | 1970 | 1980

Married couples
as proportion of
all households

35 47 100

1960 | 1970 | 1980

Divorces per 1,000
married persons
(with spouse present)

523,000 957,000 1,560,000

1970 | 1977 | 1980

Unmarried couples
living together

All these changes will affect the demand for goods and services related to housing and housekeeping. Suppliers of these goods and services cannot ignore their meaning.

The Birthrate and Age Distribution

Another important dimension of our population is its age distribution. The "baby boom" that lasted for almost two decades after World War II translates into a very large number of young adults in the 1980s. The birthrate (births per 1000 women aged 15–44) fell from more than 100 in 1960 to between 62 and 67 since 1975. Despite a slight upturn recently, the birthrate is expected to remain well below that of the postwar period. One out of every five women of childbearing age is childless and that number is growing. **The United States is very close to realizing ZPG—zero population growth—the birthrate that stabilizes the population level.** This trend affects the demand for goods and services, especially schools, food, and children's clothes.

zero population growth (ZPG)

Population shifts—
especially to the
Sunbelt and nonurban
areas—create
business opportunities
for manufacturers of
recreational equipment

Another trend that helps explain the age distribution of the population is the increasing longevity of our citizens. (See Figure 20-5.) Not only are people living longer but their later years are becoming healthier and more active because of somewhat higher incomes and Medicare. The elderly are organizing to put political and economic pressure on businesses. One of their main goals has been to combat the trend toward early retirement. They want to keep their jobs longer. In a sense, then, senior citizens are competing for jobs against you and other younger entrants into the job market.

The antidiscrimination movement has already resulted in better treatment for elderly job seekers. Recent changes in the Age Discrimination in Employment Act of 1967 have made it possible for people to postpone retirement past age 65 if they want to do so. The changes prohibit employers of 20 workers or more from forcing workers to retire before age 70 if they are capable of performing their jobs.

There are other by-products of the trend toward longer lives. For example, the construction industry will need to answer the demand for new types of housing to meet the needs of older people. Growing elderly markets are already resulting in the use of older people in ads and more careful marketing treatment of this important group of the population. Anticipating longer retirement periods, workers and their unions will probably begin to emphasize

FIGURE 20-5

Longevity in the United States

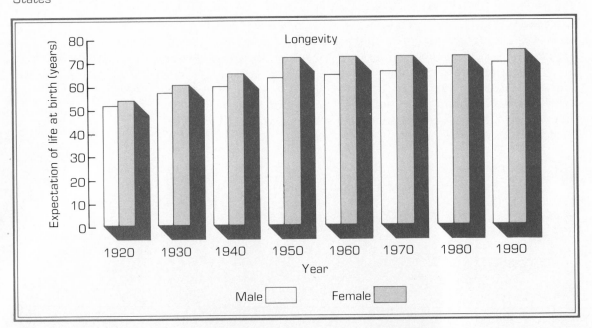

better retirement plans when they negotiate collective bargaining agreements.

Rising Education Level

The level of educational attainment has always been a major factor to consider in business planning. Figure 20-6 shows the numbers of people over 25 who have reached or who are predicted to reach various levels of education. It shows that the number of persons with only an elementary education is declining steadily and is expected to do so through the first half of the 1980s. It also shows that the numbers in all three higher educational groups are rising. By 1985, it is predicted, more than 90 million people will have a high school diploma but no college, and there will be between 20 and 25 million persons in each of the "some college" and "college graduate" categories. This fact is important for business both in terms of the labor force that will be available and in terms of the tastes of future customers.

The Income Dimension

When business managers examine the characteristics of the population to help them make better decisions they pay special attention to income. As we have seen in previous discussions about establishing wage rates (Chapter 6) and about marketing research (Chapter 9), managers need to know about the level and the distribution of income.

Chapter 2 introduced a table (Table 2-1) tracing the level of median family income in recent years. That table shows that the real spendable income of the "average" family actually declined about 10 percent between 1972 and 1980. Taxes and inflation more than

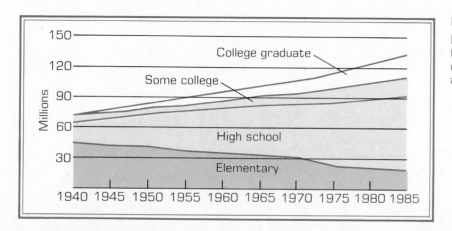

FIGURE 20-6

Educational attainment (years of school completed, persons 25 and over)

absorbed the substantial growth in pre-tax dollars received. On the average, then, it appears that the average family's standard of living stopped growing during the 1970s.

For those firms that produce or sell consumer goods, especially luxury goods, a continuation of this trend means that future sales growth will require a more vigorous marketing effort. It certainly should lead managers to examine the *distribution* of income in their geographic markets. The income level (measured by the median) tells only part of the income story. The distribution is even more significant for market planning. The distribution among households across the nation for the year 1981 is shown in Table 20-1. Similar tables are available from the Census for regions, cities, and states.

Table 20-1 shows, for example, how many households (as a proportion of the more than 83 million households in the nation in 1981) received income in the amount of less than $10,000 and how many received $50,000 or more. Firms selling luxury cars are much more interested in the upper part of the income distribution. Contractors who might build low-cost government-supported housing would be more interested in the numbers of households in the lowest income brackets. Between these extremes of income lie the great bulk of American households. The numbers of households in each income category have meaning for different groups of firms.

If you were a builder of middle-income homes—like U.S. Home—and you were planning construction of 100 homes in Baton Rouge, Louisiana, you would not do so until you had determined the household income needed to purchase, for example, an $80,000 home or a $100,000 home. You would also need to determine how many households with the appropriate income level reside in the city and how many of these are ready to purchase a new home. The income distribution is only part of the needed information, but it is essential for firms selling consumer goods.

TABLE 20-1

Household income distribution, 1981

Income level	Percent of all households
Less than $10,000	25.4
$10,000–19,999	26.7
20,000–29,999	21.1
30,000–39,999	13.1
40,000–49,999	6.5
50,000 or over	7.2

From the tangible characteristic of income we now turn to some of the more subtle human characteristics that are important to business decision makers. We will focus especially on what is happening to the things that our people think are important—their values.

Changing American Values

Anyone who has observed life in the U.S. since this century began can testify that we don't think quite the way we used to think. Even in the last three decades, the changes in values are startling.

The Protestant Ethic

As we saw in Chapter 1, the Protestant ethic is a set of beliefs that dominated the lives of this country's people at the time we became a nation and that still plays a role today. It entails a strong sense of duty and self-discipline and places great value on hard work, thrift, and self-control. The Protestant ethic flourished throughout the nineteenth century, reinforced the profit motive, and played an essential role in building the economic power of the United States. It helped make the most of two scarce commodities—labor and capital. A variety of events in this century—two world wars, a great depres-

---

WHAT DO YOU THINK?

Is Our Culture Ready for Humiliation Elimination, Inc.?

One of the most interesting examples of the application of old-fashioned entrepreneurship to an era of self-indulgence is alive and well in Washington, D.C. The idea is simple. If your car is towed away for a parking violation and your credit card is good for it, all you have to do to avoid the humiliation and inconvenience is to call Humiliation Elimination, Inc.

For a fee they will (a) send someone to the city department of transportation to stand in line and pay the ticket or tickets and towing charge; and (b) send out a limousine, complete with chauffeur, champagne, and crabmeat hors d' oeuvres to take you at a leisurely pace over to the auto pound to retrieve your vehicle.

The owner-founder of Humiliation Elimination, Inc. is planning expansion to several other major cities whose parking enforcement programs are vigorous and annoying to the affluent. What does this tell us about the Protestant ethic in today's culture? What does it say about the responsiveness of the capitalist system? Is our culture ready for Humiliation Elimination, Inc.? WHAT DO YOU THINK?

sion, expanded communication networks, and (until the 1970s) growing economic abundance—have helped dilute the force of the Protestant ethic.

Debt, leisure, and self-indulgence are no longer considered sinful. Rather, they seem to be a major part of our national character today. Advertising slogans like "When it's time to relax," "You deserve a break today!," and "Easy credit terms!" would not have been used in the previous century. Recent political changes, however, suggest that there is still some of the Protestant ethic around. Whether there is enough to bring about a serious return to more conservative values is hard to predict. If this does happen it will certainly influence the choice of advertising themes and slogans, the use of credit, and the variety of goods and services offered for sale by business.

The Role of Women

Closely tied to the Protestant ethic was the idea that "a woman's place is in the home." The shortage of men during World War II led to a major change in our society's acceptance of women in the labor force. More recently, the Women's Rights Movement, backed up by legal protection of women's rights in the courts, has had significant impact on the economic role of women in America.

Women are playing an increasing and more complex role in the labor force and in management. More women are working, and a greater percentage of them are working in managerial and professional jobs. They are also spending a greater part of their lives in the labor force. Women's impact on business from the inside is growing while their impact on household decisions decreases.

The entry of greater and greater numbers of women into the workforce (see Figure 20-7) has had some interesting effects. For one thing, it has increased the pressure for more flexible working hours (see Chapter 6) to accommodate women who have family duties as well as their employment to cope with. The states of California and Wisconsin have experimental projects in "job sharing," which allow two workers to share one job, one salary, and one set of benefits. Working wives have led to changes in store hours, lower PTA attendance, and higher family incomes. Some firms are providing day-care facilities, too. In recognition of the complementary changes occurring in the role of men, some firms are giving husbands "paternity leave" to help with the arrival of a child in their family.

Today, many women are having fewer children and they are spending less time with their children and less time shopping. This means kids learn more (including product preferences and lifestyles) from their friends and from TV. Others (husbands and older children) are doing a greater part of the job of "purchasing agent" for the

Increases in the number of working mothers have led to more company-sponsored day-care centers

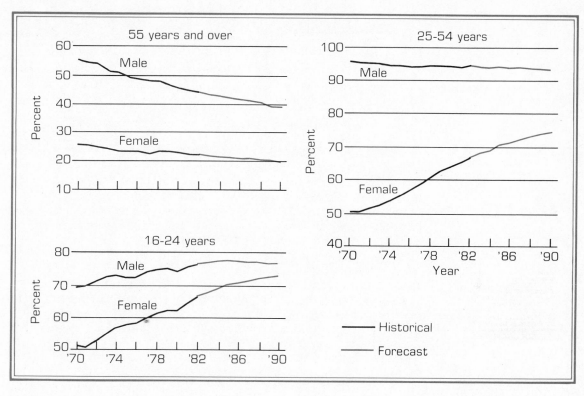

FIGURE 20-7

Proportion of men and women in the labor force

family. TV advertisers have to think about influencing these husbands and children who share in the shopping chore. An ad for Stove
Top Stuffing features teenagers preparing the meal; other food ads
show husbands doing the grocery shopping.

Changing Consumer Tastes

Despite efforts to influence their customers, firms have often found
them independent and resistant to change. Even the most carefully
planned marketing programs have gone astray. Moviegoers, for example, rejected the first version of the film *Heaven's Gate* and later
rejected a radically-changed second version despite a major promotion effort. Certain fashion designers have invested fortunes in
promoting this "look" or that and found no takers.

The American consumer can be stubborn and unpredictable.
Knowing this to be the case, modern firms maintain expensive marketing information systems to reduce the chance of error in predicting taste changes. Procter & Gamble has devoted great effort toward
understanding consumer reactions to its products. When sales of
Pringle's Potato Chips did not meet expectations P&G researched

Changes in the
Worker-Nonworker
Ratio

Some call it the economic dependency ratio. It is the number of people who work divided by the number who don't. Over the long run it can be changed by changes in working customs, by changes in labor-related laws, and by changes in the age distribution of the population. If worker productivity remains constant, this ratio is the main factor in determining the welfare of a nation.

Current trends indicate a continued rise in the worker-nonworker ratio so that workers will be supporting relatively fewer nonworkers in the next few years. Nonworkers tend to be at the two extremes of the age distribution. The number of children is expected to decline sharply and the increase in the number of older people is not enough to compensate for this. Changes in retirement laws have also slowed the rate of retirement of older people. The growing number of two- and three-earner families is also a factor.

Unless continued high unemployment levels lead to legislation restricting employment of teenagers or any other major segment of the labor force, or unless the birthrate turns around radically, the worker-nonworker ratio will continue to grow until about the year 2015 when products of the baby boom of the 1950s and 1960s begin to reach retirement. At that time, things will reverse themselves and the worker-nonworker ratio will decline rapidly.

the problem and made some changes in the product and its advertising. They turned to greater emphasis of the product's "natural" qualities because this was what their customers wanted.

Looking to the future, two New York ad agencies studied the direction consumer tastes are taking. The two agencies—Leber Katz Partners and Brain Reserve—found that the trend is toward quality buying. Consumers are willing to pay more for a product that "is first-rate, reliable and that makes them feel that they're leading quality lives." We hear clothing firms promoting "investment dressing" and see an attempt on the part of the U.S. auto makers to build more quality into cars. Consumers are looking for integrity rather than status. The implication of this finding is far-reaching if it is correct. We can expect an upgrading of quality control, an increasing emphasis on durability, and less superficial advertising appeals. The chances are that all of this will be accompanied by higher prices and greater dependence on a high-quality retail sales effort.

While firms must spend time and money to monitor customers' tastes they must also be sensitive to the long-run good of society as a whole. The social upheavals of the 1970s served notice to the large corporations that they must review their roles with respect to the public interest.

THE SOCIAL RESPONSIBILITY OF BUSINESS

Opinion regarding business's rightful role in the solution of social ills ranges widely. Two general positions have been taken, however, and we will examine them in turn.

The Traditional Business Ethic

Two of the obvious ways that business has always affected society are by creating employment and by producing useful goods and services. Most people agree that these are the basic responsibilities of business to society. Under our modified capitalist system, as we saw in Chapters 1 and 2, businesses take risks by investing in plants and equipment. They do this mainly to make profit, but in the process they create jobs.

This function of business in society is a basic part of the traditional economic theory of capitalism. Job-creation is an important by-product of the motive for profit which underlies the capitalist risk taking. **The traditional business ethic, then, says that business owes it to society only to seek profit. In so doing it creates jobs and produces goods and services.** This position has dominated our business climate for many decades. It is still supported widely by associations such as the Chamber of Commerce of the United States, and most small and medium-sized firms still feel pretty much this way.

traditional business
ethic

Traditional business ethic	Professional-managerial ethic
1. Maximum profits	1. Satisfactory long-term profits; other values are weighed
2. Minimum government control	2. Government-business "partnership"
3. Protectionism	3. Internationalism
4. Stockholder-oriented	4. Serves several masters including stockholders, customers, citizens, and employees

TABLE 20-2

Comparing the assumptions of two ethics in business

This ethic usually also calls for minimum government control of business, and it serves the interest of the business's owners or stockholders almost exclusively. It also tends to favor protective tariffs for American products. All in all, it is rather conservative and is in sharp contrast to the professional-managerial ethic (see Table 20-2).

The Professional-Managerial Ethic

professional-managerial ethic

The professional-managerial ethic[2] has become accepted in recent years by an increasing number of the largest corporations. It holds that managers represent the interests of stockholders, customers, employees, and the general public. Decisions are weighed in terms of longer-range company welfare, not immediate profit. Also, it is assumed that usually what is good for the employees and the general public is good for the company. For example, a firm that participates voluntarily in training and hiring the disadvantaged may not expect increased profits to result in the next year or two. However, the firm may expect that such activity will pay off in the long run. The society gains, and a stable, healthy society is presumed to have long-run beneficial effects on the firm. There are also indirect benefits in the form of good public relations from such activities.

Yet another important part of this ethic is the belief in a cooperative partnership relationship between business and government instead of the traditional hostility. This thinking fosters business participation in solving social problems.

The Changing Responsibility of Business

Business's attitude toward its social responsibility has changed dramatically in recent years. As we saw in the preceding section, the

Local McDonald's® Restaurants help fund over 30 Ronald McDonald Houses™ for families with children being treated for cancer-related diseases

prevailing ethic among large businesses has shifted from the traditional view that the only responsibility to society is that which springs from the profit motive to the broader professional-managerial ethic which recognizes social obligations. One of the more interesting and promising views of the role of today's business as a social problem solver is that of the public-private partnership.

The Committee for Economic Development (CED) has made a good case for a public-private partnership to attack the problem of finding jobs for the hard-to-employ. This activity can take many forms but it means drawing on the special experience of private businesses, unions, and community organizations to join with government in solving social problems such as finding jobs for the hard-to-employ.[3]

public-private
partnership

CHANGING TECHNOLOGY

The high standard of living that modern Americans enjoy depends on our desire and ability to pursue the benefits of technology. **Technology is the application of science so that people can do entirely new things or do old things in a better way.** Technology created a new home computer for the household and satellites that have revolutionized world communications.

technology

What Is Technological Progress?

Technological progress results in improvements in the state of industry, manufacturing, and commerce. For example, Boeing's 757 and 767 represent improvements over earlier models of commercial jets. Similarly, new word processors simplify inter-business communication. Not all such progress leads to the betterment of humanity, however. This is one of the most serious challenges facing us today. How do we harness our great technological know-how for human welfare?

Modern Technological Developments

Since 1940 a number of extraordinary discoveries have been made: nuclear power, space exploration, television, computers, organ transplants, and genetic engineering. Less dramatic, but of major importance to human welfare, are developments in statistical techniques, human psychology, crop yields, contraceptive methods, and marine explorations. Businesses must know about new technology and contribute to it in order to compete.

Advances in materials research suggest we may soon be able to forge ceramics the way we forge metals and that some of these ceramics will function in very high temperatures or conduct electricity. Because ceramics are made from metal oxides which are abundant throughout the world, these technological breakthroughs could be one solution to the growing shortage of many metals. Another advance affecting the use of metals is the technique of implanting atoms of corrosion-resistant substances into the surface of steel parts. This might reduce the serious problem of corrosion of thousands of structures, tools, and vehicles. This technique, called catalysis, may lead to huge energy savings.

There have also been major new breakthroughs in computers and biochemistry. Progress in miniaturizing computers is proceeding rapidly. Experts are predicting the creation of a tiny computer chip that will hold a million bits of information. Biotechnologists have created strains of bacteria that can make alcohol from wood waste materials. They hope to modify plants and livestock in such a way as to multiply agricultural productivity many times. All of these discoveries have major business opportunity implications.

The Energy Picture

Another crucial factor in the technological environment is the direction we take with respect to energy. Just a few years ago, at the time of the Arab oil embargo, OPEC (the Organization of Petroleum Exporting Countries) fixed the world price for oil. This presented the major industrial nations of the world, including the U.S., with what seemed like a very serious threat to growth.

The energy problem is still serious for the long run, but recent experience in dealing with the petroleum shortage gives the U.S.

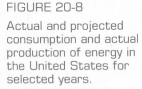

FIGURE 20-8

Actual and projected consumption and actual production of energy in the United States for selected years.

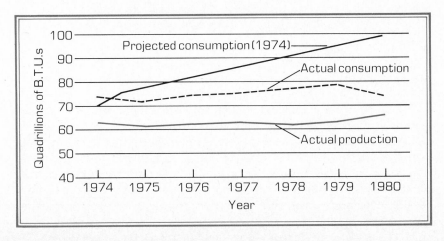

In mid–1981, four out of every five cars sold in Brazil were run on alcohol. This was all part of a long-term Brazilian government program started in 1975. The goal was to substitute alcohol made from sugar cane for nearly half the gasoline used in the country. The program included subsidies, experimentation in government-owned fleets, and a huge promotional campaign.

Although the fuel has met the goal of providing at least 75 percent efficiency of gasoline it has caused many serious problems. The worst of these is that it has a corrosive effect on engine parts. In addition, it is much harder to start the engine in the morning than with gasoline engines.

Ford and Volkswagen engineers at Brazilian factories are working on the corrosion and start-up problems and feel that they will be overcome. Meanwhile, the average Brazilian is disillusioned and is not yet convinced by industry claims that it "is still a good deal."

The lesson in all this for U.S. drivers is that technology comes to grips with problems (the fuel shortage) slowly and not without taking some false steps. Will alcohol play a major part in the future of energy consumption? What is your interpretation of the Brazilian experience? What is your point of view concerning a technological solution to the energy shortage?

reason for optimism. This is true despite the slowdown in development of nuclear power which has resulted from fears of nuclear accidents and from waste disposal problems.

What has happened, as shown in Figure 20-8, is that the market mechanism worked. Rising prices of crude oil resulted in great economies in use of energy and in a remarkable increase in production of energy from other than imported fuel. Projections of future consumption and production suggest that even by 1990 the U.S. will depend on outside sources of energy for only about one-sixth of its needs. Of course, as the past few years have shown, it is difficult to forecast events that are far in the future.

We have certainly demonstrated that we can conserve on gasoline, heating, and industrial fuel use if we have to. We have also shown that the spectre of rising petroleum costs can stimulate big increases in natural gas and coal production and improved technology for extracting oil. Some technical advances are also being made in the development of renewable sources such as biomass and solar. This gives industry greater confidence in technology than many people expressed in the early 1970s. At that time many scientists were predicting an end to growth because of shortages in power, metals, and agriculture.

Business decision making has been greatly influenced by changes in the energy picture. Many industries have begun to develop alternative strategies for energy consumption, balancing the cost, availability, and ecological factors of coal, natural gas, oil, nuclear energy, and other energy sources available to them.

Just as flexibility is essential in the case of fuel, it is also important with respect to many strategic materials such as zinc and nickel for which shortages exist and for which dependency on other nations is risky. The need for research and development is at an all-time high.

How Does Technology Affect Business Decisions?

Nearly all firms must deal with new technology. One specific problem is developing and protecting new ideas. This task requires finding, training, and holding personnel who are inventive and creative. For many firms, the hardest part of this task is recruiting top engineers and scientists from universities and from competing firms. The competition for the best talent is often fierce, because there is no substitute for creative minds. Such minds form the basis of the research and development (R&D) department of a firm.

Technology and the Need to Plan

Another outgrowth of rapid change in technology is the vital need to plan. If a firm is to succeed in the long run, it must not define its objectives too narrowly. Petroleum producers are wise to think of themselves as "energy" companies. They must consider substitutes for oil as sources of energy. Most manufacturers of containers used to be specialists in one kind of container (glass, paper, or metal). Now they produce all three types, mostly because of uncertainty about which types of container will prevail in the long run. Small new firms started by scientists and engineers are often a part of the trend toward merger and acquisition of smaller firms. This kind of merger brings new ideas into the large firm and provides the capital needed to make the new ideas flourish and reach the marketplace successfully.

Technological obsolescence, as we saw in Chapter 10, means the replacement of a technical product or product feature by a newer, better, or cheaper one. This encourages firms to reduce the risk of obsolescence by introducing their own new products. As we have seen, many firms engage in planned obsolescence; they plan to introduce new versions of products that will encourage previous buyers to replace their older (but still useful) models.

As we also saw in Chapter 10 patents provide legal protection from theft or imitation of technological ideas. They are important to this kind of planning. In many cases a large number of patents are needed to protect a new idea fully. Careful patent development is one way of planning to meet future product competition.

Technology and Social Problems

Technological change may lead to unemployment and related social problems. As we saw in Chapter 8, computerized robots are bringing great changes to manufacturing processes in the auto industry. Labor-intensive production methods are giving way to more capital-intensive methods. One effect is layoffs of some workers. Although economic theory says that improved technology will, in the long run, benefit the whole economy, this theory gives little comfort to those who will be out of work.

The problem is especially tough when a worker in such a case is not easily re-employable. If there is already an oversupply in the worker's specialty, the worker may have to be completely retrained. This problem confronts employers, unions, and governments, and there are no easy solutions for providing the training that will enable such displaced workers to get another job. This may be a fruitful area for government-industry cooperation.

We have already mentioned another technology-related problem that affects society—pollution. A specific case that relates to energy technology has become a major issue of the day. Depletion of high-grade, low-polluting fuels (natural gas and oil) makes the use of low-grade, high-polluting fuels (coal) more economically feasible. This does not necessarily make such a use socially desirable, though. Situations such as these require solutions that are not 100 percent satisfactory either in terms of ecology or of profit. We will probably design less polluting techniques for burning coal. In other words, technology will, we hope, overcome the bad side effects of other technology.

Technological advances, such as computers, are also used to combat social problems. Computers are used to spread job information among various labor markets, to improve educational systems, and to analyze law-enforcement problems.

Japanese robot technology has made great strides in recent years

Research and Development

Firms must be aware of technological change so that their processes, products, and product features will not become obsolete.

They must be more than simply "aware." They must be ready to counteract the competitive effect of such technology. If a firm is aggressive, it will be the first to introduce a new, cheaper way to make its "Gizmo." It might also introduce a "Mark II Gizmo" with features that make a competitor's product obsolete. Any of these objectives requires substantial investment in research and development (R&D). R&D, as we saw in Chapter 10, is a general name applied to those activities that are intended to provide new products and processes. It usually requires a large investment in laboratories, equipment, and scientific talent.

R&D can lengthen a product life cycle. It can also lead to the quick end of the life cycle of a firm's product or that of its competitors. R&D is the key to much competition today and represents a major class of business activity. It often results in rapid improvement in the quality of products and often causes higher prices because of development costs. It also creates an endless chain of obsolescence. Such planned obsolescence is criticized on the grounds that consumers are forced to waste their resources.

Some firms consider R&D a substitute for price competition. A few large firms who can afford major research programs use them to strengthen their hold on the market. By means of continuous product improvement and innovation, they can prevent entry of competitors.

But a small firm that gives its scientists freedom to explore and a modest budget sometimes comes up with a "breakthrough" that puts it on a competitive basis with the giants in its industry. Dr. E. H. Land's photographic genius made "Polaroid" a name to stand beside "Kodak" in an industry that was nearly a monopoly before World War II. Smaller firms are often forced to merge with others so as to be able to afford R&D. Sometimes they must purchase patent licensing rights from larger firms.

R&D and the National Interest

military-industrial
complex

One important feature of the technological environment is the great involvement of the U.S. government—especially in defense research. **Our recent history of "cold" and "hot" wars has led to the birth and growth of the military-industrial complex. This is a powerful network of military planners and industrial firms that influences the use of a large part of our nation's resources and guides research and development.** It consists of the Department of Defense, its far-flung military organization, and the major defense contractors. These include manufacturers of rockets, jets, tanks, nuclear weapons, rifles, electronic equipment, and a million other things that maintain our nation's military strength.

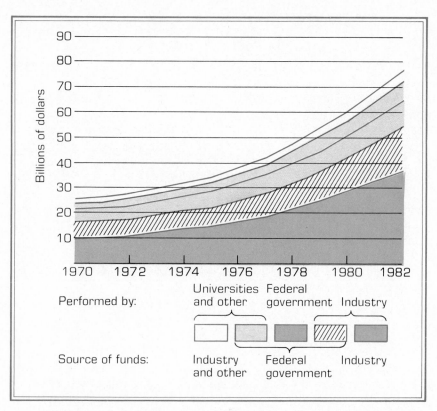

FIGURE 20-9

Funding for research and development, 1970–1982

Figure 20-9 illustrates the growth of research and development spending from 1970 to 1982. It shows who did it and who paid for it and includes defense and other research. It shows that in 1982 private industry did more than two-thirds of all R&D and paid for about half of its $80 billion cost. The federal government paid for nearly half and actually did about 12 percent. The rest was done mostly by universities.

It should be noted that R&D growth up to 1980 was not so great as Figure 20-9 might suggest. When corrected for inflation (using constant 1972 dollars) the average expenditure for the period 1970–1980 was $29.8 billion compared to $25.2 billion for the preceding decade.

The continuing argument for more defense research is that the U.S. must stay ahead of the Soviet Union in military might so as to avoid world domination by the Soviet Union and communism. This stimulates technological progress because weapons production and design have become increasingly complex and expensive. Government financing is needed to make such specialized research possible. A partnership of private industry and government is therefore essential to provide for our defense.

Cooperation between business and government has been essential to our space program

SUMMARY AND LOOK AHEAD

Business must survive and grow in a sometimes-hostile environment with important social and technological dimensions. Businesses must be sensitive to changes in society, including changes in family size and income, population shifts to the Sunbelt, changing tastes, and changing attitudes toward the role of women, toward spending, saving, and work. Of equal importance is awareness of social obligations, although there is widespread disagreement concerning the nature of that responsibility.

Firms must also learn to monitor and react to technological change. They must be alert to what is happening in computers, in communications, in atomic research, and in energy technology.

In the final chapter we will turn to the most important member of the business community—you. We will explore the question of business careers and how to evaluate and prepare yourself for a lifetime of learning and work.

FOR REVIEW . . .

1. Describe two of the techniques business uses to deal with change.

2. Which sections of the country are gaining population? How can the knowledge of population shifts affect the way that a national distributor of consumer goods plans future warehouse construction?

3. What has happened to real income of families during the 1970s? How does this affect the growth of luxury goods markets?

4. Explain the significance of the worker-nonworker ratio for economic growth. In which direction is it moving?

5. In what ways has the Protestant ethic faded in American society?

6. Describe in your own words the traditional business ethic.

7. Give two examples of major technological advances in the last twenty years. Show how they might affect the way that a small manufacturer of steel construction products does business.

8. What are the trends in use of coal and nuclear energy? How could these trends affect business's confidence in technology?

9. Explain the relationship between the military budget and the course of research and development in the U.S.

. . . FOR DISCUSSION

1. What does the distribution of income have to do with the market for luxury items? For necessities?

2. Discuss one way that the Protestant ethic still influences personnel planning.

3. Contrast the traditional business ethic and the professional-managerial ethic positions on the question of social responsibility of large corporations.

4. Identify and discuss a social problem that might stem from technological change.

5. Discuss the role you think the government should play in energy use.

INCIDENTS

The Future of Uranium Mining

From 1977 through 1979 the price of milled uranium ore was over $40.00 per pound. By mid-1981 it was down to $24.00 and employment in uranium mines was down by a third. The operations of firms like Western Nuclear, Inc. and Pathfinder Mines Corp. have been drastically curtailed.

Hopes for the industry are pinned on accelerated licensing of reactors by the federal government. Many of the towns in the uranium mining areas, such as Jeffrey City, Wyoming, have been built handsomely in anticipation of the long-range growth of uranium mining as an industry.

QUESTIONS

1. Show how the technological, social, government, and business environments are interacting in this case.

2. What strategies for survival would you suggest to these uranium mining firms? To the Chamber of Commerce of Jeffrey City, Wyoming?

From *Me* Generation to *We* Generation

A team of social scientists from Catholic University of America predicts that the pressure of making ends meet, the shortages of housing and fuel, and inflation are bringing people back to a reliance on community and sharing. They feel that the selfishness of the 1970s is being terminated by relatively hard times. As an example, they point to joint or group purchasing of homes in response to spiraling housing prices. Part of this trend will be a sharing of responsibilities between husband and wife or a further blurring of the traditional sex roles in marriage.

QUESTIONS

1. What will the trend to group rather than individual orientation mean to industries other than housing?

2. Could less emphasis on self influence the clothing industry? Explain.

3. Discuss the likelihood that the social scientists' prediction will become a reality.

CHAPTER 21

Your Career
in Business

OBJECTIVES:

After reading this chapter, you should be able to

1. Assess career opportunities in terms of the job marketplace and career values.
2. Identify sources of career information and summarize the general employment outlook for major classes of jobs and industries.
3. Analyze job growth by geographical area of the United States.
4. Analyze a methodical system for self-evaluation and understanding in preparation for securing a job.
5. Discuss the preparation of student data sheets, résumés, letters of inquiry, and the mechanics of taking job interviews.
6. Tell what is involved in the formula approach to job selection.

KEY CONCEPTS:

Look for these terms as you read the chapter

career values   résumé

student data sheet   letter of inquiry

The business world of tomorrow will be vastly different. The pace of change is expected to be rapid. In a matter of decades, whole new industries will arise because of new inventions and because of changes in resources and lifestyles. This can be a source of confusion for you, but it has its very definite positive aspect. A dynamic business world is a healthy business world. If nothing were to change, the future would be a familiar one, but it would also provide very little opportunity. You should be optimistic and you should begin to plan for the business career that lies ahead of you.

THE JOB MARKETPLACE

What you will be doing in the business world depends on job market conditions, what you have to offer, and how well you present your talents to potential employers.

There are at least two ways to examine the marketplace for jobs. One way is to look at the market for individual occupations (regardless of the industry in which it is found). Another is to check out the projected growth of whole industries in which jobs may be available. Which way you choose should depend on how clear your ideas are about a career and on the "career values" you have established.

Career Values

career values

By career values we mean those things that you feel are important in selecting a career. You may, for example, value living in a certain place or dealing with the public or using your artistic talent or having the opportunity to rise rapidly in an organization. It may be that you are excited about working in a particular industry like the communications industry but haven't decided on the specific job you want in that industry. On the other hand, you may have a clear idea about the kind of work you want to do (for example, accounting), but you don't care much about which specific industry you work in.

Sources of Career Information

The Department of Labor is a good source of information about the job market. It makes frequent analyses of the job outlook. Data from a recent study are presented in Figure 21-1. The figure shows expected growth of employment in major job classes to 1990. According to this projection, an increase of over 24 million jobs is expected. These include 4.7 million new jobs for professional and technical workers; 1.9 million for managers and administrators; 1.7 million for salesworkers; and 4.7 million for clerical workers. Among the professional and technical workers are more than 150,000 jobs as computer systems analysts and more than 150,000 as computer programmers. More than 250,000 accountants and auditors, 15,000 real estate appraisers, 47,000 retail and wholesale buyers, 36,000 personnel and labor relations specialists, 18,000 tax preparers, 25,000 travel agents, and 20,000 insurance underwriters are also in this total. Among the managers, officials, and proprietors, there are expected to be over 170,000 additional store managers, over 80,000 sales managers, and 65,000 wholesalers, as well as 143,000 restaurant, cafe, and bar managers needed. An overview of Figure 21-1 indicates a big shift toward

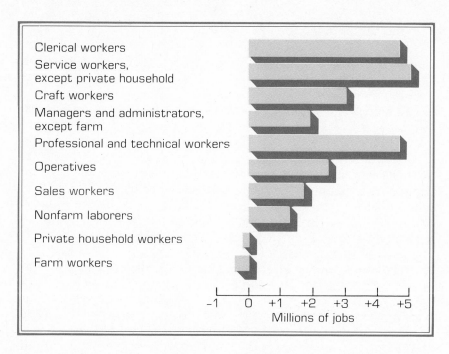

FIGURE 21-1

Projected change in
employment,
1978–1990*

white-collar and away from blue-collar jobs, especially away from jobs as laborers, farm workers, and household workers.

From what you have learned about markets you know that future demand is not the only factor to examine. It is also necessary to think about future supply. These two factors will determine the general level of wages in an occupation and how hard it is to get a certain type of job. The Department of Labor has made projections of the supply of people trained for most occupations. It is a good idea to consult the statistics released by the Labor Department in order to get a feel for the future marketplace for the job or jobs you are interested in.

You may wish to get statistics on a particular job market from trade or professional associations such as the American Marketing Association or the American Bankers Association. Some state departments of labor or state departments of commerce and industry also have current job market statistics.

Of course, statistics don't present a complete picture. You will also want to know something about these jobs—expected earnings, working conditions, advancement, etc. A good start in finding such information is the Labor Department publication, the *Occupational Outlook Handbook*. The latest edition of this publication should be available in the library. It provides a comprehensive survey of job opportunities, so it's definitely worth checking out. It reports for each job

- the nature of work
- the places of employment
- advancement, training, and other qualifications needed
- job outlook
- earnings and working conditions
- related occupations
- additional information sources

Of particular interest to students of business are the occupations listed under the general headings of clerical, computer-related, banking, insurance, administrative-related, and sales in the *Occupational Outlook Handbook*. Table 21-1 provides a complete listing of jobs in these categories. To give you an idea of the thoroughness of this coverage, Figure 21-2 provides a sample from the handbook concerning Hotel Managers and Assistants.

TABLE 21-1

Business-related occupations

Clerical occupations	Administrative and related occupations
Bookkeepers	Accountants
Cashiers	Advertising workers
Collection workers	Buyers
File clerks	City managers
Hotel front office clerks	College student personnel workers
Office machine operators	Credit managers
Postal clerks	Hotel managers and assistants
Receptionists	Industrial traffic managers
Shipping and receiving clerks	Marketing research workers
Statistical clerks	Personnel and labor relations workers
Stock clerks	Public relations workers
Stenographers and secretaries	Purchasing agents
Typists	
Computer and related occupations	Sales occupations
Computer operating personnel	Auto parts counterworkers
Programmers	Auto salesworkers
Systems analysts	Auto service advisors
	Insurance agents and brokers
Banking occupations	Models
Bank clerks	Manufacturers salesworkers
Bank officers and managers	Real estate agents and brokers
Bank tellers	Retail trade salesworkers
	Route drivers
Insurance occupations	Travel agents
Actuaries	Securities salesworkers
Claims representatives	Wholesale trade salesworkers
Underwriters	

When you refer to books such as the *Occupational Outlook Handbook* or the *Encyclopedia of Careers and Vocational Guidance*[1] you should be careful to note the date of publication. This is important because it does not take long for the supply or the demand to change. Also, it is possible that in the particular city or area you may be looking at, the job market is quite different from the national average. Population growth or new industries could mean that a given city or area has jobs open in most occupations. On the other hand, the recent closing of a large plant or a slump in tourism for a resort city could have the opposite effect.

CHOOSING AN INDUSTRY

The *Occupational Outlook Handbook* provides a rather detailed analysis of thirty-five major industries. For each industry it provides information about the nature and location of the industry, the occupations found in each, the employment outlook, and a variety of job facts similar to those provided for individual occupations. It also gives sources of career information for specific industries.

Some of the industries that are expected to grow more than the average for all industries are: communications, retail trade, services, durable goods, and finance, insurance, and real estate.

The *U.S. Industrial Outlook*, published annually by the U.S. Department of Commerce, provides even more detail concerning prospects for specific industries. Major corporations and labor unions will also gladly provide you with industry and job information. For a complete list of job information sources, you might consult the article "Where To Go for Further Information" by Helen K. Wright in the *Encyclopedia of Careers and Vocational Guidance*.

CHOOSING A GEOGRAPHIC AREA

It has been estimated that the average annual rate of employment growth from 1979 to 1990 will be 1.9 percent. This rate of growth, of course, will not be uniform around the whole country.

The majority of jobs are in the nation's metropolitan areas. How job growth is expected to vary among many of these areas has been estimated by Chase Econometrics. Some of these estimates are shown in Figure 21-3. This figure shows projected average annual job growth in various metropolitan areas and the 1980 population of these areas. Ranks among metropolitan areas are also shown both for

HOTEL MANAGERS AND ASSISTANTS

Nature of the Work

Hotel managers are responsible for operating their establishments profitably, and satisfying hotel guests. They determine room rates and credit policy, direct the operation of the food service operation, and manage the housekeeping, accounting, security, and maintenance departments of the hotel. Handling problems and coping with the unexpected are important parts of the job.

A small hotel or motel requires only a limited staff, and the manager may have to fulfill various front office duties, such as taking reservations and assigning rooms. When management is combined with ownership, these activities may expand to include all aspects of the business.

General managers of large hotels usually have several assistants or department heads who manage various parts of the operation. Because the hotel restaurant and cocktail lounge are important to the success of the entire establishment, they almost always are operated by managers with experience in the restaurant field. Other areas that usually are handled separately are advertising, rental of banquet and meeting facilities, marketing and sales, personnel, and accounting.

Large hotel and motel chains often centralize some activities, such as purchasing and advertising, so that individual hotels in the chain may not need managers for these departments. Managers who work for chains may be assigned to organize a newly built or purchased hotel or to reorganize an existing hotel or motel that is not operating successfully.

About 84,000 hotel and motel managers worked in 1980.

Working Conditions

Since hotels are open around the clock, night and weekend work is common. Hotel employees frequently must work on shifts. Managers who live in the hotel usually have regular work schedules, but they may be called for work at any time.

Hotel managers sometimes experience the pressures of coordinating a wide range of functions. Dealing with irate or non-English-speaking patrons can also be stressful. The job can be particularly hectic around checkout time.

Training, Other Qualifications, and Advancement

Experience generally is the most important consideration in selecting managers. However, employers increasingly are emphasizing college education. A bachelor's degree in hotel and restaurant administration provides particularly strong preparation for a career in hotel management. In 1980, over 80 colleges and universities offered 4-year programs in this field. Because more aspiring hotel managers seek formal training, applicants to these programs may face increasing competition in the coming years, however. Many junior colleges, technical institutes, and the Educational Institute of the American Hotel and Motel Association also have courses in hotel work that provide a good background.

Included in many college programs in hotel management are courses in hotel administration, accounting, economics, data processing, housekeeping, food service management and catering, and hotel maintenance engineering. Part-time or summer work in hotels and restaurants is encouraged because the experience gained and the contacts with employers may benefit students when they seek a job after graduation.

Managers should have initiative, self-discipline, and the ability to organize and direct the work of others. They must be able to solve problems and concentrate on details.

FIGURE 21-2

A sample job summary from the *Occupational Outlook Handbook*

Sometimes large hotels sponsor specialized, on-the-job management training programs which enable trainees to rotate among various departments and receive a thorough knowledge of the hotel's operation. Other hotels may help finance the necessary training in hotel management for outstanding employees.

Most hotels promote employees who have proven their ability, usually front office clerks, to assistant manager and eventually to general manager. Newly built hotels, particularly those without well-established on-the-job training programs, often prefer experienced personnel for managerial positions. Hotel and motel chains may offer better opportunities for advancement than independently owned establishments, because employees can transfer to another hotel or motel in the chain or to the central office if an opening occurs.

Job Outlook

Employment of hotel managers is expected to grow faster than the average for all occupations through the 1980s as additional hotels and motels are built and chain and franchise operations spread. However, most openings will occur as experienced managers die, retire, or leave the occupation. Seasonal employment opportunities will be available in resort establishments that are open only part of the year.

Applicants who have college degrees in hotel administration will have an advantage in seeking entry positions and later advancement.

Earnings

Salaries of hotel managers and assistants are particularly dependent upon the size and sales volume of the hotel, and vary greatly because of differences in duties and responsibilities. Hotel manager trainees who are graduates of specialized college programs generally start at around $13,500 a year and usually are given periodic increases for the first year or two. Experienced managers may earn several times as much as beginners. For example, salaries of hotel general managers ranged from about $20,000 to $80,000 a year in 1981, according to a survey conducted by the American Hotel and Motel Association. Hotel food and beverage managers earned from about $16,000 to $40,000. Managers may earn bonuses ranging from 10 to 20 percent of their basic salary in some hotels. In addition to salary, hotels sometimes furnish managers and their families with lodging in the hotel, meals, parking facilities, laundry, and other services.

Most employees receive 5 to 10 paid holidays a year, paid vacation, sick leave, life insurance, medical benefits, and pension plans. Some hotels offer bonuses, profit sharing plans, educational assistance, and other benefits to their employees.

Related Occupations

Hotel managers and assistants are not the only workers concerned with organizing and directing a business where pleasing people is very important. Other workers with similar responsibilities include apartment building managers, food service managers, department store managers, office managers, and sales managers.

Sources of Additional Information

Information on careers and scholarships in the lodging industry may be obtained from: The American Hotel and Motel Association, 888 7th Ave., New York, N.Y. 10019.

For a directory of colleges and other schools offering programs and courses in hospitality education, write to: Council on Hotel, Restaurant, and Institutional Education, Human Development Building, Room 118, University Park, Pa. 16802.

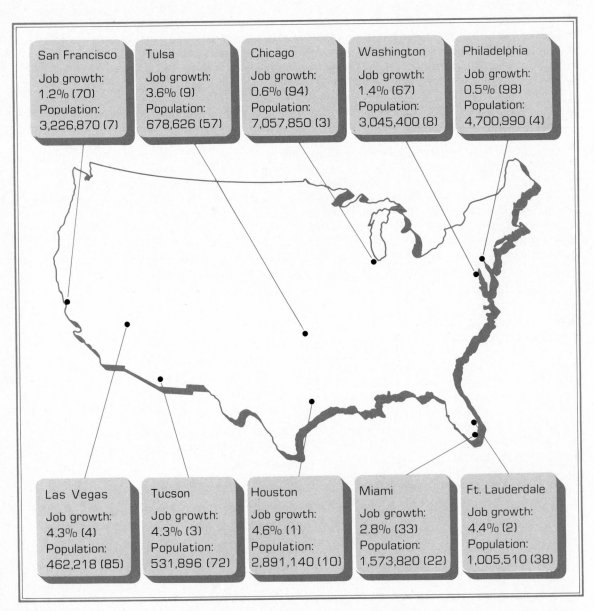

San Francisco
Job growth:
1.2% (70)
Population:
3,226,870 (7)

Tulsa
Job growth:
3.6% (9)
Population:
678,626 (57)

Chicago
Job growth:
0.6% (94)
Population:
7,057,850 (3)

Washington
Job growth:
1.4% (67)
Population:
3,045,400 (8)

Philadelphia
Job growth:
0.5% (98)
Population:
4,700,990 (4)

Las Vegas
Job growth:
4.3% (4)
Population:
462,218 (85)

Tucson
Job growth:
4.3% (3)
Population:
531,896 (72)

Houston
Job growth:
4.6% (1)
Population:
2,891,140 (10)

Miami
Job growth:
2.8% (33)
Population:
1,573,820 (22)

Ft. Lauderdale
Job growth:
4.4% (2)
Population:
1,005,510 (38)

FIGURE 21-3
Where the jobs are

Projected average annual percentage growth for nonagricultural employment, 1979–1990. Ranking among 108 metropolitan areas shown in
parentheses. United States job growth average is 1.9 percent per year.

job growth rate and population. Among the sample of cities shown here, it is clear that the average expected rate of employment growth of the Sunbelt cities is well above the average of the nation—1.9 percent. Houston, Fort Lauderdale, Tucson, and Las Vegas are all well above the 4 percent mark—more than double the growth rate for the nation. The major northern cities, on the other hand, have below-average job growth expectations. Employment in Philadelphia and Chicago, two of the nation's largest cities, will only grow at a rate of 0.5 to 0.6 percent.

Not shown in the figure, but also far below the national average in growth of employment, are the major cities of New York (0.1 percent), Boston (1.1 percent), Baltimore (0.8 percent), and Detroit (0.5 percent). Dallas-Fort Worth (4 percent), Denver (2.8 percent), and Orlando (3.6 percent) are other areas of dynamic employment expansion for the eighties. Two surprises are the recent boom areas of Los Angeles and Atlanta which are expected to grow in employment by only 1.6 and 2.1 percent respectively. With these two exceptions, though, it is clear that the South and West are expected to continue their boom in economic growth while the huge population centers of the Midwest and Northeast continue to lag in comparison. The general pattern indicates that many northern job seekers will be changing locations in the decade to come. They will probably move to the Sunbelt.

EVALUATING YOURSELF

There are several ways of looking at the career selection process. Because we have been studying markets and prices of products, why not look at yourself as a product that some business firm will "buy"? A good salesperson must know his or her product. You, then, must know yourself.

John W. Loughary and Theresa M. Ripley[2] have developed a very useful, methodical system for self-evaluation and understanding in preparation for job hunting. They recommend that the job-seeker use certain exercises to understand his or her

- evolving values
- abilities and skills
- interests as they relate to careers
- social issue attitudes
- influence of important others
- ability to identify and express feelings

What Do You Really Want Out of a Job?

A job will bring you great unhappiness and little chance for success if it conflicts with what you really are. You must, therefore, explore your own values and interests in life. What are the things that really are important to you? Do you like meeting people? Do you value security or free time or your hometown?

Career values are those things you really want to get out of a job. It may help you to examine the "Career Value Checklist" (Table 21-2). Look over each of these ten questions carefully. Can you give yourself a pretty clear answer to each question? If so, you know yourself better than most college students do! You are in an excellent position to evaluate a specific job from the "interests" or "values" perspective. If you are unsure of some answers, this is typical. You can still use this checklist to clarify your value system for a job choice.

First, try to rank the ten questions in terms of their importance to you. You should be able to rank at least six or seven of them. Once you've done this, pick out several jobs you know something about and rate them in terms of the important job values you have chosen.[3] This process should help you to understand what a job means to your life in the ways that are important to you. It will prepare you to make a final job choice.

Once you have checked this list, read the description of several of the jobs you are most seriously interested in. From the descriptions you should be able to tell which ones match up best with your "career values." Another big question besides your interests and

TABLE 21-2

Career value checklist

	YES	NO
1. Do you like meeting people?	☐	☐
2. Do you welcome responsibility?	☐	☐
3. Do you want a flexible work schedule?	☐	☐
4. Do you want to be your own boss?	☐	☐
5. Do you want security in your job?	☐	☐
6. Do you expect high starting pay?	☐	☐
7. Is rapid promotion potential important?	☐	☐
8. Is staying in your hometown important?	☐	☐
9. Do you want public recognition?	☐	☐
10. Do you expect self-fulfillment from your job?	☐	☐

values is your set of skills. How do they match the jobs you are considering?

What Are Your Skills?

Your skills and interests are usually closely related. You are more likely to be interested in those things in which you excel. If

TABLE 21-3

Hiring criteria as seen by managers

Rank	Characteristic*	Variable	Mean score
1.	P	Maturity	3.68
2.	M	Personal selling/sales mgmt. skills	3.67
3.	P	Appearance	3.60
4.	P	Cooperativeness	3.54
5.	N	Communications/public speaking	3.45
6.	P	Disposition	3.34
7.	P	Punctuality	3.30
8.	P	Mannerisms	3.28
9.	M	General mktg. skills	3.21
10.	N	English/writing skills	3.14
11.	N	Management skills	2.89
12.	P	Extroversion	2.74
13.	S	Mktg. department reputation	2.60
14.	M	Product development/mgmt. skills	2.59
15.	N	Finance skills	2.55
16.	M	Market research skills	2.51
17.	M	Market logistics skills	2.49
18.	N	Personnel mgmt. skills	2.48
19.	O	Civic functions	2.48
20.	N	Mgmt. science skills	2.47
21.	M	Advertising/advtsg. mgmt. skills	2.45
22.	M	Consumer/industrial buyer behvr. skills	2.38
23.	S	School reputation	2.38
24.	M	Pricing skills	2.36
25.	N	Accounting skills	2.36
26.	S	Internship program	2.34
27.	O	Social functions	2.30
28.	S	Recruiting success w/school	2.21
29.	N	Internship training skills	2.19
30.	O	Sports participation	2.10
31.	M	Retailing/retail mgmt. skills	1.99
32.	O	Home hobbies	1.99
33.	O	Fraternal organizations	1.99
34.	N	Social sciences/arts skills	1.93

* **P:** Personal traits. **M:** Marketing skills. **N:** Nonmarketing skills. **S:** School reputation. **O:** Outside activities.

you had trouble learning the multiplication tables, you would not be interested in a statistician's job.

While some skills are very specifically related to a job, others are required of most jobs. A skill that is needed in most jobs, particularly as you move up in a company, is the human relations skill—the ability to communicate with others and to listen to and understand what they have to say. Another general skill is skill in organizing. If you have a knack for keeping things in order and putting them in perspective, there are a great many jobs in which this skill will prove valuable. More specific skills include skill in writing, skill in calculation, mechanical skills such as typing and shorthand, and skills relating to memory and precise observation. The descriptions in the *Occupational Outlook Handbook* will tell you which skills are needed in various jobs.

As a rough guide to the importance of various skills, traits, interests, values, etc., Table 21-3 on page 637 is worth examining. It shows how a group of 87 marketing/sales managers weighed a variety of factors in judging applicants for marketing jobs.

Now that you have surveyed the general job market to discover the occupations and industries that show promise for you, and have seen the importance of self-evaluation in terms of interest and competence, we can turn to the process of finding a particular job.

CONDUCTING THE JOB SEARCH

The type of thinking you do about career opportunities is perhaps the most important type of analysis you will ever engage in. It affects your entire future lifestyle. Needless to say, you should approach this with a great deal of careful thought.

There is, however, a big difference between firming up your ideas about career opportunities and landing a job that is related to your career plans. Here we narrow our sights; we assume that you have some rather specific career choices in mind and are seeking employment.

Most of you will not be seeking a full-time job until after completing your studies. As a college student, however, you may be looking for a part-time job right now. Our discussion of student data sheets, résumés, letters of inquiry, and job interviews is helpful in getting both part-time and full-time jobs.

The Student Data Sheet

Many schools have on-campus services to help you in career preparation. For example, many schools have a student testing and guidance counseling center that can help you formulate more concrete career plans.

The student placement office is another service offered by many schools. Placement office personnel can help you find a job in the career field of your choice. Find out what services are offered. The personnel there are trained to help you make a smooth and productive transition from student to employee.

Your student placement office schedules on-campus interviews with prospective employers. These employers (business firms, government agencies, and other organizations) send campus recruiters to interview students who are about to complete their courses of study. Later in this chapter we will discuss in detail the

COLLEGE/UNIVERSITY INTERVIEW FORM
(Do not include information where prohibited by law.)

UNIVERSITY OF NEW ORLEANS
CAREER PLANNING & PLACEMENT CNTR.
Lakefront, New Orleans, La. 70122

☐ Regular Employment ☐ Other Employment

Personal Data

Name Last First Middle Initial		Social Security No.
Present Address (Street, City, State, ZIP)	Present Phone, Area Code	Check one: U.S. Citizen ☐
Permanent Address	Perm. Phone, Area Code	Permanent Resident ☐ Student Visa ☐

Work Preference

Brief Statement of Job Interests and/or Description of Work Desired

Date Available for Employment	Geographical Preference	Geographical Objections

College Information

Name and Location of Colleges Attended	Dates (Mo./Yr.) From	To	Degree Earned or Expected	Grad. Date Month	Year	Academic Major	Other courses studied 15 or more hours.
	/	/					
	/	/					
	/	/					

Honors, Activities and Organizations

Employment Information

Employment and Business Experience (Include Permanent, Cooperative, Intern, Volunteer, Summer work and any prior U.S. military service.)

Work Experience (Name and Address of Employer)	Description of Work (Descriptive Title)	Hours per Week	Dates (Mo. Yr.) From	To
			/	/
			/	/
			/	/
			/	/

General Information

References: such as faculty members who know you well and past supervisors; name, title, business address and telephone number

Other Information: Community Activities, Hobbies, Interests, etc.

THE PLACEMENT CENTER HAS MY PERMISSION TO RELEASE MY PLACEMENT CREDENTIALS IN ENTIRETY TO PROSPECTIVE EMPLOYERS. THE PLACEMENT CENTER SHALL IN NO WAY BE RESPONSIBLE FOR THE CONTENTS OF ANY REFERENCES OR FOR ANY INFORMATION CONTAINED THEREIN.

SIGNATURE	DATE SIGNED

FIGURE 21-4
A sample student data sheet

mechanics of interviewing. At this point our main concern is the student data sheet.

student data sheet

A student data sheet (sometimes called a college interview form) is a form prepared by the student placement office and filled out by the students who sign up for campus interviews. All students who establish placement files in the placement office fill out this form. A campus interviewer, therefore, can examine this form for each student who signs up for an interview. Figure 21-4 shows a student data sheet.

The Résumé

résumé

A résumé is a biographical summary of your education, experience, activities, interests, career goals, and so on. It contains much of the same type of data that the student data sheet contains. The major difference is that it is tailor-made by the person who is seeking employment.

Preparing a good résumé takes a lot of effort and care. Personnel departments receive many job application letters and résumés each day from people seeking jobs. A well-prepared résumé—one that is creative, neat, and complete—overshadows others.

Usually, you will want to send your résumé to several employers. Unless you are going to prepare a different résumé for each employer or if you are going to type each employer's copy of the same résumé separately, you will face the problem of reproducing your résumés. Try to produce copies that are as clean and neat as the original.

Some methods of photo reproduction are acceptable as are some offset-printed methods. You can get help here from a professional reproduction service either on campus or off campus.

Style and Format

There is no one best style and format for a résumé. If you are interested in several career options, you may want to prepare several different styles and formats for different employers. Each résumé would be tailor-made to appeal best to each employer.

There are several important guidelines for preparing your résumé. One is the "KISS" rule—keep it short and simple! Unless you have had a great deal of prior work experience, your résumé probably should not be longer than one typewritten page. To keep it short, do not use complete sentences. The reason is simple—employers are busy people.

Another good rule is to avoid creating a résumé that appears crowded. Don't try to squeeze too much on the page. You've probably seen ads in the classified section of newspapers that have a lot of "white space." They stand out against a background of ads that are practically all "black space." Skillful use of white space in a résumé enables you to draw attention to important parts of your résumé. It also increases the chance that your résumé will be read attentively.

Look at your résumé as a type of promotional effort. Your task is to create interest in you as a prospective employee. Be honest, candid, and to the point.

Contents

Remember, you are working with a limited amount of space. You cannot tell all that you might want to tell. You must concentrate on or highlight your strongest points.

Work Experience. If you think that your major appeal is your previous work experience, then stress that experience. Of course, if you are a typical student, you won't have much to highlight here. But if you are an experienced worker, then highlight your experience.

In covering your work experience, list the last job you held first. Then work backward to your earliest job. If you held summer jobs while in school, list them. If you show that you worked for the same employer for several summers, this tells the person who examines your résumé that you performed well in your job. If you got a promotion, be sure to indicate that.

Extracurricular Activities. By all means, list your extracurricular activities. Membership in a collegiate chapter of a professional association, such as the American Marketing Association, shows that you are seriously interested in professional development. Membership in an honorary organization or society shows that you are a notch above the average. Membership in social organizations shows that you work well with others and are people-oriented. If you held an office in any of these organizations, list that also. This shows leadership ability. The same is true of honors and other types of recognition that you may have earned. In other words, try to give some insight into your interests and show how well rounded you are.

Grades. While your résumé is not the place to list each course you took and each grade you earned, you should give some indication regarding your overall grade-point average. You could do this by stating "average grades in courses outside major; very good grades in courses in major"; or by stating your specific grade point average—"3.2 out of a possible 4.0."

FIGURE 21-5

A sample résumé

```
                    RESUME FOR ALFRED JOHN POWELL
                     (Date prepared:  April 15, 1983)


    Address:    3060 Avenue A, Apt. 21-C
                New Orleans, LA   70122 (to June 1, 1983)
    Telephone:  (504) 288-9543
    Home address:  2106 Myrtle Avenue
                   St. Rose, LA   70090
    Home telephone:  (504) 721-0810
    Personal data:  Age--21; Weight--175 pounds; Height--6'1"
                    Health--excellent


    Education:
         B.S., Business Administration, University of New Orleans (1983).
         Majored in marketing.  Overall grade point average of 3.2 on 4.0
         scale.  In major, 3.5.  Dean's list during my last two years.  I
         received a scholarship that paid 100 percent of my tuition during
         my last two years.  I worked during summer vacations and held
         other part-time jobs to pay 75 percent of my total expenses
         during my college career.

    Career Goal:
         Salesperson, with ultimate goal to move into sales management or
         marketing management.

    Extracurricular Activities:
         Treasurer, Collegiate Chapter (UNO), American Marketing Association
         Chairperson, Business Student Advisory Council (to the Dean,
                    College of Business Administration)
         Member, Society for Advancement of Management
         Member, Sailing Team
         Representative, College of Business Administration Student
                    Government Association

    Work Experience:
         June 1, 1981 to present, Zeppo Electronics, Inc., New Orleans,
         LA.  Part-time salesperson.  Received outstanding part-time
         salesperson award for 1980.

         Summers, 1979 and 1980, Beta Retail Stereo Systems, Kenner, LA.
         Stock clerk.  Promoted to salesperson in June, 1980.

    References:
         Mr. Donald Sykes, Director of Student Placement, University of
         New Orleans, New Orleans, LA   70122 (for references from my
         college professors).

         Mr. Anthony Pizzo, Sales Manager, Zeppo Electronics, Inc., 2001
         Laramie Avenue, New Orleans, LA   70111.

         Ms. Vera Callahan, owner, Beta Retail Stereo Systems, 7911
         Marcott Street, Kenner, LA   70031.
```

It's hard to say how much emphasis any given employer will place on grades. Some employers consider grades to be the most objective thing they have to go on in the case of a young prospect with little work experience. Others, particularly in recent years, discount grades because they believe that grade inflation is widespread.

Your grade-point average, of course, is not the only thing that employers consider. An average grade point might look very impressive if you also were involved in on-campus activities and worked part-time. A high grade-point average might be less impressive if you did nothing else but kept your nose in a book the whole time you were in school.

References. Generally, it's a good idea to include the names, titles, and addresses of persons who are in a position to evaluate your performance as a student and/or employee. Get their permission to list them on your résumé. Do not list relatives or only friends. If you have reference letters in your file in your school's placement office, you might say that your references can be obtained from that source. Figure 21-5 is a sample résumé.

The Letter of Inquiry

After preparing your résumé, you should write a letter of inquiry. **A letter of inquiry is the first written contact with a prospective employer. It introduces the applicant and is usually sent with a résumé.**

letter of inquiry

Purposes

The basic purpose of a letter of inquiry is communication. You are trying to communicate in writing your interest in working for the employer. You want it to lead to communication from the employer regarding your prospects for a job.

Your letter must first of all get the employer's attention. Second, it should spark the employer's interest in you as a prospective employee. Third, it should motivate the employer to respond to your letter—by sending a job application form and/or contacting you to set up a preliminary employment interview.

When to Send One

There are two situations in which you might write a letter of inquiry. The first is in response to an employer's ad in a newspaper (or any other medium) seeking applicants for a job in which you are interested. In your letter you would refer to the ad and express your desire to apply for that job. In a sense, this type of letter is solicited (or asked for) by the employer.

The second type of situation exists when you want to apply for a job with an employer even though you are unsure whether that employer is seeking job applicants. Your task of creating employer interest in you is tougher in this situation than in the case where an employer asks for such letters.

Contents

In a letter of inquiry written in response to a job ad, you should refer to the ad and where you saw or heard it. This is important because the employer may be advertising for several types of jobs. By referring to the specific ad, you leave no doubt about the job you want.

In an unsolicited letter of inquiry, your task is a little tougher. The task of specifying where you might fit into the employer's organization is entirely yours. Furthermore, the employer may be less interested in receiving such letters. You must overcome this barrier in order to avoid getting a polite rejection letter. You must do an extra good job of motivating the employer to respond.

FIGURE 21-6

A sample letter of inquiry

```
                                        3060 Avenue A, Apt. 21-C
                                        New Orleans, LA    70122
                                        April 18, 1983


Mr. Charles H. Browning
Personnel Manager
Nationwide Electronics, Inc.
P.O. Box 1475
Dallas, TX    75221


Dear Mr. Browning:

I read your advertisement for sales trainee applicants in the NEW
ORLEANS TIMES, April 17, 1983.

Your company came to my attention during the time I have been employed
as a part-time salesperson with Zeppo Electronics, Inc., in New Orleans,
Louisiana.  Ms. Barbara Rollins handles Zeppo's account with Nationwide.
We have talked about sales career opportunities with your firm on several
occasions.  Those conversations, along with some reading I have done on
Nationwide in business periodicals, have made me very interested in
working for Nationwide.

Although I have been very satisfied with my part-time position with
Zeppo, I want to relocate with a larger firm after graduating from
college next month.  As you can see from my resume, I majored in
marketing.  I will graduate in the top 15 percent of those students
receiving B.S. degrees in Business Administration at the University of
New Orleans.

A career in selling has been my goal since my sophomore year in college.
Eventually, I want to be a sales manager or a marketing manager, and am
willing to work hard to reach that goal.

Please consider my qualifications for employment with Nationwide.
I am looking forward to hearing from you regarding an interview.


                                        Sincerely,



                                        Alfred J. Powell
```

Regardless of the situation that prompts you to write a letter of inquiry, it must be brief and to the point. Put yourself in the employer's shoes. Show your interest and qualifications in a manner that motivates the employer to answer your letter favorably.

You indicate your interest by either referring to a specific job ad or to the employer in general. Again, it is easier to show interest when you are applying for a specific job. When sending an unsolicited letter, avoid being too narrow in stating your career goals. That narrows your appeal. But don't be too broad either. Leave some room for the employer to fit you into the organization.

Flexibility is good. It's much easier to fit a promising applicant who states his or her career interest as "bookkeeper" than it is to fit the applicant who states his or her career interest as "accounts payable clerk." If the employer doesn't need an accounts payable clerk, the applicant's letter may be answered with a "sorry, we can't use your talents now" letter. But the applicant for a bookkeeping job may be considered for an opening in the employer's accounts receivable department.

In general, try to communicate your career goals, education, experience, and personal qualifications as briefly as possible. Try to stimulate the employer to take the time to review your résumé. Figure 21-6 is a sample letter of inquiry.

The Job Interview

No matter what career you want, before you can actually land a job you will have to have a job interview. In fact, before landing a job, you will probably have several interviews.

The Preliminaries

A good way of looking at a job interview is to think of it as a sales pitch. You are trying to sell yourself to the interviewer. As any good salesperson knows, you don't go into a selling situation without being prepared.

For campus interviews it's a good idea to start interviewing three or four months before you complete your program of study. Starting too early lessens the interviewer's interest in you since you will not be available for employment in the short run. Few employers can accurately predict their employee needs beyond several months. But don't wait to start interviewing until two weeks before you need a job. That will greatly limit your chances of finding a good job.

A campus interview is an ideal opportunity for you. Prospective employers, in effect, come to you. After you leave school, you will have to find them on your own.

How many interviews should you schedule? In general, it's a good idea to sign up only for those that you are really interested in. If you have never taken an interview, however, you should sign up for two or three to learn what it's all about. Experience is a good teacher of how to interview. But even these practice interviews should be with employers who are looking for people to fill jobs that you are interested in. There is always the chance that you could "pull it off" in your first interview. Your attitude is also better when you are really interested in the job.

Do Your Homework. Above all, an interview is an exercise in face-to-face communication. You are the major communicator. An interviewer is not there to sell you on the employer as much as you are there to sell the interviewer on your value to that employer. It's a good idea to look at it as a buyer's market. Remember, the interviewer is the buyer. You are the seller.

If you have an interviewing opportunity, make the most of it. Jot down the place and time where the interview is to be held. That is basic but often overlooked, forgotten, or incorrectly noted.

Gather some information on the prospective employer. If it's a company, go to the library and check reference works such as *Dun & Bradstreet Reference Book*. If the firm is a corporation, try to locate and to read its recent annual reports to stockholders. Ask your instructors and any others who might be familiar with the firm about its operations. If it's a government agency or nonprofit organization, check the *U.S. Government Organization Manual*, encyclopedias, or other pertinent publications. You'd be surprised how many interviewees don't have the foggiest notion of the type of business or service the prospective employer is engaged in.

After you have a basic knowledge of the employer's operations (products sold, services performed, size, position in its industry, etc.), your next step is to learn something about the employer's representative—in this case, the interviewer. Don't overlook earlier interviewees as a source of information here. Knowing the interviewer's age, sex, hair style, style of dress, mannerisms, types of questions asked, and so on can help you relate better in the interview. Some interviewees will go into an interview and mispronounce the interviewer's name—and, even worse, the company's name. That does little for the interviewer's ego and even less for his or her first impression of you as a person.

Finally, try to anticipate and be prepared for one or more hard questions. Many interviewers ask questions such as "Why do you want to work for ____?" "What can you do for ____?" "Why are you here?" If you walk in cold, chances are that you will "blow it."

Be Relaxed. Don't be nervous. Some people get so uptight about interviews that they fall apart at the seams. Try your best to get the butterflies out of your stomach before you go into the interview.

But don't be so relaxed that you give the impression of not really caring whether or not you get the job. What is needed is a mild amount of anxiety—enough to keep you alert and responsive during the interview, but not so much as to make you "uptight."

Going to the Interview. Take a note pad and pencil and have questions prepared. An interviewer is always impressed when an interviewee has meaningful questions prepared in advance.

Be careful about your appearance. In recent years, many employers and their interviewers have adjusted to some of the newer clothing styles and have modified or done away with dress codes. But you are wise not to appear in a "way-out" outfit. Cleanliness, neatness, and moderation are very desirable.

Most important, be on time!

"You can start on Monday, Miss Creel. No bluejeans."

The Interview

Your preparation for the interview will pay off once you go through the door to be interviewed. But that was only preparation. You did not rehearse for a part in a play. Interviewers are too diverse a group to permit you to walk in prepared for everything.

Introducing Yourself. By introducing yourself, you avoid the chance that the interviewer will mispronounce your name. Beyond that, it's a good idea to consider yourself a guest. Don't rush to sit down unless you are asked to. Don't walk in with your hand outstretched for a handshake. Let the interviewer make the invitation.

Interviewer-Interviewee Interaction. As we said earlier, an interview is an exercise in face-to-face communication. But who dominates the conversation depends on the interviewer's style of interviewing. Some interviewers like to do most of the talking. Others like the interviewee to do most of the talking. Regardless of how much you did or did not prepare, you will have to play it by ear once you are in the interview room.

If the interviewer asks simple, direct questions, that does not mean that "yes" or "no" answers are all that is expected of you. Elaborate, but not to the point of "running off at the mouth." The interviewer's reactions are your best guide here. They tell you how much to say if you are observant.

If there is a noticeable break in the conversation, it's a good clue that you are slipping. Pick up the ball and run with it! It's a good chance to stress your good points, to reinforce and to elaborate on items in your résumé. But don't "blow your horn" so loud that it forces the interviewer to "tune you out."

Above all, be honest and sincere in answering questions. Be creative in asking them. Don't give the impression that you dropped in because you had nothing better to do.

Things to Avoid. There are several interviewing "don'ts." Don't chew gum, smoke, squirm in your chair, stare at the ceiling, or crack your knuckles. Don't take notes as if you were in a lecture class. Don't try to "butter up" the interviewer. Don't be phoney. Don't give the impression that you believe that the business world has been waiting too long for you to become available.

Don't try to be a comedian. On the other hand, don't be overly serious and pompous. Don't try to hide the "real you." Don't accept a job or schedule further interviews with higher-ups unless you really want the job. Don't give up if you get the feeling that you aren't making it. That's instant death to your chances of landing the job. Finally, don't emphasize an interest in the firm's retirement plan. That says nothing good about your motivation and enthusiasm.

Getting to Specifics. There are certain important questions that you will want answered. A major one, of course, is the nature of the job. What does it involve? What about the chances for promotion to higher jobs? What is the starting salary? A discussion of the salary often is the most ticklish part of an interview. You may be asked what you would expect. You should have a floor salary in mind—what you need to get by on, given your personal circumstances. You should also have an idea of what the going rate for that particular job is in the area. But don't give the impression that you're interested only in the salary. Mention the job's challenge to you and your desire to see how you measure up to it. Emphasize that you want to learn.

If asked whether you are willing to relocate, give an honest answer. But you do limit your appeal when you say that you want to stay close to home. If you want to relocate in a city that is very desirable to a lot of interviewees, be prepared for stiffer competition for jobs in that city.

A much-asked question is "Where do you see yourself 10 years from now?" How well you can answer this question depends largely on how well you did your homework on the job and the company. The main thing to get across is that you want to move up in the firm. But be realistic about how far and how fast you expect to go.

When asked what kind of employees they want, many top-level

executives answer in very general terms. "I want people who can think" is a typical response. In most cases, however, you are not interviewed by a top-level executive. An interviewer has more specific qualities and skills in mind when looking for prospective employees. This is why it's a good idea to try to learn as much as you can about the interviewer before and during the interview. He or she is a "gate keeper." The "gate" will be closed to you if you do not make a good impression on the interviewer.

Closing the Interview.   When you sign up for a campus interview, notice how far apart the interviews are spaced. That gives you an idea about how long a typical interview will last. Make sure you get all your questions answered in the allotted time.

Many people leave interviews in a total state of confusion. Very rarely is a person hired during the first interview. Few are even definitely offered a job. This, of course, is disappointing to many interviewees who expect to "sew it up" during the interview. They often leave feeling frustrated, rejected, or unsure of themselves.

Before leaving, however, you will get some indication as to your status. Usually, you will be told that the interviewer will be in touch with you in a couple of weeks. Thank the interviewer and leave.

After the Interview.   Be patient! When the letter arrives, it will be either: (1) an outright rejection; (2) a notice that your skills are not needed now but that your résumé is being placed in the active file; or (3) a letter expressing a desire to arrange another interview with higher-ups.

If, however, you do not hear from the interviewer within a reasonable period after the interview, write a follow-up letter. If you get a letter saying that your résumé is being placed in the active file, write a follow-up after two or three months to keep your résumé active. If you get an outright rejection, do not become discouraged. If you get a letter or phone call for the purpose of setting up another interview, respond tactfully and promptly.

Remember, during your career you will probably work for several employers. Your choice of a first job and employer is not a choice that will commit you to a lifetime with one employer. Approach that first job with a desire to learn all that you can. That increases your mobility and promotability.

Job Search Time-Line

Loughary and Ripley have developed a novel "time-line" for implementing the job hunt.[4] (See Figure 21-7.) This analysis of the

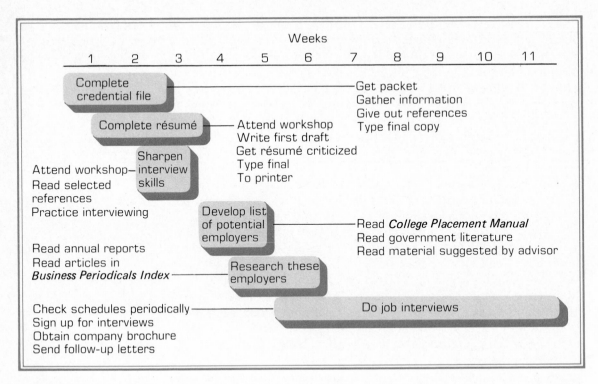

FIGURE 21-7

A job search time-line

job search shows that it is neither simple nor quick. A thorough, well-planned job search and selection process may take eleven weeks or more to complete.

The stages in a thorough job search, according to these authors, are as follows: 1) complete credential file, 2) complete résumé, 3) sharpen interview skills, 4) develop list of potential employers, 5) research these employers, and 6) do job interviews. These major steps include several substeps, as shown in Figure 21-7. For a complete discussion of each step, refer to a copy of *A Career Planning Program.* Such attention to detail in job hunting can result in a much better "matching" of your personal skills, aptitudes, and interests with those work opportunities available in the marketplace. If economic conditions in the area are favorable at the time you are looking, you will have a choice to make.

MAKING THE FINAL CHOICE

If you are in a position to choose between or among job offers, it is wise to set up a practical system to reach a decision. To do this

TABLE 21-4

A job selection formula illustrated

Directions: Rate each job by each value factor on a 1 to 10 scale. Multiply scores by indicated weights and then total the products for each job.

Value factors and weights	Job A	Job B	Job C
Self-fulfillment	3	5	8
× 5 =	(15)	(25)	(40)
Promotion opportunity	5	9	6
× 4 =	(20)	(36)	(24)
Starting pay	4	8	7
× 3 =	(12)	(24)	(21)
Prestige	10	6	8
× 2 =	(20)	(12)	(16)
Location	3	4	10
× 1 =	(3)	(4)	(10)
Total score	70	101	111

Note: This concept was developed from suggestions offered by Professor Robert S. Ristau of Eastern Michigan University.

you need a standard—a set of values—to guide your choice. You will also need all the facts about each job. We have already discussed what you want out of a job. These are the standards, or values. We assume you have gained the facts about each job from the job-search process.

A job-selection formula could look like Table 21-4. Assume that you have three jobs to choose from. These are labeled A, B, and C at the top of the three columns of the table. Assume further that you have honestly searched your values and that only five factors are important to you in choosing: the degree of self-fulfillment you expect from the job, the opportunity for promotion, the starting pay, the prestige of the job, and the location. You have assigned relative importance, or weights, of 5, 4, 3, 2, 1, respectively, to each of these five factors. This means that, for example, self-fulfillment is five times as important to you as location and that promotion opportunity is twice as important as prestige. Assigning your own weights will require careful thought.

Next, you start to rate each job on a 1 to 10 scale according to each of your value factors. Table 21-4 shows your degree of self-fulfillment in job A is only rated 3, while in job B it is rated 5, and in job C it is rated 8. Because the weight, or importance, of the factor self-fulfillment is 5, you multiply the job ratings times 5 and score them 15, 25, and 40 in that order. (These scores are circled.) Next, you do the same in terms of the promotion opportunity. In this case, job A rates a 5, job B, a 9, and job C, a 6. Multiply these by 4—your "weight" for promotion opportunity. The scores appear circled below the ratings. They are 20, 36, and 24. Do the same for the other value factors and add up the scores for each job—all the circled values in each column. The total scores in this illustration are 70, 101, and 111.

The results in Table 21-4 indicate that you should choose job C. However, since job B is so close, you might want to go through the process once more for jobs B and C. Remember—no formula is perfect. There may be something about one of these jobs that attracts you but you can't put your finger on it. It may be enough to make you select the "close second" choice according to the formula.

The formula approach to job selection should not be looked upon as either automatic or fool-proof. Its chief merit lies in the fact that it causes you to think through your values and examine as many facts about the jobs as you can. It can't stop you from fooling yourself about what you really want.

Whether all of this works or not will not become apparent until you have been hired and are doing (or trying to do) the work that you are assigned.

A FINAL WORD

You now have a taste of what the business world is like. It is such a huge and complicated set of industries and firms that it is almost impossible to describe adequately. Even if we could describe it well, you would still have to become a part of it to begin to fully appreciate it. And even after you're in it for a while, you'll realize that because it's changing so rapidly, you'll never really learn all there is to know. You'll probably take other business courses in school that will concentrate on specific aspects of operating businesses to prepare you more completely for a specific job. They will also help you in choosing a career.

CASE STUDY

YANKEE INNOVATION PAYS OFF

The one-story, cement-block building that houses Black & Webster Inc., of Waltham, Mass., nestles in a wooded hollow, unspoiled by the soot of sprawling factories. From his white-marble-top desk, President Peter T. Webster, 41, can watch pheasants dart across the lawn. But the rustic setting is deceptive. Webster and his staff of eighty-three people, including six engineers and ten highly skilled machinists, turn out such space-age products as orbital riveters and vibratory feeders.

Like many small high-technology companies, B & W has parlayed astute innovation and aggressive marketing into rapid growth. In 1945 the firm started out manufacturing the valves used to mix soda water and syrup in Coca-Cola machines at soda fountains. Since then it has made machine tools for General Electric, R.C.A. and Texas Instruments. Between 1975 and 1979 business expanded by 25 percent annually.

But not in 1980. As towering interest rates and inflation clobbered the economy, B & W's sales grew by a disappointing 6 percent, to $6.2 million. Profits were off 60 percent. And during the final three months of 1980 the firm barely broke even.

The uncertainties generated by the current economic turmoil have trapped Webster in a tense guessing game. He must pick a price level low enough to stimulate new sales but high enough to cover soaring costs. In 1980 the prices of his raw materials, including steel and plastic, jumped anywhere from 7 percent to 20 percent. Says Webster: "Every decision has a bearing on the bottom line. During inflationary times my margin for error is erased."

At the top of Webster's worry list is the high cost of energy, and so he has sought a number of ways to cut fuel use. Sine 1977 the company has invested $1,500 for ceiling fans to blow hot air down to the floor of the plant and $10,000 for a miniature computer that governs the heating and air-conditioning system to regulate air temperature for maximum energy efficiency. Even with these and other tough conservation measures, the firm's heating oil and electricity bills have gone up by 54 percent since 1977, to $37,000 a year.

High interest rates have severely slowed Webster's efforts to boost productivity through capital investment. Two years ago he spent $80,000 for a "machining center" that can wield up to twenty-five different tools while making B & W products. The firm is now large enough to use a second machining center, but the price has jumped to $150,000 in the past three years. Webster has delayed borrowing the money because his bank demands a staggering 20½ percent interest. Says he: "I have to guess how soon

I should go to the bank. If I wait too long because of interest rates, it's going to cost us business."

Despite his current troubles, Webster remains confident that his firm will not stay down for long. In fact, he boldly predicts a sales surge of 25 percent in 1982. His reason: members of the baby boom generation born in the '50s are reaching the age at which they buy houses and the major appliances to go in them. Many of those products will be made with his equipment. Says Webster: "Unless we really foul up the economy, expansion is inevitable." It is just that kind of optimism and vision that has made small businesses such powerful engines of growth.

QUESTIONS

1. What is a "high-technology company"?

2. Why did Black & Webster Inc. experience a 60 percent decline in profit in 1980 despite the 6 percent increase in sales?

3. Explain how high interest rates would affect the firm's efforts to boost productivity.

4. Why is Mr. Webster optimistic about the future?

CAREER PROFILE

My name is Robert F. Simpson. Currently, I am manager of the International Division of Russell Corporation.

In 1968 I received a bachelor's degree in Business and Management Studies. After two-years in the U.S. Army, I entered business school and received an M.B.A. degree in 1971. Prior to my graduation I interviewed with many companies. Most of the companies did not satisfy my objectives of: a small to medium sized company; a location in the Southeastern United States; a starting salary commensurate with my previous work experience and level of formal education; and, opportunity for advancement.

I met the president of Russell Corporation socially and was invited to visit the company in Alabama. After meeting the three division general managers and reviewing their operations, I was offered and accepted a position with the Knit Apparel Division.

Upon completing a training program that concentrated on each phase of the vertically integrated manufacturing operation, I was promoted to manager of a sales territory. The next advancement was to the position of Assistant Sales Manager. In 1973 I was transferred to the New York office as a salesman. It was during this time that I began dealing with foreign customers. As international business began to grow, its tremendous sales potential became apparent to me. At a meeting with top management in 1975 the decision was made to establish an International Division.

As manager of the International Division, my primary responsibility is to solicit export sales and to develop markets outside the United States to which Russell can profitably ship products. The products include those normally sold by two of the three operating divisions. In executing responsibilities I have the authority to select, hire, and terminate agents to assist in the selling effort. I travel to foreign countries 2 or 3 times each year for a period of 2–3 weeks per trip to meet foreign buyers and learn their marketing techniques and business customs.

Last year sales from the International Division represented about 10 percent of the gross sales of the Corporation. My objective is to increase this percentage continually until the 20–25 percent range is met. Allied to this goal is the expansion of our overseas salesforce. My personal objective is to continue growing professionally and financially with Russell Corporation.

GLOSSARY

absenteeism The failure of workers to report to work.

absentee ownership A term usually applicable to a corporation owned by a large number of stockholders who do not actively participate in managing its affairs.

absolute advantage A country has an absolute advantage in producing a product when it is the only country that can produce that product or when it can produce it at a lower cost than any other country. (p. 534)

acceptance sampling A procedure to control the quality of purchased items; it involves examining a sample and deciding to accept or reject the shipment based on inspection of the sample.

accessory equipment A category of industrial goods. Accessory items are less costly than installations (for example, manufacturing equipment) and their useful lives are shorter. Like installations, they do not become a physical part of the goods they are used to produce. Typewriters and fork-lift trucks are examples.

account A register of financial value. There are four basic kinds of accounts: asset, equity, revenue, and expense accounts. Account balances are changed by transactions. (p. 348)

accountability The requirement for subordinates to report results to their superiors. (p. 137)

account executive A person in charge of the relationship between the client and the advertising agency who coordinates the work of several professional agency employees in preparing the client's advertising effort. (p. 316)

accounting The recording, gathering, manipulating, auditing, and interpreting of information that describes the assets and operation of a firm. The two main types of accounting are financial and managerial. (p. 344)

accounts payable Money owed to creditors who supplied the firm with goods and services on credit. Listed in the current liabilities section of the balance sheet.

accounts receivable Money owed to a firm by its customers. Listed in the current assets section of the balance sheet.

accrual The process of holding over expenses or income to another period.

accrued expense A liability created by incurring an expense in one period but not paying for it until the next. (p. 353)

acid-test ratio A ratio that measures a firm's liquidity. Cash and near-cash items divided by current liabilities.

acquisition The purchase by one firm of a controlling interest in another. (p. 490)

Active Corps of Executives (ACE) An advisory service of the Small Business Administration. Members are currently employed executives who volunteer their services to small firms. (p. 527)

Ada A programming language developed by the U.S. military. It is intended to replace other languages used by the Department of Defense. It can be used both for business and scientific applications. (p. 384)

actuary Loss-predicting expert who helps determine premiums for insurance companies by examining past occurrence of loss.

administered pricing The process of determining pricing policies that guide the actual setting of prices on a firm's output rather than relying only on the daily market forces of supply and demand to determine prices. Common in market structures other than pure competition.

administrative law   A body of law under which administrative officials (for example, the FTC) act as judges and legislators. (p. 579)

advertising   All nonpersonal promotional activity for which a fee is paid by an identified sponsor. It is complementary to personal selling. (p. 314)

advertising agency   A firm that produces and places advertisements in media and may arrange total programs of advertising for its clients. (p. 316)

advertising department   A separate department within a firm that oversees the firm's advertising activities. It may deal with the firm's advertising agency, which is outside the firm.

advertising media   Any means by which advertising can be carried: radio, television, print, etc. (p. 316)

affirmative action plan   A detailed statement by a firm describing how the firm will implement a program of actively recruiting members of minority groups and women and upgrading jobs currently held by them. (p. 171)

agency-principal relationship   Exists when one party (the agent) is authorized and consents to act on behalf of another (the principal). (p. 595)

agency shop   A type of union security. All employees for whom the union bargains must pay dues but need not join. (p. 205)

agent middleman   A middleman who does not take title to the goods he or she offers for sale and who earns a commission.

aggregate demand   Overall or total demand for all goods and services in an economic system.

aggregate supply   Overall or total supply of goods and services in an economic system.

AIDA process   Short for attention, interest, desire, and action—the process of selling sought by advertising and personal selling. (p. 317)

alien corporation   A corporation that operates in countries in addition to the country in which it was chartered. It is an alien corporation in those foreign countries.

AMEX   The American Stock Exchange.

antitrust laws   Laws designed to maintain competition, including the Sherman Act and the Clayton Act. (p. 588)

applied research   Research effort that in contrast to basic research has immediate and practical application.

apprenticeship training   Training that occurs when an employee works under the direct supervision of an experienced and skilled worker in order to learn a trade.

aptitude tests   Tests used to tell if a person is likely to do well in a particular kind of work. They estimate the ability to learn a skill.

arithmetic mean   A kind of "average" computed by adding a group of values and dividing the total by the number of values. (p. 392)

array   A list of all values in a statistical series, usually from lowest to highest.

articles of copartnership   A written agreement between or among partners that specifies the rights and duties of each.

assembly language   A low-level language (close to machine language) specific to a given computer manufacturer. Used for system programs. (p. 383)

assessment center   A systems approach based on the use of group techniques to diagnose and assess individual performance. Useful in determining individual training and development needs of present and potential workers and managers.

assets   A firm's resources such as land, cash, and accounts receivable. They have a positive dollar value. (p. 348)

asset redeployment   The action of selling company divisions. (p. 492)

audit   A periodic check of accounting, financial, or marketing records and/or performance either to verify compliance with generally accepted principles and/or to make recommendations for improving performance.

auditor   An accountant who inspects and reviews accounting records of firms and individuals and verifies the accuracy of the data recorded.

authority   The right to take the action necessary to accomplish an assigned task. Power to make decisions. (p. 137)

autocratic leader   A leader who makes decisions without consulting subordinates or without allowing them to participate in the decision making that affects them.

automation   A process for performing repeated tasks in which little human supervision is needed. Computer systems monitor performance. (p. 227)

background investigation   Checking up on a job applicant's references to help in assessing his or her suitability to the job. (p. 175)

backward vertical integration   A term that describes a firm's integration backward from its present type of operation. Examples are a retailer who goes into wholesaling or an electric utility that goes into coal mining.

bailor-bailee relationship   A common occurrence in business. A bailor gives possession and control of his or her property to a bailee. The bailor still owns the property but the bailee holds it in trust. In bailment, the bailor is the person who delivers goods in trust to a bailee, who is the person to whom the goods are committed in trust. A bailment is a transfer of possession without sale. (p. 595)

bait and switch advertising   Advertising one inexpensive item that is really not available and then convincing those persons who want to buy it to buy a more expensive substitute.

balance of payments   The difference between money flowing into a country and money flowing out of that country as a result of trade and other transactions. An unfavorable balance means more flowing out than flowing in. (p. 545)

balance of trade   The difference between the money values of a country's imports and exports. An unfavorable balance means that the money value of imports is greater than the money value of exports. (p. 545)

balance sheet   A statement or list of the assets and equities of a firm at one point in time. Also called a statement of financial position. (p. 351)

bankruptcy   A firm that cannot meet its maturing financial obligations is insolvent. If, in addition, its liabilities are greater than its assets, the firm is bankrupt. Such a firm is said to be in bankruptcy. (p. 493)

bargainable issues   Aspects of the work or job environment that are subject to collective bargaining between union representatives and management representatives. Examples are wages and fringe benefits. (p. 208)

barter   A simple type of trade or exchange. Trading one kind of good or service for another kind of good or service. Money is not involved in the trade, or exchange.

BASIC   Language widely used in instruction and with microcomputers. Stands for Beginners' All-purpose Symbolic Instruction Code. (p. 384)

basic accounting equations   Two equations that explain the basic system of financial accounting:
(1) Assets = Equities
(2) Revenues − Expenses = Net Profit (p. 350)

basic research   Research effort to study general relationships among phenomena in order to understand them. In contrast to applied research, basic research is conducted with no immediate concern for practical application.

batch processing   Entering data into a computer in large groups on an intermittent basis.

bear market   A market for securities in which prices are falling and investors expect falling prices to continue. There is little buying of securities in a bear market. Investors are pessimistic.

belonging needs   In Maslow's hierarchy of needs they include social belonging, love, affection, affiliation, and membership needs.

Better Business Bureau (BBB)   The Council of Better Business Bureaus, Inc. is made up of local BBBs in many cities. A BBB is a nonprofit organization of business firms that join together to help protect consumers and businesses from unfair business practices. (p. 516)

blacklists   Lists circulated among employers containing the names of workers who were known to be in favor of unions. Blacklisted workers were denied employment. The use of blacklists is now illegal. (p. 195)

big board   The New York Stock Exchange.

block diagram   A flowchart. A method of presenting a computer program that shows visually the functions performed and their sequence; a means of documentation.

blue chip stock   Common stock of corporations able to produce profits and pay dividends in both good times and bad.

blue-collar workers   Workers who perform manual labor.

"blue skies" unit   An independent unit in a firm which has the responsibility of bringing in new ideas. (p. 602)

blue-sky laws   State laws that apply mainly to the sale of new securities. Their purpose is to prevent corporations from issuing securities that have nothing of value to offer the buyer. (p. 481)

board of directors   The group of people, elected by a corporation's stockholders, that is ultimately responsible for the management of that corporation. (p. 78)

board officers   Officers of the board of directors elected by the board. They include a chairperson, vice-chairperson, and a secretary.

bona fide occupational qualification (BFOQ)   An occupational qualification based on sex, age, religion, or national origin. Allowed by the Equal Employment Opportunity Commission if the qualification is job related and can be justified. (p. 176)

bond   A bond is a written promise to pay. It indicates that the borrower will pay the lender, at some stated future date, a sum of money (the principal) and a stated rate of interest. (p. 471)

bond indenture   The agreement under which bonds are issued. It designates the trustee.

boom period   That period in the business cycle during which the volume of business activity is at a high level. Consumers and businesses are very confident and optimistic.

boycott   In labor relations a boycott is a union's attempt to get people to refuse to deal with the boycotted firm. Also used by other groups to get people to unite against another person, business, nonbusiness organization, or country and to agree not to buy from, sell to, or associate with that person, organization, or country. (p. 215)

brand   A name, term, symbol, or design, or a combination of them used to identify the goods or services of one seller or a group of sellers and to differentiate them from those of competitors. (p. 294)

breakeven analysis   A technique for estimating the relationships among volume of operation, costs, and sales revenue. Costs are divided into fixed and variable parts. When sales revenues equal total costs, the firm breaks even. (p. 395)

breaking down   A production process that involves removing or separating some of the original input (raw material), as when logs are cut into boards. (p. 226)

brokerage house   A firm that buys and sells securities that have previously been issued by businesses and governments. It buys and sells on behalf of its investor-clients. (p. 472)

budget   A financial forecast showing expected income and expenditures for a given period of time. (p. 363)

bull market   A market for securities in which prices are rising and investors expect rising prices to continue. There is a lot of buying of securities in a bull market. Investors are optimistic.

business   All profit-directed economic activities that are organized and directed to provide goods and services. (p. 27)

business cycle   The cyclical changes that occur as the level of economic activity varies over time: boom, decline, recession or depression, and recovery.

business opportunity   A set of circumstances that may enable a person or firm to reap some benefit or profit. (p. 56)

business trust   A business arrangement, created by an agreement, in which a trustee holds the property, runs the business, and accepts funds from investors. These investors receive trust shares, have limited liability, but do not vote for the trustee. A mutual fund is an example. (p. 87)

call provision   A provision sometimes included in preferred stock and bond issues. It permits the corporation to retire preferred stock by paying the stockholder the call price. For bonds, it permits the corporation to redeem the bond before its maturity date.

"canned program"   A computer program that has been placed in storage and is available for use by anyone who so desires.

capital   A factor of production. Tools and machinery or anything made by humans that aids in producing and distributing goods and services. Human-made productive capacity. (p. 14)

capital budget   A projection of capital needs for from five to twenty years. (p. 485)

capital formation   The process of adding to the productive capacity of an economy. (p. 20)

capital-intensive   Production processes depending more heavily on machinery, plant, and equipment than on labor. Capital investment is a major part of production costs. (p. 228)

capital investment   A firm's financial commitment to buildings, land, machinery, and other productive assets.

capitalism   An economic system based on private ownership of the factors of production. The bulk of economic decision making is in the hands of individuals and privately owned business firms. (p. 16)

career values   Those factors that have an important effect upon the choice of a career or a job. (p. 628)

cartel   A group of firms or countries that agrees to operate as a monopoly to regulate prices and production. (p. 556)

cash discount   A discount off list price for prompt payment. Used to speed up collection of accounts receivable. (p. 328)

cash dividend   Cash payments made to a firm's common and preferred stockholders as a return on their investment in the firm.

cashier's check   A check written by a bank's cashier and payable to a specified payee.

cash trading   In the commodities markets, cash trading means the actual buying and selling of commodities for delivery in the cash market. In the securities exchanges, purchases of securities for cash.

caveat emptor   "Let the buyer beware." The philosophy of business during the 1800s. The consumer is responsible for his or her purchase behavior.

cease and desist order   An order handed out by a federal agency that informs a business that it must stop a questionable practice.

CED (Committee for Economic Development)   A national group of representatives of major American corporations. It is concerned with optimum resource allocation and is viewed as a supporter of the professional-managerial ethic for business.

centralization   The concentration of decision-making power at the top level of an organization. Managers in centralized organizations disperse very little authority throughout the organization. (p 138)

centralized organization   An organization in which decision-making power and authority are concentrated in the hands of a few upper-level managers.

central planning   Practiced in collectivist economic systems. The government decides how productive resources will be used and how output will be distributed. (p. 17)

central processing unit (CPU)   The device which performs the actual calculations and logic in a computer system. It includes an internal memory, an arithmetic unit, a logic unit, and a control unit. (p. 377)

certificate of deposit (CD)   A deposit made for a certain period of time by individuals, business firms, or other organizations. The interest rate is higher than that on regular passbook accounts. There is a penalty for early withdrawal.

certified check   A check that is stamped "certified" by a bank, which immediately withdraws the amount of the check from the drawer's checking account.

Certified Public Accountant (CPA)   An accountant who has fulfilled the legal requirements of his or her state for knowledge in accounting theory, practice, auditing, and law and who is licensed to sign legally required financial reports. (p. 345)

chain of command   The authority relationship that exists between superiors and subordinates. It is a command relationship in which line authority has the right to direct the work of subordinates.

chain store   A unit in a group of stores that are centrally owned and managed; each unit is engaged in the same type of business. A&P is a chain store organization. A particular A&P supermarket is a chain store.

channel of distribution   The set of firms directly involved in selling a product. (p. 298)

chattel mortgage bond   A bond that is secured by movable property.

checkoff   The employer's deduction of the employee's union dues from his or her paycheck to give to the union.

class action suit   A lawsuit by a single consumer that may result in recovery by a number of similarly injured parties.

clearing checks   Process by which checks are returned to the bank upon which they were drawn and to the originator or drawee.

close corporation   A corporation owned by only a few stockholders. Its shares are not sold to the public.

closed shop   A type of union security. Only members of the union can be hired by an employer. Outlawed in interstate commerce by the Taft-Hartley Act. (p. 205)

COBOL   A specialized language that is extremely close to English and is used for business data processing. (Common Business Oriented Language.) (p. 384)

coinsurance clause   A clause in a fire insurance policy that requires the insured to carry adequate insurance (usually 80 percent) on the market value of the property.

collateral   Assets of a borrower pledged as security against the amount of money lent him or her.

collateral trust bond   A bond secured by stocks and bonds in other corporations that are owned by the issuing corporation.

collective bargaining   The process of negotiating a labor contract between union representatives and employer representatives and the on-going process of administering an existing labor contract. The parties bargain in good faith on bargainable issues. (p. 194)

collective bargaining agreement   The contract negotiated between employer and union representatives which sets forth the terms and conditions under which union members will offer their labor services to an employer. (p. 194)

collectivism   An economic system in which the government owns the factors of production and controls social and economic decision making. (p. 16)

combination   A production process that involves bringing things together into a new arrangement. (p. 226)

combination export manager   A domestic agent middleman who serves as the export department for several noncompeting manufacturers on a commission basis. (p. 553)

commercial bank   A privately owned, profit-seeking firm that serves individuals, businesses, and nonbusiness organizations. Major services are accepting deposits and making short-term loans. It also provides many other services such as exchanging foreign currency for U.S. currency and giving financial advice. (p. 411)

commercial finance company   A company that helps firms finance their accounts receivable. It may buy a firm's accounts receivable at a discount or lend money on accounts receivable that are pledged as security for a loan. Also makes loans secured by inventory or equipment. (p. 418)

commercial paper   Promissory notes issued by corporations that are backed only by the firm's promise to pay.

commercial paper house   A company that buys commercial paper directly from issuing corporations and resells it to buyers or acts as a middleman who, for a commission, brings the issuing corporation and a buyer together. Commercial paper is a promissory note written by a business firm to obtain short-term working capital from a lender. (p. 419)

committee organization   A type of organization structure in which several persons share authority and responsibility for accomplishing an objective. This form of organization, where it does exist, usually exists within the overall line and staff organization. Also called project management, program management, team management, and group management.

commodity exchanges   Voluntary trade associations whose members engage in trading commodities. Provide a market for commodities such as copper, pork, cotton, etc.

common carrier   A carrier that offers its services to the general public at uniform rates to all, for example, railroads. (p. 304)

common law   Law that is built on precedents, or the previous opinions of judges. (p. 593)

common market   A term often used for the European Economic Community, which was founded in 1958 by Belgium, France, Italy, Luxembourg, the Netherlands, and West

Germany. Denmark, Ireland, the United Kingdom, and Greece have since joined. See *regional trading bloc.*

common stock   A certificate showing ownership in a corporation. All shares are equal in value and all common stockholders enjoy the same rights. Common stockholders are the residual owners of a corporation. (p. 76)

communication   A transfer of information between people that results in a common understanding between them. (p. 110)

community property   Property husbands and wives own together under the laws of community property states.

comparative advantage   According to the principle of comparative advantage, the people of a country will enjoy a higher standard of living if the country specializes in producing those goods in which it has the greatest comparative advantage or the least comparative disadvantage in relation to other countries. It should import the other goods it needs. A country's natural resources, labor and capital cost, nearness to markets, labor skills, technological skills, and so on determine where its relative or comparative advantage lies. (p. 534)

comparative advertising   Advertising which makes comparisons of the advertised brand to named competitive brands.

competition   Rivalry among firms to attract and serve customers in the hope of making a profit.

competitive bidding   A purchasing department's invitation to sellers to submit bids to fulfill its purchase requirements. It requires the buyer to specify in detail what is needed. A purchase contract will be awarded to the lowest bidder who can meet the specifications.

competitive structures   Variations in the market framework that imply variations in the degree and type of competition that the firm must face (for example, oligopoly, monopoly).

component parts and materials   A category of industrial goods. They become part of the goods they are used to produce. Examples are car batteries, car tires, and cement.

compulsory arbitration   A method of settling a dispute between labor and management. A neutral third party decides how the dispute is to be settled and it is binding on both parties. Used only when essential public services are involved. Compelled by federal or state law. (p. 213)

computer   An electronic data processing system that stores great amounts of data and manipulates data quickly and accurately. (p 370)

computer program   A detailed set of instructions to a computer in a special computer language. (p. 376)

computer programmer   A person who writes programs for computers.

conciliation   A method of settling a dispute between labor and management. A neutral third party tries to prevent negotiations from breaking down. If negotiations break off, the third party (conciliator) tries to get the disputants back to the bargaining table. (p. 212)

conglomerate   A firm involved in a number of noncompetitive industries.

consent order   An agreement by a firm to stop doing something that a regulatory agency has found to be illegal. (p. 580)

consignment   Goods bought by a wholesaler or retailer but are not paid for until they are sold.

Consumer Credit Protection Act   The "Truth in Lending Act" of 1968. Requires firms that sell on credit to consumers to state the charges for loans and installment purchases in terms of the annual percentage rate (APR).

consumer finance company   A company that makes personal loans to individuals, often on a signature basis that involves no collateral. This type of company does not make loans to businesses. (p. 418)

consumer goods   Products and services used by consumers for their own satisfaction, not for producing other products or services. (p. 263)

consumerism   A movement to enhance the power of consumers relative to that of business firms. Motivation for any action taken or legislation that shows concern for the welfare of consumers. (p. 20)

consumer power   The consumer power concept means that, because consumers are free to do business with whomever they choose, businesses must consider consumer needs and wants in making decisions. (p. 20)

consumer price index   A measure of inflation. A figure that measures the change in the dollar value of a selected group of consumer goods from a base period.

Consumer Product Safety Commission   A commission created by the Consumer Product Safety Act of 1973. It enforces consumer protection laws. Its main concern is preventing unsafe products from reaching the market.

containerization   The method of shipping products in standard container units. It simplifies handling at points of transfer, loading, and unloading.

continuous production   Production carried out routinely and without interruption. The opposite of intermittent production. (p. 227)

contract   A mutual agreement between two or more people to perform or not perform certain acts. Consists of an offer seriously and clearly made by one party (the offeror) to another party (the offeree) who must accept it in a serious and unambiguous manner. To be valid a contract must include an agreement, consideration, competence of parties, and a legal objective. (p. 594)

contract carrier   A carrier that makes temporary contracts with individual shippers to move their freight. (p. 305)

control chart   Any of a variety of charts or illustrations guiding the sequence of steps required in production or in the flow of paperwork. (p. 239)

controller   A device to regulate the flow of multiple sources of data (terminals, etc.) into the CPU (central processing unit) of a computer system. (p. 383)

controlling   The management function of setting standards of performance, measuring actual performance and comparing it to performance standards, and taking corrective action, if necessary. (p. 115)

convenience goods   Items bought frequently, demanded on short notice, and often habitually purchased, like cigarettes or gasoline. (p. 268)

convertible bond   A bond that can be converted to common stock at the bondholder's option.

cooperative advertising   The sharing by a manufacturer and middlemen in the channel of distribution, mainly retailers, of the costs of advertising the manufacturer's product.

cooperative association   Also called a co-op. An association formed and owned by a group of persons who act together to accomplish some purpose. It is a collective undertaking, and any revenues in excess of costs are returned to the owner-member. A co-op is incorporated and the members elect a board of directors. Each member has one vote. Employee credit unions and consumer co-ops are examples. (p. 87)

corporate campaign   An approach to organizing workers whose employers resist unionization. Involves the use of picketing, boycotting, and encouraging the firm's outside directors to pressure the firm's management to cease its interference or resistance to the organizing effort.

corporate charter   A document that states the purpose for which a corporation is being formed, the nature of its business, its founders, and the number of shares of stock it can issue. Granted by the state in which it is being formed, or incorporated. Authorizes the formation of a corporation. (p. 74)

corporate officers   The top managers of a corporation who are selected by the board of directors. They usually include the president, vice-president(s), secretary, and treasurer. They are employees of the board.

corporate PAC   A political organization composed of the employees of an incorporated firm. It often supports candidates and causes that are thought to be favorable to business.

corporation   The legal entity (thing) created by law that is granted rights set out in the corporate charter. A separate and legal entity apart from its owners. (p. 68)

corporation bylaws   The rules by which a corporation operates. Usually state place and time of stockholders' meetings, procedure for calling those meetings, duties of the corporate officers, procedure for changing the bylaws, etc. (p. 79)

corrective advertising   Advertising done by an advertiser to correct previous advertising that is considered deceptive by a regulatory agency such as the Federal Trade Commission.

cost of living   A measurement often used to assess the impact of inflation. It compares the prices of goods bought by consumers to their wages.

cost per contact   An expression of the cost of reaching a prospective buyer with the advertising message. It is often used in selecting among advertising media.

cost-push inflation   An increase in the price level due to increases in the cost of the factors of production.

Council of Economic Advisers   A three-member group that advises the President of the United States on economic problems. Established in 1946 to help the President to achieve the goals set out in the Employment Act of 1946.

countervailing power   The term used to describe the balance of power between big labor, big business, and government. The theory is that each is large and powerful enough to prevent any one of them from becoming too powerful and dominant in our society. (p. 84)

coupon bond   A bond for which the owner's name is not registered and does not appear on the bond. The owner clips coupons from the bond and presents them to the corporation's bank for payment of interest due.

"cowboy economy"   A phrase referring to unplanned and careless use of resources.

CPM (Critical Path Method)   A planning and control tool used by managers to estimate the time needed to complete various parts of a project, and focusing on the longest or "critical" path. (p. 241)

craft unions   Unions organized by crafts or trades—plumbers, carpenters, machinists, etc. Membership is restricted to workers with specific skills. (p. 200)

credit union   A cooperative savings association that is owned by its depositors who work for the same employer or are members of the same nonbusiness organization. Also makes loans to members. (p. 417)

cumulative quantity discount   A discount on purchases that is figured on the total volume of purchases made during a certain period of time. It encourages buyer loyalty.

cumulative voting   A requirement in some states that the number of votes a stockholder has is the number of shares owned times the number of directors to be elected. (p. 78)

current assets   Cash or property that can be quickly converted to cash. Examples are accounts receivable, inventories, short-term notes receivable. (p. 352)

current liability   Debts that must be paid in less than one year. (p. 353)

current ratio   Measure of liquidity. Current assets divided by current liabilities. (p. 359)

customary price   Long-used price level which is difficult to change because consumers are used to it.

data processing   The accumulation, storage, sorting, interpretation, and reporting of facts, mostly in numerical form. (p. 375)

debenture   A corporate bond that is backed only by the general credit and strength of the issuing corporation.

debt capital   Borrowed funds, as distinguished from equity capital or equity financing provided by the owners of the firm.

debt financing   Obtaining funds by going into debt (for example, issuing bonds). (p. 438)

decentralization   The dispersion of decision-making power in an organization. Managers in decentralized organizations disperse considerable authority throughout the organization. (p. 138)

decentralized organization   An organization in which decision-making power and authority are dispersed throughout the organization as a result of the delegation process.

decision-making process   Involves recognizing an opportunity or a problem, gathering information, developing and analyzing alternatives, choosing the best alternative(s), implementing the decision, and evaluating the decision. (p. 116)

decision rules   Rules to guide the movement of orders through various manufacturing processes.

delegation   The process of entrusting part of a superior's job (or activities) to a subordinate. Involves the three actions of assigning responsibility, granting authority, and establishing accountability. (p. 137)

demand   Exists when there are people who desire a product or a service, they have the buying power to purchase it, and they are willing to part with some buying power in order to buy it. The quantity demanded is the number of units of a product or service that people will buy at a certain price at a given point in time. (p. 36)

demand curve   A curve showing the number of units of a product or a service that will be demanded (bought) at each price at a given point in time. Usually slopes down and to the right. (p. 47)

demand deposit   Checking accounts of individuals, businesses, and other organizations. (p. 423)

demand-pull inflation   An increase in the price level due to excess demand for goods and services in relation to their supply.

demarketing   A term referring to a firm's efforts to decrease the demand for its products or services due to supply shortage. An electric utility that urges its customers to "turn off unnecessary lights" is practicing demarketing.

democratic leader   A leader who consults with his or her subordinates and allows them to participate in the decision making that affects them.

demographic   Relating to population size, characteristics, or distribution.

departmentation   The process of identifying, grouping, and assigning organizational activities to specific departments within the organization. The result is a departmented, or departmentalized, organization. (p. 132)

deposit expansion   Process by which bank deposits expand the money supply by a factor equal to the reciprocal of the reserve ratio.

depreciation   A deduction in the balance sheet to indicate a decline in value of a fixed asset over time. (p. 353)

depression   That period in the business cycle during which the volume of business activity is at a very low level. Consumers and businesses are extremely pessimistic. Unemployment is high as is the rate of business failures.

diminishing marginal utility   The greater the number of items of a particular type a person has, the less he or she is willing to pay to acquire additional units of that item.

deregulation movement   Movement during the early 1980s that sought to reduce the level of regulation at the federal level.

directing   The management function of encouraging subordinates to work toward achieving organizational objectives. Also called leading, guiding, motivating, or actuating. (p. 108)

discharge   A permanent involuntary separation due to permanent layoff or firing of an employee. (p. 189)

disciplinary action   Action which is administered by the worker's supervisor when the worker fails to adhere to employee discipline policy. It ranges from oral reprimands to discharge from the company.

discount rate   The rate at which the Federal Reserve System discounts the notes it buy from member banks that desire to increase their deposits with the system. The higher the rate, the less willing member banks are to borrow.

discouraged workers   The "hidden unemployed." Persons who want jobs but do not seek them because they believe that jobs are not available to them.

discretionary income   The amount of income a household has left after paying taxes and making expenditures for necessary goods and services. (p. 37)

dismissal   A temporary or permanent involuntary separation of an employee. (p. 188)

distribution of income   The way in which the aggregate income of a nation, region, or area is allocated among individuals or households. It determines the number of potential customers for products other than basic necessities and the number of persons eligible for welfare assistance.

Disposable Personal Income (DPI)   The incomes of people minus taxes paid by them. (p. 10)

distributed data processing   A multiple systems approach to information handling. Contrasts with large, centralized systems. (p. 382)

diversification   The involvement of a firm in a variety of products or activities at the same time.

documentation   Explanation or illustration of a computer program. (p. 385)

domestic corporation   A corporation that operates in the state in which it was chartered.

domestic international sales corporation (DISC) A tax-shelter subsidiary. By setting up a DISC, an American firm that exports goods can defer some of its taxes on export earnings.

dormant partner   A partner, in a partnership, who does not actively participate in managing the firm and whose identity is not disclosed to the public.

"double-breasted" company   A nonunion subsidiary set up by a firm whose employees are unionized.

draft   A written order made by one party (the drawer) addressed to a second party (the drawee) ordering the drawee to pay a certain amount of money to a third party (the payee). Examples are ordinary checks drawn on banks, trade acceptances, certified checks, and cashier's checks.

dumping   Shipping substantial quantities of a product to a foreign country at prices that are below either the home-market price of the same product or the full cost (including profit) of producing it. (p. 543)

echelons of management   The different layers, or levels, of management in an organization— upper, middle, and lower. (p. 99)

economic development   A process by which a nation improves its production per capita. It depends largely upon technology.

economic development council   An organization of business firms and government officials that promotes the economic development of an area. (p. 516)

economic freedoms   These include individual initiative and self-interest, private property, profit incentive, consumer power, freedom to

compete, occupational freedom, freedom of contract, and limited role of government.

the economic problem   The problem of trying to satisfy our unlimited wants with limited resources. (p. 4)

economies of scale   Savings realized by an increase in the volume of production or size of the productive unit.

ecology movement   A movement for cleaner air, water, and cities.

effective demand   (See *demand.*)

egalitarian   Pertaining to the belief that all people are equal and are entitled to the same standard of living. One who holds this belief.

embargo   Legal prohibition on the import and/or export of certain products into or out of a country. (p. 540)

employee benefits   (See *fringe benefits.*)

employee orientation   The process of introducing a new employee to the job and to the firm. Also called induction or indoctrination. (p. 177)

Employment Act of 1946   This law imposes on the federal government the responsibility to promote full employment, maximum economic growth, and price stability.

encounter groups   (See *T-group training.*)

endowment insurance   A type of insurance that emphasizes savings over protection. It is in effect for a stated number of years. If the insured dies during the period, the face value is paid to the beneficiary. If the insured lives, the insured receives the face value.

entrepreneur   A person who assumes the risk of organizing and managing a business in the hope of making a profit. (p. 14)

entrepreneurship   Bringing land, labor, and capital together and managing them productively to produce a good or service to make a profit. (p. 14)

environment   All the outside factors that may come into contact with and influence the behavior or success of an organization or any entity. (p. 574)

equal opportunity employer   An employer who hires, promotes, and pays people without regard to race, sex, or national origin.

equipment trust certificates   These are like short-term bonds and are backed by the equipment purchased with reveneus from the sale of the certificates. (p. 489)

equity   Claims on resources or assets. The two major types of equity are owner's equity and liabilities. (p. 348)

equity financing   The provision of funds by the owner(s) of a firm. For example, issuing stock or using retained profits. (p. 439)

equity theory of compensation   Equity is the perceived fairness of what a worker does compared to what he or she receives from the employer. Inequity results when the worker perceives imbalances between the inputs (such as skills) and the outputs (tangible and intangible rewards from the employer).

escalator clause   A provision in a collective bargaining agreement that wage hikes will be granted on the basis of changes in the cost of living. These hikes are called cost-of-living adjustments (COLA). (p. 210)

esteem needs   In Maslow's hierarchy of needs they include social-esteem needs such as prestige and status, and self-esteem needs such as competence and self-respect.

ethics   A system of "oughts." A way of defining obligations and rights among people.

European Economic Community (EEC)   (See *common market.*)

exchange   Makes specialization, or division of labor, possible. A specialist trades part of his or her output for part of the output of other specialists. Trading one thing for another thing. (p. 7)

exchange control   Government control over access to a country's currency by foreigners. (p. 541)

exit interview   An interview conducted with an employee who is leaving the firm. Its purpose is to find out the reasons for leaving. (p. 188)

expense   The using up of resources. Expenses are deducted from the revenues in the pursuit of which they were incurred. (p. 349)

exports   Goods produced in country A and sold in country B are an export of country A. The opposite of imports. (p. 535)

expropriation   In international business expropriation occurs when a government takes over ownership of a foreign-owned subsidiary. The firm may or may not be compensated, and it may be run by the government or sold to private citizens in the expropriating country. (p. 556)

facilitating middleman   One who participates in transporting and storing a product as it moves through its distribution channel, but who does not participate in the actual buying and selling of it. Examples are railroads and public warehouses.

factoring company   Also called a factor. A company that buys accounts receivable from a firm. It pays less than the face value of the accounts (it buys them at a discount) but collects the face value of the accounts from its client's customers. The difference, minus the factor's cost of doing business, is the factor's profit. (p. 417)

factors of production   The elements needed for producing goods and services. The inputs of the productive system: land, labor, capital, and entrepreneurship. (p. 12)

Fair Labor Standards Act   A 1938 law that defines the normal working week, requires time-and-a-half pay for all hours over forty worked by an employee during a week, and establishes a federal minimum wage. (p. 197)

fashion obsolescence   Obsolescence of a product due to a change in fashion.

featherbedding   Paying for work which workers do not perform or offer to perform.

Federal Advisory Council   A council of 12 members who advise the board of governors of the Federal Reserve System. There is one member from each Federal Reserve Bank.

Federal Communications Commission (FCC)   Established in 1939, this agency regulates the broadcast media and communications carriers.

Federal Deposit Insurance Corporation (FDIC)   An agency of the U.S. government created to insure national banks' depositors (up to $100,000 for each account). Insured banks pay a fee. Open to state banks. (p. 412)

Federal Fair Packaging and Labeling Act of 1966   A law requiring that consumer goods be clearly labeled in order to provide consumers with product-related information.

Federal Open Market Committee (FOMC)   A committee composed of 12 members (7 from the board of governors and 5 from Federal Reserve banks) who set the Federal Reserve's open-market policy. It directs the Federal Reserve banks either to buy or to sell government securities.

Federal Power Commission (FPC)   This commission has jurisdiction over interstate electric transmission lines, the sale of electric utilities, and the transmission of natural gas by pipeline; it also regulates interstate electric rates.

Federal Reserve System (the "Fed")   A banking system created by the Federal Reserve Act of 1913 to regulate the nation's money supply. Its 12 Federal Reserve Banks are privately owned, but their operations are controlled by the board of governors of the Federal Reserve System. (p. 427)

Federal Savings and Loan Insurance Corporation (FSLIC)   An agency of the U.S. government that insures accounts in member savings and loan associations up to $100,000 for each account.

Federal Trade Commission (FTC)   The FTC Act of 1914 created the FTC, which regulates competition and controls unfair or deceptive practices in interstate commerce.

fee simple   A person is the owner in fee simple of real property when he or she owns the entire estate.

fidelity bond   Insurance that protects, up to the policy limits, the employer from employee theft of company funds.

final selection interview   The last in a series of interviews of a prospective new employee. It comes after the in-depth interview. (p. 176)

financial accounting   The accounting process directed toward the flow of resources, communicating with people outside the firm. (p. 344)

firm's publics   Those groups in society that have an interest in the affairs of a firm—its owners, employees, labor unions, suppliers, creditors, government, etc.

fixed asset   An asset which, when originally acquired, is expected to have a lifetime of more than one year. (p. 353)

fixed cost   Costs that do not vary in total as the volume of business varies (for example, executive salaries and fire insurance premiums).

flex time   Flexible, as opposed to fixed, working hours.

floor planning   A special type of secured financing in which title to inventories passes to the lender, who pays the bill. (p. 449)

flowchart   (See *block diagram.*)

focus group interview   Marketing research tool whereby a group of people is interviewed informally so as to generate ideas for further research regarding a product or service. (p. 279)

Food and Drug Administration (FDA)   The federal agency charged with protecting the people from dangerous foods and drugs.

foreign assembly   The assembling of a finished product by a subsidiary or licensee in a host country from parts exported to it by a parent firm.

foreign corporation   A corporation that operates in states other than the one in which it was chartered.

foreign exchange   Money transactions in international trade. International trade requires that firms in different countries transact business in different currencies.

foreign exchange rate   The ratio of one currency to another. It tells how much a unit of one currency is worth in terms of a unit of another. (p. 548)

foreign freight forwarder   A middleman who consolidates small export shipments into large ones, arranges for transportation and insurance, and handles both export and import documentation for clients. (p. 553)

foreign licensing   The licensing of a firm in one country by a licensor in another country to make and sell the licensor's product in the licensee's country. (p. 558)

form utility   The increase in value of products because form has been changed or separated parts have been combined, which increases the usefulness of the products. (p. 279)

FORTRAN   Short for "Formula Translator." FORTRAN is a science-oriented computer language. (p. 384)

forward vertical integration   A term that describes a firm's integration forward from its present type of operation. Examples are a wholesaler who goes into retailing or a raw-materials supplier who goes into manufacturing.

formal leader   One who is delegated authority or power over his or her subordinates.

formal organization   The structure created by management so that human, financial, and physical resources of the firm can be related to each other. Depicted by the organization chart.

franchised retailer   A retail firm operating under a licensing agreement with a franchise grantor. Examples include car dealerships and fast-food restaurants. (p. 301)

franchisee   A person or firm that is licensed by a franchiser to sell its products or services in a specific territory under a franchising agreement. (p. 519)

franchiser   A person or firm that licenses franchisees to sell its products or services in specified territories under a franchising agreement. (p. 519)

franchising   Licensing of a name, design, process, or symbol by its owner for use by others. Also applies to setting up small retail or service firms under such a licensing agreement.

franchising agreement   The contract between a franchiser and his or her franchisees. (p. 519)

frequency distribution   A means of describing a large group of values. Intervals or ranges of values are established first. Then the number of values falling within each interval is computed and listed next to the interval. (p. 393)

fringe benefits   Paid vacations, retirement plans, sick leave, and so on that accompany the wage or salary the employee receives.

functional authority   Authority of the staff to issue orders directly to line managers. This authority is granted only in the staff's area of expertise. (p. 142)

functional discount   A discount given to a channel member (middleman) for performance of a specific marketing function. An example is an advertising allowance. (p. 329)

functions of management   Planning, organizing, staffing, directing, and controlling. Together, they constitute managerial work. (p. 104)

future estate   Property owned but that cannot be enjoyed until some future time. A wife owns a future estate in property that her husband owns but that will go to her upon his death.

futures markets   The buying and selling of contracts to receive or deliver a certain quantity and grade of commodity at a specified future date. Most futures trading does not result in the physical exchange of goods. Buyers of futures contracts try to protect themselves against adverse future price changes or try to make speculative profits from those price changes.

Gantt Chart   A control chart used to schedule production that involves a number of interdependent processes.

General Agreement on Tariffs and Trade (GATT)   A treaty among the world's major trading nations that is administered by a permanent secretariat through which member countries act jointly to reduce tariff and nontariff trade barriers. (p. 544)

general partner   A partner with unlimited liability for the debts of the partnership and who actively participates in the management of the firm.

generic brand   A product identifed by the name of the product class to which it belongs rather than by a manufacturer or a middleman brand. For example, "laundry detergent" rather than Tide or Topco.

"givebacks"   Concessions made by unions to existing collective bargaining agreements in order to protect their members' jobs.

goal congruence   The coincidence of personal and corporate goals.

"going public"   Phrase referring to a small private corporation that is preparing to offer its shares of ownership (stock) for sale to the general public.

goodwill   An intangible asset which a firm acquires when buying a business which has built up a good reputation so that its value is greater than the book value at the time of purchase.

grievance   A complaint about the job that is taken up with management. A simple complaint is not a legitimate grievance unless it violates the worker's rights.

grievance procedure   The sequence of steps a grieved employee should follow in seeking to correct the cause of the grievance. A grievance is a complaint about an alleged violation of a collective bargaining agreement or the law as it applies to a worker. Included in most collective bargaining agreements. (p. 214)

Gross Domestic Product   A country's Gross National Product minus net property income from abroad.

gross margin   Total dollar sales minus the cost of goods sold.

Gross National Product (GNP)   The market value of all final products and services produced by a nation during a given year. (p. 9)

gross profit   Sales minus cost of goods sold. The amount of profit before operating expenses are deducted to compute net operating profit. (p. 355)

gross working capital   Total current assets.

group norms   Standards of behavior established by groups. An example is an upper limit on production that workers set.

group sanctions   The rewards or punishments that a group confers upon its members for living up to or violating group norms of behavior.

guaranteed annual wage   A provision in a collective bargaining agreement that maintains the worker's income at some agreed-on level during a year. (p. 205)

hard-to-employ   A term which describes persons who, because of education, race, physical handicap, or background, are unemployed.

hardware   The electronic and mechanical components of a data processing system. (p. 376)

hierarchy of needs   A. H. Maslow's ranking of human needs: physiological, safety, belonging, esteem, and self-actualization needs. The lowest level of needs, the physiological needs, are the most prepotent. They are the first to emerge. (p. 148)

hierarchy of organizational objectives   A breakdown of broad, overall organizational objectives into divisional, departmental, work-group, and individual worker objectives. (p. 132)

histogram   A graphic representation of a frequency distribution, using bars or columns to indicate frequency. (p. 394)

horizontal integration   The buying out by a firm at one level in a distribution system of other firms on that same level. An example is a supermarket chain buying out another supermarket chain.

human resource   The personnel who staff a firm, including both workers and managers. (p. 164)

Humphrey-Hawkins Full Employment Act   A 1978 law that reenforces previous government policy to maintain employment. It includes emphasis on economy in government and greater reliance on the private sector.

imports   Goods produced in country A and bought by people in country B are imports of country B. The opposite of exports. (p. 535)

import quota   A limit set by the government on the amount of a product that can enter the country. (p. 539)

import surcharge   A tax on goods imported into a country that makes them more expensive to buy. The purpose is to reduce imports.

incentive pay   Payments made to a worker who exceeds his or her quota under a piece-rate system. In general, the purpose is to encourage and reward increased employee productivity. (p. 182)

income distribution A statistical illustration of the numbers of persons or families or households found in each of several income brackets covering the entire range of incomes.

income statement A financial statement showing revenues, expenses, and profits of a firm during a given period of time. (p. 355)

in-depth interview The interview given to an applicant who passes the selection tests. It is conducted by trained specialists to shed light on the applicant's motivation, ability to work with others, ability to communicate, etc. (p. 175)

individualism The idea that the group, the society, and the government are necessary but are less important than the individual's self-determination. A characteristic of a free enterprise, or capitalist, economic system. (p. 17)

Individual Retirement Account (IRA) Account that any employed person with earned income can establish at various types of financial institutions. The money in an IRA—and the interest it earns—is tax-free until the person begins to make withdrawals after age 59 $1/2$.

industrial goods Products sold to business firms, such as installations, accessory equipment, component parts and materials, supplies, and raw materials to make another product or to provide a service. Industrial services also are included. (p. 263)

industrial services A category of industrial goods. They are often necessary to support plant or office operations. Examples are maintenance services and food services purchased from other firms.

industrial unions Unions organized according to industries—steel, auto, clothing, etc. Include semiskilled and unskilled workers. (p. 200)

inflation An increase in the prices of goods and services over a period of time that has the effect of reducing the purchasing power of a nation's currency. (p. 9)

inflationary psychology A widespread belief among the people in an economic system that prices will rise rapidly, resulting in little incentive to save money rather than spend it.

informal groups Face-to-face groups created by their members to satisfy needs that are not being satisfied on the job by management. They arise naturally as a result of human interaction on the job. (p. 151)

informal leader One who enjoys influence over others because they want and accept him or her as leader.

informal organization The entire complex of informal groups that exists within the framework of the formal organization but is separate from it. (p. 151)

informative labeling A marketing practice that describes for the consumer in simple terms the content, nutrition, precautions, durability, or other special features of a product. (p. 296)

injunction An order issued by a court. A mandatory injunction requires performance of a specific act. A prohibitory injunction orders the defendant to refrain from certain acts. In labor relations, an injunction granted to an employer orders employees to return to work or not to strike. (p. 196)

input-output device Any piece of equipment that allows information to be fed into a computer or permits the computer to make information available to its user (for example, a typewriter terminal). Also called peripheral equipment. (p. 378)

inside directors Members of the board of directors of a corporation who are also officers of the corporation.

"insider" A person who owns more than 10 percent of the stock of a publicly-held corporation. Must register with the Securities and Exchange Commission.

insolvency A firm or person is insolvent when its debts exceed its ability to pay them off with readily available funds.

installations A category of industrial goods. They are costly and do not become a physical part of the goods they are used to produce. Major equipment and buildings are examples.

installment credit A type of credit that involves making regular monthly payments (installments) on credit purchases, usually of durable products such as cars.

institutional advertising Advertising that is intended to promote the advertiser's organization as a whole rather than one of its products. An example is the slogan "GM Mark of Excellence."

institutional investors Professional investors who invest in the securities of other firms and government securities (for example, mutual funds, pension funds, investment clubs, insurance companies).

insurable interest People or firms have an insurable interest when they can show that they would suffer a loss from the thing insured against. (p. 458)

insurable risks Dangers or perils against which insurance firms are willing to insure. (p. 458)

insurance company A firm that shares pure risk with its policyholders (customers) for the payment of a premium.

insurance premium The price paid for insurance protection.

intangible assets Assets that do not have a tangible form but are still valuable, for example, goodwill.

intelligence tests   Tests used to measure a person's general verbal abilities and specific abilities such as reasoning.

intelligent terminals   Remote input-output devices that are also computers in themselves. They can "talk" back and forth with the main computer.

interest   The amount paid for using borrowed money.

intermediate-term financing   One to ten year financing. (p. 489)

intermittent production   Production that stops and starts. This happens because the products may require several different kinds of treatments or because stocks must be replenished from time to time. (p. 227)

intermodal service   Transportation that uses the facilities of two or more modes of transportation as complements or supplements to one another, for example, piggyback truck/train transportation.

international business   The business activities of a firm that involve persons or firms outside the home nation of that firm.

international trade   The exchange of goods and services among countries. (p. 534)

interstate commerce   Commerce between or among states.

Interstate Commerce Commission (ICC)   This agency, created by law in 1889, regulates rates of all forms of interstate public transportation except air carriers, pipeline companies, and certain intraurban carriers.

intrastate commerce   Commerce within a particular state.

inventory   Items of value kept in stock for sale (merchandise inventory) or use (supplies or parts inventory). A major type of asset. Also applies to the process of accounting for the level of such assets.

inventory turnover rate   The cost of goods sold divided by the average inventory. A high turnover rate indicates efficiency in the use of resources. (p. 330)

investment   Process of putting money into business firms in order to try to make a profit. (See *capital formation.*)

investment bank   A bank that does not accept deposits from the general public, but helps corporations sell new issues of stocks and bonds. Also called an underwriting house. (p. 472)

isolationism   Noninvolvement with other countries. An isolationist country limits its social and economic contact with other countries.

job analysis   Defining the jobs that must be done if a firm is to reach its goals. (p. 168)

job application form   A form prepared by an employer to be completed by a job applicant. The applicant gives a written summary of his or her education, experience, skills, etc. Also called an application blank or a biographical inventory. (p. 173)

job costing system   Computer-based cost accounting system to keep track of various costs of doing a specific job.

job description   A listing and description of the nature and requirements of a job. Prepared from the job analysis. (p. 169)

job enlargement   The addition of new tasks to a worker's job.

job enrichment   The process of redesigning jobs to satisfy the worker's higher-level needs and organizational needs by improving worker satisfaction and task efficiency. It gives workers more responsibility, authority, and autonomy in planning and doing their work. (p. 112)

job evaluation   A part of wage and salary administration. A method for determining the relationship between pay rates for particular job classifications. Considers factors such as the desirability of the work, amount of skill, and education needed to perform a given job.

job rotation   Involves periodically assigning workers to new jobs in order to reduce boredom.

job selection formula   A system of value-weighting and scoring to help someone decide the kind of job he or she wants.

job sharing   A new working arrangement to accommodate people who cannot work full time. Two workers share one job, salary, and set of benefits.

job-skill training   Training an employee how to do a job. It can be done on the job or away from the job. Its main purpose is to teach specific job skills. (p. 178)

job specification   A statement of the personal qualifications (education, skill, experience, etc.) needed by the person who is to fill each job. Prepared from the job analysis. (p. 169)

joint liability   Liability for debts that exists in a general partnership. Each general partner is responsible for the business debts incurred by the other general partner(s).

joint tenancy   The sharing by two or more persons of title to personal or real property. Each has equal rights to use and enjoy the property during their lives. When one owner dies, the entire estate goes to the surviving title holder(s), not to that owner's heirs.

joint venture   A special type of temporary partnership arrangement that is set up for a specific purpose and ends when that purpose is accomplished. (p. 87) In international business, a partnership of two or more partners that are based in different countries. They share ownership and control of the venture's operations and property rights. (p. 558)

journal   In accounting, books in which original

entries are recorded in chronological order and then transferred to ledgers.

jurisdictional dispute　Controversy between or among labor unions regarding which union should perform which jobs or which union should represent workers in a given industry or firm.

keypunch machine　A machine used to record information on computer punch cards by punching holes in them. Similar to a typewriter.

key ratio　A financial ratio computed from items on the financial statements of a firm and used to evaluate the credit risk or financial strength of a firm. Typical ratios are published by Dun & Bradstreet. (p. 358)

label　That part of the total product which describes the content and other features (durability, precautions, etc.) of the product.

labor　A factor of production. Human mental and physical effort needed to produce goods and services. (p. 13)

laboratory training　(See *T-group training.*)

labor force　Persons able and willing to work and actively seeking jobs or currently employed.

labor-intensive　A production process involving relatively large amounts of human input. Wages are a major production cost. (p. 228)

labor relations　The relationship between management and unionized employees.

labor turnover　Employees quitting their jobs.

labor union　An organization of employees formed for the purpose of dealing collectively with their employers in order to further the interests of those employees. (p. 194)

laissez faire　Let people do as they please. As an economic philosophy, it means let the owners of business set the rules of competition without governmental regulation or control. (p. 15)

land　A factor of production. Includes all natural resources. (p. 12)

Landrum-Griffin Act　A 1959 law that requires unions and employers to file financial reports with the Secretary of Labor and that contains provisions to ensure democratic operation of unions. A labor-reform amendment to the Taft-Hartley Act. (p. 198)

law of demand　More of a product or service is demanded (will be bought) at a lower price than at a higher price. Graphically depicted as a demand curve. (p. 36)

law of large numbers　A probability calculation of the likelihood of the occurrence of perils on which premiums are based. (p. 456)

law of supply　More of a product or service is supplied (offered for sale) at a higher price than at a lower price. Graphically depicted as a supply curve. (p. 43)

layoff　Temporary separation of an employee from his or her job due to variation in the demand for the products the company markets. Also used to discipline employees.

layout　The arrangement of parts in a printed advertisement—illustration, headline, and copy.

leader pricing　Pricing a widely bought item at a low price to attract buyers to a retail store.

leadership　The manager's ability to get subordinates to develop their capabilities by inspiring them to achieve. (p. 112)

lease　An agreement to grant use of an asset for a period of time for stated regular payments.

leasing　The act of renting buildings, equipment, etc., rather than buying them. The lessor is the party who rents to the lessee.

ledger　Account books of final entry. Each ledger shows a current balance. Examples are cash, accounts receivable, and accounts payable ledgers.

legal reserves　The amount of money that member banks of the Federal Reserve System must maintain in the form of cash or deposits with a Federal Reserve Bank.

legal tender　Coins and paper money. Creditors must accept them in payment of debts that are expressed in money terms.

letter of inquiry　Letter sent to a possible employer to inquire about a job opportunity. (p. 643)

leverage　Using borrowed funds to earn more than their cost. (p. 440)

liability　A nonowner's claim against a firm. (p. 348)

life estate　An interest in property that is granted to or willed to a person and that lasts only during the possessor's lifetime.

life insurance　This provides a degree of financial security to the insured's family or firm. The insurer pays a cash benefit to a surviving person or firm upon the death of the person insured. (p. 462)

life insurance company　A mutual or stock company that shares risk with its policyholders for payment of a premium. A source of long-term funds for some business firms. (p. 417)

lifestyle　A pattern of work, leisure, sexual habits, and tastes.

limited liability　Stockholders of a corporation enjoy limited liability for debts of the corporation. Unlike proprietors and partners whose personal, and in some cases, real property can be taken to satisfy company debts, the stockholder's liability is limited to the amount he or she paid for the shares of stock. Limited partners also may enjoy limited liability.

limited partner　A partner who enjoys limited liability for the debts of the partnership and who does not actively participate in the management of the firm.

limited partnership   A type of partnership in which there is at least one general partner and one or more others (limited partners) whose financial liability is limited to their financial investment in the firm. (p. 86)

limited payment life insurance   Insurance for which the insured pays premiums only for a stated number of years, at the end of which his or her policy is paid up.

line and staff organization   A type of organization structure comprised of line managers in the chain of command who are advised and served by staff personnel who are outside the chain of command.

line authority   The right to direct subordinates' work. The authority relationship that exists between superiors and subordinates. The chain of command. (p. 139)

line functions   Organizational functions that contribute directly to reaching primary firm goals. Production and marketing are line functions in a manufacturing firm. (p. 141)

line of credit   An unsecured bank loan in which the bank stands ready to lend up to a particular amount with some restrictions. (p. 449)

line organization   The oldest and simplest type of organization structure in which a person in the chain of command takes orders from people higher in the chain and gives orders to people lower in the chain.

linear programming   A mathematical tool used to allocate resources in the "best way" so that a desired objective is maximized or minimized. (p. 397)

liquidity   The ability to pay bills, wages, and other current payments when they fall due. (p. 442)

listed securities   Stocks and bonds that are traded on organized stock exchanges such as the New York Stock Exchange.

load mutual fund   The purchase price of a share that includes a sales commission.

lobbying   Efforts to influence the passage, administration, or enforcement of laws. (p. 202)

local development company   A corporation set up by citizens of a community for the purpose of improving their local economy by promoting and assisting the development of small business firms.

local union   The basic unit of union organization. A local of a craft union is made up of artisans in the same craft in a relatively small geographical area. A local of an industrial union is made up of workers in a given industry in a relatively small geographical area. (p. 200)

lockout   An employer's tool in labor disputes. Employees are locked out or denied access to their place of employment until they accept the employer's terms of employment. (p. 216)

logistics   (See *physical distribution*.)

long run   Usually a period of time that exceeds one year; equivalent of long term.

machine language   Set of instructions in binary form designed for use in a specific computer model. (p. 384)

maintenance factors   In Frederick Herzberg's theory of motivation, maintenance (or hygiene) factors include pay, working conditions, and job security. They are job context, or extrinsic, factors that are not part of the work itself. They tend to be dissatisfiers if they are absent or inadequate.

make-or-buy decisions   Decisions about the economy of making a product or a component part or buying it. (p. 232)

management   The process of achieving goals by bringing together and coordinating the human, financial, and physical resources of an organization. (p. 98)

management by exception   Also called the exception principle. Managers who practice this grant authority to lower-level managers to make routine decisions. This enables upper-level managers to devote more time to nonroutine decisions. (p. 121)

management by objectives (MBO)   Also called managing by results. The manager gets together with each subordinate to set his or her objectives. Allows the subordinate to participate in goal setting. The subordinate is considered to have performed well if he or she accomplishes those objectives. (p. 105)

management development   Training present and potential managers to improve their managerial abilities. It focuses mainly on developing the manager's conceptual and human relations skills. (p. 179)

management information system (MIS)   A firm's MIS is made up of people and machines. People feed in data that are deemed necessary for decision-making purposes. These data are processed and fed out as information to decision makers who need it.

manager   A person who works through other people (subordinates). A manager "brings together" their efforts to accomplish goals. (p. 98)

managerial accounting   The accounting process when internally directed to facilitate the firm's management. (p. 344)

managerial skills   Conceptual skills, people skills, and technical skills. All managers need all three skills. (p. 101)

manufacturers' agent   An agent middleman representing a manufacturer or manufacturers in a specific region for a given commission. (p. 299)

margin requirement   The percentage that buyers of securities must put up in cash when they buy them. It is set by the board of governors of the Federal Reserve System. (p. 431)

margin trading   A person who buys securities partly on credit financed by his or her stockbroker engages in margin trading. (p. 479)

market economy   An economic system in which relative prices determine how productive resources (the factors of production) will be allocated and how the goods and services produced will be distributed. These prices are determined in markets through the interaction of supply and demand. (p. 34)

marketing   A set of activities undertaken to find, influence, and serve customers for goods and services. Includes product design, place, promotion, and pricing activities. (p. 260)

marketing concept   The guiding philosophy that says a firm must be consumer-oriented and that the entire firm must recognize this fact in order to make a profit. (p. 262)

marketing mix   A certain combination of the elements of price, product, promotion, and place (or distribution) manipulated by a firm in order to achieve its marketing objectives. (p. 286)

marketing research   The systematic gathering, recording, and analyzing of data concerning the marketing of products and services. (p. 276)

market penetration pricing   A pricing strategy for introducing a new product. Setting a price low to secure a market share for the product. (p. 329)

market segment   A subgroup within a market that is made up of people who have one or more characteristics in common. For example, one segment of the market for motels is made up of young couples who take vacations with children.

market segmentation   Designing a special marketing mix for a special segment of the market or several mixes for several different segments. (p. 271)

market share   The proportion of the total market for a type of product held by a given seller.

market skimming pricing   A pricing strategy for introducing a new product. Setting a high initial price in order to get maximum quick return on product development costs, often in anticipation of entry of competition into the market within a short period. (p. 330)

market system   An economic system in which prices are determined in markets. The market forces of supply and demand determine relative prices.

markup   An addition to cost by a middleman. A middleman adds a markup to the cost of an item in order to compute selling price. It can be expressed in money terms or as a percentage. (p. 325)

mass production   The application of technology and scientific management to the continuous production of a large volume of goods.

materials management   Management of inventories of raw materials, partly finished products, finished products, and maintenance of capital goods.

matrix organization   An organizational structure that includes horizontal reporting requirements in addition to the traditional vertical chain of command. Organizational activities are structured in both functional and project arrangements and functional and project managers have authority over the same subordinates. (p. 145)

maturity   The factor of time repayment. When a debt matures it must be paid. (p. 440)

mechanization   Changing from manual operation to machine operation.

median   The middle value of a group of values ranked in order of magnitude. (p. 392)

mediation   A method of settling a labor-management dispute. A neutral party suggests a possible compromise of the dispute. (p. 212)

mercantilism   An economic philosophy that advocated building strong national states and that viewed a nation's strength to be in its supply of precious metals, such as gold and silver. (p. 15)

merchandise inventory   All goods purchased for sale but not yet resold are reported in this account. A current asset on the balance sheet.

merchant middlemen   Those who actually take title to the merchandise that they offer for resale.

merger   Two firms join together, or combine, to create a new firm. The new firm is usually created under friendly terms and the stockholders of each merger partner usually get newly issued stock of the new firm. (p. 490)

merit rating system   An approach to evaluating employee performance. Performance is appraised periodically by each worker's supervisor. Performance criteria include personal traits and work habits. (p. 181)

microcomputer   A desk-top sized computer system with variable memory capabilities that includes a video display terminal and a keyboard. Priced between $1500 and $10,000 it is used in schools, homes, and offices.

microprocessor   Small, special-purpose computer such as might be used on a car to control fuel consumption or in computer games.

middlemen   Firms that participate in buying and selling products as part of a channel of distribution. (p. 263)

military-industrial complex   A powerful network of military planners and industrial firms that influences the use of a large part of our nation's resources and guides research and development. (p. 622)

minicomputer   The next-to-smallest sized computer that has substantial memory capability and a larger core memory. Priced between $25,000 and $100,000, it is used primarily by businesses.

minority enterprise   The ownership of their own businesses by ethnic or racial minorities.

Minority Enterprise Small Business Investment Company   A small business investment company that is created to further minority enterprise. It is privately owned and privately operated and is licensed by the Small Business Administration to provide long-term financing and management assistance to small, minority-owned business firms. (See *Small Business Investment Company.*)

mixed economic system   A system that is not purely capitalist or purely collectivist. Such a system has a private and a public sector.

mode   The most frequent value in an array. (p. 393)

modem   A device that converts direct current (DC) signals to tones and then converts them back to DC signals. This makes it possible to use ordinary telephone cables for transmission of computer programs and data. (p. 380)

modes of transportation   Ways of transporting goods and people—air, water, rail, motor carrier, and pipeline.

money   Paper currency, coins, checkable deposits at banks and other financial institutions, and traveler's checks of nonbank issuers. (p. 410)

money market mutual fund   A pool of funds invested in Treasury bills, commercial paper, and "jumbo" ($100,000 or more) certificates of deposit. The interest rate investors in a fund receive varies with the returns received from the average of the fund's various investments. (p. 425)

monopolistic competition   A market condition existing when many sellers compete for customers by offering differentiated products. (p. 325)

monopoly   A market condition in which the single producer could theoretically demand as high a price as "the market will bear," or as high a price as buyers will pay before seeking substitutes for the product.

morale   Employee attitudes about the work environment.

motivation   The result of the drive to satisfy an internal urge. Managers must structure jobs so that they provide incentives that will satisfy workers' needs if those workers apply effort on the job. By doing this, managers can motivate their subordinates to work toward company objectives. (p. 110)

motivational factors   In Frederick Herzberg's theory of motivation, motivational factors (motivators) include achievement, recognition, and responsibility. They occur as part of the work itself and are job content, or intrinsic, factors that make work rewarding in and of itself.

multinational company (MNC)   A firm having production and marketing operations spread over several countries. The ultimate commitment to international business. A global enterprise. (p. 554)

mutual company   A firm that is owned by its user members. An example is a life insurance company that is owned by its policyholders. (p. 88)

mutual fund   The owners of a mutual fund pool their investment dollars and buy securities in other businesses. Buying one share in a mutual fund makes you part owner of all the securities owned by the fund. (p. 481)

National Credit Union Administration   A U.S. government agency that insures accounts in member credit unions up to $100,000 per account.

nationalization   In international business, nationalization occurs when a government expropriates a foreign-owned firm and the government runs the nationalized firm. The owners of the firm may or may not be compensated.

National Labor Relations Board (NLRB)   Created by the Wagner Act, the board investigates cases of alleged unfair labor practices committed by employers and unions and issues orders to prevent them. It is responsible for holding elections to determine whether or not a firm's employees want a union and, if so, which one. (p. 198)

national union   The organization set up to bring all the member local unions of a particular craft or industry together for bargaining purposes. (p. 200)

near cash   Assets that can be quickly converted into cash. An example is short-term Treasury bills.

negotiable instruments   Checks, promissory notes, etc., the ownership of which may be transferred from one party to another.

negotiable order of withdrawal (NOW)   Account that is available in commercial banks and savings and loan associations as well as savings banks. It permits payment of interest on a checking account as long as a minimum balance is kept. (p. 414)

net annual household formation   Number of households formed minus the number disbanded. (p. 606)

net profit   What remains after expenses are deducted from revenues. (p. 350)

net working capital   Total current assets minus current liabilities.

New Deal   Term applied to the set of national programs introduced by the Franklin D. Roosevelt administration during the Great Depression of the 1930s.

new product committee   Consists of personnel from several different departments, such as production, marketing, finance, and research and development. Reviews and acts on new product ideas generated by the firm. An example of the matrix form of organization. (p. 293)

noise   Any barrier that interferes with the communication process.

no-load mutual fund   A fund in which the purchase price of a share is net asset value (no sales commission).

nominal partner   A person who is not an actual partner in a firm but whose name is identified with the firm. Usually a well-known personality.

noncumulative quantity discount   A discount on purchases that is figured on the size of each individual order, not on the total volume purchased during a certain period of time. Encourages the buyer to place larger orders.

noninstallment credit   A type of credit that involves paying in full credit purchases at the end of the credit period, usually 30 days.

nonprice competition   Competition among firms based upon advertising, product differentiation, service, and so on, rather than price differences.

nonroutine decision   A nonrecurring decision. The two types are strategic and tactical. (p. 120)

norms   Standards of behavior. (See *group norms*.)

Norris-LaGuardia Act   A 1932 law that prohibits employers from using an injunction in labor disputes unless employers can meet the strong requirements set out in the act. Also outlaws the yellow-dog contract. (p. 196)

nutritional labeling   The practice of including nutritional information on the label of a food product.

NYSE   The New York Stock Exchange; "the big board."

obsolescence   Growing old, becoming outdated or not as efficient as newer products; applied to technological or fashion products. (p. 244)

Occupational Outlook Handbook   Publication by the U.S. Department of Labor which provides a general overview of occupations and opportunities therein. Revised every two years.

Occupational Safety and Health Act (OSHA)   A 1970 federal law. Passed to help ensure that every working man and woman in the nation has a safe and healthful work environment. Enforced by the Occupational Safety and Health Review Commission. (p. 186)

odd lot   Less than 100 shares of stock.

oligopoly   A market condition existing when a few firms sell highly similar products and dominate a market. (p. 325)

online real-time system   A computer system that permits direct and continuous access by employees to stored information. (p. 383)

open-book account   A type of credit arrangement in which the seller of merchandise bills the buyer when the ordered merchandise is shipped. No credit instruments are involved. The seller includes the bill along with the shipment of merchandise.

open corporation   A corporation whose stock is widely held by investors and is actively traded.

open market operations   Federal Reserve banks' buying and selling of government securities to control member bank reserves and, consequently, the money supply.

open shop   An employer may hire either union and/or nonunion workers. Employees need not join or pay dues to a union. (p. 206)

operational planning   Planning for the day-to-day survival of a firm. A major responsibility of middle- and lower-level managers. (p. 105)

operations management   A general term applied to production, financial, and marketing management with an emphasis on the treatment of all three as parts of a system that is subject to improvement by scientific management methods. The focus is on current operations and control. (p. 248)

operations research (OR)   Various complex quantitative techniques used by managers to assist them in decision making. (p. 397)

opportunity costs   Costs of losing an option to use funds in another way. (p. 447)

optimum   Pertaining to the best result possible under given conditions.

organization   Something that is structured so that human activity can be coordinated to accomplish objectives. The three basic components (people, activities, and physical resources) are related to each other through the organizing process. (p. 129)

organizational objectives   The goals that the formal organization is structured to accomplish. Examples are "to increase market share" (economic objective) and "to be a good community citizen" (social objective).

organization chart   A diagram showing an organization's formal structure at a given point in time. It indicates the functions that must be performed if the organization is to accomplish its objectives, the chain of command, how the firm is departmented, how the departments relate to each other, the various positions in the organization, and the titles of these positions. (p. 138)

organization development   A re-education process that is used to change the values and behavior of the entire organization in order to improve its effectiveness in reaching its objectives and in solving problems. Uses knowledge in the fields of psychology and sociology to improve organizations. (p. 180)

organization manual   The handbook given to employees that contains information on company policies and procedures.

organized labor   That part of the total workforce that is unionized.

organizing   The management function of relating people, tasks (or activities), and resources to each other so that a firm can accomplish its objectives. (p. 107)

outside data storage systems Means of storing data other than in the CPU itself. Magnetic tape and disks are examples. (p. 377)

outside directors Members of the board of directors of a corporation who are not corporate officers.

overhead cost (See *fixed cost.*)

over-the-counter market (OTC) A complex of securities dealers who are in constant touch with one another. Stocks and bonds of locally owned corporations, as well as new issues of stocks and bonds, most government bonds, and the stocks of most banks, mutual funds, and insurance companies are traded here. (p. 476)

owner-managers People who own and directly manage their business firms.

owners' equity The claim of owners against resources of the firm. Often referred to as *capital.* In a corporation it is called *shareholders' equity.* (p. 349)

ownership utility The actual transfer of title to a product creates the utility of ownership. (p. 280)

package An important part of the "total product." The container or wrapper for the physical product. Protects the product, divides it into convenient units, and serves a promotional role.

participative management The manager encourages and allows his or her subordinates to involve themselves directly in the decision making that will affect them. (p. 109)

partnership Defined by the Uniform Partnership Act as "an association of two or more persons to carry on as co-owners of a business for profit." (p. 65)

partnership agreement Also called Articles of Partnership or Articles of Copartnership. An oral, but preferably written, contract between the owners of a partnership that states the name, location, and business of the firm and the names of the partners along with their duties, obligations, and rights in running the business and sharing in the profits. (p. 66)

par value The value printed on the stock certificate. Many stock certificates do not show a par value (no-par value stock). Par value may represent the price of the stock when it was originally issued or it may be a completely arbitrary amount.

Pascal Relatively new high-level computer language (close to ordinary spoken language) that uses structured programming and is used with microcomputers. (p. 384)

patent Legal protection of a process, invention, or formula by the federal government. Protects against imitation for a period of 17 years in the United States. (p. 296)

peer group A group composed of one's contemporaries (for example, people of the same age) who interact regularly.

perception How an individual interprets a situation or a message or how he or she "sees" somebody else.

perfect competition A competitive state with many buyers and many sellers, a uniform product, perfect market information, and no excess profit.

performance appraisal system A system used by management to measure and evaluate employee performance on the job. (p. 180)

performance rating A part of wage and salary administration. Setting a series of rates (steps, or pay ranges) for each job. New employees start at the base rate and advance to higher rates as they gain experience, proficiency, and seniority.

performance tests Tests used to measure a person's proficiency in a given type of work, such as typing.

peripheral equipment Input and output equipment accompanying the central processing unit in a computer or data processing system.

personal property All property except land and its permanent attachments. Examples are cars, furniture, and office machines. (p. 595)

personal selling Direct contact of salesperson with a prospective buyer and a face-to-face sales effort. (p. 319)

personal staff A staff person who performs duties at the request of his or her line boss. Usually designated by the title "assistant to."

personnel department A staff department headed by a personnel manager which advises and assists line managers in managing their personnel. Performs personnel tasks such as recruiting and training. (p. 165)

personnel management The task of implementing top management's policies regarding human resource management. Includes activities such as recruiting, selecting, training, developing, compensating, and terminating employees. (p. 164)

PERT (Program Evaluation and Review Technique) A planning and control tool used by managers to estimate how much time it takes to complete various parts of a project so that bottlenecks can be avoided and the project can be done on time. (p. 241)

Peter Principle The promotion of a competent person for good performance until he or she winds up in a position in which he or she is incompetent, because the demands of the position exceed the person's capacities. Developed by J. L. Peter.

physical distribution The physical movement and storage of products. This has provided the main opportunity to apply technology to reduce costs of marketing. Also called logistics. (p. 303)

physiological needs   The most prepotent needs in Maslow's hierarchy of needs: food, clothing, shelter, and sex.

picketing   A means of communicating with others. People (pickets) form a picket line and walk around a plant or office building with signs informing other workers and the general public that the employer is held unfair to labor. (p. 215)

piece rate   A method of paying workers. Each worker is paid a certain rate for each acceptable unit of output produced. (p. 182)

piggyback exporting   The use by one firm (the carrier) of its overseas distribution network to sell noncompetitive products made by other firms (riders). (p. 553)

place (distribution)   An element in the marketing mix concerned with the movement of products through a channel from producer to consumer or industrial user. (p. 297)

place utility   The increase in the value of a product by changing its location. (p. 279)

planned obsolescence   Intentionally scheduled replacement of a product or model with a new product or model produced by the same firm. (p. 291)

planning   The management function of preparing a firm to cope with the future by relying on knowledge of present and past conditions and forecasting probable future developments. Setting a firm's objectives over different time periods and deciding on the methods of achieving those objectives result in a plan to be followed to reach desired goals. (p. 104)

plant capacity   The limits of the output of a production facility. A major subject of production planning. (p. 235)

plant layout   The internal design of a factory, including the arrangement of the machines used in the manufacturing process. (p. 235)

portfolio   The set of securities owned by a person or a firm.

postindustrial society   A society that has progressed beyond the industrial society. Instead of manufacturing being the dominant form of business activity, the service industries are predominant.

precedent   A previous case decided in the same legal jurisdiction, for which there was no explicit written law or statute and whose circumstances and issues were the same as those in a subsequent case, which will therefore be decided in the same way as the earlier case.

preemptive right   The right of old stockholders to buy new shares issued by a corporation before anyone else. It enables a stockholder to maintain his or her same proportionate ownership of the corporation.

preferred stock   A certificate showing ownership in a corporation. It has preference over common stock in dividends and liquidation of the corporation's assets. Preferred stockholders usually do not have the right to vote. (p. 76)

preliminary employment interview   A job applicant's first interview with a prospective employer. (p. 174)

prepaid expense   A current asset representing an expenditure of funds the benefit of which has not yet been realized in the firm's operations.

preventive maintenance   The inspection and/or replacement of certain critical machines and parts on a regular basis to avoid downtime. (p. 243)

price   The amount of money (or other goods and services) that is paid in exchange for something else. (p. 35) Price also is an element in a firm's marketing mix. It includes monetary cost and the terms of sale. (p. 324)

price discrimination   Charging different prices to competitive buyers of the same product for reasons not associated with costs.

price/earnings (P/E) ratio   The present price of a share of stock divided by the current earnings per share.

price index   The ratio of prices in the current period (or year) to prices in a base period (or year); a measure of inflation.

price leadership   A situation common in oligopoly markets in which one firm sets a price and others follow suit in the interest of price stability and avoidance of price competition. (p. 325)

price lining   Setting retail prices at standard preset levels, such as $6.95, $8.00, etc., for items bought at a variety of wholesale prices to simplify consumer decisions and pricing administration. (p. 331)

price system   (See *market economy.*)

pricing model   A mathematical formula to help firms set the best basic price. (p. 327)

primary demand   The demand for a product category rather than the demand for a particular brand of product within that category (selective demand). For example, the demand for milk and the demand for Borden's milk.

primary research   Obtaining original information for a specific research objective. In marketing, it often requires use of questionnaires directed toward the target market. (p. 277)

prime rate of interest   Rate charged to best customers of large commercial banks. Especially important as an indicator of money supply conditions, but variable between banks and regions. (p. 426)

principle of indemnity   A principle of insurance. The insured cannot collect more than the actual cash value of a loss. (p. 459)

private brand   Also called middleman brand, local brand, or dealer brand. A brand owned by a wholesaler or retailer as opposed to a manufacturer.

private carrier   A transportation system owned by a manufacturer or middleman for exclusive use in moving its own products. (p. 305)

private corporation   A corporation that is organized, owned, and operated by private investors.

private enterprise   Private ownership of business firms. (p. 16)

private trading company   A privately owned business that buys and sells goods in many different countries, either in its own name or as an agent for its buyer-seller clients. (p. 536)

process-organized plant   Plant designed to accommodate a specific process. Distinguished from product-organized plant.

product   An element in the marketing mix consisting of the entire bundle of satisfactions made available for sale. In addition to the physical product itself, it includes the package, brand, warranty, and so on. Also included are the psychological satisfactions associated with it. (p. 288)

product cost accounting   Systems for allocating costs to products by a firm. (p. 365)

product differentiation   Making products or services appear different from those of competitors, thereby attracting buyers or commanding higher prices. (p. 271)

production   An activity that results in the creation of goods and services. (p. 224)

production for stock   Production kept in inventory in anticipation of receipt of orders.

production management   The application of the functions of management to a production process. A narrower concept than operations management (see above). (p. 231)

production to order   Production as required on demand from the firm's customers. Also called jobbing.

product life cycle   The evolution of a product through periods of introduction, growth, maturity, and decline/obsolescence. (p. 288)

product mix   All products offered for sale by a firm. (p. 293)

product obsolescence   The replacement of one product or product feature by a newer, better, or cheaper one.

product offering   The product element of the marketing mix that includes not only the physical product but also the guarantee, service, brand, package, installation, alteration, etc., that accompanies the physical product.

product-organized plant   Plant designed to handle production of more than one product with separate layout for each. Distinguished from process-organized plant.

product liability insurance   A policy designed to protect a company from claims made by users of its products.

professional-managerial ethic   The position that corporate managers represent the interests of stockholders, employees, and the general public. (p. 616)

professional managers   Hired managers. Most often used when there is a separation of ownership and management in a firm. Persons whose career is management. (p. 84)

profit   What remains after a business deducts its costs of doing business (expenditures) from the sales revenues (receipts) it receives from selling its goods or services. (p. 27)

profit sharing   The receipt by an employee of a portion of the profits earned by the employer.

progressive tax   A tax that taxes higher incomes at a higher rate. (p. 590)

promissory note   A written promise to pay a certain sum of money (principal and interest) made by a borrower (maker) to a lender (payee) at a certain time in the future. (p. 450)

promotion   In personnel management, promotion means moving up a higher position on a firm's job ladder. Usually involves more pay and more challenge. (See page 185.) In marketing, promotion is an element in the marketing mix. It includes all communication a firm has with its present or potential customers for the purpose of expanding sales, either directly or indirectly. (p. 312)

property and casualty insurance   A general category of insurance other than life insurance. Includes the perils of firm, windstorm, flood, theft, burglary, accident, loss of health, and liability due to negligence. (p. 458)

prospecting   That part of a salesperson's job that involves developing a list of prospective customers.

prospectus   A summary of the registration statement that is filed with the Securities and Exchange Commission when a company proposes to issue new securities. It includes information about the firm and the purpose of the proposed issue. It must be made available to prospective buyers before they buy the issuing corporation's securities. (p. 483)

the Protestant ethic   A tradition stressing the values of hard work, accumulation of property, and self-reliance. (p. 17)

proxy   A person appointed to represent another person. A stockholder transfers his or her right to vote at a stockholders' meeting to a proxy by signing a proxy form. (p. 78)

public bidding   Process used in many government purchasing situations which permits general access to government contracts within specification limits.

public corporation   A corporation organized, owned, and operated by government.

publicity   Information about a company or its product that is considered "news" by the media and is reported by them at no charge to the company. (p. 323)

public-private partnership   A collaboration

between government and business to solve social problems. (p. 617)

public relations   Communication with the public or with the government that seeks to create goodwill for the firm as a whole. (p. 323)

public securities market   Individual and institutional investors who buy stocks and bonds. Also includes the various securities middlemen who bring buyers and sellers of securities together. (p. 468)

punched card   A paper card that is used in computers to store and transmit information by means of specially arranged holes made in the card.

pure risk   An opportunity for financial loss without opportunity for financial gain. (p. 455)

quality control   Means by which the level of quality of inputs and outputs is known and monitored so that it can be kept within a certain range of acceptable quality standards. (p. 242)

quality of life   A concept used as an indicator of the "real" effects of modern society on human life as opposed to the more narrow, traditional economic indicator such as GNP per capita. The idea is that higher income can be offset by such things as pollution or obsolescence.

quality-of-work-life (QWL) programs   Forms of work organization whose underlying idea is that worker participation with managers in decisions at the bottom level of the organization through problem-solving committees will result in increased job satisfaction and raise product quality and labor productivity. (p. 148)

quantitative tools   Methods of using mathematics and statistics to help solve business problems and understand facts. (p. 392)

quantity discount   As the size of the order increases, unit prices are reduced. In a noncumulative quantity discount, the discount percentage applies to each individual order. In a cumulative quantity discount, the discount percentage applies to the total purchases made over a period of time. (p. 329)

quasi-public corporation   A corporation that is organized, owned, and operated jointly by government and private investors.

quick ratio   (See *acid-test ratio.*)

raw materials   A category of industrial goods. They become a physical part of the goods they are used to produce. Examples are farm products such as cotton and natural products such as lumber.

real estate mortgage bond   A bond that is secured by real property.

real income   Current income expressed in terms of buying power; current income adjusted for the decline in buying power due to inflation. (p. 38)

real property   Land and its permanent attachments. (p. 595)

recapitalization   Occurs when a firm changes its capital structure to meet changing conditions. An extraordinary financial circumstance that may require drastic financial action on the firm's part and may require it to amend its charter or receive permission of the Securities and Exchange Commission. (p. 493)

recession   That period in the business cycle during which the volume of business activity is declining. Consumers and businesses are losing confidence and are becoming pessimistic about the future.

reciprocity   A "you buy from me and I'll buy from you" purchasing policy. Two firms agree to supply each other. (p. 247)

recovery   That period in the business cycle during which the volume of business activity is expanding after a recession or depression. Businesses begin investing again and consumers begin buying again. Optimism prevails.

recruiting   The task of attracting potential employees to a firm. (p. 170)

recycling   Means developed in order to turn pollution sources into economic resources by reusing them.

redeemable bonds   Also referred to as callable bonds. They can be redeemed or called in prior to maturity.

reference groups   Groups that help define a person's place in society, his or her goals, and his or her aspirations.

regional trading bloc   A group of nations that reduces or eliminates trade barriers among themselves. (p. 556)

registered bond   A bond on which the owner's name appears; his or her name is registered with the issuing corporation.

regression analysis   An estimate, arrived at by use of an equation, of the form of the relationship between a dependent variable and one or more independent variables.

regressive tax   A tax that places a relatively greater burden on the poor than on the wealthy (like a sales tax). (p. 591)

reorganization   An involuntary process that occurs when a firm is in very serious financial trouble and the court steps in to protect creditors. (p. 493)

research and development   (R&D) A general category of activities that are intended to produce new products and processes.

reserve requirement   The percentage of deposits that member banks of the Federal Reserve System must keep in vault cash or as deposits with their Federal Reserve Banks. It is set by the board of governors of the Federal Reserve System. (p. 431)

resignation   An employee's announcement that he or she is voluntarily leaving an employer's service. (p. 188)

responsibility   The obligation of a subordinate to perform an assigned task. (p. 137)

responsibility accounting   A method of classifying cost information and thereby evaluating the performance of the components of the firm (responsibility centers) and their managers. (p. 364)

résumé   A brief statement of a person's qualifications for employment. (p. 640)

retailer   A firm selling goods to households or other ultimate consumers.

retained earnings   Profits that have been held in the business as capital. A major source of funds.

revenue   Inward flow of value to a firm, mostly from sales. (p. 349)

revolving credit   Commercial bank credit under a formal agreement. It guarantees the borrower funds for a period of time under strict rules. (p. 449)

right-to-work laws   State laws permitted under the Taft-Hartley Act that outlaw the union-shop type of union security. (p. 205)

risk   The chance of loss. All business activity involves risk. (p. 57)

Robinson-Patman Act   A 1936 federal law designed to curb unfair marketing practices. It outlaws price discrimination and other anticompetitive forms of behavior.

rolling over   Successive renewals of short-term notes as a substitute for longer-term financial commitments. (p. 489)

round lot   A unit of 100 shares of stock.

routine decision   A recurring decision, often set up as a policy. (p. 120)

safety needs   Needs that emerge after the physiological needs in Maslow's hierarchy of needs. They include the need to feel that you will survive and that your physiological needs will continue to be met.

salary   Fixed compensation to an employee who is regularly paid on a weekly, biweekly, or monthly basis. (p. 183)

sales finance company   A firm that specializes in financing installment purchases made by individuals and firms. (p. 418)

sales forecast   An estimate of the sales that will be made in a future period of time, thus making budget construction easier. (p. 364)

sales promotion   Any of a variety of devices to increase sales, including trading stamps, contests, and special attractions. (p. 324)

sales quota   The number of units or the dollar sales volume that is set as a target for salespersons. Often, sales above quota result in the salesperson earning a bonus.

sales revenue   The total amount of money a firm receives from the sale of its product(s). Price per unit multiplied by the number of units.

sample   A part of a larger group that represents the larger group. (p. 394)

sampling   The use of a part (sample) of a larger group (universe or population) to represent that larger group.

savings and loan association   Accepts deposits from the general public and makes mortgage loans mainly on homes and other real estate. (p. 414)

savings bank   A bank that serves small savers by accepting their deposits and paying them interest on their savings. (p. 414)

secondary research   Research into materials previously developed by someone other than the present researcher. The present researcher benefits from work done earlier for another purpose. Libraries are a frequent source for this kind of research. (p. 276)

secret partner   In a partnership, a partner who actively participates in managing the firm but whose identity is not disclosed to the public.

secured loans   A loan which is guaranteed by a pledge of the borrower's assets or collateral. (p. 449)

Securities and Exchange Commission (SEC)   An agency that polices the operation of national exchanges, the over-the-counter market, and corporations whose securities are traded on them.

securities exchange   Place where buyers and sellers of securities deal with each other through members of the exchange. Exchanges are set up by brokerage houses to reduce the cost and increase the efficiency of financial investment. (p. 474)

selection tests   Tests given to job applicants whose preliminary employment interview and job application forms were satisfactory. Their purpose is to select the best applicants and to reject the others. They include aptitude tests, intelligence tests, performance tests, personality tests, and interest tests. (p. 175)

selective demand   The demand for a particular brand of product within a product category. For example, the demand for Borden's milk as opposed to the demand for milk in general (primary demand).

self-actualization   In Maslow's hierarchy of needs, it is the drive for achievement, creativity, and the need to achieve your potential in life.

self-insurance   The practice of preparing for losses by saving systematically instead of buying an insurance policy. (p. 454)

seniority   An employee's length of service. The longer that service, the greater the seniority. It can be computed on the basis of length of service with the firm, length of service in a particular job or department, or length of membership in a labor union. (p. 181)

sensitivity training   (See *T-group training.*)

serial bonds   A large issue of bonds with varying maturity dates.

Service Corps of Retired Executives (SCORE)   An advisory service of the SBA. Members are retired executives who volunteer their services to small firms. (p. 527)

services   Services are a type of consumer good. They provide consumer satisfactions and benefits but they are not physical objects. Examples are the services of physicians, beauticians, banks, and restaurants.

severance pay   A payment to the worker above his or her wage or salary that is due when he or she terminates employment with the employer.

shipper's export declaration   A document that is required for all goods that are to be exported from the United States. It declares the quantity and dollar value of the goods and must be filed with the collector of customs at the port of exportation. (p. 550)

shopping goods   Consumer products whose purchase is taken seriously enough to require comparison and study. (p. 268)

short run   A period of time of one year or less; equivalent of short term.

short selling   The selling of a security that a person does not own by borrowing it from his or her broker. At some time in the future, the person must buy the security to "cover" the short sale. (p. 480)

short-term debt   Notes issued by a firm or any debt that it has incurred that will require one year or less for repayment.

short-term capital   (See *working capital.*)

silent partner   In a partnership, a partner who does not actively participate in managing the firm but whose name is identified with the partnership.

sinking fund   A fund set aside over the lifetime of bonds for their retirement. (p. 487)

sinking fund bonds   The annual deposit of funds by the issuing corporation with a trustee so that those deposits, along with earned interest, will be available to redeem bonds upon maturity.

sleeping partner   (See *dormant partner.*)

small business   As defined by the Small Business Administration, a firm that is independently owned and operated for profit (except sheltered workshops), not dominant in its field, and that meets certain standards of size in terms of employees or annual receipts. (p. 504)

Small Business Administration (SBA)   An independent agency of the U.S. government created in 1953 to promote and protect the interests of small business firms. (p. 524)

SBA direct loans   Loans made to entrepreneurs entirely with SBA funds. (p. 525)

SBA guaranteed loans   Loans made to entrepreneurs by commercial banks and guaranteed up to 90 percent by the SBA. (p. 525)

SBA participating loans   Loans made to entrepreneurs with SBA funds and with funds secured from private sources. (p. 525)

Small Business Institute (SBI)   An SBA program that provides counseling of small business owners by faculty members and senior and graduate students from collegiate business schools. (p. 527)

Small Business Investment Company (SBIC)   A privately owned and privately operated company that is licensed by the SBA to provide long-term financing and management assistance to small firms. (p. 526)

social cost   In pursuing profit expressed in dollars, a firm may incur great social cost in the form of polluted streams, air, or blight of cities.

Social Darwinism   The nineteenth-century political and economic philosophy that advocated the survival of the economically fittest in an unregulated competitive environment.

social responsibility of business   Refers to the general idea that a business firm has obligations to individuals and groups (its publics) other than its owners.

social stratification   Division of members of a society into recognized classes or groups of varying status (that is, upper class, middle class, lower class).

society   A large group of people who are bound together by a complex set of relationships.

software   The programs, languages, and routines used in electronic data processing. Software complements hardware. (p. 382)

sole proprietorship   A business firm owned by one person. The firm and the proprietor are the same. (p. 63)

source document   Evidence of a transaction, such as an invoice or a sales slip.

"spaceship economy"   Phrase referring to planned and careful use of resources. Includes conservation and recycling of resources.

span of control   (See *span of management.*)

span of management   A term that refers to the number of subordinates an individual manager supervises. Also called span of control. (p. 134)

specialization   Concentrating on a specific task instead of dividing one's efforts among a greater number of tasks. Dividing work into several tasks and having one person perform only a limited number of those tasks. Each person can make better use of his or her limited time and talents and become more efficient in performing a specialized task. (p. 5)

specialized staff   Staff personnel who serve the entire firm, not just one line manager. The director of marketing research is an example.

specialty goods   Items for which strong conviction as to brand, style, or type already exists in the buyer's mind and for which he or she will make a great effort to locate and purchase a specific brand. (p. 269)

speculative risk   "Gambles," which offer the possibility of gain as well as loss. (p. 455)

speculative trading   Buying or selling securities in the hope of profiting from near-term future changes in their selling prices. Common especially in bull markets.

staff   Persons who advise, serve, assist, and support line managers in their work of achieving primary company goals. Personal staff perform duties for one line executive; specialized staff serve the entire firm. (p. 141)

staff functions   Organizational functions that help the line to achieve primary firm goals. Quality control and market research are staff functions in a manufacturing firm. (p. 141)

staffing   The management function of recruiting, selecting, training, and promoting personnel to fill both managerial and operating positions. (p. 108)

stagflation   A peculiar economic condition under which inflation and depressed economic activity occur at the same time.

standard   A predetermined level of quality, speed, strength, or size pertaining to some aspect of a firm's operation. Could relate to product or people or finance.

standard metropolitan statistical area (SMSA)   An integrated social and economic unit with one city (or twin cities) of 50,000 or more inhabitants. It includes the county of this central city and adjacent counties that are socially and economically integrated with the central city.

standard of living   A measure of economic well-being; often expressed as per capita Gross National Product. (p. 9)

standard product cost   In standard cost accounting, the cost that should have been incurred in a production process.

state development company   A corporation organized by state government to operate statewide in assisting the growth and development of business firms.

statement of financial position   (See *balance sheet.*)

state trading company   A government-owned operation that handles a country's trade with other governments or firms in other countries. (p. 536)

statistics   Data; also the science of manipulating, interpreting, and summarizing data. (p. 392)

status   A person's rank in a social system as perceived by others.

status symbols   Symbols often used to affect how others will perceive a person's status. An executive with a plush carpet on the office floor enjoys more status than another executive with cheap tile on the office floor.

statutory law   Written or codified law as developed in city councils, state legislatures, and the Congress of the United States and supported by city charters, state constitutions, and the federal Constitution. (p. 594)

steward   A union official selected by the employees in a plant to represent them.

stock and bond averages   Indices used to tell what is happening on the securities exchanges, that is, prices advancing or declining.

stockbrokers   Middlemen who buy and sell securities for their investor-clients. They work for brokerage houses.

stock dividend   A payment to stockholders in additional shares of stock. Enables a corporation to conserve its cash.

stockholders   Also called shareholders. A corporation's stockholders are the persons who own it. The owners of the entity that is the corporation. (p. 69)

stock split   An action that gives a shareholder a greater number of shares but maintains his or her same proportionate ownership in the corporation.

straight life insurance   A type of insurance for which the insured pays premiums until his or her death, at which time the face value of the policy is paid to the beneficiary. Has savings and protection elements.

straight line depreciation   Charging equal parts of the original cost of an asset in each year of its expected life.

strategic planning   Planning for the long-range future. A major responsibility of top-level managers. (p. 105)

strike   A temporary withdrawal of all or some employees from an employer's service. (p. 215)

student data sheet   Also called a college interview form. A form prepared by the student placement office and filled out by the student for inspection by employers who send campus interviewers to a school. (p. 640)

Subchapter S Corporation   A corporation with no more than 25 stockholders that elects to be taxed somewhat like a partnership. It pays no income tax as a firm. The owners pay income tax on the dividends they receive from the corporation. (p. 72)

suboptimize   Pertaining to being satisfied with something less than the best. In trying to integrate personal and organizational objectives, management frequently must suboptimize.

subsidiary   A company owned by a parent company.

subsistence economy   A nation or region in which the people have a very low standard of living, barely enough to survive.

supplemental unemployment benefits (SUB)   Payments to laid-off workers made by their employers. (p. 207)

supplies   A category of industrial goods. They are relatively inexpensive items that do not become a physical part of the goods they are used to produce. Examples are light bulbs, nuts and bolts, and paper clips.

supply   The quantity of a product or a service that is made available for sale as the result of effort by producers. Price induces supply. The quantity supplied is the number of units of a product or service that sellers are willing to offer for sale at a certain price at a given point in time. (p. 43)

supply curve   A curve showing the number of units of a product or a service that will be supplied (offered for sale) at each price at a given point in time. Usually slopes up and to the right. (p. 47)

supply-side economics   The basic idea is that an economy can be managed by adjusting the supply side of the supply-and-demand equation. Advocates tax cuts to leave consumers with more money to spend and business people with more money to invest. The desired result is that the economy would expand, employment would increase, supply would increase, demand would adjust to supply, and prices would stabilize.

surety bond   A bond that insures a person or firm against loss if the other party to a contract does not fulfill a contractual obligation.

surrender value   The amount the insured gets back from the insurance company if the insured cancels his or her life insurance policy. Not applicable to term life insurance policies.

systems concept   A way of looking at a firm as a complex of interacting parts, or subsystems. The firm itself is a subsystem of its industry and the socioeconomic system. Management effort focuses on integrating the firm's subsystems to improve overall performance. (p. 107)

Taft-Hartley Act   A 1947 law that outlaws the closed shop, permits states to pass right-to-work laws, provides for injunctive processes in national emergency strikes and in illegal strikes, requires unions to bargain in good faith with employers, and makes it illegal for unions to discriminate against workers who do not join unions if they are not required to do so as a condition of continued employment. (p. 198)

target market   The set of customers, present and potential, to which a firm directs its attention when it designs its marketing mix and the policies associated with it. (p. 263)

tariffs   Duties or taxes that a country's government imposes on products imported into or exported from that country. (p. 538)

tax control   The practice of a country's government of using its taxing authority to control foreign investments in that country. Involves applying discriminatory taxes to foreign-owned firms. (p. 541)

technological obsolescence   The obsolescence of a product or production process because of technological progress. The alternator made the generator technologically obsolete for cars.

technology   The application of science so that people can do entirely new things or do things in a new way. (p. 617)

technology forecasting   A technique used to predict technological change. It involves gathering bits of evidence from professional meetings, technical journals, etc. Specially-trained experts interpret this evidence to diagnose the direction of technological change and its implications for their firms. (p. 602)

tenancy in common   The sharing by two or more persons of title to real property. Each tenant's share passes to his or her heirs at the tenant's death.

tenants by the entirety   A form of joint tenancy of real property. It can be ended only by death of one party. The other partner becomes sole owner.

term life insurance   A type of insurance written to cover a certain number of years. If the insured dies during that period, the beneficiary receives the face value of the policy. If not, all premiums paid belong to the insurance company. It is pure protection.

T-group training   A T-group is a laboratory where trainees come together in small discussion groups to deal with real (not simulated) problems that exist within the training group itself. Rather than only teaching skills, the purpose is to help trainees learn about their individual weaknesses, how groups work, and how to behave more effectively in interpersonal relations. Also called sensitivity training, laboratory training, or encounter groups.

theory X manager   A term developed by Douglas McGregor to describe a manager who assumes that the average person inherently dislikes work and is, by nature, lazy, irresponsible, self-centered, security oriented, indifferent to the needs of the organization, and unambitious, and wants to avoid responsibility.

theory Y manager   A term developed by Douglas McGregor to describe a manager who assumes that the average person is capable of developing interest in his or her work, committing himself or herself to working to reach company goals, and working productively with a minimum of control and threat of punishment.

time deposit   A deposit that is made for a period of time. Savings accounts and certificates of deposit are examples. Interest is usually paid on a time deposit. (p. 423)

time sharing   A method whereby a number of users may utilize the facilities of a single computer at one time. (p. 383)

time utility   The increase in value resulting from the passage of time. (p. 280)

total cost concept   A concept applicable to a firm's physical distribution, or logistics, management. It involves consideration of all

Orleans Better Business Bureau. Ad p. 518—Courtesy of Marquette National Bank, Chicago, Illinois. Cartoon p. 520—*Funky Winkerbean*, by Tom Batiuk © 1979 Field Enterprises, Inc., Courtesy of Field Newspaper Syndicate. Photo p. 520—Ken Buck/Picture Cube. p. 528—*Statistical Abstract 1980*, 101st edition, p. 558. Photo p. 529—Eric Roth/Picture Cube. Incident p. 530—Excerpt from Sanford Jacobs, "Turning an Airy Pastime into a Business," *The Wall Street Journal*, November 16, 1981, p. 25. Reprinted by permission of *The Wall Street Journal*, © Dow Jones & Company 1981. All rights reserved. Incident p. 531—Excerpt from Gail Bronson, "Going Public has its Rewards, as Liz Claiborne, Inc. Discovers," *The Wall Street Journal*, August 10, 1981, p. 19. Reprinted by permission of *The Wall Street Journal*, © Dow Jones & Company 1981. All rights reserved. p. 536—U.S. Department of Commerce, Bureau of Economic Analysis, *Survey of Business*, July 1983, p. 5–17. pp. 536–537—*Survey of Current Business*, November 1981.

Chapter Eighteen: Cartoon p. 541—*Pepper . . . and Salt:* From *The Wall Street Journal*, permission—Cartoon Features Syndicate. Ad pp. 546–547—Courtesy of Westinghouse Credit Corporation. Photo p. 548—Daniel Brody/Stock, Boston. Photo p. 550—Richard Wood/Picture Cube, p. 551—U.S. Department of Commerce. p. 555—"The International 500" *Fortune* August 22, 1983, p. 172. Reprinted from *The Fortune Directory*; © 1982 Time Inc. All rights reserved. Photo p. 557—Larry Lawfer. Photo p. 558—Barbara Alper/Stock, Boston. Case Study pp. 564–565—Excerpt from John M. Geddes, "Small U.S. Firms use European Trade Fairs as an Inexpensive Way to tap new Markets," *The Wall Street Journal*, November 12, 1981, p. 25. Reprinted by permission of *The Wall Street Journal*, © Dow Jones & Company 1981. All rights reserved.

Section Eight: SO Duotone p. 571—Cary Wolinsky/Stock, Boston.

Chapter Nineteen: Photo p. 576—Eric Roth/Picture Cube. Photo p. 578—Culver Pictures. *Point of View* p. 579—Excerpt from "AT & T's Access to new Markets Backed by Court," *The Wall Street Journal*, September 8, 1981, p. 12. Reprinted by permission of *The Wall Street Journal*, © Dow Jones & Company 1981, All rights reserved. p. 582—U.S. Senate Subcommittee on Federal Regulations, *The Federal Paperwork Burden, The 92nd Congress, Part 1*, pp. 124–128. p. 583—"The Record: Major Changes in Auto Deregulation," *The New York Times*, November 1, 1981. © 1981 by The New York Times Company. Reprinted by permission. *What Do You Think?* p. 586—Excerpt from Monica Langley, "Government's Staggering Leasing Expense Stirs Debate on Whether to Rent or Buy," *The Wall Street Journal*, © Dow Jones & Company 1981. All rights reserved. Photo p. 587—Larry Lawfer. p. 590—Data from U.S. Office of Management and Budget. Photo p. 592—Eric Roth/Picture Cube. Incident p. 598—Excerpt form George Anders, "We Have Play-Offs, Runoffs, Bake-Offs: Now, a Compute-Off," *The Wall Street Journal*, September 21, 1981, p. 1. Reprinted by permission of *The Wall Street Journal*, © Dow Jones & Company 1981. All rights reserved.

Chapter Twenty: Chapter opening p. 601—Excerpt from Steve Lohr, "New In Japan: The Manless Factory," *The New York Times*, December 13, 1981, Section 3, p. 1. © 1981 by The New York Times Company. Reprinted by permission. Ad p. 604—Reprinted with permission of Triangle Publications, Inc. p. 605—*Statistical Abstract 1981*, 102nd edition, p. 6. p. 606—*The Consumer: A Graphic Profile* (New York: The Conference Board). p. 607—Based on data from *Current Population Reports*, P-20, No. 365 (Washington, D.C.: U.S. Bureau of the Census, 1981), p. 3. p. 608—*White House Conference on the World Ahead*, Washington, D.C., 1973. p. 609—*The Consumer: A Graphic Profile* (New York: The Conference Board). *What Do You Think?* p. 610—The Conference Board based on Census Bureau's Current Population Survey. p. 611—Excerpt from Laurie McGinley, "So What if Your Car's Been Towed?," *The Wall Street Journal*, October 15, 1981. Reprinted by permission of *The Wall Street Journal*, © Dow Jones & Company 1981. All rights reserved. Photo p. 612—Courtesy of Stride-Rite Corporation. Cartoon p. 616—Drawing by Dana Fradon; © 1978 The New Yorker Magazine, Inc. Photo p. 616—Larry Lawfer. p. 618—Data from The Conference Board, September 1981, numbers 1910–1911. *Point of View* p. 619—Excerpt from Eduardo Gentil, "Brazil's Alcohol Car Binge Dries Up," *The Wall Street Journal*, October 15, 1981, p. 33. Reprinted by permission of *The Wall Street Journal*, © Dow Jones & Company 1981. All rights reserved. Photo p. 621—George Fischer/Visum. p. 623—*Statistical Abstract 1981*, 102nd edition, p. 596. Based on data from the National Science Foundation. Photo p. 624—Courtesy of NASA. Incident p. 625—*bottom:* Excerpt from Patricia McCormack, "We Generation: Spirit of Interdependence Replacing 'Me Cult', Experts Say," *New Orleans Times-Picayune*, February 22, 1981, Section 4, p. 15. Reprinted by permission of United Press International.

Chapter Twenty-One: p. 629—Based on data from *Occupational Outlook Handbook 1982–1983*, pp. 632–633—*Occupational Outlook Handbook 1982–1983*, pp. 38–40. p. 634—Data from Chase Econometrics. © 1982 The New York Times Company. Reprinted by permission. p. 637—Kenneth Schneider, "Hiring Criteria as Seen by Managers," *Marketing News*, 11 (January 13, 1978):5. Reprinted by permission of American Marketing Association. p. 639—Reproduced with permission of the College Placement Council, Inc. Cartoon p. 647—Drawing by Weber; © 1981 The New York Magazine, Inc. p. 650—From *A Career Planning Program for Colleg Students* by John Loughary and Theresa Ripley, Copyright 1978. Used with permission of Follett Publishing Company, a division of Follett Corporation. Case Study pp. 653–654—Excerpt from "The Little Engines of Growth," *Time*, January 26, 1981, p. 53. Copyright 1981 Time Inc. All rights reserved. Reprinted by permission from *Time*.

Endsheets: Top row, left to right—Ewing Galloway; Camerique; Alvis Upitis/Image Bank; Shostal Associates; Bottom row, left to right—William Herbeck/After-Image; © Michael Melford 1981; J. Adanson/Sygma; Roger Tully/After-Image.

Section One
OUR BUSINESS SYSTEM

Section Two
MANAGEMENT AND ORGANIZATION

Section Four
MARKETING MANAGEMENT

Section Three
HUMAN RESOURCES AND
PRODUCTION MANAGEMENT